Principles of
Micro Economics

third edition

John E. Sayre
Capilano College

Alan J. Morris
Capilano College

 **McGraw-Hill
Ryerson**

Toronto Montréal Boston Burr Ridge, IL Dubuque, IA Madison, WI
New York San Francisco St. Louis Bangkok Bogotá Caracas
Kuala Lumpur Lisbon London Madrid Mexico City Milan
New Delhi Santiago Seoul Singapore Sydney Taipei

McGraw-Hill
Ryerson Limited
A Subsidiary of The **McGraw·Hill** Companies
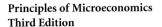

Principles of Microeconomics
Third Edition

ISBN: 0-07-087546-4

1 2 3 4 5 6 7 8 9 10 TRI 0 9 8 7 6 5 4 3 2 1

Printed and bound in Canada.

Photo Credits: Images on pages 94, 101, 164, 179, 330, and 396 copyright © 1998 PhotoDisc, Inc.

Statistics Canada information is used with permission of the Ministry of Industry, as Minister responsible for Statistics Canada. Information on the availability of the wider range of data from Statistics Canada can be obtain from Statistics Canada's Regional Offices, its World Wide Web site at *http://www.statcan.ca*, and its toll-free access number 1-800-263-1136.

Care has been taken to trace ownership of copyright material contained in this text; however, the publisher will welcome any information that enables them to rectify any reference or credit for subsequent editions.

Vice President and Editorial Director: Pat Ferrier
Senior Sponsoring Editor: Lynn Fisher
Editorial Consultant: Ron Doleman
Developmental Editor: Maria Chu
Copy Editor: Erin Moore
Production Supervisor: Nicla Dattolico
Senior Marketing Manager: Jeff MacLean
Page Layout: Leanne O'Brien/ArtPlus Limited
Cover Design: Sharon Lucas
Cover Image Credit: Bill Frymire/Masterfile
Printer: Tri-Graphic Printing

Canadian Cataloguing in Publication Data

Sayre, John E., 1942-
  Principles of microeconomics

3rd ed.
Includes index
ISBN 0-07-087546-4

Microeconomics. I. Morris, Alan J. (Alan James). II. Title.

HB172.S354 200   338.5   C00-931961-1

With love to my two daughters:

Alison and Meridith

(JES)

and

To the ones I love:

Wakako, Daniel, and Christian

(AJM)

About The Authors

Alan Morris, though loath to admit it, first worked as an accountant in England, where he became an Associate of the Chartered Institute of Secretaries and obtained his first degree in 1971 in Manchester, U.K. He subsequently obtained his Master's degree at Simon Fraser University, B.C., in 1973. He worked on his doctorate at Leicester University, U.K., and returned to work in business in Vancouver, B.C., until his appointment at Capilano College in 1988. He currently resides in North Vancouver with his wife and two sons and is an avid devotee of classical music, mountaineering, soccer, and beer. To his knowledge, he has never been an adviser to the Canadian government.

John E. Sayre earned a B.S.B.A. at the University of Denver and an M.A. from Boston University. He began teaching principles of economics while in the Peace Corps in Malawi. He came to Vancouver to do Ph.D. studies at Simon Fraser University and ended up teaching at Capilano College for the next 30 years. As a balance to the rigours of economics, John is an avid cyclist and jogger who has all too little time left over for golfing.

Photograph by Jan Westendrop

Brief Contents

Contents

Preface

To the Students

So, one may well ask, why are you taking a course in economics? For many of you, the obvious answer to this question is: "Because it is a requirement for the program or educational goal that I have chosen." Fair enough. But there are other good answers to this question. It is a simple truth that if you want to understand the world around you, then you have to understand some basic economics. So much of what goes on in the world today is driven by economic considerations, and those who know no economics often simply cannot understand why things are the way they are. In this age of globalization, we are all becoming citizens of the world and we need to function effectively in the midst of enormous changes that are sweeping across almost every aspect of the social/political/economic landscape. You can either be part of this, and all the opportunities that come with it, or not part of it because you can't make any sense of it.

It is quite possible that you may be a little apprehensive because you have heard that economics is a difficult subject. Nonetheless, we are convinced that almost any student can succeed in economics. But it will require some real work and effort. Here are some tips on the general approach to this course that you might find helpful. First, read the Economics Toolkit that appears at the beginning of the book. The section titled "Canadian Reality" gives basic information on Canada and its economic picture. "Graphing Reality" gives a quick lesson on graphs, which are an essential part of economics. These two sections will give you a solid foundation on which to build your economics knowledge.

Second, before each lecture quickly look over the chapter that will be covered. At this point you don't need to worry about the glossary boxes, the self-test questions, or the Study Guide. Third, take notes as much as you can in the lecture, because it is the process of forcing yourself to express ideas *in your own words* that is a crucial stage in the learning process. Fourth, re-read the chapter, again taking notes and using your own words (don't just copy everything word for word from the text). While doing this, refer to your classroom notes and try to integrate them into your reading notes. Having done this, you are now ready to take on the Study Guide. As painful as it may be for you to hear this, we want to say loud and clear that you should do all of the questions in the Study Guide. You may be slow at first, but you will be surprised at how much faster you become in later chapters. This is a natural aspect of the learning process. It might be helpful for you to get together with one or two other students and form a little study group that meets once or twice a week to do economics Study Guide questions. You will be amazed at how explaining an answer to a fellow student is one of the most effective learning techniques there is. If you ever come across a question that you simply can't understand, this is a sure sign that you need to approach your instructor (or teaching assistant) for help. Don't get discouraged when this happens, and realize that it will probably happen more in the beginning of your process of learning economics than later on in the semester. We are convinced that if you follow this process consistently, beginning in the very first week of class, you will succeed in the course—and not only succeed, but most likely do well. All it takes is effort, good time management, and consistent organization.

Finally, a great deal of what becoming educated is all about involves gaining self-confidence and a sense of accomplishment. Getting an A in a "tough" economics course can be a great step in this direction. We wish you all the best.

To the Instructors

Philosophy

Over the years, we have become increasingly convinced that most economics textbooks are written to impress other economists as much as they are to enlighten beginning students. Such books tend to be encyclopedic in scope and intimidating in appearance. It is no small wonder that the average student too often emerges from an economics course feeling that the discipline really does earn its reputation of being daunting and unapproachable. The study of economics is challenging, but our experience is that students can also see it as intriguing and enjoyable if the right approach is used. It is our belief that this right approach starts with a really good textbook that is concise without sacrificing either clarity or accepted standards of rigour.

In writing this text we attempted to stay focused on five guiding principles. The first is to achieve a well-written text. We have tried to write as clearly as possible, to avoid unnecessary jargon, to speak directly to the student, and to avoid unnecessary abstraction and repetition.

Our second principle has been to avoid an encyclopedic text. It seems that in an effort to please everyone, textbook authors often include everything. The result is that students have difficulty separating the important principles of economics from mere applications and illustrations of those principles. In contrast, we have made a conscious decision to stay focused on time-honoured principles and to spend the necessary effort to explain those principles thoroughly.

Our third principle is to put the emphasis on student learning. Many years of teaching the principles courses have convinced us that students learn economics "by doing economics." To this end, both review questions and self-test questions are positioned throughout each chapter. This encourages students to apply what they have just read and gives them continuous feedback on their comprehension of the material being presented. Further, we feel that we offer the most comprehensive Study Guide on the market—six different types of questions, and up to sixty questions for each chapter. In addition, each chapter's Study Guide has a carefully crafted section of Chapter Highlights as well as a section of study tips for the student.

The fourth principle is to avoid problems of discontinuity that can occur when different groups of authors do separate parts of a total package. To this end, we are the sole authors of the entire package of material—text, Study Guide, instructor's manual, and test bank.

Finally, we have tried to ensure that as much care and attention has gone into the ancillary materials as went into the writing of the text.

Few things are more satisfying than witnessing a student's zest for learning. We hope that this textbook adds a little to this process.

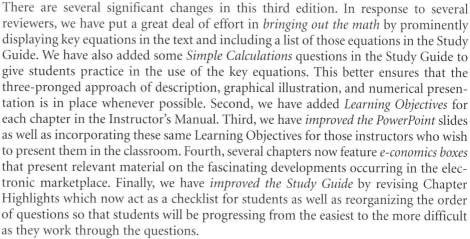

Third Edition

There are several significant changes in this third edition. In response to several reviewers, we have put a great deal of effort in *bringing out the math* by prominently displaying key equations in the text and including a list of those equations in the Study Guide. We have also added some *Simple Calculations* questions in the Study Guide to give students practice in the use of the key equations. This better ensures that the three-pronged approach of description, graphical illustration, and numerical presentation is in place whenever possible. Second, we have added *Learning Objectives* for each chapter in the Instructor's Manual. Third, we have *improved the PowerPoint* slides as well as incorporating these same Learning Objectives for those instructors who wish to present them in the classroom. Fourth, several chapters now feature *e-conomics boxes* that present relevant material on the fascinating developments occurring in the electronic marketplace. Finally, we have *improved the Study Guide* by revising Chapter Highlights which now act as a checklist for students as well as reorganizing the order of questions so that students will be progressing from the easiest to the more difficult as they work through the questions.

Let's now take a quick walk through each chapter as well as highlighting some of the more specific changes to this third edition. The *Economics Toolkit* is designed for students who need help in upgrading their skills in basic math as well as general literacy about Canada. In response to several reviewers, we have added a study guide component to the *Toolkit* as well as some new material on deriving straight line equations. *Chapter 1* introduces some of the important themes in microeconomics and sets the stage for further development of these themes in later chapters. Here, we added a brief discussion of capitalism compared to socialism as well as a new table illustrating the point that economists do, in fact, agree on many things. The pivotal *Chapter 2* is a basic introduction to supply and demand analysis in which we introduce the concept of equilibrium as early as possible before getting into a discussion of why either demand or supply might change. Here, we changed the language of "productively related products" to "substitutes in production" as well as adding several highlight boxes and an e-conomics box. In addition, we have added an *Appendix to Chapter 2* which uses algebra to help analyze the concepts of supply and demand. *Chapter 3* is designed to help the student better understand real world events using these same concepts. *Chapter 4* is a basic treatment of elasticity and here we have made a special effort at surfacing the math to better enable the student to apply this important concept. *Chapter 5* (as well as the *Appendix* to 5) examines consumer behaviour by looking at the theory of marginal utility and has additional highlight boxes and e-conomics boxes. *Chapter 6* introduces the costs of production and, again in response to reviewers, we put more emphasis on the point that normal profits can validly be viewed as a necessary expense of doing business and we have repositioned the Total Product and Marginal/Average Product to emphasis their relationship to each other. *Chapter 7* is a basic discussion of long run costs in which we added some highlight boxes. *Chapter 8* introduces the topic of market structure by focusing on perfect competition and here we have added highlight boxes and an e-conomics box. *Chapter 9* examines the implications, strengths, and failures of a perfectly competitive market in which we again add emphasis of important points with more highlighted boxes. *Chapter 10* examines the pros and cons of monopoly markets where we added highlighted boxes and new e-conomics boxes. In *Chapter 11*, we examine both monopolistically competitive and oligopoly markets. Again in response to reviewers, we dropped the discussion of the Cournot model and added a section entitled "Pricing Strategies for Firms with Market Power." In addition, we clarified the point that the figures in the various game theory pay-off matrixes are not derived in any way but simply assumed. We also updated the Added Dimension box on the world's largest economic entities and were amazed at how much had changed in just a few years. In *Chapter 12* we shift attention to factors markets and give a brief but clear exposition of the markets for labour, natural resources, capital, and entrepreneurial ability. We also clarified the substitution/income effect discussion with reference to the supply of labour and added highlighted boxes. *Chapter 13* is an investigation of international trade and we, again, focused on surfacing the math, which we believe will help the student better understand the more difficult concepts. This last chapter is duplicated in the macro text as Chapter 9 to accommodate those instructors who teach trade in their macro courses.

Textbook Features

We have provided a number of features to help the student come to grips with the subject matter. **Glossary** terms indicate the first use of any term that is part of the language of economics. The term itself is in bold print and the definition is provided in the margin. The page number on which the definition appears is supplied at the end of the chapter for quick and easy reference, and a complete glossary of terms appears at the end of the book.

Review boxes contain very straightforward questions that cover the most basic material of each chapter. Students should be able to answer these questions directly from the text and must master these basics before they will be able to comprehend the more abstract concepts that are at the heart of economics.

E-conomics boxes are brief snippetts which are designed to give a glimpse of what is coming to be known as the "new economy."

Added Dimension boxes identify material that is either general information or supplementary material that we hope adds a little colour to the student's reading.

Self-Test question boxes have been integrated into the text and are scattered at important points throughout each chapter. Their purpose is to give students immediate feedback on how well they understand the more abstract concept(s) discussed. In doing this, we have tried to establish what we believe to be a minimum standard of comprehension that all students should strive to achieve. Students can check their own progress by comparing their answers with those in the Answer Key, which is included with the book.

Study Guide Features

We believe that answering questions and doing problems should be an active *part of the learning process*. For this reason, we chose to integrate a complete **Study Guide** under this same cover. Thus a Study Guide section, with pages screened in colour, immediately follows each chapter. We were careful to write the questions in the Study Guide to cover all the material, but *only* the material, found in the text itself. We have chosen a colourful, user-friendly design for the Study Guide sections, and we hope this will encourage significant student participation.

Within each Study Guide section we begin with **Chapter Highlights** which are designed to provide the student with a quick checklist of the main points of each chapter. In a similar vein, **New Glossary Terms** and **Key Equations** are presented next. These are followed by **Study Tips** which are our suggestions to the students for managing the material in the chapter.

Next, we reinforce the Review Questions and Glossary boxes from the text with a true–false section entitled **Are You Sure?** These questions obviously require students to make a choice, but if they choose false, they are required to explain why. Then comes a series of multiple-choice questions entitled **Choose the Best**. These questions increase in difficulty and in number of optional answers offered as the student works through the twenty questions. Next, where appropriate, is a section of **Simple Calculations** which are designed to ensure that the student is able to handle the basic numerical questions. A number of other longer questions follow in a section entitled **Problems**.

The **Translations** section requires students to translate a graph or other mathematical material into words or to translate words into a mathematical presentation. Finally, comes the **Key Problem**. This problem encompasses the fundamental idea or ideas in the chapter. Students are then given the opportunity to really test their understanding with an additional, very similar, problem called **More of the Same**.

The answers to all the Study Guide questions, as well as answers to the self-test questions found in the text itself, can be found in the **Answer Key**, included with the text under a separate cover. We chose to provide the answers in this way so that the student can have the text open to the question page and the Key open to the answer at the same time.

The **Unanswered Questions** in the Study Guide section contain a number of short essay, analytical, and numerical problems for which there are no answers in the Key. Instructors therefore have the option of using these questions for exams, out-of-class assignments, or other types of tests. The answers to the analytical and numerical questions are found in the *Instructor's Manual to accompany Principles of Microeconomics and Principles of Macroeconomics*.

Finally, the **Web-Based Activities** are included to give students the opportunity to apply what they've learned through the exciting and dynamic World Wide Web. The Web addresses were correct at the time of printing, but these may change; changes to any addresses will be posted on McGraw-Hill Ryerson's *Principles of Microeconomics* Web site.

Supplements For Instructors

Instructor's Manual

There are three parts to each chapter of the *Instructor's Manual*. First is a brief overview of the chapter, with some rationale for the topics included. Second is a description of how we think the material found in the chapter is best presented. Between the two of us, we have taught the micro principles course over two hundred times, and we pass on helpful hints gained from this extensive experience to instructors who may not have been at it so long. More-experienced instructors who have found a comfortable groove will simply ignore these suggestions.

The third part contains the answers to the analytical and numerical questions that appear in the Unanswered Questions section of the Study Guide as well as answers to the Web Based Activities. We have not included answers to the essay questions of this section because a basic answer can be found directly in the text and a more sophisticated answer would become rather subjective.

Computerized Test Bank

Much effort went into writing the *Test Bank to accompany Principles of Microeconomics* in order to ensure that the questions cover all topics in the textbook, but *only* those topics. Questions are written in plain English and in true question form to minimize any misunderstanding by students as to what is being asked. There are approximately one hundred questions per chapter. They come in the order of the topics covered in the chapter and include a mixture of both four- and five-answer questions. In addition, certain clearly marked questions are repeats of multiple-choice questions from the Study Guide section. This gives the instructor the option of including multiple-choice questions on an exam that students have, or have not, seen before.

Instructors receive special software that lets them design their own examinations from the test bank questions. It also lets instructors edit test items and add their own questions to the test bank. A printed version of the test bank is available to instructors upon request.

PowerPoint® Presentations

Instructors who adopt *Principles of Microeconomics*, Third Edition, receive, on request, a PowerPoint presentation package. This package has been significantly improved and includes a complete file of PowerPoint "slides" for each chapter, as well as a PowerPoint Viewer to display and print this material from the instructor's computer. Each file has several slides relating to the chapter, including some graphs and figures from the text.

Acknowledgements

We wish to thank the following economists who participated in the formal review process during the creation and revision of this book: Terri Anderson, Fanshawe College; Doug Beatty, Lambton College; Dale Box, University College of the Fraser Valley; Larry Brown, Selkirk College; Tom Chambers, Canadore College; Jean Guy Cormier, New Brunswick Community College; Brian Coulter, University College of the Fraser Valley; Doug Curtis, Trent University; Fidelis Ezeala-Harrison, University of New Brunswick—Saint John; Greg Flanagan, Mt. Royal College; Ron Gallagher, New Brunswick Community College; Bill Gallivan, University College of Cape Breton; Barbara Gardner, SAIT; Anthony Goss, Niagara College; David Gray, University of Ottawa; Dean Haggerty, Sir Sandford Fleming College; Ibrahim Hayani, Seneca College; James Hnatchuk, Champlain College; Gordon Holmes, Mohawk College; Lionel Ifill, Algonquin College; Peter Jacobs, Champlain College; Witold Jankowski, Lakehead University; Cheryl Jenkins, John Abbot College; Peter Kaglik, Red River Community College; Susan Kamp, University of Alberta; Zafar Kayani, University of Northern British Columbia; Peter Kennedy, Simon Fraser University; Hans Krueger, Loyalist College; Ivo Kvarda, Confederation College; Joe Luchetti, Sault College; Peter MacDonald, Cambrian College; Sharam Manouchehri, Grant MacEwan College; Chris McDonnell, Malaspina University College; Mark Moore, University of British Columbia; Martin Moy, University College of Cape Breton; Paul Pieper, Humber College; Wimal

Rankaduwa, University of Prince Edward Island; Neil Ridler, University of New Brunswick – Saint John; Chris Sarlo, Nipissing University; Joe Selby, College of the Rockies; James Sentance, University of Prince Edward Island; Cal Shaw, George Brown College; William Sinkevitch, St. Clair College; Ken Strand, Simon Fraser University; Warren Wain, Keewatin Community College; Lewis Soroka, Brock University; Bob Weil, Sir Sandford Fleming College; and Ian Wilson, St. Lawrence College.

We would like to acknowledge our colleagues in the Economics Department of Capilano College—Nigel Amon, Ken Moak, Mahak Yaseri, and Zu Fromm—for their encouragement and vigilance in spotting errors and omissions in the first edition. Numerous colleagues in other departments also gave us encouragement, and sometimes praise, which is greatly appreciated. Jim Walker provided valuable assistance with the Web-Based Activities and with many of the questions.

The administration at the college were very accommodating and supportive, while the staff of the computer services and social sciences division were always helpful.

Most particularly, we wish to acknowledge the help and support of Ron Doleman, our editorial consultant. Ron provided the original framework for revisions to the third edition and provided the follow up work and encouragement necessary to ensure that this framework became reality. He was persistent in putting forth needed changes while, at the same time, respecting the integrity of the authors' work. We greatly appreciate his efforts.

Erin Moore's editing has been superb, while Maria Chu and Kelly Dickson at McGraw-Hill Ryerson offered excellent professional skills, and Lynn Fisher once again demonstrated her faith in our work which is greatly appreciated.

In the end, of course, whatever errors or confusions remain are our responsibility.

Finally, we wish to acknowledge the help and support of our families, who patiently and good-humouredly took over many additional tasks in order to provide us with "free" time. We are deeply moved by this support.

McGraw-Hill Ryerson **Online Learning Centre**

McGraw-Hill Ryerson offers you an online resource that combines the best content with the flexibility and power of the Internet. Organized by chapter, the Sayre/Morris Online Learning Centre (OLC) offers the following features to enhance your learning and understanding of Economics.

- Online Quizzing
- Web Links
- Microsoft® PowerPoint® Presentations
- Internet Application Questions

By connecting to the "real world" through the OLC, you will enjoy a dynamic and rich source of current information that will help you get more from your course and improve your chances for success, both in economics and in the future.

For the Instructor

DOWNLOADABLE SUPPLEMENTS

All key supplements are available, password-protected for instant access!

WEB COMMUNITY

Access to a dynamic brain trust of resources, information, ideas and opportunities coming from faculty! Content includes such topics as current events, Web links, lecture suggestions and more, all discipline-specific! Visit www.communities.mcgrawhill.ca

PAGEOUT

Create your own course Web page for free, quickly and easily. Your professionally designed Web site links directly to OLC material, allows you to post a class syllabus, offers an online gradebook, and much more! Visit www.pageout.net

A New Way to Deliver

For the Student

ONLINE QUIZZING

Do you understand the material? You'll know after taking an Online Quiz! Try the Multiple Choice and True/False questions for each chapter. They're auto-graded with feedback and you have the option to send results directly to faculty.

WEB LINKS

This section references various Web sites including all company Web sites linked from the text.

MICROSOFT® POWERPOINT® PRESENTATIONS

View and download presentations created for each text. Great for pre-class preparation and post-class review.

INTERNET APPLICATION QUESTIONS

Go online to learn how companies use the Internet in their day-to-day activities. Answer questions based on current organization Web sites and strategies.

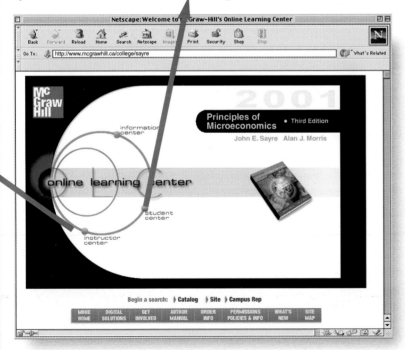

Your Internet companion to the most exciting educational tools on the Web!

The Online Learning Centre can be found at:
www.mcgrawhill.ca/college/sayre

EDUCATIONAL CONTENT

Economics Toolkit

Some students take economics because it is a requirement for a program they have chosen or a degree that they are working toward. Some are interested in a career in business, and taking economics seems like a natural choice. Some even take it because they think that they might like it. Whatever might be the reason you chose to take it, we are glad that you did and hope that you will not be disappointed. Economics is a challenging discipline to learn, but it is also, potentially, one of the most rewarding courses you will ever take. The logic and analysis used in economics is very powerful, and successfully working your way through the principles of economics over the next semester will do for your mind what a serious jogging program will do for your body. Bon voyage!

The Canadian Reality

The Land

Canada is a huge country—in fact, it is the second-largest country on this planet. It contains 7 percent of the world's land mass. It stretches 5600 kilometres from the Atlantic to the Pacific Oceans and encompasses six time zones. Ontario alone, which is the second-largest province after Quebec, is larger than Pakistan, or Turkey, or Chile, or France, or the United Kingdom. Canada's ten provinces range in size from tiny Prince Edward Island to Quebec, which is nearly 240 times as large. In addition, its three territories–the Northwest Territories, the Yukon, and the recently formed Nunavut—demand that we describe this country's reach as from sea to sea to sea.

Within Canada there are at least six major mountain ranges: the Torngats, Appalachians, and Laurentians in the East, and the Mackenzie, Rocky, and Coast ranges in the West, each of which rivals the European Alps in size and grandeur. In addition, Canada has vast quantities of fresh water—9 percent of the world's total—in tens of thousands of lakes and numerous rivers, of which the St. Lawrence and the Mackenzie are the largest.

Canada is richly endowed in natural resources, including gas, oil, gold, silver, copper, iron ore, nickel, potash, uranium, zinc, fish, timber, and, as mentioned above, water—lots of fresh water. The conclusion is inescapable: Canada is a big, beautiful, and rich country.

The People

The word *Canada* comes from the Huron–Iroquois word meaning *village*. In a sense this is very appropriate, because big as the nation is geographically, it is small in terms of population. Its 30 million people make up only 0.5 percent of the world's population. In fact, there are more people in California or in greater Tokyo than there are in the whole of Canada. Interestingly, Canada's population growth rate, at 1.1 percent, is the highest among the G-8 countries of the world primarily because of Canada's high rate of immigration. Thirty-six percent of Canadians live in the province of Ontario, and 25 percent in Quebec. On the other hand, Prince Edward Island has a population of only 140 000, which is less than that of the cities of Sherbrooke, Quebec, or North Vancouver, B.C.

Despite the popular images of the small Maritime fishing village, the lonely Prairie grain farmer, or the remote B.C. logger, Canada is, in fact, an urban nation. A full 77 percent of Canadians live in what Statistics Canada calls "urban" areas. There are four Canadian metropolitan areas with populations of over one million: Toronto, with 4.3 million; Montreal, 3.3 million; Vancouver, 1.8 million; and Ottawa–Hull, 1.1 million. It is also true that the vast majority of the 30 million Canadians live in a narrow band stretching along the border with the United States, which, incidentally, is the longest unguarded border in the world.

Approximately one half of the Canadian population of 30 million are active in the labour force. The labour-force participation rate for males is 73 percent, and for females, 58 percent.

Multiculturalism

Within this vast, thinly populated country there is a truly diverse, multicultural mix of people. This reality was officially recognized in 1988 when Parliament passed the Multiculturalism Act.

There are two official languages in Canada, yet 18 percent of Canadians speak a language other than English or French. In fact, sixty languages are spoken in this country. In each year of the 1990s, more than 200 000 new immigrants arrived in Canada. Over 15 percent of all Canadians are first-generation immigrants. In both Toronto and Vancouver, over one half of the students in the public school system are from non–English-speaking homes. There are over 100 minority-language publications in Toronto, and Vancouver has three daily Chinese-language newspapers.

Canada's First Nations people number 533 000 (1.8 percent of the total population), and almost half of them live in Ontario.

Government

Canada is a constitutional monarchy with a democratic parliament made up of the House of Commons, with 301 elected members, and the Senate, with 104 appointed members. In addition to Parliament, the other two decision-making divisions of the federal government are the cabinet, comprised of the prime minister and his or her twenty-five (or so) ministers and their departments, and the judiciary, which includes the Supreme, Federal, and Tax courts.

Just as there are two official languages in this country, Canada has two systems of civil law—one uncodified and based on common law in English Canada, and the other as codified civil law in Quebec. Canada's constitution, the Canadian Charter of Rights and Freedoms, came into being in 1982, a full 115 years after Confederation created the country in 1867.

The fact that Canada is a confederation of ten provinces results in the federal government sharing responsibilities with the provinces. For example, while the federal government has jurisdiction in national defence, international trade, immigration, banking, criminal law, fisheries, transportation, and communications, the provinces have responsibility for education, property rights, health, and natural resources. Inevitably, issues arise from time to time that do not fit neatly into any one of these categories, with the result that federal–provincial disputes are a continuous part of the Canadian reality.

Canada the Good

Most Canadians are well aware that they live in a good country. But perhaps many don't realize just how good. The average household income is currently over $54 000, which puts the Canadian living standard sixth in the world behind that of the United States, Switzerland, Luxembourg, Germany, and Japan.

The United Nations maintains a "Human Development Index" that uses other factors in addition to average income levels, including crime rates, life spans, income distribution, and the presence of human rights. This index ranks Canada as the number one nation in the world in which to live. One reason for this high ranking is that Canadian governments spent $1700 per person on health care (in 1994, a representative year), which is nearly 10 percent of the country's gross domestic product (GDP), a measure of the total output of all goods and services.

Nearly 65 percent of Canadians own their homes, well over 90 percent are literate, and 25 percent of all Canadians have access to the Internet. All three of these statistics are among the highest in the world.

Canada the Odd

Canada *is* a good country in which to be born or to have emigrated to. However, it does have its oddities. In 1965, 98 years after its "birth," it was decided that Canada really should have a national flag. The Parliamentary selection committee set up to choose one received no less than two thousand designs, and the flag debate was acrimonious, to say the least. Today, however, most Canadians seem quite comfortable with the Maple Leaf. The English-language lyrics of Canada's national anthem, "O Canada," were formally approved only in 1975. Canada adopted the metric system of measurement in the 1970s, but the imperial system is still in wide use; for example, Statistics Canada still reports the breadth of this country in miles, we still sell lengths of wood as "2 × 4s" (inches), and football fields are still 110 yards long.

In this bilingual country, it is odd to note that there are more Manitobans who speak Cree than British Columbians who speak French. In this affluent country of ours, it also interesting to note that 4 percent of Canadian homes are heated exclusively by burning wood. Canada has an official animal—the beaver.

On a more serious note, it is a sad fact that the trade of many goods, and even some services, between any one province and the United States is freer than trade between provinces. There is an interesting history concerning trade patterns in North America. At the time of Confederation, trade patterns on this continent were mostly north–south. The Maritimes traded with the New England states, Quebec with New York, Ontario with the Great Lakes states to its south, and the West Coast traded with California. Canada's first prime minister, John A. Macdonald, was also elected as its third, after having lost his first re-election bid, on the basis of a campaign promise known as the National Policy. This policy had three aspects: a) to build a railway to the West Coast and coax British Columbia into joining Canada; b) to offer free land to new immigrants on the prairies in order to populate this area; and c) to force trade patterns into a east–west mode by erecting a tariff wall against U.S. imports. British Columbia did join Confederation; people did come to Manitoba, Saskatchewan, and Alberta; and the pattern of trade did become more east–west.

So was the National Policy a success? Some would argue yes, pointing out that it built a nation and that just possibly Canada, as we know it, would not exist today without it. Others aren't so sure and would argue that it set back Canada's development by encouraging and protecting new, less efficient industries through the creation of a branch-plant economy. This occurred because American firms that had previously exported to Canada simply jumped over the tariff walls and established Canadian branch plants. This in turn promoted Canadian regionalism and aggravated relations between regions because both the West and the Maritimes felt that most of the economic benefits of the National Policy favoured central Canada.

In any case, as a result of the North American Free Trade Agreement (NAFTA) of 1992, trade with the United States (and Mexico) is now without tariffs and north–south trade patterns are re-emerging. Historically, Canadian policy has come full circle. However, the interprovincial trade barriers between provinces, which were built piece by piece over 100 years, still remain.

The Economy

Canada is among the ten largest economies in the world, despite its small population. In 1999, Canada's GDP was $949 billion. This figure can be broken down as illustrated in **Table T.1**.

TABLE T.1

Category	Amount ($ billion)
Personal expenditures	554
Investment spending	167
Government spending	200
Exports	412
Less imports	(384)
Total GDP	949

Source: Adapted from Statistics Canada, CANSIM database, matrix 6548.

The provincial breakdown of the 1998 GDP figure of $896 billion is shown in **Table T.2**.

TABLE T.2

Province	Population (millions)	GDP ($ billions)	GDP per capita ($ thousands)
Newfoundland	0.54	11.3	20.7
Prince Edward Island	0.14	2.9	21.2
Nova Scotia	0.94	20.7	22.1
New Brunswick	0.75	17.2	22.8
Quebec	7.3	193.2	26.4
Ontario	11.4	371.9	32.7
Manitoba	1.1	29.9	26.3
Saskatchewan	1.0	28.8	28.1
Alberta	2.9	105.0	36.1
British Columbia	4.0	110.9	27.7
Yukon	0.3	1.1	34.2
Northwest Territories (pre-Nunavut)	0.4	2.5	26.3

Source: Adapted from Statistics Canada, CANSIM database, matrices 9015–9026.

This table illustrates the wide disparity in average incomes between provinces, from a low of $20 700 per person in Newfoundland to a high of $36 100 in Alberta.

In most years, the economy grows and the GDP figure rises. To accurately compare growth in GDP, however, we need to use a common set of prices so that a simple rise in prices isn't confused with an actual increase in the output of goods and services. Using *real* GDP figures, which corrects for any inflation, accomplishes this. **Table T.3** looks at some recent real GDP figures, using 1992 prices.

TABLE T.3

Year	Real GDP ($ billion)	Increase ($ billion)	% Increase
1995	769	—	—
1996	782	13	1.7
1997	813	31	4.0
1998	838	25	3.1
1999	873	35	4.2

Source: Adapted from Statistics Canada, CANSIM database, matrix 6549.

Next, let's look at an industry breakdown of Canada's GDP in **Figure T.1**.

FIGURE T.1 Canada's GDP at Factor Costs, 1999

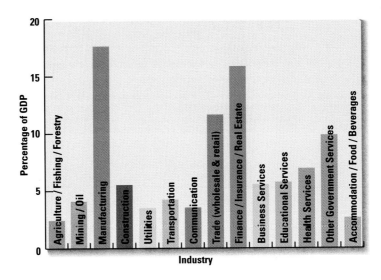

Source: Adapted from Statistics Canada, CANSIM database, matrix 4677.

This information is helpful in many ways. For example, it is certainly time to put to rest the idea that Canada is a resource-based economy and that Canadians are simply "hewers of wood and drawers of water," as many of us were taught in school. In fact, agriculture/fishing/forestry and mining/oil make up less than 7 percent of our economy's GDP. Another figure that makes the same point is that only 5.6 percent of working Canadians are in primary industries, which is dramatically down from 13 percent a quarter of a century ago.

In contrast, one can marshal an argument that Canada is a quite sophisticated and technologically advanced economy. For example, it is not generally recognized that Canada was the world's third nation to go into space with the Alouette I satellite in 1962. Canadian industries pioneered long-distance pipeline technology, and Canada is a world leader in several areas of aviation, including turboprop, turbofan, and fire-fighting aircraft, not to mention the well-known Canadarm used on space shuttles. Canada is also a world leader in commercial submarine technology, and it routinely maintains one of the world's longest and most efficient railway systems. One can also point to many outstanding Canadian companies that are truly world leaders in technology and performance, including Bombardier in transportation equipment, Ballard Power in fuel cell technology, SNC Lavalin in aluminum plant design, Northern Telecom in cellular communications, Trizec Hahn in real estate development, and Magna International in automobile parts manufacturing.

Exports: The Engine that Drives the Economy

Exports are a fundamental part of the Canadian economy. Over 40 percent of its GDP is exported, which makes Canada one of the world's greatest trading nations. Exports to the United States alone directly support over 1.5 million Canadian jobs, and a $1 billion increase in exports translates into 11 000 new jobs. Again, contrary to historical wisdom, only 20 percent of Canadian exports are resources—this figure was 40 percent a quarter of a century ago.

Figure T.2 breaks down the $412 billion of Canadian exports in 1999 into nine categories.

FIGURE T.2 Canada's Exports by Category, 1999

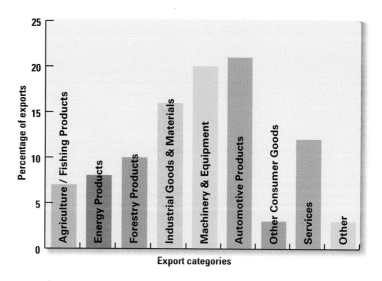

Source: Adapted from Statistics Canada, CANSIM database, matrices 3685 and 3651.

A Mixed Economy

As we enter the twenty-first century, the market system dominates most of the world's economies, and Canada is no exception to this. Yet, government also plays a big role in our economy. For example, in the fiscal year 1998–99 the three levels of government collected $392 billion in tax revenue, which represents over 44 percent of Canada's 1999 GDP. **Figure T.3** shows the sources of this revenue.

FIGURE T.3 Tax Revenue for All Canadian Governments, 1999

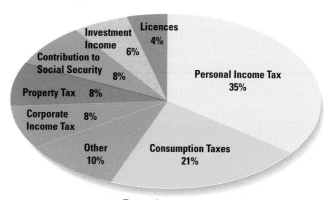

Source: Adapted from Statistics Canada, CANSIM database, matrix 3315.

The largest single source of the government's tax revenue, 35 percent, was personal income taxes. Consumption taxes include, most significantly, the GST (goods and services tax) and the PST (provincial sales tax) as well as gasoline, alcohol, and tobacco taxes, customs tax, and gaming income. These indirect taxes accounted for 21 percent of total revenue. Thus we can see that a majority of the government's tax revenue comes from individual Canadians in the form of direct income taxes or consumption taxes.

And how does government spend its nearly $392 billion of tax revenue? **Figure T.4** shows us.

FIGURE T.4 Expenditures by All Canadian Governments, 1999

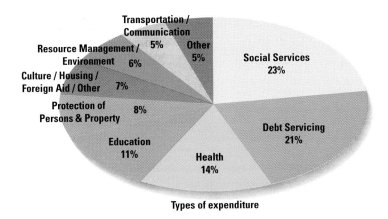

Source: Adapted from Statistics Canada, CANSIM database, matrix 3315.

Here we see that government's largest single category, which is 23 percent of spending, was on payments to individuals. The lion's share of this expenditure, 68 percent, was social assistance (welfare) payments. Thus we see that a large percentage of spending by government is an attempt to direct income to poorer Canadians. Since it is all Canadians who pay for most of these expenditures, we can see that the government is actively involved in *transferring* income from higher-income to lower-income families and individuals. This income distribution role is seen by many Canadians as an important function of government.

On the other hand, some Canadians take the view that government has gone too far in its interventionist role and yearn for less government involvement in the economy. They often point to the United States as an example of a economy in which both welfare, unemployment, and pension payments to individuals and direct government aid to poor regions of the country are lower. The difference in the general approach of the two governments may well lie in historical differences in the attitudes of Canadians and Americans toward government. Over the years, Canadians, by and large, have trusted governments to act in their best interest and been more tolerant of government attempts at income redistribution. Americans, on the other hand, have a history of being suspicious of big government and have repeatedly rejected attempts to expand its role. The recent rejection in the United States of attempts to implement a national health-care policy is an example. Another is the Canadian government's direct aid to cultural endeavours, including the funding of a national television and radio network, while no such efforts exist in the United States.

Interest on the national debt was the second-largest category of spending, at 21 percent. Over the years, government has borrowed over $500 billion to finance budget deficits, and the interest paid on this borrowing totalled $44 billion in 1999. Most Canadians believe that expenditures on health (the universal medical plan) and education make up government's largest spending categories. However, though these two are large—a combined total of 25 percent—they rank only third and fourth. The fifth category, protection of persons and property, includes expenditures on police, fire departments, the court system, and prisons. The sixth category includes a host of items such as culture (the Canada Council), housing, foreign affairs, immigration, labour, and research.

This completes our brief look at the Canadian economic reality. We hope that it has helped to fill in some of the gaps in your knowledge of the country. We are confident that you will come to know your country much better after a thorough grounding in the principles of economics, for, in a very real sense, economics is about understanding and improving on what we already know.

Graphing Reality

Let's face it: a lot of students hate graphs. For them a picture is not worth a thousand words. It may even be true that they seem to understand some economic concepts just fine until the instructor draws a graph on the board. All of a sudden, they lose confidence and start to question what they previously thought they knew. For these students, graphs are not the solution, but the problem. This section is designed to help those students overcome this difficulty. For those other, more fortunate, students who can handle graphs and know that they are used to illustrate concepts, a quick reading of this section will help reinforce their understanding.

It's probably true to say that if an idea can be expressed clearly and precisely with words, then graphs become an unnecessary luxury. The trouble is that from time to time, economists find themselves at a loss for words and see no other way of getting a certain point across except with the use of a graph. On the other hand, by themselves, graphs cannot explain everything; they need to be accompanied by a verbal explanation. In other words, graphs are not a substitute for words, but a complement. The words accompanied by a picture can often give us a much richer understanding of economic concepts and happenings.

Graphing a Single Variable

The graphing of a single variable is reasonably straightforward. Often economists want to concentrate on a single economic variable, such as Canada's exports, or consumers' income, or the production of wine in Canada. In some cases they want to look at the composition of that variable, say different categories of exports. In other cases they are interested in seeing how that variable changed over a period of time, say total exports for each of the years 1992 through 1999. In the first instance, we would be looking at a *cross-section*; in the second instance we are looking at a *time series*.

Cross-Sectional Graphs

One popular way of showing cross-sectional data is in the form of a **pie chart**. Figure T.5, for instance, shows the composition of Canada's exports for 1999 in terms of the type of goods or services that Canada sells abroad.

FIGURE T.5A Composition of Canadian Exports, 1999

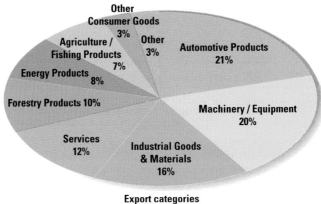

Export categories

The size of each slice indicates the relative size of each category of export. But the picture by itself is not always enough. We have added the percentage of total exports that each type represents. Notice, however, that there are no dollar amounts for the categories.

Alternatively, the same information could be presented in the form of a **bar graph**, as in Figure T.5B.

FIGURE T.5B Composition of Canadian Exports, 1999

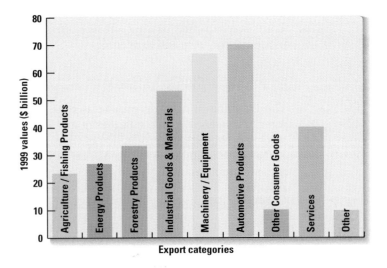

Looking at the bar graph, you'll notice that it's possible to estimate the dollar amounts, but it would be difficult to know the percentage share of the category without a lot of tedious calculation.

Time-Series Graphs

Time-series data can also be presented in the form of a bar graph. **Figure T.6A** shows a bar graph of how the dollar amount of Canada's total exports (ignoring its composition) has changed over a six-year period.

FIGURE T.6A Total Canadian Exports, 1992–99

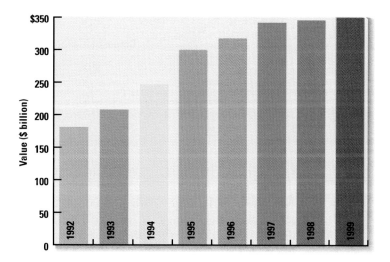

The same information can be presented in a **line graph**, as is done in **Figure T.6B**.

FIGURE T.6B Total Canadian Exports, 1992–99

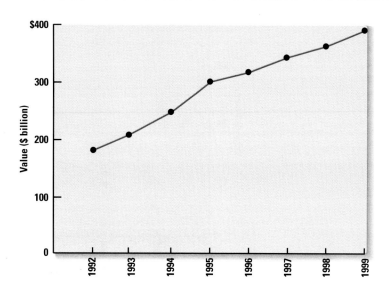

Note that, in both cases, the years (time) are shown on the horizontal axis; early years are on the left, and later years on the right. This is because graphs are always read from left to right.

Graphing Two Variables

Things get a little trickier when we want to deal with two variables at the same time. For instance, suppose we want to relate Canada's disposable income, which is the total take-home pay of all Canadians, and the amount spent on consumer goods (these numbers are in billions and are hypothetical). One obvious way to do this is with a table, as is done in **Table T.4**.

TABLE T.4

Year	Disposable Income	Spending on Consumer Goods
1995	$100	$ 80
1996	120	98
1997	150	125
1998	160	134
1999	200	170

A time-series graph, using the same data, is presented in **Figure T.7**. You can see that the two lines in Figure T.7 seem to be closely related, and that is useful information. However, to more clearly bring out the relationship we could plot them against one another. But if you look again at Table T.4, you will see that there are really three different variables involved: the time (six years), the values of disposable income, and the values of spending. However, it is very difficult to plot three variables, all three against each other, on a two-dimensional sheet of paper.

FIGURE T.7 Disposable Income and Spending on Consumer Goods, 1995–99 (hypothetical numbers)

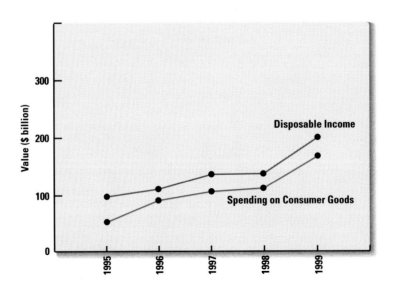

Instead, in **Figure T.8**, we will put disposable income on the horizontal axis (also called the X-axis), and consumer spending on the vertical axis (also called the Y-axis) and indicate time with written notation. There is a rule about which variable goes on which axis, but we will leave that for later chapters.

Next, we need to decide on a scale for each of the two axes. There is no particular rule about doing this, but just a little experience will enable you to develop good judgement about selecting these values. We have chosen to give each square on the axes the value of $20. This can be seen in Figure T.8.

FIGURE T.8: Spending on Consumer Goods

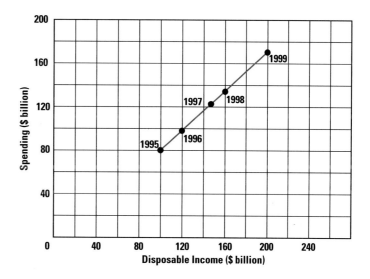

We started plotting our line using the 1995 data. In that year disposable income was $100 and consumer spending was $80. Starting at the origin (where the vertical and horizontal axes meet), which has an assigned value of zero, we move five squares to the right. Now from an income of $100, we move up vertically four squares, arriving at a value of $80 for consumer spending. This is our first plot (or point). We do the same for 1996. First, we find a value of $120 on the horizontal (disposable income) axis and a value of $98 (just less than five squares) on the vertical axis. Where these two meet gives us our second point to plot. We do the same for the three next years, and join up the five points with a line. Notice that the relationship between income levels and consumer spending plots as a straight line.

Direct and Inverse Relationships

Next, if you look back at Table T.4, you will see that disposable income and consumer spending rise together over time. When two variables move together in this way, we say that there is a **direct** relationship between them. Such a direct relationship appears as an upward-sloping line. On the other hand, if you see that two variables move in opposite directions, so that as one variable increases, the other variable decreases, we say there is an **inverse** relationship between them. In that case plotting the two variables together would result in a downward-sloping line.

(When we talk about upward- and downward-sloping, by the way, remember that we are reading the graphs from left to right.)

One last point: the income–consumer-spending line in Figure T.8 is a straight line. There is no reason this has to always be the case. Some data might plot as a straight line, and other data might be non-linear when plotted (as in Figure T.7). Either, of course, could still be downward- or upward-sloping.

Measuring the Slope of a Straight Line

As you proceed with this course, you will find that you need to go a bit further than merely being able to plot a curve—in economics, by the way, all lines are described as curves, whether they are linear or non-linear. You will also need to know just how steep or how shallow the line is that you have plotted. That is, you will need to measure the slope of the curve. What the slope in effect shows is how much one variable changes in relation to the other variable as we move along a curve. In graphic terms, this means measuring the change in the variable shown on the vertical axis (known as the **rise**), divided by the change in the variable shown on the horizontal axis (known as the **run**). The rise and the run are illustrated, for our disposable income/consumer spending example, in **Figure T.9**.

FIGURE T.9 Rise Over Run

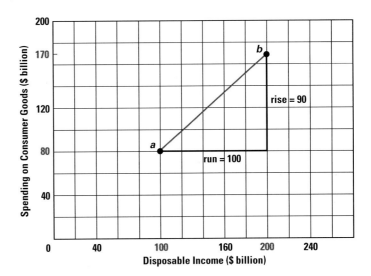

Notice that as we move from point *a* to point *b*, consumer spending increases by 90 (from 80 to 170). This is the amount of the rise. Looking along the horizontal axis, we see that disposable income increases by 100 (from 100 to 200). This is the amount of the run.

In general, we can say:

$$\text{Slope} = \frac{\text{Rise}}{\text{Run}} = \frac{\text{Change in the value on the vertical axis}}{\text{Change in the value on the horizontal axis}}$$

Specifically, the slope of our line is therefore equal to:

$$\frac{+90}{+100} = 0.9$$

Figure T.10 shows four other curves, two upward-sloping and two downward-sloping, with an indication for each on how to calculate the various slopes. In each case we measure the slope by moving from point *a* to point *b*.

FIGURE T.10 Four Different Slopes

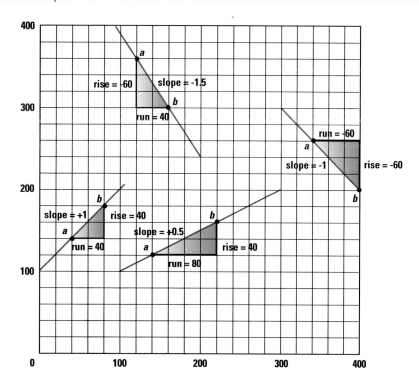

The Slope of Curves

In measuring the slope of a straight line, it doesn't really matter where on the line we choose to measure it, the slope is constant throughout its length. But this is not true of a curve. The slope of a curve will have different values at every point along its length. However, it is possible to measure the slope at any point by drawing a straight line that touches the curve at that point. Such a line is called a tangent to the curve. Figure T.11, for instance, shows a curve that has a positive slope (the upward-sloping portion), a zero slope (the top of the curve), and a negative slope (the downward-sloping portion). We have drawn in three tangents at different positions along the curve. From these straight lines we can calculate the value of the slope at each of these points.

FIGURE T.11 The Slope of a Curve

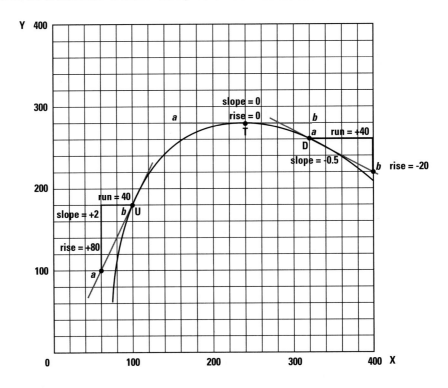

At point U, the curve is rising quite steeply. So what is its slope? Well, its slope at this point is the same as the value of the slope of the straight line tangent. As we already know:

The slope of the straight line is: $\dfrac{\text{Rise}}{\text{Run}}$

At point U, this is equal to: $\dfrac{+80}{+40} = +2$

And this is also the value of the slope of the curve at point U.

At point T, the tangent is a horizontal line, which, by definition, does not rise or fall. The rise/run at this point therefore is equal to 0. Finally, at point D, both the curve and the tangent are downward sloping, implying a negative slope. Its value is calculated, as before, as rise/run, which equals $-20/40$ or -0.5.

Equations For A Straight Line

In economics, graphs are a very important and useful way to present information. Thus you will find the pages of most economics books liberally sprinkled with graphs. But there are other equally useful ways of presenting the same data. One way is in the form of an algebraic equation. You will often find it very useful to be able to translate a graph into algebra. In this short section we will show how to do this. Just to keep things simple we will restrict our attention to straight line graphs.

In order to find the equation for any straight line you need only two pieces of information: the slope of the line and the value of the Y-intercept. You already know how to calculate the value of the slope. The value of the Y-intercept is simply the value at which the line crosses Y (the vertical axis). In general, the algebraic expression for a straight line is given as:

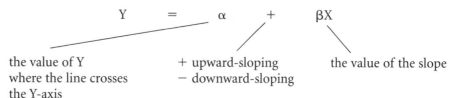

$$Y \quad = \quad \alpha \quad + \quad \beta X$$

the value of Y
where the line crosses
the Y-axis

+ upward-sloping
− downward-sloping

the value of the slope

For instance in **Figure T.12**, line 1 has a slope of +1 (the line is upward-sloping and therefore has a positive slope and rises by 10 units for every run of 10 units). The line crosses the Y-axis at a value of 50. The equation for line 1 therefore is:

$$Y \quad = \quad 50 \quad + \quad (1)X$$

Armed with this equation, we could figure out the value of Y, for any value of X. For example, when X (along the horizontal axis) has a value of 40, Y must be equal to:

$$Y \quad = \quad 50 \quad + \quad 40 \quad = \quad 90.$$

You can verify this in Figure T.12.

In addition, we can work out values of X and Y which are not shown on the graph. For example, when X equals 200, Y equals: 50 + 200 = 250.

FIGURE T.12 Equations for Straight Lines

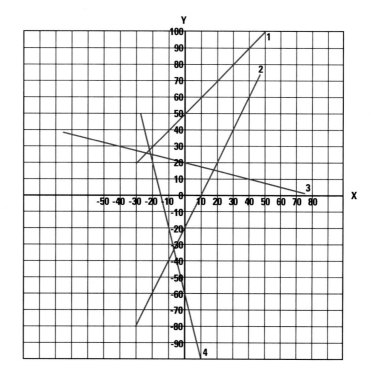

Let us work out the equations for the other lines shown in Figure T.12. Line 2 is also upward-sloping but is steeper than line 1 and has a slope of $+2$ (it rises by 20 for every run of 10). Its intercept however is in the negative area of the Y axis and crosses at the value of -20. The equation for line 2 then is:

$$Y \quad = \quad -20 \quad + \quad 2X$$

Again, you can check that this is correct by putting in a value for X, finding the corresponding value of Y, and looking on the graph to see if it is correct. For instance, when X has a value of 40, the equation tells us that:

$$Y \quad = \quad -20 \quad + \quad 2(40) \quad = \quad 60.$$

You can confirm in Figure T.12 that this is indeed the case.

In contrast, line 3 has a negative slope of 0.25 and a Y-intercept at 20. Its equation therefore is:

$$Y \quad = \quad 20 \quad - \quad 0.25X$$

Finally, line 4 has the equation:

$$Y \quad = \quad -60 \quad - \quad 4X$$

Graphs and Logic

There are some potential problems in illustrating data with graphs. For example, the relationship between income and consumer spending in the earlier Table T.4 is hypothetical, since we created it to plot well on a graph. However, any real-world relationship between two variables may not be as neat and simple. Data doesn't always plot into a nice straight line. Even more seriously, we can never be totally certain of the *nature* of the relationship between the variables being graphed. There's often a great danger of implying something that's not there. You need therefore to be on guard against a number of logical fallacies. Suppose for instance that you were doing a survey of women's clothing stores across the country. Reviewing the data you have collected, you notice that there seems to be a close relationship between two particular sets of numbers: the rent paid by the owners of the store and the average price of wool jackets sold. The data is shown in **Table T.5**.

TABLE T.5

Monthly Rent (per 100 m²)	Average Jacket Price
$1500	$80
1600	90
1700	100
1800	110
1900	120
2000	130

The higher the monthly rent, the higher the price of jackets charged in that store. It seems clear, therefore, that the higher rent is the *cause* of the higher price, and the higher price is the *effect* of the higher rent. After all, the store owner must recoup these higher rent costs by charging a higher price to her customers. If you think this, then you are guilty of the logical fallacy of **reverse causality**. As you will learn in economics, although the rent of premises and product prices are indeed related, the causality is the other way around. This is because stores in certain areas can charge higher product prices because of their trendy location, and landlords charge those stores higher rents for the same reason—it is a desirable location. Higher prices, therefore, are the *cause*, and high rents the *effect*. This is not obvious, and suggests that using raw economic data without sound economic theory can lead to serious error.

A second logical fallacy is that of the **omitted variable**, which can also lead to confusion over cause and effect. **Table T.6** highlights this error. Here we see hypothetical data on rates of alcoholism and on annual income levels of individuals:

TABLE T.6

Income Levels ($)	Alcoholism (per thousand of population)
Below 10 000	40
10 000 – 19 000	35
20 000 – 29 000	30
30 000 – 29 000	25
40 000 – 49 000	20
Over 50 000	15

There certainly seems to be a very close relationship between these two variables. Presented in this form, without any commentary, one is left to wonder if low income causes alcoholism or if alcoholism is the cause of low income. Some people with low incomes may drink in order to try to escape the effects of poverty. Or is it that people who drink to excess have great difficulty in finding or keeping a good job? In truth, it is possible that neither of these views is true. Simply because two sets of data seem closely related doesn't necessarily imply that one is the cause of the other. In fact, it may well be the case that both are effects of an omitted variable. In the above example, it is possible, for example, that both high alcoholism and low incomes are the result of low educational attainment.

A third fallacy can occur when people see a cause and effect that doesn't really exist. This is known as the fallacy of **post hoc, ergo propter hoc**, which literally means after this, therefore because of this. That is to say, it is a fallacy to believe that just because one thing follows another, the one is the result of the other. For example, just because my favourite soccer team always loses whenever I go to see them doesn't mean that I am the cause of their losing!

There is a final fallacy you should guard against, a fallacy, unfortunately, that even the best of economists commit from time to time. This is the **fallacy of composition**, which is the belief that because something is true for the part, it is true for the whole. You may have noticed, for instance, that fights occasionally break out in hockey games. These fights often occur in the corners, which makes them difficult to see. The best way for the individual to get a better view is by standing, and of course when everybody stands, then most people cannot see. Thus, what is true for a single fan—standing up to see better—is not true for the whole crowd. Similarly, a teacher who suggests that in order to get a good grade, a student should sit at the front of the class is also guilty of the same kind of logical fallacy!

We hope that this little primer on Canada and on graphing has been helpful. It is now time to move on to the study of economics.

STUDY GUIDE

Are You Sure?

Indicate whether the following statements are true or false. If false, indicate why they are false.

1. Canada is the world's largest country in area and has 1 percent of the world's population.

   T or F   If false: _____

   _____

2. Ontario has the largest provincial economy, the largest provincial population and is Canada's largest province in area.

   T or F   If false: _____

   _____

3. Over 50 percent of Canada's exports are resources.

   T or F   If false: _____

   _____

4. The largest single source of government tax revenue is personal income taxes.

   T or F   If false: _____

   _____

5. Spending on social services is the largest category of spending by (all) governments in Canada.

   T or F   If false: _____

   _____

Simple Calculations

6. The following data shows the results of market research done on the latest Guns n' Butter CD. The numbers indicate the total quantity of CDs that fans would purchase at the various prices.

TABLE T.7

Price per CD ($s)	Quantity (hundreds of thousands)
$20	20
19	30
18	40
17	50
16	60
15	70
14	80

   a) Graph the table with the price on the vertical (y) axis and the quantity on the horizontal (x) axis.
   b) What is the slope of the line?
   c) What is the value of the Y-intercept?
   d) What is the equation for this line?

7. What are the values of the slopes of the four lines shown in **Figure T.13**?

8. What are the equations for the four lines shown in **Figure T.14**?

9. Graph the following equations using the same scale for each axis:
   a) $Y = 5X$ b) $Y = 20 + 2X$ c) $Y = 30 - 3X$ d) $Y = -10 + 4X$

FIGURE T.13

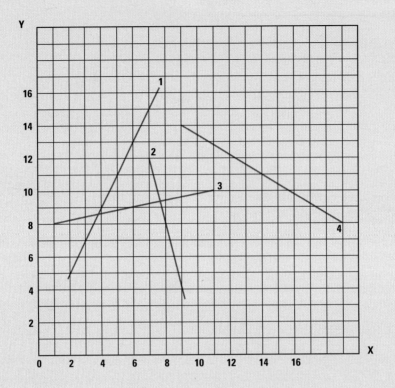

FIGURE T.14

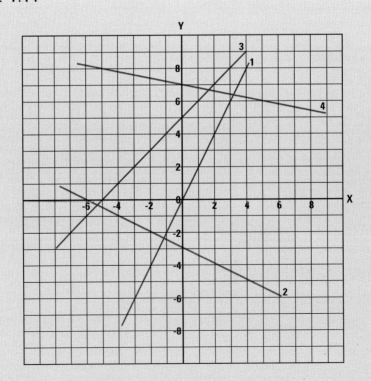

The Economic Problem

What's ahead... In this first chapter we introduce you to the study of economics and hope to arouse your curiosity about this fascinating discipline. We first look at scarcity and choice, define economics, make the distinction between macro- and microeconomics, and examine three fundamental economic questions. We then take a brief look at different types of economies and discuss the methodology and language of economics. The important role of models is emphasized with a simple example. Finally, we develop the idea of production possibilities to help you understand some of the fundamental choices facing all economies.

A QUESTION OF RELEVANCE...

Jon and Ashok are both avid soccer fans and play for local teams. They both like old movies, chess, and *Star Trek*. They are both seventeen years of age, neither has a steady girl friend, and both are vegetarians. The other thing that they have in common is that their fathers are in banking. Jon's father is the executive vice-president of customer relations for the Royal Bank in Toronto. Ashok's father is a night janitor at a branch of the Bank of India in the dock area of Bombay. All of these points are relevant in forming a mental picture of a person, but you will probably agree that a person's economic circumstances are the most relevant of all. In truth, economics is one of the most relevant subjects you can study.

W hat might you expect from a course in economics? Well, it will not help you balance your cheque book and may not be directly helpful in your choice of the right stock to buy. But the study of economics will give you a broad understanding of how a modern market economy operates and what the important things are within one. If you see yourself as a budding businessperson, the study of economics can offer some general insights that will be helpful. Yet you will not find specific tools or instructions. Economics is an academic discipline, not a self-help or how-to course. The common conception that economics is about money is only partly true. We study money, but more in the sense of what it is and the effects of different central-bank money policies, than in the sense of how to make it. The study of economics may not help you to function better in the world in any specific sense, but it will probably help you to understand better how the world functions.

Scarcity, Choice, and Technology

Economists put a great deal of emphasis on scarcity and the need to economize. Individual households face a scarcity of income and therefore must budget expenditures. Most individuals also face a scarcity of time and must somehow decide where to spend time and where to conserve it. In the same sense, an economy as a whole has limited productive resources and must allocate those resources among competing uses.

Productive resources is a term that economists use interchangeably with the term **factors of production** or, sometimes, simply "inputs." Factors of production are traditionally divided into four categories: land, labour, capital, and enterprise. **Land** is defined as anything natural such as fertile soil, deep harbours, good climate, or minerals in the ground. **Labour** refers to a broad spectrum of human effort, ranging from that of a skilled naturopathic physician to that of a construction labourer. **Capital** is made up of the tools, equipment, factories, and buildings used in the production process. Finally, **enterprise** is that very special human talent that is able to put abstract ideas into practical application.

Economists see such productive resources (the factors of production) as *scarce* in the sense that no economy has sufficient resources to be able to produce all of the goods and services that everyone wants. This is not to say that there aren't some people who would say they have all that they want, but there are millions of people who possess a seemingly endless list of wants, and millions more like them waiting to be born. Since the economy cannot produce all that everyone wants, the resources available for production are scarce, and some kind of mechanism must be put into place to *choose* what will be produced and, thereby, by implication, what will not be produced. And this is why economics is sometimes called the *science of choice*.

The term *technology* means the process of using the factors of production, in one of an infinite variety of combinations, to create physical goods and services of an endless variety of types. The output of these goods and services gives the citizens of an economy the ability to meet their wants and needs. In this sense, an economy that produces a large quantity of goods and services is more successful than one that is able to produce only a small quantity.

The success or failure of any economy depends a great deal on whether the individuals, firms, and institutions within it can make the necessary choices in order to adapt to the technological and social changes that inevitably occur over time. For example, we have seen that economies that use an economic system which relies on individual choice and enterprise (for example, Canada, the United States, Japan, and

factors of production: the productive resources that are available to an economy, categorized as land, labour, capital, and enterprise.

land: any natural resource that can be used to produce goods and services.

labour: human physical and mental effort that can be used to produce goods and services.

capital: all human-made resources that can be used to produce goods and services.

enterprise: the human resource that innovates and takes risks.

Some industry insiders say there are just too many choices for consumers shopping for music these days. Some labels have so many acts on their roster that they can't give them the proper attention.

Germany) continue to enjoy success while economies that, until recently, relied on centrally controlled systems (such as Poland, Hungary, and the USSR) faltered.

Another aspect of choice that economists consider important is that any society, much like an individual household, always has a choice between consumption now or in the future. A household could choose to consume less now and save more, enabling it to consume more in the future. Societies that consume less now can use scarce productive resources to build more capital goods with which to produce even more consumer goods and services *in the future*. We will return to this point later in this chapter.

Economics: A Definition

In the light of this discussion we can now venture a definition of economics:

> Economics is the study of the allocation of scarce productive resources to produce goods and services that are used to maximize human satisfaction in the face of unlimited human wants.

macroeconomics: the study of how the major components of an economy interact; it includes the topics of unemployment, inflation, interest rate policy, and the spending and taxation policies of government.

microeconomics: the study of the outcomes of decisions by people and firms through a focus on the supply and demand of goods, the costs of production, and market structures.

We now need to make the distinction between macro- and microeconomics. Many colleges and universities offer a separate course for each of these subjects, but this is not always the case. **Macroeconomics** is the study of how the major components of the economy, such as total investment spending or exports, interact; it includes most of the topics a beginning student would expect to find in an economics course. These include unemployment, inflation, interest rates, tax and spending policies of government, and national income determination. **Microeconomics** studies the outcomes of decisions made by people and firms and includes topics like supply and demand, the study of costs, and the nature of market structures. This distinction can be described metaphorically as a comparison between the use of a wide-angle lens and a telephoto lens of a camera. In the first instance we see the big picture. In the second instance a very small part of that big picture appears in much more detail.

Is Economics Relevant?

As we enter the twenty-first century, we find ourselves living in a society filled with a host of problems and a wide variety of issues that bombard us every day in the media and dominate many of our conversations. Will Quebec separate from the rest of Canada? Will governments reduce their spending on education, and will this drive up the cost of tuition? Are the threats to our environment too serious for us to adequately cope with them? What kinds of jobs will there be in the future, and will there be enough of them to meet the aspirations of our youth? Will Canada's health care system continue to meet people's expectations? Will this country's history of tolerance toward minorities continue, or will prejudice and hatred raise their ugly heads? Will productivity in Canada grow rapidly enough for Canadian firms to thrive in an increasingly globalized marketplace?

These questions are broad and diverse. Yet there is an economic dimension to every one of them. In fact, economics is one of the *most relevant* subjects that a student might study. Strangely, however, not everyone shares this view. There are a variety of reasons for this. One is that people often see economics as being too theoretical. However, let's remember that the most effective way to say something intelligent about nearly all the issues of the day is to use theory and abstraction. Another observation that students often make about the discipline of economics is that it seems too narrow in its focus. Yet a precise focus is sometimes needed to identify cause and effect.

Trying to understand economic theory can be challenging and certainly does not come easily, but the rewards, in terms of a better understanding of the world in which we live, are great. Economics is the study of ideas, and in a very real way this is the most important thing that a student can pursue. One of the most famous of twentieth-century economists, John Maynard Keynes, said:

> The ideas of economists, both when they are right and when they are wrong, are more powerful than is commonly understood. Sooner or later, it is ideas, not vested interests, which are dangerous for good or evil.[1]

The Three Fundamental Questions of Economics

A broad perspective on the discipline of economics can be obtained by focusing on what can be called the three fundamental questions of economics: what, how, and for whom? That is, economics is about what gets produced, how it is produced, and who gets it.

What to Produce?

Underlying the question of what should be produced is the previously mentioned reality of scarcity. Any society has only a fixed amount of resources at its disposal, and therefore must have a system in place to make millions of decisions about production. For example, should 50 new military helicopters be produced, or should the limited resources available be used to produce 10 new hospitals with (or without?) research facilities for the study of genetics? Should society exploit natural resources faster to create more jobs and more tax revenue, or slower to conserve these resources for the future? Should human effort, capital, and land be directed toward more preschool

---

[1] John Maynard Keynes, *The General Theory* (1936).

In this 1995 protest in Toronto, parents walked with children to protest day-care cuts proposed by the Ontario government.

day-care facilities so that women are not so tied to the home? Or, instead, should those same resources be directed toward increasing the number of graduate students studying science and technology so that the Canadian economy can win the competitive international race in the twenty-first century?

No economist would claim to have the right answer to even one of these questions. That is no more the role of an economist than it is of any other member of society. What the economist can do, however, is identify and measure both the benefits and the costs of any one answer—of any one choice. Let's review what we have said so far.

> **In the face of people's unlimited wants and society's limited productive resources, choice becomes a forced necessity. Because of these choices, the decision to produce one thing means that some other thing will not be produced.**

opportunity cost: the value of the next-best alternative that is given up as a result of making a particular choice.

This last point is so fundamental that economists have invented a special term to identify it: **opportunity cost**. For instance, suppose that the production of 50 new helicopters carries a price tag of $5 billion. In the conventional sense, that is their cost. However, economists would argue that it is more revealing to measure the cost of the helicopters in terms of the 10 hospitals that can't be built because the helicopters were produced. Opportunity costs can thus be defined as what must be given up as a result of making a particular choice; in this case, the hospitals instead of the helicopters. In addition we should recognize that the $5 billion could be spent on other things besides hospitals—say, colleges and universities or mass-transit systems. At this point society would presumably choose what it considers to be its *next best* alternative. Thus our definition of opportunity costs needs to be modified to: the next best alternative that is given up as a result of making a particular choice.

Why is it better to think of costs in terms of opportunity cost rather than simply as money payments? Economists argue that using the concept of opportunity costs captures the true measure of any decision. If we use money payments as the true measure, then we seemingly have unlimited means to produce goods, since governments can always print more money. But no matter what any government might wish, any society has only a limited amount of resources. When we realize this, there is no such thing as a "free lunch"—any decision (to produce helicopters, for example) necessarily means less of something else (hospitals). Recognizing that there are opportunity costs involved also forces us to rethink our idea of what we mean by "free." Simply because money does not change hands does not mean that a product is free. A free lunch is never free, because the provision of any meal involves the use of resources that could have been put to some other use.

The concept of opportunity cost can be applied not only at the level of the overall society, as we just saw, but also at the individual level. For the individual, the constraint is not the limited quantity of productive resources but, instead, a limited amount of income. For example, you could think of the cost of going to two movies on the weekend as the sacrifice of one new CD. If you want to think of both of these choices (two movies or one CD) as each costing about $16, that is fine. But thinking of the one as costing the other is often more effective. In general, your income will not allow you to have everything you may want, so you are forced to make choices about what you buy. And the cost of these choices can be measured in what must be given up as a result of making the choice. In the same sense, a society faces a similar set of choices imposed not by limited income but by a constraint on the quantity and quality of the factors of production available.

How to Produce?

Let's move on to the second fundamental economic question that every society must somehow answer: what is the most appropriate technology to employ? We could reword this question by asking: how should we produce what we choose to produce?

For example, there are a variety of ways to produce 10 kilometres of highway. At one extreme, a very labour-intensive method of production could be used involving rock crushed with hammers, roadbed carved from the landscape with shovels, and material moved in wheelbarrows. The capital equipment used in this method is very minimal. The labour used is enormous, and the time it will take is extensive. At the other extreme, a very capital-intensive method could be used involving large earth-moving and tarmac-laying machines, surveying equipment, and relatively little but highly skilled labour. In between these two extremes are a large variety of capital–labour mixes that could also produce the new highway.

The answer to the question of how best to build the highway involves, among other things, knowing the costs of the various resources that might be used. Remember that technology means the way the various factors of production are combined to obtain output. The most appropriate technology for a society to use (the best way to combine resources) depends, in general, on the opportunity costs of these resources. Thus, in the example above, the best way to build a highway depends on the opportunity costs of labour and of capital as well as the productivity of each factor.

For Whom?

We are now ready to move to the third fundamental economic question that every society must somehow answer: For whom? Here we ask: how should the total output of any society's economy be shared among its people? Should it involve an equal share for all, or should it, perhaps, be based on people's needs? Alternatively, should it be based on the contribution of each member of society? If so, how should this contribution be measured—in numbers of hours, or in skill level, or in some other way? Further, who should define what is an important skill and which ones are less important?

Wrapped up in all this is the question of the ownership of resources and whether it is better that certain resources (like land and capital) be owned by society as a whole or by private individuals. In short, the "for whom" question (as well as the "what" and "how" questions) cannot be adequately addressed unless we look at the society's attitude toward the private ownership of resources and the question of who has the power to make crucial decisions.

Thus, you can see that in addressing the "for whom" question, other questions about the fairness of income distribution, incentives, and the ownership of resources all come into play. John Stuart Mill pointed out, nearly 150 years ago, that once an economy's goods are produced and the initial market distribution of income has occurred, society can intervene in any fashion that it wants to redistribute such income; that is, there are no laws of distribution other than the ones that society wants to impose. Whether this observation by Mill gives enough consideration to the incentive for productive effort remains an open question to this day.

Thus, to a large extent the way in which each of the three fundamental questions is answered by a society depends on how that society organizes itself. We will now turn to a discussion about this topic.

ADDED DIMENSION

John Stuart Mill: Economist and Philosopher

John Stuart Mill (1806–73) is considered the last great economist of the classical school. His *Principles of Political Economy*, first published in England in 1848, was the leading textbook in economics for 40 years. Raised by a strict disciplinarian father (James), John Stuart began to learn Greek at the age of three, authored a history of Roman government by eleven, and studied calculus at twelve, but didn't take up economics until age thirteen. Not surprisingly, this unusual childhood later led to mental crisis. Mill credits his decision to put his analytical pursuits on hold and take up an appreciation of poetry as the primary reason for his recovery. He was a true humanitarian who held a great faith in human progress, had a love of liberty, and was an advocate of extended rights for women.

Types of Economies

Throughout history, humankind has coordinated its economies by using some blend of the four Cs: cooperation, custom, command, or competition. Thousands of years ago, members of small groups of hunter-gatherers undoubtedly relied on cooperation with each other in order to survive the dual threats of starvation and predators. They decided cooperatively what work needed to be done, how it was to be done, and who was to obtain what share of the produce. On the other hand, European feudal society in the Middle Ages was dominated by custom, which dictated who performed which task—sons followed the trade of their fathers—and implied that traditional technology was superior to new ways of doing things. Also, serfs were required, by tradition, to share a portion of their produce with the feudal lord.

One need only think of an ancient civilization, such as Egypt 4000 years ago, as an example of how society answered the three fundamental questions by using the command method. There, most of the important economic questions were answered by the orders of those in power, such as the pharaohs and priests. In this century, command has been the prevailing coordinating mechanism in fascist and communist regimes, in which a central committee (or presidium) makes most of the fundamental economic decisions.

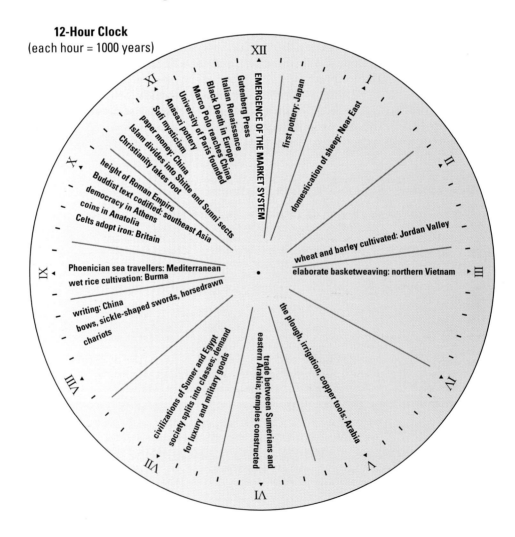

12-Hour Clock
(each hour = 1000 years)

Market societies, such as we see in most of the industrial countries around the globe today, did not begin to emerge until approximately *200 years ago*. Here we find a large role played by competition, while the roles of custom and cooperation have faded. Yet, in small ways we can still witness the role of custom. For example, there are probably as many people in a typical movie theatre audience who use the restrooms as there are people who eat popcorn. However, the theatre charges for the popcorn but not for the use of the restrooms. Why? Because it is customary. The command aspect certainly appears in market societies, in the form of government involvement in the economy. As an aside, it is interesting to note that custom and command totally replace the use of competition within the family unit, even in the most market-oriented societies.

To a large extent the essence of each of these different blends of the four Cs is found in the patterns of ownership and control of the factors of production. It is important to note that ownership of the factors doesn't always mean control over them. Land and capital was communally owned by the people in the former Soviet Union, but control of them was in the hands of a very few powerful Communist Party officials. Conversely, what we call capitalism today stresses the private ownership of the factors of production, but society's laws often place extensive controls on how they can and cannot be used.

wages: the payment made and the income received for the use of labour.

interest: the payment made and the income received for the use of capital.

rent: the payment made and the income received for the use of land.

profits: the income received from the activity of enterprise.

Most modern economies today are referred to as mixed economies because they comprise elements of the two dominant types: command and competition. In such an economy, incomes are earned through the payment of **wages**, **interest**, **rent**, and **profits** to the private owners of the factors of production: labour, capital, land, and enterprise. The higher the market value of the factor of production owned by a person, the more income that individual receives. Thus the "for whom" question is answered by the distribution of ownership of the factors of production that the market considers valuable. The "what" question in a modern market economy depends on the way that people choose to spend their income, since it is this spending that makes up the demand for the various goods and services. The "how" question is answered by firms finding the most appropriate technology to produce their output, knowing that success brings profits and that if they fail to do this they will not long be in business.

You have no doubt heard the terms capitalism and socialism used in the media and conversation. Just what do these terms mean to an economist? Basically they distinguish different degrees in the competition/command mix used by society to organize its economic affairs and answer the three fundamental questions. In "socialist" Sweden, for example, the state (government) plays a much larger role in the economy than in "capitalist" Hong Kong. While Sweden does *not* have central planning, as found in the former Soviet Union, and does have private property, it also has high taxes and high levels of social spending . Eighty percent of the workforce is unionized, everyone receives a minimum of 37 days of paid holiday per year, and unlimited sick leave benefits at nearly full pay. It has a generous unemployment insurance plan which also includes mandatory retraining. Until very recently, the government mandated an investment fund which required that corporations give a percentage of their profits to the central bank, which would then release these funds back to the companies in times of recession, with stipulations on how it was to be spent. By contrast, Hong Kong has almost none of this and relies, instead, on a policy of *laissez-faire*, which minimizes the role of government and emphasizes the role of the market in the economy. The U.S. leans towards the Hong Kong end of the spectrum and Canada towards the Swedish example.

The Methodology and Language of Economics

Let's now turn to a brief discussion on the methodology used in economics. Earlier, we discussed the *concept* of opportunity cost. We used the word concept, but we could have conveyed the same meaning with the word *idea*. Concepts (or ideas) become the building blocks for the more general terms *theory* or *principle*. In building a theory, a concept is first identified as a hypothesis. Consider, for example, the hypothesis that people will buy more of a good if its price falls. Along with this simple hypothesis, we need to define the terms involved, such as, what is the price we are considering—wholesale? retail? an average over time? a sale price? Also, we need to ask under what conditions this hypothesis is true: for every type of product or just certain types? any time of the year or only certain times? After the terms have been clearly defined and conditions (assumptions) spelled out, the hypothesis is ready to be tested with empirical data gathered by observing actual events. On the basis of this test of data, the theory is accepted, revised, or rejected.

In addition to terms like concept, principle, and theory, you will also find that the discipline of economics has developed its own very specialized language. When we think about this, it really shouldn't be a surprise since every specialty, from sailing to the arts, from pottery to chemistry, has its own language. Such specialized language is, in fact, quite necessary because the development and use of concepts, as well as the use of logic to draw conclusions, often requires language that is either not in general use or requires a more precise definition than is generally understood. As you proceed with your study of economics, the point that you need to first learn the language of economics cannot be overemphasized. Only then will you begin to understand the concepts of economics.

There may be times when the beginning student will think that economics is very abstract and theoretical. If this happens, try to remember that the purpose of theory is analogous to the purpose of a map—to compress a mass of detail down into a highly summarized, but manageable, form. Just as a map on the scale of 1:1 is useless, so too would be a theory that tries to explain every possible reality all at once. Building good theories involves identifying basic underlying relationships between crucial variables and reaching conclusions that point us in the right direction to answer important questions.

To better accomplish this task, economists often build models. Let's look at what we mean by this. Imagine walking into the sales office of a condominium project under construction. Part of the sales presentation is a model of the entire project sitting on a table. You would have no trouble recognizing the model as a representation of what the building will eventually look like. This is true despite the fact that many of the details, such as the elevators, furniture, and appliances, are absent from the model.

Similarly, an economic model uses a scaled-down version of that big picture. However, economists cannot construct a physical representation as is used in the example of the building. Instead, the level of abstraction is even greater, in that the model is all on paper and in the form of concepts, numbers, equations, and graphs. The economist's model also ignores the details that really aren't that important. Constructing such models helps us to understand important relationships between variables.

A Simple Model: The Circular Flow

We can take even the little bit that we have learned so far and build a very simple model of the whole economy. We use **Figure 1.1** to help us.

In Figure 1.1 we identify two sectors in the economy—the business sector and the household sector. In a market economy like Canada the four factors of production,

FIGURE 1.1 The Circular Flow

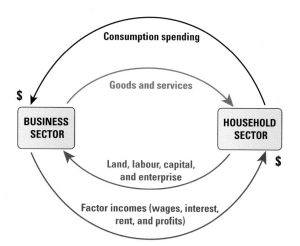

which we spoke of earlier, are owned by individuals who make up the household sector. These factors flow to the business sector, as represented by the red line identifying land, labour, capital, and enterprise. The business sector uses these factors to produce goods and services, which then flow to the household sector, as seen in green. Economists refer these as the physical (or real) flows—land, labour, capital, and goods.

Now of course, the business sector must pay for the use of the factors of production. These factor incomes, in the form of wages, interest, rents, and profits, are shown in blue. It is these payments that are the income of individuals in the household sector.

And what do people do with their income? They pay for the goods and services that they have received from the business sector. This payment, shown in black, is called consumption spending.

The income flow, made up of wages, interest, rents, and profits, and the consumption spending flow are made with money and are thus referred to as financial flows.

Needless to say, our economy is far more complex than this. However, even a very simple model like this can help us to better understand how it works. Chapter 3 of the macroeconomics text will take this circular flow model several steps further. For now, we need to remember that every model is an abstraction from reality. It doesn't intend to capture all possible relationships or details. In fact, it is often true that the more realistic we try to make our models, the more complex and thus the more confusing and distracting they become.

Agreements and Disagreements in Economics

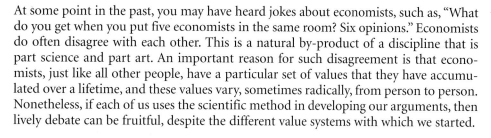

At some point in the past, you may have heard jokes about economists, such as, "What do you get when you put five economists in the same room? Six opinions." Economists do often disagree with each other. This is a natural by-product of a discipline that is part science and part art. An important reason for such disagreement is that economists, just like all other people, have a particular set of values that they have accumulated over a lifetime, and these values vary, sometimes radically, from person to person. Nonetheless, if each of us uses the scientific method in developing our arguments, then lively debate can be fruitful, despite the different value systems with which we started.

It is also true, however, that there is wide agreement among economists on many questions, and this is remarkable given that economists ask such a wide variety of questions, many of which do not get asked in other disciplines. For example, why do firms produce some goods internally and buy others in the market? Why do nations sometimes both export and import the same good? Why does society provide some things to children without charge (education) but not other things (food)?

ADDED DIMENSION

To illustrate the point that there is a great deal of agreement by economists, here are five examples of issues with the percentage of economists who agree with the statement:

1. A ceiling on rents reduces the quantity and quality of housing available. (93%)

2. Tariffs and quotas generally reduce economic welfare. (93%)

3. A tax cut or an increase in government expenditure has a stimulative effect on a less than fully employed economy. (90%)

4. The government should restructure the social assistance system along the lines of a negative income tax. (79%)

5. Effluent taxes and marketable pollution permits represent a better approach to pollution control than imposition of pollution ceilings. (78%)

Source: Richard M. Alston, J. R. Kearl, and Michael B. Vaughn, "Is There Consensus among Economists in the 1990s?" *American Economic Review,* May 1992, 230–239.

To help sort out the kind of thing that economists will probably agree on, and what they may well disagree on, we need to make the distinction between what is called a *positive statement* and a *normative statement*. Positive statements are assertions about the world that can be tested by using empirical data. Normative statements are based on a value system of beliefs and cannot be tested by using empirical data.

An example of a positive statement would be: The quantity purchased of any commodity will rise if its price falls. There will be little or no disagreement among economists on the importance of this kind of statement, and all will agree that such a statement can be verified with data. An example of a normative statement is: Canadians should save more. Such a statement is normative because it implies a definite value judgment and cannot be verified. This does not make such a statement unimportant, but it does mean that there is likely to be much more disagreement over it.

When building new theories and principles within the discipline, economists tend to work with positive ideas and statements and avoid the normative ones. None of this implies that economists should not enter the legitimate debate over controversial issues, such as the benefits and costs of free trade, but they should be careful and use only sound economic principles in their thinking and then clearly identify the points at which they leave the positive behind and enter the world of normative judgment, advocacy, and value systems.

Production Possibilities

Let's now construct another very simple model of a country's production possibilities. This allows us to return to a point that we made earlier, that every economy is faced with the constraint of limited resources. Imagine a society that produces only two products—cars and wheat. First, we want to figure out what this economy is capable of producing if it works at maximum potential. What exactly does this mean? Well, it certainly means that it is making use of all its resources: the labour force is fully employed, and all of its factories, machines, and farms are fully operational. But it means more than this. It also means that it is making use of the best technology of which it is aware and is working as efficiently as possible. So what, then, is it capable of producing? Since it can produce either cars or wheat, the output of each depends on how much of its resources it devotes to each. **Table 1.1** shows six possible output combinations, as well as the percentage of the economy's resources used in producing each combination. These possible outputs are labelled A through F.

The finite resources available to this economy allow it to produce up to a maximum of 20 tonnes of wheat per year, if 100 percent of its resources are used in wheat production. Notice that this can be done only if no cars are produced (combination A). At the other extreme, a maximum of 30 cars per year can be produced, if all available resources are used in car production. This, of course, would mean that no wheat is produced (combination F). There are many other possible combinations in between these two extremes, and Table 1.1 identifies four of these (B, C, D, and E).

TABLE 1.1 Production Possibilities for Cars and Tonnes of Wheat (in millions of units)

Possible Outputs	CARS		WHEAT	
	% of Resources Used	Output	% of Resources Used	Output
A	0	0	100	20
B	20	10	80	19
C	40	18	60	17
D	60	24	40	13
E	80	28	20	8
F	100	30	0	0

production possibilities curve: a graphical representation of the various combinations of maximum output that can be produced.

We can take the data from Table 1.1 and use it to graph what is called a **production possibilities curve**, which is a visual representation of the various outputs that can be produced. What appears in **Figure 1.2** is simply another way of presenting the data in Table 1.1.

FIGURE 1.2 The Production Possibilities Curve I

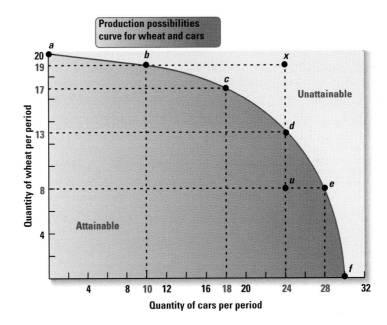

This society's limited resources allow for the production of a maximum of 20 tonnes of wheat if no cars are produced, as represented by point *a*. Moving down the curve from point *a*, we find other combinations of fewer tonnes of wheat and more cars until we reach point *f*, which is 30 cars and no wheat. Point *u* indicates either the underemployment of resources, inefficiency in resource use, or the use of inappropriate technology. Point *x* is unobtainable.

We should pause here and note that what is shown on the production possibilities graph are the various combinations of *outputs* that this economy is capable of producing. It does not show the *inputs* (the percentage of productive resources) that are necessary to produce those outputs.

Now, recall the three assumptions that lie behind our production possibilities curve:
- **full employment**
- **the use of the best technology**
- **efficiency**

If any one of these three assumptions does not hold, then the economy would be operating somewhere inside the production possibilities curve as illustrated by point *u*, 24 cars and 8 tonnes of wheat. On the other hand, point *x* represents an output of 24 cars and 19 tonnes of wheat, which, given this economy's current resources and technology, is unobtainable.

Next, let's address the actual shape of the curve. Why is it bowed out such that it is concave to the origin? We need to understand the implication of this particular shape. **Figure 1.3** will help.

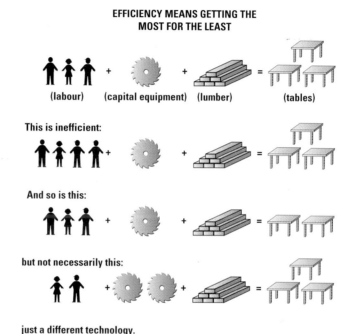

EFFICIENCY MEANS GETTING THE MOST FOR THE LEAST

(labour)   (capital equipment)   (lumber)   (tables)

This is inefficient:

And so is this:

but not necessarily this:

just a different technology.

FIGURE 1.3 Production Possibilities Curve II

At point *b*, 19 tonnes of wheat and 10 cars are being produced. If society decided that it wanted 8 more cars (point *c*), then 2 tonnes of wheat would have to be sacrificed. Thus, 1 more car would cost 0.25 tonnes of wheat. Moving from point *c* to *d* would increase car production by 6 (18 to 24) at a sacrifice of 4 tonnes of wheat (from 17 to 13). In this instance, one more car costs 0.67 tonnes of wheat. Moving from point *d* to *e* would increase car production by only 4 (from 24 to 28), while wheat production would drop by 5 (from 13 to 8). Thus, the cost of 1 more car rises to 1.25 tonnes of wheat.

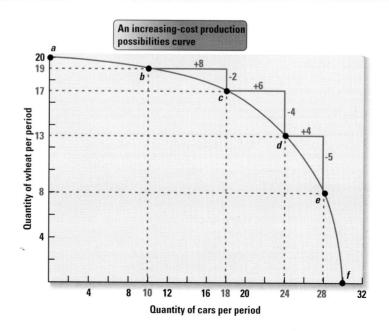

An increasing-cost production possibilities curve

Assume that our hypothetical economy is currently producing 19 tonnes of wheat and 10 cars, as illustrated by point *b* on the production possibilities curve. Then let's assume that production decisions are made to reallocate 20 percent of the productive resources (labour, machines, materials) from wheat production to car production. This new output is illustrated by point *c*. Note that here the opportunity costs of producing the additional 8 cars is *not* the additional 20 percent of resources that must be allocated to their production *but* the decreased output of wheat that these resources could have produced. That is to say, the additional 8 cars could only be obtained by reducing the output of wheat from the original 19 tonnes to the new 17 tonnes. Thus, 8 more cars cost 2 tonnes of wheat. This can be restated as: 1 more car costs 0.25 tonnes of wheat (2 divided by 8). This seems clear enough, but we are not done.

Next, assume that society, now at point *c*, decides to produce even more cars as illustrated by moving to point *d* (24 cars and 13 tonnes of wheat). This time an additional 20 percent of the resources produces only 6 more cars (18 to 24) at a cost of 4 units of wheat (17 to 13). This can be restated as: 0.67 tonnes of wheat for every additional car. This is considerably more than the previous cost of 0.25 units of wheat per car. Another shift of 20 percent of resources would move the economy from point *d* to *e*, with the result of an addition of only 4 more cars at a cost of 5 tonnes of wheat. Now, each additional car costs 1.25 (5/4) units of wheat.

law of increasing costs:
as an economy's production level of any particular item increases, its per unit cost of production rises.

We have just identified what economists call the **law of increasing costs**. This law states that as the production of any single item increases, the per unit cost of producing additional units of that item will rise. Note that this law is developed in the context of a whole economy and, as we will see in later chapters, need not apply to the situation of an individual firm.

Thus, you can see that as the total production of cars is increased, the rising *per unit* cost of cars gives the production possibilities curve its bowed-out shape.

SELF-TEST

3. Below is a list of economic goods. You are to decide whether each is a consumer good (C), or a capital good (K), or possibly both, depending on the context in which it is used (D):

A) A jackhammer.
B) A carton of cigarettes.
C) An office building.
D) A toothbrush.
E) A hammer.
F) A farm tractor.

4. Given the accompanying figure:

A) If the society produces 1000 units of butter, how many guns can it produce?
B) Suppose that the society produces the combination shown as point *b* on the production possibilities curve; what is the cost of 1000 additional units of butter?
C) Would the cost of 1000 additional units of butter be greater, the same, or smaller as the society moves from point *c* to *d*, compared with a move from point *b* to *c*?

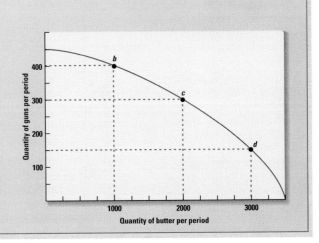

But why does the per unit cost of cars increase—what is the reason behind the law of increasing costs? The answer is that not all resources are equally suitable for the production of different products. Our hypothetical society has a fixed amount of resources that are used to produce different combinations of both wheat and cars. However, some of these resources would be better suited to producing cars, whereas others would be better suited to producing wheat. An increase in the production of cars requires that some of the resources currently producing wheat would need to be reallocated to the production of cars. It is only reasonable to assume that those resources that are reallocated first are the ones that are relatively well suited to the production of cars, whereas those resources not so suited to the production of cars would continue to produce wheat. After all this has taken place, if even *more* cars are to be produced, the only resources left to reallocate will be ones that are not very well suited for the production of cars. Therefore, a larger quantity of less well suited resources will have to be reallocated to obtain the desired increase in car production. This will increase the per unit cost of cars since a larger sacrifice of wheat production will be required.

Perhaps the way to really nail down this idea of increasing costs is to imagine another economy that produces only two products—leather shirts and leather moccasins. Assume that the leather and tools used to make both goods are exactly the same. Further, assume that all the people involved are clones of a long-deceased expert leatherworker and are therefore equally skilled. The production possibilities data for this economy are shown in **Table 1.2**. (This time the percentage of resources used to produce each combination is omitted.)

TABLE 1.2 Production Possibilities for Shirts and Pairs of Moccasins

			QUANTITIES PRODUCED PER DAY			
	A	**B**	**C**	**D**	**E**	**F**
Shirts	20	16	12	8	4	0
Moccasins	0	8	16	24	32	40

From the data in Table 1.2, we see that 8 additional pairs of moccasins can, in all instances, be obtained by giving up 4 shirts, which is a ratio of 2 pairs of moccasins for 1 shirt. This can also be stated as 1 additional shirt costing 2 pairs of moccasins. Taking this data and plotting it as a production possibilities curve yields a straight line, as can be seen in **Figure 1.4**.

Thus, we can see that a straight-line production possibilities curve is conceivable. The implications of a straight-line production possibilities curve is that the law of increasing costs does not apply. In fact, what we have above are constant costs—the cost of two pairs of moccasins is always one shirt.

Notice, however, what we had to assume in order to obtain such a result: homogeneous inputs to the production process—the same material (leather), identical tools, and labour that is equally skilled—and the very similar outputs of leather shirts and moccasins. If resource inputs are not homogeneous and if products are quite different, which is almost always the case, then we could not expect the production possibilities curve to be a straight line. Therefore, we would expect the law of increasing costs to prevail in the real world.

It is not difficult to find examples of this law. Thirty years ago, when there were very few air pollution controls in effect, the costs of obtaining a 10 percent reduction

FIGURE 1.4 Production Possibilities Curve III

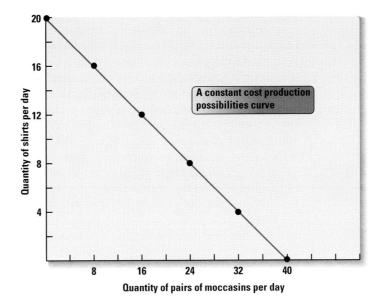

The opportunity cost of additional pairs of moccasins in terms of shirts sacrificed is constant; that is, 4 additional shirts always costs 8 pairs of moccasins. This yields a straight-line production possibilities curve.

in air pollution was relatively cheap. Today, when air pollution levels have been substantially reduced in many industries, an additional reduction of 10 percent would be much more costly because the most cost-effective reductions have already been made.

Consider another example. Assume that the infant mortality rate in a less-developed country is 55 out of every 1000 births. The reduction of this level by five (to 50 out of 1000) could been achieved relatively cheaply—say, with a smallpox vaccination campaign that would require only a small quantity of resources. However, once the rate dropped to, say, 25 out of 1000, then the resources required to gain an additional drop of five points, to 20 out of 1000, would probably be substantial and the costs involved would be much greater. This is the law of increasing costs.

Technological Change and Capital Accumulation

Earlier in the chapter we spoke of the important role that technology plays in economic performance. Technology is the application of human knowledge to lower the cost of producing goods and services. To illustrate the effects of technological change, imagine a society that produces only two categories of goods—capital goods and consumer goods. Economists define **capital goods** as the buildings, tools, machinery, and equipment that are used to produce other goods. **Consumer goods** are those goods used by consumers to satisfy their wants and needs.

Let's start, in **Figure 1.5**, with the economy operating efficiently on the production possibilities curve PPI at point *a*. Now let's assume that a new technology becomes available that has application *only* in the consumer goods industry. This is represented by a shift outward in the curve, with the new production possibilities curve becoming PPII. There are three possible results. First, the same quantity of capital goods, but more consumer goods, can be produced as represented by *b*. Second, more of *both* goods can also be produced, as represented by point *c*. And third, this economy could now achieve an increase in the production of capital

capital goods: things used to aid in the production of other goods, such as buildings, tools, equipment, and machinery.

consumer goods: goods used by consumers to satisfy their wants and needs.

goods if the same number of consumer goods were produced (point *d*) *despite* the fact that this new technology could only be applied to the consumer goods industry. This emphasizes the important role of technological change. It widens the choices (there's that word again) available to society and is often seen in a positive light. Alas, technological change also carries costs, and this is another subject that will receive our attention later.

Now, look at Figure 1.5 and ask yourself the following question: Which of the three new possible combinations is preferable? If the choice had been between two consumer goods, such as wheat and cars, then we could not give a definitive answer to this question without knowing something about the country's wants and needs. But the choices illustrated in this figure are between capital goods and consumer goods, and choosing combination *d*—more capital goods—leads to significantly different effects than does choosing combination *b*.

FIGURE 1.5 The Effect of Technological Change on the Production Possibilities Curve

Start at point *a*, which is a point of efficient production on PPI. An improvement in technology in the consumer goods industry shifts the production possibilities curve to PPII. This creates three possible results. First, the same quantity of capital goods, and more consumer goods, can now be produced as represented by point *b*. Alternatively, more of *both* consumer goods and capital goods can be produced as represented by point *c*. Point *d* represents the third possible result, which is more capital goods and the same quantity of consumer goods, despite the fact that the technological change was in the consumer goods industry.

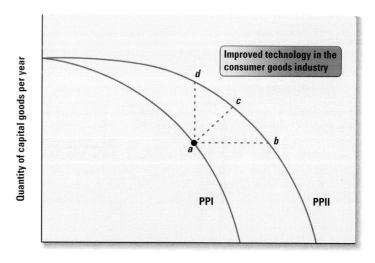

This point is illustrated in **Figure 1.6**, in which we show two different economies. Atlantis places greater emphasis on the production of capital goods than does Mu. This can be seen by comparing point a_1 (40 units of capital goods) with point b_1 (20 units of capital goods). This emphasis on capital goods production also means a lower production of consumer goods (30 units in Atlantis, compared with 50 in Mu). The emphasis on capital goods production in Atlantis means that it will experience more economic growth in the future. This faster growth is illustrated by the production possibilities curve shifting to the right more in the case of Atlantis than in Mu. After the increase in production possibilities, Atlantis can continue producing 40 units of capital goods but now can produce 70 units of consumer goods (a_2). Mu, by contrast, can produce only 60 units of consumer goods while maintaining capital goods production at the original 20 units (b_2). All of this is a result of a different emphasis on the output choices by the two economies.

FIGURE 1.6 Different Growth Rates for Two Economies

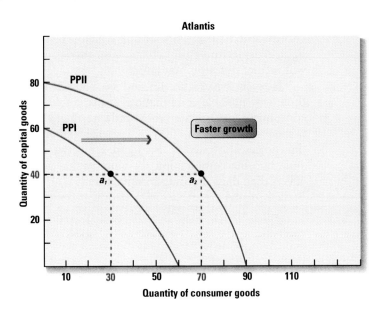

We begin with Atlantis and Mu being the same size, as indicated by the same PPI curves. However, since Atlantis chooses to emphasize the production of capital goods (point a_1) while Mu emphasizes the production of consumer goods (point b_1), Atlantis will grow faster. The result of this faster growth is that, over time, PPII shifts out more in the case of Atlantis than it does in the case of Mu.

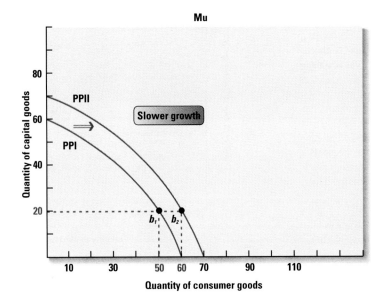

SELF-TEST

5. Assume that the economy of Finhorn faces the following production possibilities:

QUANTITIES PER YEAR

	A	B	C	D
Grain	50	40	25	0
Tools	0	4	8	12

A) Draw a production possibilities curve (PPI) with tools on the horizontal and grain on the vertical axis. Now assume new technology that can be used only in the tool industry is developed, which increases tool output by 50 percent.

B) Draw a new production possibilities (PPII) curve that reflects this new technology.

C) If Finhorn produced 12 units of tools per year, how many units of grain could be produced after introduction of the new technology?

This completes your introduction to the study of economics. If there is only one thing that you retain from this chapter, it should be the idea that society must continually make difficult choices about what, how, and for whom to produce, and that these choices invariably involve costs. Perhaps the following story will help.

A sage of some bygone age said that there is no such thing as a free lunch. We can now make some sense out of this idea. Producing more of anything—a lunch, for example, since it involves the use of scarce resources—necessarily means producing less of something else. The lunch might be provided free to the people who eat it, but from the point of view of the society as a whole, it took scarce resources to produce it and therefore is not free.

REVIEW

1. What is a *production possibilities curve*?
2. Define *the law of increasing costs*.
3. What does a straight-line production possibilities curve imply?
4. Define *capital good*.
5. Define *consumer good*.
6. How would you shift the production possibilities curve if you wanted to illustrate technological change or the accumulation of more capital goods?

STUDY GUIDE

Chapter Highlights

In this introductory chapter you gained an insight into the scope and depth of economics. You learned that economists are very focused on the choices, and the related costs of those choices, that individuals, organizations, and governments face when making decisions. A very simple model using production possibilities is a powerful tool in analyzing choice.

1. The factors of production are:
   - land, labour, capital, and enterprise;

   and the payments made to these factors are:
   - rent, wages, interest, and profits.

2. The discipline of economics is subdivided into:
   - microeconomics which studies the outcomes of decisions by people and firms;
   - macroeconomics which studies how the major components of an economy interact.

3. The three fundamental questions that all societies must somehow answer are:
   - *What* is the right combination of consumer goods to produce and what is the right balance between consumer goods and capital goods;
   - *How* should these various goods be produced;
   - *Who* is to receive what share of these goods once they are produced?

4. The *economic organization* of all societies are based on one or more of the following:
   - custom, cooperation, command, and competition;

   and *modern (mixed) economies* use, primarily:
   - competition along with a varying amount of command in the form of government intervention.

5. The *production possibilities* model is an abstraction and simplification that helps to illustrate:
   - the opportunity cost involved in making a choice;
   - the necessity of choice in deciding what to produce;
   - inefficient production and the consequences of unemployed resources;
   - economic growth.

New Glossary Terms

capital   2
capital goods   18
consumer goods   18
enterprise   2
factors of production   2
interest   9
labour   2
land   2

Study Tips

1. Since this is your first chapter, you should not be overly concerned if it seems to contain so much new terminology that it feels overwhelming. Mastering the principles of economics requires that you first learn the language of economics, and the best way to do this is to use it over and over. Let this study guide help you do this. Conscientiously work through all of the questions before proceeding to the next chapter.

2. Opportunity cost is one of the most important concepts in economics. As a start, make sure that you understand the basic idea that cost can be measured not just in dollars and cents but also in what has to be given up as a result of making a particular decision.

3. This chapter introduces you to the use of graphs with the production possibilities curve. If you have any difficulty understanding graphs, you should practise with the simple PP graphs until you become more comfortable using them, because graphs are an integral part of economics.

4. For many of you, economics will be one of the more difficult courses in your undergraduate studies. Yet it can be mastered, and doing so can be very rewarding. You will probably be much more successful if you work a little on economics several times a week rather than have one long session a week. This will enable you to gain mastery over the language more quickly through repetition and thereby gain confidence. You might consider buying a pack of 3" × 5" index cards and writing two or three definitions or simple ideas on each card. Carry several cards around with you so that you can glance at them several times a day. The authors found this technique helpful when—oh, so many years ago—they started to learn the discipline.

Are You Sure?

Indicate whether the following statements are true or false. If false, indicate why they are false.

1. Individual households face scarcity because of limited household income.

    T or F   If false: _____

    _____

2. An economy as a whole faces scarcity because of limited national income.

    T or F   If false: _____

    _____

3. The three fundamental questions in economics are what, how, and how many.

   T or **F**   If false: _____

   _____

4. Opportunity cost is the value of the next-best alternative that is given up as a result of making a particular choice.

   T or **F**   If false: _____

   _____

5. There are only three Cs that humankind has used to coordinate its economies: cooperation, custom, and competition.

   T or **F**   If false: _____

   _____

6. Wages, interest, rent, and profits are the four factors of production.

   T or **F**   If false: _____

   _____

7. A production possibilities curve is a graphical representation of the various combinations of output that are wanted.

   T or **F**   If false: _____

   _____

8. A straight-line production possibilities curve and the law of increasing costs are not consistent.

   T or **F**   If false: _____

   _____

9. Technological improvement can be illustrated graphically by a rightward shift in the production possibilities curve.

   T or **F**   If false: _____

   _____

10. Macroeconomics focuses on the outcomes of decisions by people and firms, whereas microeconomics is a study of how the major components of an economy interact.

    T or **F**   If false: _____

    _____

Choose the Best

11. The building blocks of a theory are:
    a) Concepts and mathematics.
    b) Concepts and ideas.

12. An economist's model comes in the form of:
    a) A physical representation of reality.
    b) Concepts, numbers, and equations.

13. A decision to produce more capital goods and fewer consumer goods now means:
    a) Less consumption of consumer goods now and in the future.
    b) Less consumption of consumer goods now but more consumption in the future.

14. "Factors of production" is a term that can be used interchangeably with:
    a) Models.
    b) Consumer goods.
    c) Either productive resources or inputs.

15. What is the distinction between a positive and a normative statement?
    a) Positive statements are assertions that can be tested with data, whereas normative statements are based on a value system of beliefs.
    b) Normative statements are assertions that can be tested with data, whereas positive statements are based on a value system of beliefs.
    c) The distinction depends on the context in which each statement is used.

16. Meridith had only $16 to spend this last weekend. She was, at first, uncertain about whether to go to two movies she had been wanting to see or to buy a new CD she had recently heard. In the end she went to the movies. Which of the following statements is correct?
    a) The choice of the two movies and not the CD is an example of increasing costs.

b) The opportunity cost of the two movies is one CD.

c) The opportunity cost of the two movies is $16.

17. What does the term technology mean to an economist?
    a) The way the various factors of production are combined to obtain output.
    b) The most recent methods of production.
    c) High-tech methods of production as found, for example, in the computer industry.

18. All of the following *except one* is a capital good. Which is the exception?
    a) An office building.
    b) A boiler in a pulp mill.
    c) A mobile home.
    d) An airport runway.

19. A simple model of the circular flow includes reference to all but one of the following. Which is the exception?
    a) Spending on exports and imports.
    b) Both physical and financial flows.
    c) The factors of production.
    d) Both the business and the household sectors.

20. What are the factors of production?
    a) Land, labour, money, and enterprise.
    b) Land, labour, money, and capital.
    c) Land, labour, capital, and enterprise.
    d) Competition, command, custom, and cooperation.

21. J. S. Mill argued that:
    a) It is ideas, not vested interests, that are dangerous for good and evil.
    b) The distribution of money is dictated by the pattern of resource use.
    c) As technology changes, what gets produced also necessarily changes.
    d) Society can intervene in any fashion that it may wish to redistribute income.

Figure 1.7 shows Mendork's production possibilities curve for the only two goods that it produces—quirks and quarks. Refer to this figure to answer questions 22–27.

FIGURE 1.7

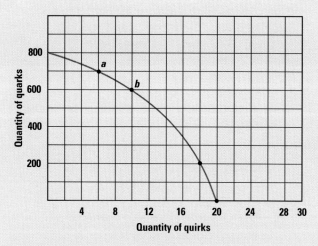

22. Refer to Figure 1.7 to answer this question. If this society chooses to produce 10 quirks, what is the maximum quantity of quarks it can produce?
    a) 500 quarks.
    b) 800 quarks.
    c) No quarks.
    d) 600 quarks.

23. Refer to Figure 1.7 to answer this question. What is the opportunity cost of producing 200 quarks?
    a) 10 quirks.
    b) 18 quirks.
    c) 2 quirks.
    d) The answer cannot be determined from the information given.

24. Refer to Figure 1.7 to answer this question. If Mendork's production is currently that indicated by point *a*, what is the (approximate) cost of producing one more quirk?
    a) 100 quarks.
    b) 50 quarks.
    c) 25 quarks.
    d) 200 quarks.
    e) 1 more quark.

25. Refer to Figure 1.7 to answer this question. What is the opportunity cost of one more quark as output changes from point *b* to *a*?
    a) 0.04 quirks.
    b) 4 quirks.
    c) 400 quirks.
    d) 1 quirk.
    e) 0.4 quirks.

26. Refer to Figure 1.7 to answer this question. If new technology increased the output of quirks by 50 percent, how many quirks could be produced if 600 quarks were produced?
    a) 18 quirks.
    b) 20 quirks.
    c) 15 quirks.
    d) 10 quirks.
    e) 0 quirks.

27. Refer to Figure 1.7 to answer this question. Which of the following statements is correct if Mendork is currently producing 500 quarks and 8 quirks?
    a) This society is using competition to coordinate its economic activities.
    b) This society is experiencing either unemployment or inefficiency.
    c) This economy is experiencing full employment.
    d) This society is not adequately answering the "for whom" question.
    e) This economy is growing quickly.

28. Which of the following statements describes the law of increasing costs as it relates to the whole economy?
    a) As the quantity produced of any particular item decreases, its per unit cost of production rises.
    b) As the quantity produced of any particular item increases, its per unit cost of production rises.

c) The prices of consumer goods always rise and never fall.
d) If you wait to make a purchase, you will pay a higher price.
e) The total cost of production rises as output goes up.

29. Which of the following statements is implied by a straight-line production possibilities curve?
    a) The law of increasing cost doesn't apply.
    b) The resources being used are homogeneous.
    c) The two goods being produced are very similar.
    d) The opportunity cost of both goods is constant.
    e) All of the above are correct.

30. Which of the following statements is correct for a society that emphasizes the production of capital goods over that of consumer goods?
    a) The society could enjoy the same quantity of capital goods and a larger quantity of consumer goods in the future.
    b) The society will have to save more now than a society that did not emphasize the production of capital goods.
    c) The society could enjoy the same quantity of consumer goods and a larger quantity of capital goods in the future.
    d) The society will grow faster than a society that emphasizes the production of consumer goods.
    e) All of the above are correct.

Problems

31. Match the letters on the left with the blanks on the right.
    a) capital good
    b) consumer good
    c) land
    d) labour
    e) enterprise
    f) factors of production
    g) ways of coordinating an economy
    h) the fundamental questions in economics

    1. cooperation, custom, command, and competition   _____
    2. the services of a brain surgeon   _____
    3. an apple   _____
    4. a satellite   _____
    5. land, labour, capital, and enterprise   _____
    6. what, how, and for whom   _____
    7. abundant clean water   _____
    8. the original marketing of a new power cell   _____

32. Change the following two positive statements into normative statements.
    a) The rate of savings in Canada is approximately 10 percent of national income.

    _____

    _____

b) Unemployment has increased by 2 percentage points over the last year.

_____

_____

33. Change the following two normative statements into positive statements.

a) All students should take a course in economics.

_____

_____

b) Economic growth is a desirable goal for a country.

_____

_____

34. Jennifer is planning how to spend a particularly wet Sunday, and the choice is between watching video movies (each lasting 2 hours) or studying her economics textbook. She has 10 hours available to her. If she decides to study, she could read the following numbers of pages:

2 hours   80 pages
4 hours   130 pages
6 hours   160 pages
8 hours   175 pages
10 hours   180 pages

a) Given this information, draw Jennifer's production possibilities curve between movies watched and pages studied on the grid in **Figure 1.8.**

FIGURE 1.8

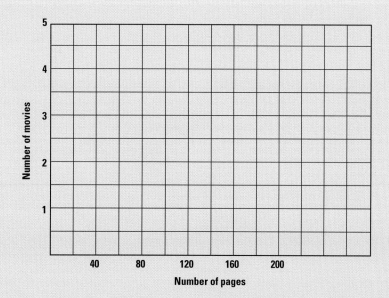

b) What happens to the opportunity cost of watching movies as more movies are watched?

_____

_____

c) Could Jennifer watch 3 movies and study 150 pages of her textbook?

_____

_____

d) If Jennifer has already watched 4 movies, what is the opportunity cost of watching the fifth movie?

_____

_____

Translations

Assume that a piece of land can produce either 600 bushels of corn and no soybeans or 300 bushels of soybeans and no corn. You may further assume that this corn–beans ratio of 2:1 is constant.

On the grid in **Figure 1.9**, draw a production possibilities curve for this piece of land. Next, indicate with the letters *a* and *b* an increase in bean production of 50 bushels. Finally, illustrate with a triangle the cost of this additional 50 bushels of beans.

FIGURE 1.9

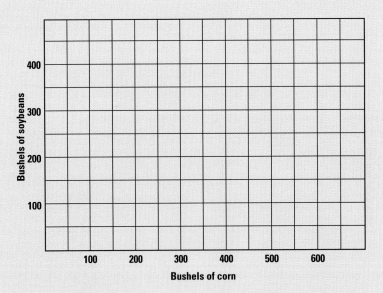

Key Problem

Table 1.3 contains the production possibilities data for capital goods and consumer goods in the economy of New Harmony.

TABLE 1.3

	A	B	C	D	E
Capital goods	0	3	6	9	12
Consumer goods	30	27	21	12	0

a) Use the grid in **Figure 1.10** to draw the production possibilities curve for New Harmony, and label it PPI. Label each of the five output combinations with the letters *a* through *e*.

FIGURE 1.10

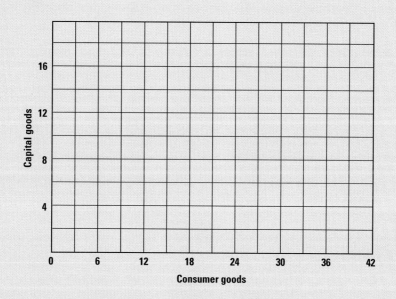

b) Assume that the people of New Harmony have decided to produce 12 units of capital goods. How many units of consumer goods could be produced?

Answer: _____.

c) Assuming the economy is producing combination C, what would be the opportunity cost of 3 more units of capital goods?

Answer: _____.

d) Assuming the economy is producing combination D, what would be the opportunity cost of 3 more units of capital goods?

Answer: _____.

e) What law is illustrated by your answers to c) and d)?

Answer: _____.

f) Fill in **Table 1.4** assuming that, 10 years later, the output potential of capital goods has increased by 50 percent while the output potential for consumers goods has risen by 12 for each of combinations A through D.

TABLE 1.4

	V	W	X	Y	Z
Capital goods	___	___	___	___	___
Consumer goods	___	___	___	___	___

g) Using the data from this table, draw in PPII in Figure 1.10.

h) Given the new table in f), how many units of consumer goods could be produced if 9 units of capital goods were produced? Label it point *x* on Figure 1.10.

   Answer: _____ .

i) Given the new PPII in Figure 1.10, approximately how many units of capital goods could be produced if 12 units of consumer goods were produced? Label it point y^*.

   Answer: _____ .

j) Given PPII, is the combination of 13.5 units of capital goods and 24 units of consumer goods possible?

   Answer: _____ .

k) Given PPII, is the combination of 8 units of capital goods and 40 units of consumer goods possible?

   Answer: _____ .

l) Given PPII, what could you say about the economy of New Harmony if 8 units of capital goods and 30 units of consumer goods were being produced?

   Answer: _____ .

m) What are three possible reasons that would explain the shift from PPI to PPII?

   Answer: _____ .

More of the Same

Table 1.5 contains the production possibilities data for capital goods and consumer goods in the economy of Waldon.

TABLE 1.5

	A	B	C	D	E
Capital goods	0	2	4	6	8
Consumer goods	20	19	16	10	0

a) Draw a PPI for Waldon on **Figure 1.11**.

FIGURE 1.11

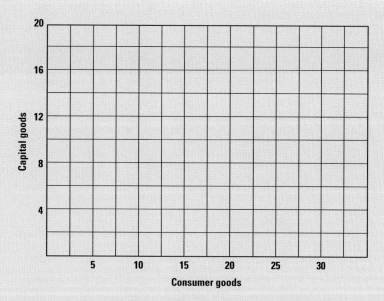

b) Assume that the people of Waldon have decided to produce 2 units of capital goods and 19 units of consumer goods and indicate this combination with the letter *b* on the graph.

c) Assuming the economy is currently producing combination B, how many more units of consumer goods could be obtained if 2 less units of capital goods were produced?

d) Again starting from combination B, what would be the opportunity cost of 2 more units of capital goods?

e) What is the opportunity cost of the very first 2 units of capital goods? Of the last 2 units?

f) Make a table assuming that, 10 years later, the potential output of both capital and consumer goods increases by 25 percent.

g) Draw the data (from the table you constructed in f) above) on Figure 1.11 as PPII.

h) Given PPII, approximately how many units of consumer goods could be produced if 2 units of capital goods were produced?

i) Given PPII, approximately how many units of capital goods could be produced if 19 units of consumer goods were produced?

j) In this problem, the shift out of PPII was much less than it was for New Harmony in the Key Problem. Why would this be, if we assume that technological change and any increase in the quantity of resources in the two economies were similar?

UNANSWERED QUESTIONS

Short Essays

1. Identify the four factors of production, and give two examples of each.

2. What does the term "technology" mean, and how would you describe the effects of an increase in technology?

3. Why is economics sometimes described as the science of choice?

4. Comment on the following statement: "While society does have a choice about what types of goods to produce, it has no choice about the total quantity that can be produced."

5. Why do economists often disagree with one another?

6. Do you think studying for long periods is subject to increasing opportunity costs?

Analytical Questions

7. Below is a list of resources. Indicate whether each is land (N), labour (L), capital (K), or enterprise (E).
   a) Fishing grounds in the north Pacific.
   b) An irrigation ditch in Manitoba.
   c) The work done by Jim Plum, a labourer who helped to dig the irrigation ditch.
   d) The work done by Yves Gaton, a symphony conductor.
   e) A fish farm in Nova Scotia.
   f) A water reservoir.
   g) A golf course.
   h) The air we breathe.
   i) The efforts of the founder and primary innovator of a successful new software company.

8. Identify each of the following statements as positive or normative:
   a) The price of oil rose by over 10 percent last year.
   b) The price of oil will be lower this time next year.
   c) The government should try to reduce the price of oil.
   d) A decrease in taxes should help reduce the price of oil.
   e) The high price of oil in Canada is unacceptable.

9. Kant Skatte is a professional player in the National Hockey League. Because he loved the game so much, Kant dropped out of high school and worked very hard to develop his physical strength and overcome his limitations. Eventually he made it to the NHL. Estimate Kant's annual opportunity costs, in dollars, of continuing to play in the NHL.

10. Construct your own definition of economics.

11. Explain the analogy between the use of theory and the use of a map.

12. Can you think of three examples in which contemporary Canadian society uses the element of command to help coordinate production?

13. To what extent is the organization of the family based on the four Cs? Give examples of how each of the four Cs is used to assign household chores to its members. What blend of the four Cs do you think is preferable, and why?

14. Explain how a society based on custom and cooperation would answer the what, how, and for whom questions.

15. Comment on the following statement: "The 'for whom' question is the easiest of the three fundamental questions in economics to answer because it involves only positive statements."

Numerical Questions

16. Ken has just graduated from secondary school. His uncle has offered him a full-time job, for $20 000 per year, at his home improvement supply outlet. Ken, however, has his heart set on going to university for four years to get a degree in engineering, but unfortunately his uncle can't use him on a part-time basis. Tuition and books for the four years will cost Ken $14 000. What is Ken's opportunity cost of getting a degree?

17. Construct a simple circular flow model. Include two sectors, two physical flows, and two financial flows.

18. The graph in **Figure 1.12** is for the country of Leviathon:

a) What could explain the shift from PPI to PPII?

FIGURE 1.12

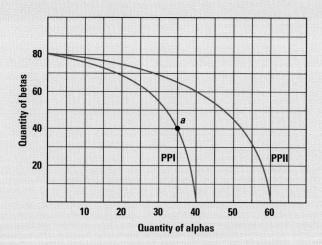

b) Given PPII, indicate with point *b*, the maximum quantity of alphas that can now be produced if 40 betas are produced.

c) Given PPII, indicate, with point *c*, the maximum quantity of betas that can now be produced if 35 alphas are produced.

d) Given point *a*, indicate, with point *d*, an increase in the production of both alphas and betas.

19. The data in **Table 1.6** are for the small country of Xanadu. Assume that the economy is originally producing combination C and technological change occurs that enables it to produce 60 percent more capital goods.

TABLE 1.6

	A	B	C	D	E	F
Capital goods	0	25	40	50	55	58
Consumer goods	50	40	30	20	10	0

a) If the economy wants to continue with the same quantity of consumer goods, how many more capital goods can it now have as a result of the technological improvement?

b) If instead the economy wants to continue with the same quantity of capital goods, how many more consumer goods can it now have as a result of the technological improvement?

c) Suppose that the economy wishes to have 30 percent more capital goods than in the original combination C. Approximately how many more consumer goods can it have?

20. **Table 1.7** presents the production possibilities for tractors (in millions) and carrots (millions of tonnes) for the country of Risa.

TABLE 1.7

	A	B	C	D	E	F
Tractors	200	180	150	110	60	0
Carrots	0	100	180	240	290	330

a) Can this economy produce 130 tractors and 140 carrots?
b) Can this economy produce 165 tractors and 210 carrots?
c) What is the *total* cost of producing 110 tractors?
d) What is the *total* cost of producing 180 carrots?
e) If the economy is producing 60 tractors and 290 tonnes of carrots, what is the *per unit* cost of producing an additional tractor?
f) In what sense (if any) could combination C be regarded as preferable to combination D?

21. Shangri-La produces only two goods: bats and balls. Each labourer comes with a fixed quantity of material and capital, and the economy's labour force is fixed at 50 workers. **Table 1.8** indicates the amounts of bats and balls that can be produced daily with various quantities of labour.

TABLE 1.8

Number of Workers	Daily Production of Bats	Number of Workers	Daily Production of Balls
0	0	0	0
10	150	10	20
20	250	20	36
30	325	30	46
40	375	40	52
50	400	50	55

a) Draw a production possibilities curve for this economy, assuming that labour is fully employed.
b) What is the opportunity cost of increasing the output of bats from 325 to 375 units a day? What is the opportunity cost of increasing the output of balls from 46 to 52 units per day?
c) Suppose that a central planning office dictates an output of 250 bats and 55 balls per day. Is this output combination possible?
d) Now assume that new technology is introduced in the production of balls so that *each worker* can produce 1/2 a ball more per day. On the same graph, draw the new production possibilities curve. Is the central planning office's output goal in c) now possible?

 ## Web-Based Activities

1. Since the early 1990s several economies in Eastern Europe have been attempting to transform command economies into market economies. Go to **www.worldbank.org/html/prddr/trans/WEB/trans.htm** and choose "Archives" and then Volume 1, Number 1, April 1990. Identify the problems associated with transforming command economies into market economies. As you identify each problem, try to classify it as a problem associated either with the "What," "How," or "For Whom" question.

2. China's economy is basically a command economy. In recent years, however, competition plays a more important role in the day-to-day economic activity. Go to **www.ccpit.org** and identify which parts of the economy are still controlled by the government and which aspect of economic activity is market determined.

Demand and Supply: An Introduction

What's ahead... This chapter introduces you to the fundamental economic ideas of demand and supply. It explains the distinction between individual and market demand and looks at the various reasons why consumers change their demand. We then take a look at things from the producers' point of view and explain what determines the amounts that they put on the market. Next we explain how markets are able to reconcile the wishes of the two groups, and we introduce the concept of equilibrium. Finally, we look at how the market price and the quantity traded adjust to various changes.

A QUESTION OF RELEVANCE...

Have you ever wondered why the prices of some products, like computers or CD players, tend to fall over time while the prices of other products, such as cars or auto insurance, tend to rise? Or, perhaps, you wonder how the price of a house can fluctuate tens of thousands of dollars from year to year. Why does a bad orange harvest in Florida cause the price of apple juice made in Ontario to rise? And why do sales of typewriters continue to fall, despite their lower prices? This chapter will give you insights into questions like these.

I f the average person were to think about the subject matter of economics, it is unlikely that she would immediately think of choice or opportunity costs, which was a principal topic of Chapter 1. More likely, she would think in terms of money or interest rates and, almost certainly, demand and supply. Most people realize, without studying the topic, that demand and supply are central to economics. In our own ways, and as a result of our experiences in life, most of us feel that we know quite a lot about the subject. After all, who are better experts on the reaction of consumers to changes in the market than consumers themselves? However, as we will see shortly, the way that economists define and use the terms "demand" and "supply" differs from the everyday usage. To make matters worse, there doesn't seem to be a consensus among non-economists about the meaning of either of these two words. This is often the case with any language, but it does lead to a great deal of confusion, which can be illustrated in the following exchange between two observers of the housing market:

> Isn't it shocking that house prices have increased so much in the past year? It makes it very difficult for first-time buyers to get into the market.

> Well, yes, but that's the law of demand. Presumably builders can get away with charging a higher price as long as people are willing to pay.

> Are you suggesting that the demand for new houses has increased, then?

> Must have done.

> But surely, higher prices are going to lead to a lower demand. I thought that was the law of demand!

> Well, yes. But, don't you see, a lower demand will lead to lower prices.

> And lower prices to a higher demand...

What's happening here? There seems to be some confusion, but what is causing it? Is it because neither of the speakers know what they are talking about? Well, that's a possibility, of course. But likely the root of the confusion surrounds that simple word "demand." As we shall see, demand is being used in two different ways, and neither speaker is aware of this. It's probably clear to you already that economists are very fussy about defining and using economic terms correctly, and this is particularly true in a discussion about demand and supply. Demand doesn't simply mean what people want to buy, nor is supply just the amount being produced. Besides the problem of definitions, another source of confusion in the above discussion is a misunderstanding of cause and effect: Is the change in house prices the effect of changing demand, or is it the cause? This chapter will clear up some of the confusion and give us a basis on which to analyze and clarify some real, practical problems. First, let us take a look at the concept of demand.

Demand

Individual Demand

demand: the quantities that consumers are willing and able to buy per period of time at various prices.

There are several dimensions to the term **demand**. First, economists use the word not in the sense of commanding or ordering but in the sense of wanting something. However, this want also involves the ability to buy it. In other words, demand refers to both *the desire and the ability* to purchase a good or service. This means that although I may well have a desire for a new top-of-the-line BMW, I unfortunately don't have the ability to buy one at current prices, and therefore my quantity demanded is zero.

Second, even though we know there are many factors that determine what products and what quantities a consumer purchases, economists would suggest that the price is usually the most important of these, and for this reason they look at how consumers might react to a change in the price assuming that all other factors remain unchanged. The Latin phrase for this perspective is **ceteris paribus**, which literally means "other things being equal." However, it is usually interpreted by economists to mean "other things remaining the same." In other words, demand is the relationship between the price of a product and the quantities demanded, *ceteris paribus*.

Third, demand is a hypothetical construct that expresses this desire and ability to purchase, not at a single price, but over *a range of* hypothetical prices. Finally, demand is also a flow concept, in that it measures quantities over a period of time. In summary, demand:

- involves both the consumers' desire and ability to purchase
- assumes that other things are held constant
- refers to a range of prices
- measures quantities over time

All of these aspects of demand are captured in **Table 2.1**, which shows the **demand schedule** for an enthusiastic beer drinker named Tomiko.

ceteris paribus: other things being equal, or other things remaining the same.

demand schedule: a table showing the various quantities demanded per period of time at different prices.

TABLE 2.1   Individual Demand

Price per Case	Quantity Demanded (Number of Cases per Week)
$12	6
13	5
14	4
15	3
16	2
17	1
18	0

Once again, what we mean by demand is the entire relationship between the various prices and the quantities that people wish to purchase, and this relationship can be laid out in the form of a demand schedule. The above schedule shows the amounts per week that Tomiko is willing and able to purchase at the various prices shown. Note that there is an *inverse* relationship between the price and quantity. This simply means that at higher prices Tomiko would not be willing to buy as much as at lower prices. In other words:

> **The higher the price, the lower the quantity demanded; and the lower the price, the higher the quantity demanded.**

Another, though less obvious, statement of this law of demand is to say that in order to induce Tomiko to buy a greater quantity of beer, the price must be lower. Tomiko's demand schedule is graphed in **Figure 2.1**.

In Figure 2.1, at a price of $15, the quantity demanded by Tomiko is 3 cases per week, while at a lower price of $12, she would be willing to buy 6 cases. The demand schedule therefore plots as a downward-sloping curve. (To economists, curves include straight lines!) Once again, note that when we use the terms "demand," or "demand schedule," or "demand curve," we are referring to a whole array of different prices and quantities.

FIGURE 2.1   Individual Demand Curve

At a price of $12 per case, Tomiko is willing and able to buy 6 cases per week. At a higher price, $15 per case, the amount she is willing and able to buy falls to 3 cases. The higher the price, then, the lower the quantity demanded. (Note that the vertical axis contains a "broken" portion. In general, an axis is often broken in this manner whenever the information about, say, low prices, is unavailable or unimportant.)

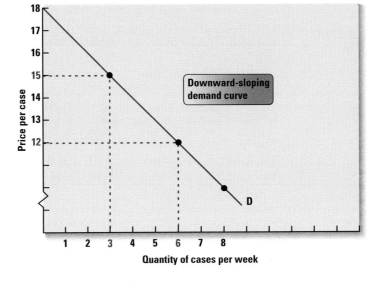

change in the quantity demanded: the change in quantity that results from a price change. It is illustrated by a movement along a demand curve.

It is very important for you to note that since price is part of what we call "demand," a change in the price cannot change the demand. Certainly it can affect the *amounts* we are willing to purchase, and we express this by saying that:

> **A change in the price of a product results in a change in the quantity demanded for that product.**

This is illustrated in **Figure 2.2**. Graphically, as we move down the demand curve, the quantity demanded increases; as we move up the demand curve, the quantity demanded decreases.

FIGURE 2.2   Changes in the Quantity Demanded

Whenever the price changes, there is a movement along the demand curve. An increase in the price from, say, P_1 to P_2, causes a decrease in the quantity demanded from Q_1 to Q_2. A decrease in the price from P_3 to P_4 leads to an increase in the quantity demanded from Q_3 to Q_4. Neither the demand nor the demand curve, however, changes.

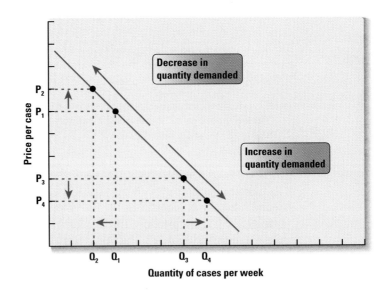

Why Is the Demand Curve Downward-Sloping?

There are a number of rationales for the proposition that people tend to buy more at lower rather than at higher prices. Most of us can confirm from our own experience that a lower price will induce us to buy more of a product or to buy something that we would not normally purchase. Witness the big crowds that are attracted to nothing more than a sign saying, "SALE." In addition, most microeconomic research done over the years tends to confirm this law of demand, and theories of consumer behaviour (such as the marginal utility theory, which we shall study in Chapter 5) lend additional support to the idea.

Sometimes, a SALE sign is all it takes to attract consumers.

Canapress/Hans Deryk

Let's begin our exploration of the question of why people tend to buy more at lower prices. Remember that our demand for products is a combination of our desire and our ability to purchase. A lower price affects both of these. The lower the price of a product, the more income a person has left to purchase additional products. Let's explain this by assuming, for instance, that the price of beer in Table 2.1 was $14, and Tomiko was buying 4 cases per week, for a total expenditure of $56 per week. Next, let's say the price decreases to $12. Tomiko could, if she wished, buy the same quantity for an outlay of $48, thus saving a total of $8. It's almost as if Tomiko had had a pay raise of $8. In fact, in terms of its effect on Tomiko's pocketbook, it is exactly the same. Or, as economists would express it, her **real income** has increased. A decrease in price means that people can afford to buy more of a product (or more of other products) if they wish. This is referred to as the **income effect** of a price change, and it affects people's *ability* to purchase. This is because a lower price means a higher real income, and as a result people will tend to buy more of a product. (Conversely, an increase in the price would effectively reduce people's real income.)

real income: income measured in terms of the amount of goods and services that it will buy. Real income will increase if either actual income increases or prices fall.

income effect: the effect that a price change has on real income, and therefore on the quantity demanded of a product.

substitution effect: the substitution of one product for another as a result of a change in their relative prices.

In addition to this, a price change also affects people's *desire* to purchase. We are naturally driven to buy the cheaper of competing products, and a drop in the price of one of them increases our desire to substitute it for the now relatively more expensive product. For instance, if the price of wine were to drop (or for that matter, if the price of beer were to increase), then some beer drinkers might well switch to what they regard as a cheaper substitute. In general, this is saying that there are substitutes for most products, and people will tend to substitute a relatively cheap product for an expensive one. This is called the **substitution effect**. A higher price, on the other hand, tends to make the product less attractive to us than its substitutes, and so we buy less.

When the price of a product drops, we will buy more of it because we are *more able* (the income effect) and because we are *more willing* (the substitution effect). Conversely, a price increase means we are less able and less willing to buy the product, and therefore we buy less. (There is a possible exception to this, which we will look at in the next chapter.)

The close relationship that exists between the price and the quantity demanded is so pervasive that it is often referred to as the *law of demand*.

Market Demand

market demand: the total demand for a product by all consumers.

Up to this point, we have focused on individual demand. Now we want to move to **market demand** (or total demand). Conceptually, this is easy enough to do. By summing every individual's demand for a product, we are able to obtain the market demand. **Table 2.2** provides a simple example.

TABLE 2.2   Deriving the Market Demand

NUMBER OF CASES PER WEEK

Price per Case	Tomiko's Demand	Meridith's Demand	Abdi's Demand	Jan's Demand	Market Demand
$12	6	3	4	9	22
13	5	2	4	7	18
14	4	2	4	6	16
15	3	0	3	3	9
16	2	0	3	1	6
17	1	0	2	0	3
18	0	0	2	0	2

Let's say we know not only Tomiko's demand but also the demands of three other friends in a small, four-person economy. The market demand then is the horizontal summation of individual demands, which simply means that to find the quantities demanded at $12 we add the quantities demanded by each individual, that is, 6 + 3 + 4 + 9 = 22. The same would be done for each price level. This particular market demand is graphed in **Figure 2.3**.

FIGURE 2.3   The Market Demand Curve

At a price of $12, the total or market quantity demanded equals 22 cases. As with individual demand, when the price increases to $16, then the quantity demanded will drop, in this case to 6. This is because at a higher price, each individual buys less, and in addition there are fewer people who can afford to or are willing to buy any at all. (Meridith has dropped out of the market.)

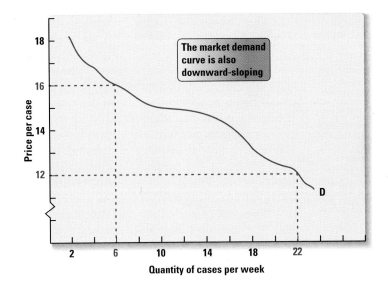

Note that, as with the individual demand curve, the market demand curve also slopes downward. This is because not only do people buy more as the price drops, but in addition more people buy. At a price of $18 in our example, only Abdi would buy any beer. As the price drops to $16, not only would Abdi buy beer, but so too would Tomiko and Jan. The price would need to drop to $14 to induce all four people to buy beer.

Finally, before we take a look at the supply side of things, note again that our demand schedule tells us only what people *might* buy; it tells us nothing about what they are actually buying, because to know this we also need to know the actual price. And to find out what the actual price of beer is, we need to know ... yes, the supply.

Supply

Individual Supply

In many ways the formulation of supply is very similar to that of demand. Both measure hypothetical quantities at various prices, and both are flow concepts. However, we now need to look at things through the eyes of the producer, rather than the consumer. We will assume for the time being that the prime motive for the producer is to maximize profits, although we will examine this assumption in more detail in a later chapter. For now we can certainly agree with Adam Smith who, in *The Wealth of Nations*, noted that few producers are in business to please consumers, nor of, course, do consumers buy products to please producers. Both are motivated, instead, by self-interest.

supply: the quantities that producers are willing and able to sell per period of time at various prices.

supply schedule: a table showing the various quantities supplied per period of time at different prices.

The term **supply** refers to the quantities that suppliers are *willing and able* to make available to the market at various different prices. **Table 2.3** shows a hypothetical **supply schedule** for Bobby the brewer.

TABLE 2.3 Bobby the Brewer's Supply

Price per Case	Quantity Supplied (Number of Cases per Week)
$12	2
13	3
14	4
15	5
16	6
17	7
18	8

Note that there is a *direct* relationship between the price and the quantity supplied, which means that a higher price will induce Bobby to produce more. Remember that Bobby's reason for being in business is to make as much profit as possible.

ADDED DIMENSION

Adam Smith: The Father of Economics

Adam Smith (1723–90) is generally regarded as the founding father of economics. In his brilliant work *The Wealth of Nations*, Smith posed so many interesting questions and provided such illuminating answers that later economists often felt that they merely were picking at the scraps he left behind. He was born and brought up in Scotland and educated at Glasgow and Oxford. He later held the Chair of Moral Philosophy at Glasgow College for many years. He was a lifelong bachelor and had a kindly but absent-minded disposition.

Smith was the first scholar to analyze in a detailed and systematic manner the business of "getting and spending." In doing this, he gave useful social dignity to the professions of business and trading. Besides introducing the important idea of the *invisible hand*, which was his way of describing the coordinating mechanism of capitalism, he examined the division of labour, the role of government, the function of money, the advantages and disadvantages of free trade, what constitutes good and bad taxation, and a host of other ideas. For Smith, economic life was not merely a peripheral adventure for people but their central motivating force.

Suppose that Bobby was asked how much she will, hypothetically, be prepared to supply if the beer could be sold at $12 per case. Knowing what her costs are likely to be, she figures that she could make the most profit if she produces 2 cases. At a higher price, there is a likelihood of greater profits, and therefore she is willing to produce more. Also, as we shall see in Chapter 6, as firms produce more, often the cost per unit tends to rise and therefore the producer needs the incentive of a higher price *in order* to increase production. For the time being, however, we can rely on the proposition that a higher price means higher profits and therefore will lead to higher quantities produced. This is illustrated in **Figure 2.4**.

FIGURE 2.4 Individual Supply Curve

At a low price of $12, the most profitable output for Bobby is 2 cases. If the price increased, she would be willing and able to produce more, since she would be able to make greater profits. At $18, for instance, the quantity she would produce increases to 8 cases.

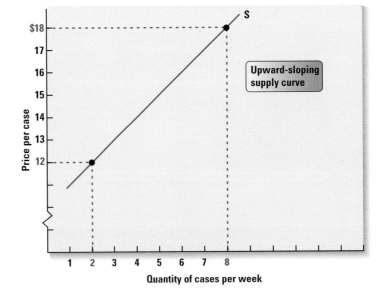

Joining together the individual points from the supply schedule in Table 2.3 gives us the upward-sloping supply curve shown in Figure 2.4. Again, we emphasize the fact that as with the term "demand," the term "supply" does not refer to a single price and quantity, but to the whole array of hypothetical price and quantity combinations contained in the supply schedule and illustrated by the supply curve.

change in the quantity supplied: the change in the amounts that will be produced as a result of a price change. This is shown as a movement along a supply curve.

Since price is part of what we mean by the term supply, a change in the price level cannot change the supply. A change in price does of course lead to a change in the quantity that a producer is willing and able to make available. Thus, the effect of a change in price we call a **change in the quantity supplied**. This is illustrated in **Figure 2.5**.

FIGURE 2.5   Changes in the Quantity Supplied

If the price changes, it will lead to a movement along the supply curve. An increase in the price from, say, P_1 to P_2 will cause an increase in the quantity supplied from Q_1 to Q_2. A decrease in the price from P_3 to P_4 will lead to a decrease in the quantity supplied from Q_3 to Q_4. The supply curve itself, however, does not change.

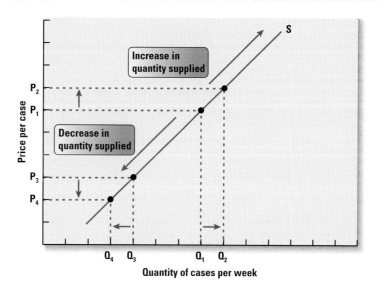

To summarize:

> An increase in the price will lead to an *increase in the quantity supplied* and is illustrated as a movement up the supply curve.

> A decrease in the price will cause a *decrease in the quantity supplied*, which is illustrated as a movement down the supply curve.

Market Supply

market supply: the total supply of a product offered by all producers.

As we did with the market demand, we can derive the **market supply** of a product by summing the supply of every individual supplier. A word of caution, however, is in order. We must make the necessary assumption that the producers are all producing a similar product and that consumers have no preference as to which supplier or product they use. Given this, it is possible to add together the individual supplies to derive the market supply. In our example, suppose that Bobby the brewer is competing with three other brewers of similar size and with similar costs. The market supply of beer in this market would be as shown in **Table 2.4**.

TABLE 2.4 Deriving the Market Supply

NUMBER OF CASES PER WEEK

Price per Case	Bobby the Brewer's Supply	Supply of Other Brewers	Market Supply
$12	2	6	8
13	3	9	12
14	4	12	16
15	5	15	20
16	6	18	24
17	7	21	28
18	8	24	32

The total quantities supplied by the three other brewers are equal to the quantities that Bobby would supply at each price, multiplied by three. The fourth column, market supply, is the addition of every brewer's supply, that is, the second column plus the third column.

The market supply of beer is illustrated in **Figure 2.6**.

FIGURE 2.6 The Market Supply

The market supply is the horizontal summation of each individual producer's supply curve. For instance, at a price of $15, Bobby would supply 5 cases; the other brewers combined would produce 15 cases. The market supply therefore is the total quantity supplied of 20 cases. In short, to derive the market supply curve, we add the totals of each supplier at each price level.

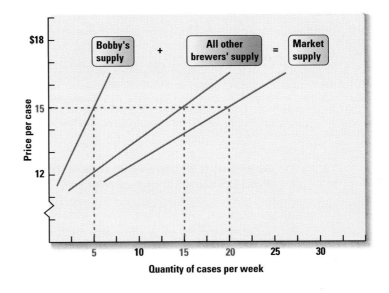

The *market* supply curve is upward-sloping primarily for the same reason the *individual* supply curve is upward-sloping: because higher prices imply higher profits and will therefore induce a greater quantity supplied. There is an additional reason. In the example we have used, we assumed for simplicity's sake that the suppliers are of similar size and have similar costs. In reality that's unlikely: costs and size are likely to differ so that a price which generates a profit for one firm may mean a loss for another. As the price of a product increases, however, some firms that previously were unable to produce will now find that they can successfully operate at a profit. Thus, as the price of the product increases, currently operating firms will produce more. In addition, other firms not previously producing will enter the market and start to produce.

In summary, then, a higher price, which deters consumers from buying more, is an incentive for suppliers to produce more. Conversely, a lower price induces consumers to buy more but is a reason for suppliers to cut back their output.

The motives of consumers and producers are very divergent, the former wishing to obtain the lowest price possible, the latter wanting to sell at the highest. How can their wishes converge? How is trade possible in these circumstances? Well, if the question means: is it possible for *all* prospective consumers and suppliers to be satisfied, the answer must be no. If the question means: is it possible for *some* of these people to be satisfied, the answer will be, almost always, yes. Of course, this will require that they are able in some sense to meet and get together. A market enables them to do just that.

The Market

market: a mechanism that brings buyers and sellers together and assists them in negotiating the exchange of products.

Most people are able to understand the terms market price and market demand but are not always clear as to what constitutes a **market**. Certainly the term includes places that have a physical location, such as a local produce or fish market. But, in broader terms, a market really refers to any exchange mechanism that brings buyers and sellers of a product together. There may be times when we feel that we need to inspect or get further on-the-spot information about a product before we buy it, and this is the purpose of the retail market. But there are other times when we possess sufficient information about a product or a producer that it's not necessary to actually see either of them before we purchase. This applies, for instance, if you wish to buy stocks and bonds or make a purchase on the Internet. Increasingly, in these days of higher costs of personal service and greater availability of electronic communication, markets are becoming both wider and more accessible. The market for commodities such as copper or gold or rubber, for instance, is both worldwide and anonymous, in that the buyers and sellers seldom meet in person.

E-CONOMICS

Re-inventing the Market

Capitalism, as we know it today, began to spread and mature about 500 years ago as commerce moved out of the occasional village markets of Europe into the age of factory-centred manufacturing which then combined with widespread systems of wholesaling and retailing. However, this transformation also introduced a less predicable chain of supply and demand. While the seller in the village market was in direct contact with the buyer, the evolution of capitalism's mass markets and mass production techniques imposed vast gaps in time and space between the two. Producers became much less sure of what the demand for their product was

and buyers were never sure if there wasn't a better deal somewhere else. In response to this, sellers used the blunt tool of a fixed-price list and adjusted output accordingly while buyers just did the best they could. The phenomenon of the Internet is re-inventing commerce as the seller's market horizon expands, buyers have more information, real-time sales become routine, and the need to stockpile inventory diminishes. In short, supply chain bottlenecks are being eradicated. What is emerging is far *more efficient markets* and the rise of dynamic pricing based on constantly fluctuating demand and supply.

By a market, then, we mean any environment in which buyers and sellers can communicate, which is relatively open and operates without preference. When we talk of the market price, then, we mean the price available to *all* buyers and sellers of a product; by market demand we mean the total quantities demanded; and market supply refers to the quantity made available by all suppliers at each possible price.

Later in the text, you will encounter a variety of different types of markets, some of which work very well and others that work poorly, if at all. The analysis in this chapter assumes that the market we are looking at is very (economists call it "perfectly") competitive. We will devote the whole of Chapter 8 to examining this type of market in more detail. For now, we need to mention that a perfectly competitive market is, among other things, one in which there are many small producers, each selling an identical product. Given this caution, let's see how this market works.

Market Equilibrium

We now examine the point at which the wishes of buyers and sellers coincide by combining the market demand and supply for beer in **Table 2.5**.

TABLE 2.5 Market Supply and Demand

	NUMBER OF CASES PER WEEK		
Price per Case	**Market Demand**	**Market Supply**	**Surplus (+)/Shortage (−)**
$12	22	8	−14
13	18	12	− 6
14	**16**	**16**	**0**
15	9	20	+11
16	6	24	+18
17	3	28	+25
18	2	32	+30

equilibrium price: the price at which the quantity demanded equals the quantity supplied such that there is neither a surplus nor a shortage.

You can see from this table that there is only one price, $14, at which the wishes of consumers and producers coincide. Only when the price is $14 will the quantities demanded and supplied be equal. This price level is referred to as the **equilibrium price**. Equilibrium, in general, means that there is balance between opposing forces; here, those opposing forces are demand and supply. The word equilibrium also implies a condition of stability, so that if this stability is disturbed, there will be a tendency to return automatically to equilibrium. To understand this point, refer to Table 2.5 and notice that if the price were, say, $12, then the amount being demanded of 22 would exceed the amount being supplied of 8. At this price there is an excess demand or, more simply, a shortage of beer to the tune of 14 cases. This amount is shown in the last column and marked with a minus sign. In this situation there would be a lot of unhappy beer drinkers. Faced with the prospect of going beerless, many of them will be prepared to pay a higher price for their suds and will therefore bid the price up. As the price of beer starts to rise, the reaction of consumers and producers will differ. Some beer drinkers will not be able to afford the higher prices, so the quantity demanded will drop. On the supply side of things, producers will be delighted with the higher price and will start to produce more—the quantity supplied will increase.

Both of these tendencies will combine to reduce the shortage as the price goes up. Eventually, when the price has reached the equilibrium price of $14, the shortage will have disappeared and the price will no longer increase. Part of the law of demand suggests, then, that:

Shortages cause prices to rise.

This is illustrated in **Figure 2.7**.

FIGURE 2.7   How the Market Reacts to a Shortage

At a price of $12, the quantity supplied of 8 is far below the quantity demanded of 22. The horizontal distance between the two shows the amount of the shortage, which is 14. As a result of the shortage, price bidding between consumers will force up the price. As the price increases, the quantity demanded will drop, but the quantity supplied will rise until these two are equal at a quantity of 16.

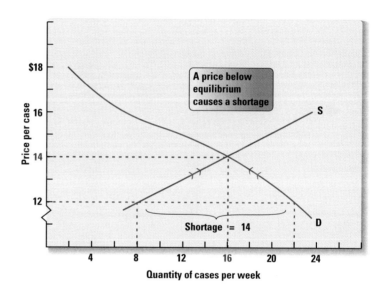

Now let's see, again using Table 2.5, what will happen if the price happens to be above equilibrium, at, say, $16 a case. At this price, the quantity demanded is 6 cases, and the quantity supplied is 24 cases. There is insufficient demand from the producers' point of view, or, more simply, there is a surplus of 18 cases. This is shown in the last column of Table 2.5 as +18. This is not a stable situation, because firms cannot continue producing a product that they cannot sell. They will be forced to lower the price in an attempt to sell more. As the price starts to drop, two things happen concurrently. Consumers will be happy to consume more, or, to use economic terms, there will be an increase in the quantity demanded. In **Figure 2.8**, note that as the price falls, the quantity demanded increases, and this increase is depicted as a movement down the demand curve. At the same time, faced with a falling price, producers will be forced to cut back production. This is what we have called a decrease in the quantity supplied. In the same figure, this is shown as a movement along (down) the supply curve. The net result of this will be the eventual elimination of the surplus as the price moves toward equilibrium. In other words:

Surpluses cause prices to fall.

equilibrium quantity: the
quantity that prevails at
the equilibrium price.

Only if the price is $14 will there be no surplus or shortage, and the quantity pro-
duced will be equal to the quantity demanded. This is the equilibrium price. The
quantity prevailing at the equilibrium price is known as the **equilibrium quantity**, in
this case 16 cases. This equilibrium quantity is the quantity both demanded and supplied (since they are equal).

FIGURE 2.8   How the Market Reacts to Surpluses

A price above equilibrium will
produce a surplus. At $16,
the quantity supplied of 24
exceeds the quantity
demanded of 6. The horizontal distance of 18 represents
the amount of the surplus.
The surplus will result in
producers dropping the price
in an attempt to increase
sales. As the price drops,
the quantity demanded
increases, while the quantity
supplied falls. The equilibrium quantity is 16.

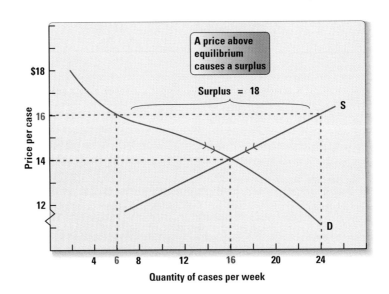

SELF-TEST

2. Can a change in the price of a product lead to a change
   in the demand? Can it lead to a change in supply? Explain.
3. The following table shows the demand and supply of
   eggs (in hundreds of thousands per day).

Price	Demand	Supply	Surplus/ Shortage
$2.00	60	30	_____
2.25	58	33	_____
2.50	56	36	_____
2.75	54	39	_____
3.00	52	42	_____
3.25	50	45	_____
3.50	48	48	_____
3.75	46	51	_____
4.00	44	54	_____

A) What is the equilibrium price and the equilibrium
   quantity?
B) Complete the surplus/shortage column. Using this
   column, explain why your answer to question A must
   be correct.
C) What would be the surplus/shortage at a price of
   $2.50? What would happen to the price and the quan-
   tity traded?
D) What would be the surplus/shortage at a price of
   $4.00? What would happen to the price and the quan-
   tity traded?

Change in Demand

change in demand: a change in the quantities demanded at every price, caused by a change in the determinants of demand.

Recall from the definition of demand that the concept refers to the *relationship* between various prices and quantities. In other words, both price and quantity make up what is known as demand. Thus, a change in price cannot cause a change in demand but does cause a change in the quantity demanded. That said, we must now ask: what are the other determinants, besides the price, that would influence how much of any particular product consumers will buy? Another way of looking at this is to ask: once equilibrium price and quantity have been established, what might disturb that equilibrium? The general answer to this question is a **change in demand**. Table 2.6 shows such a change in the demand for beer.

TABLE 2.6   An Increase in Demand

	NUMBER OF CASES PER WEEK	
Price per Case of Beer	Demand 1	Demand 2
$12	22	33
13	18	29
14	16	27
15	9	20
16	6	17
17	3	14
18	2	13

The original market demand, labelled Demand 1, is from Table 2.5 and was the demand that existed, let's say, last month. Demand 2 is the market demand for beer this month. There has been an increase in demand of 11 cases per week at each price. Put another way, whatever the price, consumers are willing and able to consume an additional 11 cases. Thus, there has been an increase in the demand. Figure 2.9 graphically illustrates an increase in demand.

An increase in demand, then, means an increase in the quantities demanded *at each price*, that is, a total increase in the demand schedule, which is illustrated by a rightward shift in the demand curve. Similarly, a decrease in demand means a reduction in the quantities demanded at each price—a decrease in the demand schedule—and this is illustrated by a leftward shift in the demand curve.

FIGURE 2.9 An Increase in Demand

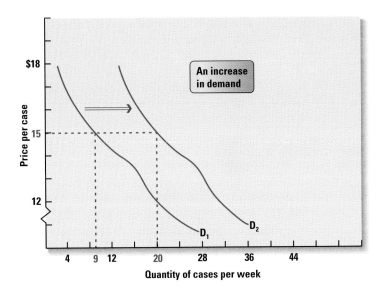

At each price, the quantities demanded have increased. In this example, the increase is by a constant amount of 11, thus producing a parallel shift in the demand curve. For example, at $15, the quantity demanded has increased from 9 to 20 (by 11).

Determinants of a Change in Demand

Having illustrated what an increase in demand looks like, we now need to look at the factors that could bring about such a change. Some of these determinants of demand affect people's willingness to purchase, others affect their ability to purchase, and still others affect both. One factor that affects our willingness to purchase a product is our own particular *preference*. An increase in demand as shown in Table 2.6 could simply have been caused by a change in consumer preferences: consumers now prefer more beer.

A host of different things could affect our preferences. Tastes change over time and are influenced by the weather, advertising, articles and reports in books and magazines, opinions of friends, special events, and many other things. These things are difficult to measure, but we know that they affect demand and are often unpredictable. They can cause the demand for a product to either increase or decrease.

The second factor affecting the demand for a product is the *income* of consumers. This will affect their ability to consume. Generally speaking, you would expect that an increase in income leads most people to increase their purchases of most products, and a decrease in income generally causes a drop in the demand, that is, there is a direct relationship between income and demand. This is true for most products that we buy, and these products are called **normal products**. But it is certainly not true for all people and products. For instance, as the incomes of most people increase, these consumers tend to buy less of such things as low-quality hamburger meats, packets of macaroni and cheese, cheap toilet-paper rolls, and so on. Instead, they start to substitute higher-quality and higher-priced articles that they could not previously afford.

normal products: products whose demand will increase as a result of an increase in income and will decrease as a result of a decrease in income.

inferior products: products whose demands will decrease as a result of an increase in income and will increase as a result of a decrease in income.

When income is low, we are forced to survive on lower-quality staple products that economists call **inferior products**. There is an inverse relationship between income and the demand for inferior products. As income levels go up, the demand goes down. It also means that as incomes fall, our demand for these inferior products will rise. In our beer example from Table 2.6, the increase in the market demand could have been caused by an *increase* in incomes because beer is a normal product.

A third important determinant of demand is the *prices of related products*. A change in the price of related products will affect both people's willingness and their ability to purchase a particular good. Products are related if a change in the price of one causes a change in the demand for the other. For instance, if the price of Pepsi were to increase, a number of Pepsi drinkers might well switch over to Coke.

substitute products: any products whose demand varies directly with a change in the price of a similar product.

There are, in fact, two ways in which products may be related. They may be related as substitutes, or they may be related as complements. **Substitute** (or competitive) **products** are products that are sufficiently similar in the eyes of most consumers that price becomes the main distinguishing feature. Pepsi and Coke, therefore, are substitute products because an increase in the price of one will cause an increase in the demand for the other. The relationship between the price of a product and the demand for its substitute is, therefore, a direct one. It also means that if the price of a product falls, then the demand for its substitute will also fall, since many consumers are now buying the cheaper product.

complementary products: products that tend to be purchased jointly and whose demands therefore are related.

Complementary products tend to be purchased together, and their demands are interrelated. Skis and ski boots are complementary products, as are cars and gasoline or beer and pretzels. If the price of one product increases, causing a decrease in the quantity demanded, then people will also purchase less of the complement. If the price of cameras were to increase so that people were buying fewer cameras, then we would also expect a decline in the demand for not only film but for other complementary products like lenses, tripods, carrying bags, and so on. There is, in this case, an inverse relationship between the price of a product and the demand for its complement, which means that an increase in price of the one product leads to a decline in the demand for the complementary product. Similarly, a decrease in the price of a product will lead to an increase in the demand for a complement.

SELF-TEST

4. The following table shows the initial weekly demand (D_1) and the new demand (D_2) for packets of pretzels (a bar snack).

Price	Demand (D_1)	Demand (D_2)
$2.00	10 000	11 000
2.50	9 800	10 800
3.00	9 600	10 600
3.50	9 400	10 400
4.00	9 200	10 200

To explain the change in demand from D_1 to D_2, what might have happened to the price of a complementary product, like beer? Alternatively, what might have happened to the price of a substitute product, like nuts?

A fourth determinant of demand is the *expectations of the future* on the part of consumers. There are many ways that our feelings about the future influence our present behaviour. Future expected prices and incomes can affect our present demand for a product, as does the prospect of a shortage. If consumers think that the price of their favourite beverage is likely to increase in the near future, they may well stock up in advance, just in case. The present demand for the product will therefore increase. Conversely, expected future price declines cause people to hold off their current purchases while awaiting the hoped-for lower prices.

In a similar fashion, an anticipated pay increase may cause some people to spend more now as they adjust to their expected higher standard of living. Similarly, it does seem likely that most people who fear a layoff or other cause of a drop in salary will cut down spending in advance of the fateful date. Finally, it should be added that the possibility of future shortages, caused for instance by an impending strike, often causes a mad rush to the stores by anxious customers trying to stock up in advance.

A Statistics Canada report released in 1996 showed that annual per capita beer sales fell to 86.5 litres from 87.1 litres: The decline in beer drinking is probably due to the aging population, lifestyle changes, and taxes, said Howard Collins of the Brewers Association of Canada.

These four determinants of demand—preferences, income, prices of related products, and future expectations—affect people's individual demand in varying degrees. If we shift our attention to the market demand, these four factors still apply. In addition, a few other factors need to be mentioned. The *size of the market population* will affect the demand for all products. An increase in the size of the population, for example, will lead to an increase in the demand for most products in varying amounts. In addition, a *change in the distribution of incomes* will lead to an increase in the demand for some products and a decrease in the demand for others, even though the total income has not changed. The same will also be true for the *age composition of the population*. An aging population will increase the demand for products that largely appeal to older people (Anne Murray CDs), and decrease the demand for those that appeal only to the young (Tragically Hip CDs).

Notice that one factor is *not* included in this list of determinants of demand, and that is supply. Economists are scrupulous in their attempts to separate the forces of demand and supply. Remember that the demand formulation is a hypothetical construct based on the quantities that consumers are willing and able to purchase at various prices. There is an implied assumption that the consumer will be able to obtain these quantities; otherwise the demand schedule itself would not be relevant. In other words, when specifying the demand, we assume that the supply will be available, just as, when formulating supply, we make the assumption that there will be sufficient demand.

In summary, the determinants of demand are:

- consumer preferences
- consumer incomes
- prices of related goods
- expectations of future prices, incomes, or availability
- population size; or income and age distribution

The Effects of an Increase in Demand

We have just seen that the demand for any product is affected by many different factors. A change in any of these factors will cause a change in demand and lead to a change in price and production levels. Let us first consider the effects of an increase in the demand for a product. In summary, any one of the following could cause such an increase in the market demand:

- a change in preferences toward the product
- an increase in incomes if the product is a normal product, or a decrease in incomes if the product is an inferior product
- an increase in the price of a substitute product
- a decrease in the price of a complementary product
- the expectation that future prices or incomes will be higher or that there will be a future shortage of the product
- an increase in the population or a change in its income or age distribution

Any of these changes could cause people to buy more of a product, regardless of its price. As an example, let us combine the data from Tables 2.5 and 2.6 into **Table 2.7.**

TABLE 2.7   The Effects on the Market of an Increase in Demand

NUMBER OF CASES PER WEEK

Price per Case	Supply	Demand 1	Demand 2
$12	8	22	33
13	12	18	29
14	16	16	27
15	20	9	20
16	24	6	17
17	28	3	14
18	32	2	13

You can see that at the old demand (Demand 1) and supply, the equilibrium price was $14 and the quantity traded was 16 cases. Assume now that the demand for beer increases (Demand 2 in Table 2.7). Since consumers do not usually signal their intentions to producers in advance, producers are not aware that the demand has changed until they have evidence. The evidence will probably take the form of unsatisfied customers. At a price of $14 a case, the producers in total have produced 16 cases. At this price, the new demand is 27 cases. There is a shortage of 11 cases, and some customers will go home disappointed because there is not sufficient beer to satisfy all customers.

The important question is: Will these brewers now increase production to satisfy the higher demand? The surprising answer is no—at least not at the present price. Brewers are not in the business of satisfying customers; they are in the business of making profits. As the dean of economics, Adam Smith, wrote over 200 years ago:

> It is not from the benevolence of the butcher, the brewer, or the baker that we expect our dinner but from regard to their own self-interest.[1]

You may object that unless firms are responsive to the demands of customers, they will soon go out of business. And you are right. But equally, a firm that is *solely* responsive to its customers will go out of business even faster. Look back at the supply schedule in Table 2.7. At a price of $14, the brewers said they are prepared to produce 16 cases. They are not prepared to produce 27 cases, the amount that consumers now want. Why is that? Because, presumably, they can make more profits from producing 16 cases than from producing 27 cases; otherwise they would have produced 27 in the first place. In fact, it may well be that if they produced 27 cases at the current price of $14, they would end up enduring a loss. Does this mean that the shortage of beer will persist? No, because we have earlier seen that *shortages drive prices up* until the shortage disappears and the new quantity demanded is equal to the quantity supplied. This will occur at a price of $15, where the quantity demanded and the quantity supplied are equal at the equilibrium quantity of 20. This adjustment process can be seen in **Figure 2.10**.

FIGURE 2.10 Adjustment to an Increase in Demand

The increase in demand from D_1 to D_2 creates an immediate shortage of 11. This will cause an increase in the price of beer. The increase affects both producers, who will now increase the quantity supplied, and consumers, who will reduce the quantity demanded. Eventually, the price will reach a new equilibrium at $15, where the equilibrium quantity is 20, and there is no longer a shortage.

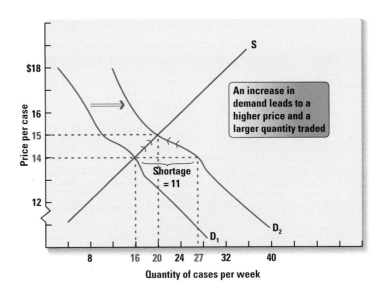

You can see in the graph that at the old price of $14, the new quantity demanded exceeds the quantity supplied. This shortage causes the price to rise. As it does so, notice that the quantity of beer that producers make also rises; that is, there will be an increase *in the quantity supplied*. Producers will produce more *not* because there is a shortage but because the shortage causes a rise in price. Note also that the increase in price

---

[1] Adam Smith, *Wealth of Nations* (Edwin Cannan edition, 1877), pp. 26–27.

causes some customers to reduce their purchases of beer; that is, there is a decrease *in the quantity demanded*. The price of beer will continue to increase as long as there is a shortage and will stop as soon as the shortage disappears. This occurs when the price has increased to $15. At the new equilibrium price, the quantity demanded will again equal the quantity supplied but at a higher quantity traded of 20 cases.

> **An increase in demand causes the price to increase and the quantity traded also to increase.**

The Effects of a Decrease in Demand

Now let's see what happens when there is a decrease in demand. Remember that a decrease in demand cannot be caused by an increase in price but is caused by a change in any of the non-price determinants, such as:

- a decrease in the preferences for the product
- a decrease in incomes if the product is a normal product, or an increase in incomes if the product is an inferior product
- a decrease in the price of a substitute product
- an increase in the price of a complementary product
- the expectation that future prices or incomes will be lower
- a decrease in the population or a change in its income or age distribution

A decrease in demand is shown in **Table 2.8** and illustrated in **Figure 2.11**.

TABLE 2.8   The Effects on the Market of a Decrease in Demand

	NUMBER OF CASES PER WEEK		
Price per Case	**Supply**	**Demand 1**	**Demand 2**
$12	8	22	16
13	12	18	12
14	16	16	10
15	20	9	3
16	24	6	0
17	28	3	0
18	32	2	0

The initial equilibrium price is $14, and the quantity traded is 16. Assume that the demand now decreases to Demand 2 in the table and D2 in Figure 2.11 on the graph. At a price of $14, producers will continue to produce 16 cases; yet consumers now wish to purchase only 10 cases. A surplus is immediately created in the market. Mounting unsold inventories and more intensive competition between suppliers will eventually push down the price. Notice in Figure 2.11 that as the price decreases, the quantity supplied also starts to decrease and the quantity demanded begins to increase. Both of these factors will cause the surplus to disappear. The price will eventually drop to a new equilibrium of $13 where the quantity demanded and the quantity supplied are equal at 12 cases. In short:

> **A decrease in demand will cause both the price and the quantity traded to fall.**

FIGURE 2.11 Adjustment to a Decrease in Demand

The drop in demand from D_1 to D_2 will cause an immediate surplus of 6, since the quantity supplied remains at 16, but the quantity demanded drops to 10. This surplus will cause the price to fall, and, as it does, the quantity demanded will increase while the quantity supplied will fall. This process will continue until the surplus is eliminated. This occurs at a new equilibrium price of $13 and an equilibrium quantity of 12.

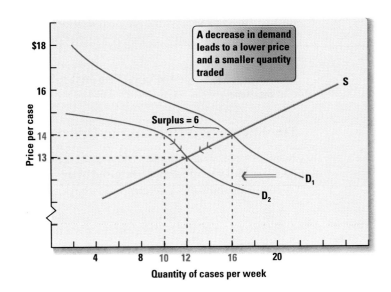

SELF-TEST

5. What effect will the following changes have upon (i) the demand for, (ii) the price, and (iii) the quantity traded of commercially brewed beer?

   A) A new medical report praising the healthy effects of drinking beer (in moderation, of course).

   B) A big decrease in the price of home-brewing kits.

   C) A rapid increase in population growth.

   D) Talk of a possible future strike of brewery workers.

   E) A possible future recession.

Change in Supply

change in supply: a change in the quantities supplied at every price, caused by a change in the determinants of supply.

Let us again be clear about what we mean by supply: it is the relationship between the price of the product and the quantities producers are willing and able to supply. Price is part of what economists call supply. In other words, supply does not mean a single quantity. What we now need to figure out is what could cause a **change in supply**. What factors will cause producers to offer a different quantity on the market even though the price has not changed—what will cause a change in supply? We begin with **Table 2.9**, where an increase in supply is illustrated. For reasons we will soon investigate, suppliers are now willing to supply an extra 6 cases of beer at every possible price. This is illustrated in **Figure 2.12**.

An increase in supply causes the whole supply curve to shift right. (Be careful if you are tempted to describe it as a downward shift because then you would be saying that as the supply goes up, the supply curve goes down, which could make things very confusing! Better to talk about a rightward shift.) This means that at each and every price, producers are now willing to produce more.

TABLE 2.9 An Increase in Supply

NUMBER OF CASES PER WEEK

Price per Case of Beer	Supply 1	Supply 2
$12	8	14
13	12	18
14	16	22
15	20	26
16	24	30
17	28	34
18	32	38

FIGURE 2.12 An Increase in Supply

At each price, the quantities supplied have now increased, that is, the supply curve has shifted right, from S_1 to S_2. For example, at a price of $14, the original quantity was 16 and has now increased to 22. Similarly, at a price of $17, the quantity supplied has increased from 28 to 34. In this example, the quantities supplied have increased by 6 units at every price level, thus causing a parallel shift in the supply curve.

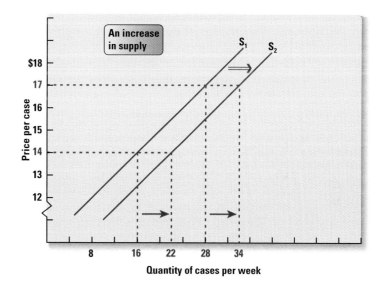

Determinants of a Change in Supply

What could have happened in the brewers' world to make them wish to produce more even though the price is unchanged? Since we are assuming that the prime motivation for the supplier is profit, then something must have happened to make brewing more profitable, which is inducing a higher supply. Profit is no more than the difference between revenue and cost, and since the price (and therefore revenue) is unchanged, then something must have affected the cost of producing beer. The first factor we will look at which might have decreased costs is the *price of productive resources*. For the brewer this includes the price of yeast, hops, malt, and other ingredients, as well as the price that must be paid for the brewing vats, bottles, and so on. If any of these should drop in price, then the cost for the brewer will fall and its profits will rise. Under these circumstances, since she is now making a bigger profit on each case of beer, she will be very willing to produce more. A fall in the price of productive resources will lead to an increase in supply. Conversely, an increase in the price of resources will cause a decrease in supply.

Another way of looking at the increase in supply, as shown in Figure 2.12, is to say that, rather than firms being willing to produce more at a given price, they are willing to accept lower prices to produce any given quantity. For instance, previously, in order to induce the brewers to supply a total of 28 cases per week, the price needed to be $17. Now that the costs of production have dropped, these same brewers are able to make the same profits by producing the 28 cases at a lower price of between $15 and $16 (presumably, $15.50 per case). This is the same thing as saying that the brewers are now willing to produce the same quantities as before at lower prices. Again, this would produce a rightward shift in the supply curve.

It is often suggested that the availability of resources is a major determinant of the supply of a product. A bad grape harvest—grapes being the key input in the making of wine—will obviously have an impact on the supply of wine. However, it's not really the difficulty in obtaining grapes that causes a decrease in the wine supply, since most things can be obtained *at a price*. But there's the rub. A bad grape harvest will cause the price of grapes to increase, and this increase will reduce the profitability and production of wine producers.

A second major determinant of supply is the *business taxes* levied by the various levels of government. They are similar to the other costs of doing business, and a decrease in them (or an increase in a subsidy) will lead firms to make higher profits and encourage them, therefore, to increase the supply; an increase in business taxes, on the other hand, will cause a decrease in supply.

A third determinant of supply is the *technology* used in production. An improvement in technology means nothing more than an improvement in the method of production. This will enable a firm to produce more with the same quantity of resources (or, for that matter, to produce the same output with fewer resources). An improvement in technology will not affect the actual price of the resources, but, because more can now be done with less, it will lead to a fall in the per unit cost of production. This means that an improvement in technology will lead to an increase in the supply.

The price of related products also affects the supply, just as it affected the demand. But here we must be careful, since we are looking at things from a producer's point of view and not a consumer's. In other words, what a producer regards as related will usually differ from a consumer's view of related. A fourth determinant of supply, then, is the *price of substitutes in production*. To a wheat farmer, for instance, the price of other grains like rye and barley will be of great interest because the production of all grain crops are related in terms of production methods and equipment. A significant increase in the price of rye, for example, may well tempt the wheat farmer to grow rye in the future. In other words, an increase in the price of one product will cause a drop in the supply of products that are substitutes in production. A decrease will have the opposite effect.

A fifth determinant of supply is the *future expectations of producers*. Again, this is analogous to the demand side of the market, but with a difference. While consumers will eagerly look forward to the drop in the price of products, producers view the same prospect with great anxiety. If a producer feels that the market is going to be depressed in the future and that prices are likely to be lower, she may be inclined to change production now, before the anticipated collapse. Lower expected future prices therefore tend to increase the present supply of a product. Higher expected future prices have the opposite effect and cause producers to hold off selling all of their present production in the hopes of making greater profits from the future higher prices.

Finally, the market supply will also be affected by the *number of suppliers*. An increase in the number of suppliers will cause an increase in the market supply, whereas a decrease in the number of suppliers will reduce the overall market supply.

Again, notice that one thing omitted from this list of supply determinants is any mention of demand. At the risk of repetition: firms are in business not to satisfy demand but to make profits. Simply because the demand for a product increases does not mean that producers will immediately increase production to satisfy the higher demand. However, the higher demand will cause the price to increase, and this increase induces firms to supply more, but this is an increase in the quantity supplied and *does not* imply an increase in the supply. That is, the supply curve remains unchanged.

In summary, the determinants of market supply are:

- prices of productive resources
- business taxes
- technology
- prices of substitutes in production
- future expectations of suppliers
- number of suppliers

The Effects of an Increase in Supply

We have just discussed six different factors that could affect the supply of a product. Let us be more specific and look at what can cause an *increase* in supply:

- a decrease in the price of productive resources
- a decrease in business taxes (or increase in subsidies)
- an improvement in technology
- a decrease in the price of a productively related product
- the expectation of a decline in the future price of the product
- an increase in the number of suppliers

Let us see the effects of an increase in supply by using the original demand for beer, and the increase in supply by using **Table 2.10**.

TABLE 2.10   The Effect on the Market of an Increase in Supply

	NUMBER OF CASES PER WEEK		
Price per Case of Beer	**Demand 1**	**Supply 1**	**Supply 2**
$12	22	8	14
13	18	12	18
14	16	16	22
15	9	20	26
16	6	24	30
17	3	28	34
18	2	32	38

At the original demand (Demand 1) and supply (Supply 1), the equilibrium price was $14 per case and the quantity traded was 16 cases. Assume that the supply now increases to Supply 2. At the present price of $14, there will be an immediate surplus of 6 cases. Before we look at the implications of this surplus, we ought to address a couple of possible qualms that some students might have. The first is this: won't customers take up this excess of beer? It is easy to see that, at this price, consumers have already given their response: they want to buy 16 cases, not 22 cases, or any other number. In other words, consumers are buying beer to satisfy their own tastes, not to satisfy the brewers. A second question is this: why would producers produce 22 cases, knowing that the demand at this price is only 16 cases? The answer is, they don't know. Each producer knows the circumstances in her own brewery and knows that, until now, she has been able to sell everything she has produced. With the prospect of higher profits coming from, let's say, a decrease in costs, the brewer wants to produce more. If all producers do the same, there will be a surplus of beer. **Figure 2.13** shows what will happen as a result of this surplus.

FIGURE 2.13   Adjustment to an Increase in Supply

The increase in the supply has the immediate effect of causing a surplus because the demand has remained unchanged. In this figure, at a price of $14, the quantity supplied has increased from 16 to 22, causing a surplus of 6. This will cause the price to drop, and as it does, the quantity demanded increases and the quantity supplied decreases, until a new equilibrium is reached at a new equilibrium price of $13 and quantity of 18.

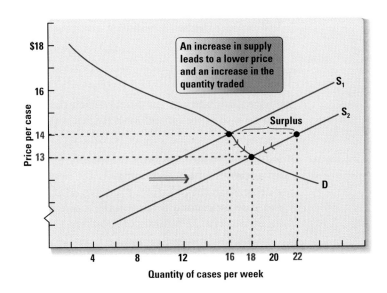

Faced with a surplus of beer, the market price will be forced down. As the price falls, the quantity demanded increases and the quantity supplied falls. Production increased initially, but because of the resulting drop in price, it is now dropping back slightly. The price will continue to drop until it reaches $13. Table 2.10 shows that, at this price, the quantity demanded and the quantity supplied are now equal at 18 cases. The effect of the increase in supply, then, is a lower price and a higher quantity traded.

SELF-TEST

6. Suppose that the demand and supply for strawberries in Corona are as follows (the quantities are in thousands of kilos per week):

Price	Demand	Supply 1	Supply 2
$4.00	140	60	_____
4.25	130	70	_____
4.50	120	80	_____
4.75	110	90	_____
5.00	100	100	_____
5.25	90	110	_____
5.50	80	120	_____

A) What are the present equilibrium price and equilibrium quantity? Graph the demand and supply curves, labelling them D_1 and S_1, and indicate equilibrium.
B) Suppose that the supply of strawberries were to increase by 50 percent. Show the new quantities in the Supply 2 column. What will be the new equilib-rium price and quantity? Draw in S_2 on your graph and indicate the new equilibrium.

7. What effect will the following changes have on the supply, price, and quantity traded of wine?
A) A bad harvest in the grape industry results in a big decrease in the supply of grapes.
B) The number of wineries increases.
C) The sales tax on wine increases.
D) The introduction of a new fermentation method reduces the time needed for the wine to ferment.
E) The government introduces a subsidy for each bottle of wine produced domestically.
F) The government introduces a quota limiting the amount of foreign wine entering Canada.
G) There is a big increase in wages for the workers in the wine industry.
H) A big increase occurs in the prices of wine coolers (an industry that is similar in technology to the wine industry).

We leave it to the student to confirm that a decrease in supply will cause a shortage that will eventually raise the price of the product. The net result will be a higher price *but* a lower quantity traded.

Final Words

To complete this introduction to demand and supply, let's use the following chart as a summary:

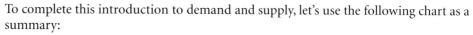

↑ Demand	→	shortage	→	↑ P	and ↑ Q traded
↓ Supply	→	shortage	→	↑ P	and ↓ Q traded
↓ Demand	→	surplus	→	↓ P	and ↓ Q traded
↑ Supply	→	surplus	→	↓ P	and ↑ Q traded

Note that when the demand changes, both the price and the quantity traded move in the same direction; when the supply changes, the quantity traded moves in the same direction, but the price moves in the opposite direction.

From this table you should confirm in your own mind that it is the supply of, and demand for, a product that determines its price, and not the price that determines supply and demand. A change in any of the factors that affects demand or supply will therefore lead to a change in the price. The price of a product *cannot* change *unless* there is a change in either the demand or the supply. It follows therefore that you cannot really analyze any problem that starts: "What happens if the price increases (decreases)...?" The reason for this, as the above chart makes clear, is that an increase in the price of a product might be caused by either the demand increasing or by the supply decreasing. But in the case of an increase in the demand, the quantity traded also increases, whereas in the

ADDED DIMENSION

The Famous Scissors Analogy

Since the time of Adam Smith, economists have continually struggled to understand how prices are determined. Toward the end of the nineteenth century, they tended to group into one of two camps: those who believed that the cost of production was the main determinant; and those who believed that consumer demand was the main determinant. Demand, in turn, was determined by what the famous economist Alfred Marshall called the utility (or satisfaction) derived from consumption.

Marshall, writing at the end of that century, was the first to present a lucid synthesis of the two views and suggest that neither demand nor supply alone can provide the answer. His famous analogy of the scissors says, "We might as reasonably dispute whether it is the upper or the under blade of scissors that cuts a piece of paper, as whether value [price] is governed by utility or cost of production. It is true that when one blade is held still, and the cutting is effected by moving the other, we may say with careless brevity that the cutting is done by the second; but the statement is not strictly accurate, and is to be excused only so long as it claims to be merely a popular and not a strictly scientific account of what happens."[1]

case of a decrease in the supply, the quantity traded falls. In the first case, we are talking about an expanding industry; in the second, we are looking at a contracting industry.

The next chapter will develop the ideas of demand and supply further and will analyze a number of diverse problems. To close this chapter, let's try to figure out a simple exercise and make some final observations.

Looking back over the past decade or so, what has happened to the prices of home computers? Generally speaking, even allowing for inflation, they have decreased. And what about the quantity of computers that are bought and sold now, compared with the situation a decade ago? Definitely, it has increased. So, according to our little chart above, what could have produced this result in the marketplace? Well, there is only one thing that could lead to a decrease in price and an increase in the quantity traded, and that is an increase in supply. And what in the computer world over the past years could have caused an increase in supply? The answer must be an improvement in technology that has significantly reduced the costs of producing computers.

As we shall see in Chapter 3, not only is the market system an efficient way of preventing persistent surpluses and shortages, but it also functions very well in rationing scarce goods, services, and resources.

SELF-TEST

8. The following are various changes that occur in different markets. Explain what will happen to either demand or supply and to the equilibrium price and quantity traded.

A) An increase in income upon the market for an *inferior product*.

B) A decrease in the price of steel on the *automobile industry*.

C) A government subsidy given to operators of *day-care centres*.

D) A government subsidy given to parents who want their children to attend *day-care centres*.

E) A medical report suggesting that *wine* is very fattening.

F) A big decrease in the amount of Middle East oil exports on the *refined-oil market*.

G) An increase in the popularity of *antique furniture*.

H) An increase in the price of coffee on the *tea market*.

---

[1] Alfred Marshall, *Principles of Economics*, 8th ed., p. 348.

However, we should mention a number of themes that we will take up in Chapter 8. In the modern world, competitive markets are few and far between, since many markets are dominated by big corporations, big trade unions, and consumer associations and are affected by government intervention. In addition, even when they are competitive, markets do not provide any guarantee that there will not be future periods of recession or inflation. Further, competitive markets cannot ensure that the right type or quantities of products are produced or that the distribution of incomes and wealth in a country are fair.

Finally, let's look back at the discussion that started this chapter and see if we can make sense of it. The one speaker started by stating that the price of houses has increased. (We presume he is talking about the market for existing, as well as new, homes.) Well, there are two major causes for a price increase: either the demand has increased (caused perhaps by lower interest rates or high immigration into the area); or the supply has decreased (caused by higher building costs or perhaps the expectation by sellers that prices will be higher in the future). In this particular conversation we are given no indication of the cause. However, the effects are going to be different. If housing prices increased because of a higher demand, you would expect to see a greater number of for-sale listings than usual; if they increased because of a lower supply, then the number of listings would be smaller than usual. It would be an easy enough job to figure out which was the cause. The rest of the conversation on the effects of a higher price is merely an exercise in confusion. Assuming that the present price is the equilibrium price, then nothing further will happen—at least until there is another change in demand or supply. Hopefully, you now realize what an important and versatile tool supply and demand analysis can be—but, like all tools, you must use it properly (and clean it off after every use!).

ADDED DIMENSION

Sales Always Equal Purchases

It is important not to confuse the terms "demand" and "supply" with "purchases" and "sales." As we have seen in this chapter, the quantity demanded and the quantity supplied are not always equal. However, purchases and sales, since they are two sides of the same transaction, must always be equal. The accompanying graph explains the differences in the terms.

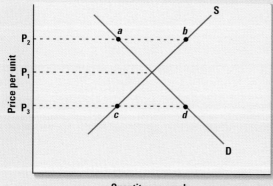

Quantity per week

P_1 is the equilibrium price, and at this price the quantity demanded and supplied are equal—this is the amount traded and is the same thing as the amount sold and purchased. If the price happened to be above equilibrium, however, at a price, say, P_2, then the quantity demanded is denoted by a, and the quantity supplied by b. Clearly, the two quantities are not equal. But how much is bought and sold at this price? The answer is quantity a. It really doesn't matter how much is being produced since, at this price, this is the maximum amount that consumers are willing to buy. The difference ab represents the amount unsold, or the surplus.

On the other hand, what is the effect of the price being below equilibrium? Suppose the price is P_3, where the quantity supplied (c) is less than the quantity demanded (d)? This time, how much is being bought and sold? The answer must be quantity c. It doesn't matter how much consumers want to buy of this product if producers are only making quantity c available. In general, the amount bought and sold is always equal to the smaller of the quantity demanded or supplied.

REVIEW

1. What are the four major determinants of individual demand?
2. Explain the difference between an *inferior* and a *normal* product.
3. What will happen to the price of a product if:
    a) the price of its substitute decreases?
    b) the price of its complement decreases?
4. Explain how future expectations can affect the behaviour of consumers.
5. What factors, aside from the determinants of individual demand, can affect the market demand?
6. Explain, step by step, how an *increase* in demand eventually affects both the price and the quantity traded.
7. Explain, step by step, how a *decrease* in demand eventually affects both the price and the quantity traded.
8. What are the six major determinants of the market supply?
9. Explain how the market adjusts to both an increase and a decrease in the supply of a product.
10. What can cause the price of a product to increase? What can cause it to decrease?

STUDY GUIDE

Chapter Highlights

In this chapter you learned that, in competitive markets, the price and quantity traded of any product depends on both the demand for, and the supply of, that product. Once equilibrium is achieved, price and quantity will not change unless either supply or demand changes first. In order to fully understand this lesson, you must also understand the following:

1. *Demand* is the price/quantity relationship of a product that consumers are willing and able to buy per period of time.

2. *Market demand* is simply the conceptual summation of each individual's demand within a given market.

3. The demand curve is *downward sloping* because of the:
   - substitution effect;
   - income effect.

4. Market demand *changes* if there is a change in:
   - consumers' preferences;
   - consumers' incomes;
   - the price of related products;
   - expectations of future prices, incomes, or availability;
   - the size of the market or income and age distribution.

5. Products can be *related* in two ways, as:
   - complements;
   - substitutes.

6. All products are *either*:
   - normal products;
   - inferior products.

7. *Supply* is the price/quantity relationship of a product that producers are willing and able to sell per period of time.

8. *Market supply* is simply the conceptual summation of each firm's supply within a given market.

9. Market supply *changes* if there is a change in:
   - the price of resources;
   - business taxes;
   - technology;
   - prices of substitutes in production;
   - future expectations of suppliers;
   - the number of suppliers.

10. An *increase in demand* will cause a shortage and result in both price and quantity traded rising.

11. A *decrease in demand* will cause a surplus and result in both price and quantity falling.

12. An *increase in supply* will cause a surplus and result in price falling and quantity traded rising.

13. A *decrease in supply* will cause a shortage and result in price rising and quantity falling.

New Glossary Terms

Study Tips

1. It is with this chapter that you will learn to appreciate the need for precision in the use of economic terms. For instance, the terms *demand* and *supply* have very clear definitions. "Demand" does *not* mean the amount a person wishes to buy or the amount she is buying. Demand is not a single quantity but a combination of different prices and quantities. Similarly, you cannot use the term "supply" synonymously with output, production, or quantity supplied. It is *not* a single quantity but, again, a range of different quantities and prices.

2. If you have understood the first point, then this next one should make sense. A change in price cannot affect the demand, since price is already part of what we mean by demand. That doesn't mean that a change in price doesn't affect consumers; generally, people change the amounts they purchase as a result of a price change, but this is what we call a change in the quantity demanded and *not* a change in demand. Similarly, a change in price leaves the supply unaffected. But it definitely affects the *quantity supplied*. These points are illustrated in the way that the demand and supply curves are affected. A change in price causes no change in the demand or supply curves but results in a movement *along* the curves. Only changes in other determinants, besides price, will cause a shift in the curves.

3. It is important for you to keep the concepts of demand and supply separate in your mind. A change in demand does *not* have any affect on the supply. This means that the supply curve will not shift when the demand curve changes. Similarly, you must disconnect the demand from the supply. A change in the supply has no impact on demand.

4. There really is no alternative to learning the factors that do affect the demand and supply. Memorize the five determinants of market demand and the six determinants of market supply. Note that, with the exception of expectations of future price changes, the factors that affect demand have no impact on supply, and vice versa. If possible, try not to be too "cute" when trying to figure out the way in

which various changes in determinants affect markets. It is possible to give a convoluted explanation of why, for example, a change in the number of suppliers can affect preferences and, therefore, the demand of customers of that product. While remotely possible, the effect would be of minor significance. Instead use common sense and focus on the main effects. Remember that usually a change in one determinant will affect *only* the demand or the supply, seldom both.

5. Don't skip the basics in this chapter even if, at times, they might seem a little simple. For example, don't try to work out the effects of changes in demand or supply until you first have a good grasp of equilibrium.

6. Finally, the most important lesson that you can get from this chapter is that the price of a product is determined by both demand and supply. Price is the effect and not the cause. This means that equilibrium price cannot change in a free market unless there has been a change in either the demand or the supply.

Are You Sure?

Indicate whether the following statements are true or false. If false, indicate why they are false.

1. The term "demand" means the quantities that people would like to purchase at various different prices.

   T or **F**   If false: _____

   _____

2. A change in the price of a product has no effect on the demand for that product.

   T or **F**   If false: _____

   _____

3. An increase in the price of a product causes a decrease in the real income of consumers.

   T or **F**   If false: _____

   _____

4. An increase in the price of a product leads to an increase in the supply.

   T or **F**   If false: _____

   _____

5. Equilibrium price implies that everyone who would like to purchase a product is able to.

   T or **F**   If false: _____

   _____

6. Surpluses drive prices up; shortages drive prices down.

   T or **F**   If false: _____

   _____

7. An increase in incomes will lead to a decrease in the demand for an inferior product.

   T or **F**   If false: _____

   _____

8. A decrease in the demand for a product will lead to a decrease in both the price and the quantity traded.

   T or **F**   If false: _____

   _____

9. An increase in business taxes causes the supply curve to shift left.

   T or **F**   If false: _____

   _____

10. A decrease in supply causes the price to fall and the quantity traded to increase.

   T or **F**   If false: _____

   _____

Choose the Best

11. What does the term "demand" refer to?
    a) The amounts that consumers are either willing or able to purchase at various prices.
    b) The amounts that consumers are both willing and able to purchase at various prices.

12. What will a surplus of a product lead to?
    a) A reduction in supply.
    b) A reduction in price.

13. What is the effect of a decrease in the price of a product?
    a) It will increase consumers' real income while leaving their actual income unchanged.
    b) It will increase consumers' actual income while leaving their real income unchanged.

14. How will a change in income affect the demand for an inferior product?
    a) The demand will increase if the income of consumers increases.
    b) The demand will increase if the income of consumers decreases.
    c) The demand for an inferior product is not affected by consumer incomes.

15. Which of the following could cause an increase in the supply of wheat?
    a) A decrease in the price of oats.
    b) An imposition of a sales tax on wheat.
    c) An increase in the price of fertilizer.

16. What is the effect of an increase in the price of coffee?
    a) It will lead to an increase in the demand for tea.
    b) It will lead to a decrease in the demand for tea.
    c) It will have no effect on the tea market.

17. What is the slope of the demand curve?
    a) It is downward-sloping because when the price of a product falls, consumers are willing and able to buy more.
    b) It is upward-sloping because when the price of a product falls, consumers are willing and able to buy more.
    c) It is upward-sloping because when the price of a product increases, consumers are willing and able to buy more.

18. Which of the following factors will shift the demand curve left?
    a) An increase in the price of a substitute product.
    b) A decrease in the price of a complementary product.
    c) An increase in income if the product is an inferior product.
    d) The expectation that future prices of the product will be higher.

19. What is the effect of an increase in the price of a productive resource?
    a) It will cause a decrease in the supply of the product.
    b) It will cause an increase in the supply of the product.
    c) It will cause a decrease in the demand for the product.
    d) It will cause an increase in the demand for the product

20. What is the effect of a shortage?
    a) It will cause a decrease in the price, leading to an increase in the quantity supplied and a decrease in the quantity demanded.
    b) It will cause a decrease in the price, leading to a decrease in the quantity supplied and an increase in the quantity demanded.
    c) It will cause an increase in the price, leading to an increase in the quantity supplied and a decrease in the quantity demanded.
    d) It will cause an increase in the price, leading to a decrease in the quantity supplied and an increase in the quantity demanded.

21. In what way are Pepsi-Cola and Coca-Cola related?
    a) They are substitute products.
    b) They are complementary products.
    c) They are inferior products.
    d) They are unrelated products.

22. A rightward shift in the supply curve for a product could be caused by all of the following *except one*. Which is the exception?
    a) The expectation by suppliers that the future price of the product will be higher.
    b) A decrease in the price of a productive resource used in its manufacture.
    c) A decrease in the price of a product that is a substitute in production.
    d) A technological improvement in manufacturing methods.

23. What is the effect of a decrease in the supply of a product?
    a) It will cause an increase in both the price and the quantity traded.
    b) It will cause an increase in the price but a decrease in the quantity traded.
    c) It will cause a decrease in both the price and in the quantity traded.
    d) It will cause a decrease in the price but an increase in the quantity traded.

Table 2.11 depicts the market for mushrooms (in thousands of kilos per month). Use this table to answer questions 24 and 25.

TABLE 2.11

Price ($)	2.50	3.00	3.50	4.00	4.50	5.00	5.50	6.00
Quantity demanded	64	62	60	58	56	54	52	50
Quantity supplied	40	44	48	52	56	60	64	68

24. Refer to Table 2.11 to answer this question. What are the values of equilibrium price and quantity traded?
    a) $3 and 52.
    b) $3 and 62.
    c) $4 and 58.
    d) $4.50 and 56.
    e) They cannot be determined from the data.

25. Refer to Table 2.11 to answer this question. What will happen if the price of the product is $3?
    a) There would be a surplus of 18, which would lead to a decrease in price.
    b) There would be a shortage of 18, which would lead to an increase in price.
    c) There would be a shortage of 18, which would lead to a decrease in price.
    d) There would be a surplus of 18, which would lead to an increase in price.
    e) There would be neither a surplus nor a shortage.

26. How will the demand and supply of a product be affected if both producers and consumers expect the future price of a product will be higher than at present?
    a) It will cause an increase in demand but a decrease in supply.
    b) It will cause an increase in both the demand and supply.
    c) It will cause a decrease in both the demand and supply.
    d) It will cause an increase in supply but will have no effect on demand.
    e) It will cause an increase in supply but a decrease in demand.

27. In what way are products A and B related if an increase in the price of product A leads to a decrease in the demand for product B?
    a) Product A must be a productive resource used in the manufacture of product B.
    b) Product B must be a productive resource used in the manufacture of product A.
    c) The two products must be complements.
    d) The two products must be substitutes.
    e) The two products must be inferior products.

Refer to **Figure 2.14** to answer questions 28, 29, and 30.

FIGURE 2.14

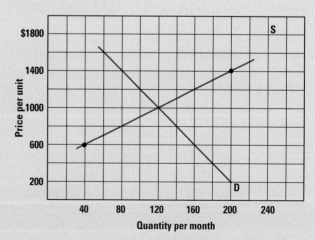

28. Refer to Figure 2.14 to answer this question. What will be the effect if the price is now $1200?
    a) There would be a surplus of 30.
    b) There would be a shortage of 30.

c) 160 would be purchased.

d) There would be a surplus of 60.

e) The price will increase.

29. Refer to Figure 2.14 to answer this question. Assume that there is a shortage of 60 units. What does this mean?

    a) Purchasers would be willing to pay an additional $600 for the quantity they are now purchasing.

    b) The price must be above equilibrium.

    c) The price must be $1200.

d) The price must be $600.

e) None of the above are correct.

30. Refer to Figure 2.14 to answer this question. Suppose that initially the market was in equilibrium and that demand increased by 60. What will be the new equilibrium as a result?

    a) A price of $1000 and quantity traded of 120.

    b) A price of $1000 and quantity traded of 160.

    c) A price of $1200 and quantity traded of 160.

    d) A price of $1400 and quantity traded of 160.

    e) A price of $1400 and quantity traded of 240.

Problems

31. In Kirin, at a market price of $1 per kilo, there is a shortage of 60 kilos of avocados. For each 50-cent increase in the price, the quantity demanded drops by 5 kilos while the quantity supplied increases by 10 kilos. What will be the equilibrium price? What will be the surplus or shortage at a price of $4.50?

    Equilibrium price: _____.

    (surplus/shortage): _____ of: _____ kilos.

32. Circle which of the following factors will lead to an increase in the demand for cranberry juice (which is a normal good).

    a) A drop in the price of cranberries.

    b) A drop in the price of apple juice.

    c) A drop in the price of cranberry juice.

    d) A decrease in consumer incomes.

    e) The expectation by consumers that the price of cranberry juice is likely to increase.

    f) An improvement in the juicing process that lowers the costs of production of cranberry juice.

33. Circle which of the following factors will lead to a drop in the price of wine, which is a normal product, regarded by consumers as a substitute for beer and a complement to cheese. (There may be more than one.)

    a) A drop in the price of grapes.

    b) An increase in the price of beer.

    c) A drop in the wage costs in the brewery industry.

    d) A drop in the tax on wine but no change to beer taxes.

    e) A drop in the tax on beer but no change to the wine tax.

TABLE 2.12

	Market	Event	D	S	P	Q
a)	Compact discs	A technological improvement reduces the cost of producing compact disc players.				
b)	Butter	New medical evidence suggesting that margarine causes migraines.				
c)	Newspapers	Because of worldwide shortages, the price of pulp and paper increases dramatically.				
d)	Low-quality toilet paper	Consumer incomes rise significantly.				
e)	Video rentals	Movie theatres halve their admission prices.				
f)	Beef	World price of lamb increases.				

34. Consider the effects of each of the events outlined in **Table 2.12** on the market indicated. Indicate by placing a (↑), (↓) or (0) under the appropriate heading to indicate whether there will be an increase, decrease, or no change in demand (D), supply (S), equilibrium price (P), and quantity traded (Q).

Translations

Explain the possible cause and the effect of the movement from point *a* to point *b* in **Figure 2.15**.

FIGURE 2.15

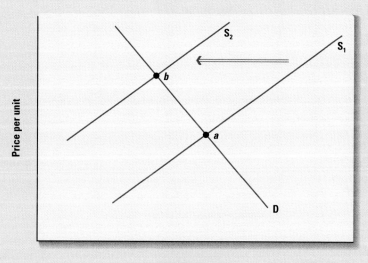

Quantity per period

Answer: _____

_____

_____.

Key Problem

Table 2.13 shows the market for wool (the quantities are in tonnes per year).

TABLE 2.13

Price ($)	100	200	300	400	500	600	700
Quantity demanded	10	9	8	7	6	5	4
Quantity supplied	1	3	5	7	9	11	13

a) Plot the demand and supply curves on **Figure 2.16**, and label them D_1 and S_1.

b) What are the values of equilibrium price and quantity? Mark the equilibrium as e_1 on the graph in Figure 2.14.

Equilibrium price: _____; equilibrium quantity: _____.

c) If the price of wool were $300, would there be a surplus or a shortage?

(Surplus/shortage): _____ of: _____.

Indicate the amount of the surplus or shortage on the graph.

FIGURE 2.16

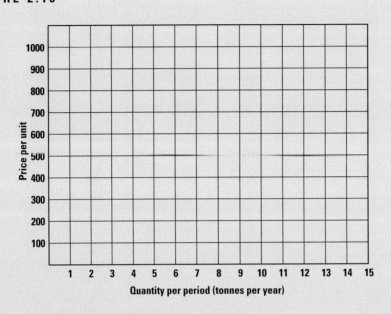

d) Suppose that the demand were to increase by 50 percent. Draw and label the new demand curve as D_2. What are the new values of equilibrium price and quantity? Mark the new equilibrium as e_2 on the graph.

Equilibrium price: _____; equilibrium quantity: _____.

e) Following the change in d), assume now that the supply decreases by 7 units. Draw and label the new supply curve as S_2. What are the new values of equilibrium price and quantity? Mark this new equilibrium as e_3.

Equilibrium price: _____; equilibrium quantity: _____.

More of the Same

Table 2.14 shows the market for olives (the quantities are in thousands of kilos per year).

TABLE 2.14

Price ($)	0	0.50	1.00	1.50	2.00	2.50	3.00	3.50	4.00
Quantity demanded	5.5	5	4.5	4	3.5	3	2.5	2	1.5
Quantity supplied	1	2	3	4	5	6	7	8	9

a) Plot the demand and supply curves, and label them D_1 and S_1.

b) What are the values of equilibrium price and quantity? Mark the equilibrium on the graph as e_1.

c) If the price of olives were $3.50, would there be a surplus or a shortage? How much? Mark the amount on the graph.

d) Suppose that the demand were to decrease by 3. Label the new demand curve D_2. What are the new values of equilibrium price and quantity? Mark the new equilibrium on the graph as e_2.

e) Following the change in d), assume now that the supply decreases by 50 percent. Label the new supply curve S_2. What are the new values of equilibrium price and quantity? Mark the new equilibrium on the graph as e_3.

UNANSWERED QUESTIONS

Short Essays

1. Explain, in terms of demand and supply analysis, why the price of maple syrup may be different in London, Ontario, from that in London, England.

2. Explain some of the factors that might reduce the price of movie theatre admission.

3. Explain what could cause a surplus and what could cause a shortage in a competitive market. How does the market eliminate them?

4. Explain the difference between a decrease in supply and a decrease in the quantity supplied.

5. What is the difference between "scarcity" and "shortage"?

6. Does the term "quantity demanded" mean the same thing as "quantity purchased"? Explain.

Analytical Questions

7. The two graphs in **Figure 2.17** show the markets for orange juice and for apple juice, which are initially in equilibrium.

FIGURE 2.17

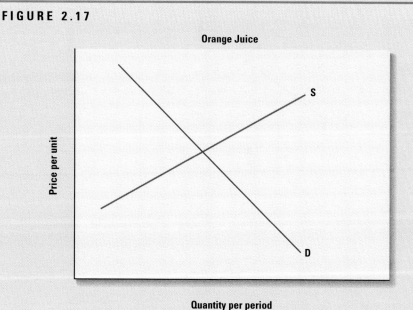

Orange Juice

FIGURE 2.17 continued

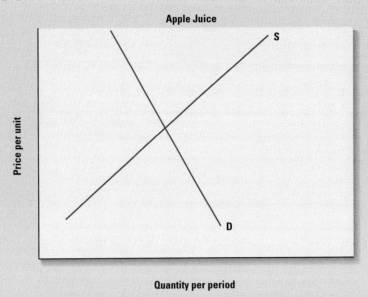

Apple Juice

Show what will happen to the prices and quantities traded of both products if a severe frost in Florida were to seriously damage the orange crop.

8. Given the graph of the market for starfruit shown in **Figure 2.18**, explain each change in terms of a shift in the appropriate curve, or movement along a curve; and for each change give an example of what might have caused the change:

FIGURE 2.18

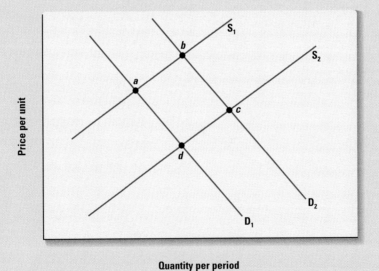

a) From point *a* to point *b*.
b) From point *a* to point *d*.

c) From point *c* to point *b*.

d) From point *c* to point *d*.

9. Consider the effects of each of the following events on the market for beef in Canada. Indicate, by placing a (↑), (↓), or (−) under the appropriate heading in Table 2.15, whether there will be an increase, decrease, or no change in demand, supply, equilibrium price, and quantity traded.

TABLE 2.15

	Event	Demand	Supply	Price	Quantity Traded
a)	Medical research indicates that cholesterol in beef is a major cause of heart attacks.				
b)	Improved cattle feeds reduce the cost of beef production.				
c)	Chicken sales are banned due to an outbreak of chicken cholera.				
d)	The price of pork decreases because the government gives a subsidy to pork producers.				
e)	A reduction in income taxes causes the incomes of Canadian consumers to rise sharply.				
f)	The price of cattle feed rises due to a drought.				

10. Suppose that in response to the high rent and low supply of affordable rental accommodation in the Toronto market, the city decides to introduce a "rental chit" system. Low-income families will receive one chit per month with a value of $200, which can only be used to help pay their rent. Draw a supply and demand graph showing the effects on the rental market.

11. "The price of houses rises when the demand increases. The demand for houses decreases when the price increases." Are these two statements each correct? Are they contradictory? Explain.

12. Suppose that new medical research strongly indicates that the consumption of coffee can cause cancer of the colon. What effect will this news have on the price and quantity traded of the following products?
   a) Coffee beans.
   b) Tea, a substitute for coffee.
   c) Danish pastries, a complement to coffee.
   d) Tea pots, a complement to tea.
   e) Cinnamon rolls, a substitute for Danish pastries.

13. Explain how each of the changes below are explained by changes in either supply or demand.
   a) The price of guitars falls, but the quantity traded increases.
   b) The price and quantity traded of saxophones decrease.
   c) The price of trombones increases, while the quantity traded falls.
   d) The price and quantity traded of clarinets increases.

Numerical Questions

14. You are given **Figure 2.19**'s demand curves for Tomi, Tami, and Timi.

FIGURE 2.19

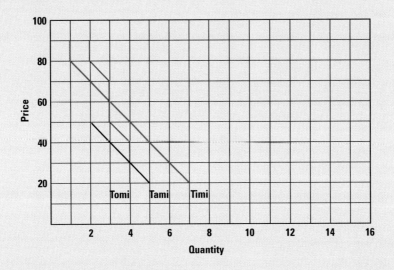

a) Draw in the total (market) demand curve.

The market supply is as shown in **Table 2.16**.

TABLE 2.16

Price	Quantity
20	6
30	7
40	8
50	9
60	10
70	11
80	12
90	13
100	14

b) Draw in the market supply curve.
c) What is the equilibrium price and quantity traded?

15. **Table 2.17** shows the market demand and supply for Fuji apples in Peterborough.

TABLE 2.17

Price	Demand	Supply
0	240	90
2	200	110
4	160	130
6	120	150
8	80	170
10	40	190

a) Graph the demand and supply curves.
b) What is equilibrium price and quantity traded?
c) Suppose the supply increases by 60. Draw the new supply curve.
d) What is price and quantity at the new equilibrium?

16. **Table 2.18** shows the demand for and supply of packaged cookies.

TABLE 2.18

Price ($)	0	1	2	3	4	5	6	7	8	9	10
Demand	10	9	8	7	6	5	4	3	2	1	0
Supply	0	1	2	3	4	5	6	7	8	9	10
Shortage/Surplus											

a) Complete the table, and then graph the demand and supply curves and label them D_1 and S_1. What is the equilibrium price and quantity?
b) Assume that the supply increases by 50 percent, that is, the quantity increases by 50 percent at every price. Draw and label the new supply curve S_2. What is the new equilibrium price and quantity?
c) Assume *instead* that the supply increases by 2 units at every price. Draw and label the new supply curve S_3. What is the new equilibrium price and quantity?
d) Now assume that the demand increases by 2 units at every price. Draw and label the new demand curve D_2. What is the new equilibrium price and quantity (D_2/S_3)?

17. **Table 2.19** shows the demand for the upcoming concert to be given by the string quartet, Guns and Butter, at the new 3000-capacity Saskatoon Auditorium.

TABLE 2.19

Price	Quantity Demanded
$10	8000
15	7000
20	6000
25	5000
30	4000
35	3000
40	2000
45	1000

a) Over what price range would there be a shortage of seats? Over what range would there be a surplus?
b) Suppose the promoters of the concert set the price at $25 per ticket. What will be the result?
c) Suppose that, in response to the great demand for the first concert, the promoters decide to add a second show open *only* to those who were unable to attend the first concert. What is the maximum price they could charge for this concert and still fill the auditorium?

18. Figure 2.20 shows the market for the new Guns and Butter compact disc, "Live at Saskatoon."
    a) Suppose that the CD producers put the disc on sale for $8 each. How much will be the surplus or shortage? How many will be sold?
    b) What is the maximum price at which the quantity actually sold in a) could have been sold?
    c) If the CD producers had actually put the CD on the market at the price mentioned in b), what would have been the resulting surplus/shortage?

FIGURE 2.20

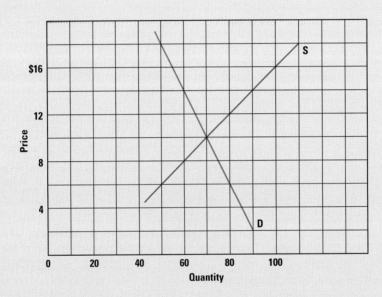

 Web-Based Activities

....

1. Draw a demand curve for public transportation. Is your hypothetical good "inferior" or "normal"? Explain. Go to the Family Expenditures section at www.tc.gc.ca./pol/en/t-facts_e/Economy_Data_menu.htm to help with this exercise. Now return to the main site of this same address to determine what has happened to disposable personal income per person in your province. Draw what you would predict to have happened to your demand curve over the period of 1961-96 if everything else was held constant.

2. Go to **www.move.de/amm/CDMarket.htm**. In 1996, what was the equilibrium price and quantity for CDs in Canada, in the United States, in Japan, and in the United Kingdom? Why do you suppose the market equilibrium differs for CDs in these countries? What is the impact on the CD market if it becomes more costly or difficult to pirate (illegally copy) CDs?

The Algebra of Demand and Supply

The Algebra of the Market

We saw in the text how can we describe the market place in terms of both tables and graphs. In this appendix we will see how we can also analyze demand and supply algebraically. Suppose that the following graph and table show the demand for soy milk in Canada:

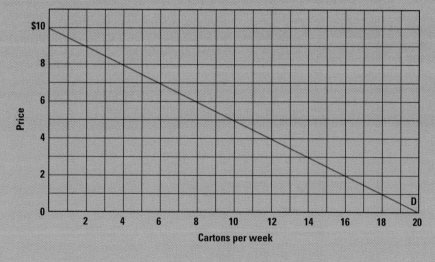

Number of cartons per week	
Price ($)	Quantity
0	20
1	18
2	16
3	14
4	12
5	10
6	8
7	6
8	4
9	2
10	0

You will remember from the toolkit that, in general, the algebraic expression for a straight line is:

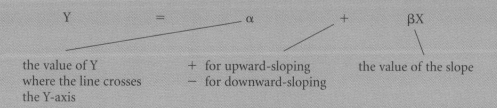

$$Y = \alpha + \beta X$$

the value of Y where the line crosses the Y-axis

+ for upward-sloping
− for downward-sloping

the value of the slope

On our graph, price is shown on the vertical (Y) axis and quantity demanded on the horizontal (X) axis. Therefore the general expression for the demand curve is given as:

$$P \ = \ \alpha \ + \ \beta Q^d$$

Here, the value of α is equal to ($)10. This is where the demand curve crosses the price axis, i.e., it is the highest price payable. The value of the slope is the ratio of change or rise/run. In terms of the demand curve, the slope shows by how much the quantity changes as the price changes, in other words:

$$\text{the slope equals} \quad \frac{\Delta \ (\text{change in}) \ P}{\Delta \ (\text{change in}) \ Q}$$

For our demand curve, that value equals:

$$\frac{1}{-2}$$

This means that each time the price changes by $1, quantity changes (in the opposite direction) by 2 units. The equation for this demand curve then is:

$$P \ = \ 10 \ - \ \frac{1}{2}Q^d$$

Though this is graphically the correct way to express it, in terms of economic logic, the quantity demanded is dependent on the price, rather than the other way about, so let us re-arrange the terms, as follows:

$$Q^d \ = \ 20 \ - \ 2P$$

Now let's look at the supply side of things: The following table and graph show the supply of soy milk in the market:

FIGURE A2

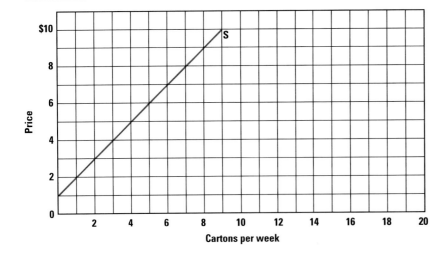

Number of cartons per week	
Price ($)	Quantity
0	—
1	0
2	1
3	2
4	3
5	4
6	5
7	6
8	7
9	8
10	9

The general equation for the supply curve is:

$$P \ = \ \alpha \ + \ \beta Q^s$$

As with the demand curve, α shows the value where the curve crosses the vertical (price) axis. This happens at a price of $1. The value of the slope is, again, the same as for the demand curve:

$$\frac{\Delta \text{ (change in) P}}{\Delta \text{ (change in) Q}}$$

For this supply curve, it equals:

$$\frac{1}{+1}$$

A $1 change in price causes a change of 1 unit in the quantity supplied. The equation for this supply curve, then is:

$$P \quad = \quad 1 \quad + \quad Q^s$$

As we did with the demand curve, let us rearrange this equation in terms of Q^s, thus:

$$Q^s \quad = \quad -1 \quad + \quad P$$

Bringing demand and supply together in **Figure A3**, allows us to find out the equilibrium values.

FIGURE A3

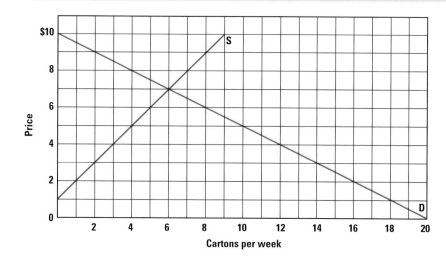

Number of cartons per week		
Price ($)	Q^d	Q^s
0	20	—
1	18	0
2	16	1
3	14	2
4	12	3
5	10	4
6	8	5
7	6	6
8	4	7
9	2	8
10	0	9

From either the table or the graph, it is easy to see that the equilibrium price is equal to $7. At this price, the quantity demanded and quantity supplied are both 6 units. Finding equilibrium algebraically is also straightforward. We want to find the price at which the quantity demanded equals the quantity supplied. We know the equations for each so we simply set them equal, as follows:

$$Q^d \quad = \quad Q^s$$

$$20 \quad - \quad 2P \quad = \quad -1 \quad + \quad P$$

This gives us:

$$3P = 21$$

Therefore,

$$P = 7$$

If we substitute $P = 7$ in either equation (and it's best to do both to make sure you are correct) gives us:

$$Q^d = 20 - 2(7) = 6$$
$$Q^s = -1 + (7) = 6$$

Doing things algebraically sometimes makes things easier. For instance, suppose that the market demand were to increase by 3 units, i.e., the quantities demanded increased by 3 units at every price. What effect would this have on the equilibrium price and quantity? Algebraically, this is quite straightforward to calculate. The increase in demand means that the value of the (quantity) intercept increases by 3, and gives us a new demand equation as follows:

$$Q^d_2 = 23 - 2P$$

The supply has not changed, so we can calculate the new equilibrium as follows:

$$(Q^d_2 = Q_s): \quad 23 - 2P = -1 + P$$

This gives us:

$$3P = 24$$

Therefore,

$$P = 8$$

and the new equilibrium quantity becomes 7.

STUDY GUIDE QUESTIONS FOR APPENDIX TO CHAPTER 2

1. If $Q^d = 40 - 2P$ and $Q^s = 10 + 3P$, what are the equilibrium values of price and quantity?

2. a) If $Q^d = 100 - 5P$ and $Q^s = 10 + P$, what are the equilibrium values of price and quantity?

   b) What will be the new equilibrium values of price and quantity if the demand increases by 30?

3. a) If $P = 11 - 0.25 Q^d$, what is the algebraic expression for Q^d?

   b) If $P = -16 + 2Q^s$, what is the algebraic expression for Q^s?

   c) What are the equilibrium values of price and quantity?

Demand and Supply: An Elaboration

What's ahead...We start this chapter by looking at circumstances that could cause simultaneous changes in demand and supply. We then ask how well markets operate and why governments often intervene. We next look at the reasons why governments sometimes introduce various types of price controls, and then we try to identify the costs and benefits of such intervention. Finally, we explore a number of variations of demand and supply and explain the situations that could cause the demand and supply to deviate from normal.

A QUESTION OF RELEVANCE...

You are probably aware that every province in Canada has legislated a minimum wage for hired labour. Do you think that this benefits you as a student looking for work to help pay for your education? Do you think that farmers should be guaranteed minimum prices for the products they sell? Are you living in a province that has rent controls? If so, who do you think benefits from such a policy? These are questions that sometimes generate a lot of debate. Make a mental note of your answers now, and see if they change as a result of studying this chapter.

When we look at the way that markets operate, there is a great danger in believing that the laws of demand and supply are immutable scientific laws that are an integral part of the natural universe. Nothing could be further from the truth. As Oser and Brue wrote, commenting on the approach of the economist Alfred Marshall:

> Economic laws are social laws—statements of tendencies, more or less certain, more or less definite.[1]

The collective behaviour of consumers and producers in the marketplace is a result of the society in which they live. Each society has its own history, economic structure, and political structure. So, while the tools of demand and supply are versatile and powerful aids for economists, we must realize that they have certain limitations that we will look at in this chapter. The results we obtain using demand and supply analysis demonstrate general tendencies that are likely to occur only under given circumstances. In the previous chapter we suggested that the price of a product is determined by demand and supply. This is only true under certain conditions. In many cases, the price of products we buy are set by the manufacturers and retailers, not by consumers and producers somehow coming together to form an agreement. Similarly, the government determines the price of a number of goods and services that it provides, and as we shall see later in this chapter, it also stipulates the minimum and maximum prices of a number of other products provided by the private sector.

ADDED DIMENSION

Alfred Marshall: The Neoclassical Giant

Alfred Marshall (1842–1924) was the son of a tyrannical father who was a cashier at the Bank of England. His father wanted him to put away such frivolous pastimes as chess and mathematics and instead devote himself to higher pursuits. To this end, he decided that Alfred would train for the church. However, Alfred rebelled, and instead of taking up a scholarship to study divinity at Oxford University, with financial help from an uncle he studied mathematics, physics, and later economics at Cambridge University. Later, as professor of economics at the same school, he influenced a whole generation of economists.

His fame was sealed with the publication of his *Principles of Economics* in 1890. Marshall was a precise and painstaking scholar, and his book was the result of years of study and research. In this text, Marshall established himself as the intellectual leader of "neoclassical economics" and provided a synthesis of the classical ideas of Smith and Ricardo, with the new ideas of marginal analysis.

Despite the fact that Marshall was an expert mathematician, he felt that mathematics should be regarded merely as a useful tool for economists rather than as the provider of fundamental economic truths. He felt that the "laws of demand" suggest what possible outcomes may result under certain circumstances and that those results may be desirable, but they are not imperative. Students of economics also owe a debt to Marshall for introducing graphical analysis into the discipline.

Under what circumstances do the forces of demand and supply determine the price of products? Strictly speaking, they do so only in what economists term a "perfectly competitive" market, a market in which there are no big dominant firms and no interference by the government. (Chapter 8 will look at this type of market in some detail.) It is important to be aware that competitive markets as described in Chapter 2 only work well if they are *truly* competitive. The existence of bigness in the marketplace, whether it is in the form of big corporations, big trade unions, or big govern-

[1] J. Oser and S. L. Brue, *The Evolution of Economic Thought*, 4th ed. (New York: Harcourt Brace), p. 273.

ment, detracts from the efficient working of the market. In essence, whenever there is a powerful participant or group of participants buying or selling in the market, the benefits of competition will be seriously reduced.

But does this also mean that if there are big firms operating they can then ignore the market and charge whatever prices they like? Well, from one point of view, yes they can—but only at their own peril. **Figure 3.1** makes this clear.

This figure illustrates the market for a particular type of four-wheel-drive car. The demand curve, as usual, shows the market demand for this vehicle at various prices. The supply curve shows the outputs that provide the greatest profit for the car manufacturer at each different selling price for the car. For information, the graph also shows what would be the equilibrium price. But this manufacturer can, if it wishes, charge any price it wants. Let's say it charges a price of $20 000 and produces 90 000 cars, since this is the quantity that will produce the greatest profit for the firm at this price.

FIGURE 3.1 An Overpriced Product

Although the car manufacturer can price its automobiles at whatever level it wishes, this graph shows that if it wants to sell *all* of its output of cars, then it must sell this particular model at a price of $16 000 or less. If it overprices it at, say, $20 000, the result will be a surplus of 20 000 unsold vehicles.

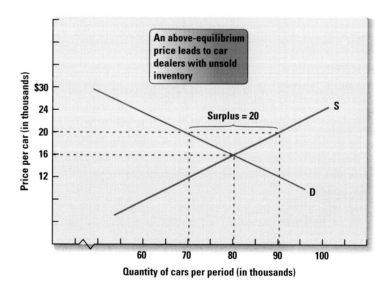

Unfortunately, the manufacturer will soon discover that consumers are not as excited about this vehicle as it had hoped. At a price of $20 000, they are only able to sell 70 000 units, leaving them with a surplus of 20 000. Obviously, they will eventually have no choice but to drop the price or reduce output. Such price decreases often take the form of dealer's rebates. The market can be a stern taskmaster.

What this example demonstrates is that even powerful producers (or for that matter, consumers or governments) must heed market forces because the market embodies the simple maxim that people cannot be forced to buy something they don't want. Similarly, producers cannot be forced to produce products that do not provide a sufficient profit.

This chapter will look at situations in which the market works well and at other situations where the government feels the need to intervene and correct what it perceives to be deficiencies in the market system. As we shall see, in some cases, markets do not always produce the right results for a number of reasons, but in other cases, interference by the government may do more harm than good. How well and how fairly markets operate is a central theme in microeconomics, and we shall look at this topic from various angles throughout this book. This chapter is a preliminary exploration into the efficiency of the market system and will help you to understand what powerful tools are provided by demand and supply analysis. First, however, we need to dig a little deeper into these concepts.

Simultaneous Changes in Demand and Supply

In the last chapter, we looked at the causes of change in demand and supply and how they affect both the price and quantity traded of a product. However, in order to deepen our understanding, we need to be able to explain what will happen if *both* demand and supply change simultaneously since, of course, this may well happen in a dynamic, ever-changing economy.

In this next example, we look at the factor market rather than the product market, but the approach remains the same. In particular, let us examine possible changes in the supply of computer programmers. The supply of computer programmers is definitely increasing these days, since a career in computers is an attractive proposition for many students, and colleges and universities offer a wide range of computer courses. In addition, the demand for programmers by software companies as well as by other businesses and government is steadily increasing. Since both the demand and the supply are increasing at the same time, what can we say about the salary of programmers and about future job opportunities in the industry? **Figure 3.2** shows the effect of a simultaneous increase in both demand and supply.

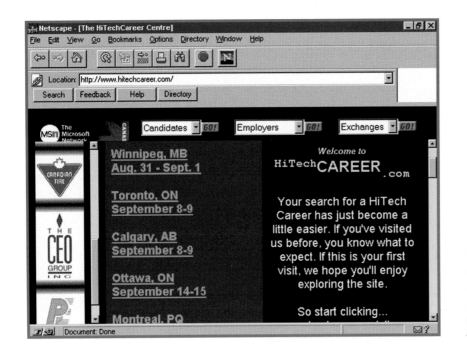

The Hi Tech Career Centre is just one of the many Web-based employment companies catering to those seeking or offering experience in the computer industry.

FIGURE 3.2 The Demand for, and Supply of, Computer Programmers

A simultaneous increase in both the demand for and supply of computer programmers will lead to an increase in the number of programmers employed, from Q_1 to Q_2. However, it is uncertain what will happen to the wage level without knowing exactly how much they each increase.

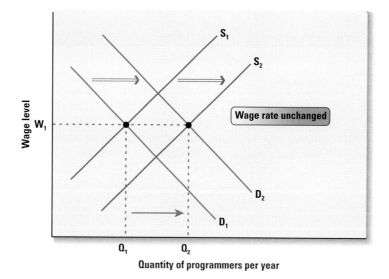

We see that the result is a definite increase in the number of employed programmers from Q_1 to Q_2; however, the wage level seems not to have changed. In contrast, Figure 3.3A and 3.3B give different results.

In **Figure 3.3A**, the shift in the demand curve is greater than the shift in the supply curve, and since the demand increases more than the supply, the wage level increases from W_1 to W_2. **Figure 3.3B** shows, in contrast, a situation in which the supply increase exceeds the demand increase, resulting in a lower wage level. Both graphs show, as does the graph in Figure 3.2, that the number of programmers employed will increase, but what happens to the wage level depends on the comparative magnitude of the change in demand and supply. In other words, to find out what will happen to the wage level, we need to know the amounts by which demand and supply increase; otherwise the effect is inconclusive (or indeterminate, as economists say).

FIGURE 3.3 Simultaneous Increases in Demand and Supply and the Effect on Wages

In Figure 3.3A, the increase in demand, from D_1 to D_2, is greater than the increase in supply, from S_1 to S_2. The result is an increase in the wage level, from W_1 to W_2. In Figure 3.3B, in contrast, the increase in the supply, from S_1 to S_2, exceeds the increase in demand, from D_1 to D_2. The result, in this case, is a drop in the wage level, from W_1 to W_2.

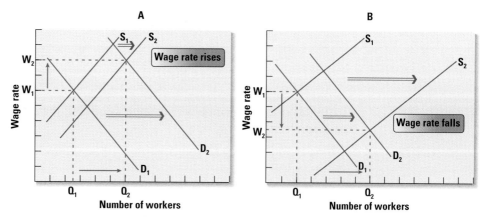

It is important to remember that many factors can affect the demand for and supply of a product. To refresh your memory on these determinants, **Table 3.1** might be helpful.

TABLE 3.1 Determinants of Demand and Supply	
Determinants of Demand	**Determinants of Supply**
Consumer preferences	Prices of productive resources
Consumer incomes	Business taxes
Prices of related products	Technology
Expectations of future prices, incomes, or availability	Prices of substitutes in production
Population size; or income and age distribution	Future expectations of suppliers
	Number of suppliers

Since there are many determinants, it is hardly surprising that in reality more than one could change at the same time. It is important, therefore, to be able to correctly identify whether the demand or supply has been affected, and in what manner.

Whenever multiple shifts are analyzed graphically, the result will always be uncertain unless the amount of each change is known. Because of these indeterminate results, it's often a good idea to analyze the changes in terms of arrows rather than graphs. For instance, from Chapter 2 we know that an increase in demand and supply will produce the following results:

$$\uparrow D \quad \rightarrow \quad \uparrow P \quad \uparrow Q$$
$$\uparrow S \quad \rightarrow \quad \downarrow P \quad \uparrow Q$$

As you can see, both changes will tend to push up the quantity traded. However, the increase in demand will push the price up, whereas the increase in supply will push the price down. The net result on the price is therefore indeterminate. It therefore follows that:

$$\left. \begin{array}{l} \uparrow D \\ \\ \uparrow S \end{array} \right\} \quad \rightarrow \quad ? P \quad \uparrow Q$$

Similarly, we can analyze the effects of a decrease in both demand and supply as follows:

$$\left. \begin{array}{l} \downarrow D \quad \} \quad \rightarrow \quad \downarrow P \quad \downarrow Q \\ \\ \downarrow S \quad \} \quad \rightarrow \quad \underline{\uparrow P \quad \downarrow Q} \\ \quad \rightarrow \quad} ? P \quad \downarrow Q \end{array} \right.$$

In this case, the quantity will definitely decrease; the effect on the price, as in our last example, is indeterminate.

Next, let's look at what happens when the demand and supply move in opposite directions. Suppose that the demand for a product were to increase while, at the same time, the supply decreases—what effect would this have on the market? In terms of arrows, the result is clear though, as usual, indeterminate.

$$\uparrow D \quad \} \quad \rightarrow \quad \uparrow P \quad \uparrow Q$$
$$\}$$
$$\underline{\downarrow S \quad \} \quad \rightarrow \quad \uparrow P \quad \downarrow Q}$$
$$\uparrow P \quad ?Q$$

It's the change in the quantity this time which is indeterminate; the price will definitely increase.

Finally, let's take a look at the last combination: a decrease in demand accompanied by an increase in supply:

$$\downarrow D \quad \} \quad \rightarrow \quad \downarrow P \quad \downarrow Q$$
$$\}$$
$$\underline{\uparrow S \quad \} \quad \rightarrow \quad \downarrow P \quad \uparrow Q}$$
$$\downarrow P \quad ?Q$$

As in the previous case, the effect on the quantity is indeterminate; the price, however, will definitely decrease.

SELF-TEST

1. In each of the following cases, explain what effect the changes will have on the equilibrium price and quantity in the following markets:

Market	Change
A) Day-care services	More mothers with small children are returning to the labour force; at the same time, the government decides to introduce subsidies for day-care operators.
B) Rubber tires	The price of automobiles drops significantly; at the same time, the price of rubber increases.
C) Marijuana	The government severely increases the penalties for both buying and selling marijuana.
D) Compact discs	A new processing method significantly reduces the costs of producing CDs; at the same time, consumers are switching to high-resolution tapes, which are cheaper and can be recorded on.
E) Beef	Vegetarianism increases as a result of medical reports extolling its health benefits; at the same time, tariff barriers on the importation of foreign beef are totally removed.

Returning to our market for computer programmers, we can now pose a practical problem that many students have to address: what are the prospects for a good job or a decent salary, given the present trends? The answer depends to a great extent on the number of graduating students and the number of new jobs being created in industry. Suppose, in **Figure 3.4**, that the number of graduates exceeds the increased demand.

FIGURE 3.4 When the Increase in Supply Exceeds the Increase in Demand

The original wage is W_1, and the number of employed programmers is equal to *a*. The demand and supply now simultaneously increases, from D_1 to D_2 and from S_1 to S_2, respectively. As a result, the number of programmers wanting jobs (*c*) exceeds the number of jobs available (*b*). The result is a number of unemployed programmers, indicated by the distance *bc*. As a result of this surplus of programmers, the wage will drop to W_2 and the new equilibrium number of programmers will be quantity *d*.

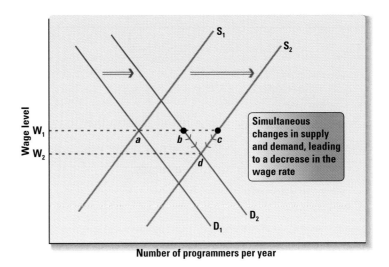

Simultaneous changes in supply and demand, leading to a decrease in the wage rate

Number of programmers per year

The initial wage level is W_1, and the quantity of programmers employed is shown as quantity *a*. Suppose that there is an increase in the demand from D_1 to D_2, and at the same time an increase in the supply from S_1 to S_2. The increase in the supply of programmers, however, exceeds the increase in the demand from industry. The number of new programmers wanted by industry is represented by the increased quantity *b*; the number of qualified programmers however has now increased to quantity *c*. There are a number of unemployed programmers (a surplus of programmers) in the amount *bc*. The competition among programmers for jobs may cause the wage level to eventually drop to a lower wage level, W_2. This lower wage level has eliminated the unemployed programmers, some of whom presumably gave up trying to find a job in computers and started looking for other types of work. The workings of the marketplace therefore do not ensure that everyone will be happy with the results. The number of employed programmers, however, has definitely increased from quantity *a* to the new equilibrium quantity *d*.

SELF-TEST

2. If the demand for a product were to decrease more than the supply decreases, will the result be a surplus or a shortage at the original equilibrium price? What will happen to the price level and the quantity traded as a result?

What this programmer example is designed to show is how markets operate and how, by changing the price (the wage level, in this case), surpluses and shortages are eliminated. Does this describe, then, how markets always work? Well...not entirely. Certainly, it's true that if the number of graduates exceeds the number of new jobs created, many of these graduates are going to be unemployed. The market's cure for this would be a reduction in wage levels. However, the market solution is not always a popular solution. Throughout the centuries, people have often attempted to circumvent or impede the workings of the market because they have either doubted the efficiency of the marketplace or not liked the results it produces. The rest of this chapter investigates this interference.

How Well Do Markets Work?

Suppose that a devastating tidal wave were to hit a major (coastal!) North American city, resulting in the total destruction of half of its housing stock. Let's assume that this was a particularly benign tidal wave, in that nobody was actually killed; however, half the residents find themselves without a place to live. The situation is illustrated in **Figure 3.5.**

FIGURE 3.5 Market Adjustment to a Decrease in Supply

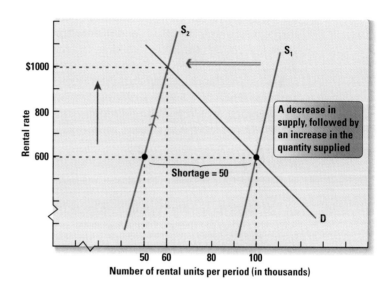

The initial equilibrium rental value was $600, and the number of rental units occupied was 100 000. A tidal wave demolishes half the units, which is reflected in the supply curve shifting left from S_1 to S_2. With a resulting shortage of 50 000 units, rents are forced up, and in time a new equilibrium is reached at a rent of $1000 and with 60 000 units now occupied.

Before the tidal wave struck, the average monthly value of housing stock (rented and owned, houses and apartments) was $600 per month and the number of occupied units was 100 000. The effect of the tidal wave has been to reduce the supply of housing units to 50 000, leading to the current shortage of 50 000 units at the present monthly value of $600. What we now want to look at is the way in which the market addresses changes in supply of this nature. The severe shortage of accommodation is definitely going to cause rents to increase appreciably because many families left homeless are only too willing to pay more than the present $600. As the monthly value starts to increase, the quantity supplied will also go up. How can this happen? Well, there are a variety of ways: many homeowners will be willing to rent out their basements; some shopkeepers may be willing to convert their shops into rented accommodation; many landlords and tenants will be very happy to subdivide their premises; at the low end of the accommodation scale, warehouses, stables, sheds, and garages will become available—all at a price. As rents continue to skyrocket, the quantity demanded will fall as many people will simply be unable to afford the higher rents. (These people will have to find someone, like a parent or a room-mate, to live with, or be forced to live on the streets or leave the city.) Rents will continue to rise as long as there is a shortage and will stop when the market has eliminated that shortage. This occurs, in Figure 3.5, when the average value of accommodation has increased to the new equilibrium price of $1000. At this figure, the number of units now occupied has increased to 60 000.

Yet, this is not the end of the story. This adjustment process probably occurs over a short period of time, maybe a few weeks. In the long run, more lasting change will come about in the market. The high value of rents and of property in general will encourage developers to start building more units. As new units are built, the supply of houses will increase, which we could have shown as a rightward shift in the supply curve. In time, as a result of the increased supply, the price of accommodation will drop and the number of housing units on the market will increase. It could well be that eventually the number of units will return to 100 000 and the price of accommodation back to $600.

Now, consider the question that faces the government. Should it sit back and allow the market to cure the problem, or should it step in and effect its own cure? Certainly, the competitive market can eliminate shortages; the problem is that, since it works through economic incentives and disincentives on a voluntary basis, it may not always work fast enough for society's liking. In emergency situations, governments have the power to effect change far quicker than can the marketplace. In times of national disasters such as floods or earthquakes, we expect the government to step in immediately and take charge to alleviate suffering. Similarly, in wartime we take it for granted that a government would and should mobilize industry on behalf of the war effort. It generally will not leave it to market incentives to produce sufficient armaments or military personnel. In other words, we expect a government to conscript workers and factories because this is the fastest method of mobilizing resources. On the other hand, it is certainly possible that governments might intervene in situations where they should not, or might use inappropriate methods in situations where they should.

Markets do not always adjust as quickly as we would like, and this can be a problem. In addition, there is an additional problem—markets do not always produce equitable results, as far as society or the government is concerned. Let's look at this aspect.

In our example of the tidal wave, the market's short-run solution was to increase the price of accommodation. Suppose, admittedly an extreme scenario, that the destroyed houses were all in the richer section of the city; the houses in the poorer section were all left intact. As the price of accommodation starts to increase, a number of tenants will no longer be able to afford to rent their homes and will be evicted by their landlords, who will gladly see them replaced by new tenants from the rich side of town. In time, we may well find that the rich now totally inhabit the poor side of town and that the former tenants are now homeless, forced to double up or relocate. Notice in Figure 3.5 that when the price of accommodation reaches $1000, there is no longer a shortage; this despite the fact that there are now only 60 000 units occupied, compared with the 100 000 prior to the tidal wave. There is technically no shortage of housing, despite the fact that 40 000 families have had their lives disrupted. (Remember that a shortage means insufficient supply at a particular price. There is sufficient supply at $1000. The fact that many people cannot afford accommodation at $1000 is a different point and is true of many products in our society.)

In a sense the marketplace, like justice, is blind. Resources and products are allocated according to the forces of demand and supply. Whether the results are desirable or not is not the concern of the market. The fact that most people cannot afford everything they would like is a fact of economic life. A number of things are unavailable to most of us, from luxury yachts to summer cabins, from the latest CD-ROM computer to this year's model of car. The market allocates these products according to supply conditions and according to people's desire *and ability* to purchase. The market does not allocate on the basis of who should or who should not get things. That is not the function of markets. However, most people believe that it is the job of governments to see that a certain amount of fairness prevails. Throughout history, governments have attempted to correct what they perceive to be inequities in the marketplace. In addition, they often intervene where a competitive market just doesn't exist.

The problem here is not so much the goals of the government (which is obviously a matter of some debate), but the methods used to achieve those goals. It is these methods to which we now turn.

REVIEW

1. **Explain why even a powerful producer has to pay attention to market forces.**
2. **What will be the effect on the equilibrium price and quantity of a product if the demand increases at the same time that the supply decreases? What would happen if the demand decreases and the supply increases?**
3. **Explain the effect on the price of the product if the demand increases more than the supply. What happens if the supply increases more than the demand?**
4. **Explain how a competitive market adjusts to a sudden decrease in supply.**
5. **Why are governments often forced to take charge of allocating goods and services in times of emergency?**

Price Controls

price controls: government regulations to set either a maximum or minimum price for a product.

A favourite method chosen by governments to correct what is seen by those in power as undesirable market prices is through the introduction of **price controls**. These are legally imposed minimum or maximum prices on various types of privately produced goods and services. Failure to observe these controls usually carries fines or imposes other punishments on the buyer or seller.

> **A price ceiling is a maximum price at which a product can be sold; a price floor is a minimum price at which the product can be sold.**

In both cases, the government is establishing limits; it is not establishing a fixed price. Let's start by looking at price ceilings.

Price Ceilings

price ceiling: a government regulation stipulating the maximum price that can be charged for a product.

Suppose, in our tidal wave example, that under pressure the government decides to introduce a **price ceiling**, for example, a maximum price on rented accommodation, so that more people will still be able to pay the rental rate. **Figure 3.6** shows the effect of the introduction of such a price ceiling which is:

> **Price ceilings result in a shortage.**

rent control: a government regulation making it illegal to rent accommodation above a stipulated level.

This type of price ceiling is known as **rent control** and has been introduced in many cities around the world wherever market rents are felt to be too high, for whatever reason. Assume that the government sets the rent control price at the old rent of $600. (In reality, of course, there could be a number of ceilings, depending on the size of the accommodation, the number of bedrooms, and so on.) Landlords are not allowed to charge a higher rent, though they may charge lower, if they wish. The shortage of units at this rent is 50 000, and since rents are not allowed to increase, the shortage will remain. Remember that without the rent controls, in the short run higher rents would induce people to make more accommodation available (moving up the existing supply curve). This will not happen now. But worse than this, since rents are not allowed to increase, there will be no inducement for developers to even replace existing units that wear out. In addition, unless the government periodically increases the controlled rents to compensate landlords for future cost increases, it's very likely that the future stock of rented accommodation will *fall*. This is because many landlords will not be able to make as good a profit as in alternative investments and will try to sell off the apartments or perhaps convert them into condominiums, if they can, rather than rent them out. Or they may convert the accommodation into shops or warehouses or do what many landlords in New York City have done—simply board up their properties and leave them empty because this alternative is more attractive than renting out.

With rent control, abandoning a building may be a better economic option than renting it.

FIGURE 3.6 The Effect of a Price Ceiling on Rented Accommodation

Suppose that the market rent is $1000. The equilibrium number of rental units is 60 000. However, the government, believing the level of rents to be too high, introduces a price ceiling of $600. At this lower rent, the quantity demanded is 100 000 while the quantity supplied is 50 000, leaving a shortage of 50 000 units.

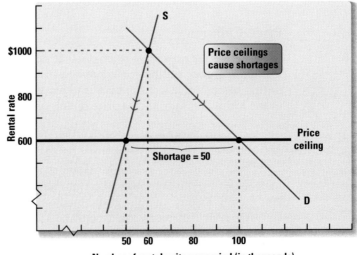

If all this is not bad enough, there is another serious problem with rent controls. If anyone gains from rent controls, it is those people who are currently renting, because they are paying below-market rents. This may include not only those in need but also many professionals who could easily afford to pay the market rate. However, in this situation, landlords are in a very strong position because there are many people desperate to find accommodation. Because of this, single mothers, members of visible minorities, low-income students, and other disadvantaged groups will find themselves in a very vulnerable position because landlords can now pick and choose the types of tenants they want. This leads to a great deal of unfairness and discrimination.

Another situation in which price ceilings are introduced is during national emergencies such as wartime. In World War II, most of the belligerent nations felt it necessary to introduce price controls. During wars, economies have to be mobilized for the war effort, which means that productive resources are conscripted by the government away from their peacetime activities: certain factories are either taken over directly by the government or ordered to start producing armaments and other military requirements; workers are redirected into various industries or directly into the military. The effect will be to reduce the amount of resources available to produce civilian goods and services. The result of this sudden reduction in the supply will be an increase in the prices of most civilian products, including the prices of most foodstuffs. Under these circumstances, the government may well feel obligated to introduce price ceilings so as to keep the price within the range of most people. The effect of price ceilings, any price ceiling, will be to cause a shortage, as **Figure 3.7** shows.

FIGURE 3.7 The Effects of a Price Ceiling on Butter

Suppose that the initial equilibrium price of butter is $5 and that the equilibrium quantity being traded is 1000 kilos per week. The government now introduces a price ceiling at the lower price of $3. The result of the price being set below equilibrium will be a shortage of 400 kilos since, at $3, the quantity demanded has increased to 1200 while the quantity supplied has declined to 800 kilos. The dashed line shows the maximum (illegal market) price at which this smaller quantity could be sold. In this case, it is $7 per kilo.

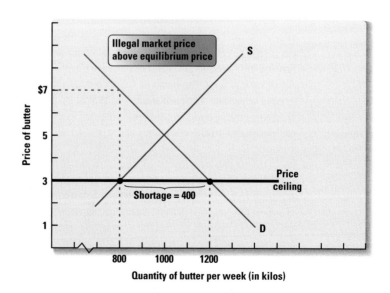

Assume that the graph illustrates the market for butter. The equilibrium price is $5, and the quantity being traded is 1000 kilos per week. Unfortunately, the price is far higher than the peacetime price of $3 per kilo, so the government decides to establish a price ceiling for butter at this former price. This lower price is looked on very favourably by consumers, and the quantity demanded rises to 1200 kilos. For many farmers, however, the lower price spells disaster: a number of them are forced to cut back production, and some are forced out of the business of producing butter. At $3, the quantity supplied falls to 800 kilos. The price ceiling, therefore, has caused a shortage of 400 kilos of butter per week.

Shortages, whether or not they are caused by price ceilings, often produce illegal markets. This means that some people, who can get their hands on commodities that are in great demand, will be willing to risk the fines and penalties from breaking the law and will sell these items above the price ceiling. Figure 3.7 shows that if illegal marketeers could get their hands on the total supply of 800 kilos, they could sell this quantity for as high as $7 per kilo—well above the equilibrium price.

SELF-TEST

3. The following table shows the demand for, and supply of, milk in the land of Apollo (the quantities are in thousands of litres per day):

Price (per litre)	Demand	Supply
$0.80	60	42
0.90	56	44
1.00	52	46
1.10	48	48
1.20	44	50
1.30	40	52
1.40	36	54

A) Suppose that the government of Apollo were to introduce an effective price ceiling that is 20 cents different from the present market equilibrium price. Would the result be a surplus or a shortage? Of what quantity?

B) If an illegal market were to develop as a result of the price ceiling, what would be the maximum illegal market price?

What the butter example above demonstrates is that if the market is not allowed to allocate goods and services in the normal manner, then someone or something else must perform that task. At the price ceiling of $3 per kilo, the supply of 800 kilos must somehow be allocated to consumers who are demanding 1200 kilos. One way of allocating this short supply is on the basis of "first come, first served." But this is not a fair system, since people who have time on their hands will be able to line up more easily than, say, a parent with young children to look after. Another method is to leave the allocation decision to **producers' preference**, that is, leave it to the seller to decide which customers get what amount of butter and which customers go without. Unfortunately, this method opens itself up to the possibility of favouritism, bribery, and corruption. For instance, sellers may demand extra payments or services from customers before selling, or may decide to sell only to favourites or refuse to sell to anyone they don't like, and so on.

For this reason, governments are usually forced to undertake the allocation process themselves through the introduction of a **rationing** scheme. This means that butter, for instance, would be distributed equally among all families, each family being given ration coupons that allow it to purchase a specified quantity. In our example, each family would get ration coupons entitling it to 2/3 kilo of butter per week. (We are assuming that at $3 per kilo, there would be 1200 families, each wanting to buy 1 kilo of butter. Therefore, each family's allocation would be 800/1200, or 2/3 kilo to each family.) Certainly this seems a much fairer method than allowing producers to decide on the allocation. But is it a fair system? On the surface it would seem so. But remember that people are being given an allowance of butter regardless of whether they would normally buy it or not. Imagine the plight of coffee drinkers and smokers if those two products were rationed (beer is not usually rationed in wartime—it's watered down instead). Their allowance would be the same

producers' preference: an allocation system in which sellers are allowed to determine the method of allocation on the basis of their own preferences.

rationing: a method of allocating products that are in short supply by the use of ration coupons issued by the government, guaranteeing a certain quantity per family.

as that of non-addicts. In contrast, the market normally takes intensity of desire into account; a rationing system does not. Given these circumstances, it's understandable that people might well trade away coupons they don't want for those they do. Since, however, bartering is a cumbersome exchange method, usually a market in ration coupons develops. This means that people will have to pay for extra coupons as well as paying for the product itself. In summary, the four possible methods of allocation are:

- the market
- first come, first served
- producers' preferences
- rationing

From this you can see that, with its faults, the market system usually works better than any alternative. Price ceilings are usually introduced when supplies of a product are limited, and prices consequently are high. But ceilings only address one problem—high prices; and they usually exacerbate the limited supply by causing it to shrink further. Many economists suggest that if the problem is affordability, then it might better be attacked by giving direct income relief to those in need rather than helping rich and poor alike by artificially depressing the price.

SELF-TEST

4. Given the demand and supply shown in the previous Self-Test, suppose that the government of Apollo were to impose a price ceiling of $1.20 per litre of milk. What impact would this have?

Let's now see what happens when the government introduces price controls, not to depress prices, but to increase them.

Price Floors

price floor: a government regulation stipulating the minimum price that can be charged for a product.

Figure 3.8 shows a market in which the government feels that the price, rather than being too high, is in fact too low. It has therefore introduced a **price floor** above equilibrium. The price floor represents a minimum price: sellers can sell at a higher price if they wish; however, it is illegal to sell at a lower price.

It's obvious in this situation that by increasing the price above equilibrium, the government is assisting the producers and not the consumers. A higher price is going to mean a higher income for the producers. Which type of producers would the government help in this way, and why? The answer is often farmers, because farming has always been regarded as a special type of industry. Agriculture is different from other types of production for a number of reasons. First, unlike, say, manufacturing, the supply cannot be totally controlled by farmers. The size of the harvest can fluctuate greatly from year to year and, with it, the income of farmers. A second reason is that farmers produce a very basic and important commodity: food. Throughout history, countries have tried to ensure that they are not totally dependent on others for their foodstuffs. If they were so dependent, and if the supply were interrupted because of war, civil unrest, drought, or other disaster, then their position would become precarious. Finally, governments have often been reluctant to allow agricultural land to be traded freely in the marketplace. It's felt that this particular resource is very precious because, once it is used for other purposes like a housing development or shopping mall, reconverting it back to farming is virtually impossible. For these reasons and others, governments in most countries have tried to protect and encourage their agricultural communities. One way of doing this is through a price floor on agricultural products, which will guarantee farmers a minimum price.

Figure 3.8 illustrates a basic principle:

> ### Price floors cause surpluses.

The graph shows the market for wheat where the equilibrium price is $10 a bushel and the quantity being traded is 20 million bushels. Suppose that the government now introduces a price floor of $12 a bushel. At this higher price, the quantity demanded drops to 15 million bushels. The higher price will, on the other hand, induce present farmers to produce more and others to start up new wheat farms. As a result, the quantity supplied increases to 25 million bushels. Consequently, there is now a surplus of 10 million bushels of wheat. This surplus belongs to the government, since by introducing the price floor it must take responsibility for any surplus thus created.

FIGURE 3.8   The Effects of a Price Floor on the Wheat Market

A price set above equilibrium will always produce a surplus. In this figure, the price floor of $12 causes a drop in the quantity demanded from the original 20 down to 15; it also causes the quantity supplied to increase from 20 to 25. Therefore, buyers want to purchase less, but sellers want to produce more. The result is a surplus of 10 million bushels.

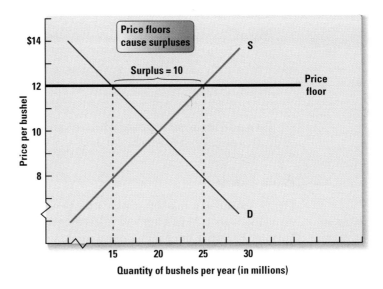

The problem for the government now is how to get rid of the surplus that a price floor will inevitably produce. A number of possibilities exist. If the surplus is storable, which is true of most grains, then it could be stored in grain elevators and used in the future, when the supply may be lower. In this way, the grain elevators are being used as reservoirs, taking in grain whenever there is a surplus and releasing it whenever it is in short supply. If the agricultural surplus is perishable, as in the case of milk or eggs or produce, then the government may be able to convert it into other foodstuffs or freeze, dry, or can it. But all such methods are likely to be expensive. Failing this, the government will have to dispose of the surplus. But this is more difficult than it sounds. Selling it to other countries may not be feasible since, in order to do so, the price may have to be reduced. But this is forbidden by many international conventions and is termed **dumping**. Donating it to countries in need is similarly difficult, except in times of natural disasters, because doing so will undermine the receiving country's own agricultural industry or disturb its present trading arrangements. The last option may be simply to destroy the sur-

dumping: the sale of a product abroad for a lower price than is being charged in the domestic market or for a price below the cost of production.

plus by burning it, burying it, or literally dumping it in the ocean. Understandably, this last alternative is politically embarrassing to governments and is also unacceptable to many people. In summary, there are five ways to deal with a surplus:

- store it
- convert it
- sell it abroad at a reduced price (dump)
- donate it
- destroy it

subsidy: a payment made by the government to a firm (or others), which may be a lump-sum grant or depend on the amount produced.

An alternative method, which has been tried by some governments, is to get farmers to stop producing a surplus! In other words, in our example from Figure 3.8, farmers would be asked to produce no more than 15 million bushels so that no surplus results. The farmers, in compensation for voluntarily complying with this quota, would still get paid as though they had produced 25 million bushels. In return for giving such a **subsidy**, the government no longer has the problem of trying to dispose of an embarrassing surplus.

ADDED DIMENSION

Farm Marketing Boards

The governments of most countries involve themselves in their agricultural sectors; the European Community and Japan do so more extensively than most. In Canada, there are more than 100 farm marketing boards regulating such produce as milk, eggs, wheat, peanuts, grains, poultry, and so on. In total, they exercise control over more than 50 percent of total farm sales in the country and include such federal bodies as the Canadian Wheat Board, the Canada Livestock Feed Board, and the Canadian Dairy Commission. In addition, there are a number of provincial boards. Besides price floors, the other main methods of enhancing and stabilizing farm incomes are by way of quotas (which, by restricting output, increase the market price) and through subsidies granted to farmers (which give them an additional sum of money for each unit of output produced).

It should be clear from this that price floors in agriculture can lead to serious problems. Again, many economists would suggest that rather than interfering directly with the market, governments might be better advised to give direct income assistance to farmers because that is the main problem they are trying to address.

SELF-TEST

5. Given the market for corn described in the figure below:

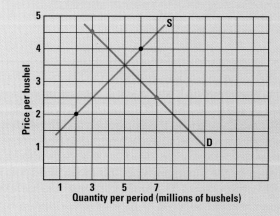

A) In equilibrium, what is the total sales revenue being received by producers?

B) Suppose that the government now imposes a price floor of $4 per kilo. What quantity will now be demanded? What quantity will farmers produce? What quantity will the government purchase?

C) How much will it cost the government to purchase the surplus?

The Minimum Wage

minimum wage: the lowest rate of pay per hour for workers, as set by government.

Finally, we will take a look at another type of price floor that is used in many countries—a minimum price for labour, or, in other words, a **minimum wage**. Minimum-wage legislation is often introduced for the commendable reason of ensuring that all working people are guaranteed a minimum income. The goal is generally not criticized by economists; it is the method chosen by governments that is in question. Whenever the free workings of the marketplace are interfered with, a number of harmful side effects are usually produced. Let's look at the situation, with the help of **Figure 3.9**.

This figure illustrates a particular labour market, one in which the equilibrium wage ($5 per hour in our graph) is considered by the government as too low. Suppose that the government therefore introduces minimum-wage legislation forbidding the payment of any wage at a rate below $7 per hour. The following graph therefore describes a market in which the going wage is generally below the minimum wage, as, for instance, in fast-food restaurants, fruit picking, and so on. These fairly low-skill occupations often attract disadvantaged members of society: the young, the old, the poorly educated, recent immigrants without sufficient language skills, and so on. The effect, as we shall see, rather than helping these groups, may well be to cause additional harm.

FIGURE 3.9 Labour Markets and Minimum Wages

The imposition of a minimum wage of $7 means that firms will economize on the use of labour. In this figure, the quantity demanded will drop from the equilibrium quantity of 100 000 to 90 000. At the same time the higher wage will attract more people to want a job, that is, the quantity supplied increases from 100 000 to 110 000. The result will be a surplus of 20 000 workers. In other words, more workers will be wanting jobs than there are jobs available, that is, there will be 20 000 unemployed workers in this particular labour market.

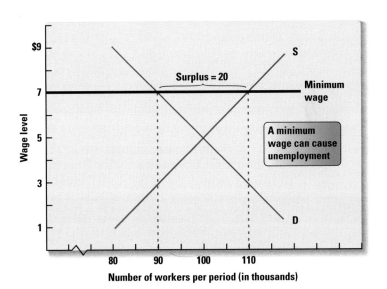

Figure 3.9 demonstrates the effect of a wage above equilibrium. The higher wage means that employers will be forced to economize on labour and will cut back on employment; that is, the quantity demanded by firms falls from 100 000 to 90 000. At the same time, the now higher wage will attract more workers in this occupation and the quantity supplied will increase to 110 000. The net result is that there will be a surplus of labour or, the same thing, unemployment to the tune of 20 000 workers. The 90 000 workers who have retained their jobs are obviously helped by the minimum-wage legislation, though it is possible that they are required to work harder now that the number of employees has been reduced. But in our example, the legislation has resulted in an increase in unemployment,

Do you want fries with that?

and it is this aspect of minimum wages that has been seriously criticized by some econo-mists, who feel that the poor may be better assisted by providing direct income relief than by doing it indirectly through the marketplace. It is also highly likely that, since employers now have a big pool of unemployed workers from which to choose, some of them may be inclined to discriminate on the basis of age, gender, race, religion, or on other non–work-related grounds. As an example of the effects of such discrimination, a recent study in the United States found that over half of the minimum-wage workers in that country came from families with *above*-average incomes. This astounding statistic can only be under-stood when one thinks of the thousands of teenagers, mostly from higher-income homes, who work for minimum wages at restaurants, gas stations, and retail shops.

A number of supporters of minimum-wage legislation, however, consider that the benefits far exceed the costs. They suggest that it's not so much the case that many work-ers are paid low wages because they are unproductive, but that they are unproductive because they are paid such low wages. If this is so, then the imposition of a minimum wage would actually increase productivity and as a result lead to an increase in the demand for labour by firms. This would consequently reduce the amount of unemployment.

Regardless of which version is the correct one, the point of this analysis is that all methods of allocation, whether done by the government or by the market, impose costs. These costs are not always obvious. What economic analysis does is to help us identify and understand the nature of these costs.

Some Elaborations

A great deal of economic analysis and theorizing is the result of observing the real world. However, much progress has been made as a result of economists abstracting from reality rather than merely reporting on it. In the context of demand and supply, economists are forever speculating on scenarios that obviously do not exist. They ask themselves the question: theoretically, what would happen if...? Having worked out the consequences of their analysis, they often discover that their conclusion exactly coin-cides with what happened in a particular situation.

What we want to do in the final section of this chapter is to look a little more closely at the shape and position of the demand and supply curves. In doing this we are exploring possibilities. But in this way, it may help to give you a deeper understanding of demand and supply.

Do All Demand Curves Slope Downward?

The law of demand suggests that a lower price will produce a higher quantity demanded than will a higher price, but is this always true? Can the law of demand be broken? **Figure 3.10**, for instance, shows a vertical demand curve: is such a construct a figment of some economist's imagination, or can it really exist?

FIGURE 3.10 A Vertical Demand Curve

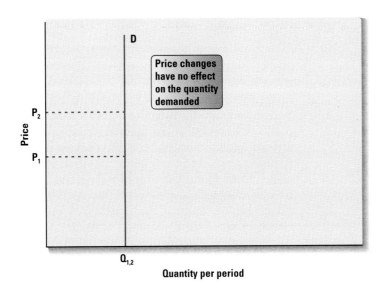

Whatever the price happens to be, the quantity demanded remains at Q_1. In this case, the price is irrelevant; this consumer does not react to a change in the price because, whether it drops or rises, he will buy the same quantity. Here, the price is not a determinant of how much is bought.

The demand curve in Figure 3.10 seems to suggest that for these particular consumers or in this particular market, the price of the product is irrelevant—the quantity remains the same regardless of the price. It says that no matter how high or how low the price, the quantity demanded remains constant. It would seem that this product is an "ultra" necessity, so that no matter how high the price goes, the same quantity would still be purchased. Perhaps it describes the demand for cigarettes by smokers or for gasoline by drivers? But doesn't it seem ludicrous to suggest that they wouldn't reduce consumption a little if the price got astronomically high? Or for that matter that they wouldn't consume more if the price were zero? What about drugs, then—either life-preserving drugs like insulin or life-taking drugs like cocaine? Isn't the demand for these products unlimited because people have to have them, regardless of price? But, again, need alone does not determine demand. Consider the unfortunate fact that even though humans need to eat food to stay alive, many millions die of starvation every year. Our demand, in other words, is limited by our income, that is, by our ability to purchase. There is a maximum price for all of us, whether we are rich or poor. Therefore, although our demand for certain products may remain constant over a range of prices, eventually, above a certain price, the quantity demanded will decrease, which means that the demand curve must eventually slope backward.

The next example seems even more perverse and totally contradicts the law of demand. **Figure 3.11** shows an upward-sloping demand curve.

FIGURE 3.11 An Upward-Sloping Demand Curve

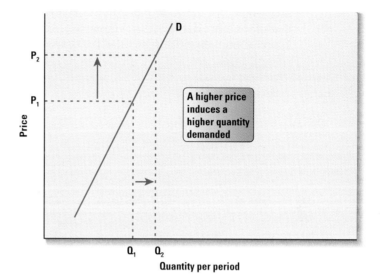

With this demand curve, the quantity demanded increases as the price increases: the lower the price, the lower the quantity demanded; the higher the price (without limit), the higher the quantity demanded. This direct relationship results in an upward-sloping demand curve.

This demand curve suggests that as the price increases, consumers purchase more. Surely, this is nonsensical? Well, certainly it is unlikely that the *whole* market would buy increasing quantities at increasing prices. However, it may be true for *certain individuals* over a limited range of prices. There are certain products whose values to some people are determined by their prices. The higher the price, the more attractive such products as jewellery, furs, and perfumes may become for some people, simply because the price is now higher. A higher price means that only an exclusive few people can now afford to buy such products. It is this exclusivity that makes such products attractive and invites these customers to "conspicuously consume," to use a phrase made popular by the iconoclastic American economist Thorstein Veblen. But again, there is still a limit to this conspicuous consumption, and eventually at some high price, one would imagine, even for the few individuals involved, the quantity demanded will start to fall so that the demand curve again becomes downward-sloping.

ADDED DIMENSION

Giffen Goods: Are They for Real?

There is another explanation sometimes given for an upward-sloping demand curve, which relates to what are termed *Giffen goods*. In the nineteenth century the economist Sir Robert Giffen, as the result of research he had done into the consumption of potatoes in Ireland following the 1856 famine, discovered an interesting paradox. As the price of potatoes rose, the consumption of potatoes actually increased, instead of falling. The reason for this is that purchases of potatoes in those days represented a big portion of the average working person's food budget. The increase in price meant a sharp drop in real incomes, which meant that for many families the price of meat, for instance, was out of reach. Instead of buying meat they substituted even more potatoes, which at least guaranteed a full stomach. Not all economists, however, trust Giffen's data, and few believe that there is any evidence of an upward-sloping market demand curve.

Economics is generally concerned with products that have a positive (above-zero) price. Figure 3.12, in contrast, illustrates a market for a free good. The reason it is a free good is that the supply is so great that it does not require the inducement of a higher price in order to elicit a higher quantity. It might describe the supply of air, perhaps, or certain types of goods called public goods, which we will look at in a later chapter. For these types of product the equilibrium price is zero, and for that reason they would not be worth a private company producing. Note, however, that the fact that the product is free does not imply that the quantity demanded is unlimited. There is a maximum quantity demanded for most things in life.

FIGURE 3.12 A Free Product

At a price of zero, the supply is unlimited. Regardless of the position of the demand curve, this must be a free good, that is, demand plays no part in determining the price. However, the quantity demanded is still limited—in this case to a quantity Q_1.

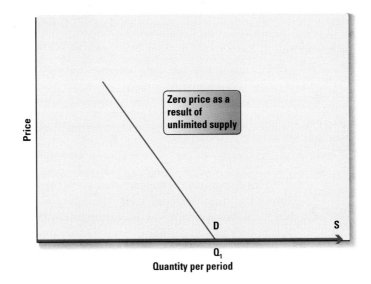

The graph in Figure 3.13 is straightforward, though the interpretation of the slope is a little more difficult. It describes the demand for water. To obtain a small quantity of water (at a life-preserving quantity like quantity Q_1), we would be prepared to pay a high price, such as price P_1. At quantities higher than quantity Q_2, on the other hand, people are not prepared to pay more than a very low price like P_2. What price and quantity they are actually paying depends not only on the demand, of course, but also on the supply. In most countries the supply is usually fairly abundant, as shown by the supply curve S_2 in the diagram, so that the price tends to be quite low. In addition, a charge in supply to S_{2A} has very little impact on the price (P_2 to P_{2A}). In desert areas of the world, on the other hand, the supply will be like S_1 and will therefore result in a comparatively high price. In such places, even a small change in supply, such as from S_1 to S_{1A}, can have a great impact on the price (P_1 to P_{1A}).

FIGURE 3.13 The Demand for Water

The effect on price of a change in supply depends very much on the shape of the demand curve. This figure depicts the demand curve for water that is very steep at low quantities but quite flat at high quantities. If the present supply is S_1 giving a price of P_1 and a quantity of Q_1, then it requires only a small change in the supply to S_{1A} to bring about a big change in the price (though the quantity will not change greatly). On the other hand, if supply is abundant, as in curve S_2, then a change in supply (to S_{2A}) will not greatly affect the price (but will lead to a big change in the quantity).

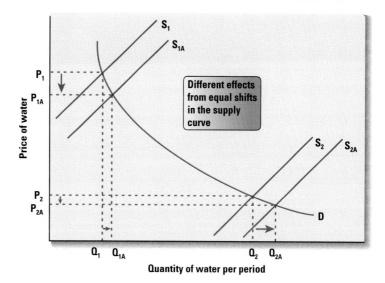

This completes our look at various aspects of demand and supply. However, as you may have become aware in this chapter, demand and supply analysis can be used, and is used, in so many different situations that it would be presumptuous to suggest that this is the end of the discussion. The tool of demand–supply analysis is so powerful and its application is so pervasive that, to an extent, much of economics is merely an elaboration and amplification of its basic principles.

SELF-TEST

6. A) Under what circumstances would an increase in supply have no effect on the price of a product?
   B) Under what circumstances would it have no effect on the quantity traded of a product?
7. Below is the demand for water in the country of Isis (price per 50 litres):

Price	$2	3	4	5	6	7	8	9	10	11	12	13	14
Demand	1000	500	200	150	110	80	60	50	43	38	34	31	30

A) Suppose the present supply of 200 is cut by 50. What effect will it have on the price?
B) Suppose, instead, that the present supply is 80, and it is now cut by 50. What effect will this have on the price?

REVIEW

1. What is meant by a *price ceiling*? What effect does a price ceiling have on the market?
2. Who gains and who loses from rent control?
3. What is an *illegal market*? What is meant by the term *illegal market price*?
4. In what way is the market's allocation of products preferable to that of producers' or government's allocation?
5. What is a *price floor*? What effect does it have on the market?
6. Give three reasons why agriculture is often regarded as a special industry.
7. In what ways can agricultural surpluses be disposed of?
8. What types of markets are affected by the imposition of minimum-wage legislation?
9. Explain how the imposition of minimum-wage legislation might cause unemployment.
10. What are the implications of a vertical demand curve?
11. Is it possible for a demand curve to be upward-sloping? Explain.
12. Describe and explain the shape of the demand curve for water.

STUDY GUIDE

Chapter Highlights

In this chapter we first explored the effects of simultaneous changes in supply and demand. The analysis involved here is simply an extension of what you learned in the previous chapter. Next, the example of a disaster wiping out a large portion of a city's housing stock was used to illustrate the fact that a market will reach equilibrium under any conditions although many may feel that sometimes the equilibrium arrived at is objectionable. We then looked at three specific examples of price controls and ended the chapter by speculating on some "what if" questions in reference to the shape of demand and supply curves.

1. In a non-competitive market, a seller is able to set any price desired, but if a price above equilibrium is chosen then a surplus will result and the seller will have to either:
   - reduce price to the equilibrium level;
   - sell less than he or she would like.

2. The four possible combinations of *simultaneous changes in demand and supply* are:
   - an increase in both demand and supply which results in an increased quantity traded but an indeterminate change in price;
   - a decrease in both demand and supply which results in a decrease in the quantity traded but an indeterminate change in price;
   - an increase in demand with a decrease in supply which results in an increase in price but an indeterminate change in the quantity traded;
   - a decrease in demand with an increase in supply which results in a decrease in price but an indeterminate change in the quantity traded.

3. An uncontrolled market will always find *equilibrium* although such a result may be seen as undesirable on the grounds of fairness.

4. *Rent controls* are an example of price ceilings imposed on the market and create shortages which force the use of some other form of allocation such as:
   - first come, first serve (the queue);
   - sellers' preferences;
   - rationing.

5. *Price controls* on agriculture products imposed on the market are an example of price floors and creates surpluses which must then be:
   - stored;
   - converted to another product;
   - sold abroad;
   - given away; or
   - destroyed.

6. The *minimum wage* is another example of a price floor and is controversial since many economists believe that, while it does benefit those who remain working, it creates unemployment which works against those that it is mainly intended to help.

7. It is possible to conceive of a perfectly *vertical demand* curve and even an upward sloping one, and we can think of examples where the supply of a good is so abundant that its equilibrium price is zero.

8. The *shape of the demand* curve for a product like water probably changes significantly as the quantity in question increases.

New Glossary Terms

dumping   98
minimum wage   100
price ceiling   93
price controls   93
price floor   97
producers' preference   96
rationing   96
rent control   93
subsidy   99

Study Tips

1. In the first part of the chapter we take some of the principles from the last chapter and apply them to real-world examples, whereas the last part deals with abstractions and may not necessarily describe a real-life example. However, you need to become familiar with the process of abstraction. This simply means exploring various possibilities, for example, what if the demand curve looked like this, or if the supply curve took this shape? This process often uncovers a number of interesting insights. In other words, don't be afraid of abstractions and don't try to immediately find practical uses; they may not always exist.

2. The chapter does not really introduce any new ideas; it simply extends the ideas developed in the last chapter. This means that even though the analysis, especially when we are dealing with multiple curve shifts, might seem forbidding at first, the principles behind things are ones you are familiar with.

3. Many students confuse the terms *scarcity* (or short supply) and *shortage*. Remember that although all products and resources are "scarce," the markets for them may well be in equilibrium, in that the demand and supply are equal. A shortage, on the other hand, describes a disequilibrium situation, in which the quantity demanded exceeds the quantity supplied.

4. Remember that a price ceiling is a *maximum price* but is imposed *below* the equilibrium price and results in a *shortage*. On the other hand, a price floor is a *minimum* price but is imposed *above* the equilibrium price and results in a *surplus*.

Are You Sure?

Indicate whether the following statements are true or false. If false, indicate why they are false.

1. Economic laws are social laws—statements of tendencies, more or less certain, more or less definite.

   T or **F**   If false: _____

   _____

2. If both the demand and the supply increase, it is impossible to say whether the price will rise or fall.

   T or **F**   If false: _____

   _____

3. If the demand increases and the supply decreases, it is impossible to say what will happen to the price.

   T or **F**   If false: _____

   _____

4. A shortage is caused by either a decrease in demand or an increase in supply.

   T or **F**   If false: _____

   _____

5. A price floor, to be effective, must be set below the equilibrium price.

   T or **F**   If false: _____

   _____

6. A price ceiling is a government regulation stipulating the maximum price that can be charged for a product.

   T or **F**   If false: _____

   _____

7. Illegal markets and rationing schemes are often the result of the imposition of a price ceiling.

   T or **F**   If false: _____

   _____

8. Invariably, price floors cause shortages and price ceilings cause surpluses.

   T or **F**   If false: _____

   _____

9. If the demand curve is vertical, then an increase in supply will have no effect on the price.

   T or **F**   If false: _____

   _____

10. Since water is a necessity, its demand is unlimited.

    T or **F**   If false: _____

    _____

Choose the Best

11. A minimum wage is an example of a:
    a) Price floor.
    b) Price ceiling.

12. Rent control is an example of a:
    a) Price floor.
    b) Price ceiling.

13. Under what circumstances can a illegal market exist?
    a) When a price ceiling is imposed.
    b) When a price floor is imposed.

14. What will happen if both the demand for and supply of a product increase simultaneously?
    a) The effect on the price is indeterminate.
    b) The price will increase.
    c) The price will decrease.

15. What will happen if both the demand for and supply of a product decrease simultaneously?
    a) The effect on the price is indeterminate.
    b) The price will increase.
    c) The price will decrease.

16. What will happen if both the demand for and supply of a product increase simultaneously?
    a) The effect on the quantity traded is indeterminate.
    b) The quantity traded will increase.
    c) The quantity traded will decrease.

17. All of the following, *except one*, are examples of price ceilings. Which is the exception?
    a) Minimum-wage legislation.
    b) Rent controls.
    c) Wartime price controls on the price of consumer necessities.

18. Which of the following type of firm would be most affected by minimum-wage legislation?
    a) A company of management consultants.
    b) An airline company.
    c) A fast-food restaurant.
    d) A hospital.

19. Which of the following is an example of a price ceiling?
   a) Minimum-wage legislation.
   b) Dumping.
   c) Rent controls.
   d) Agricultural price supports.

20. What does a vertical demand curve suggest?
   a) That producers are unable to adjust the quantity they produce.
   b) That the price is not a determinant of the quantity demanded.
   c) That consumers will not buy the product unless it is free.
   d) That a change in supply has no effect on the price.

21. What is the term used to describe certain goods whose demand curve is upward-sloping?
   a) Inferior goods.
   b) Giffen goods.
   c) Complementary goods.
   d) Substitute goods.

Refer to **Figure 3.14** when answering question 22.

FIGURE 3.14

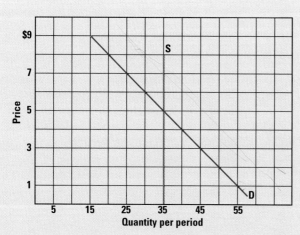

22. Refer to Figure 3.14 to answer this question. If this market is originally in equilibrium and demand increases by 10, what will be the new equilibrium price and quantity?
   a) $3 and 45 units.
   b) $5 and 35 units.
   c) $5 and 45 units.
   d) $7 and 35 units.

Refer to **Figure 3.15** when answering questions 23 and 24.

FIGURE 3.15

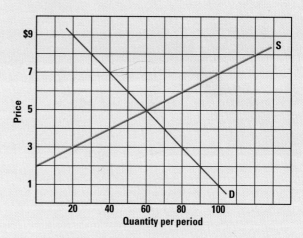

23. Refer to Figure 3.15 to answer this question. What would be the result if an effective price floor is set that is $2 different from the equilibrium price?
   a) The price would be above equilibrium, and a surplus of 60 would be produced.
   b) The price would be below equilibrium, and a shortage of 60 would be produced.
   c) The price would be above equilibrium, and a shortage of 60 would be produced.
   d) The price would be below equilibrium, and a surplus of 60 would be produced.

24. Refer to Figure 3.15 to answer this question. What would be the result if an effective price ceiling is set that is $2 different from the equilibrium price?
   a) The price would be above equilibrium, and a surplus of 60 would be produced.
   b) The price would be below equilibrium, and a shortage of 60 would be produced.
   c) The price would be above equilibrium, and a shortage of 60 would be produced.
   d) The price would be below equilibrium, and a surplus of 60 would be produced.

25. Under what circumstances would an increase in the supply of a product have no effect on the price?
   a) If the demand curve is vertical.
   b) If the supply curve is vertical.
   c) If the demand curve is horizontal.
   d) If both the demand and supply curves are vertical.
   e) If the demand curve is upward-sloping.

26. If the demand curve is upward-sloping, what would be the effect of an increase in supply?
    a) An increase in supply would be impossible.
    b) It will reduce both the price and the quantity traded.
    c) It will increase both the price and the quantity traded.
    d) It will increase the quantity traded but will reduce the price.
    e) It might or might not increase the price and quantity traded, depending on which curve is steeper.

27. Why is the market's allocation of products preferable to that of either the producers or of the government?
    a) Because it ensures that even the poor will be able to afford to buy everything.
    b) Because it ensures that only people who really need certain products will be able to afford them.
    c) Because it ensures that both demand and supply factors are taken into consideration.
    d) Because it will mean that scarce resources are available at low prices.
    e) Because it ensures that the income distribution of the population is ignored.

Table 3.2 describes the market for day-care workers in the city of Vishna (quantity of workers in hundreds). Refer to this table to answer questions 28, 29, and 30.

TABLE 3.2

Hourly Wage ($)	5.00	5.50	6.00	6.50	7.00	7.50
Quantity demanded	17	16	15	14	13	12
Quantity supplied	13	14	15	16	17	18

28. Refer to Table 3.2 to answer this question. What is the result if this market is in equilibrium?

a) The wage rate would be $5 an hour, and there would be 400 unemployed workers.
b) The wage rate would be $5.50 an hour, and there would be 200 unemployed workers.
c) The wage rate would be $6 an hour, and there would be no unemployed workers.
d) The wage rate would be $6.50 an hour, and there would be 200 unemployed workers.
e) The wage rate would be $5 an hour, and there would be 1,300 unemployed workers.

29. Refer to Table 3.2 to answer this question. What would happen if the government were to establish a minimum wage of $6.50 an hour?
    a) The wage would stay at $6, and there would be no unemployment.
    b) The equilibrium wage would rise to $6.50, and there would be no unemployment.
    c) The number employed would increase by 100.
    d) There would be 200 day-care workers unemployed.
    e) The day-care centres would have difficulty finding sufficient workers.

30. Refer to Table 3.2 to answer this question. Suppose that after the imposition of a minimum wage of $6.50, a number of new day-care centres opened up, increasing the demand for workers by 400. In what way would this market be affected?
    a) The wage would increase to $7, and there would be no unemployment.
    b) The wage would remain at $6.50, but there would now be no unemployment.
    c) The wage would remain at $6.50, and there would now be 200 unemployed day-care workers.
    d) The wage would remain at $6.50, and there would now be 200 job vacancies.
    e) The wage would drop to $5, and there would be no unemployment.

Problems

31. **Figure 3.16** shows the market for mandarin oranges in Odin for the month of November (in thousands of kilos).

FIGURE 3.16

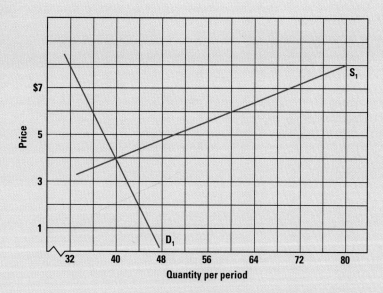

Suppose that in December the supply of mandarin oranges increases by 20 percent while the demand doubles. Draw and label the new curves D_2 and S_2. What will be the new equilibrium price and quantity?

New equilibrium price: _____; equilibrium quantity: _____.

32. **Table 3.3** shows Osiris's market for olive oil (in thousands of litres per month).

TABLE 3.3

Price ($)	1	2	3	4	5	6	7	8
Quantity demanded	70	60	50	40	30	20	10	0
Quantity supplied	10	20	30	40	50	60	70	80

Suppose that olive oil increases in popularity, and Osiris's buyers are willing to pay an additional $1 for each of the eight quantities demanded in Table 3.3. At the same time, as the result of improved technology, oil producers are willing to accept $1 less for each of the eight quantities supplied. What will be the new equilibrium price and quantity?

New equilibrium price: _____; equilibrium quantity: _____.

33. Suppose that a number of coincidental changes were to occur in the following markets. In each case, indicate what will happen to the price and quantity traded as a result. ($\uparrow$ = increase; $\downarrow$ = decrease; 0 = no change; ? = indeterminate.)

Changes affecting demand

1. Incomes increase.
2. Price of substitute product increases.

Changes affecting supply

A. The price of inputs (productive resources) falls.
B. Price of productively related product increases.

a) Assume that changes 1 and A occur, and the market is for an inferior product.

Equilibrium price: _____; equilibrium quantity: _____.

b) Assume that changes 1 and B occur, and the market is for a normal product.

Equilibrium price: _____; equilibrium quantity: _____.

c) Assume that changes 2 and A occur, and the market is for a normal product.

Equilibrium price: _____; equilibrium quantity: _____.

d) Assume that changes 2 and B occur, and the market is for a normal product.

Equilibrium price: _____; equilibrium quantity: _____.

34. Suppose that a number of coincidental changes were to occur in the following markets. In each case, indicate what will happen to the price and quantity traded as a result. ($\uparrow$ = increase; $\downarrow$ = decrease; 0 = no change; ? = indeterminate.)

Changes affecting demand

1. Price of complementary product increases.
2. Population increases.

Changes affecting supply

A. Technological improvement increases.
B. Number of suppliers falls.

a) Assume that changes 1 and A occur, and the market is for a normal product.

Equilibrium price: _____; equilibrium quantity: _____.

b) Assume that changes 1 and B occur, and the market is for a normal product.

Equilibrium price: _____; equilibrium quantity: _____.

c) Assume that changes 2 and A occur, and the market is for a normal product.

Equilibrium price: _____; equilibrium quantity: _____.

d) Assume that changes 2 and B occur, and the market is for a normal product.

Equilibrium price: _____; equilibrium quantity: _____.

Translations

"Technological improvements over the last 10 years have so reduced the costs of producing compact disc players that, although they have greatly increased in popularity, the average price has dropped." Illustrate the changes in the compact disc market on the graph in **Figure 3.17**.

FIGURE 3.17

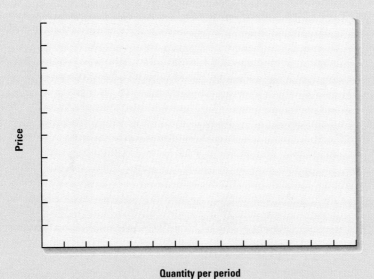

Key Problem

Figure 3.18 depicts the market for rice in the country of Shiva.

FIGURE 3.18

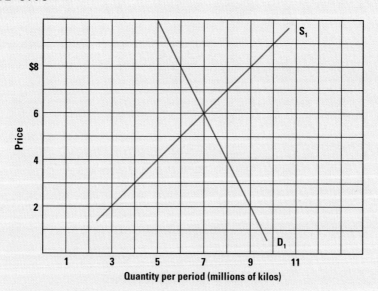

a) What is the present equilibrium price and quantity traded in this market?

Price: _____; quantity traded: _____.

b) How much, in total, are rice buyers paying for this quantity? Total spending: _____.

c) Suppose that the government introduces a price floor of $8 per kilo. How much in total will rice buyers now be paying? Total spending: _____.

d) As a result of the price floor, what will be the total amount of the surplus? What will be the dollar amount of this surplus? Who will be responsible for buying this surplus?

Surplus: _____ kilos of rice; dollar amount of surplus: $ _____;

surplus is the responsibility of _____.

e) Suppose that after the imposition of the price floor, the demand in Shiva increases by 1.5 million kilos. Draw the new demand on Figure 3.18, and label it D_2. Now, how much in total will rice buyers be paying?

Price: _____; quantity traded: _____; total spending: _____.

f) What will be the total amount of the new surplus? What will be the dollar amount of this surplus?

Surplus: _____ kilos of rice; dollar amount of surplus: $ _____.

g) After the change in demand, what would happen if, as a result of a bad harvest, the supply now drops by 3 million kilos? Draw the new supply curve on Figure 3.18, and label it S_2. What will be the new price, the quantity traded, the total spending of buyers, the surplus and the dollar amount of the surplus?

Price: _____; quantity traded: _____; total spending: _____;

surplus: _____ kilos; dollar amount of surplus: $ _____.

More of the Same

Figure 3.19 depicts the market for potatoes in the country of Ahura Mazda.

FIGURE 3.19

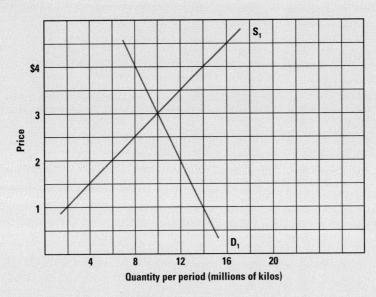

a) What is the present equilibrium price and quantity traded in this market?

b) How much in total are buyers paying for these potatoes?

c) Suppose that the government introduces a price floor of $4 per kilo. How much in total will potato buyers now be paying?

d) What will be the total amount of the surplus? What will be the dollar amount of this surplus? Who will be responsible for buying this surplus?

e) Suppose that after the imposition of the price floor, the demand in Ahura Mazda increases by 3 million kilos. Draw the new demand curve on Figure 3.19, and label it D_2. Now, how much in total will potato buyers be paying?

f) What will be the total amount of the new surplus? What will be the dollar amount of this surplus?

g) After the change in demand, what would happen if, as a result of a bad harvest, the supply now drops by 3 million kilos. Draw the new supply curve on Figure 3.19, and label it S_2. What will be the new price, the quantity traded, the surplus and the dollar amount of the surplus?

UNANSWERED QUESTIONS

Short Essays

1. In what way are buyers' willingness and ability to purchase affected by a price change?

2. In what way are sellers' willingness and ability to produce affected by a price change?

3. If the government considers the price of a product too high for consumers, it could subsidize consumers rather than introduce a price ceiling. Discuss.

4. If the government considers the price of a product too low for producers, it could subsidize producers rather than introduce a price floor. Discuss.

5. Who gains and who loses from the imposition of rent controls?

6. Explain why the supply of rented accommodation tends to drop with the imposition of rent controls.

7. Discuss the pros and cons of minimum-wage legislation.

Analytical Questions

8. Show graphically how a change in the *same direction* of both the demand and supply curves can produce the following results.
   a) Price increases; quantity traded increases.
   b) Price is unchanged; quantity traded increases.
   c) Price decreases; quantity traded increases.
   d) Price decreases; quantity traded decreases.
   e) Price is unchanged; quantity traded decreases.
   f) Price increases; quantity traded decreases.

9. In each of the following cases, explain what effect the changes will have on the equilibrium price and quantity traded in the following markets:

Market	Change
a) Rental accommodation	The government introduces a subsidy for both apartment owners and renters.
b) Cars	The city abolishes bus fares throughout the region; at the same time, the government increases gasoline taxes.
c) Snowboards	Youth employment increases; at the same time, snowboard manufacturers introduce a more flexible and lower-cost snowboard.
d) Membership in aerobics clubs	The government introduce a new excise tax on exercise; at the same time, the popularity of keep-fit increases.

10. Explain clearly why a price ceiling imposed above the equilibrium price is as ineffective as a price floor imposed below the equilibrium price.

11. If the government were to impose an effective price ceiling on beer, what would happen to the demand for a substitute product like cider? What would happen to the demand for a complementary product like pretzels? Suppose that the government had instead imposed a price floor on beer. What effect would it have on the demands for cider and pretzels?

12. Suppose that both the quantities demanded and supplied of an exclusive French perfume called "Eau de Bière" increased with its price. Would there be a surplus or a shortage of this perfume if it was priced above its equilibrium price? What would happen to its price as a result? Does your answer depend on the comparative slopes of the two curves?

13. As in the previous question, suppose that both the quantities demanded and supplied of an exclusive French perfume called "Eau de Bière" increased with its price. Imagine that the market price is at equilibrium, and both the demand and supply were to increase. Draw the corresponding curves. What would happen to the price as a result? Does your answer depend on the comparative sizes of the increases? Explain. Does your answer depend on knowing which of the two curves is steeper? Explain.

Numerical Questions

14. Table 3.4 shows the demand and supply per year for freezers in Antarctica. Graph and label the curves and find the equilibrium price. Explain this market verbally.

TABLE 3.4

Price	Quantities Demanded	Price	Quantities Supplied
$200	30	$500	0
300	20	600	10
400	10	700	20
500	0	800	30
600	0	900	40

15. Table 3.5 shows the market for kumquats in the country of Poseidon.

TABLE 3.5

Price per Kilo	Quantities Demanded	Quantities Supplied
$0.50	100	10
1.00	95	20
1.50	90	30
2.00	85	40
2.50	80	50
3.00	75	60
3.50	70	70
4.00	65	80
4.50	60	90
5.00	55	100

a) What are the equilibrium values of price and quantity?

b) Suppose the government now imposes a price floor on kumquats that is $1 different from the present equilibrium price. What would be the resulting surplus/shortage?

c) Suppose the government instead imposes a price ceiling that is $1 different from the present equilibrium price. What would be the resulting surplus/shortage?

16. **Table 3.6** shows the market for milk in the country of Pegasus (in thousand of litres).

TABLE 3.6

Price ($)	0	0.25	0.50	0.75	1.00	1.25	1.50	1.75	2.00	2.25	2.50
Demand	120	115	110	105	100	95	90	85	80	75	70
Supply	0	15	30	45	60	75	90	105	120	135	150

a) What is the present equilibrium price and quantity traded?

b) Suppose the government introduces a price floor of $2 per litre. What would be the resulting surplus/shortage?

c) What would be the result if, after the introduction of the price floor, both demand and supply were to increase by 25 percent?

d) What would happen if, instead, the demand and supply were to decrease by 25 percent?

17. **Figure 3.20** depicts the international market for the Canadian dollar (priced in terms of the U.S. dollar).

FIGURE 3.20

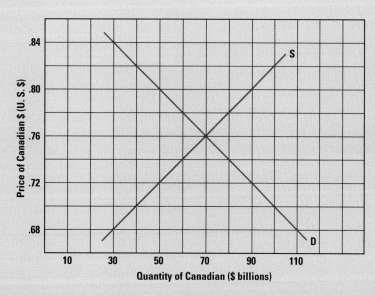

a) Assuming that the market is in equilibrium, suppose that the demand increased by $40 billion and the supply by $20 billion. What happens to the value of the Canadian dollar? How many Canadian dollars are now traded?

b) Suppose that the Bank of Canada had fixed the value of the Canadian dollar at its previous equilibrium level so that no one was allowed to trade Canadian dollars at any other price. What would be the surplus/shortage resulting from the increase in demand and supply mentioned in a)?

18. Figure 3.21 depicts the market for rice in the country of Ran.

FIGURE 3.21

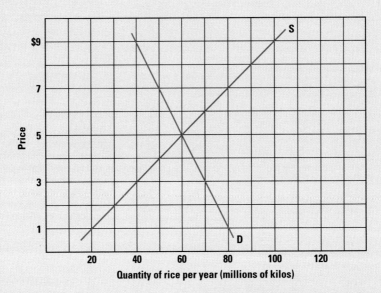

Quantity of rice per year (millions of kilos)

a) Suppose that, in an effort to boost the price of rice for its farmers, the government of Ran introduces a quota that limits the total amount that farmers can produce to 50 million kilos per year. What is the maximum price at which this quantity could be sold?

b) What would be the result if this government decides, instead of using a quota, to introduce a price floor of $7 per kilo? What difference, if any, is there between the two schemes?

 Web-Based Activities

1. Go to **www.millennianet.com/glondon/rent.html**, and **www.slip.net/~cjwarren/rent.html**. Based on these articles, should any city council consider implementing or continuing to maintain rent controls? Why or why not?

2. Anti-poverty groups argue that minimum-wage laws are necessary to help keep people out of poverty. Others believe that minimum-wage laws actually end up causing more people to fall below the poverty line because these laws actually result in fewer poor (low-income) people being employed. Go to **www.fraserinstitute.ca/publications/forum/1997/june/coverstory.html** and **www.ccsd.ca/es_left.htm**. Based on these articles, write a short essay about the pros and cons of minimum wages.

Elasticity

What's ahead... This chapter focuses on how consumers respond to a change in the price of any particular good. Such responsiveness is called price elasticity of demand. We begin by showing how the seller's total revenue is directly tied to elasticity. Next, we use the idea of elasticity to analyze four popular myths that are widely held by the general public. Finally, we see how elasticity is also used in the contexts of supply, income, and interproduct comparisons.

A QUESTION OF RELEVANCE...

Have you ever noticed that most people make some purchases seemingly without thinking about it, yet agonize, sometimes for days, over the purchase of other things? Do you realize that there may well be a dozen or so different prices paid by people who board the same plane for a transcontinental flight? We are all aware that almost everything we purchase in Canada is taxed. It may seem clear that an increase in the GST is simply passed on to the consumer, while the retailer and producer are nothing more than disinterested bystanders. But do consumers really pay these taxes, or is it possible that the supplier shares some of the burden? Do the ticket scalpers you see outside the buildings of high-profile events like playoff hockey games or a Celine Dion concert always make a profit from the resale of the tickets they hold? Although these questions seem unrelated, they have a common link that we will explore in this chapter.

total revenue: the total amount of income a firm receives from its sales; formally, it is price multiplied by the quantity of the product sold.

I f a business raises the price of its product, will its revenue rise? Most people instinctively answer "yes" to this question. However, such an answer is correct only under certain conditions. You will recall that Chapter 2 introduced the law of demand and established the inverse relationship between price and quantity. Thus we know that a decrease in the price of, say, an airline ticket from Toronto to Montreal would result in an increase in the quantity of tickets sold. Obviously, this would be beneficial to consumers, but what we have not yet discussed is whether this would or would not be beneficial to the airline company selling the tickets. What is involved here is whether the airline would receive more or less total revenue as a result of selling more tickets at a lower price per ticket. **Total revenue** (TR), not to be confused with total profit, is simply the total dollar value of selling some quantity of an item at a certain price. Formally, it is:

$$TR = P \times Q$$

price elasticity of demand: the responsiveness of quantity demanded to a change in price.

Here, P stands for the price of the product and Q stands for the quantity sold. The effect of lowering price by itself will decrease total revenue. At the same time, however, the lower price will result in the quantity sold going up, and this will tend to increase total revenue. So what will be the net effect of these opposing pressures? The answer to this question depends on the concept economists call **price elasticity of demand**. The dictionary defines elasticity as "the state of being elastic or flexible," and our focus is on the flexibility of consumers' reactions to a change in price.

Price Elasticity of Demand

Price elasticity of demand, which for the time being we will simply call elasticity, can also be defined as a measure of how much quantity demanded changes as a result of a change in price. The measurement of elasticity is obtained by taking the percentage change in quantity and dividing it by the percentage change in price. Note that we use percentage changes because price is expressed in dollars and quantity in units, so that using just the absolute change in quantity divided by the absolute change in price would not work. Also, showing elasticity in percentage terms means that we can ignore the units in which the quantity is measured. Let's look at some hypothetical data, shown in **Table 4.1**.

TABLE 4.1 Demand for Airline Tickets I

Vancouver to Edmonton			Vancouver to Calgary		
Price	Quantity of Tickets	Total Revenue	Price	Quantity of Tickets	Total Revenue
$650	1000	$650 000	$650	1000	$650 000
550	1100	605 000	550	1250	687 500

Suppose the Vancouver to Edmonton ticket price is $650 and the quantity of tickets sold per day is 1000. This would yield total revenue to the airline of: $650 × 1000 = $650 000. Next, assume that the price of a ticket falls to $550. As a result, the quantity of tickets sold rises to 1100. Total revenue, however, actually *drops* to: $550 × 1100 = $605 000. In contrast, for the Vancouver to Calgary flight the same price change results in quantity rising from 1000 to 1250. As a result, total revenue also *rises* to: $550 × 1250 = $687 500. From these examples we can conclude that the effect on total revenue can vary greatly, depending on how quantity responds to a price change. It also means that one cannot predict the effect on total revenue of a price decrease without knowing how responsive the quantity demanded will be. This is what is meant by the concept of elasticity.

Let's use the same information in Table 4.1 to do some calculations of elasticity. To obtain what is called the **elasticity coefficient** we use the general equation mentioned above, where elasticity is symbolized by the Greek upper-case letter epsilon, the subscript ρ indicates that it is the price elasticity of demand that is being referred to, and Δ means "change in":

elasticity coefficient: a number that measures the responsiveness of quantity demanded to a change in price.

$$\epsilon_\rho = \frac{\% \; \Delta \; \text{quantity demanded}}{\% \; \Delta \; \text{price}}$$

This basic equation can be expanded as follows:

$$\epsilon_\rho = \frac{\dfrac{\Delta \, Q_d}{\text{average } Q_d} \times 100}{\dfrac{\Delta \, P}{\text{average } P} \times 100}$$

To obtain the elasticity coefficient in the Vancouver to Edmonton example, we first need to determine the percentage change in quantity as the quantity changes from the original 1000 to the new 1100. The absolute increase is 100, and we need to put this 100 over a base to get the percentage increase. This raises the question of whether that base should be the original 1000 or the new 1100. Since 100 ÷ 1000 is 0.1 and 100 ÷ 1100 is 0.09, it clearly does make a difference as to which base is chosen. To resolve this question we take the *average* of the original base and the new base, which, in this case, is:

$$\frac{1000 + 1100}{2} = 1050$$

(Using averages ensures that we get the same result if the quantity goes down from $1100 to $1000 or up from $1000 to $1100.) Thus, the percentage change in quantity is the absolute change of 100 divided by the average base of 1050 multiplied by 100. Let's show this explicitly:

$$\% \, \Delta \, Q_d = \frac{100}{1050} \times 100 = 9.5\%$$

The 9.5 percent result is the numerator in the above equation. Next we calculate the percentage change in price by dividing the absolute change of $100 by the average of the original and new prices. The percentage change in the price is:

$$\% \, \Delta \, \text{Price} = \frac{\$100}{\$600} \times 100 = 16.7\%$$

Actually, the technical answer is −16.7 percent, but, with appropriate apologies to mathematicians, we simply ignore the minus sign. The reason economists do this is that price and quantity always move in opposite directions, and thus *any* calculation of price elasticity of demand would result in a negative coefficient. We can now obtain the elasticity coefficient:

$$\epsilon_p = \frac{\% \, \Delta \, Q}{\% \, \Delta \, P} = \frac{9.5\%}{16.7\%} = 0.57$$

inelastic demand:
quantity demanded that is
not very responsive to a
change in price.

So, the Vancouver to Edmonton market has an elasticity coefficient of 0.57, which is less than 1 and is referred to as **inelastic demand**. This means that the quantity demanded is not very responsive to a price change. Specifically, a 1 percent change in price leads to only a 0.57 percent change in quantity. Note that because the demand is inelastic, total revenue will fall as a result of the decrease in price. In the calculation above we saw that total revenue decreases from the original $650 000 to $605 000. We are now able to make our first generalization involving elasticity:

> **If demand is inelastic and price falls, then total revenue will also fall.**

Let's make the same calculation using the figures in the Vancouver to Calgary example. Here the absolute change in quantity is 250 and the average base is:

$$\frac{1000 + 1250}{2} = 1125$$

Next is the following calculation:

$$\frac{250}{1125} = 22.2\%$$

To obtain the denominator we put the absolute change in price, $100, over the average base of:

$$\frac{\$650 + \$550}{2} = \$600$$

This gives a denominator of:

$$\frac{100}{600} = 16.7\%$$

Thus, the elasticity coefficient is:

$$\frac{22.2\%}{16.7\%} = 1.32$$

elastic demand: quantity
demanded that is quite
responsive to a change in
price.

The Vancouver to Calgary market, therefore, has an elasticity coefficient of 1.32, which is greater than 1 and is referred to as **elastic demand**. Here, the quantity demanded is much more responsive to a change in price. A 1 percent change in price leads to a 1.32 percent change in quantity demanded. Since the increase in quantity, which pushes total revenue up, is stronger than the decrease in price, which pushes total revenue down, we would expect that the net effect will be an increase in total revenue and this is verified by our earlier calculation of total revenue increasing from the original $650 000 to $687 500. We can now make our second generalization about elasticity:

> **If demand is elastic and price falls, then total revenue will rise.**

Do we get the same kind of result if the price increases instead of decreases? Let's examine this by going to **Table 4.2**, in which we see price increasing from the original $650 to $750.

SELF-TEST

1. Shown below are three sets of prices and their related quantities. Calculate the elasticity coefficients for each set.

	Price	Quantity
Set I	$1.50	200
	2.00	100
Set II	120.00	1600
	100.00	1800
Set III	18.50	48
	22.50	40

TABLE 4.2 Demand for Airline Tickets II

Vancouver to Edmonton			Vancouver to Calgary		
Price	Quantity	Total Revenue: C	Price	Quantity	Total Revenue: D
$650	1000	$650 000	$650	1000	$650 000
750	900	675 000	750	750	567 500

We see from Table 4.2 that a $100 price increase in each market ($650 to $750) results in a decrease in the number of tickets sold for the Vancouver to Edmonton flights of only 100, but for the Vancouver to Calgary flights the decrease is 250.

You should be able to verify that the elasticity coefficient in the Vancouver to Edmonton market is 0.74 and in the Vancouver to Calgary market is 2. These figures are different from the coefficients calculated previously, and there is a lesson in this. Moving up or down a demand curve results in the elasticity coefficient changing because the average base changes. Recall that the elasticity coefficient in the Vancouver to Edmonton example was 0.57 in the $550–$650 price range (Table 4.1), whereas it is 0.74 in the $650–$750 price range (Table 4.2). This, despite the fact that the absolute change in price is $100 and the absolute change in quantity is 100 tickets in both cases. However, the two average bases are not the same. The average quantity in the first instance is 1050 but only 950 in the second. Similarly, the average price is $600 in the first instance but $700 in the second.

SELF-TEST

2. Below are two sets of prices and their related quantities. Calculate the elasticity coefficients for each set.

In each set the change in price is $1 and the change in quantity is 1 unit. Why aren't the coefficients the same?

	Price	Quantity
Set I	$9	1
	8	2
Set II	2	8
	1	9

Despite the difference in elasticity coefficients at different price ranges, one thing remains consistent: the Vancouver to Edmonton market is an example of inelastic demand, and the Vancouver to Calgary market is an example of elastic demand. We saw earlier that if price *decreases* and demand is inelastic, then total revenue would fall. Thus, if price were to rise, we would expect the opposite, a *rise* in total revenue, and this is exactly what we get as total revenue increases from $650 000 to $675 000.

Similarly, Table 4.1 indicated that if price *falls* and demand is elastic, we would experience an increase in total revenue. Thus, we would expect that a price *rise* in combination with elastic demand would cause a decrease in total revenue, and this is exactly what happens in Table 4.2, as total revenue falls from $650 000 to $567 500.

Table 4.3 summarizes the effect of elasticity on total revenue as a result of a price change.

TABLE 4.3 Relationship Between Price and Total Revenue

Elasticity Coefficient	Price	Total Revenue
inelastic (<1)	falls	falls
inelastic (<1)	rises	rises
elastic (>1)	falls	rises
elastic (>1)	rises	falls

We could also summarize the effects of a price change by saying that:

If the demand is inelastic, price and total revenue move in the same direction. If the demand is elastic, price and total revenue move in opposite directions.

SELF-TEST

3. What would happen to total revenue in each of the circumstances below:
   A) $\epsilon > 1$ and price falls?
   B) $\epsilon < 1$ and price rises?
   C) $\epsilon < 1$ and price falls?
   D) $\epsilon > 1$ and price rises?

4. Suppose that the price of four different products all increased by 20 percent. Given the elasticity coefficients shown below, what is the percentage change in the quantity of each product?
   A) $\epsilon = 4$.
   B) $\epsilon = 0.5$.
   C) $\epsilon = 1$.
   D) $\epsilon = 0$.

Determinants of Price Elasticity

Before we examine the determinants of elasticity, let's identify some commodities that typically have elastic demands and some that typically have inelastic demands (see **Table 4.4**).

TABLE 4.4 Examples of Products with Different Elasticities of Demand

Commodities That Have Elastic Demands	Commodities That Have Inelastic Demands
fresh tomatoes (4.60)	household electricity (0.13)
movies (3.41)	eggs (0.32)
lamb (2.65)	car repairs (0.36)
restaurant meals (1.63)	food (0.58)
china and tableware (1.54)	household appliances (0.63)
automobiles (1.14)	tobacco (0.86)

Source: H.S. Houthakker and Lester D. Taylor, *Consumer Demand in the United States* (Cambridge, MA: Harvard University Press, 1970).

A major determinant of elasticity is the *availability of close substitutes*. For example, in most people's eyes almost any other vegetable is a substitute for tomatoes. Home videos and other forms of entertainment are substitutes for movies, whereas pork and beef are close substitutes for lamb. The substitute for a restaurant meal is to cook at home. Many households find that the substitute for furniture or china and tableware is to simply make do with less of what many consider to be non-essential items. Automobiles have the least elastic demand of those on our list because many people do not consider public transit or bicycling to be a close substitute. A clear conclusion comes out of all this. The more substitutes available for any particular commodity, the greater is the elasticity of demand for that commodity.

ADDED DIMENSION

What Is a Necessity?

It is not uncommon for people to think of products as either luxuries or necessities. There is then a temptation to conclude that luxury products are elastic in demand, whereas necessities must be inelastic. While there is undoubtedly validity in this rule of thumb, we must be careful. To some, wine with a meal is an absolute necessity, while to others it is a seldom-bought luxury. What is a bottle of brandy—a necessity for evening relaxation or a luxury used only in holiday times? What really matters when we are talking about the elasticity of demand is that normally we are looking at market elasticity, that is, the preferences of the majority of people.

Let's now go through the list of commodities that have inelastic demands. Candles can be used as a substitute for electric light, but this is not an attractive option to most people. Eggs are an essential ingredient in baking and cooking. The only real substitutes for auto repairs are to repair the car yourself or to buy a new one, and both of these options are impractical most of the time. Food, as a category, has no substitutes. To the users of tobacco, this item involves an addiction for which there is simply no substitute. To most families, significant price swings in household appliances such as a hot-water heater will not change the quantity demanded much.

Before leaving this discussion of the availability of substitutes, we should note that a great deal depends on how the commodity in question is defined. The demand for food is an example of a broadly defined category and as such it is highly inelastic, since there is no substitute for food. Yet the elasticity of demand for any one food item, such as green beans, is much more elastic because there are many close substitutes. As another example, the elasticity of demand for housing in general is quite low because all of us have to live somewhere whereas, the elasticity of demand for home ownership is much greater since there is the alternative of renting.

A second determinant of elasticity is the *percentage of household income spent on the commodity*. In general, we can say the larger the percentage of one's income that is spent on a particular commodity, the more elastic is the demand for that commodity.

For this reason the elasticity of demand for a high-priced automobile or for a top-of-the-line stereo system will be high. On the other hand, the elasticity of demand for ordinary spices or hand soap will tend to be inelastic simply because the total percentage of a household's budget that is spent on such items is small and the price change will have little impact on our budgets.

The third determinant of elasticity involves the *amount of time that has elapsed since the price change*. The classic example here is that of gasoline. When the OPEC oil embargo of l973 resulted in the halting of (most) oil shipments to North America, the price of gasoline increased fourfold in just 18 months. Measurements of elasticity made over this period of time indicated a very inelastic demand. This was because in the immediate aftermath of such a price shock, very few close substitutes to gasoline were available. This fact became much less true as time wore on, and a number of substitutes were developed. The most significant of these was the development and marketing of much more fuel-efficient automobiles that became increasingly popular in the later 1970s. In addition, given enough time to adjust, people moved closer to their place of employment and the established patterns of driving long distances for a holiday or for a casual visit were changed. Subsequent measurements of the elasticity of demand for gasoline over a time period of 5 or 10 years after the price shock showed elasticity coefficients that were much higher than those taken in the first 18 months. All of this can lead us to conclude that the elasticity of demand tends to be greater the longer the time period involved. In summary, the demand for a product is more elastic:

- the more substitutes there are available
- the larger the percentage of one's income that is spent on the product
- the longer the time period involved

E - C O N O M I C S

A New Way of Shopping

Wired magazine reports that the following scenario is not far off. Imagine yourself walking into a supermarket and instead of picking a shopping cart to hold your purchases you pick up your Personal Digital Assistant (PDA). This new electronic device allows you to walk up and down the aisles and obtain your individually tailored price for every item you pass. But this initially-quoted price is just the starting point of the process. You could, for example, "have a conversation" with a tube of toothpaste by saying something like: "I understand that the price for one is $2.89 but what if I buy six units?" The response might be: "$2.73 for six and $2.59 for twelve." You would then indicate your choice and move on without actually picking up any toothpaste. When your shopping was done, you would proceed to a checkout area where your goods would be waiting for you, along with your bill. After several shopping experiences like this, the store would have a very good idea of what you buy and in what quantities. In short, it would know your demand elasticity for scores of products. Having this knowledge, the store could then pattern individual prices for each item and for each customer. Currently, obtaining such information is very expensive for the seller and can only be applied to large groups of people; e.g. young families, older singles, etc. The PDA will change all that by personalizing each customer's preferences.

Price Elasticity Graphically

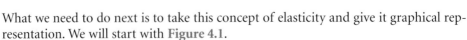

What we need to do next is to take this concept of elasticity and give it graphical representation. We will start with **Figure 4.1**.

FIGURE 4.1 The Demand for Airline Tickets: Vancouver to Edmonton

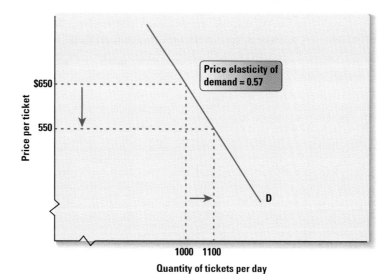

When the price of an airline ticket from Vancouver to Edmonton is $650, 1000 tickets per day are sold. If the price falls to $550, then the quantity demanded rises to 1100 tickets.

Using the data from Table 4.1, Figure 4.1 shows that a price decrease of $100 in the Edmonton fare results in an increase in the quantity demanded of 100 tickets. You may recall that the elasticity coefficient in this case is 0.57. This indicates that demand is inelastic. This is reflected in the relatively steep demand curve in Figure 4.1. Contrast this demand curve with the one in **Figure 4.2**.

FIGURE 4.2 The Demand for Airline Tickets: Vancouver to Calgary

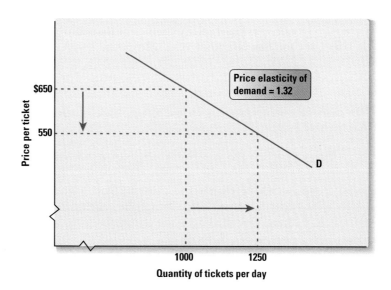

When the price of an airline ticket from Vancouver to Calgary is $650, 1000 tickets per day are sold. If the price falls to $550, the quantity demanded rises to 1250 tickets.

In Figure 4.2, using the Vancouver to Calgary data from Table 4.1, the demand curve plots out an increase of 250 tickets demanded as a result of a $100 decrease in price. This is an elastic demand. Notice that the demand curve is not as steep as was the one in Figure 4.1 but is, instead, relatively shallow. Does this mean that all demand curves that appear steep are inelastic and all that appear shallow are elastic—that is, is there a relationship between the slope of the demand curve and elasticity?

We must be very careful here because the technical answer is no, but the practical answer is maybe. To sort this out, let us go to Figure 4.3.

FIGURE 4.3 A Constant-Slope Demand Curve

Both of the movements *a* to *b* and *c* to d involve a change in price of $2 and a change in quantity of 2 units. Yet, the elasticity coefficient for the *a* to *b* movement is much larger than that for the *c* to *d* movement. Since the slope of this demand curve is constant and the elasticity is not, we can conclude that slope and elasticity are not the same concepts.

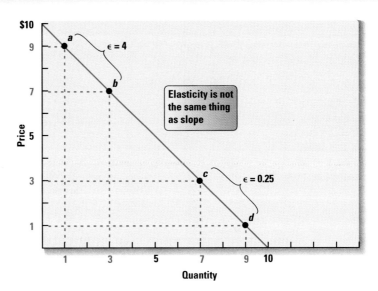

You may recall from high school math that the slope of any straight line is equal to the rise over run. Note in the demand curve in Figure 4.3 that an increase in price of $1 always results in a quantity decrease of 1. Thus the slope of the demand curve is constant and equal to 1 (again the negative sign is ignored). Is elasticity also constant? Let's calculate the elasticity coefficient for a movement along the curve first for point *a* to *b* and then for point *c* to *d*. Movement *a* to *b* would yield a coefficient of:

$$\epsilon_p = \frac{\%\ \Delta Q}{\%\ \Delta P} = \frac{2/2 \times 100}{2/8 \times 100} = \frac{100\%}{25\%} = 4$$

On the other hand, movement from point *c* to *d* would yield:

$$\epsilon_p = \frac{2/8 \times 100}{2/2 \times 100} = \frac{25\%}{100\%} = 0.25$$

Quite clearly the elasticity coefficient is different at different points on the demand curve. Thus, it must be concluded that slope and elasticity are *not* the same thing. One final note: the changes in price and quantity in Figure 4.3 are rather large. Technically, elasticity can be measured for very small changes — in the extreme at a single point by multiplying the inverse of the slope by the ratio P/Q.

SELF-TEST

5. Imagine that elasticity coefficients were recently measured in Canada over a period of one year for the following products. Indicate whether you think such a measurement would be elastic (>1) or inelastic (<1) demand.

    A) Sugar   D) Restaurant meals
    B) Gasoline   E) Women's hats
    C) Ocean cruises   F) Alcohol

There is more that we can learn from a simple demand curve such as that shown in Figure 4.3. Let's calculate, in **Table 4.5**, the total revenue associated with each price.

TABLE 4.5 Demand and Total Revenue Schedule

Price	Quantity	Total Revenue
$10	1	10
9	2	18
8	3	24
7	4	28
6	5	30
5	6	30
4	7	28
3	8	24
2	9	18
1	10	10

Notice how total revenue *rises* as price decreases from $10 to a price of $6. Since price is falling and total revenue is rising, we know this means that demand must be elastic. Further, as price continues to fall from $5 to $1, total revenue *falls*, indicating that demand is inelastic in this range of the demand curve. The price–quantity combinations of $5 and 6 units along with $6 and 5 units are also of particular interest because total revenue is the same $30, which is maximum total revenue.

It is also evident that this $6/$5 price range is the midpoint of the demand curve. This is no coincidence. If total revenue ceases to rise as price falls, we can no longer be on the elastic portion of the demand curve. If total revenue has not yet begun to fall as price decreases, we cannot yet be on the inelastic portion of the demand curve. Thus, if demand is no longer >1 and not yet <1, then it can only be exactly equal to 1. From this we can conclude that:

> **The upper half of any straight-line demand curve is elastic and the lower half is inelastic.**

unitary elasticity: the point where the percentage change in quantity is exactly equal to the percentage change in price; that is, the point where the elasticity coefficient is equal to 1.

Furthermore, the midpoint is where we experience what is called **unitary elasticity**. This can be defined as the point where the percentage change in quantity is exactly equal to percentage change in price, and thus total revenue does not change.

We can now give a practical answer to the question we asked above concerning the relationship between the slope of a demand curve and the elasticity. When we look at a shallow sloped demand curve like D_1 in **Figure 4.4**, what we are looking at is the upper half of what would be a much longer curve if it were extended all the way to the horizontal axis of the graph.

Since the upper half of any straight-line demand curve is the elastic portion, we can look at D_1 and say that it is an elastic demand curve even though we know that the lower half of the curve (most of which we do not see) is the inelastic portion. Similarly, when we look at D_2 we are looking at the lower portion of a much longer demand curve, and this lower portion is inelastic.

In summary, one can make some conclusions about elasticity from the appearance of a demand curve but must always remain aware that slope and elasticity are not the same thing.

FIGURE 4.4 An Elastic and an Inelastic Demand Curve

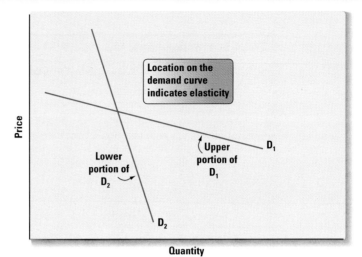

Demand curve D_1 is the elastic (upper) portion of a curve that could be extended downward, while D_2 is the inelastic (lower) portion of demand curve that could be extended upward.

SELF-TEST

6. A) Graph a demand curve using the data from the accompanying demand schedule.
   B) What is the slope of this demand curve?
   C) How could you demonstrate that the elasticity of demand was not the same as the slope?

Price	Quantity
1	18
2	16
3	14
4	12
5	10
6	8
7	6
8	4
9	2

REVIEW

1. **How is *total revenue* calculated?**
2. **Write the formula used to calculate *price elasticity of demand*.**
3. **Distinguish between *inelastic* and *elastic* demand.**
4. **List the three determinants of elasticity.**
5. **Is it valid to say that the slope and the elasticity of a demand curve are the same things? Why or why not?**
6. **Define *unitary elasticity*.**

Applications of Price Elasticity

Misconception One: The Consumer Always Pays a Sales Tax

Sales taxes can take the form of a tax imposed by (federal or provincial) governments on a *specific* product such as alcohol, gasoline, or a movie ticket (these are often referred to as excise taxes). Sales taxes can also take the form of a *general* tax on a wide category of goods, as in the case of the GST. It is the seller who is, by law, responsible for collecting these taxes and actually sending the money to the government. But who really pays these taxes—the seller or the consumer? Most people believe it is the consumer because they assume that the seller simply adds whatever amount the tax might be on to the price of the product and thus passes the tax on to the buyer. Is this correct?

We can use basic supply and demand analysis and the concept of elasticity of demand to answer this question. In **Figure 4.5** we show the demand and supply curves, D_1 and S_1, for movie tickets before the imposition of an excise tax. The equilibrium price initially is $6, and the equilibrium quantity is 10 million tickets per month.

Now let's look at the effect on both equilibrium price and quantity of a $2 per ticket excise tax. The effect on the supply curve would be to shift it up by the same $2, which gives us the new supply curve S_t. The reason for this is that it is the seller who must actually send payment to the government. Movie-house owners were previously willing to supply 10 million tickets per month at a price of $6. If they must now pay the government $2 for each ticket sold, they must collect $8 per ticket in order for them to continue to be willing to supply the same 10 million tickets. The same reasoning would apply to any price (not just $6), so we get the supply shifting up by the amount of the tax—$2.

FIGURE 4.5 The Effect of an Excise Tax on the Price and Quantity of Movie Tickets

The effect of a $2 per ticket excise tax is to shift the supply curve up from S_1 to S_t. The result is that equilibrium price increases from $6 to $6.75 and equilibrium quantity decreases from 10 million to 8 million tickets per month.

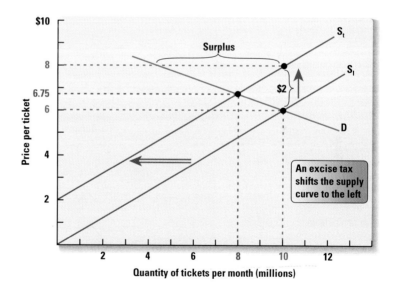

After the shift in the supply curve, we have a new equilibrium price of $6.75 and a new equilibrium quantity of 8 million tickets per month. Thus, the $2 per ticket excise tax increases equilibrium price from the original $6 to $6.75, and it is the consumer who pays an extra $0.75 (or 37.5 percent of the $2) and the seller must be paying $1.25 (or 62.5 percent).

But why does the price not simply increase from $6 to $8? The answer is that while movie-house owners will continue to supply 10 million seats per week just as they did before, moviegoers simply not will attend in the same numbers as they did before the price increase. The theatre owners will be forced to reduce the $8 price until the number of empty seats is reduced. In our example, a new equilibrium will not occur until the price is reduced to $6.75.

But does the seller always pay the bigger part of an excise tax? Not at all. We obtained this particular result because we assumed that the demand for movie tickets is elastic and drew our demand curve accordingly. If demand was inelastic, we would have obtained a different result. We can see this in **Figure 4.6**. In both graphs the shift in supply, S_1 to S_t, is the same. However, the demand, D_1, in graph A is inelastic while demand, D_2, in graph B is elastic. The initial price, P_1, in both instances is the same. But notice how much more price increases (P_1 to P_2) in the circumstances illustrated in graph A compared with that in graph B. Since the price increase is a result of the sales tax, consumers are paying a larger percentage of the tax in graph A than they are in graph B. Further, the larger the percentage paid by the consumers, the smaller the percentage of the tax paid by the sellers of the product.

FIGURE 4.6 The Effect of an Excise Tax on Two Different Demand Curves

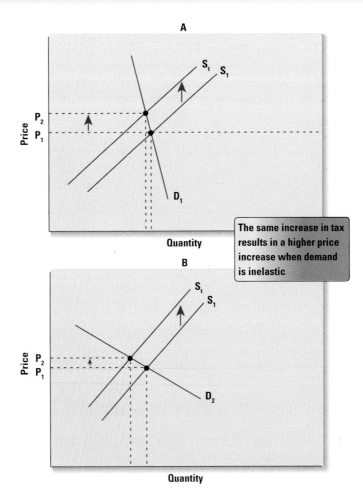

The same increase in tax results in a higher price increase when demand is inelastic

Here the supply curve shifts by the same amount, from S_1 to S_t, in both graph A and graph B as a result of the imposition of a sales tax. The two demands, however, are quite different— inelastic in the case of graph A and elastic in the case of graph B. The resulting increase in price is much greater in graph A than in graph B. Thus consumers are paying a larger percentage of the tax in graph A than they are in graph B.

Thus, we can generalize to say:

The more inelastic the demand for a product, the larger the percentage of a sales (or excise) tax the consumer will pay.

Another way to look at this is that since there are few substitutes for products with inelastic demand, the higher price will not have a big effect on consumers and they will be more willing to pay a higher price.

SELF-TEST

7. The following data are for packages of razor blades.

Price	Demand (D₁)	Supply (S₁)	Supply (tax)
$3	80	40	_____
$4	70	50	_____
$5	60	60	_____
$6	50	70	_____
$7	40	80	_____

A) What are equilibrium price and quantity, assuming demand schedule D_1 and supply schedule S_1?
B) Fill in the blanks in the Supply (tax) column assuming that a $2 per unit excise tax was placed on this product.
C) What is the new equilibrium price and quantity after the imposition of the tax?
D) What proportion of the tax is paid by the consumer, and what proportion is paid by the seller in this case?
E) Draw D_1, S_1, and S_t, and verify your answers above.

Misconception Two: Governments Tax Products Like Cigarettes and Alcohol Heavily Because They Are Concerned About People's Health

Cigarettes cost smokers about $5 to $6 per pack in Canada—the price varies because both the federal and provincial governments impose taxes and the rate of taxation varies from province to province. Generally, the tax on a pack of cigarettes is between $4 and $5. In addition, about 80 percent of the price of beer, wine, and other types of alcohol is tax.

The reason for these high rates of taxation is not complicated. Both of these products have very inelastic demand, and governments discovered, a long time ago, that they could raise their tax revenues by simply raising the tax rate.

The graphical effect of increasing the tax rate on a product with an inelastic demand is illustrated in **Figure 4.7**. A higher tax rate shifts the supply curve to the left, and the price goes up much more than the quantity traded goes down.

A block from Parliament, where the government is working on anti-smoking legislation, teens in the Rideau Centre shopping mall light up. Fifteen percent of Canadian teenagers smoke, according to a Statistics Canada survey.

Canapress/Fred Chartrand

FIGURE 4.7 The Effect of an Increase in the Tax on Cigarettes

An increase in the tax on cigarettes has the effect of shifting
the supply curve to the left,
from S_{t1} to S_{t2}. Since the
demand for cigarettes is
inelastic, the resulting increase
in price, P_1 to P_2, is greater
than the decrease in the quantity demanded, Q_1 to Q_2.

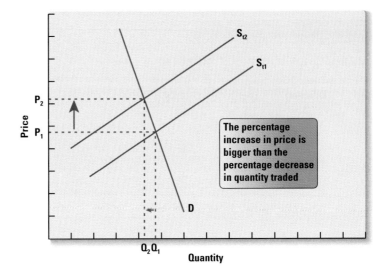

This same point can be shown, perhaps even more effectively, by using some
actual numbers, as is done in **Table 4.6**.

TABLE 4.6 The Effect on Tax Revenue of a Higher Tax Rate When Demand Is Inelastic

Tax Rate per Pack	Quantity Traded (millions of packs)	Tax Revenue to Government ($ millions)
$3.50	20	$70
4.00	19	76
4.50	18	81
5.00	17	85
5.50	16	88

Two things are evident in the table. First, as the tax rate rises, the number of cig-
arette packs bought declines. This is simply a reflection of the law of demand: a higher
tax rate means a higher price for cigarettes and, therefore, a lower quantity sold.
Second, the percentage decline in the quantity traded is much less than the percentage
increase in the tax rate. This is simply a reflection of the inelasticity of demand for cigarettes. The result is clear, as is shown in the third column of Table 4.6. Government
tax revenues rise as the tax rate increases.

To really clinch this idea, let's consider a tax on a product with an elastic demand,
say higher-priced automobiles, and see what happens to government tax revenues.
This is done in **Table 4.7**.

TABLE 4.7 The Effect on Tax Revenue From a Higher Tax Rate When Demand Is Elastic

Tax Rate per Automobile	Quantity Traded (in thousands)	Tax Revenue to Government ($ millions)
$1000	500	$500
2000	200	400
3000	100	300
4000	50	200
5000	25	125

Here you can see that tax revenue declines as the tax rate increases. This is a reflection of the fact that demand is elastic, which means that the percentage decrease in equilibrium quantity is greater than the percentage increase in price, which, of course, rises as the tax rate rises.

In summary, we can conclude that, while some members of governments may have a genuine concern for people's health, the main reason governments put "sin" taxes on goods with inelastic demands is because they can increase their tax revenues.

Misconception Three: A War on Drugs Will Reduce Crime

Most people feel that crime rates in our society are high and seem to rise year after year. Furthermore, the effects of crime appear to be spreading into the middle class of our society and are no longer confined to the underworld. The mood of the general public is becoming more intolerant of all this, and some politicians are responding by calling for tougher laws against criminal activity. The criminal activity that often gets targeted in any get-tough-on-crime campaign is the selling of illegal drugs such as cocaine and heroin.

What is ignored in any such anti-crime policy is the fact that heroin and cocaine have highly inelastic demands. This has serious consequences when we consider that even if the anti-crime policy is effective, the supply of illegal drugs will not be eliminated. This is illustrated in **Figure 4.8**.

A front-line community worker patrols the lanes and parks of Vancouver's Downtown Eastside and picks up used syringes and other drug paraphernalia.

FIGURE 4.8 The Cocaine Market

If D_1 and S_1 are the demand and supply curves for cocaine, the equilibrium price and quantity will be $100 per gram and 500 000 grams per week. One outcome of an effective campaign against the drug trade is that the supply of cocaine will be reduced and the supply curve will shift to the left, as in S_2. This will greatly increase the price (for example, to $180) because, when demand is inelastic, a reduction in supply has a far greater impact on the price than on the quantity.

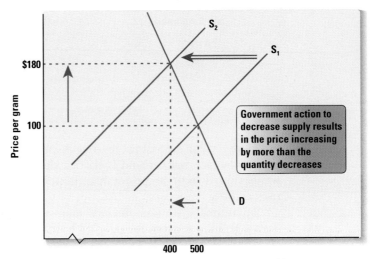

Quantity (thousands of grams per week)

Let's assume that D_1 is the (inelastic) demand for cocaine and that S_1 is the original supply which results in a price of $100 per gram and a quantity traded of 500 000 grams per week. Next, let's assume that the government launches a campaign to crack down on drug imports with the result that the supply decreases, as illustrated by the curve shifting back to S_2. This causes the price of cocaine to rise to $180 per gram while the quantity demanded decreases to 400 000 grams per week.

What is important in all this is the amount that is spent by the consumers of cocaine in the two instances. When the price is $100 per gram, a total of $50 million per week is spent ($100 × 500 000) while $72 million is spent after the rise in price caused by the decrease in supply ($180 × 400 000). A large percentage of this money is obtained by the users of cocaine through various types of crime such as robberies, car thefts, muggings, and hold-ups as well as white-collar crimes such as embezzlement and fraud. In our example, $22 million more per week is spent on cocaine than before the decrease in supply. We would have to conclude that it is highly likely that more crime will be committed to obtain these additional funds.

What we are left with is the seeming paradox that this policy aimed at reducing crime, in fact, increases the incidence of crime. This provides an insight into why some types of crime seem to continue to rise despite (or because of?) our anti-crime policies and the efforts of our police.

Misconception Four: A Bumper Harvest Is Good News for Farmers

A bumper harvest is one in which crop yields are high and farmers are able to bring large quantities of what they grow to market. For example, a typical wheat farmer might harvest 25 000 bushels in a bumper year, whereas an average harvest would be only 20 000 bushels. Wouldn't this be cause for celebration on the part of the farmer? The answer is no, and the reason, again, involves the price elasticity of demand.

The elasticity of demand for some agricultural products is certainly elastic—tomatoes, lettuce, and plums, for example—since there are many close substitutes available. However, the elasticity of demand for the more basic commodities such as wheat is more inelastic.

If we combine an inelastic demand with the fact that a bumper harvest would increase supply and shift the supply curve to the right and thus decrease price, the total revenue that would flow to the farmers as a group would decline. This is illustrated in **Figure 4.9**. In Figure 4.9, we assume that the normal-year equilibrium price and quantity is $3.50 per bushel and 80 million bushels. This would give wheat farmers total revenue of $280 million. In the bumper-harvest year the supply curve shifts to the right and the new equilibrium price and quantity is $2.50 and 100 million bushels. This results in price dropping far more than the quantity increases so that the total revenue decreases to $250 million. The bumper harvest results in farmers losing $30 million in revenue. This illustrates the old adage that farmers ask the gods for a poor harvest—for everyone except themselves.

FIGURE 4.9 The Effect of a Bumper Harvest on the Wheat Market

A bumper harvest increases the supply of wheat and shifts the supply curve from S_1 to S_2. Given the inelastic demand for wheat, the decrease in price is substantial and the total revenue going to farmers as a group decreases.

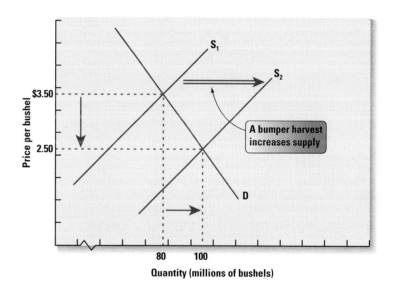

SELF-TEST

8. The data below is for economy-line bicycles.

Demand (D_1) per Week	Price per Unit	Supply (S_1) per Week
2 000 000	$260	800 000
1 800 000	320	1 200 000
1 600 000	380	1 600 000
1 400 000	440	2 000 000
1 200 000	500	2 400 000

A) What is the equilibrium price and quantity?
B) What is the total expenditure at equilibrium?
C) If the supply was increased by 50 percent, what would be the new equilibrium price and quantity?
D) What is the total expenditure at this new equilibrium?
E) What is the price elasticity of demand between these two equilibrium points?

Elasticity of Supply

elasticity of supply: the responsiveness of quantity supplied to a change in price.

The concept of elasticity can be applied to supply as well as to demand. The definition of **elasticity of supply** is analogous to that of demand:

$$\epsilon_s = \frac{\% \, \Delta \text{ quantity supplied}}{\% \, \Delta \text{ price}}$$

As we did with the demand curve, we can make some generalizations about the elasticity of supply from the position and slope of the curve as seen in **Figure 4.10**.

FIGURE 4.10 Elasticity of Supply

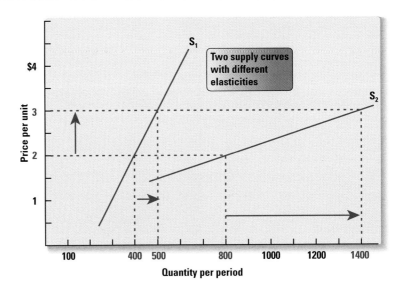

Supply curve S_1 is inelastic, as can be seen from the fact that only a small quantity change (from 400 to 500) results from the price increasing from $2 to $3. S_2, on the other hand, is an elastic supply curve since quantity increases from 800 to 1400 as a result of the same price increase.

Here, we have two supply curves, S_1 and S_2, and a common price change from $2 to $3. In the case of supply curve S_1, the quantity supplied rises from 400 to 500, while in the case of supply curve S_2 the quantity supplied doubles from 800 to 1400. We can therefore legitimately conclude that the elasticity of supply of S_2 must be larger than that in S_1. This allows us to generalize that the elasticity of supply of more shallow curves is greater than that of steeper curves, although we again caution that elasticity does change as we move along any supply curve, just as it did in the case of the demand curve. Given that producers would like to increase the quantity they supply as much as they can in response to an increase in price, what might explain the kind of difference in response indicated by S_1 and S_2? The first possible explanation involves the *level of technology* in use. If it is a sophisticated technology, such as one that requires complicated tool and die making, then S_1 is probably more representative. The use of a very simple technology, such as in cardboard carton production, would more likely be represented by S_2. Implied in this explanation, however, is an even more important determinant of supply elasticity, and that is the *time period involved*.

SELF-TEST

9. Calculate the price elasticity of supply in the $2 to $3 range for both supply curves S_1 and S_2 in Figure 4.10.

Alfred Marshall recognized the importance of time in the determination of supply elasticity with his famous fish market example. In **Figure 4.11A** we see a perfectly inelastic supply curve, representing what Marshall called the momentary market period but is now usually referred to simply as the market period. As an example, he talked about the day's fish catch, in the quantity of Q_1, having been landed at the docks. This is all the fish that will be supplied until the next day (momentary supply), no matter how high the price might go. Marshall called the supply curve S_2 in **Figure 4.11B** the short-run supply curve, which is more elastic than S_1 and is reflective of the various responses that fishers might be able to make in the short run to a higher price. This might include putting on extra crew, staying out longer, or using more nets. The supply curve in **Figure 4.11C** is the long-run supply curve, reflecting long-term adjustments to higher price, such as training additional crew and building more boats, which could take a number of months or years to accomplish.

FIGURE 4.11 Supply Elasticity in Three Time Periods

A
Market Period

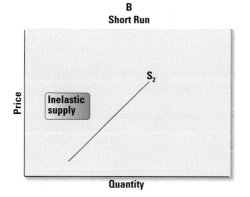

B
Short Run

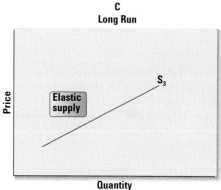

C
Long Run

Supply is perfectly inelastic in graph A. Marshall called this the momentary or market period. In graph B, the short run, supply is still inelastic but not perfectly inelastic. In graph C, the long run, supply is elastic.

From Marshall's fish market example we can conclude that:

The longer the time frame involved, the more elastic will be the supply.

Ticket Scalping

An interesting application of supply elasticity involves ticket scalping. This occurs when individuals who have purchased tickets at the regular price resell those tickets for a higher price. Consider any popular event, such as a hockey playoff game or a high-profile concert, for which only a limited number of tickets are available for sale. In this case, the owners of the home team (or the promoters of the event) must set the regular ticket price in advance by trying to estimate, as best they can, the demand for the event. **Figure 4.12** gives us three possibilities.

The fact that there is only a limited number of tickets for sale results in the supply curve being perfectly inelastic, as reflected by S_1. Now assume that the price, which must be fixed before the tickets go on sale, is set at \$40. If the demand for tickets to this event happens to be that represented by D_1, then we would have equilibrium with 17 000 tickets sold. If instead demand turns out to be higher, as represented by D_2, the general public will wish to buy 5000 more tickets than are available for sale. These are the circumstances of a shortage that ticket scalpers thrive on. Such individuals will get into the line to buy tickets as early as possible and then buy as many tickets as they can so that they can later resell them at a higher price. Whether such activity is or is not legal varies from province to province in Canada but undoubtedly goes on everywhere.

FIGURE 4.12 Perfectly Inelastic Supply

A concert hall or hockey rink has a fixed number of seats, which gives us the perfectly inelastic supply curve S_1. Here, the price per seat is preset at \$40. If demand turns out to be exactly as indicated by D_1, this \$40 price will be equilibrium. If, however, demand turns out to be higher than anticipated, D_2, 5000 people who wanted a ticket will have to do without. Finally, if demand proves to be that represented by D_3, there will be unsold seats for the event.

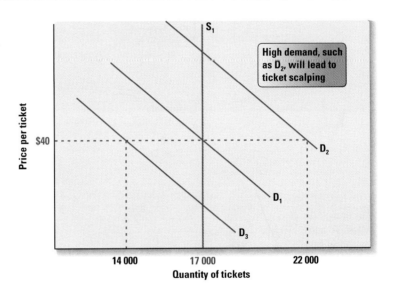

Does the activity of scalping tickets always pay off? The answer is clearly no if both the ticket-price setters and the scalper overestimate the demand. This situation is represented by D_3 in Figure 4.12. Here, 3000 tickets will remain unsold and the scalper will have no option but to dump the \$40 tickets at a greatly reduced price. This probably does not often happen, however, because there is evidence that event organizers prefer to set the official price a little below what they think they could sell at in order to reap the publicity that results when there are big line-ups for tickets. In any case, it is clear that the phenomenon of a perfectly inelastic supply curve and a fixed preset price does generate some interesting twists in our analysis.

Income Elasticity

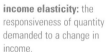

income elasticity: the responsiveness of quantity demanded to a change in income.

As we have seen, the concept of price elasticity of demand involves the responsiveness of the quantity demanded to a change in price. Another important idea is the responsiveness of quantity demanded to a change in income, which is called **income elasticity** (of demand). In the case of price elasticity, our measurement involves moving up or down on a single demand curve as illustrated in **Figure 4.13A**, whereas income elasticity involves the whole demand curve shifting since, as you recall from Chapter 2, a change in income causes a change in demand.

The increase in the quantity demanded in **Figure 4.13B** is a result of the shift in the demand curve from D_1 to D_2, and the higher the income elasticity the greater will be this shift.

The mechanics of measurement of the coefficient of income elasticity are quite analogous to that of price elasticity:

$$\epsilon_Y = \frac{\% \Delta \text{ quantity}}{\% \Delta \text{ income}}$$

FIGURE 4.13 Price Elasticity and Income Elasticity

In 4.13A, the movement along the demand curve from point *a* to point *b* involves the price elasticity of demand. In contrast, income elasticity of demand involves a shift in the demand curve such as D_1 to D_2 in 4.13B.

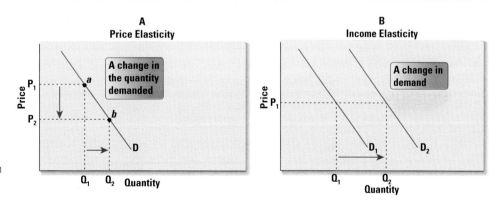

Once again, if this coefficient turns out to be greater than 1 the demand is said to be income elastic, and if it turns out to be less than 1 but greater than 0 we use the term income inelastic. Examples of products that tend to be income elastic are air travel, restaurant meals, hairstyling services, and private swimming pools. Examples of products that tend to be income inelastic are tobacco, food, newspapers, and telephone hook-ups.

If these examples suggest to you that the distinction between products that are income elastic and income inelastic is one of luxuries and necessities, you are correct. Households with limited income tend to buy only necessities. If the household's income rises, almost all of that additional income would be spent on the luxuries that previously could not be purchased. An undeniable characteristic of a postindustrial economy is that the percentage of total consumption of services rises while that of physical goods declines. This is a reflection of the fact that most people consider services such as travel, dining out, and hiring a gardener as little ways that they might give themselves a treat, and this kind of expenditure undoubtedly becomes a greater part of one's total expenditures as income rises.

Most products, be they income elastic or inelastic, have an income elasticity coefficient that is greater than zero and are therefore the normal products that were defined in Chapter 2. However, for inferior products the quantity demanded of the product actually declines in response to an increase in income, and, therefore, the income elasticity is negative. Staple foods such as rice, flour, and cabbage are the most likely candidates for examples of inferior goods. Imagine a family so poor that it eats rice three times a day. This family then experiences a rise in income. It is feasible that this family may in fact consume less rice (and greater quantities of more expensive foodstuffs) as a result. If the experience of this hypothetical family was typical of the families in society generally, rice would be an inferior good and conform to our definition of negative income elasticity.

SELF-TEST

11. You are given the following data and may assume that the prices of X and Y do not change:

A) Calculate the income elasticity for products X and Y.
B) Are products X and Y both normal goods?

Income	Quantity Demanded of X	Income	Quantity Demanded of Y
$10 000	200	$50 000	50
15 000	350	60 000	54

Cross-elasticity of Demand

cross-elasticity of demand: the responsiveness of the change in the quantity demanded of product A to a change in the price of product B.

Finally, in addition to price elasticity of demand, income elasticity, and elasticity of supply, we also have the concept of **cross-elasticity of demand**. Here we are comparing the quantity response in one product, A, with a change in the price of another product, B. The formal definition is:

$$\epsilon_{AB} = \frac{\% \, \Delta \text{ quantity demanded of product A}}{\% \, \Delta \text{ price of product B}}$$

Consider the two products, butter and margarine. An increase in the price of margarine will lead to an increase in the demand for butter, as indicated in **Table 4.8.**

TABLE 4.8 Cross-elasticity of Margarine and Butter

Margarine		Butter	
Price	Quantity Demanded per Week (lbs.)	Price	Quantity Demanded per Week (lbs.)
$1.50	5000	$3.00	1000
2.10	3200	3.00	2000

Given the data in Table 4.8, it seems clear that the increase in the demand for butter is the result of the change in the price of margarine. The cross-elasticity of demand of butter for margarine therefore is:

$$\epsilon_{BM} = \frac{\dfrac{+1000}{1500} \times 100}{\dfrac{+0.60}{1.80} \times 100} = \frac{+67\%}{+33\%} = +2$$

When we are looking at cross-elasticity the sign of the coefficient is important. The fact that the coefficient is a positive number verifies that these two goods are substitutes and reinforces something that we learned in Chapter 2, that is, a rise in the price of a product (margarine) will increase the demand of a substitute product (butter).

It stands to reason that if substitute products have a positive cross-elasticity, then complementary products will have a negative cross-elasticity. We can easily verify this. What would you expect to happen to the demand for film as a result of a price *decrease* in the price of cameras? Surely, it would *increase*, and as a result the cross-elasticity calculation between the two would have a negative sign, as we would expect in the case of complementary products.

As we have seen, elasticity is a concept with wide application and one that extends our understanding of supply–demand analysis in many useful ways.

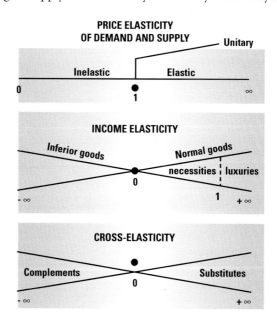

SELF-TEST

12. Given the following data:

Year	Income	Price of Cameras	Quantity of Cameras Demanded	Price of Tripods	Quantity of Tripods Demanded
1	$50 000	$200	80	$50	300
2	50 000	225	70	50	280
3	50 000	225	60	75	250
4	60 000	225	70	75	260
5	70 000	250	50	100	200

A) Calculate the price elasticity of demand for cameras for years 1 and 2.
B) Calculate the income elasticity of tripods for years 3 and 4.
C) Calculate the cross-elasticity of demand of cameras for tripods for years 2 and 3.
D) Is it possible to calculate the price elasticity of demand for cameras and tripods between years 4 and 5?

REVIEW

1. How would you show the effect of a new excise tax on a supply and demand graph?
2. If the government increases the excise tax on a product whose demand is inelastic, what would happen to tax revenues?
3. If the supply of a product decreases and its demand is inelastic, what happens to total expenditures on the product?
4. Define *elasticity of supply*. What determines the elasticity of supply?
5. What is the difference between Marshall's momentary market, short-run supply, and his long-run supply?
6. What is the major characteristic of supply–demand analysis as it applies to concerts, live theatre, and sporting events?
7. Define *income elasticity*.
8. What is the difference between a *normal good* and an *inferior good*?
9. What is the formula for *cross-elasticity of demand*?

STUDY GUIDE

Chapter Highlights

The focus of this chapter was elasticity which is one of the more powerful concepts in microeconomics. Price elasticity of demand is the responsiveness of the quantity demanded to a change in price. Elasticity determines whether the consumer's total expenditure and, more importantly, the seller's total revenue rises or falls as price changes. The chapter presented four specific applications of this concept to illustrate its relevance and importance in microeconomic analysis. We saw how the concept of elasticity can be applied to supply, income, and prices changes of related products.

1. The *measurement of elasticity* involves a standard formula that relates the percentage change in the quantity demanded (or supplied) to the percentage change in price (or income, or the price of a related product) which yields an elasticity coefficient.

2. The price elasticity of demand is *inelastic* if:
    *   the coefficient is less than 1;

    and it is *elastic* if:
    *   the coefficient is greater than 1.

3. If the price elasticity of demand is *inelastic*:
    *   price and the firm's total revenue move in the same direction;

    and if it is *elastic* then:
    *   price and the firm's total revenue move in opposite directions.

4. The *determinants* of the price elasticity of demand are:
    *   the number of substitutes available;
    *   the percentage of income that is spent on the product;
    *   the time period involved in the measurement.

5. While it can be easily demonstrated that the *slope of a demand curve* and its elasticity are not the same thing, we can, nonetheless, generalize and say that:
    *   a relatively steep demand curve is mostly inelastic;
    *   a relatively shallow demand curve is mostly elastic.

6. The *four applications* of the concept of price elasticity of demand show that:
    *   consumers pay a larger portion of a sales tax the more inelastic the demand curve;
    *   governments raise a great deal of revenue from excise taxes on products with high inelastic demand such as cigarettes;
    *   any attempt to crack down on crime by focusing on the supply of illegal drugs will likely increase crime;
    *   a bumper harvest for farmers is not always good news for this group.

7. The *elasticity of supply* depends primarily on the time period involved with the result that:
    *   supply is perfectly inelastic in the market period;
    *   supply is inelastic, but not perfectly so, in the short run;
    *   supply is elastic in the long run.

8. The case of *ticket scalping* is a classic application of the concept of supply elasticity.

9. *Income elasticity* involves a shift in the demand curve as a result of a change in income (rather than a movement along the demand curve as in the case of price elasticity of demand) and:
   - a negative coefficient indicates an inferior product;
   - a positive coefficient which is less than 1 indicates a necessity;
   - a positive coefficient which is more than 1 indicates a luxury product.

10. *Cross elasticity* of demand involves the percentage change in the quantity demanded of one product as a result of a percentage change in the price of another product and a positive elasticity coefficient indicates a:
    - substitute product;

    while a negative coefficient indicates a
    - complementary product.

New Glossary Terms and Key Equations

cross-elasticity of demand   142
elastic demand   122
elasticity coefficient   121
elasticity of supply   138
income elasticity   141
inelastic demand   122
price elasticity of demand   120
total revenue   120
unitary elasticity   129

Equations:

1. Total revenue (TR)   =   price (P)   ×   quantity (Q)

2. $$\epsilon_p = \frac{\% \Delta Q_d}{\% \Delta P} \quad \text{or} \quad \frac{\frac{\Delta Q_d}{Q_d} \times 100}{\frac{\Delta P}{P} \times 100}$$

3. $$\epsilon_s = \frac{\% \Delta Q_s}{\% \Delta P} \quad \text{or} \quad \frac{\frac{\Delta Q_s}{Q_s} \times 100}{\frac{\Delta P}{P} \times 100}$$

4. $$\epsilon_y = \frac{\% \Delta Q_d}{\% \Delta Y} \quad \text{or} \quad \frac{\frac{\Delta Q_d}{Q_d} \times 100}{\frac{\Delta Y}{Y} \times 100}$$

5. $$\epsilon_{AB} = \frac{\% \Delta Q_B}{\% \Delta P_A} \quad \text{or} \quad \frac{\frac{\Delta Q^B_d}{Q_d} \times 100}{\frac{\Delta P^A}{P^A} \times 100}$$

Study Tips

1. It may be helpful to think of elasticity as a concept that measures the responsiveness of one variable to a change in a related variable. As a way of summary, you can think of the most common application being the responsiveness of quantity demanded to a change in price, which is called price elasticity of demand or, simply, demand elasticity.

2. Bear in mind that the concept of elasticity can also be applied to the ways that a change in income or a change in the price of a related good affects the quantity demanded of a particular product. Similarly, it can be applied to the way a change in price affects quantity supplied. These applications are called income elasticity, cross-elasticity (of demand), and supply elasticity.

3. You must learn the formulas for calculating elasticities in the same way you learned your phone number—use them until they stick. The recipe-card suggestion made earlier would really work here.

4. Since elasticity involves price and quantity, it also directly relates to a seller's total revenue. The effect of a price increase on total revenue will be to either increase or decrease it, depending on elasticity. The same can be said for a price decrease. The exact relationships are, again, something you simply have to memorize.

5. The power of the concept of elasticity is illustrated in the analysis of the four myths presented in the chapter. If you follow the arguments in each of these, you can be reasonably assured that you have grasped the basic ideas of elasticity.

Are You Sure?

Indicate whether the following statements are true or false. If false, indicate why they are false.

1. A firm's total revenue is equal to price times demand. quantity

   T or F   If false: _____

   _____

2. The price elasticity of demand coefficient is, technically, always negative, but for convenience economists ignore the minus sign.

   T or F   If false: _____

   _____

3. If demand is inelastic and price falls, then total revenue will rise.

   T or F   If false: _____

   _____

4. If demand is elastic and price rises, then total revenue will rise.

   T or F   If false: _____

   _____

5. If the elasticity of demand is unitary and the price rises, then total revenue will rise.

   T or F   If false: _____

   _____

6. A major determinant of demand elasticity is the number of complementary products available.

   T or F   If false: _____

   _____

7. A straight-line (constant-sloped) demand curve does not imply constant elasticity.

   T or F   If false: _____

   _____

8. Supply elasticity is measured by percentage change in quantity supplied divided by percentage change in quantity demanded.

   T or F   If false: _____

   _____

9. If a calculation of cross-elasticity of demand is positive, we could conclude that the two products are substitutes.

   T or **F**   If false: _____

   _____

10. If income elasticity is positive, we could conclude that the product in question is an inferior good.

   T or **F**   If false: _____

   _____

Choose the Best

11. What is the effect on total revenue if demand is elastic and price rises?
    a) Total revenue will fall.
    b) Total revenue will rise.

12. What is the effect of a rise in income on the quantity demanded of a product ?
    a) It will rise if the product is an inferior product.
    b) It will rise if the product is a normal product.

13. How will the imposition of a sales tax shift the supply curve?
    a) The supply curve will shift to the left.
    b) The supply curve will shift to the right.

14. What is the elasticity of supply of seats for a one-night concert in an auditorium?
    a) It is elastic.
    b) It is inelastic.
    c) It is perfectly inelastic.

15. What is the effect on tax revenue if the government increases the excise tax on a product that has an inelastic demand?
    a) It will rise.
    b) It will fall.
    c) It may rise or fall, depending on the size of increase.

16. What is a normal good?
    a) It is a good whose income elasticity of demand is < 0.
    b) It is a good whose demand will rise as income rises.
    c) It is a good that has many substitutes.

17. What is the elasticity of Marshall's short-run supply curve?
    a) It is perfectly elastic.
    b) It is elastic.
    c) It is inelastic.

18. A local transit authority has just applied to its regulatory board for a fare increase on its rail-transit system, arguing that the increase is needed to cover rising costs. A citizens committee is opposed to the proposed increase, arguing that the company could increase its revenue by decreasing fares. Which of the statements below is correct?
    a) The company thinks that the demand is inelastic, whereas the committee thinks it is elastic.
    b) The company thinks that the demand is elastic, whereas the committee thinks it is inelastic.
    c) Both the company and the committee think that elasticity is unity.
    d) It is possible that both the company and the committee are correct.

19. Under which of the following situations will total revenue rise?
    a) If elasticity is >1 and price falls.
    b) If elasticity is >1 and price rises.
    c) If elasticity is <1 and price falls.
    d) If elasticity is = 1 and price falls.

20. What will happen to the quantity demanded if the price elasticity of demand is 2 and the price increases by 10 percent?
    a) It will increase by 10 percent.
    b) It will decrease by 10 percent.
    c) It will decrease by 20 percent.
    d) It will increase by 20 percent.

21. If a product has many substitutes, which of the following statements is correct?
    a) Its income elasticity is high.
    b) It is likely that it is an inferior product.
    c) Its supply elasticity is high.
    d) Its price elasticity of demand is high.

22. If people spend a large percentage of their income on a particular product, which of the following statements is true?
    a) The product has a large number of substitutes.
    b) The elasticity of demand for the product is high.
    c) The income elasticity for the product is low.
    d) The elasticity of supply for the product is low.

23. What will cause the elasticity of demand for a product to be high?
    a) A low percentage of income is spent on the product.
    b) There are a small number of available substitutes.
    c) The elasticity of supply for the product is high.
    d) A long time period is used to measure elasticity.

24. Graphically, what is the effect of imposing an excise tax on a product?
    a) It will shift both the supply and the demand curve for the product to the left.
    b) It will shift the supply curve for the product to the left.
    c) It will shift the supply curve for the product to the right.
    d) It will shift both the supply and the demand curve for the product to the right.
    e) It will shift the supply curve for the product to the left and the demand curve to the right.

25. If the government puts a $2 excise tax on a product and, as a result, price rises by $0.75, which of the following statements is correct?
    a) The sellers pay more of the tax than do the buyers.
    b) The buyers pay more of the tax than do the sellers.
    c) The government's tax revenue falls.
    d) The quantity demanded of the product falls by 37.5 percent.

26. What is the likely effect of the government reducing the supply of illegal drugs?
    a) The total amount spent on drugs will decrease.
    b) The total amount spent on drugs will increase.
    c) The quantity of drugs consumed will remain unchanged.

    d) The demand for drugs will fall.
    e) The demand for drugs will increase.

27. Which of the following circumstances will raise the total revenue of oat farmers?
    a) A bumper harvest, combined with inelastic demand.
    b) A poor harvest, combined with inelastic demand.
    c) A poor harvest, combined with elastic demand.
    d) A bumper wheat and oat harvest, combined with inelastic demands.
    e) A poor wheat and oat harvest, combined with elastic demands.

Refer to **Table 4.9** to answer questions 28, 29, and 30.

TABLE 4.9

Income	Quantity of K Demanded	Quantity of L Demanded	Quantity of M Demanded
$50 000	200	40	80
60 000	260	50	85

28. Refer to Table 4.9 to answer this question. What is the income elasticity of product K?
    a) 1.5.
    b) 15.
    c) Approximately 14.
    d) Approximately 1.4.
    e) Approximately 0.7.

29. Refer to Table 4.9 to answer this question. What is the income elasticity of product L?
    a) Approximately 12.
    b) Approximately 1.2.
    c) Greater than the income elasticity of product K.
    d) Approximately 0.8.
    e) 8.

30. Refer to Table 4.9 to answer this question. Which of the following is correct about product M?
    a) It has an income elasticity of approximately 6.7.
    b) It has an income elasticity of approximately 0.2.
    c) It has an income elasticity of approximately 0.6.
    d) It is a normal good.
    e) It is an inferior good.

Simple Calculations

31. You are given the following data for the pencil market:

Original price (per box): $4.25   new price: $3.75
Original quantity sold: 980   new quantity sold: 1020

What is the value of the price elasticity of demand over this price range? _____ .

32. Suppose that the price of a kilo of bananas drops from $.50 to $3.50 and as a result the quantity sold increases from 85 to 115 kilos.
a) What is the value of total revenue before and after the price change? _____ .
b) What is the percentage change in the price? _____ .
     What is the percentage change in the quantity? _____ .
c) What is the value of the price elasticity of demand over this price range? _____ .
     Is the demand elastic or inelastic? _____ .

33. If the quantity of bread supplied increased by 12 percent when the price of bread increased by 10 percent, what is the value of the elasticity of supply? _____ .

34. Suppose that household incomes in Sherbrooke rose from $50 000 to $54 000 and assuming no change in price, the quantity of Kraft macaroni cheese dinners rose from 156 to 164 cases per week.
a) What is the value of the income elasticity of demand for Kraft dinners? _____ .
b) What does this suggest about the type of product it is? _____ .

35. Suppose that the price of President's Choice macaroni cheese dinners decreased from $9 to $7 per case while at the same time the quantity of Kraft macaroni cheese dinners dropped from 192 to 128 cases. What is the cross elasticity of demand between the two products? _____ .

Problems

36. Given the demand curve in **Figure 4.14**:

FIGURE 4.14

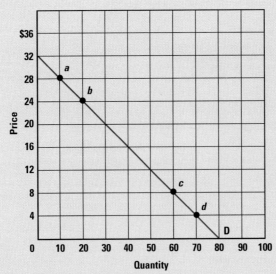

a) What can you say about the slope of the demand curve?

Answer: _____ .

b) What is the elasticity of demand between points *a* and *b*, and between points *c* and *d*?

a and *b*: _____; *c* and *d*: _____.

c) At what price is the elasticity of demand equal to one?

Price: _____.

d) At what price would consumers spend the most on this product?

Price: _____.

e) Between what prices is demand inelastic?

Between: _____ and _____.

37. Fill in the blanks in **Table 4.10**, which relates to a particular market.

TABLE 4.10

Year	Average Income	Price of M	Quantity of M	Price of N	Quantity of N	Price ε for M	Price ε for N	Income ε for M	Income ε for N	Cross ε M for N
1	$50 000	$2.50	100	$20	800	X	X	X	X	X
2	50 000	2.80	90	20	800	_____	X	X	X	X
3	50 000	2.80	80	30	700	X	_____	X	X	_____
4	55 000	2.80	90	30	720	X	X	_____	_____	X

38. The data in **Table 4.11** are for 5-kilo boxes of lobsters.

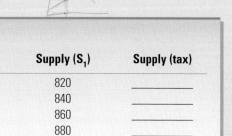

TABLE 4.11

Price	Demand	Supply (S₁)	Supply (tax)
$100	900	820	_____
110	880	840	_____
120	860	860	_____
130	840	880	_____
140	820	900	_____
150	800	920	_____

a) If the supply is S₁, what is equilibrium price and quantity?

Price: _____; quantity: _____.

b) Fill in the Supply (tax) column, assuming that a $20 per unit excise tax is put on the product.

c) What is the new equilibrium price and quantity?

Price: _____; quantity: _____.

d) What portion of the $20 excise tax is paid by the seller, and what portion is paid by the consumer?

Paid by seller: _____; paid by consumer: _____.

39. **Table 4.12** shows the demand for haircuts by seniors and other customers on an average weekday in the local hairdressing shop.

TABLE 4.12

Price of Haircut	Quantity Demanded by Seniors	Quantity Demanded by Other Customers
$20	1	9
18	4	10
16	7	11
14	10	12
12	13	13
10	16	14
8	19	15
6	22	16
4	25	17
2	28	18

a) Between the prices of $16 and $20, which of the two demands is more elastic? Explain.

b) What is the price that would give the shop the greatest sales revenue?

Price: _____.

Translations

Describe in words the demand curve illustrated in **Figure 4.15**. Include in your answer references to elasticity and to the revenue of the seller(s).

_____

_____

_____

FIGURE 4.15

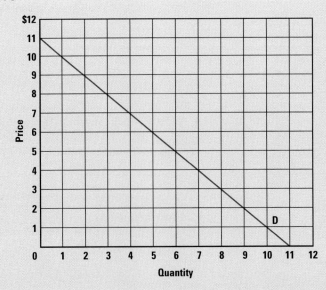

Key Problem

Assume that there is only one movie theatre and only one video rental outlet in a small mining town in northern Manitoba. The weekly demand, by all the townspeople, for movies and video rentals is given in **Table 4.13**.

a) Fill in the total revenue columns.

b) What would be the most advantageous price for the sellers to charge?

Movie price: _____; video price: _____.

TABLE 4.13

Price of Movies	Quantity of Movies Demanded	Total Revenue	Price of Videos	Quantity of Videos Demanded	Total Revenue
$3	450	_____	$2.00	950	_____
4	400	_____	2.50	900	_____
5	350	_____	3.00	825	_____
6	300	_____	3.50	750	_____
7	250	_____	4.00	650	_____
8	200	_____	4.50	550	_____
9	150	_____	5.00	425	_____

c) What is the elasticity of demand for movies if the seller changes the price from $6 to $5, and what is the change in total revenue? What if the price changes from $6 to $7?

From $6 to $5: _____; change in revenue: _____.

From $6 to $7: _____; change in revenue: _____.

d) What conclusions can you draw from your answers in c)?

e) Suppose that the video store was charging the price that maximized revenue, and then the city government imposed an excise tax on videos that resulted in the price of videos rising to $4.50. As a result, the demand for movies increased by 20 at each price. Would the movie seller now want to charge the same price for movies?

Yes: _____. No: _____.

f) Given the circumstances in e), what is the cross-elasticity of movies for videos? And what does this say about the relationship between the two products?

Elasticity: _____; relationship: _____.

g) Referring back to the original data in Table 4.13, assume now that the average weekly earning of the townspeople rises from $500 to $550 and that, as a result, the demand for movies increases 20 percent. If the price being charged was $6, what would be the income elasticity of demand? And what does this suggest about the product, movies?

Elasticity: _____; it suggests: _____.

More of the Same

The (weekly) local demand for mangos and pineapples is given in **Table 4.14**. The quantities are in thousands.

TABLE 4.14

Price of Mangos	Quantity of Mangos Demanded	Total Revenue	Price of Pineapples	Quantity of Pineapples Demanded	Total Revenue
$0.60	27	_____	$2.25	17	_____
0.70	24	_____	2.50	16	_____
0.80	21	_____	2.75	14	_____
0.90	18	_____	3.00	12	_____
1.00	15	_____	3.25	9	_____
1.10	12	_____	3.50	6	_____
1.20	9	_____	3.75	3	_____

a) Fill in the total revenue columns in Table 4.14.

b) What would be the best prices for the sellers of mangos and pineapples?

c) What is the price elasticity of demand for mangos if the price changes from $0.80 to $0.90, and what is the change in total revenue? What if the price changes from $0.80 to $0.60?

d) Given the total revenue data you calculated in a), what conclusion can you make about elasticity in the $0.70 to $0.80 price range?

e) Assume that the price of pineapples rises from $2.50 to $3.50 and that, as a result, the demand for mangos increases by 50 percent. If the price of mangos was $0.80, what is the cross-elasticity of mangos for pineapples? What does the coefficient tell you?

f) Assume that average incomes rose by 10 percent and that, as a result, the demand for pineapples increased by 2 at every price level. If the price of pineapples was $3.50, what is the income elasticity of pineapples? What does the coefficient tell you?

UNANSWERED QUESTIONS

Short Essays

1. Give a definition of the price elasticity of demand, and explain why the slope of a demand curve and the elasticity are not the same thing.

2. What is the relationship between the elasticity of demand and the revenue received by the sellers of the product?

3. Why is the elasticity of demand for carrots different from the elasticity of demand for cigarettes?

4. Why is the elasticity of demand for toothpicks different from the elasticity of demand for housing?

5. Under what conditions will the consumer pay all of the excise tax placed on a particular product?

6. Under what conditions will the sellers pay all of the excise tax placed on a particular product?

7. What would happen if all of Canada's dairy farmers joined together and reduced the supply of milk by 50 percent?

Analytical Questions

8. Which of the demand curves in **Figure 4.16**, D_1 or D_2, is more elastic at price P_1? At price P_2?

FIGURE 4.16

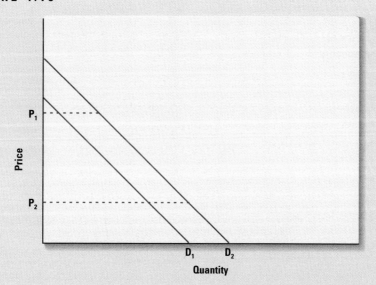

9. Which of the demand curves in **Figure 4.17**, D_1 or D_2, is more elastic at price P_1? At price P_2?

FIGURE 4.17

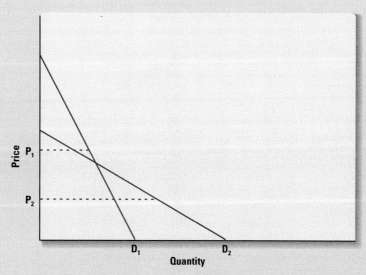

10. Below is a list of six products. What do you think each product's income elasticity is, in terms of high, low, or negative?
    a) Skiing holidays.
    b) Postage stamps.
    c) Potatoes.
    d) Scuba diving equipment.
    e) Prescription drugs.
    f) Low-priced, single-ply toilet paper.

11. Do you think there is a big difference between the price elasticity for kitchen stoves in the long run and in the short run? For paper towelling?

12. Suppose that you are a researcher attempting to calculate the price elasticity of demand of products A and B. Your research associate has collected the data in **Table 4.15** to assist you.

TABLE 4.15

Year	Price of Product A	Quantity Traded of Product A	Price of Product B	Quantity Traded of Product B	Average Consumer Income
1	$ 8	1000	$25	300	$32 000
2	10	1100	22	350	34 000

Suppose that you have calculated the price elasticities of demand for products A and B. Comment on the validity of your calculations.

13. What do you think will happen to the government's tax revenues if it decides to increase the excise tax on cigarettes by $1 a pack? Would your answer change if the increase was $10? Why or why not?

14. What would be the effects of a war on drugs that targeted drug users rather than drug suppliers?

15. The dean of arts at a large university recently said that she felt that the demand for post-secondary education must be very inelastic because enrollment has decreased very little despite a doubling in tuition fees (after inflationary effects have been removed) over the last ten years. Do you agree with the dean? Why or why not?

16. The Vancouver Folk Music Festival is held each summer in a very large, fenced-in park that gives people ample room to wander from stage to stage or to go off and find a quiet spot for a picnic. In effect, the supply curve for admission to the festival is perfectly elastic. What is the best price of admission for the festival organizers to charge?

Numerical Questions

17. Nelson runs a small, specialized furniture-making business out of his basement at home. His daily sales revenues average $600 when he charges $30 for his sliding keyboard holders and $630 when his price is $35. What is the price elasticity of demand for Nelson's product?

18. Suppose that the price of product A decreases from $22 to $18 and, as a result, the quantity traded of A increases from 200 to 250, the quantity traded of product B increases from 50 to 60, and the quantity traded of product C falls from 600 to 550.
    a) What is the price elasticity of demand of product A?
    b) What is the cross-elasticity of product A for product B?

   c) What is the cross-elasticity of product A for product C?

   d) Comment on the three elasticity measures.

19. Suppose that the quantities demanded for five different products all increased by 20 percent. Given the elasticity coefficients shown below, what must be the percentage change in the price for each product?

   a) $\varepsilon = 4$.   **b)** $\varepsilon = 0.5$.   **c)** $\varepsilon = 1$.

   d) $\varepsilon = 1.2$.   **e)** $\varepsilon = 0$.

20. The data in **Table 4.16** are for electricity, measured in megawatts.

TABLE 4.16

Price	Demand
$97	103
98	102
99	101
100	100
101	99
102	98

   a) At what price is the total expenditure by consumers at a maximum?

   b) What is the price elasticity of demand at this price?

21. Given **Figure 4.18**:

FIGURE 4.18

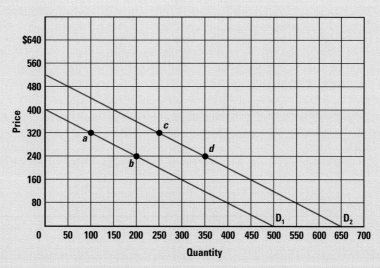

What is the elasticity of demand between *a* and *b* and between *c* and *d* on D_2? Which is bigger, and why?

22. The data in **Table 4.17** are for bags of Ultra Grow lawn fertilizer.

TABLE 4.17

Price	Demand	Supply (S$_1$)	Supply (tax)
$50	660	420	_____
55	600	440	_____
60	540	460	_____
65	480	480	_____
70	420	500	_____
75	360	520	_____

a) What is the equilibrium price and quantity?
b) Fill in the Supply (tax) column assuming that a $10 per unit excise tax is imposed on this product.
c) What is the new equilibrium price and quantity?
d) What portion of the $10 excise tax is paid by the seller, and what portion is paid by the consumer?

23. Draw a straight-line demand curve that illustrates zero quantity demanded at a price of $50 and a quantity demanded of 200 at a price of zero. Calculate the price elasticity of demand if the price decreases from $50 to zero. Next, draw another straight-line demand curve that illustrates zero quantity demanded at a price of $200 and a quantity demanded of 50 at a price of zero. Calculate elasticity of demand if the price decreases from $200 to zero. What conclusion can you draw from this exercise?

 Web-Based Activities

1. Go to **www.health.org/pubs/qdocs/tobacco/state.htmp.** Do you think that the information presented here indicates that the elasticity of demand for cigarettes among youth is different than that of the market overall? If so, in what way is it different and why?

2. "The Utility of Drug Pricing" is the title of a web page published by the Rand's Drug Policy Research Center. The drug market is examined in terms of the basic demand and supply model. In this context, the workings of the market may be inferred from the historical trend in drug prices. Go to **www.rand.org/centers/dprc/DPRCnews.6.97/drugprices.html** and then answer the following questions.
   a) What is the consensus estimate on the price elasticity of demand for cocaine?
   b) If price increased by 10 percent, the average percentage change in the quantity demanded would be approximately what?
   c) If the price decreased by 10 percent, the average percentage change in the quantity demanded would be approximately what?
   d) Given the Rand's estimate of the price elasticity of demand, what would happen to total expenditure on drugs if the supply decreases?
   e) Suppose the police observe a 20 percent increase in the price of street drugs. By how much do you think supply has changed?

Consumer Demand

What's ahead...This chapter looks at the theory of consumer behaviour known as marginal utility theory. This theory helps us to better understand how the rational consumer allocates income toward the purchase of various products. It also gives us a different perspective on the meaning of demand. We explain the idea of consumer surplus and look at attempts by producers to acquire this surplus through price discrimination.

A QUESTION OF RELEVANCE...

Suppose the government of Canada were to give a $200 holiday bonus to every citizen of the country with the proviso that it must be spent immediately. What are the odds that any two individuals would buy exactly the same products? One in a thousand? One in a million? Probably more like one in 20 million. The point is that each individual is unique, and this uniqueness is reflected in each person's tastes and spending behaviour. What determines individual tastes is more a subject for the psychologist than the economist. But how tastes are translated into purchases is very much the province of the economist and is the subject of this chapter.

Y ou do not need to be a student of economics to appreciate that people's tastes differ: one person's paradise is another person's prison! And even where people buy the same products, we cannot be sure that they receive the same amount of satisfaction from them. Yet our formulation of an individual's demand is predicated on the basis that it measures, or is an indicator of, that person's desire as well as her ability to purchase. An increase in either would presumably cause her to purchase more. Measuring ability to purchase is easy enough: it can be gauged by that person's income and wealth. But how do we measure intensity of desire? Well, a number of economists in the latter part of the nineteenth century attempted to do just that; in doing so, they introduced the important new idea called the **margin**.

margin(al): the extra or additional unit.

The marginal revolution shifted the focus of economists away from totals, such as total profits or total costs or total utility, and toward the marginal, which means the extra or additional profit or cost or utility. The English economist Alfred Marshall believed that concentrating on people's actions *at the margin* provided a better understanding of their behaviour. If we are trying to understand why a consumer buys one particular basket of goods rather than any other, it is more instructive conceptually to look at each purchase one at a time than to try to evaluate the total result of a morning's shopping. The basket of goods is, after all, the result of a number of individual decisions rather than one single decision. Using this approach, Marshall developed the concept of marginal utility, and with it the important law of diminishing marginal utility. The theory of consumer behaviour, which uses this concept, is the focus of this chapter. Before we look at it, we should mention that the idea of the marginal is not always easy to grasp at first acquaintance. It is definitely worth the effort, however, since it lies at the heart of so much economic analysis and is the basis of many of the ideas contained in later chapters.

The Law of Diminishing Marginal Utility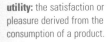

utility: the satisfaction or pleasure derived from the consumption of a product.

Suppose I wished to communicate to you the immense satisfaction I get from my first beverage of the day. I could use words like "greatly" or "fantastically" or even "indescribably" refreshing, but no words could accurately capture the degree of my pleasure, or **utility**, as economists call it. Suppose instead that I attempted to assign a number to indicate the amount of my utility, say, 100 utils. Does this communicate my pleasure any more accurately? Probably not, since you have no idea what a util is and we have no instrument with which to measure it. However, if I then tell you that the second beverage of the day gives me only 50 utils of pleasure, you have a very clear indication of how I rate these two drinks. On the other hand, my friend Cleo might suggest that she gets 200 and 100 utils from her first two drinks. Since neither of us can objectively measure the amount of utility, we cannot conclude that she derives twice as much utility as I do. In other words, we cannot make interpersonal comparisons of utility. Nevertheless, we can still draw some interesting conclusions about consumer behaviour by pursuing this idea of utility.

For example, assume that an almost frantic student is beginning an all-night cram session for finals at her local coffee bar. Further, assume that our student, whose name is Anna, keeps score of the amount of pleasure (measured in utils) that she derives from successive lattés that keep her going through the night. (Of course, this is her subjective evaluation, and it might change from time to time.) It seems reasonable to suppose that the very first latté would give her the greatest satisfaction, and each one afterward would give less and less pleasure, as shown in **Table 5.1**.

TABLE 5.1 Total and Marginal Utility

Quantity	Marginal Utility (MU)	Total Utility (TU)
1	120	120
2	90	210
3	65	275
4	45	320
5	25	345
6	23	368
7	10	378
8	4	382
9	0	382
10	−2	380

marginal utility: the amount of additional utility derived from the consumption of an extra unit of a product.

law of diminishing marginal utility: the amount of additional utility decreases as successive units of a product are consumed.

The column headed **marginal utility** shows the amount of pleasure or satisfaction, measured in utils, that Anna derives from each latté consumed. We can express marginal utility in terms of an equation:

$$\text{marginal utility (MU)} = \frac{\Delta \text{ total utility}}{\Delta \text{ number of units}}$$

Since Table 5.1 shows the quantity changing by 1 unit each time, the denominator in the above equation is equal to 1. It can be seen that Anna derives decreasing marginal utility from each successive latté. Although every latté, at least until the ninth cup, gives her positive marginal utility, each one is less satisfying than the previous one. This is known as the law of **diminishing marginal utility.** It seems reasonable to suppose that this law is applicable to most of us most of the time. Our knowledge of life and our personal experiences alone can validate the law of diminishing utility:

More may be better, but additional units do not give the same degree of pleasure.

Furthermore, in time there will come a point where more becomes worse. For Anna, whose consumption we see illustrated in Table 5.1, that point comes with the tenth cup. Since the first unit of anything we consume gives us positive utility, and the last one gives us negative utility, marginal utility must be declining with successive amounts.

The last column in Table 5.1 shows Anna's total utility derived from consuming the various quantities. Total utility can be found by summing the marginal utility from each unit. For example, the total utility from consuming five units is equal to:

$$\text{TU}_{5 \text{ units}} = \text{MU}_1 + \text{MU}_2 + \text{MU}_3 + \text{MU}_4 + \text{MU}_5$$

From Table 5.1, we can see that the total utility from five units equals:

$$\text{TU}_{5 \text{ units}} = 120 + 90 + 65 + 45 + 25 = 345.$$

You can see, looking at the same table, that Anna's total utility increases with the amount consumed, but the rate of increase slows down with increasing quantities. This is the same thing as saying that marginal utility diminishes. Table 5.1 is illustrated in **Figure 5.1**.

FIGURE 5.1   Total and Marginal Utilities

Total utility (TU) increases as more of this product is consumed—at least, up to the ninth unit. However, the rate at which it increases gets smaller and smaller, that is, the slope of the total utility curve gets smaller (or the curve gets flatter). The slope of the TU curve is the same thing as the marginal utility. In other words, starting from a high of 120 utils when one unit is consumed, the MU declines with increased consumption until it eventually becomes 0 with the consumption of the ninth unit. Note that the TU curve is at a maximum when MU equals 0.

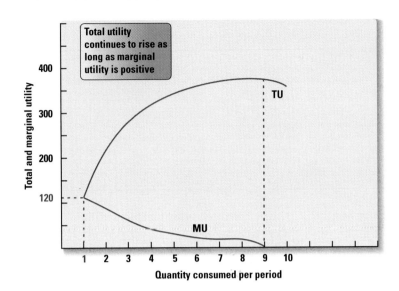

Before we start to develop this theory of utility a bit further, it is important to understand that, as with most economic theories, we need to be careful to state the conditions under which it operates. First of all, we take it for granted that the consumers we are describing act rationally. By this, we mean that they will wish to consume more as long as total utility increases. This point bears repeating: a rational consumer will want to consume more so long as increased consumption adds to total satisfaction.

The objective of the consumer, it is assumed, is to maximize the pleasure derived from consumption, that is, to maximize total utility.

In addition, this idea of diminishing marginal utility makes sense only if we are considering a particular period of time. If Anna were to consume the 10 lattés over 10 evenings, then it's likely that her marginal utility would remain constant. Finally, as Alfred Marshall pointed out, certain products are indivisible; thus, a small quantity may be insufficient to meet certain special wants. For example, three automobile tires would not give a great deal of utility without the fourth. In summary, marginal utility theory applies when:

① • the consumer is behaving rationally
② • the consumer's objective is maximum satisfaction
③ • purchases and consumption takes place over a short period of time
④ • products are not divisible

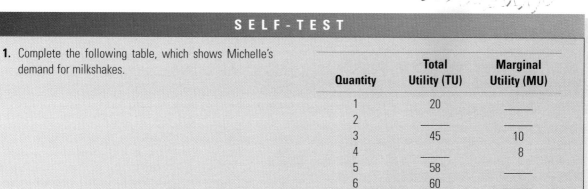

SELF-TEST

1. Complete the following table, which shows Michelle's demand for milkshakes.

Quantity	Total Utility (TU)	Marginal Utility (MU)
1	20	___
2	___	___
3	45	10
4	___	8
5	58	___
6	60	___
7	___	0
8	___	−5

Optimal Purchasing Rule

From the information contained in Table 5.1, it is apparent that if Anna had unlimited income or if the refreshment were free, there would still be a limit to how much she would drink. She would never drink more than 9 lattés, since no rational consumer would consume a unit that gives negative marginal utility. In other words, if we wanted to develop some rule of rational consumer behaviour, we might suggest that a person with unlimited income should consume every product to the point of satiation! The problem with this little rule is that it doesn't apply to any known consumer because all people, no matter how rich or poor, have limited incomes (not to mention limited time) and therefore have to make choices.

To derive a more relevant rule of consumer behaviour, let's suppose that Anna has a limited budget of $36 and has a choice of buying two products: lattés or pieces of pastry, each costing $4. The utility of both products is shown in **Table 5.2**.

TABLE 5.2 Comparison of the Utilities of Lattés and Pastries

CUPS OF LATTÉ			PIECES OF PASTRY		
Quantity	Marginal Utility	Total Utility	Quantity	Marginal Utility	Total Utility
1	120	120	1	60	60
2	90	210	2	50	110
3	65	275	3	35	145
4	45	320	4	21	166
5	25	345	5	16	182
6	23	368	6	10	192
7	10	378	7	0	192
8	4	382	8	−5	187
9	0	382	9	−10	177
10	−2	380	10	−15	162

The question now is, how should Anna best allocate her evening's budget if she wishes to maximize her total utility? She certainly cannot consume to the points of maximum total utility of both products, since that would cost her $36 for the 9 cups of latté and $28 for 7 pieces of pastry, for a total of $64—more than her budget. We need to figure out (on her behalf) what combination of the two goods, costing $36, will produce the maximum total utility. One way to do this would be to work out every possible combination, given the $36 constraint, and see which particular combination maximizes utility. The procedure is a little tedious, but not particularly difficult, as **Table 5.3** shows.

A glance at the last column of Table 5.3 shows that the best combination is 6 cups of latté and 3 pieces of pastry because this yields the maximum total utility of 513 utils.

TABLE 5.3 Utility Obtained from Combinations of Lattés and Pastries

LATTÉS		PIECES OF PASTRY		BOTH
Quantity	Total Utility	Quantity	Total Utility	Total Utility
0	0	9	177	177
1	120	8	187	307
2	210	7	192	402
3	275	6	192	467
4	320	5	182	502
5	345	4	166	511
6	**368**	**3**	**145**	**513**
7	378	2	110	488
8	382	1	60	442
9	382	0	0	382

If we were to compare the two products from Anna's point of view, we would tend to suggest, based on the evidence of Table 5.2, that she prefers lattés to pastries. However, this could be a misleading statement because, if we were to categorize products in terms of absolute favourites, it would seem reasonable to spend all our incomes on our favourite products. We don't do this, for one obvious reason: even our favourite product lose its attractiveness if we buy it to the exclusion of all other products. Translated into marginal utility theory, this idea suggests that we would buy a product until its marginal utility falls below that of some other product, at which point we would switch purchases to that other product. We now have a new insight into our spending behaviour and a better method of solving the previous budget problem. Instead of trying to decide in advance how Anna should spend her budget, let's look at choices one at a time, that is, marginally.

Suppose that, on entering the coffee bar, Anna takes $4 from the $36 out of her purse, and walks up to the counter to place an order. What should she buy? Table 5.2 shows us that a latté looks more attractive because the marginal utility of the first latté exceeds that of the first piece of pastry. Having downed her drink, should Anna now buy her *second* latté or should she buy her *first* piece of pastry? Well, the lattés still look more attractive, since the MU of a second latté is 90, compared with 60 from the first piece of pastry. Third purchase: another latté, the third, or the first piece of pastry? Answer: another latté, since the MU of the *third* latté (65) still exceeds that of the *first* piece of pastry (60). Not until the fourth purchase does pastry look as attractive as lattés. The *first* piece of pastry now yields more utility than does the *fourth* latté. All of this means that since marginal utility declines with consumption, the comparative attractiveness of any two products depends on how much of each has been consumed. After 3 cups of latté, pastries now look more attractive to Anna. We continue in a similar fashion until Anna's $36 has been exhausted. This is shown in **Table 5.4**.

At the end of the evening Anna will have purchased a total of 6 lattés and 3 pieces of pastry, and in doing so she will have maximized her utility at 513 utils (Table 5.2 shows that 6 lattés gives 368 utils and 3 pieces of pastry gives 145 utils). We have already seen from Table 5.3 that this combination will ensure maximum utility.

TABLE 5.4 Successive Purchase Choices

	Total Spent	Purchases of Lattés	Purchases of Pastries
First purchase	$ 4	1st latté	
Second purchase	8	2nd latté	
Third purchase	12	3rd latté	
Fourth purchase	16		1st pastry
Fifth purchase	20		2nd pastry
Sixth purchase	24	4th latté	
Seventh purchase	28		3rd pastry
Eighth purchase	32	5th latté	
Ninth purchase	36	6th latté	

From this knowledge, we could perhaps adopt a new optimal purchasing rule: in order to maximize utility, a consumer should allocate spending by comparing the marginal utility of each product and purchase the product that gives the greatest marginal utility. There is, however, a very serious defect in this rule. Suppose, for example, that I were to compare the marginal utilities of two following products, and, according to this rule, purchase the one that gives the greatest marginal utility:

1st bottle of beer: MU = 120 utils

1st Porsche car: MU = 10 000 000 utils

So, I would buy the Porsche because it has a higher MU for me! Our purchasing rule obviously needs a little more refinement, since I can't afford a Porsche, and therefore we need to take the price of products into consideration. What we really need to compare in order to make a rational decision is the amount of utils per dollar spent. Or, expressing it more colloquially, we are trying to find out which product gives the most bang for the buck! In terms of a formula, it is:

$$\text{MU per \$ spent} = \frac{\text{MU}}{\text{Price}}$$

Next, suppose that in our last example the price of a pastry happened to be $2 instead of $4. The MU per dollar spent for Anna's first purchases of both lattés and pastries would then be equal for her, and she would, therefore, be indifferent as to which she purchased:

$$\text{MU per \$ spent on 1st latté} = \frac{120}{4} = 30$$

$$\text{MU per \$ spent on 1st pastry} = \frac{60}{2} = 30$$

SELF-TEST

2. Given the following marginal utilities and prices, which product would a rational consumer choose?

	Apple	Beer	Ice Cream	Hot Dog
Marginal Utility	120	300	140	150
Price	$1.50	$4.00	$2.00	$3.00

What this suggests is that a rational consumer would continue to purchase a product as long as its MU per dollar spent is greater than that of any other product. Of course, as the consumer increases the consumption of any given product, its MU is going to fall, so some other product will then become a more attractive proposition. Let's stay with the latté–pastry example but this time, in **Table 5.5**, assume that the management of the coffee bar decides to increase the price of lattés to $5 but leaves the price of pastry unchanged at $4. Now how would Anna spend her budget of $36?

TABLE 5.5 Marginal Utility per Dollar Spent

	LATTÉS			PIECES OF PASTRY	
Quantity	MU	MU per Dollar (price = $5)	Quantity	MU	MU per Dollar (price = $4)
1	120	24	1	60	15
2	90	18	2	50	12.5
3	65	13	3	35	8.75
4	45	9	4	21	5.25
5	25	5	5	16	4
6	23	4.6	6	10	2.5
7	10	2	7	0	0
8	4	0.8	8		
9	0	0	9		

To figure out the optimal allocation of Anna's $36 budget, we will proceed as we did before, by looking at each separate purchase. To start with, each of the first two lattés give a higher MU per dollar spent than does the first pice of pastry (24 and 18 respectively, compared with 15 for the first pastry), so these would be her first two purchases. The first pastry, however, does give a higher MU per dollar spent than does the third latté, so she would at this point switch to a piece of pastry. We can continue in this fashion, purchase by purchase, and the result is summarized in **Table 5.6**.

TABLE 5.6 Choice of Lattés and Pastries, Purchase by Purchase

	Total Spent	Purchases of Lattés	Purchases of Pastries
First purchase	$5	1st latté	
Second purchase	10	2nd latté	
Third purchase	14		1st pastry
Fourth purchase	19	3rd latté	
Fifth purchase	23		2nd pastry
Sixth purchase	28	4th latté	
Seventh purchase	32		3rd pastry
Eighth purchase	36		4th pastry

The best way for Anna to spend her $36 is to purchase 4 lattés and 4 pieces of pastry. This would give her (check back to Table 5.2) a total utility of 486 (320 + 166) utils, which is higher than could be produced by any other combination that could be purchased with $36. Note also the effect of this increase in the price of lattés: the number of lattés purchased dropped from 6 to 4, whereas the quantity of the related product, pieces of pastries, increased from 3 to 4. We will look at this aspect in more detail later.

The optimal spending choice for the rational consumer, then, is that he should purchase the product that yields the greatest marginal utility per dollar.

optimal purchasing rule: in order to maximize utility, a consumer should purchase the product that yields the greatest marginal utility per dollar spent.

The procedure we have just developed enables us to derive an **optimal purchasing rule.** It suggests that whenever the MU per dollar spent on product A is greater than that for product B, we would buy and consume more of A. As this is done, of course, the MU per dollar spent on product A starts to decline, until we get to the point where other products, B or C, become more attractive; that is:

$$\text{if } \frac{MU_A}{P_A} > \frac{MU_B}{P_B} \Rightarrow \text{consume more A}$$

$$\text{if } \frac{MU_A}{P_A} < \frac{MU_B}{P_B} \Rightarrow \text{consume more B}$$

Our conclusion then is that:

we should buy and consume products to the point at which the MU per dollar spent on each product is more or less equal for all products.

The optimal purchasing rule then is:

$$\frac{MU_A}{P_A} = \frac{MU_B}{P_B} = \text{........} \frac{MU_Z}{P_Z}$$

If we didn't purchase products in this fashion, we would be acting irrationally. For instance, suppose that the MU per dollar spent on the last apple we bought is 15 utils (and it doesn't matter if this is the 1st, 5th, or 100th apple) and an additional pear gives an MU per dollar spent of 25 utils—we would gain 10 utils by giving up one apple and buying an additional pear instead.

SELF-TEST

3. Given the following MU per dollar curves for apples and pears, how many of each would a rational consumer purchase if she could only afford nine purchases?

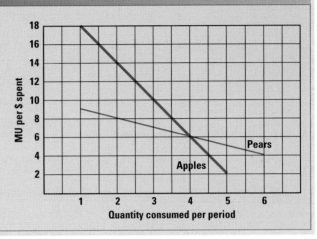

REVIEW

1. **What does the term *utility* mean?**
2. **What does *marginal utility* mean, and what is the *law of diminishing marginal utility*?**
3. **Explain why total utility is at a maximum when marginal utility is zero.**
4. **What does the term *utility per dollar* spent mean?**
5. **Explain why a rational consumer does not spend all of her income buying only her favourite product.**
6. **What is the *optimal purchasing rule*? Explain it.**

Applications of Marginal Utility Theory

Marginal utility theory, as esoteric as it might at first appear, does provide us with some interesting insights into consumer behaviour. It can explain some obvious, and some not so obvious, activities. First, it explains why none of us spends all our income on one single product. Even our favourite product is only a favourite *up to a point*. After consuming a certain quantity, its MU per dollar spent drops to the point where other things become more attractive.

Second, it is an interesting experiment to imagine how one would spend additional increments of income starting off, say, with a basic $100 per week, and increasing it by increments of $100. Let's say you did have only $100 per week; what would you spend the money on? Presumably, you would spend it on those things that have the greatest marginal utility for you; for most of us, this would mean using our money on food and shelter. Income would need to increase appreciably before any allocations are made for clothes, and be higher still before any entertainment dollars are spent.

The way in which we adjust our purchases to higher income levels is what is meant by the concept of income elasticity that we encountered in the last chapter. You can imagine that products with low income elasticities (water, food) have the highest initial marginal utilities and thus will be highest in terms of priority. Similarly those products with high income elasticities (airline travel, movies) will have lower initial marginal utilities and must be of a lower priority. Research has consistently demonstrated that poorer families spend by far the largest proportion of their incomes on the

How Income Affects Our Spending Patterns

In the nineteenth century, a German statistician named Ernst Engel did a survey among working people in England to find out how the average person's income was allocated to different forms of spending, and how this changed as income changed. He discovered that the percentage spent on food (though not the actual amount) tended to decline with increasing incomes, whereas the percentage spent on housing remained constant; the percentage spent on clothing remained the same or declined, and other items increased. These results (often graphed in the form of an Engels Curve) have been repeated in many other surveys over the years. In Canada, StatsCan publishes a periodical survey of consumer spending. The following table shows an extract from a recent survey:

Family Income Quintile Group, Percentage of Total Consumption Spending

	All Classes	Lowest 20%	4th 20%	3rd 20%	2nd 20%	Top 20%
Food	19	24	20	19	19	17
Shelter	22	31	24	22	21	19
Clothing	8	6	7	8	8	11
Travel	18	11	17	18	19	20

Source: Statistics Canada, *Family Expenditure in Canada*, 1996

basic necessities like food and shelter (often well over 50 percent), whereas richer families spend proportionately less (sometimes less than 30 percent).

A third intriguing aspect of marginal utility theory is trying to think of situations in which the law of diminishing marginal utility may not apply. The law is applicable to all products and all people, but maybe not at all times. For example, it's certainly possible to think of certain things for which the MU seems to increase the more that is consumed. (Think of a CD of new music; it often takes repeated hearings before you get full enjoyment from it.) This may be true also of fine wines and paintings and so on. However, Alfred Marshall cautioned his readers that the idea of diminishing marginal utility only makes sense if the product is consumed over a reasonably short period of time. Furthermore, our rule applies only to the purchasing of the product, not to its repeated "consumption," as is the case with CDs and artwork.

A fourth aspect is that diminishing marginal utility takes an interesting twist when we look at another fascinating commodity: money. Is money also subject to the law of diminishing marginal utility? In other words, is it true that the more money you have, the less valuable additional amounts become for you? Since money is just one form of wealth, often the question is amended to ask: does the MU of wealth or income decline as more is obtained? For example, imagine a rich person and a poor person walking toward each other on the street; halfway between them lies a $10 bill. Which would gain the greater utility from its possession—the rich person, for whom it might be the hundred-thousandth $10 bill of the year, or the poor person, for whom it could be the difference between a good week and a bad one? Intuition suggests that the MU of the poor person is likely to be far higher than the MU of the rich person, for whom the gain (or loss, for that matter) of $10 might well go unnoticed. Here, intuition seems to confirm the law of diminishing marginal utility even for the product, money. If this is so, some might argue that this is strong grounds for advocating a more equitable distribution of income and wealth, since the gain in MU by the poor would greatly exceed the loss of MU by the rich so that overall utility (or social welfare) is increased.

Note that the above idea need not imply an equal distribution, only a more equitable or fairer one. The idea would be to take from the rich and give to the poor as long as the MU of the former is smaller than the MU of the latter. This would continue until (figuratively) the screams of the rich person (who may no longer be rich) are equal to the whoops of joy coming from the poor person (who may no longer be quite so poor). It may well be that their MUs become equalized when the rich person now has an income reduced to $5000 per week, while that of the poor person has been increased to $500. However, you might protest such a scheme. After all, you may well ask, what is fair about a system that takes income from one person, who may have worked extremely hard to earn it, and gives it to another who may have done nothing to deserve it? Nevertheless, modern governments do try to increase the overall well-being of their communities by transferring income from the rich to the poor. It is most likely that those individuals with higher incomes (a lower MU of money) tend to save more and receive, in turn, relatively more of their income from their investment sources. Governments have typically imposed higher taxes on this type of income, which is a de facto acceptance of the argument that these marginal income dollars yield a lower MU for their recipients than the higher MU gained from labour by lower income earners when they sell their labour.

There is another issue in all of this. As pointed out earlier, we simply cannot compare utilities between people. Thus, while we might well be inclined to believe that the rich person's MU is less than the poor person's, there is simply no way of measuring this.

From all of this, however, we should not conclude that the theory of marginal utility is of little use or that it should be discarded. One of its most important uses is to give a strong underpinning to the law of demand, which is the topic of the next section.

SELF-TEST

4. The table below shows the total utility that two children, Jan and Dean, derive from various amounts of weekly allowance.

As their parent, you can afford to pay them a total allowance of only $10. How would you divide this amount between the two children so as to maximize their combined total utility? What will be the combined total utility?

Amount of Weekly Allowance	Jan's Total Utility	Dean's Total Utility
$1	200	400
2	380	500
3	540	595
4	680	685
5	800	770
6	900	850
7	980	925
8	1040	995
9	1080	1060
10	1100	1120

Marginal Utility and Demand

We saw earlier in our latté–pastry example that marginal utility theory suggests that an increase in the price of one product leads to a decrease in the quantity purchased of that particular product while increasing the quantity purchased of the competitive product. We need to look at this aspect in more detail.

We know that the particular numbers we assign to utility are quite arbitrary. Thus, any set of numbers would do. However, there is one particular measuring unit with which we are all familiar, and that is money. We could, if we wished, measure utility in dollars. For instance, Akio could suggest that his first drink after a hard game of tennis gives him, say, $8 worth of utility; another way of expressing it would be to say that, irrespective of its actual price, he would be willing to pay $8 for it. Let's table Akio's utility for his favourite drink in terms of *dollar marginal utility* ($MU) in **Table 5.7**.

TABLE 5.7 Akio's Dollar Marginal Utility

Quantity Consumed	$MU
1	$8
2	5
3	4
4	3
5	2
6	1
7	0

Although they look similar, do not confuse our previous term, MU per dollar spent, which measures the number of utils obtained for each dollar spent, with $MU, which is measuring utility itself in terms of dollars. Table 5.7 shows that Akio's $MU declines with increasing quantities; this simply reflects the law of diminishing marginal utility. However, with this information we can work out exactly how much Akio would purchase at different prices. Suppose, for instance, that the price of his drink was $10 a bottle; how much would he purchase? The answer must be zero, since even his first drink of the day is worth only $8 for him, so why would he pay $10 for the product? We would get the same result if the price was $9. What if the price dropped to $8; now how many would he buy? The answer will be one, since he would surely pay $8 for something he felt was worth $8. However, he would not purchase a second drink, since he rates it at only $5, which is less than the price. Let's continue to drop the price. Say the price is $7; now how many will he purchase? Presumably, he still wouldn't be prepared to buy more than one, since the price is still higher than his valuation of the second drink. The same is true at $6. Not until the price drops to $5 would Akio be prepared to buy two drinks. Continuing to drop the price by $1 each time would produce the results in **Table 5.8**.

What Table 5.8 spells out is Akio's demand schedule, which relates the quantities demanded at various different prices. This is graphed in **Figure 5.2**.

TABLE 5.8 Demand Curve, Derived

Price of Drinks	Quantity Demanded
$10	0
9	0
8	1
7	1
6	1
5	2
4	3
3	4
2	5
1	6

FIGURE 5.2 Marginal Utility and the Demand Curve

To induce Akio to buy one drink, the price cannot be higher than $8, since that is how much he values the first drink. To get him to buy a second drink, the price must drop to $5 because that is his evaluation of the second drink. If the price drops to $4, Akio would be prepared to buy 3 drinks. The price must continue to drop in order to encourage Akio to buy more. His $MU curve is the same thing, then, as his demand curve.

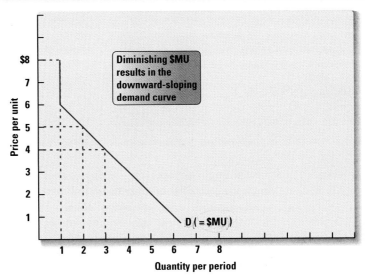

The derivation of the demand curve in this manner, while not being particularly ingenious, does provide a very different perspective on demand. In a sense it shifts the emphasis away from the price and onto the quantity. Instead of asking the question: "How many would you buy at this price?" it asks, "What is the maximum price you would pay to buy this quantity?" From Akio's point of view, the price cannot be more than $8 to induce him to buy one drink. In order to get him to buy two drinks, the price of the second drink must drop, simply because we know that the MU of his second drink will be lower. In other words, to induce people to buy increasing quantities of any product that they value less and less, the price must be lower. To get Akio to buy 6 drinks, the price must be as low as $1. In a sense, it is the value of the last one purchased and not the total value of them all that determines how much is bought.

The fact that it is the marginal utility *of the last unit* purchased which determines the price you are prepared to pay for a product and the quantity you are buying is a very subtle idea, one that is difficult to grasp at first. It does, however, provide a solution to the famous diamond–water paradox, which was first introduced by Adam Smith in his 1776 work, *Wealth of Nations*.

The Famous Diamond–Water Paradox

Smith was interested in finding out what determines the value of products and realized that the rather elusive term "value" is used in two different contexts. It could mean what he termed "value in use," which is what we mean by utility, that is, the amount of satisfaction the individual derives on the basis of her individual evaluation. Alternatively, the word might mean what Smith termed "value in exchange." This is the value the market places on the product, that is, in exchange for other products (or for money). Most things we buy have similar values in use and in exchange. However, a number of products, like water, have a very high value in use but are worth almost nothing in exchange. Conversely, other products like diamonds have a very high exchange value but quite a low value in use. Smith tried, unsuccessfully, to resolve this seeming paradox. It took almost a century and the introduction of marginal utility theory before economists were able to provide a solution. In the following example, instead of considering diamonds, let us look at the contrast between water and another very precious commodity, oil. Suppose we are comparing the utilities derived from 50-litre drums of each. **Table 5.9** presents the preferences of Karl, an average consumer.

TABLE 5.9 The Utilities of Water and Oil

WATER			OIL		
Quantity	$MU	$TU	Quantity	$MU	$TU
1	$1000	$1000	1	$30	$30
2	500	1500	2	29	59
3	200	1700	3	28	87
4	100	1800	4	27	114
5	50	1850	5	26	140
6	25	1875	6	25	165
7	10	1885	7	24	189
8	5	1890	8	23	212
9	2	1892	9	22	234
10	1	1893	10	21	255

The first thing that strikes one is how highly valuable water is when compared with oil. Its total utility (value in use) far exceeds that of oil. Suppose that you literally had no water; how much would you be prepared to pay for it? Karl would pay almost anything—$1000 for the first drum of water. This may be his whole income, but it would be worth spending to stay alive. But notice how dramatically the $MU of water drops. After 9 drums Karl not only has enough to drink, but enough to wash his clothes, his body, and his house and still have plenty left over to water the garden. The value of a tenth drum of water to Karl is only $1. In contrast, though, note how gradually the $MU of oil drops.

Now, suppose that Karl has a budget of $300 and that the price of both oil and water is $25: how much of each would he purchase? You can see that his first $125 would be spent on 5 drums of water, but the next $125 would go on 5 drums of oil. Then he would buy one of each, for a total of 6 drums of water and 6 drums of oil. After spending $300 he values the oil and water equally, despite the fact that 6 drums of water gives him a total dollar utility of $1875, compared with only $165 for oil— over 11 times as much. But the total utility is irrelevant when deciding on the next purchase, and Smith's idea of value in exchange centres on the marginal and not the total utility. If Karl had another $100 to spend, you can see that he would buy only oil. Thus, we can see that the answer to Smith's paradox is that:

> **Value in use is reflected in the *total utility* of a product, whereas the value in exchange (the price) is determined by its *marginal utility.***

In conclusion, we should emphasize that it is the marginal utility of a product that determines just how much of a product we will buy.

Consumer Surplus

consumer surplus: the difference between the consumer's evaluation of a product and the price paid for it.

Our water–oil paradox showed that the total value a consumer derives from consuming products usually exceeds the total expenditure on them. Table 5.9 shows, for instance, that if the price of water is $25 a drum, Karl would consume 6 drums at a cost of $150. Karl's total dollar utility of those 6 drums, however, is $1875. In dollar terms, then, Karl obtains a bonus amounting to the difference of $1725. This bonus is called **consumer surplus**. This surplus is not a sum of money received but the additional satisfaction that we receive for free. It comes about from the fact that normally we can obtain as much or as little of a product as we want at a single constant price. Karl could obtain 1 drum or 5 drums or 100 drums, and they would still have cost him $25 each. However, except for the last one, every unit he buys is worth more than the price. He obtains a consumer surplus on each one, as **Table 5.10** shows.

TABLE 5.10 Marginal and Total Consumer Surplus

Drums of Water	$MU	Price	Marginal Consumer Surplus	Total Consumer Surplus
First	$1000	$25	$975	$975
Second	500	25	475	1450
Third	200	25	175	1625
Fourth	100	25	75	1700
Fifth	50	25	25	1725
Sixth	25	25	0	1725

SELF-TEST

5. Given Akio's utility for beverages as shown in Table 5.7, if the price was $2, what quantity would he purchase and what would his total consumer surplus be as a result?

The marginal consumer surplus is the difference between the price paid for a unit of a product and the dollar marginal utility of that unit, i.e., $MU - Price

$$\text{marginal consumer surplus (MCS)} = \text{Price} - \$MU$$

And total consumer surplus is the sum of the marginal consumer surplus derived from each successive unit consumed (5 units in this case), i.e.,

$$\text{total consumer surplus}_{5 \text{ units}} = MCS_1 + MCS_2 + MCS_3 + MCS_4 + MCS_5$$

Since all of us derive consumer surplus from our purchases, we can illustrate the idea in terms of the market demand. **Figure 5.3** shows the demand curve for CDs.

FIGURE 5.3 Consumer Surplus, Graphically

The demand curve shows the maximum price that could be charged at various different quantities; for example, 10 000 CDs could be sold at a price of $30, 20 000 CDs could be sold at $28 each, and so on. The demand curve, therefore, represents how much people would be willing to pay. Let's assume that the price is $20. The vertical distance between the price line and the demand curve represents the amount of consumer surplus at each quantity. The total area between the price line and the demand curve represents the total amount of consumer surplus for all quantities up to the present quantity.

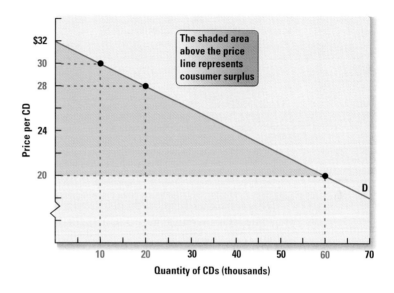

Mark Colburne, owner of the Urban Sound Exchange, a used-CD store, displays his wares in Halifax. A tough economy and a wide range of available products make the business viable and have caused the music industry to take notice.

Suppose that the present price is $20 for this particular recording and that 60 000 CDs are being sold at this price. The demand curve tells us, though, that if the price had been $30, the quantity demanded would have been only 10 000 CDs; 10 000 people would have been prepared to pay $30 for this CD. The fact that they only have to pay $20 means that each of them obtains a consumer surplus of $10. If instead the price had been $28, then 20 000 people would have bought the CD. But we already know that 10 000 of those 20 000 would have paid $30; the other 10 000 weren't prepared to pay $30, but they are willing to pay $28. Members of this latter group, then, are enjoying a consumer surplus of $8 each. If we continue this exercise down to the $20 price level, we will discover that the total consumer surplus is $300 000, as shown in **Table 5.11**.

TABLE 5.11 Calculating Consumer Surplus

Consumers	would have paid:	but only pay:	therefore get a consumer surplus of:	for a total consumer surplus of:
1st 10 000	$30	$20	$10	$100 000
2nd 10 000	28	20	8	80 000
3rd 10 000	26	20	6	60 000
4th 10 000	24	20	4	40 000
5th 10 000	22	20	2	20 000
6th 10 000	20	20	0	0
			Total Consumer Surplus	$300 000

This consumer surplus, then, can be represented by the triangular area above the price line, as shown in Figure 5.3. A higher price will of course mean that consumers will enjoy a smaller total consumer surplus; a lower price means a higher total consumer surplus from that product. In addition, **Figure 5.4** shows that consumers enjoy a bigger consumer surplus from products with inelastic demands than from those that have elastic demands.

FIGURE 5.4 Consumer Surplus Varies with Elasticities

If the price is P_1, then the quantity purchased of each of the two products is quantity Q_1. At lower quantities, however, buyers of product 1 (demand curve D_1) would have been prepared to pay higher prices than would buyers of product 2 (demand curve D_2). The area between the price line and the demand curve represents the total amount of consumer surplus. The graph shows that this area is much greater in the case of the inelastic demand curve, D_1, than it is with the elastic demand curve, D_2.

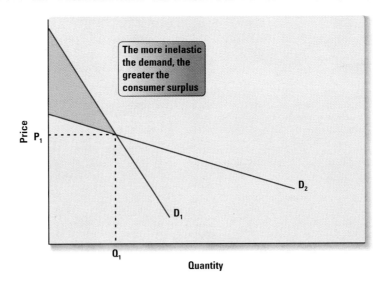

The more inelastic the demand, the greater the consumer surplus

The idea that consumers derive a greater surplus from products with inelastic demands conforms with our idea of what is meant by inelastic, that is, that buyers are not particularly resistant to price changes, presumably because they derive a greater benefit from the product than is represented in the price of the product. For example, the benefit that most smokers get from cigarettes usually far exceeds even the very high prices they have to pay for them.

It is easy to see why producers would like to, if they could, capture this consumer's surplus for themselves. At the present price of $20 per CD, producers in our last example (Figure 5.3) are deriving an income of 60 000 × $20 = $1 200 000 from the sales. However, as Table 5.11 shows, consumers are enjoying an additional psychic benefit, or consumer surplus, of $300 000. The temptation for sellers to try to capture this surplus is great. Let us examine the ways in which sellers might try to do this.

One thing that sellers need to do in order to capture the consumer surplus is try to identify just how much individual consumers are prepared to pay for the product. One way of doing this is through an auction. Here, customers bid up the price to the point where (ideally from the seller's point of view) the sole remaining customer is being forced to pay what she really thinks it is worth. An example of this is the e-commerce web sites that have recently become popular. A "Dutch auction" works even better from the seller's point of view and captures even more of the consumer surplus. Here, the auctioneer starts the bidding at a very high price, which is then lowered, step by step, until someone indicates she is willing to pay the last price mentioned. In order to avoid missing out on a purchase, customers may well end up paying the maximum they are prepared to go. In addition, you will notice that if an auctioneer has four identical items to sell, he will sell them one at a time so as to get the maximum consumer surplus from each. Another way of capturing this consumer surplus is to recognize that consumers value the first item purchased far more than they do subsequent purchases. A seller of CDs then might charge $25 for a single CD, but sell 2 for $40 and 3 for $50, and so on. You might think of this as receiving a discount from bulk-buying, but alternatively you could look on it as having to pay a premium for short-buying!

Price Discrimination

price discrimination: the selling of an identical product at a different price to different customers for reasons other than differences in the cost of production.

A final example of the way in which producers attempt to capture this consumer surplus is through **price discrimination**. Price discrimination means that the same product, with the same costs of production, is being sold to different consumers at different prices. It recognizes the fact that consumers have different demands for the same product and are therefore prepared to pay different prices in order to obtain the product. As we shall see, in order for a seller to practise price discrimination, she must be able to recognize that there are different groups of buyers with different demand elasticities, and somehow she must be able to separate those groups. Furthermore, if people are being charged different prices, then the seller must try to find a way of preventing resales of the product.

Suppose that you are the owner of a movie theatre and you estimate that the demand for movie tickets is as shown in **Table 5.12**.

TABLE 5.12 Demand for Movie Tickets

Price of Admission	Number of Daily Tickets Sold
$8	200
6	250
4	300

Suppose that at present you are charging $8 admission and receiving a daily revenue of $1600. Of course, you would like to increase your revenue by attracting more customers. You realize, however, that a number of people are not willing to pay $8 on a regular basis and that the only way to attract them is to reduce the price. The trouble is that if you do reduce the price, your total sales revenue will fall to $1500 at $6 (that is, $6 × 250) and to $1200 at $4 ($4 × 300). This is so because if you do reduce the price, you will have to reduce the price for everyone. Or do you? What if you could charge different prices to different groups of people? Well, what you first need to find out is: who are the people who are reluctant to pay $8 but would be willing to pay, say, $4? Included in this group are low-income people, many of whom would happily visit the theatre for $4 but are unable to afford a price of $8. However, you have no way of recognizing such people. But there are identifiable groups who are not always poor. This includes young people and retired people. So what you would do is charge a lower price for these groups but continue the high price for your regular patrons. In this way, you can increase your revenue appreciably. Your regular 200 patrons continue to pay $8, but you attract an additional 100 patrons who each pay $4. Your total revenue increases by $400 per day as a result. On the surface, it looks as though you are offering discount prices to certain identifiable groups and, of course, that is how you would probably advertise it. The truth of the matter is that you are, in fact, charging a premium price to the other identifiable group (the higher income group).

In order to practise price discrimination, then, it is necessary:

- to identify groups of customers with different demands
- to separate them from the others
- to ensure that those obtaining the lower prices cannot resell the product

E-CONOMICS

Extracting Consumer Surplus

You may recall from the e-conomics box in the previous chapter that some supermarkets are on the verge of being able to record data that would give them the individual demand elasticities for scores of products for most of their customers. What do you think that these sellers might do with this information? Ideally, from the store's perspective, they could adjust the price charged to each customer so as to extract the maximum possible consumer's surplus from each individual. Will this be the outcome? If the supermarket was a monopolist, the answer would probably be "yes." However, much more likely, several stores will offer the PDA method of shopping and this competition will keep the prices paid by consumers down and, in the end, work to the consumer's benefit. The other way that a seller might succeed in extracting consumer surplus is through an auction process. If only one unique item is up for auction and there were many bids, then the highest bidder presumably bid up the price to the maximum that she was willing to pay. The buyer then has no consumer surplus from this purchase. This is the idea behind the many auction sites that are now on the web. It doesn't always work this way, especially if there is a large number of the same product for sale. But this is why you see these sites try and focus on selling unique items.

This is true of theatre admissions, because a young person cannot resell the seat to an older person. For this reason, price discrimination is mostly practised with personal services rather than goods. Other examples of discrimination on the basis of *age* occur in the area of transportation, where, in most countries and cities, seniors and students travel at reduced fares on buses, trains, and planes.

Special ticket prices for seniors are one form of price discrimination.

Price discrimination is also practised on the basis of *time*. Suppose I own a coffee shop and I have no trouble attracting customers between 7 and 10 o'clock in the morning, the time when most people are desperate for coffee. However, business falls off considerably after 10 o'clock. In order to attract more customers in the off-peak periods, I would have to drop my prices, but why should I give everyone the benefit of lower prices when they are quite happy to pay my regular prices? The answer, of course, is to have two-tiered prices: a higher price in peak periods than in off-peak periods. Again, this is method is practised by many transport companies and other businesses, such as hairdressers and movie theatres, that have times of the day or whole days when sales are sluggish. Similarly, many telephone and hydro companies have different rates at different times of the day.

Another case in which customers are charged different prices for the same item is that of bulk-buying. This is discrimination on the basis of the *volume of purchases*. As we saw earlier, it is true that often if you wish to buy a single item of a product you may have to pay more than if you buy a dozen, for instance. However, this practice may not always be price discrimination, since the costs per unit in terms of packaging, storing, and merchandising are often much higher for single items than for bulk. In a sense, when you buy in bulk, the costs are lower per item for the seller, and as a result the savings are passed on to the buyers (witness the success of warehouse-style stores opening up in many countries). On the other hand, it is certainly true that big customers often get charged lower fees for many services, such as banking and legal services, than is the case for small customers, who only use these services infrequently or not extensively. These are almost certainly examples of price discrimination. To sum up, price discrimination is practised on the basis of:

- age
- time
- volume of purchases

SELF-TEST

6. The following table shows the demand for haircuts on an average weekday in your hairdressing salon. Investigation into the market has revealed to you that the demand from seniors differs greatly from that of your other customers, as follows:

Price of Haircut	Quantity Demanded by Seniors	Quantity Demanded by Other Customers
20	1	9
18	4	10
16	7	11
14	10	12
12	13	13
10	16	14
8	19	15
6	22	16
4	25	17
2	28	18

A) Which of the two demands is the more elastic? Why?

B) If you could only charge one price to all customers, which price would give you the greatest sales revenue?

C) Suppose, however, that you charged a different price for seniors from that of your other customers. What prices would you charge each group in order to maximize your sales revenue?

REVIEW

1. In what way is marginal utility related to income elasticity?
2. Is it possible for marginal utility to increase with increased consumption of a product?
3. What does the term *dollar marginal utility* mean?
4. Explain the relationship between marginal utility and the demand for the product.
5. What did Adam Smith mean by the terms *value in use* and *value in exchange*? Explain with examples.
6. What is *consumer surplus*? What is the difference between marginal consumer surplus and total consumer surplus?
7. Which produces a greater total consumer surplus: products with elastic demands or products with inelastic demands? Why?
8. What does the term *price discrimination* mean? Give three examples of price discrimination.
9. What conditions must exist in order for price discrimination to be practised?
10. What are the different bases on which price discrimination is founded?

STUDY GUIDE

Chapter Highlights

This chapter examined the theory of consumer behaviour using the concept of marginal utility. You learned that, given a fixed income or budget, consumers will maximize their total utility (satisfaction) by equating the marginal utility per dollar spent of each product purchased with the marginal utility per dollar spent of every other product. You then learned that the law of diminishing marginal utility can be used to explain down-ward-sloping demand curves and this opened the discussion of consumers' surplus and price discrimination.

1. *Marginal utility* is the amount of extra satisfaction derived from the consumption of one more unit of a product. It can be expressed as:

$$MU = \frac{\Delta \text{ total utility}}{\Delta \text{ quantity}}$$

   and can be measured in:

   • hypothetical numbers of utils; or

   • in terms of dollars.

2. The *law of diminishing marginal utility* states that the extra satisfaction derived from one more unit of a product declines as more of that product is consumed.

3. The *optimal purchasing rule* can be expressed as:

$$\frac{MU_A}{P_A} = \frac{MU_B}{P_B} = \text{......... } \frac{MU_Z}{P_Z}$$

4. The law of diminishing marginal utility explains why individual consumers are willing to buy more of a product only if its price is lower and this, in turn, explains why *demand curves* are downward-sloping.

5. The realization that consumers' purchasing decisions are based on marginal utility and not total utility can be used to explain why *water*, essential to life itself, has a low price but *diamonds* have a high price.

6. The fact that consumers are able to buy all they want of most products at a fixed price, but base their decisions on how much to buy on marginal utility, leads to the concept of *consumer surplus* which is the difference between the consumer's evaluation of a product and the price paid for it.

7. If sellers could *price discriminate* by charging a higher price to certain groups and a lower price to oth-ers, then most (all) consumer surplus would be expropriated. In order to do this the seller would have to:

   • identify customers with different demands;

   • separate them from the others;

   • ensure that those obtaining the lower prices cannot resell the product.

New Glossary Terms and Key Equations

Equations:

1. marginal utility (MU) $= \dfrac{\Delta \text{ total utility}}{\Delta \text{ quantity}}$

2. $\text{TU}_{n \text{ units}} = \text{MU}_1 + \text{MU}_2 + \text{MU}_3 + \dots \text{MU}_n$

3. MU per \$ spent $= \dfrac{\text{MU}}{\text{Price}}$

4. marginal consumer surplus (MCS) $=$ Price $-$ \$MU

5. total consumer surplus $_{n \text{ units}} = \text{MCS}_1 + \text{MCS}_2 + \text{MCS}_3 + \dots \text{MCS}_n$

Study Tips

1. Do not be discouraged if on a first reading you become dismayed by the level of abstraction in this chapter. It may seem to you that all that economists do is to make the commonplace seem unnecessarily esoteric and complicated. But think of the level of abstraction that a physicist brings to her job. Imagine you are trying to find out how a five-year-old successfully negotiates a steep curve without falling off his bike. The boy might give you a very graphic and comical description of his achievement. A physicist, on the other hand, is likely to enter into a serious and pedantic discourse involving factors like centrifugal force, the velocity of the bike, the weight of the child, angle of declension, and so on. Both are describing the same phenomenon: the child's description is likely to be more interesting, but the physicist's will be more illuminating and helpful in the long run—once you understand it. In a sense, this is what an economist is trying to do with the mundane tasks of buying and selling. She is not dealing in abstractions to make things incomprehensible, but to make them, eventually, more comprehensible.

2. If, initially, you have difficulty grasping the optimal purchasing rule, try working through a number of problems. You may find, in this case, actually "doing" economics is preferable to simply reading it.

3. One of the most important lessons in this chapter is that it is the marginal and not the total utility that determines consumer behaviour. This simply means that asking a person to name his favourite product doesn't make sense except in context. In other words, my favourite product at any moment depends on how much of it I have recently consumed. If I have recently consumed very little, I am likely to rate it highly (it has a high marginal utility); if I have consumed a great deal recently, then I am not likely to rate it as highly (its marginal utility is small) and will likely prefer other products.

4. Bear in mind that economic theories of consumer behaviour try to explain people's actions and do not try to figure out the reasons for that behaviour; this, after all, is the role of the psychologist. It is sufficient for economists to conclude that, faced with identical prices, a consumer who buys product A rather than product B does so because it possesses a higher marginal utility; that is, because she prefers it. This is not a particularly profound observation. However, its implications are reasonably fruitful.

Are You Sure?

Indicate whether the following statements are true or false. If false, indicate why they are false.

1. The term "marginal" means the difference between averages.

   T or **F**   If false: _____

   _____

2. Utility is defined as the satisfaction or pleasure derived from the consumption of a product.

   T or **F**   If false: _____

   _____

3. Marginal utility is the additional utility derived from the consumption of one more unit of a product.

   T or **F**   If false: _____

   _____

4. The law of diminishing marginal utility suggests that as successive units of a product are consumed, total utility declines.

   T or **F**   If false: _____

   _____

5. If the MU per dollar spent on product A is greater than on product B, then a rational consumer should consume more of product B to compensate.

   T or **F**   If false: _____

   _____

6. It is the marginal utility of the *last* unit consumed that determines how much a consumer is prepared to pay for a product.

   T or **F**   If false: _____

   _____

7. Consumer surplus is the additional amount that consumers have to pay if they really need a particular product.

   T or **F**   If false: _____

   _____

8. The consumer surplus derived from products that have an inelastic demand is greater than that from products with an elastic demand.

   T or **F**   If false: _____

   _____

9. Price discrimination is the practice of charging different prices for different products.

   T or **F**   If false: _____

   _____

10. Price discrimination cannot be practised if consumers are able to resell the product.

    T or **F**   If false: _____

    _____

Choose the Best

11. Which is the correct expression for marginal utility?
    a) It is equal to total utility divided by quantity consumed.

    b) It is the change in total utility resulting from a change in the quantity consumed.

12. If total utility is falling, then:
    a) marginal utility must be negative.
    b) marginal utility must also be falling.

13. When is total utility at a maximum?
    a) When marginal utility is maximum.
    b) When marginal utility is zero.

14. What does the diamond–water paradox refer to?
    a) The fact that water is far more plentiful than diamonds, even though people need more diamonds.
    b) The fact that water is far more valuable than diamonds, yet its price tends to be far lower.
    c) The fact that although people don't necessarily want diamonds, they are prepared to pay a high price for them.

15. Which of the following is correct in reference to the law of diminishing marginal utility?
    a) The amount of additional utility decreases as successive units of a product are consumed.
    b) Marginal utility increases at first, but after some point starts to decline.
    c) Total utility declines at first, but after some point starts to increase.

16. Suppose that the price of a plate of sushi is $10 and that Jan's marginal utility is 8 while Jin's marginal utility is 12. What can be deduced from this information?
    a) That Jin should buy the sushi, but Jan should not.
    b) That Jin likes sushi better than does Jan.
    c) No deductions can be made from this information.

17. Which of the following is a correct statement of the optimal purchasing rule?
    a) $MU_A/MU_B = P_B/P_A$.
    b) $MU_A/P_A = MU_B/P_B$.
    c) $P_A/MU_A = P_B/MU_B$.

18. Which of the following products are likely to yield the greatest amount of consumer surplus?
    a) Water.
    b) Diamonds.
    c) Ice cream.
    d) A Persian carpet.

19. What will happen if $MU_A/P_A > MU_B/P_B$?
    a) The price of A will be forced to drop.
    b) The price of B will be forced to drop.
    c) The consumer will purchase more of product A.
    d) The consumer will purchase more of product B.

Refer to **Table 5.13** when answering questions 20 and 21.

TABLE 5.13

Quantity Consumed	Total Utility
1	30
2	55
3	75
4	90
5	100
6	105
7	105
8	100

20. Refer to Table 5.13 to answer this question. What is the marginal utility of the 5th unit?
    a) 10.
    b) 20.
    c) 100.
    d) Cannot be answered from this information.

21. Refer to Table 5.13 to answer this question. If the price of this product is $5, how many units should this consumer purchase?
    a) 4.
    b) 5.
    c) 6.
    d) Cannot be answered from this information.

22. In order for price discrimination to work, three conditions must be fulfilled. Which of the following is not one of those conditions?
    a) The seller must be able to identify and separate different groups of buyers.
    b) The different groups of buyers must have different elasticities of demand.
    c) The product must be a necessity.
    d) It must be impossible to resell the product.

Refer to **Figure 5.5** to answer questions 23 and 24.

FIGURE 5.5

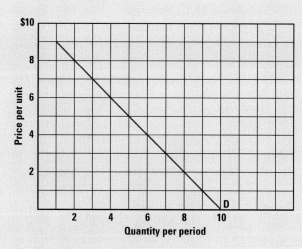

23. Refer to Figure 5.5 to answer this question. If partial units cannot be purchased, what is the value of total consumer surplus at a price of $5?
    a) $10.
    b) $12.
    c) $20.
    d) $35.

24. Refer to Figure 5.5 to answer this question. If partial units cannot be purchased, at what price is the total consumer surplus equal to $21?
    a) $3.
    b) $4.
    c) $5.
    d) $6.
    e) $9.

25. Suppose that Jon is purchasing the optimal amounts of apples and oranges. The marginal utility of the last apple is 8 and of the last orange is 6. If the price of an apple is $1, what must be the price of an orange?
    a) 50 cents.
    b) 75 cents.
    c) $1.33.
    d) $1.40.
    e) Cannot be determined from this information.

26. Suppose that, for a certain consumer, the marginal utility of product A is equal to 40 and its price is $42, while the marginal utility of product B is 30 and its price is $40. What conclusion can be inferred from this?

a) This consumer should buy more of product A and less of product B.
b) This consumer should buy more of product B and less of product A.
c) This consumer should buy more of product B because it is cheaper.
d) This consumer should buy neither product since the prices exceed the marginal utilities.
e) This consumer should buy more of product B because it gives greater value for money.

Refer to **Figure 5.6** to answer questions 27 and 28.

FIGURE 5.6

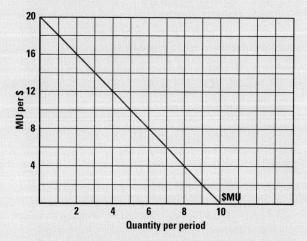

27. Refer to Figure 5.6 to answer this question. What is the maximum price that would be paid by this consumer, assuming that partial units cannot be purchased?
    a) $9.
    b) $10.
    c) $16.
    d) $18.
    e) Cannot be determined from this information.

28. Refer to Figure 5.6 to answer this question. At what quantity would this consumer maximize her total utility?
    a) 5.
    b) 9.
    c) 10.
    d) 18.
    e) Cannot be determined from this information.

Refer to **Table 5.14** when answering questions 29 and 30.

TABLE 5.14

Quantity Consumed	MU Apples	MU Bananas
1	20	18
2	18	17
3	16	14
4	14	11
5	12	8
6	10	5
7	8	2
8	6	0

29. Refer to Table 5.14 to answer this question. Suppose that the price of both apples and bananas is $1 each and this consumer has $8 to spend. In order to maximize her total utility, how many of each should she purchase?

a) 3 apples and 5 bananas.
b) 4 apples and 4 bananas.
c) 5 apples and 3 bananas.
d) 8 apples.
e) 8 bananas.

30. Refer to Table 5.14 to answer this question. Suppose that the price of an apple is $2 and the price of a banana is $1 and this consumer has $8 to spend. In order to maximize her total utility, how many of each should she purchase?
a) 1 apple and 6 bananas.
b) 2 apples and 4 bananas.
c) 3 apples and 2 bananas.
d) 4 apples.
e) 8 bananas.

Simple Calculations

31. Given Jan's total utility from consuming packets of potato chips below, calculate her marginal utility for each unit:

Quantity	1	2	3	4	5	6	7	8	9	10
Total utility	60	110	140	155	167	177	186	192	195	196
Marginal utility										

32. Given Jon's marginal utility from consuming packets of potato chips below, calculate his total utility for each quantity:

Quantity	1	2	3	4	5	6	7	8	9	10
Total utility										
Marginal utility	38	26	22	18	14	10	8	5	3	2

33. Joan is undecided whether to buy a packet of potato chips, cheese whirls, or nacho chips, whose marginal utilities are 50, 36, and 42, respectively. The prices of the snacks are $1.25, $0.80, and $1.20, respectively.
a) Calculate the MU per $ spent for the three products. _____ ; _____ ; _____ .
b) If Joan can afford to buy only one packet, which should she buy? _____ .

34. June's evaluation of packets of nacho chips in terms of $MU is as follows:

1st packet: $3; 2nd packet: $2.50; 3rd packet: $1.80; 4th packet: $1.50; and the 5th packet: $1.25.

If the price of nacho chips is $1.20, and June buys 5 packets, calculate her marginal consumer surplus for each packet and the total consumer surplus from all 5.

Problems

35. **a)** Suppose that Daniel is willing to pay a maximum of $5 for his first slice of pizza. For each additional slice, he would be prepared to pay up to 50 cents less. If Daniel could obtain the pizza for free, how many slices would he eat?

    Number of slices: _____

    b) If the price of a slice of pizza happened to be $2, how many slices would he purchase (assuming his budget allowed it)? What would be his total consumer surplus as a result?

    Number of slices: _____; consumer surplus $_____.

36. **Figure 5.7** depicts Christian's dollar marginal utility for ice creams and for giant chocolate cookies.

FIGURE 5.7

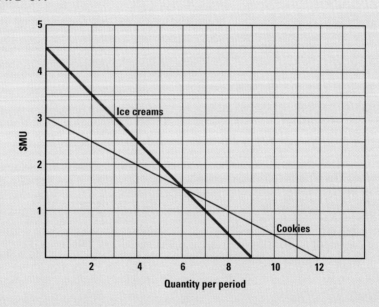

a) If Christian's budget only allowed him to make a total of 6 purchases, how many of each product would he buy?

_____ ice creams, and _____ cookies.

b) What if he found he could afford 10—how many of each product would he buy?

_____ ice creams, and _____ cookies.

37. **a)** Chika has calculated the marginal utility that she derives from her earned income and from leisure. This is presented in **Table 5.15.** In her ideal world, where she could work as few or as many hours as she wished, how would she allocate her 16 waking hours? (She does need to sleep.)

TABLE 5.15

Hours	Paid Employment MU	Leisure MU
1	100	80
2	90	75
3	80	70
4	70	65
5	60	60
6	50	55
7	40	50
8	30	45
9	20	40
10	10	35

_____ working hours, and _____ leisure hours.

b) Unfortunately, Chika begins to realize that unless she gets an education, she won't enjoy a high salary and therefore won't be able to afford more leisure time. She therefore decides to spend 6 hours each day studying (in addition to her 8 hours' sleep). How will she now devote the 10 hours between work and leisure?

_____ working hours, and _____ leisure hours.

38. Sam's drive-in movie theatre attracts two main groups of customers: teenagers and parents with young children. The demand of the two groups is shown in **Table 5.16**.

TABLE 5.16

	Teenagers			Parents		Both Groups
Admission Price ($)	Quantity Demanded	Total Revenue ($)	Quantity Demanded	Total Revenue ($)	Total Revenue ($)
8	100	_____	0	_____	_____
7	150	_____	5	_____	_____
6	180	_____	15	_____	_____
5	200	_____	30	_____	_____
4	210	_____	55	_____	_____
3	215	_____	80	_____	_____
2	218	_____	100	_____	_____
1	220	_____	150	_____	_____

a) If Sam charges a single admission price and wants to maximize his total revenue, what price should he charge and what will be his total revenue?

Price: $_____; total revenue: $_____.

b) Suppose, instead, that Sam is able to discriminate between the two groups and charge different prices to each. How much would he charge each, and what would be his total revenue now?

Price to teenagers: $_____; price to parents: $_____;

total revenue: $_____.

Translations

Explain in words what the following expression means. What action on the part of the consumer would it lead to?

$$\frac{MU_A}{P_A} > \frac{MU_B}{P_B}$$

Answer: _____

_____

_____

_____

_____

Key Problem

Suppose that you are vacationing at a resort in the Caribbean and you are trying to determine how to spend your time and money on two activities, windsurfing and snorkelling, which both cost $10 per hour. The marginal utility of the activities are shown in **Table 5.17**.

TABLE 5.17

	WINDSURFING			SNORKELLING	
No. of Hours	**Marginal Utility**	**Total Utility**	**Marginal Utility**	**Total Utility**	
1	85	_____	100	_____	
2	80	_____	90	_____	
3	65	_____	75	_____	
4	60	_____	70	_____	
5	55	_____	50	_____	
6	40	_____	25	_____	
7	30	_____	20	_____	
8	5	_____	10	_____	

a) Complete the columns of total utilities.

b) Assume that you have a budget of $60. To maximize your total utility, how would you allocate your spending between the two activities? What is the resulting total utility?

$_____ (_____ hours) on windsurfing; and (_____ hours)

$_____ on snorkelling. Total utility: _____ utils.

c) At the end of the day, you dig deep in your pocket and discover an extra $20. If you allocate this additional spending between the two activities so as to maximize your total utility, what will be the utility of the $80 spent?

$_____ (_____ hours) on windsurfing; and $ _____

(_____ hours) on snorkelling. Total utility: _____ utils.

d) Suppose that your utility from the two activities remains unchanged the next day, when you arrive with $80 in you pocket. Unfortunately, you discover that the hourly charge for snorkelling has increased to $15. How will you now allocate your expenditures to maximize your total utility, assuming that partial hours cannot be purchased? (Completing the columns in **Table 5.18** marked "marginal utility per dollar spent" will be helpful.)

TABLE 5.18

| | WINDSURFING | | | | SNORKELLING | |
No. of Hours	Marginal Utility	Total Utility	Marginal Utility per Dollar Spent	Marginal Utility	Total Utility	Marginal Utility per Dollar Spent
1	85	_____	_____	100	_____	_____
2	80	_____	_____	90	_____	_____
3	65	_____	_____	75	_____	_____
4	60	_____	_____	70	_____	_____
5	55	_____	_____	50	_____	_____
6	40	_____	_____	25	_____	_____
7	30	_____	_____	20	_____	_____
8	5	_____	_____	10	_____	_____

$_____ (_____ hours) on windsurfing; and $_____

(_____ hours) on snorkelling. Total utility: _____ utils.

e) Show the effects of the price change on the two products on the graphs in Figure 5.8.

FIGURE 5.8

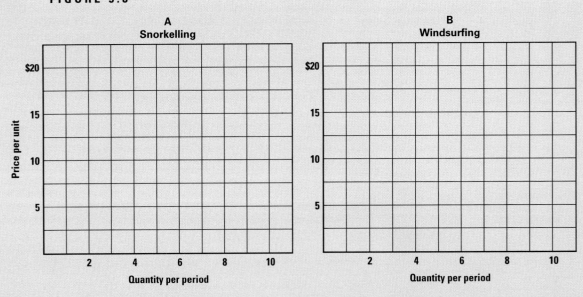

f) The next year you are vacationing at a resort in Buffalo and, with your utility unchanged, discover to your joy that windsurfing and snorkelling are free. How will you allocate your 8-hour day between the two activities in order, as usual, to maximize your total utility?

_____ hours on windsurfing; and _____ hours on snorkelling.

Total utility: _____ utils.

More of the Same

Suppose Jean spends recreation time and money on two leisure activities: tennis and fishing. The cost per hour of tennis (court fees) and per hour of fishing (boat rentals) are both $2. **Table 5.19** shows the total utility that Jean derives from the two activities.

TABLE 5.19

FISHING			TENNIS		
No. of Hours	Total Utility	Marginal Utility	No. of Hours	Total Utility	Marginal Utility
1	31	_____	1	38	_____
2	60	_____	2	72	_____
3	87	_____	3	102	_____
4	111	_____	4	130	_____
5	131	_____	5	152	_____
6	149	_____	6	170	_____
7	161	_____	7	184	_____
8	167	_____	8	194	_____

a) Complete the columns of marginal utilities.

b) Assume that Jean has a budget of $8. To maximize her total utility, how would she allocate her spending between the two activities? What is the resulting total utility?

c) At the end of the day, Jean digs deep in her pocket and discovers an extra $4. If she allocates this additional spending between the two activities so as to maximize her total utility, what will be the final totals?

d) Suppose that Jean's utility from the two activities remains unchanged the next day, when she arrives with $12 in her pocket. To her pleasure, she discovers that the hourly charge for boat rentals has decreased to $1. How will she now allocate her expenditures in order to maximize her total utility?

e) Show the effects of the price change on the two products graphically.

UNANSWERED QUESTIONS

Short Essays

1. What are total and marginal utility, and how are they related? Explain the law of diminishing marginal utility.

2. Explain the optimal purchasing rule. In what way do you think it helps explain observed consumer behaviour?

3. Explain how the demand curve for the individual can be derived from knowledge of her marginal utility curve.

4. What is meant by consumer surplus? How does it relate to the individual's demand curve and to the market demand curve?

5. How is consumer surplus related to the price elasticity of demand?

6. What is price discrimination? What conditions are necessary for it to be practised? Give three examples, and explain what the grounds are for the discrimination.

Analytical Questions

7. "If marginal utility is decreasing, then total utility must also be decreasing." Is this correct?

8. Why is the cost per game of a season's pass for the Toronto Raptors so much cheaper than a ticket for a single game?

9. Explain why the total utility derived from the consumption of a product is not relevant as far as purchasing decisions are concerned.

10. If a nightclub charges a higher entrance fee after 10 p.m. than before, do you think that latecomers are being penalized or early-comers are being favoured?

11. If two people are both willing to pay the same price to watch a soccer game, does that imply that their marginal utilities are equal? Why or why not?

12. To what extent is time a factor when examining the law of diminishing utility? Why? Can you name products that might give increased rather than decreased marginal utility over time? Does this invalidate the law?

13. Does the law of diminishing marginal utility apply to increased purchases of a product or increased consumption of a product, or both?

14. Explain why a higher elasticity of demand results in a smaller consumer surplus. Under what circumstances would consumer surplus be zero?

15. If you buy more than one unit of any product, you will always obtain some consumer surplus. Is this true? Why, or why not?

Numerical Questions

16. **Table 5.20** shows Juanita's demand for rented videos.

TABLE 5.20

Q	MU	TU
1	50	
2		90
3		125
4	25	
5	20	
6		188
7		200
8	6	
9		206
10		200

a) Complete the above table.

b) At what quantity is total utility maximized, and what is marginal utility at this quantity?
c) Is Juanita's TU curve a straight line or not? Explain.

17. Suppose you are trying to decide whether to play an hour of squash, which will cost you $6, or instead go swimming for an hour, at a cost of $4. The marginal utility of squash is 180 utils and swimming is 140 utils. Which is a better buy for you? What does the marginal utility of swimming need to be to make you indifferent between the two?

18. Yoko has $14 to spend on lunch. Unfortunately, the deli doesn't have a very extensive menu: apples at $1 each, bagels at $2 each, and cappuccino at $3 each. Given her utility figures in **Table 5.21**, how should she allocate her $14?

TABLE 5.21

	APPLES	BAGELS	CAPPUCCINO
Quantity	Total Utility	Total Utility	Total Utility
1	80	200	270
2	145	350	480
3	200	470	630
4	240	560	735
5	260	610	825
6	275	630	840

19. Mina is wondering how to spend her $12 evening budget. She has decided she wants to watch videos and eat pizza. A movie rental and a slice of pizza each cost $2. Her total utility for the two products is shown in **Table 5.22**, parts A and B.

TABLE 5.22

A VIDEO MOVIES		B PIZZA SLICES	
No. of Videos	Total Utility	No. of Slices	Total Utility
1	34	1	40
2	64	2	76
3	88	3	108
4	106	4	136
5	118	5	162
6	126	6	184

a) How should she allocate her budget between the videos and pizzas to maximize her total utility?
b) Suppose that the pizza shop has a deal whereby Mina can buy a 6-slice pizza for the price of $10. How will she allocate her $12 budget now?

20. In Ajax, milk drinking seems to be related to hair colouring (or is it vice versa?). The demand for milk by the three different hair-colour groups is shown in **Table 5.23**.

TABLE 5.23

LITRES OF MILK	REDHEADS	BRUNETTES	BLONDES
Price ($)	Daily Quantity	Daily Quantity	Daily Quantity
3	10	20	60
2.50	20	26	62
2	30	32	64
1.50	40	38	66
1	50	44	68
0.50	60	50	70

The country's milk is provided by a single dairy farmer.

a) What price should the farmer charge if he wishes to maximize his total sales revenue? What is the farmer's total revenue?

b) Suppose that the government of Ajax allows the dairy farmer to price-discriminate on the basis of hair colour. If he wishes to maximize his total revenue, how much should he charge each group? What will be his total sales revenue now?

c) What is the price elasticity of demand for these three groups for a price change from $3 per litre to $2.50? What do you think is the connection between price discrimination and price elasticity?

21. Akira's pleasure from eating sushi and drinking sake is shown in **Table 5.24**, which shows his marginal utility measured in terms of dollars, that is, in $MU.

TABLE 5.24

SUSHI		SAKE	
No. of Pieces	$MU	No. of Drinks	$MU
1	10	1	6
2	8	2	5
3	5	3	4.50
4	3	4	4
5	2	5	3.50
6	1	6	1
7	0.50	7	0
8	0	8	−2

a) Suppose Akira has a budget of $16 and the prices of both sushi and sake are $2. How many of each will Akira consume so as to maximize his total utility? How much total utility will he derive? How much consumer surplus will he obtain from each product, and what will be the total consumer surplus?

b) Suppose Akira is not restricted to any budget. How much of each will he buy, and how much will his total dollar utility and his total consumer surplus be?

22. **Figure 5.9** indicates Sara's marginal utility for two products, A and B.

FIGURE 5.9

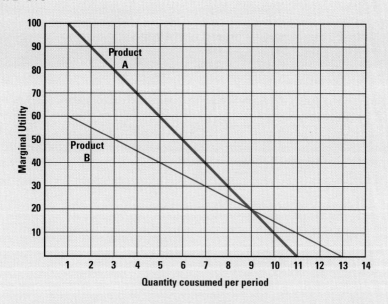

a) If $P_A = P_B = \$2$, what quantity of each good would be purchased by Sara if her budget was $20?

b) Suppose P_A increased to $3. If Sara's budget remains at $20, what quantities of each good would now be purchased?

23. Figure 5.10 indicates Becky's demand for bus tickets.

FIGURE 5.10

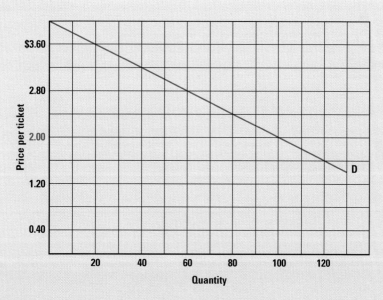

a) What is Becky's total consumer surplus if the price of tickets is $2 each and she can only buy tickets in books of 10?

b) What is her total consumer surplus if the price per ticket is $2 and she can buy any quantity, including single tickets?

Web-Based Activities

1. Go to **www.fraserinstitute.ca/publications/forum/1999/04/apr99ff.html.** How does the opening paragraph's use of the term "consumer surplus" differ from the way it is used in this chapter? Do you think the AirCare example gives meaning to the idea of negative consumer surplus?

2. Changes in tastes (and preferences and values) are neglected in much of economic analysis, but they are the keys to many aspects of human behaviour. Advertising may have the ability to alter tastes and preferences or to help identify existing (yet-unknown to the consumer) tastes and preferences. Read **www.demographics.com/ publications/mt/98_mt/9804_mt/mt980415.htm,** and **www.demographics.com/publications/mt/95_mt/9511_mt/mt388.htm** and discuss whether tastes and preferences can be easily changed by advertisers.

Indifference Curve Analysis

Sasha was a financially struggling student who spent all his hard-earned savings (plus the proceeds of his student loans) on the bare essentials of life—food, rent, tuition, books, bus pass, and so on. Then one day he received a very pleasant surprise in the mail. An understanding aunt wrote to tell him that henceforth she would send him $64 per month on the condition that he promise to spend all of it only on whatever gave him a little pleasure. Since Sasha loved both music (he had been given a CD player to take with him to college) and movies, he decided that he would spent this monthly gift on only those two items. Sasha was a little out of touch with prices but he did know that CDs cost more than movies, so he asked himself what would be his ideal combination to purchase. He felt that 5 movies and 3 CDs sounded right (Combination B). But then he thought a little more about it and asked himself: "If I wanted to buy one more CD, how many movies would I be prepared to sacrifice?" His answer was only 1, since the prospect of fewer than 4 movies per month was not appealing (Combination C). Sasha then asked the same question in reverse: "If I had to sacrifice one of these CDs, how many more movies each month would compensate me?" He decided that the answer to this question was 3 (Combination A). In effect, Sasha now identified three combinations of the two goods that gave him equal satisfaction (or pleasure) as summarized in Table A1.

TABLE A1

Combination	CDs	Movies
B	3	5
C	4	4
A	2	8

The Indifference Curve

indifference curve: shows the combinations of goods that would give the same satisfaction (or total utility) to an individual (or household)

An economist, observing Sasha's thought process, would say that Sasha was attempting to maximize total utility from his spending on entertainment and had identified three points on his **indifference curve**.

Figure A1 illustrates this indifference curve.

FIGURE A1

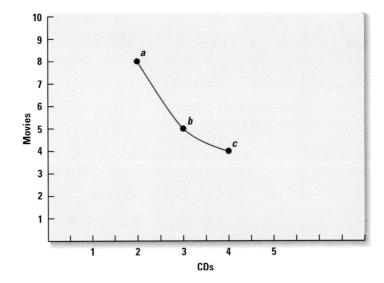

Sasha's preferences for movies and CDs are such that he is indifferent between the three possible combinations indicated by points *a*, *b*, and *c*. Connecting these points yields an indifference curve.

marginal rate of substitution: the amount of one good a consumer is willing to give up to get one more unit of another good.

law of diminishing marginal rate of substitution: the more of one good a person has, the less of another good he will be willing to give up to gain an additional unit of the first good.

There are two important aspects to this indifference curve that we need to emphasize. First, it is downward-sloping, which is to say that Sasha will be willing to give up CDs only if he gets more movies, and vice versa. This seems eminently reasonable. Second, the rate at which he is willing to give up movies for a CD or CDs for a movie is crucial. Economists call this the **marginal rate of substitution**, or, as we will call it, the MRS.

If we focus on point *a* in Figure A1 we see that this is the combination of 8 movies and 2 CDs. If we move from point *a* to point *b*, we see that Sasha is willing to give up 3 movies (8 down to 5) to gain 1 more CD (2 up to 3). Between these two points, the value of Sasha's MRS of a CD for movies is 3/1 or 3. Notice, however, what happens as we move from point *b* to *c*. Here, Sasha is willing to give up only 1 movie (5 down to 4) to gain 1 more CD (3 up to 4). Thus, here the value of his MRS of CDs for movies is only 1/1 or 1. What we have just identified is the **law of diminishing marginal rate of substitution**. This is quite analogous to the law of diminishing marginal utility that we encountered in Chapter 5 and reflects the fact that the more CDs that Sasha already has, the fewer movies he is willing to give up to gain yet another CD. Again this seems reasonable because we know that Sasha loves both CDs and movies.

The effect of the law of diminishing MRS is that the indifference curve will be "bowed in" (convex), and because we have already established that it is downward-sloping, we now have the basic shape of all indifference curves. Furthermore, we can point out two more things about the indifference curve: its slope is equal to the MRS and this slope becomes less steep as we move down the curve, since the MRS of CDs for movies diminishes the more CDs Sasha has. We thus know that Sasha's indifference curve in Figure A1 would become less steep to the right of point *c* and more steep to the left of point *a*.

The Budget Line

Let us now return to Sasha's story to report that he has just made a trip downtown to price out both CDs and movies (remember his previous financial situation had made him a little out of touch). He was surprised, and more than a little disappointed, to learn that movies were now $8 and the type of CDs that he wanted averaged $16. He then returned to his dorm and made **Table A2**, which lists the combinations of the two goods that he could *afford to buy* with his budget of $64 per month.

TABLE A2

Movies	CDs
8	0
6	1
4	2
2	3
0	4

We can now graph the data in Table A2 and obtain what economists call the budget line (BL) or budget constraint line, since Sasha's limited budget constrains him to only these combinations (he could, of course, buy fewer quantities of either goods, but his aunt's condition was that he spend all of the $64). The budget line is illustrated in **Figure A2**.

FIGURE A2

The budget line, BL, identifies the various combinations of movies and CDs that Sasha is able to afford given his financial constraint of $64. The budget line begins with the combination of 8 movies and zero CDs and has a slope of −2. Any combination of the two goods in the shaded area is unobtainable.

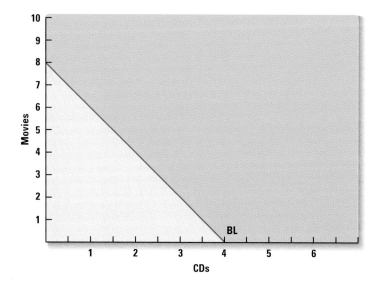

We need to point out that the slope of the budget line is a reflection of the prices of the two goods. If we put the price of CDs, which is $16, over the price of movies, which is $8, we get 16/8 or 2. Technically this slope needs to be expressed as −2 because the budget line must be downward-sloping.

It was clear to Sasha that he simply couldn't obtain any of the combinations he had first listed in Table A1. He would therefore need to construct another indifference curve, which, although it would result in lower total utility, would fit his budget. He could see that a combination of 4 movies and 2 CDs per month was within his budget, so he started there (Combination E). He then asked himself how many more movies would compensate him for reducing the number of CDs from 2 to 1. He decided that this would be 3 movies, giving him a second combination of 7 movies and 1 CD (Combination D). He then asked himself, alternatively, how many movies would he sacrifice in order to have 3, rather than 2, CDs. The answer is only 1, which gives him a third combination (F) of 3 movies and 3 CDs. These new combinations are summarized in Table A3.

TABLE A3

Combination	Movies	CDs
D	7	1
E	4	2
F	3	3

Since Sasha is indifferent between these three (new) combinations we can take this information and plot a new indifference curve (I_2) on **Figure A3**.

FIGURE A3

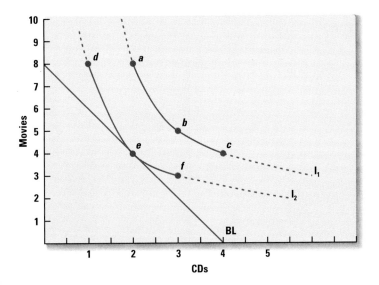

Sasha is indifferent to the combinations represented by points *d*, *e*, and *f* because they all are on the same indifference curve, I_2. Given his budget line, BL, only combination *e* is affordable.

Let's examine what Figure A3 is telling us. First, points *d*, *e*, and *f* are all combinations of the two goods to which Sasha is indifferent since they are all on the same indifference curve, I_2, and give him equal utility. Second, Sasha would prefer any combination of the two goods on indifference curve I_1 since it higher than (or is to the right of) I_2. Third, he is limited by his budget to the points that lie on the budget line, BL. And finally, of all these points only *e* is within Sasha's budget, and this will then be his obvious choice.

Utility Maximization

There is something very fundamental about point *e* that you need to fully understand. At this point the indifference curve and the budget line are tangent, and this means that their slopes are the same. Since we know that this slope is −2 and since we have established that the budget line is equal to the relative prices of the two goods and that the slope of the indifference curve is equal to the MRS, we have:

$$\frac{P_{CDs}}{P_M} = MRS$$

Furthermore, we know that the MRS is a reflection of Sasha's marginal utility for the two goods. Therefore, the above equation can be expressed as follows:

$$\frac{P_{CD}}{P_M} = \frac{MU_{CD}}{MU_M}$$

This second equation can be rewritten to be:

$$\frac{MU_M}{P_M} = \frac{MU_{CD}}{P_{CD}}$$

You will recognize that this is the optimal purchasing rule that we obtained in Chapter 5. Sasha will maximize his utility, given a budget constraint, by equating the marginal utility per dollar spent on movies with the marginal utility per dollar spent on CDs. What is different about the indifference curve approach, however, is that we got here without having to assign values for the marginal utilities of either good. Interesting, isn't it?

The Income and Substitution Effect

In Chapter 2 we learned that if the price of a particular good increases, then the quantity demanded will decrease for two reasons—the income effect and the substitution effect. This can be illustrated nicely using indifference curves, as illustrated in **Figure A4.**

FIGURE A4

Point *a* illustrates the original maximization of utility, which results in the consumer purchasing quantity Q_1 of good B. An increase in the price of good B results in the budget pivoting from BL_1 to BL_2 and a new maximization illustrated by *b*. Budget line BL_3 passes through the original combination *a* but is now tangent to a higher indifference curve, I_3, at point *c* and quantity purchased of Q_2. Thus Q_1 to Q_2 is the substitution effect and Q_2 to Q_3 is the income effect.

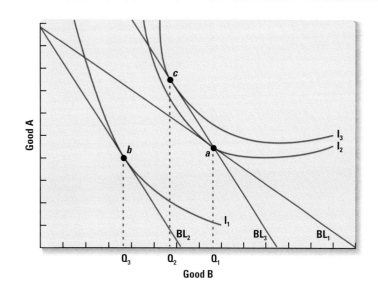

Given budget line BL_1 and indifference curve I_2, the consumer's maximization point is *a*, which results in quantity Q_1 of good B being purchased (as well as some of good A). An increase in the price of good B pivots the budget line to the left, as seen in BL_2. As a result, the consumer changes her purchases to point *b* and quantity Q_3. This is quite consistent with the idea that an increase in the price of good B will lead to a decrease in the quantity demanded. But how much of the decrease (Q_1 down to Q3) is because the consumer's real income has decreased, and how much is due to the consumer substituting the now relatively cheaper good A for good B? To answer this question, we conceptually give the consumer enough additional income to enable her to purchase the original combination of the two goods. This is illustrated by the budget line BL_3, which has been shifted right and passes through the original combination at point *a*. You should note that BL_3 is parallel to BL_2 since BL_3 represents the same price level as BL_2 with a higher income level. BL_3 is tangent to a higher indifference curve, I_3 at point *c*. Note that the consumer could purchase the original combination *a* but has instead chosen combination *c*. This latter combination must yield a higher level of utility and is thus on a higher indifference curve. The point of tangency between BL_3 and I_3, point *c*, yields quantity Q_2. Thus, this consumer has decreased her purchases of good B from Q_1 to Q_2 because she is substituting good A for good B, which is the *substitution effect*. The decrease in the quantity of good B purchased, Q_2 to Q_1, is the result of the decrease in real income and thus is the *income effect*.

This completes our brief discussion of indifference curve analysis.

STUDY GUIDE

New Glossary Terms

law of diminishing marginal rate of substitution   198
marginal rate of substitution   198

Are You Sure?

Indicate whether the following statements are true or false. If false, indicate why they are false.

1. The budget line is bowed out from the origin.

   T or F   If false: _____

   _____

2. An increase in the price of the product on the vertical axis will make the BL steeper.

   T or F   If false: _____

   _____

3. It is logically inconsistent for any two indifference curves to cross.

   T or F   If false: _____

   _____

4. Lower indifference curves represent lower levels of income.

   T or F   If false: _____

   _____

5. The point at which the budget line is tangent to the indifference curve is where the consumer derives equal utility from both products.

   T or F   If false: _____

   _____

Choose the Best

6. Suppose that a consumer has a budget of $30 and the price of a can of pop is $2 while pizza slices are $3. Which of the following combinations is on the budget line?
   a) 15 cans of pop and 10 slices of pizza.
   b) 6 cans of pop and 6 slices of pizza.
   c) 0 cans of pop and 15 slices of pizza.

Table A4 shows combinations of CDs and movies that give a consumer equal amounts of total utility.

TABLE A4		
Combination	**CDs**	**Movies**
A	0	16
B	1	9
C	2	5
D	3	3
E	4	2

7. Refer to Table A4 to answer this question. How many movies is the consumer prepared to give up in order to obtain a second CD?
   a) 3.
   b) 4.
   c) 5.

8. Suppose that John's budget doubles and the prices of both of the goods he spends this budget on also double. What will happen to his budget line?
   a) It will shift out but not change slope.
   b) It will shift in but not change slope.
   c) It will remain unchanged.

9. If the price of one good changes but the price of the other good does not, how can the income and substitution effects be identified graphically?
   a) By drawing in a third budget line, parallel to the original one, which is tangent to the original indifference curve.
   b) By drawing in a third budget line, parallel to the original one, which passes through the original point of utility maximization.
   c) By drawing in a third budget line, parallel to the second one, which is tangent to the original indifference curve.
   d) By drawing in a third budget line, parallel to the second one, which passes through the original point of utility maximization.

10. Suppose that a consumer has a budget of $64 and the price of a CD is $16 while a movie costs $8. If CDs are measured on the vertical axis, what is the slope of the budget line?
    a) 4.
    b) 2.
    c) −4.
    d) −2.
    e) −1/2.

Problems

11. **Table A5** shows three indifference schedules for Barbara.

TABLE A5

INDIFFERENCE CURVE 1		INDIFFERENCE CURVE 2		INDIFFERENCE CURVE 3	
Apples	**Bananas**	**Apples**	**Bananas**	**Apples**	**Bananas**
9	2	10	4	12	6
6	3	6	6	8	7
5	5	5	9	6	8
4	9	4	13	5	11
3	14	3	18	4	16

The price of each fruit is $1 and Barbara's budget is $12.

a) Draw the three indifference curves and the budget line on **Figure A5**.

FIGURE A5

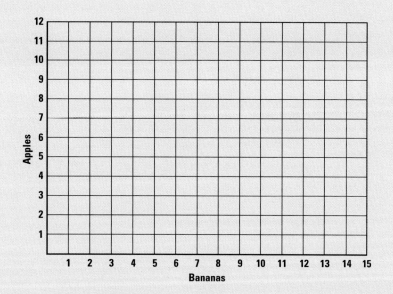

b) What quantities of each will maximize Barbara's utility if she spends all of her budget?
_____ apples;   _____ bananas.

Suppose that the price of apples increases to $1.50.

c) Draw the new budget line in Figure A5.

d) What quantities of each will now maximize Barbara's utility if she spends all of her budget?
_____ apples;   _____ bananas.

12. Figure A6 shows an indifference map for Alan.

FIGURE A6

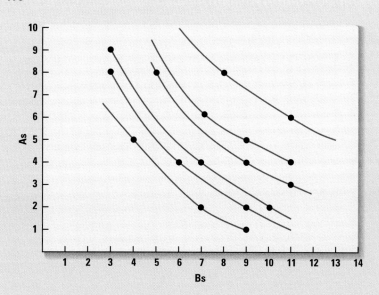

The price of As is $3, and Bs have a price of $2. Alan has a budget of $30.

a) Draw Alan's budget line in Figure A6.

b) What quantities of each product will maximize Alan's utility if he spends all of his budget?
_____ As;   _____ Bs.

Suppose that the price of Bs increases to $3.

c) Draw in the new budget line in Figure A6.

d) What quantities of each will maximize Alan's utility if he spends all of his $30 budget?
_____ As;   _____ Bs.

e) In Figure A6, draw a budget line (BL3) which reflects the new price but with the same real income as before the price change.
_____ As;   _____ Bs.

f) How much does the quantity of B decline due to:

the substitution effect _____;   the income effect _____?

The Costs of Production

What's ahead...In this chapter we look at the costs of production faced by a typical firm. First, we make a distinction between explicit cost and implicit cost. Later, we see that there are seven ways to measure costs and that each is interrelated with the others in specific ways. This gives us the necessary understanding to be able to study the behaviour of firms in different market structures that comes in subsequent chapters. A thorough understanding of the costs of production requires that we first explore the meaning of the term *productivity*, because it is the firm's productivity that underlies its costs. Finally, we address the question of just what is meant by a cut in a firm's cost of production.

A QUESTION OF RELEVANCE...

Have you even been given a free ticket to a concert or ball game? Did it cost you anything? Did it cost the person who gave it to you anything? Did it cost the organizers of the event anything? Who said (besides the Beatles) that the best things in life are free? And does this include a free lunch? How to identify free goods and "unfree" goods, and how we measure the cost of the latter, are the subjects of this chapter.

W̶e now need to shift our focus from supply–demand analysis to that of the business organization—what economists call "the firm."

We will be discussing the firm and its behaviour in the next five chapters. As a general introduction to the study of the firm, consider some of the types of decisions the typical firm must make: What is the right product(s) to produce? What is the right level of production for now, and how might this change in the future? What methods of distribution and marketing approaches are the most appropriate? And what is the right price to charge?

Out of this come two fundamental questions that economists ask about the behaviour of firms. The first is, how do firms decide on the price of their products, and second, how do they determine the level of production? In the process of answering these questions we will look (in Chapters 8–11) at what economists call market structure. But first we need to understand all that falls under the general topic called the *costs of production.*

Production is the activity of a business organization or firm using inputs to obtain output of some product. We see examples of production every day. For example, think of inputs like sand, gravel, cement, water, machines, and labour, which are used to produce the output concrete. Now, of course, the inputs used in production have to be paid for, and this payment becomes the firm's cost.

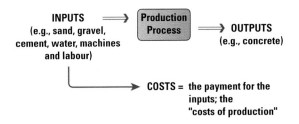

When most students hear the word "costs," they think of the dollars and cents actually paid out by the firm. Many costs can be thought of in just this way, but this is by no means the whole story. For example, a firm may buy a machine for $200 000 that it expects to be able to use for 8 years. What is the cost of this machine in the first year of its use? Surely, the answer is not the full $200 000. Instead, it could be thought of as the portion of the machine that is used up or worn out during that year. What is called **depreciation** is the annual amount of this wear. In this example, the cost of depreciation could be equal to, say, one-eighth of $200 000, or $25 000.

depreciation: the annual cost of any asset that is expected to be in use for more than one year.

ADDED DIMENSION

Why Do Firms Exist? The Coase Answer

One of the truly intriguing questions in economics is: why do firms exist? Ronald Coase (1910–), a Nobel laureate who spent many years at the University of Chicago, offered an elegant answer in the late 1930s. Consider the situation in which I want a new house. I could locate a lot and arrange to buy it; then hire someone to prepare the lot for construction; locate and hire someone to dig a hole for the basement; hire still someone else to prepare and pour the concrete foundation; others to frame the building, after someone else has been found to design the structure; still others to do the roofing, plumbing, electrical, and finishing work.

At each stage I would have to seek bids, negotiate prices, decide on product types and schedules, and hope that everyone delivered on what they promised. All of this would take a lot of time and money—that is, it has *transactions costs*.

Alternatively, I could simply buy a house that some firm has put onto the market. In putting a house up for sale, the firm has absorbed all the transactions costs, and since it has produced dozens (hundreds) of houses, as well as the one I buy, it has been able to reduce the *per-house* transactions costs. That is why a firm exists—it is more efficient.

Explicit and Implicit Costs

Let's take another example, this time the case of smaller firms of the mom-and-pop variety, in which the owners often contribute their own money and time to the firm. Is the contribution of money to the firm free? Should we consider the time put into the firm by its owners as having no costs? The answer to both questions is no, and this once again raises the concept of opportunity costs, which was introduced in Chapter 1. Let's say that our hypothetical owners, Otto and Melissa, put $100 000, which they obtained from an inheritance, into their own soup-and-sandwich shop, the Moonlight Cafe. The costs to the firm, economists would argue, must include what this couple could have done with the $100 000 instead of putting it into their own business. One clear alternative would be to buy some mutual funds, from which they could earn, let us say, 10 percent per year. Therefore, the cost to the firm of using this $100 000 is the sacrifice of the lost return of $10 000 per year (or $833 per month). Similarly, we could ask what Otto and Melissa could do instead of putting 18 hours a day of work into their own business. Well, both of them could hire their labour out to someone else in a similar business who wanted the skills that our hypothetical couple possess. Let us assume that the going market wage for this type of labour (short-order cook and waiter) is $8 an hour. We should then assign a cost to the firm of this couple putting their time into the business of $144 a day ($16 an hour times, let's say, 9 hours a day). The important thing for you to note is that neither the $10 000 in interest per year nor the $144 per day in wages need necessarily be actually paid out by the firm, but each is a legitimate cost of doing business using the concept of opportunity cost. In other words, to an economist, there is a cost involved—even if no payment is made—if an activity involves the use of productive resources, since those resources could have been used elsewhere.

explicit cost: a cost that is actually paid out in money.

implicit cost: a cost that does not require an actual expenditure of money.

We can see that there are two distinct types of costs in our example of the Moonlight Cafe: **explicit costs**, the costs paid to non-owners; for example, wages to employees and payments to suppliers; and **implicit costs**, the costs of using the owners' resources (whether or not any payment is made).

Table 6.1 shows a typical month's accounting of the business activity for the cafe.

TABLE 6.1 Profit and Loss Statement (For a Typical Month)

Total Revenue:	Cash sales (excluding sales tax)		$14 445
Explicit Costs:	Rent	$ 900	
	Food	5750	
	Sundries	1000	
	Insurance and licences	1095	
	Hired labour	1600	
	Advertising	1600	
	Depreciation on equipment	500	
Total Explicit Costs:			12 445
Accounting Profit:			2 000
Implicit Costs:	Opportunity costs of the $100 000 put into business	833	
	Labour put in by owners (25 days)	3600	
Total Implicit Costs:			4 433
Total Explicit and Implicit Costs:			16 878
Economic Profit or (Loss):			(2 433)

We should mention that an accountant and an economist treat the depreciation on equipment calculation differently. Let's assume that the $500 depreciation expense is the maximum amount that the tax laws allow in this particular year and this is the figure used by the accountant. The economist would argue, however, that the actual cost of equipment this year is the decline in its market value that results from it being one year older. This might or might not be equal to $500, but for expediency we will assume that it is.

As you can see from Table 6.1, if we considered only direct out-of-pocket expenses (explicit costs) we would conclude that Otto and Melissa had made a profit of $2000 in this month. In fact, this is the way that an accountant would report the month's activities, i.e.,

Total accounting profit = total revenue − total explicit costs

Economists, however, recognizing the concept of opportunity costs, argue that rather than making a $2000 profit, the Moonlight Cafe in fact lost $2433 in this month. In other words,

Total economic profit = total revenue − total costs (implicit and explicit)

Another way of looking at this is that if Otto and Melissa had put their money into a mutual fund and hired themselves out at the going market wage rate, they would have been $2433 ahead for this month. However, they do enjoy the benefit of working for themselves, which is attractive to many people. In addition, there is the prospect of better months in the future, which Otto and Melissa will weigh before becoming too depressed about their business decisions.

1. Judy, who has two young daughters in day care, is currently working as an activities facilitator at a nearby community centre. She is unhappy with her job, but the idea of not being able to work and having to stay home all day with the kids makes her even more unhappy. Therefore, she is contemplating returning to college for a two-year certificate in computer technology. Judy has collected the following facts:

a) College tuition per year	$860
b) Two-year estimate for textbooks	$1200
c) Cost for day care per child per year	$4800
d) Judy's present per-month income (after taxes)	$1056
e) Transportation to and from college per year	$600
f) Judy's contribution to the household budget per month	$656

What would be an economist's estimate of the cost for Judy to take the two-year program at the college?

There is another aspect of opportunity cost that is also interesting. Consider the following scenario. You are walking through the local mall and come upon the food fair section and decide to buy something to eat. At first, you cannot decide between a taco platter for $4.99 or a soup-and-sandwich combo for the same price. You understand (from Chapter 1) that the opportunity cost of the one is the sacrifice you make by not buying the other, but there is more. Let's assume that you decide on the taco platter and sit down to enjoy your purchase. After a single bite, you realize that you made the wrong choice and you really don't want to eat even another bite. What is the cost of leaving the platter uneaten and simply walking away? To an economist, the answer is zero because the $4.99 you spent on the taco platter is a **sunk cost**, the historical cost of buying something that has no current resale value. Sunk costs are absolutely irrelevant to decision making. Even if a firm has spent millions of dollars on equipment, if that money has already been spent and the equipment has no resale value, then throwing it away has no cost. What we are really saying here is that if an asset is a sunk cost, it no longer carries any opportunity cost.

sunk costs: the historical costs of buying plant, machinery, and equipment that are unrecoverable.

Normal Profits and Economic Profits

We need to say something about the different possible definitions of profit. We saw that economists include both explicit and implicit costs when calculating profit. These costs are often referred to by economists as necessary *expenses*. If Otto and Melissa are not prepared to pay the necessary wage and interest costs, then those resources would not be available. Similarly, what economists refer to as **normal profit** can also be viewed as a necessary cost and earning at least normal profits is considered a necessary part of doing business. Normal profit, then, is regarded as sufficient profit to keep the owners in that particular line of business.

normal profit: the minimum profit that must be earned to keep the entrepreneur in that type of business.

economic profit: revenue over and above all costs, including normal profits.

Economic profit, on the other hand, is not a necessary expense. It is a true surplus. It is the amount earned after all costs, explicit and implicit (which includes a normal profit), have been deducted from revenues. Otto and Melissa don't have to make any economic profits to keep them in business. As long as they are earning normal profit, they will be reasonably pleased. Of course, they would like to make economic profit, and the more the better, but it is a true bonus for them, not a necessity.

Theory of Production

It is clear that increased production will involve higher costs, and this output–cost relationship is one that we need to explore fully. First, however, we need to understand some basic relationships *within* the concept of production itself.

Total, Average, and Marginal Product

Common sense would lead one to think that if more inputs were added to the production process, more output would be obtained. Yet to leave things at that would skirt over some of the most important aspects of the production process.

Not all inputs can be increased at the same time. For example, a farmer can add more variable inputs such as water and fertilizer to his fields this season, but he cannot increase the size of his fields. Thus, we need to recognize that, within any given time period, some inputs will be fixed. This leads us to the very important point that as long as any one input is fixed, we are in what economists call the short run. This chapter will be entirely in the context of the **short run**. The next chapter will look at the long run, in which all inputs are considered variable.

short run: any period of time in which at least one input in the production process is fixed.

Let's now look at a simple model of production by using some hypothetical data for grain production in **Table 6.2**, which we assume requires only two inputs. The first of these two inputs is land, which we assume is a fixed size of 10 hectares, and the second is labour, which we assume comes equipped with some fixed complement of seed, fertilizer, water, and tools.

TABLE 6.2 Total Product Data

Units of Labour (L)	Total Product (TP), in Bushels
0	0
1	8
2	20
3	45
4	75
5	100
6	120
7	130
8	135
9	135
10	130

total product: the total output of any productive process.

marginal product: the increase in total product as a result of adding one more unit of input.

The right-hand column in Table 6.2 indicates the output, which is what economists call **total product** (TP). Here we see what happens to total product as we add successive units of labour. What is important to notice about this data is that total product does not rise proportionately with the increase in labour. The explanation for this involves the use of a concept that economists call **marginal product** (MP), which is defined as the change in total product as a result of adding one more unit of input, in this case labour. Formally then, the marginal product of *labour* is:

$$MP_L = \frac{\Delta TP}{\Delta L}$$

average product: total product (or total output) divided by the quantity of inputs used to produce that total.

It is important not to confuse marginal product with **average product** (AP), which is nothing more than total product divided by the number of inputs. Average product is often called productivity per worker. Formally, the average product of *labour* is:

$$AP_L = \frac{TP}{L}$$

Let's go to **Table 6.3** to examine these new concepts in detail.

TABLE 6.3 Marginal and Average Product Data

Units of Labour	Total Product (TP)	Marginal Product (MP)	Average Product (AP)
0	0	—	—
1	8	8	8
2	20	12	10
3	45	25	15
4	75	30	18.8
5	100	25	20
6	120	20	20
7	130	10	18.6
8	135	5	16.9
9	135	0	15
10	130	−5	13

division of labour. the dividing of the production process into a series of specialized tasks, each done by a different worker.

The data in the third column of Table 6.3 indicate that the marginal product of the first unit of production is 8, whereas that of the second production unit rises to 12. Why might the marginal product of labour rise? Does it mean that the second worker is better than the first? No, because we assume that each worker is equally good. So what is the explanation? An analogy may help here. Can you imagine trying to build a fence by yourself? It could be done, but it would be slow and awkward. You would have to set each post temporarily and then step back to see if it was straight and then readjust it and step back again and so on and so on. Clearly, two people (each with tools and material) could build a fence at a rate that is *more than* twice as fast as one person. That is to say, the marginal product of the second person would be higher than that of the first person.

Adam Smith referred to this phenomenon as the **division of labour** in his famous example of the pin factory. Smith marvelled at the fact that a state-of-the-art factory in eighteenth-century England, which employed only ten workers, was able to produce 48 000 ordinary straight pins in a single day by dividing the process of pin-making into 10 distinct functions in which each worker performed only one task. The emphasis here is on the word *process*, as distinct from the situation where each worker separately and independently would make a whole pin from start to finish. In Smith's estimation, doing it this way would result in the production of less than 1000 pins in a day.

This production line is a modern-day example of Adam Smith's division of labour.

ADDED DIMENSION

Division of Labour: The Key to the Industrial Revolution

Adam Smith saw five distinct reasons for the productive power of the division of labour:

a) the ability to fit the best person to the right job;

b) the increased dexterity achieved when the worker makes a single operation his sole employment;

c) the time savings gained from not having to change tools;

d) the time savings gained that would otherwise be lost in moving from one operation to another (what we would today call assembly-line production);

e) the machine specialization that can be developed around specific, discrete operations.

This last aspect is a vital step in the industrial process. Without the division of labour, the extensive use of machines that has occurred over the past two centuries simply would not have been possible.

We can now see how the marginal product of labour will, at first, increase as more labour is added to a production process. Next we need to ask the question: why, after a point, does marginal product decline? (We see this in Table 6.3, beginning with the addition of the fifth unit of labour.) The answer to this question involves one of the

law of diminishing returns: as more of a variable input is added to a fixed input in the production process, the resulting increase in output will, at some point, begin to diminish.

most important concepts in all of microeconomics: the **law of diminishing returns**, a concept first popularized by David Ricardo. This law states that as more and more units of a variable resource (in this case, labour) are added to a production process, at some point the resulting increase in output (MP) begins to decrease, assuming that at least one other input (in this case, land) is fixed. A more accurate term would be the law of diminishing *marginal productivity*, but in this chapter we will stick with the more commonly used law of diminishing returns.

INCREASING amount of labour added to: $\Longrightarrow$ A FIXED amount of land $\Longrightarrow$ Output increasing, but the rate of increase DIMINISHES

A D D E D   D I M E N S I O N

David Ricardo: The Businessman Economist

Regarded in his time as the natural heir to Adam Smith, David Ricardo (1772–1823) was the acknowledged leader of classical economics. The third of seventeen children born to Jewish immigrants to England, he trained in his father's successful brokerage firm. When he was 21, he fell in love with a Quaker woman and left his faith to become a Unitarian, so his father disowned him. Undaunted, he married and, supported by friends, entered the brokerage business on his own. By the time he was 25, his personal fortune had surpassed his father's. He retired at age 43 and devoted himself full time to his real love—the study of economics.

Though he was a hardheaded businessman, his contributions to economics were the result of abstract reasoning rather than of experience and observation. He is known for his theories of trade, rent, and income distribution and for elegantly stating the law of diminishing returns, which he developed. His *Principles of Economy and Taxation* (1817) quickly replaced Smith's *Wealth of Nations* as the standard text in economics.

The law of diminishing returns is a technological reality that must be valid; otherwise we could grow the world's food in a flowerpot by simply adding more and more variable inputs until production rose to the necessary level. We can't do this, and the reason we can't is because of the law of diminishing returns.

We now need to make four points of clarification. First, while the fixed input in our example above happens to be land, it could have been *any* input—the only necessity for the law of diminishing returns to apply is that at least one input be fixed. Second, our example had only one variable input, labour, and we illustrated the law of diminishing returns by showing that the marginal product of labour declines. However, if there had been two variable inputs instead of one, both would have manifested diminishing returns. Third, any discussion of the law of diminishing returns assumes that technology is unchanging. If technological change does occur, we would get a new set of output numbers, but those numbers would still be subject to diminishing returns. Finally, while our example is in the context of agriculture, the law of diminishing returns applies in all productive activities.

It is very important to note that even after the point of diminishing returns has been reached, the total product *continues to rise*. However, the *rate of increase* in the total product does begin to fall. Those of you who have taken calculus will recognize that marginal product is the first derivative of total product. Those of you who have not need only realize that total product can continue to rise even though marginal product has started to decline.

SELF-TEST

3. Assuming that amount of capital is fixed:
   A) Fill in the blanks in the table.
   B) Diminishing returns begin with the addition of which unit of labour?
   C) The average product of labour is at a maximum when how many units of labour are used?
   D) What is the value of marginal product when total product is at a maximum?

Units of Labour	TP	MP_L	AP_L
0	0	—	—
1	80	___	___
2	170	___	___
3	___	80	___
4	310	___	___
5	___	___	70
6	370	___	___
7	370	___	___

The data in Table 6.3 can also be put into graphical form. Let's go to **Figure 6.1** to illustrate this.

Note three things about this curve. First, total product rises quickly at first because of the advantages gained from the division of labour. Second, at the point of diminishing returns (with the use of the fifth unit of labour) the rate of increase in the curve decreases. Third, the rise in total product continues despite having passed the point of diminishing returns.

Let us now turn to a discussion of average product. There is a marginal–average relationship reflected in the data in Table 6.3 that needs to be emphasized. All students intuitively know what this relationship is, but many are not aware that they do. Imagine that you are taking a course in which your class mark is made up of ten quizzes worth 10 points each. You know that if you got 4 points on the first quiz and 6 points on the second quiz, your average quiz score is, at that point, 5. You also know that in order to raise your average test score, you will have to get a mark on the third quiz that is above 5. The mark on the third quiz is the marginal mark, and if the marginal is above the average, the average will rise. If, however, your third test mark is less than 5, your average of all three quizzes would fall, that is, if the marginal is below the average, the average will fall.

Let's take this marginal–average relationship and look back at the data in Table 6.3. Notice that the third, fourth, and fifth units of labour all have a marginal product that is above the average product, and therefore average product rises. The addition of the sixth unit of labour, which has a marginal product that is exactly the same as the previous average (20), results in the average product neither increasing nor decreasing, but remaining constant at 20. The seventh unit of labour has a marginal product of 10, which is below the average, and therefore average product falls to 18.6. We can generalize as follows:

Average product will rise if marginal product exceeds it and will fall if marginal product is less than it.

Figure 6.2 illustrates this relationship graphically. In this figure, you can see that marginal product is at a maximum when four units of labour are used. Further, when marginal product equals average product, average product is at its maximum. Because of the way these particular set of numbers work out, this maximum average product *appears* (see Table 6.3) to occur with the addition of the fifth unit of labour. But we must be careful here because, technically speaking, it is with the sixth unit that average product is maximized, since this is where average product is equal to marginal product.

The Costs of Production

FIGURE 6.1 The Total Product Curve

As more units of the variable input labour are used (up to 9 units), total product rises, but the rate of increase slows with the use of the fifth unit of labour. This is the point of diminishing returns. Maximum *total* product of 135 is reached when 9 units of labour are employed (where MP = 0).

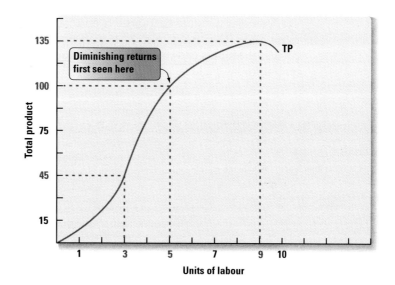

FIGURE 6.2 The Average Product and Marginal Product Curves

As long as the marginal product curve lies above the average product curve, the latter continues to rise. Similarly, if the marginal product curve is below the average product curve, the average declines. Finally, at the point where the marginal product curve intersects the average product curve, the average is at its maximum, which is 20 bushels per unit of labour. Recall that total product is at a maximum when 9 units of labour are being used, which is where MP = 0.

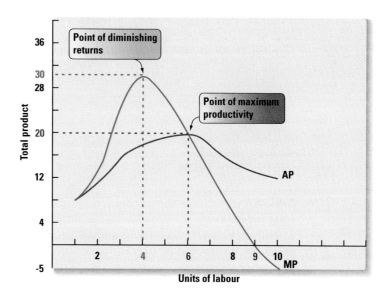

We have now identified three maximums: of total product, which was achieved with the addition of the ninth unit of labour; of marginal product, which was achieved with the addition of the fourth unit of labour; and of average product, which is at a maximum with the sixth unit of labour. So which is the most productive point? When economists use the term most productive or mention *highest productivity*, they are referring to maximum *average* product. This is an engineering concept that refers to the point where the most output *per unit of input* is achieved.

A similar question that involves an economic concept is: what is the best output to produce? The answer is that we have no way of telling without knowledge of the costs of the inputs and the price of the output. We will leave discussion of the price of output for later and take up discussion of the costs of production next.

SELF-TEST

4. Given the data in the table, calculate both the MP_L and the AP_L for each unit of labour used.

Quantity of Labour	Total Output
1	400
2	1000
3	1500
4	1800
5	1900

REVIEW

1. What do we mean by the term *production*?
2. What are *depreciation costs*?
3. Distinguish between *explicit costs* and *implicit costs*.
4. What is the difference between *normal profits* and *economic profits*?
5. What is the *short run*?
6. Identify and define the terms TP, AP, and MP.
7. What is meant by the term *division of labour*?
8. Define the *law of diminishing returns*.

Marginal and Variable Costs

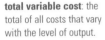

total variable cost: the total of all costs that vary with the level of output.

marginal cost: the increase in total variable costs as a result of producing one more unit of output.

Table 6.4 reproduces the first four columns from Table 6.3 and adds a fifth column, **total variable cost** (TVC), which is the sum of all costs that vary directly with the level of output. Variable costs would normally include the cost of variable inputs, such as materials, power, and labour. However, in our simplified example, we have assumed that labour is the only variable cost. Suppose in our example that labour can be obtained for $100 per unit per day. The figures in the total variable costs column are then obtained by simply multiplying the number of units of labour by $100.

The sixth column introduces the very important concept of the **marginal cost** (MC). Marginal cost is the increase in total variable cost as a result of producing one more unit of output. Ignore the seventh column for the moment.

TABLE 6.4 Cost Data for a Firm

Units of Labour	TP	MP	AP	TVC	MC	AVC
0	0	—	—	0	—	—
1	8	8	8	$100	$12.50	$12.50
2	20	12	10	200	8.33	10.00
3	45	25	15	300	4.00	6.67
4	75	30	18.8	400	3.33	5.33
5	100	25	20	500	4.00	5.00
6	120	20	20	600	5.00	5.00
7	130	10	18.6	700	10.00	5.38
8	135	5	16.9	800	20.00	5.93
9	135	0	15	900	—	6.67
10	130	-5	13	1000	—	7.67

To obtain the value for marginal cost, we need to remember that the definition of marginal cost involves the cost of each additional *unit* of output produced. Therefore, we need to divide the $100 increase in total variable cost, which results from using one more unit of labour, by *marginal product* in order to find the cost of an additional *unit of output* produced. For example, the first unit of labour can produce 8 units at a cost of $100. Each unit therefore costs $100 divided by 8, or $12.50 per unit.

Similarly, the second unit of labour increases total product by (has a marginal product of) 12 at a cost of $100. This yields a marginal cost of $8.33 ($100 divided by 12). The third unit of labour has a marginal product of 25, and therefore the marginal cost of production when three inputs are employed is $4.00, and so on.

In summary, each unit of labour that is hired costs an identical $100. However, the amount of output that each unit produces (MP) is different. The cost of producing additional units of output (the marginal cost) therefore will also vary.

We will see later, in this and subsequent chapters, that this concept of marginal cost is at the centre of a great deal of microeconomics analysis.

The formal definition of marginal cost can be expressed as:

$$MC = \frac{\Delta TVC}{\Delta \text{ output}} \text{ or } \frac{\Delta TVC}{MP}$$

average variable cost: total variable cost divided by total output.

Let's now look at the seventh column of our data in Table 6.4. Here, we have **average variable cost** (AVC), which is simply the total variable cost divided by the total output. Formally, this is:

$$AVC = \frac{TVC}{\text{output}}$$

To illustrate this calculation assume, in Table 6.4, that 8 units of labour were being used, which result in an output of 135 and total variable cost of $800. Dividing the $800 by 135 yields an average variable cost of (approximately) $5.93.

We should point out that the same marginal–average relationship we discussed in reference to the marginal and average product also applies to marginal–average costs. Thus, just as the average product was at a *maximum* when it was equal to marginal product, average variable cost will be at a *minimum* when it is equal to marginal cost. **Figure 6.3**, which uses the data from Table 6.4, will help you understand this.

SELF-TEST

5. A) Assuming that all units of labour cost the same, fill in the blanks in the table.
   B) When is marginal cost at a minimum?
   C) What is the marginal product of labour when four units of labour are used?

Units of Labour	Total Output	TVC	MC	AVC
0	—	—	—	—
1	100	_____	_____	_____
2	220	_____	_____	_____
3	320	_____	_____	_____
4	400	_____	_____	_____
5	460	_____	_____	_____
6	480	1200	_____	_____

FIGURE 6.3 The Marginal Cost and Average Variable Cost Curves

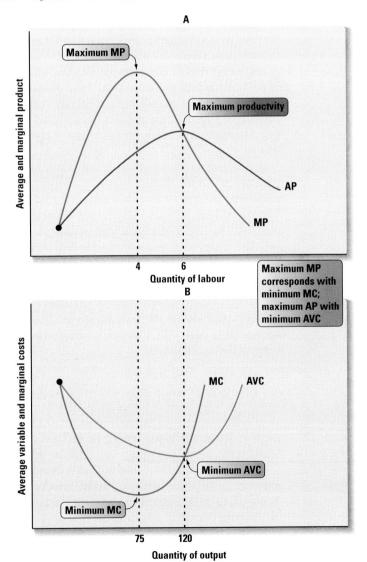

In 6.3A the MP curve intersects the AP curve at its maximum point when 6 units of labour are being used. In 6.3B the MC curve intersects the AVC curve at its minimum, which occurs at an output of 120. This is the output that 6 units of labour can produce.

In Figure 6.3A you see the marginal product and average product curves. They are, roughly, two inverse-U-shaped curves with the marginal product curve intersecting the average product curve at the latter's *maximum* point. This occurs when six units of labour are being used and is the firm's *most productive* point for this size of plant. Next, look at the graphing of the marginal cost and average variable cost curves in Figure 6.3B. What you see there are two U-shaped curves, with marginal cost intersecting average variable cost at the latter's *minimum* point. This is at an output of 120, which is the output that six units of labour are able to produce. In short, when the average product of the variable *input* is at a maximum, the average variable cost will be at its minimum. It is also true that when the marginal product is at a maximum, marginal costs will be at a minimum.

As mentioned above, this is not a coincidence. Average variable cost and marginal cost are upside-down images of average product and marginal product. That is to say:

> **Variable costs of production are a reflection of productivity.**

This is what lies behind the observation that an increase in productivity is equivalent to a decrease in costs.

Earlier in this chapter we talked about how the advantages of the division of labour and the law of diminishing returns gave the marginal product curve its inverse-U shape. We can now apply these same ideas to costs and say that the marginal cost curve initially declines because of the production advantages gained by the division of labour and later rises as these advantages are outweighed by the law of diminishing returns. This is a basic law of production:

> **As long as at least one input is fixed, an increase in output eventually means an increase in both marginal and average costs.**

Total Costs and Average Total Costs

total fixed costs: costs that do not vary with the level of output.

We have established the fundamental relationship between productivity and costs. Our next step is to complete our discussion of costs by reminding ourselves that, in the short run, any production process involves at least one fixed factor, and we therefore need to add the concept of fixed cost to our analysis. **Total fixed costs**, in contrast to variable costs, do not vary with the level of output. In fact, fixed costs are the same regardless of whether output is 0, 100, 1000, or 100 000. Examples of fixed costs would include a long-term lease, a business licence, or an insurance policy.

We are now going to introduce a new set of figures, which are those experienced by Rosemary, who runs a small pottery business out of her home. Rosemary faces very low fixed costs because she is able to rent kiln time at the local school. Notice that the new data in **Table 6.5** below (unlike Table 6.4) shows what happens to costs as we increase *output* one unit at a time rather than investigating the effects of increasing *inputs* one unit at a time. This will make our calculations much easier.

TABLE 6.5 The Complete Table of Costs

Output (per week)	TVC	AVC	MC	TFC	AFC	TC	ATC
0	—	—	—	$30	—	$30	—
1	$20	$20.00	$20	30	$30.00	50	$50.00
2	28	14.00	8	30	15.00	58	29.00
3	42	14.00	14	30	10.00	72	24.00
4	60	15.00	18	30	7.50	90	22.50
5	82	16.40	22	30	6.00	112	22.40
6	110	18.33	28	30	5.00	140	23.33
7	148	21.14	38	30	4.28	178	25.43
8	198	24.75	50	30	3.75	228	28.50

average fixed cost: total fixed cost divided by the quantity of output.

The first column is simply the output (or total product) per week of the large vases in which Rosemary specializes. Columns two, three, and four have been explained. The fifth column is the total fixed cost which, in this example, we assume to be $30 per week. Next, we have **average fixed costs** (AFC), which are simply:

$$AFC = \frac{TFC}{output}$$

total cost: the sum of both total variable cost and total fixed cost.

Notice that average fixed cost declines continuously as output rises. To obtain **total cost** (TC), we simply do a summation:

$$TC = TVC + TFC$$

Total cost rises continuously as output rises, and the *rate* of rise also begins to increase once diminishing returns set in.

average total cost: total cost divided by quantity of output.

Finally, **average total cost** (ATC) is:

$$ATC = \frac{TC}{output}$$

Also note that since we know that:

$$TC = TVC + TFC$$

it then follows that:

$$ATC = AVC + AFC$$

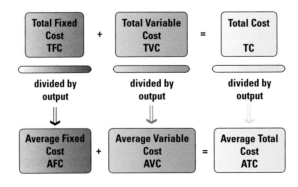

SELF-TEST

6. Fill in the blanks in the table below.

Output (per day)	TC	TVC	AVC	TFC	AFC	ATC	MC
0	$200	—	—	—	—	—	—
1	280						
2	340						
3	420						
4	520						
5	640						
6	780						

The relationship between marginal cost and *average variable* cost that we stressed earlier in this chapter also applies to the interaction between marginal cost and *average total* cost. As long as marginal cost is below average total cost, average total cost will fall (as it does for the first five units of output in Table 6.5). But as soon as marginal cost rises above average total cost, the latter will begin to rise. Given this basic relationship, it is also true that the marginal cost curve will intersect the average total cost curve at the latter's minimum point. This can be seen at point *b* in **Figure 6.4.**

FIGURE 6.4 The MC, ATC, AVC, and AFC Curves

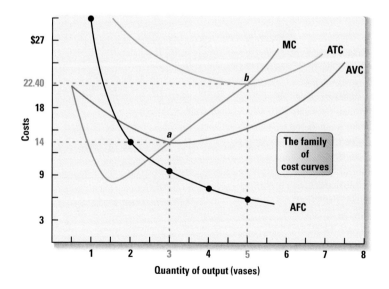

The U-shaped marginal cost curve intersects the average variable cost curve at its minimum point (*a*), which is an output of 3 units and a cost of $14. It also intersects the average total cost curve at its minimum point (*b*), which is 5 units and $22.40. The average fixed cost curve declines continuously.

Using this figure as a visual representation, let's pull things together:

- The U-shaped marginal cost curve reflects the advantages of the division of labour as it declines, and then, as it rises, the law of diminishing returns.
- Marginal cost is initially below the average variable cost curve and the average total cost curve but then rises above each of these, which explains their basic U shape.

- The marginal cost curve intersects the average variable cost curve at its minimum point and the average total cost curve at its minimum point.
- The average fixed cost curve continuously declines.

Let's now focus on point *a*, the minimum point of the average variable cost curve. Note that this occurs at an output of three vases. Since the average variable cost curve is an upside down image of the average product curve, we know that the average product curve must be at its maximum. Next, notice that the minimum point on the average total cost curve is at an output of five vases (point *b*). Comparing these two points enables us to emphasize that the most productive point, where average product is at a maximum, is *not* the lowest-cost point, where average total cost is at a minimum. This is simply a reflection of the fact that fixed costs are part of average total costs, but they are not part of average variable costs.

Figure 6.5 is a graphing of the total cost (TC), total variable cost (TVC), and total fixed cost (TFC) curves. The TVC curve starts at the origin because variable costs are zero when output is zero and rises slowly at first (reflecting declining average variable cost) but then more quickly later (reflecting rising average variable cost). The TC curve starts at $30 because total fixed costs are equal to this level even when output is zero. The TFC curve starts at the same $30 and does not vary with output.

FIGURE 6.5 The TC, TVC, and TFC Curves

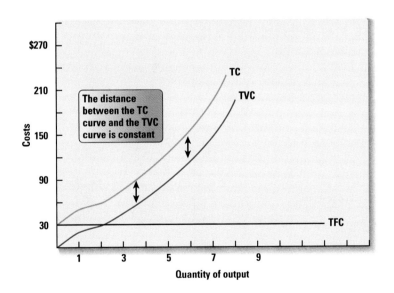

The total cost curve begins at $30 (the amount of fixed cost) and rises from there. The total variable cost curve starts at the origin since variable cost is zero when there is no output. The total fixed cost curve is horizontal, reflecting the fact that the fixed cost of $30 does not vary with output. The difference between the TC and TVC is this constant $30.

Let's now ask how many vases per week Rosemary would want to produce. The lowest ATC is achieved when she produces five a week. Would she ever choose to produce six, seven, or even more? We hope you can see that the answer to this question depends on how much she gets for each vase when she sells them. Putting what we have now learned about costs together with revenue analysis, which will come later, will eventually allow us to get to an answer to the question of what is the best output.

Can Cost Fall in the Short Run?

There is a great deal of discussion in today's media about the need for firms to "cut costs." Unfortunately this phrase is, by itself, ambiguous. A firm can always cut *total* cost by decreasing output. But surely this is not what is meant by the urgent calls for reductions in costs. It seems likely that when firms are planning to cut costs, what they intend is a reduction in *average* costs rather than total costs. But first, we need to make one point clear. Our presentation of costs so far is based on the assumption that the firm is already producing at the lowest possible cost *for each output level*. In other words, it is producing efficiently. Given this, is it possible for average costs to get any lower? Yes, if the firm is able to buy its inputs cheaper. The firm often has little control over the prices of the inputs it buys, but these prices can and do change from time to time. It is possible that the price of either the fixed or the variable inputs might change. Let us consider the effect of a decrease in the price of a variable input.

In graphical terms, such a decrease would shift down the marginal, average variable, and average total cost curves. We will isolate in our analysis only the average total and the marginal cost curves in **Figure 6.6** to illustrate such a shift.

FIGURE 6.6 A Shift in the Marginal and Average Total Cost Curves

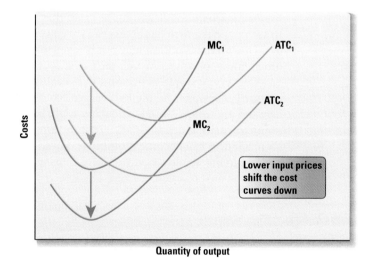

The shift down in the marginal cost curve from MC_1 to MC_2 and in the accompanying average total cost curve—ATC_1 to ATC_2—is the result of input prices decreasing.

In Figure 6.6 the marginal cost curve shifts down as a result of a decrease in the input price of the variable input such that the minimum point of the curve occurs at a lower dollar cost and at a higher level of output. There is also a corresponding shift in the average total cost curve. We have not shown the average variable cost curve, but if we had it too would shift down. The basic shape of the curves remains unchanged, however, since the law of diminishing returns still applies. Would the average fixed cost curve also shift down? Only if the price of the fixed input(s) decreased. Similarly, the curves would shift up if input prices increased.

There is another possibility that we need to mention. Recall that the marginal cost of output is determined by the marginal product of the factor inputs. What if marginal product were to increase? This would decrease marginal cost, which would pull both average variable and average total cost down as well. And what might cause this increase in productivity leading to a decrease in costs? It might be as simple as a firm replacing, within the same plant, older inefficient machines with newer, more efficient ones. Even something as simple as a new photocopying machine might make the small staff in a law firm more productive. We do need to be careful with this analysis, however, since we are getting very close to a discussion of technological change, and applying new technology often involves a new size of plant—that is a subject of the long run, which we will deal with in the next chapter. We can say, however, that if the marginal product of a productive process increases, then the cost of production will decrease, even in the short run.

If neither resource prices nor productivity change, is there any other way that it can reduce average costs? Certainly, this will *not* be possible if the firm is producing the output that results in the lowest average cost. Such an output level is defined by economists as **economic capacity**. Graphically this simply means the lowest point on the average total cost curve. This level of output does not, however, imply maximum physical capacity. This is because most production processes probably reach minimum average total cost at about 75–80 percent of physical capacity.

Would firms ever want to operate at an output that is less than economic capacity output? No, they would not want to, but firms are sometimes forced to reduce output because of market conditions. The consequences of this are illustrated in **Figure 6.7**. In Figure 6.7 we assume that market conditions have forced this firm to choose an output of Q_2 with average total costs of ATC_2, which are higher than they would be at economic capacity (ATC_1). This is what economists describe as **excess capacity**, defined as the situation in which the firm's output is less than economic capacity. Excess capacity is inefficient in the sense that average total costs are not at a minimum. In summary, if a firm has excess capacity, average costs could be cut by *increasing* output. However, this option may not be available to the firm if it does not have sufficient orders for its product. We will refer to this concept again in Chapter 11.

Conversely, would firms want to operate at an output level above this capacity, say output Q3, despite the higher average cost? Perhaps in the short run they would, if demand and prices were particularly high, but no firm wants to produce above economic capacity indefinitely. The cost in terms of overtime pay and the wear and tear on machinery can become prohibitive. Given this, it is likely that the firm will soon be looking to move into larger premises. This is what we mean by the long run, the subject of the next chapter.

economic capacity: that output at which average total cost is at a minimum.

excess capacity: the situation in which a firm's output is below economic capacity.

FIGURE 6.7 A Firm Experiencing Excess Capacity

If market conditions force a firm to operate at output level Q_2, then its average total costs (ATC_2) will be higher than they would be if the firm operated at economic capacity (Q_1). Similarly, a firm will have a higher average cost if it is operating above economic capacity, such as Q_3.

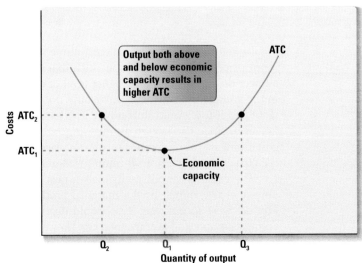

Output both above and below economic capacity results in higher ATC

ATC

ATC_2

ATC_1

Economic capacity

Costs

Q_2 Q_1 Q_3

Quantity of output

SELF-TEST

Inputs	Total Output	TC_1	MC_1	ATC_1	TC_2	MC_2	ATC_2
1	0	$150	—	—	—	—	—
2	10	175	___	___	___	___	___
3	25	200	___	___	___	___	___
4	35	225	___	___	___	___	___
5	40	250	___	___	___	___	___
6	40	275	___	___	___	___	___

7. A) Fill in the blanks in the MC_1 and ATC_1 columns above.
   B) Assuming that the price of the input decreases by 20 percent, fill in the TC_2, MC_2, and ATC_2 columns.
8. Given the accompanying graph:
   A) At what output is MP at a maximum?
   B) At what output is AP at a maximum?
   C) At what output is ATC at a minimum?
   D) What is the most productive output?
   E) What output is economic capacity?
   F) When output is 250, what does *ab* represent?

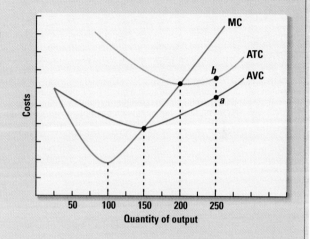

REVIEW

1. Identify and define TVC, MC, and AVC.
2. Write a mathematical expression for marginal cost and average variable cost.
3. What is the relationship between the AP/MP curves and the AVC/MC curves?
4. What are *fixed* costs?
5. How would you calculate AFC?
6. Which curves are affected by an increase in the price of variable inputs? The price of fixed inputs?
7. What is *capacity output*?
8. What is *excess capacity*?

STUDY GUIDE

Chapter Highlights

The focus of this chapter was on the crucial relationship between the productivity of the factors of production (inputs) and the costs of production. Productivity involves the output of the final product that results from using various amounts of factor inputs. Costs involve the dollar amount that is incurred in producing that output.

1. The chapter begins by making the distinction between:
   - explicit cost;
   - implicit cost;

   and this distinction leads to the definitions of:
   - normal profit;
   - economic profit.

2. Total product (output) is the end result of *adding inputs* to the production process and from this we get:

$$MP_L = \frac{\Delta TP}{\Delta L}$$

$$AP_L = \frac{TP}{L}$$

3. Advantages gained from the *division of labour* explains why:
   - MP initially rises as more inputs are used;

   while the *law of diminishing returns* explains why:
   - MP eventually declines as even more units of input are used.

4. AP will:
   - rise if MP is above it;
   - fall if MP is below it.

5. *Total variable cost* is the dollar amount of variable inputs incurred in producing output and from this we get:

$$MC = \frac{\Delta TVC}{\Delta \text{ output}} = \frac{\Delta TVC}{MP}$$

$$AVC = \frac{TVC}{\text{output}}$$

6. Two very important *relationships* are:
   - MP is at a maximum when (the number of inputs being used are able to produce an output where) MC is at a minimum;

- AP is at a maximum when (the number of inputs being used are able to produce an output where) AVC is at a minimum.

7. *Total cost* is:

$$TC \quad = \quad TVC \quad + \quad TFC$$

and from this we get:

$$AFC = \frac{TFC}{output} \; ; \qquad ATC = \frac{TC}{output}$$

and:

$$ATC \quad = \quad AVC \quad + \quad AFC$$

8. Graphically, the *MC curve* is U-shaped and intersects:
   - the AVC curve at its minimum;
   - the ATC curve at its minimum.

9. MC, AVC, and ATC *decrease* (and, graphically their respective curves shift down) if:
   - input prices fall;
   - productivity increases.

10. *Economic capacity* is always below physical capacity and occurs when ATC are at a minimum.

New Glossary Terms and Key Equations

Equations:

1. Total economic profit $(T\pi)$ = total revenue (TR) − total costs (TC)

2. $$MP_L = \frac{\Delta TP}{\Delta L}$$

3. $$AP_L = \frac{TP}{L}$$

4. $$MC = \frac{\Delta TVC}{\Delta\ output} \quad or \quad \frac{\Delta TVC}{MP}$$

5. $$AVC = \frac{TVC}{output}$$

6. $$AFC = \frac{TFC}{output}$$

7. $$ATC = \frac{TC}{output}$$

8. $$TC = TVC + TFC$$

9. $$ATC = AVC + AFC$$

Study Tips

1. There are many new terms and definitions for you to learn in this chapter—probably more than in any other chapter. None of the terms are complex, however, so you should be able to handle them if you simply learn a few at a time.

2. Students usually find the distinction between explicit costs and implicit costs quite straightforward but get a little puzzled over how these concepts tie in with normal and economic profits. Simply remember that if both explicit and implicit costs are being covered, then the firm is earning a normal profit. Revenues in excess of explicit and implicit costs result in economic profits.

3. Two of the more important concepts in the whole of microeconomics are the division of labour and the law of diminishing returns. They are used in this chapter to explain the relationship between the use of factors of production and their productivity. Once you understand marginal and average productivity, you can understand marginal and average variable cost. This is crucial and is, therefore, the focus of the Key Problem.

4. Adding fixed cost and average total cost to the analysis is quite straightforward. Once this is done, a graph like that found in Figure 6.4 can be constructed. Here is a prime example of the phrase "a picture is worth a thousand words."

5. Always remember that the amount of total cost when output is zero is the total fixed cost that the firm faces.

6. We hear a great deal about the importance of firms cutting their costs. Just what is meant by this phrase is ambiguous. A firm can always cut its total cost by reducing output, and it might be able to decrease its average cost by changing its output level. The only unambiguous way "cutting costs" makes sense is as a reduction of marginal and average cost *at each level of output*. This is illustrated graphically by a downward shift in the two curves.

7. The introduction of the concepts of economic capacity and excess capacity in this chapter provide a springboard into the discussion of long-run costs, which is the focus of the next chapter.

Are You Sure?

Indicate whether the following statements are true or false. If false, indicate why they are false.

1. Marginal cost equals average variable cost when the latter is minimized.

   T or **F**   If false: _____

   _____

2. Depreciation is the annual cost of any asset that is expected to be in use for more than one year.

   T or **F**   If false: _____

   _____

3. Implicit costs are the amounts actually paid out in money.

   T or **F**   If false: _____

   _____

4. Sunk costs are the historical costs of an asset that has no current resale value.

   T or **F**   If false: _____

   _____

5. If a firm is making economic profits, then it must also be making normal profits.

   T or **F**   If false: _____

   _____

6. The short run is any period of time in which at least two inputs are fixed.

   T or **F**   If false: _____

   _____

7. Marginal product is the increase in total product as a result of adding one more unit of output.

   T or **F**   If false: _____

   _____

8. Total product and total output are the same thing.

   T or **F**   If false: _____

   _____

9. The division of labour is the dividing of the production process into a series of specialized tasks, each done by a different worker.

   T or **F**   If false: _____

   _____

10. The short run is a period of time in which the output is fixed.

    T or **F**   If false: _____

    _____

Choose the Best

11. Which of the following statements about the MP of labour is correct?
    a) It may either rise or fall as more labour is used.
    b) It always falls as more labour is used.

12. Which of the following statements about marginal cost is correct?
    a) It is always below average costs.
    b) It can be either above or below average costs.

13. Which of the following statements is true about the average product of labour?
    a) It is equal to total output divided by the quantity of labour inputs used.
    b) It is equal to the increase in total output divided by the quantity of labour used.

14. Which of the statements below is true about the marginal product of labour?
    a) It is total output divided by the quantity of labour used.
    b) It is the increase in total output resulting from the use of one more unit of labour.
    c) It is the increase in total output divided by the quantity of labour used.

15. What is the sum of the marginal costs of all of the units produced?
    a) Total cost.
    b) Average cost.
    c) Total variable cost.

16. What is average fixed cost?
    a) It is all the costs that do not vary with the level of output.
    b) It is total cost less total variable cost.
    c) It is total fixed cost divided by the level of output.

17. What is the sum of total variable costs and total fixed costs?
    a) It is equal to the sum of average product and marginal product.
    b) It is the sum of all marginal costs.
    c) It is total cost.

18. All the items below are explicit costs, *except one*. Which is the exception?
    a) The weekly cost of a lease on a building.
    b) The total wages paid each week.
    c) The monthly hydro bill.
    d) The wages withdrawn by the owner each week.

19. Which of the following conditions is necessary in order to consider a cost a sunk cost?
    a) It must have occurred over six months ago.
    b) It must have occurred as a result of the purchase of a fixed asset.
    c) It must have occurred as a result of the purchase of a fixed asset and have no resale value.
    d) It must have occurred as a result of the purchase of a fixed asset and be fully paid for.

20. Which of the following statements is true about the division of labour?
    a) It causes the marginal product of labour to increase, but it has no effect on the average product of labour.
    b) It was first thought of by David Ricardo in his example of a hat factory.
    c) It is an idea that has little application in the real world.
    d) Its application results in both the marginal and average product of labour increasing.

21. What is significant about the level of output at which marginal product begins to decline?
    a) It is the point of maximum average product.
    b) It is the point of minimum average cost.
    c) It is the point at which the division of labour begins.
    d) It is the point at which diminishing returns begins.

22. What will happen to total product after the point of diminishing returns has been reached?
    a) It will continue to rise until marginal product becomes zero.
    b) It will continue to rise until marginal product begins to decline.
    c) It will begin to fall.
    d) It will start to rise for the first time.

23. What is the significance of the maximum point on the total product curve?
    a) It is the point where the increase in output begins to slow down.
    b) It is the point where diminishing returns sets in.
    c) It is the point of maximum marginal product.
    d) It is the point where marginal product becomes zero.

24. If marginal product is declining, which of the following statements is correct?
    a) Average product must be falling.
    b) Average product could be rising or falling.
    c) Marginal cost must be falling.
    d) Average variable cost must be rising.
    e) Average variable cost must be falling.

25. What do economists mean by the term "the most productive output"?
    a) The output where total product is at a maximum.
    b) The output where average product is at a maximum.
    c) The output where marginal product is at a maximum.
    d) The output where marginal cost is at a minimum.
    e) The output where average total cost is at a minimum.

26. Which of the following statements regarding total fixed costs is correct?
    a) When total fixed costs are graphed, the curve will rise from the origin at a constant rate.
    b) When total fixed costs are graphed, the curve will be horizontal.
    c) Total fixed costs equal total variable costs less total average costs.
    d) Total fixed costs rise slowly at first, but then more quickly as output increases.
    e) Total fixed costs equal total marginal costs plus total variable costs.

27. If we assume that the level of output remains unchanged, which of the following could cause a decrease in average total, average variable, and marginal costs?
    a) A decrease in the price of the variable factor.
    b) An increase in the price of the variable factor.
    c) An increase in the firm's capacity output.
    d) A decrease in the firm's capacity output.
    e) A decrease in the firm's fixed cost.

28. All of the following statements, *except one*, are correct. Which is the exception?
    a) If the marginal cost curve shifts down, then the average total cost curve will also shift down.
    b) If the marginal cost curve shifts down, then the average variable cost curve will also shift down.
    c) The average fixed cost curve will be unaffected by a shift in the marginal cost curve.
    d) If the marginal product curve shifts up, then the marginal cost curve will shift up.
    e) If the marginal product curve shifts up, then the average product curve will shift up.

29. How do economists define capacity output?
    a) The maximum physical output possible.
    b) The output that maximizes total cost.
    c) The output that maximizes total product.
    d) The output that minimizes marginal cost.
    e) The output that minimizes average total cost.

30. Which of the following statements would be true about a firm that is operating under conditions of excess capacity?
    a) The firm's average total cost would be at a minimum.
    b) The firm's average total cost would not be at a minimum.
    c) The firm's average total cost may or may not be at a minimum, but the firm would not be at capacity output.
    d) The firm would not be at capacity output, but its average total cost would be at a minimum.
    e) The firm would need to reduce output to achieve minimum average total cost.

Simple Calculations

31. Given the following information calculate total profit: a) according to an accountant and b) according to an economist:

Explicit costs: $79 500   Total revenue: 117 500
Implicit costs: $18 000
(including normal profits)

a) Accountant: _____ ;   b) Economist: _____ .

32. The following table shows the total product for a firm. Complete the average and marginal products.

Units of labour	0	1	2	3	4	5	6	7
Total product	0	12	30	54	68	80	84	78
Average product								
Marginal product								

33. The following table shows the total fixed and variable costs of a firm. Complete the table.

Output	1	2	3	4	5	6	7	8
TFC	1200	1200	1200	1200	1200	1200	1200	1200
TVC	400	600	720	800	1500	3000	5250	8000
TC								
AFC								
AVC								
ATC								
MC								

Problems

34. David recently graduated with a B.A. in economics and was offered a job with a large company which would have paid $36 000 per year. At about the same time, David's grandfather died and left him an inheritance of $40 000. David decided to pass up the job, and using $30 000 from the inheritance, he purchased a tool rental business. (David put the other $10 000 into a savings account that pays 6 percent per year interest.) He put his full effort into the new business, and in the first three months of operation he had total sales revenues of $25 600 and total explicit costs of $12 400. What was David's economic profit or loss for the three months?

35. a) Complete **Table 6.6** for Louis Inc.

TABLE 6.6

Output	TFC	TVC	TC	AFC	AVC	ATC	MC
0	$60	_____	_____	—	—	—	—
1	_____	_____	_____	_____	_____	_____	45
2	_____	_____	145	_____	_____	_____	_____
3	_____	_____	_____	_____	_____	_____	35
4	_____	_____	_____	_____	_____	_____	30
5	_____	185	_____	_____	_____	_____	_____
6	_____	_____	_____	_____	_____	_____	40
7	_____	_____	_____	_____	_____	_____	45
8	_____	325	_____	_____	_____	_____	_____
9	_____	_____	_____	_____	_____	_____	65
10	_____	_____	525	_____	_____	_____	_____

b) At what level of output is average product at a maximum?

Answer: _____.

c) What is average total cost at this output?

Answer: _____.

d) If fixed costs were to double, what would be the marginal cost of the fifth unit of output?

Answer: _____.

e) What is the level of economic capacity?

Answer: _____.

36. a) Fill in the blank columns in **Table 6.7** for the firm Bannister Railings, assuming that the cost of variable inputs decreases by 50 percent.

TABLE 6.7

Output	TVC_1	TVC_2	AVC_1	AVC_2	MC_1	MC_2
1	$44	_____	$44.00	_____	$44.00	_____
2	64	_____	32.00	_____	20.00	_____
3	78	_____	26.00	_____	14.00	_____
4	88	_____	22.00	_____	10.00	_____
5	100	_____	20.00	_____	12.00	_____
6	120	_____	20.00	_____	20.00	_____
7	150	_____	21.42	_____	30.00	_____
8	200	_____	25.00	_____	50.00	_____

b) Draw AVC_1, MC_1, AVC_2, and MC_2 on the grid in **Figure 6.8**.

FIGURE 6.8

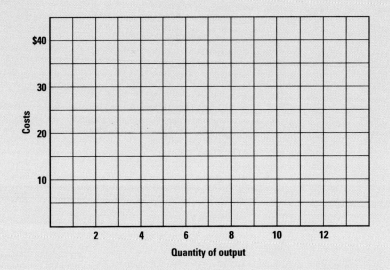

37. **a)** On Figure 6.9, draw AVC, AFC, and ATC curves that have the following characteristics:
    –AVC is $30 and AFC is $20 when output is 10.
    –AVC declines $5 for every increase in output of 10, up to a output of 50.
    –Above output levels of 50, AVC rises $5 for every increase in output of 10.
    b) What is the level of economic capacity?

    Answer: _____ .

    c) What is the most productive output?

    Answer: _____ .

FIGURE 6.9

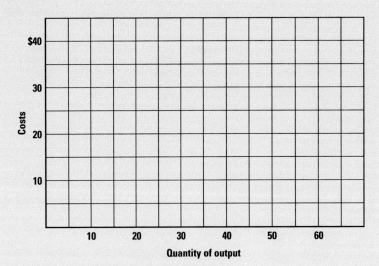

Translations

Explain the graph in **Figure 6.10** in words.

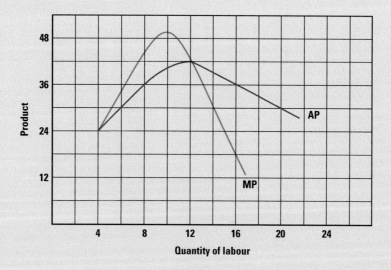

FIGURE 6.10

Key Problem

Last summer Daniel started the Custom Made Fencing Company, which specializes in building fences to meet the specific needs of his customers. Since Daniel works out of his parents' basement, uses an old pick-up, and needs only a few simple tools, his fixed costs are minimal. He measures the firm's output in terms of the number of feet per day of fence that is built. Experience has shown Daniel that different crew sizes can build fences as shown in **Table 6.8**.

TABLE 6.8

Number of Workers in Crew	TP_L (feet per day)	MP_L (feet per day)	AP_L (feet per day)
1	20	_____	_____
2	80	_____	_____
3	150	_____	_____
4	200	_____	_____
5	230	_____	_____
6	246	_____	_____

a) Fill in the marginal and average product of labour columns in the table above.

b) On the graph in **Figure 6.11**, draw the two curves.

FIGURE 6.11

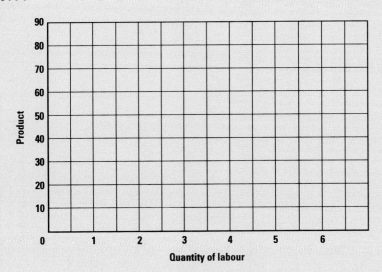

c) Assuming that each worker costs $240 a day (wages and materials), fill in **Table 6.9.**

TABLE 6.9

Number of Workers in Crew	TP (feet per day)	TVC (feet per day)	AVC (feet per day)	MC (feet per day)
1	20	_____	_____	_____
2	80	_____	_____	_____
3	150	_____	_____	_____
4	200	_____	_____	_____
5	230	_____	_____	_____
6	246	_____	_____	_____

d) On the graph in **Figure 6.12**, draw the average variable and marginal cost curves.

FIGURE 6.12

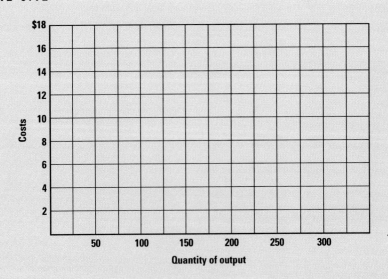

e) Looking back at Figure 6.11, determine how many workers are used to achieve maximum average product. (Remember that the definition of maximum AP is where it equals MP.)

Answer: _____ .

f) What output can this number of workers produce?

Answer: _____ .

g) Now, from Figure 6.12, what is true at the output level you gave as your answer in f)?

Answer: _____ .

h) Return to Table 6.8 and, this time, determine how many workers are used to achieve maximum marginal product.

Answer: _____ .

i) What output can this number of workers produce?

Answer: _____ .

j) Look at Figure 6.12 again and determine what is true at the output level you gave as your answer in i).

Answer: _____ .

k) What conclusion can you make from your answers in e) through j)?

More of the Same

Table 6.10 provides some data for the output of sugar beets (tonnes per year) in the agriculturally rich land of Marino.

TABLE 6.10

Quantity of Labour	Total Output	MP_L	AP_L
1	200	_____	_____
2	600	_____	_____
3	900	_____	_____
4	1,000	_____	_____
5	1,040	_____	_____

a) Fill in the marginal and average product of labour columns in Table 6.10.

b) On the graph in **Figure 6.13**, draw the two curves.

FIGURE 6.13

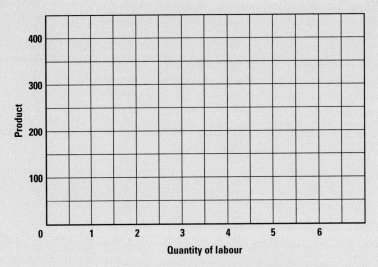

c) Assuming that each worker costs $160 a day (for wages and materials), fill in **Table 6.11**.

TABLE 6.11

Quantity of Labour	Total Output	TVC	AVC	MC
1	200	____	____	____
2	600	____	____	____
3	900	____	____	____
4	1000	____	____	____
5	1040	____	____	____

d) On the graph in **Figure 6.14**, draw the average variable and marginal cost curves.

e) Looking back at Figure 6.13, determine how many workers are used to achieve maximum average product.

FIGURE 6.14

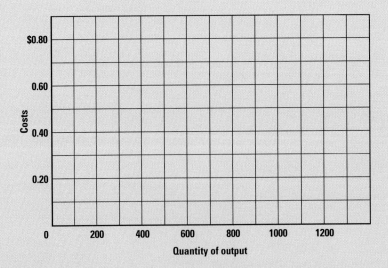

f) From Table 6.11, what output can this number of workers produce?

g) Now, from Figure 6.14, what is true at the output level you gave as your answer in f)?

h) Return to Figure 6.13 and, this time, determine how many workers are used to achieve maximum marginal product.

i) From Table 6.11, what output can this number of workers produce?

j) Look at Figure 6.14 again and determine what is true at the output level you gave as your answer in i).

k) Does this exercise verify the conclusion that you reached in answer k) of the Key Problem?

UNANSWERED QUESTIONS

Short Essays

1. To an economist, costs include profit. Discuss.

2. Comment on the following statement: "If a firm wants to cut costs, it must first increase productivity."

3. Explain the difference between an explicit cost and an implicit cost.

4. What is the most productive output level for a firm to produce? Why would it ever produce less than this output?

5. What is the meaning of the term *economic capacity*? Does it represent the maximum output that the firm can produce?

6. Comment on the following statement: "A decrease in the prices of factor inputs makes a firm more productive."

Analytical Questions

7. Which of the following are fixed costs, and which are variable costs?
    a) Utilities expenses such as power, heat, and light.
    b) The set-up costs for a computerized payroll accounting system.
    c) Production cost for materials and supplies.
    d) Production staff wages.
    e) Leasehold costs for the firm's land and buildings.
    f) The cost of a one-minute TV advertisement for six minutes per week over the next three months.
    g) Supervisory staff salaries.

8. Suppose you and a friend are thinking of going into the business of home delivery of rented videos. You plan on obtaining the videos from an existing video store, with whom you have made arrangements to pay $3 each for the videos you plan to deliver. Can you think of three fixed costs and three variable cost associated with this business idea?

9. What is the cost for the Toronto Maple Leafs to give a local boys' club 50 free tickets to a hockey game? Does it matter for what game the tickets are offered?

10. Make a list of what you consider to be the explicit costs of a college providing parking spaces for faculty and students on land that it owns. Is there an implicit cost in providing the spaces?

11. It has been observed that all the members of peasant families in Third World countries often work intensively on small pieces of land. What do you think the MP_L is in these cases? Is this rational?

12. Assume that you paid, in advance, $400 tuition for a course in microeconomics.
    a) What is the cost of sleeping in and missing one of the lectures?
    b) How would you answer a) if the tuition was $200?
    c) How would you answer a) if tuition was free?

13. Suppose that the Innovative Cab Company announced that in the future its rates within the downtown area of Vancouver would be half price on all sunny days. Is this pricing decision related to the firm's cost of production? Is it related to the opportunity costs of cab users?

Numerical Questions

14. a) Complete Table 6.12 for Landry Ltd.

TABLE 6.12

Number of Workers	Total Product	Average Product	Marginal Product
0	0	—	—
1	1	___	___
2	3	___	___
3	___	2	___
4	___	___	4
5	15	___	___
6	___	3	___
7	___	___	2
8	21	___	___
9	___	___	−2

    b) How many workers are being used when the point of diminishing returns first begins?
    c) How many workers are being used when total product is at a maximum?
    d) What is the most productive point?

15. The data in Table 6.13 are for the Steady Stitch Sewing Company. The quantities are for the number of women's wool suits per day.

TABLE 6.13

Quantity	Total Cost
0	$200
1	240
2	260
3	300
4	360
5	440
6	560

    a) What is the level of fixed cost?
    b) What is the marginal cost of the fifth suit produced?
    c) What is the total variable cost of producing three suits?
    d) What is the average total cost of producing four suits?

16. Figure 6.15 is for the Grow 'Em Right Nursery company.

FIGURE 6.15

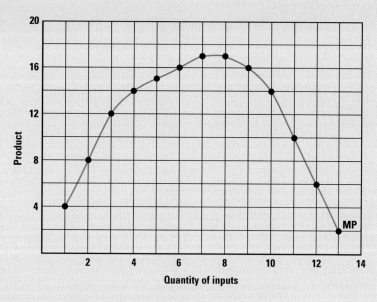

a) Calculate Grow 'Em Right's total product and average product.
b) Add the AP curve to the graph above.
c) What is the value of maximum AP?

17. Table 6.14 shows data for Big Bob's Brewing Company. The quantities are for large vats of beer.

Fill in the blanks in the table.

TABLE 6.14

Quantity	TFC	TVC	TC	MC	AFC	AVC	ATC
1	$210	___	___	$100	___	___	___
2	___	___	___	60	___	___	___
3	___	___	___	50	___	___	___
4	___	___	___	80	___	___	___
5	___	___	___	100	___	___	___
6	___	___	___	126	___	___	___
7	___	___	___	156	___	___	___
8	___	___	___	190	___	___	___
9	___	___	___	242	___	___	___
10	___	___	___	296	___	___	___
11	___	___	___	381	___	___	___
12	___	___	___	529	___	___	___

18. A firm has the choice of two different technologies to produce its product. The first technology has total fixed costs of $50 and a constant marginal cost of $10. The second technology has a total fixed cost of $100 and a constant marginal cost of $5. Draw the ATC curve for both technologies on the same graph, using quantities of 1 through 12 on the horizontal axis. At what levels of output is it better to use the high-fixed-cost technology, and at what levels would it be better to use the low-fixed-cost technology?

19. **Table 6.15** gives data for a firm named Crystal Clear Speech Writing Services. Fill in the blanks in the table.

TABLE 6.15

Quantity	AFC	AVC	ATC	MC	TVC	TC
1	___	___	___	40	___	___
2	___	___	___	___	70	___
3	___	___	90	___	___	___
4	40	___	___	___	___	320
5	___	___	___	70	___	___
6	___	55	___	___	___	___
7	___	___	___	___	480	___
8	___	___	___	___	___	840

20. Suppose the following data describes the cost data of a furniture manufacturer named Don's Legacy.
   a) Complete **Table 6.16** by assuming that labour costs $10 an hour.
   b) Describe the shapes of the AFC, AVC, and ATC curves.
   c) What is the most productive output? What are AVC and ATC at this quantity?
   d) What is capacity output?

TABLE 6.16

Output of Tables	Total Hours	Average Hours per Table	Marginal Hours per Table	TVC($)	AVC($)	TFC($)	TC($)	ATC($)	MC($)
1	40	___	___	___	___	$600	___	___	___
2	70	___	___	___	___	___	___	___	___
3	95	___	___	___	___	___	___	___	___
4	120	___	___	___	___	___	___	___	___
5	160	___	___	___	___	___	___	___	___
6	210	___	___	___	___	___	___	___	___

 ## Web-Based Activities

1. Visit **www.agr.ca/pfra/sidcpub/sidpub4.htm**. Select an agricultural product from the list found in the article. In your opinion, have the authors estimated all of the explicit and implicit costs of production? Explain.
   For spearmint production, what is the average total cost, average variable cost, and average fixed costs of production? Given your calculations, sketch a diagram that illustrates the costs of production as well as where the marginal cost curve lies in relation to the average cost curves.

2. Suppose you are thinking of going into soybean farming. But before you can decide, you need to do some research into the profitability of soybean farming. Visit **www.ag.uiuc.edu/~stratsoy/97soystats/pg2.html** and develop a profile of the soybean industry. Include in your profile total explicit and implicit costs as well as an estimate of economic profits.

Costs in the Long Run

What's ahead...In this chapter we continue the discussion of costs, but now we shift the focus from the short run to the long run. We define what economists mean by the long run and develop the long-run average cost curve. In making this shift, the concepts of returns to scale and economies of scale are introduced, and their crucial role is emphasized in the context of several examples. Finally, we discuss the idea of the right size of firm by looking at the concept of minimum efficient scale.

A QUESTION OF RELEVANCE...

If you think of all the different products that you and I purchase, it's clear that some of them are quite easy to produce, such as tomatoes or cookies or even a birdhouse. Other products, however, involve such complexity that we wouldn't dream of trying to make them for ourselves. Examples of these products include microwave ovens, calculators, or airplanes. Now ask yourself, why is it that something as comparatively simple to make as a cardboard box is produced in giant factories, whereas highly complex computers are produced in small workshops that dot the countrysides of Asian countries? Why, for that matter, aren't furniture factories as big as car assembly plants, or why aren't aluminum smelters as small as dairy plants? The answers to these questions involve the concept of economies of scale, the central theme of this chapter.

long run: the period of
time during which all inputs
are variable.

I n the discussion about the costs of production in the previous chapter, we made the assumption that at least one factor of production was fixed. This is what we referred to as the short run. In contrast, economists define the **long run** as a period of time in which the producing firm has the option of varying all of its inputs. Put another way, in the long run there are no fixed factors of production.

There is a technique to thinking about the long run. You should recognize that at any one *point in time* the firm must always be in the short run. Imagine a factory manager as he steps out of his office onto the shop floor. Are any of the factor inputs used in production fixed? The answer is yes, of course. At least one input, and probably several, would be fixed—the square footage of the plant, or the number of machines, or the quantity of some crucial raw material. Firms are always operating in the short run. Now, imagine our factory manager walking back into his office and closing the door as he sits down to ask himself: where do we want to be in five years? As he proceeds to answer this question, he is able to treat all inputs as variable. He is able to conceptualize the long run. It is in this sense that economists describe the long run as a planning horizon. In summary:

> **All production processes operate in the short run and diminishing marginal productivity is an unavoidable reality.**

> **In the long run there are no fixed factors and diminishing marginal productivity does not apply.**

**long-run average cost
curve**: a graphical
representation of the per
unit costs of production in
the long run.

We now need to elaborate on this very important short-run/long-run distinction by carefully developing the **long-run average cost curve** (LRAC). (Note that for the balance of this chapter we will use the term "average cost" to refer to the short run and "long-run average cost" for the long run.)

We begin this discussion by imagining a firm, called Rising Sun Products Limited, which produces high-quality CDs and operates in a small-sized plant, which we shall call plant 1. Further, we will assume that there are also three other plant sizes available to Rising Sun: plant 2, which is exactly twice the size of plant 1; plant 3, which is exactly three times the size of plant 1; and plant 4, which is exactly four times the size of plant 1. Some short-run average cost data is presented in **Table 7.1**.

Inventory is just one of the costs of
production.

TABLE 7.1 Rising Sun's Plant Size Alternatives

Output of CDs per Day	AC in Plant 1	AC in Plant 2	AC in Plant 3	AC in Plant 4
100	$ 6.00	$ 7.00	7.50	$8.00
200	5.00	6.00	6.50	7.10
300	6.00	5.50	6.00	6.50
400	8.00	5.00	5.70	6.00
500	11.00	5.50	5.30	5.80
600	15.00	6.00	5.00	5.50
700	20.00	7.00	5.30	5.20
800	26.00	8.00	5.70	5.00
900	33.00	9.50	6.00	5.20
1000	41.00	11.00	6.50	5.50

Remember from the previous chapter that the definition of economic capacity is that output at which (short-run) average costs are at a minimum. From Table 7.1 we can see that in plant 1 (the present plant) economic capacity is achieved with an output of 200 CDs per day. However, Rising Sun's reputation for producing a quality product has been steadily growing within the industry, and it has had to increase production to 400 a day for the last couple of months just to meet customers' orders. The consequence of this strong demand, which the firm welcomes, is that its average costs have been running at $8 per unit, which is far above the minimum average cost level of $5. Something has to be done. Rising Sun must either refuse some customers' orders, which is undesirable; raise prices, which might have negative long-run consequences; or build a bigger plant that can handle the 400 per day output and still maintain average costs of $5.

Suppose the firm decides to build a larger plant. This decision leads to debate among management about the size of the new plant. One option is to go conservative and opt for plant 2, which achieves minimum average total costs of $5 at the current output level of 400 units per day. The second option is to anticipate even *more growth* in the future and opt for plant 3, which would require an output of 600 units a day to achieve the desired minimum average costs of $5. There are, however, two drawbacks associated with plant 3. The first is that it is more expensive to build, and the second is that if plant 3 is chosen, the current rate of production of 400 per day would only lower average costs to $5.70. Thus, building plant 3 would prove to be the right decision only if the future brings in further increases in orders to justify a production run that is higher than the current level. Since no one can predict the future with certainty, let's assume that a decision is made to stay conservative and build plant 2.

In time the new plant is ready, and Rising Sun is able to handle the runs of 400 units per day at a reduced average total cost of $5. But, of course, the story does not end here. Our firm's fortunes continue to grow, and sales rise to the point that production runs of 600 units a day are needed to keep up with commitments made to customers. As we can see in Table 7.1 (plant 2 column), this raises average cost to $6, and Rising Sun is again faced with a major decision about what is the correct plant size for its operations. Now it could upgrade to plant 3 and reduce average costs (at current rates of output) to $5, or it could get really bold and build a new plant 4 in anticipation of even more growth in sales in the future. If it does this, it takes the risk that sales in the future might decline, and it could again face high average costs.

As you can see, the long run involves planning, which in turn requires firms to try to anticipate the future. This is, by its very nature, risky. Businesspeople do not always like taking risks, but doing so is often unavoidable.

FIGURE 7.1   Average Costs of Production in Four Sizes of Plant

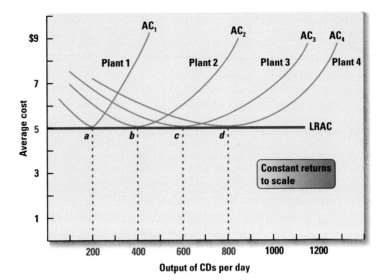

a, b, c, and *d* are each points of minimum average costs in four different sizes of plant. By connecting these four points, we obtain the long-run average cost curve.

Figure 7.1 is a graphical presentation of the average costs data from Table 7.1. Points *a, b, c,* and *d* in Figure 7.1 identify economic capacity in each of the four plant sizes, that is, where (short-run) average costs are at a minimum. By connecting these four points, can we obtain a long-run average cost curve? Technically the answer is no, if these four different-sized plants are the *only* options. This is because the LRAC curve would be the AC_1 curve up to output 300 and the AC_2 curve between outputs 300 and 500. However, if we assume that there are many other possible plant sizes, then there would exist many other AC curves that have not been shown. Each of these unseen cost curves would have a minimum point, and connecting these many minimum points would give us something close to a horizontal LRAC curve, as shown in Figure 7.1. Let's make this assumption and proceed with our focus remaining on the four mentioned plant sizes.

In its long-run planning, Rising Sun must choose one of these four points as its daily production target. Which of the four it chooses would, of course, depend on its estimates of its long-run production requirements, and that would depend on its estimates of its future sales. However, once a decision is made, be it plant 1, 2, 3, or 4, the firm finds itself on one of the four (short-run) average cost curves. That is, the firm finds itself in the short run where, at output levels above economic capacity, average cost rises. Thus we say, once again:

> A firm can *plan* as if it is in the long run, but it always *operates* in the short run.

Constant Returns to Scale

constant returns to scale: the situation in which a firm's output increases by the same percentage as the increase in its inputs.

Let's return to Figure 7.1 and point out that the horizontal long-run average cost curve shown there is a reflection of the concept of **constant returns to scale**. This term is used only in the context of the long run and refers to the situation in which output increases in exact proportion to an increase in inputs.

You will recall that in this example we assumed that plant 2 was exactly twice as large as plant 1. If we also assume that the amount of labour and materials being used in plant 2 is also exactly twice the quantity used in plant 1, and if we assume that the prices of these inputs do not change, then the total cost of producing 400 units per day would be exactly twice the total costs of producing 200 units per day. This means that the average costs will be the same in both cases. You can verify that this is so by looking back at Table 7.1. These are the conditions that result in a horizontal long-run average cost curve, that is, constant returns to scale.

SELF-TEST

1. The accompanying table shows some cost data pertaining to Caravan Motors plant size 1. Complete the table. Suppose that plant 2 is exactly twice the size of plant 1 and uses (at economic capacity) twice the amount of labour and materials. Further, assume that the prices of these inputs are the same and that plant 2 can produce 3000 units of output at economic capacity.

A) At what output is economic capacity achieved in plant 1?

B) How much is total fixed cost in plant 1?

C) If plant sizes 1 and 2 are the only two possible plants, what is the shape of the long-run average cost curve?

Output	Average Total Cost	Total Cost
0	$0	$5000
500	50	____
1000	45	____
1500	40	____
2000	45	____
2500	50	____
3000	65	____
3500	85	____

Increasing Returns to Scale

To take our discussion of long-run costs one step further, we introduce a new firm, Deep Sea Cement, which is currently producing 1000 cubic metres of concrete a day in plant 1. We will assume that the total cost of doing this is $40 000, which means that Deep Sea's average cost of production is currently $40 a metre.

Next, let's assume that Deep Sea builds a larger plant 2, in which both its inputs and its total costs are exactly double. The crucial question at this stage is: what will happen to its output level? Would output exactly double, as it did in the case of Rising Sun? It could, of course, but it is also quite possible that Deep Sea's output will *more than* double, and these are the circumstances of **increasing returns to scale**. Increasing returns to scale exist if a doubling of inputs result in output more than doubling.

Let's assume that as a result of doubling its inputs, Deep Sea's output level increased from the original 1000 cubic metres up to 2500 cubic metres per day. Remember that costs have doubled from $40 000 to $80 000. If we divide the new output level of 2500 cubic metres into $80 000, we obtain a new per-cubic-metre cost of $32, which is one point on plant 2's (short-run) average cost curve. This is well below the original $40, which is one point on plant 1's (short-run) average cost curve. If we connect these two average cost curves, we see a portion of the long-run average cost curve, and this (partial) curve will be downward-sloping. This leads us to the conclusion that when a firm experiences increasing returns to scale, per unit costs of pro-

increasing returns to scale: the situation in which a firm's output increases by a greater percentage than do its inputs.

duction fall as output increases. **Figure 7.2** is a graphical illustration of the long-run average cost curve when increasing returns to scale are present.

FIGURE 7.2 Long-Run Average Costs under Conditions of Increasing Returns to Scale

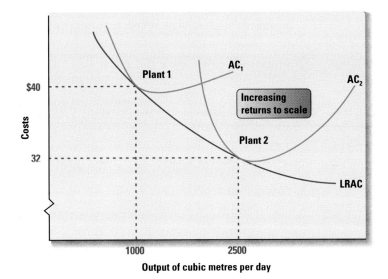

AC_1—plant 1, and AC_2— plant 2, are both short-run average cost curves. We have identified one point on each curve representing two output levels used in our example. Connecting these two points gives us a portion of the long-run average cost curve, which declines as output rises.

Firms in industries characterized by assembly-line production of standardized products, such as automobiles, television sets, refrigerators, or railway cars, are likely to experience declining long-run average cost. In these cases, such firms become formidable competitors because increased output means lower unit costs. As we will examine in much more detail in later chapters, this is the reason why these industries are often dominated by a few large firms.

Economies of Scale

economies of scale: cost advantages achieved as a result of large-scale operations.

We now need to look at the reasons behind increasing returns to scale. Increasing returns to scale are often referred to as technical **economies of scale**, which are very closely related to the advantages gained from the *division of labour* discussed in the previous chapter. In many contexts, production workers save time if they do not have to switch job functions during the day or if they can develop special skills as a result of performing only one particular operation. Small plants also utilize the division of labour, but big plants are able to exploit it on a far greater scale. In addition to using the division of labour, large-scale production also encourages *management specialization*. Two examples of this are a supervisor who is just as capable of handling 12 workers as 8, or an accounting department that does not grow in size despite a 30 percent increase in the output of the firm. Further, as a firm grows in size, rather than increasing the number of general managers, it would make sense for the firm to hire specialized managers, such as controllers, marketing managers, production managers and so on. A third type of technical specialization, *machine specialization*, is also possible. A classic example is the use of robots on a expensive assembly line, something that would probably not be an option for a firm that produces a small output.

We have now established that technical economies of scale lead to decreasing long-run average cost. We need to take one more step, however. In addition to benefiting from technical economies of scale, large firms also enjoy pecuniary economies of scale. These come in four forms. The first involve the *cost of borrowing*. Large firms with large output often need, and are able, to borrow large sums of money, and the interest rate they have to pay is often lower than the rate charged when smaller amounts are borrowed. Second, high-volume firms can *buy inputs in bulk*, which also often means at a lower per-unit price. In addition, their *bulk selling* lowers their per-unit sales cost. Third, a large volume of output often means that previously wasted *by-products can be sold*—think of a fruit canning operation. Once volume is high enough, the firm is also able to sell canned fruit juice using what was previously a waste by-product. Fourth, large firms have advantages of pecuniary economies of scale in *marketing and advertising*. A thirty-second national television advertisement costs the big firm no more than it does the small firm, but the per-unit output cost of the advertisement is much lower.

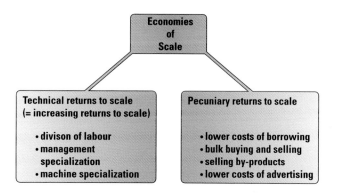

As a way of summary, let's return to the example of Rising Sun Products, which experiences constant returns to scale. This means that there must have been no economies of scale present. However, in the case of Deep Sea Concrete, it enjoys economies of scale, which means that its long-run costs are falling and the long-run average cost curve is downward-sloping. The reason for this is that economies of scale, whether technical or pecuniary, are present.

REVIEW

1. Define the *long run*.
2. Identify and define the *LRAC curve*.
3. What happens to average costs as output rises above economic capacity?
4. What is the shape of the long-run average cost curve under conditions of constant returns to scale?
5. Define *increasing returns to scale*.
6. What are *economies of scale*?
7. Distinguish between technical economies of scale and pecuniary economies of scale.

Decreasing Returns to Scale

decreasing returns to scale: the situation in which a firm's output increases by a smaller percentage than its inputs.

The Deep Sea Cement example illustrated *increasing* returns to scale. Is it possible for *decreasing* returns to scale to exist? The answer is yes. Let's explore this further. **Decreasing returns to scale** exist if a doubling of inputs results in output increasing by less than double. The presence of decreasing returns to scale means that long-run average cost increases as output levels increase. This is illustrated in **Figure 7.3**, where decreasing returns to scale are experienced for output levels above 4000 units and result in a rising long-run average cost curve.

FIGURE 7.3 The LRAC Curve under Conditions of Decreasing Returns to Scale

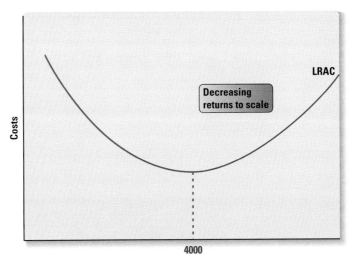

Decreasing returns to scale are present for all output levels above 4000 units, as indicated by the rising long-run average cost curve.

diseconomies of scale: bureaucratic inefficiencies in management that result in decreasing returns to scale.

What could be the explanation of such decreasing returns to scale? Since it is difficult to imagine how *pecuniary* **diseconomies of scale** could exist, we have to conclude that the only reason for decreasing returns to scale would be *technical* diseconomies of scale. Such technical diseconomies would most likely occur as a result of bureaucratic inefficiencies in management that all larger firms (as well as non-profit organizations and governments) experience. This is due to size and does not necessarily imply incompetence. The main reason for such diseconomies is that interpersonal communication passes through more channels and becomes subject to interpretation by many more people. Since the lines of communication increase exponentially with the number of personnel, the cost of communication can increase dramatically. Misinterpretation thus becomes more likely, especially if the information is complicated and technical in nature. Further, as the management organization within the firm becomes larger, the points of responsibility and decision making become blurred. If the problem of miscommunication and uncertain responsibility become serious enough, diseconomies of scale would occur.

If such technical diseconomies of scale outweighed the pecuniary economies of scale that might be present, then diseconomies of scale would result and the long-run average cost curve would begin to rise.

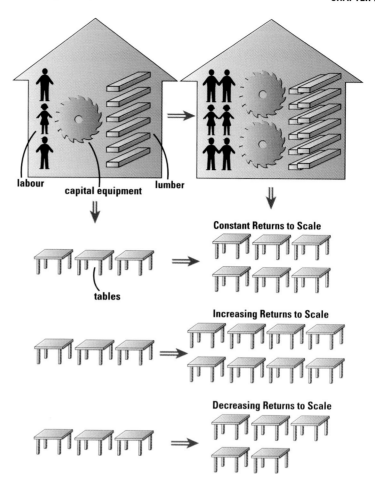

labour   capital equipment   lumber

tables

Constant Returns to Scale

Increasing Returns to Scale

Decreasing Returns to Scale

Changes in Short- and Long-Run Costs

technological improvement: changes in production techniques that reduce the costs of production.

We pointed out at the end of Chapter 6 that if the price of factor inputs decreases, then short-run average cost, as well as marginal cost, would decrease. This would result in the average cost curves shifting down. Such a shift in the short-run average cost curve would result in a corresponding shift in the long-run average cost curve. Recall that the long-run average cost curve is derived from a family of short-run cost curves. If any one of these curves shifts down, then all of the short-run curves that make up the "family" will shift down and, thus, so will the long-run average cost curve. Besides a decrease in input prices, there is another way that costs can decrease at all levels of output and thus cause the average and marginal cost curves to shift down. Improvements in technology have this effect. In fact, one of the possible definitions of **technological improvement** is change that reduces the costs of production at all output levels. This point emphasizes the importance of technological improvement for the firm in this modern, competitive world. Improved technology means lower costs of production, and lower costs of production means more success.

We can add one more point in the discussion of reducing costs. As you are aware, the takeover by one firm of another or the merger of two firms is quite popular these days. Why is this? One explanation involves fixed costs. If the new, larger firm that results from a takeover or merger can keep its fixed cost below the *combined* fixed costs of the original two firms, then average costs of production will have been reduced and the profitability of the new firm will be enhanced.

E·CONOMICS

Increased Rates of Productivity Growth

One of the truly phenomenal trends in recent years has been the impressive growth rates in output per capita in the U.S., which have occurred without rates of inflation becoming worrisome. Underlying this trend has been increases in labour productivity in the 3 to 4 percent range, something that has not been seen for years. Quotes such as "productivity growth is the cornerstone of economic growth and wealth creation" can be found in popular publications as well as in academic journals. Most economists agree that at the root of these productivity increases is the *technological change* associated

with the computer and information "revolution." What this technological change does, in terms of the analysis of this chapter, is decrease both short-run and long-run average (as well as the marginal) cost which allows firms to increase output without having to raise prices. This same trend seems to have eluded Canada however. In fact, labour productivity increases in this country were a poor 1 to 1.5 percent in the 70s, 80s, and most of the 90s. While recent evidence suggests that there has been an increase in these rates in the last few years, they still appear to lag behind those in the U.S.

SELF-TEST

2. Assuming that the prices of all inputs remain fixed, decide in each of the cases below whether constant returns to scale or increasing returns to scale exist.

	Total Cost	Output
A:	$420 000	620
	840 000	1240
B:	$ 80 000	40
	160 000	82
C:	$ 80 000	40
	120 000	61

3. Assume that a firm's total cost of producing an output of 600 units is currently $24 000. If total cost increases to $48 000 and the price of inputs and technology remain unchanged, explain what must happen to the quantity of output under conditions of:
   A) Constant returns to scale.
   B) Increasing returns to scale.
   C) Decreasing returns to scale.

What Is the Right Size of Firm?

In the previous chapter, when we looked at a firm's operations in the short run, we pointed out that the most important question faced by the firm is: what is the best output level? Similarly:

The most important question in the long run is: what is the best size of firm?

Can a firm be too small? Can it be too big? Our discussion of returns to scale allows us to answer questions like these. **Figure 7.4** will help.

Firms in many industries are not subject solely to constant, increasing, or decreasing returns to scale. In fact, for many, all three may be present over different output ranges. Figure 7.4 illustrates a situation in which increasing returns to scale exist for any output level up to quantity Q_1. Output levels that are greater than Q_1 but less than Q_2 are subject to constant returns to scale, and any output level above quantity Q_2 is subject to decreasing returns to scale.

FIGURE 7.4 The Complete Long-Run Average Cost Curve

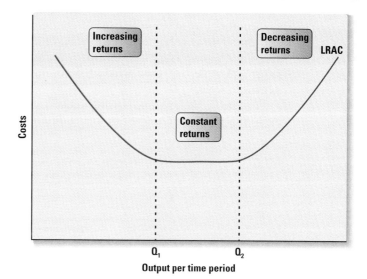

Increasing returns to scale exist for output levels up to Q_1. Constant returns to scale prevail for output levels between Q_1 and Q_2. Finally, decreasing returns to scale prevail for output levels above Q_2.

If this long-run average cost curve were typical for a particular industry, we would conclude that any firm that has an output level below quantity Q_1 is probably too small. Output levels below Q_1 would put any firm at a cost disadvantage compared with its competitors. Similarly, we would also conclude that any firm whose output level was above quantity Q_2 was probably too big and could lower its average cost of production by scaling down the size of its operations.

Notice that the long-run average cost curve in Figure 7.4 has the same general U shape as the short-run average cost curve found in the previous chapter. The similar shapes of the two curves, however, are the result of quite different reasons. In the case of the short-run average cost curve, the reasons involve the division of labour and dimin-

---

ADDED DIMENSION

Does Size Matter? The Merger Phenomenon

There is a perceptible shift in thinking among economists about the question of firm size. For most of the twentieth century conventional wisdom suggested that the bigger a firm became, the more likely it would be successful. General Motors, Imperial Oil, and IBM are big and successful and are likely to remain so. But recently things have started to change. Small CNN is giving the big three American TV networks the fits. Small mini-mill companies in the steel industry are more profitable than the large mainstream firms. The giant car companies of the world are knocking on the door of small Ballard Power to try to make deals. What is happening here? Don't economies of scale count any more?

In many cases the answer is still yes, but that is not the whole story. Technology is changing in ways that lower the barriers to entry for new firms into industries despite the presence of economies of scale. Financial capital is much more mobile and, therefore, more available to small firms. Growing affluence is leading customers to demand higher-quality goods that are more customized to meet specific needs. The result is that a firm's flexibility is becoming more important, and giant established firms, which might well enjoy economies of scale, often aren't very flexible.

An even more intriguing question is: are we moving to a time when size will not matter at all? Smaller companies show signs of trying to act like big ones by forming alliances with other firms, whereas bigger firms are contracting out (out-sourcing) many of their functions to smaller ones or, alternatively, subdividing into small autonomous profit centres.

To quote Bob Dylan, the times they are a-changin'— especially when it comes to the right size of firm.

ishing marginal productivity. The long-run average cost curve, on the other hand, takes on this shape because of increasing, constant, and decreasing returns to scale.

Another way to view the issue of the right size of firm is to ask the rather significant question: is bigger better? We will see that it really depends on the industry in question. Appropriately sized firms are able to take advantage of any increasing returns to scale that exist without becoming too big and experiencing decreasing returns to scale.

Figure 7.5 shows three possible LRAC curves for different industries, each resulting in the appropriate-sized firm being different.

FIGURE 7.5 Three Possible LRAC Curves

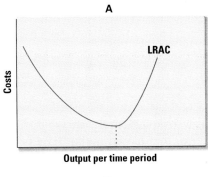

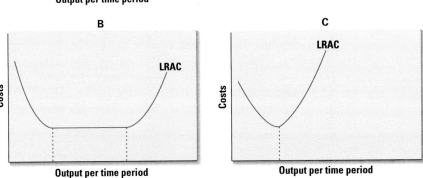

Given the LRAC curve in 7.5A, the appropriately sized firm would need to be large. In 7.5B, a variety of firm sizes would be appropriate. However, the LRAC curve in 7.5C would indicate that only small firms would be appropriate.

Figure 7.5A illustrates the case in which a firm would have to be quite large to capture all of the economies of scale available. In this type of industry, small and medium-sized firms, because of their comparatively higher average costs, are simply not able to compete with larger firms. Thus, this type of industry tends to be dominated by large firms. Examples of such industries are automobiles, pipelines, satellite data transmission, cable distributors, television transmission, and petrochemicals.

In Figure 7.5B, we can imagine a variety of different-sized firms, all of whom are able to capture economies of scale. This is because costs remain constant over a wide range of outputs, and therefore an appropriately sized firm could be either relatively small or large. Examples here would be industries such as computer software, real estate services, and meat packing.

Finally, Figure 7.5C illustrates an industry in which only relatively small firms would be appropriate. This is the case with vegetable growing and small-scale retailing, such as the corner convenience store.

Can a Market Be Too Small?

minimum efficient scale: the smallest-size plant capable of achieving the lowest long-run average cost of production.

Adam Smith observed, over 200 years ago, that the division of labour was limited by the size of the market. Is it possible that a limited size of market can restrict the extent to which firms achieve increasing returns to scale? In Canada, with its small population and, therefore, small market, the answer is yes, at least for some industries.

This leads us to the concept of **minimum efficient scale** (MES), which is the smallest level of output at which a firm is able to minimize long-run average costs. If a small market results in firms being unable to achieve minimum efficient scale, then inefficiency can become widespread throughout the industry. The Canadian economy has historically faced this problem. Its market is too small for those industries in which the MES dictates that a large output is necessary to minimize average cost. As a result, such firms are inefficient by world standards. This situation is illustrated in Figure 7.6.

FIGURE 7.6 Minimum Efficient Scale

If a small market limits the firm's output to Q_1, then plant AC_1 is not able to achieve minimum efficient scale. A larger market that allowed an output of Q_2, and thus plant AC_2, would enable the firm to achieve its minimum efficient scale.

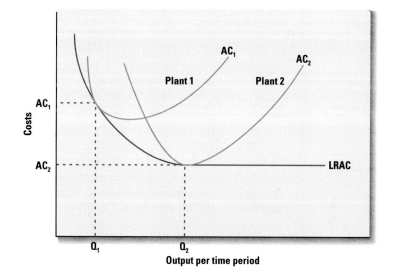

ADDED DIMENSION

Free Trade Agreements and MES

Proponents of both the Canada–U.S. Free Trade Agreement and of NAFTA argued in the late 1980s that a failure to achieve minimum efficient scale was hindering the success of many Canadian firms. The logical extension of this argument was that both agreements would extend the size of the market considerably for Canadian producers, and this would allow these firms to increase output and achieve minimum efficient scale. For this to happen, Canadian exports would have to rise substantially. In fact, Canadian exports to the United States and, to a lesser extent, Mexico, have increased significantly in the 1990s.

Does this mean that more Canadian firms have achieved minimum efficient scale? We cannot answer "yes" on the evidence of increased exports alone, but greater exports and lower long-run average costs following an expansion in the size of the market are certainly consistent with one another.

A small market may force a firm to limit its output to Q_1 and experience average total cost of AC_1, as illustrated in Figure 7.6. This is above the level of minimum long-run average cost. A larger market would allow the firm to build a larger plant, as represented by the AC_2 curve, and thereby achieve minimum long-run average costs.

Thus, we can see that Adam Smith was correct in his observation that the division of labour can be limited by the size of the market in both the short-run and the long-run sense. In the short run, a limited-sized market can force a firm to operate at an output below economic capacity. More significantly, a limited-sized market can prevent firms from building large-scale plants and capturing available economies of scale through increased output levels. This inability to increase output levels limits the firm's ability to gain all of the possible advantages of the division of labour.

Are the Advantages of Economies of Scale Changing?

Let's consider what is probably the economist's favourite example of technical economies of scale. The cost of a pipeline is roughly proportional to its circumference—the larger the circumference, the more steel needed to build it. However, the carrying capacity of a pipeline is determined by its area, which means that larger pipelines have disproportionately increased capacity and thus lower per-unit costs. For instance, a 12-inch-diameter pipe requires twice the steel of a 6-inch pipe but can carry four times the volume. This illustrates the classic relationship between bigger volume and lower long-run average cost.

However, the invention of the microchip raises the possibility that this classic relationship can, in many cases, be inverted. As technology advances, smaller and smaller computers can do what could previously only be done with a room-sized mainframe. Thus, unlike the pipeline, increased efficiency comes from *reductions* in the size of the means of production. This new concept, that smaller is better, fits well with emerging evidence that market demand for many products is shifting away from standardized and toward customized products. More and more, consumers are demanding unique products that meet highly specialized needs. Thus, production must become much more flexible, and the emphasis is shifting to customized products.

Photo courtesy of Intel Corporation

Computer chips like these are getting smaller and more powerful every year.

Next, consider the fact that networks of small computers can quickly be expanded or scaled back. Thus firms can deploy *many* assembly lines, each one turning out a customized variant of the same basic product, rather than only *one* huge assembly line that stamps out a standardized product in massive volumes.

The fundamental question this raises is whether this new technology will alter the scale of the firm that uses it. In other words, as production becomes more customized and computers become more sophisticated, will efficient production mean smaller firms? Are huge corporations finding it cheaper to farm out work to lower-cost specialists, who are often more flexible, rather than retain the bureaucratic organizational structure necessary to manage the entire process within a single operation?

Evidence suggesting such downsizing comes from the fact that small automotive-parts firms have been growing in the last decade, while large automobile manufacturers have been laying off workers. This leads some economists to argue that as production becomes significantly more specialized and products more customized, the growth in the numbers of efficient small firms will come at the expense of giant firms.

Not all economists agree that this is the trend. They point out that what can be done efficiently in a small firm can also be done in the corner of a General Motors plant. However, if the trend of smaller is better does prove valid, then a great deal will change and this chapter on long-run average cost and the related advantages of economies of scale will have to be rewritten.

SELF-TEST

4. A) Draw a short-run average total cost curve for Firm X on a graph, label it, and indicate with point *a* an output level, Q_1, that results in excess capacity.

B) If output was increased to achieve economic capacity, would the firm necessarily also have achieved minimum efficient scale?

REVIEW

1. Define *decreasing returns to scale.*
2. What is the most likely cause of decreasing returns to scale?
3. In what sense might a firm be too small?
4. In what sense might a firm be too big?
5. Identify and define *minimum efficient scale.* Indicate on a graph the point of minimum efficient scale.
6. In Canada, what is the likely cause of production being below MES?

STUDY GUIDE

Chapter Highlights

In this chapter you focused on the long-run average costs and on the three types of "returns to scale" that are associated with them. This opened the door for a discussion of two questions: what is the right size of firm; and can a market be too small?

1. Firms always operate in the *short run* where at least one factor of production (input) is fixed and diminishing marginal productivity is inevitable.

2. Firms can plan as if they are in the *long run* where, conceptually, there are no fixed factors of production and diminishing marginal productivity does not apply.

3. If a firm increases its *scale of operation* by proportionally increasing all of its inputs, one of three results are possible:
   - constant returns to scale where output increases proportionally;
   - increasing returns to scale where output increases more than proportionally;
   - decreasing returns to scale where output increases less than proportionally.

4. The economies of scale involves either *technical economies* as a result of:
   - the division of labour;
   - management specialization;
   - machine specialization;

   (these three factors result in increasing returns to scale)

   or *pecuniary economics* of scale such as:
   - lower cost of borrowing;
   - bulk buying and selling;
   - the selling of by-products;
   - lower costs of advertising.

5. Both short-run and long-run average costs can *decrease* if:
   - the price of factor inputs decreases;
   - technological improvement occurs;
   - mergers can reduce the average fixed costs of the new firm.

6. *Diseconomies of scale* can occur if bureaucratic inefficiencies within large firms are significant.

7. A firm can be considered to be of the *right size* only if it is big enough to capture economies of scale but not so big as to suffer diseconomies. The right size is called the minimum efficient scale.

8. A market can be *too small* if it limits the size of the firm to an output level that is either:
   - below economic capacity in the short run;
   - below minimum efficient scale in the long run.

New Glossary Terms

Study Tips

1. Students often think that the terms "increasing returns to scale" and "economies of scale" refer to the same phenomena. This is not quite correct. Increasing returns to scale refers to the increase in output that results from the increase in inputs associated with a larger plant size. These cost advantages are also called technical economies of scale. Economies of scale, on the other hand, includes both these technical economies *and* the pecuniary advantages that sometimes go with a larger scale of operations.

2. Students who come to understand the law of diminishing returns (or diminishing marginal product) wonder what explains the often observed phenomenon of both rising output levels and falling prices for things like VCRs, computers, and CD players. Surely, if the law of diminishing returns applies, then higher output would be associated with higher marginal and average costs and, therefore, higher prices. Yet, we actually see prices for these products fall as output increases *over time*. An understanding of the long run, where diminishing MP does not apply but increasing returns to scale often do, reconciles this apparent contradiction.

3. Many students are thrown by the word "pecuniary." It simply means: pertaining to money.

4. Remember that, for the sake of convenience, we often refer to average total cost in the short run as "average cost," or AC, and to average total costs in the long run as LRAC.

5. The value of graphical analysis to help one understand concepts is quite apparent in this chapter. Do take the time to draw the graphs in the questions where you are asked to, and keep in mind the concept being illustrated. You will find yourself beginning to "think in graphs" as well as in words.

Are You Sure?

Indicate whether the following statements are true or false. If false, indicate why they are false.

1. The long run is the circumstance in which at least one input is variable.

   T or **F**   If false: _____

   _____

2. While a firm can plan for the long run, it must always operate in the short run.

   T or **F**   If false: _____

   _____

3. Constant returns to scale is the situation in which a firm's output increases by the same percentage as the increase in its inputs.

   T or **F**   If false: _____

   _____

4. Increasing returns to scale is the situation in which a firm's output increases by the same percentage as the increase in its inputs.

   T or **F**   If false: _____

   _____

5. The long-run average cost curve declines continuously as output levels increase.

   T or **F**   If false: _____

   _____

6. Labour, management, and machine specialization are examples of pecuniary economies of scale.

   T or **F**   If false: _____

   _____

7. Economies of scale are divided into those cost advantages that are technical and those that are pecuniary.

   T or **F**   If false: _____

   _____

8. A firm's economic capacity and its most productive output level are the same.

   T or **F**   If false: _____

   _____

9. Pecuniary diseconomies of scale probably do not exist.

   T or **F**   If false: _____

   _____

10. The right size of firm is determined by the minimum point on its short-run average cost curve.

   T or **F**   If false: _____

   _____

Choose the Best

11. Which of the following is correct in reference to the long run?
    a) All inputs are variable.
    b) Only one input is variable, whereas all others are fixed.

12. If increasing returns to scale are present, then:
    a) Economies of scale are also present.
    b) Economies of scale may or may not be present.

13. Which of the following statements is correct?
    a) A firm can operate in either the short run or the long run.
    b) While a firm can plan as if it is in the long run, it can operate only in the short run.

14. What is meant by the term "economic capacity"?
    a) An output level at which the firm is physically unable to increase output.
    b) The output level at which average variable cost is at a minimum.
    c) The output level at which average total cost is at a minimum.

15. Which of the following statements is correct if constant returns to scale are present?
    a) A doubling of inputs will lead to output more than doubling.
    b) A doubling of inputs will lead to output also doubling.
    c) A doubling of output will lead to inputs more than doubling.

16. Economies of scale:
    a) Is another term for constant returns to scale.
    b) Are cost advantages achieved as a result of large-scale operations.
    c) Only come in pecuniary forms.

17. The ability of a person to supervise 12 workers just as well as 8 is an example of:
    a) The division of labour.
    b) Labour specialization.
    c) Management specialization.

18. All of the following, *except one*, are examples of pecuniary economies of scale. Which one is the exception?
    a) A lower interest rate paid on money borrowed.
    b) The ability to sell the by-products of production.
    c) The ability to use specialized inputs such as a robotics assembly line.
    d) The ability to obtain lower prices by buying in bulk.

19. The fact that a one-minute television commercial costs a large firm no more than a small firm is an example of which of the following?
    a) Increasing returns to scale.
    b) Pecuniary economies of scale.
    c) Technical economies of scale.
    d) Management specialization.

20. Which of the following is the most likely cause of diseconomies of scale?
    a) Increasing returns to scale.
    b) A small scale of operations and output.
    c) Low productivity.
    d) Bureaucracy.

21. Which of the following statements is correct if a firm's capacity output increases from 400 to 800 and its total costs rise from $60 000 to $110 000?
    a) The firm is experiencing constant returns to scale.
    b) The firm is experiencing decreasing returns to scale.
    c) Both the firm's short-run and long-run average costs must have decreased.

    d) The firm's long-run average cost must have decreased, but its short-run average cost could have either decreased or increased.

22. If a firm builds a larger plant and constant returns to scale apply, which of the following statements is correct?
    a) The capacity output of the larger plant has a lower average cost.
    b) The capacity output of the larger plant has the same average cost.
    c) Economies of scale are present.
    d) LRAC will decrease as output increases.

23. Which of the following statements is correct if a firm builds a larger plant and, at any particular output, its short-run average cost increases?
    a) Decreasing returns to scale must be present.
    b) Increasing returns to scale must be present.
    c) Constant returns to scale must be present.
    d) Decreasing, increasing, and constant returns to scale are all possible.

24. Which of the following statements is correct if the appropriately sized firm is one with a large output?
    a) Constant returns to scale must begin at low levels of output.
    b) Increasing returns to scale must prevail until high levels of output are reached.
    c) Decreasing returns to scale must begin at low levels of output.
    d) Constant returns to scale must be absent.

25. What does the term "minimum efficient scale" mean?
    a) The smallest level of output at which a firm is able to minimize both short-run and long-run average costs.
    b) The smallest level of output at which a firm is able to minimize short-run marginal cost.
    c) The smallest level of output at which a firm is able to minimize short-run average cost.
    d) The smallest level of output at which a firm is able to minimize long-run marginal cost.
    e) The smallest level of output at which a firm is able to minimize both short-run and long-run marginal cost.

26. Suppose a firm builds a larger plant and increases its output. Which of the following statements is correct?
    a) Its MES output must increase.
    b) Its MES output must decrease.
    c) It will be able to achieve its MES output only if it also achieves economic capacity.
    d) Its short-run average cost curve for the original plant will have shifted down.
    e) Its long-run average costs must have increased.

27. Adam Smith observed that the division of labour is limited by the size of the market. Which one of the following statements contradicts this observation?
    a) A limited-sized market can prevent firms from achieving economic capacity.
    b) A limited-sized market can prevent firms from achieving their minimum efficient scale.
    c) A limited-sized market can prevent firms from achieving minimum short-run average cost.
    d) A limited-sized market can prevent firms from achieving minimum long-run average cost.
    e) A limited-sized market can prevent firms from achieving excess capacity.

28. Graphically, what is the effect of technological change?
    a) The long-run average cost curve will shift down, but the short-run curves will not change.
    b) Both the long-run and short-run average cost curves will shift down.
    c) The long-run average cost curve will shift up, but the short-run curves will not change.
    d) Both the long-run and short-run average cost curves will shift up.
    e) It will reduce the size of the average firm.

Refer to **Figure 7.7** to answer questions 29 and 30.

FIGURE 7.7

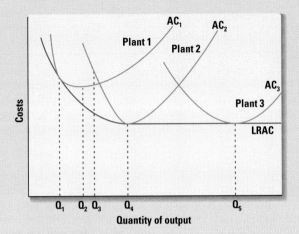

29. Refer to Figure 7.7 to answer this question. All of the following statements, *except one*, are correct. Which is the exception?
    a) Plant 1 has excess capacity at output level Q_1.
    b) Output level Q_2 is economic capacity for plant 1.
    c) Output level Q_3 can be produced cheaper in plant 2 than in plant 1.
    d) Plant 2 achieves minimum efficient scale.
    e) Increasing returns to scale are experienced when output is increased from Q_1 to Q_4.

30. Refer to Figure 7.7 to answer this question. All of the following statements *except one* are correct. Which is the exception?
    a) AC_1, AC_2, and AC_3 are short-run average cost curves.
    b) The long-run average cost curve illustrates both increasing and constant returns to scale.
    c) Constant returns to scale exist between outputs Q_4 and Q_5.
    d) An increase in output from Q_1 to Q_3 would require that a larger plant be built.
    e) Both the short run and the long run are illustrated in this graph.

Problems

31. **Table 7.2** shows cost data for three different-sized plants—1, 2, and 3—which are the only three plants possible.

TABLE 7.2

Output	Plant 1	Plant 2	Plant 3
100	$12	$15	$19
200	11	12	16
300	10	8	12
400	11	11	9
500	12	15	10

a) In what plant size is MES achieved?

Answer: _____.

b) What is economic capacity for plant 3?

Answer: _____.

c) What is the right-sized plant to produce an output of 400?

Answer: _____.

32. **Figure 7.8** illustrates a series of short-run average cost curves numbered AC_1 through AC_5 which correspond to five different plant sizes.

FIGURE 7.8

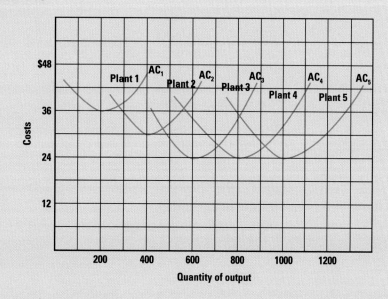

a) What is true about output levels 200, 400, 600, 800, and 1000?

Answer: _____.

b) What is the right-sized plant to produce an output of 900?

Answer: _____.

c) Between what output levels do increasing returns to scale prevail?

Answer: _____.

d) At what output levels do decreasing returns to scale prevail?

Answer: _____.

33. Figure 7.9 illustrates a series of short-run average cost curves numbered AC_1 through AC_4, which correspond to the only four different automobile plant sizes possible.

FIGURE 7.9

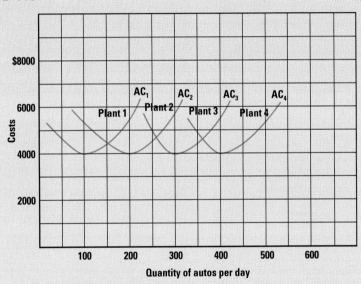

a) What can you say about returns to scale?
Answer: _____.

b) Are economies of scale present?
Answer: _____.

c) If it takes 40 workers and 100 units of capital to produce 200 automobiles a day, how much labour and capital is involved in producing 600 automobiles a day?
Answer: _____.

d) At what output is economic capacity and MES the same?
Answer: _____.

34. On the graph in Figure 7.10, sketch average cost curves that illustrate a firm facing a very small market size that limits its output (labelled Q_1), which results in it being unable to achieve either economic capacity or MES.

FIGURE 7.10

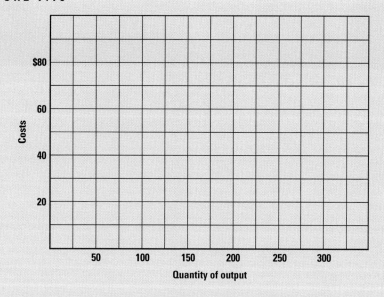

Translations

On **Figure 7.11**, draw and label the curves needed to illustrate the following passage (don't forget to label the axes too).

Sketch in a short-run average cost curve, and label it AC1. Also label its minimum point as output Q_3. Next, show an increase in output from Q_1 to Q_2 that results in excess capacity at both points. Now illustrate a larger-sized plant with AC2 that shows a lower minimum average cost at a higher output level than is possible given AC1. With the letters *c* and *d*, show an increase in output from Q_4 to Q_5 on AC2 in which excess capacity is eliminated. Now, sketch in an LRAC curve that is just tangent to AC1 and 2. This LRAC curve should illustrate that increasing returns to scale are present for output levels up to Q_5.

FIGURE 7.11

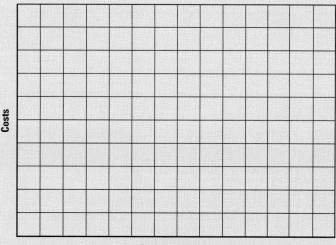

Key Problem

Table 7.3 contains short-run cost data for five different plant sizes for the R2D2 Robotics Company.

TABLE 7.3

Output	Plant 1	Plant 2	Plant 3	Plant 4	Plant 5
10	$ 8.00	$10.50	–	–	–
20	7.00	9.00	–	–	–
30	6.00	7.50	$10.00	–	–
40	6.50	6.00	8.00	–	–
50	7.50	5.00	6.50	$10.30	–
60	9.00	5.80	5.00	8.50	–
70	10.50	7.00	4.00	7.00	–
80	–	8.20	4.90	5.10	$6.50
90	–	10.00	6.00	4.00	6.00
100	–	–	7.80	4.30	5.40
110	–	–	8.50	5.60	5.00
120	–	–	–	7.70	5.30
130	–	–	–	10.00	6.00
140	–	–	–	–	7.10

a) On the grid in Figure 7.12, graph the short-run average cost curves for the five plants.

b) What is the best size of plant if output is:

    30? Plant: _____ .

    40? _____ .

    50? _____ .

    60? _____ .

    70? _____ .

    80? _____ .

    90? _____ .

    100? _____ .

    110? _____ .

    120? _____ .

c) Roughly sketch in the long-run average cost curve in Figure 7.12.

d) What plant size would the firm need in order to achieve minimum efficient scale (MES)?

    Answer: _____ .

e) What is the output level that achieves MES?

    Answer: _____ .

FIGURE 7.12

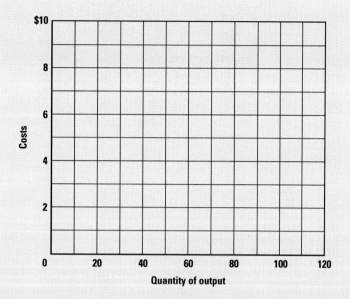

f) If R2D2 is producing an output of 80 in plant 4, does excess capacity exist?

Answer: _____.

g) What would be the economic capacity for plant 5?

Answer: _____.

h) Given the LRAC curve in Figure 7.12, between what output levels does increasing returns to scale exist?

Answer: _____.

i) Given the LRAC curve in Figure 7.12, between what output levels does constant returns to scale exist?

Answer: _____.

j) Given the LRAC curve in Figure 7.12, between what output levels does decreasing returns to scale exist?

Answer: _____.

k) If R2D2's sales are limited to 50, we can say that the market is too small for which plant sizes?

Answer: _____.

More of the Same

Table 7.4 contains short-run cost data for five different plant sizes for C3PO Technologies Ltd.

TABLE 7.4

Output	Plant 1	Plant 2	Plant 3	Plant 4	Plant 5
2	$0.50	$0.70	–	–	–
4	0.45	0.55	–	–	–
6	0.50	0.45	$0.65	–	–
8	0.60	0.40	0.50	–	–
10	0.75	0.45	0.40	$0.60	–
12	–	0.55	0.35	0.45	–
14	–	0.70	0.40	0.35	$0.60
16	–	–	0.50	0.30	0.45
18	–	–	0.65	0.35	0.35
20	–	–	–	0.45	0.30
22	–	–	–	0.60	0.35
24	–	–	–	–	0.45

a) On the grid in **Figure 7.13**, graph the short-run average cost curves for the five plants.

FIGURE 7.13

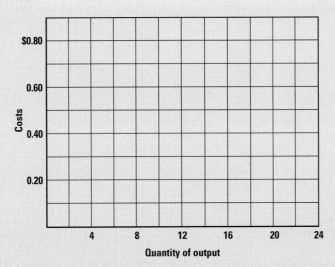

b) What is the best size of plant for each of the following output levels: 4, 6, 8, 10, 12, 14, 16, 18, 20, 22, 24?

c) Do a rough sketch of the long-run average cost curve in the graph above.

d) What plant size would C3PO need to use in order to achieve minimum efficient scale?

e) What is the output level that achieves MES?

f) If C3PO is producing an output level of 10 in plant 3, does excess capacity exist?

g) What is economic capacity for plant 2?

h) Given the LRAC curve in Figure 7.13, between what output levels do increasing returns to scale exist?

i) Given the LRAC curve in Figure 7.13, at what output level do constant returns to scale begin?

j) Given the LRAC curve in Figure 7.13, is there any evidence of decreasing returns to scale?

k) What is the smallest level of sales that could exist in order to conclude that C3PO is not constrained by a limited size of market?

UNANSWERED QUESTIONS

Short Essays

1. Discuss the distinction between increasing returns to scale and economies of scale.

2. Discuss the effects of technological change on the short-run and the long-run average cost curves.

3. What does it mean to suggest that a firm is the "right size"?

4. Explain in what sense the domestic market in Canada might be too small.

5. The advantages of economies of scale are changing. Discuss this statement.

Analytical Questions

6. Discuss the difference between diminishing returns and decreasing returns to scale.

7. Which of the following adjustments do you consider to be long-run, and which are short-run changes?
    a) The Bay hires an additional 50 sales staff in four of its downtown stores.
    b) The National Bus Line adds 10 buses to its fleet.
    c) Central Island Brewing Company opens its own retail outlet.
    d) A canola farmer doubles her seed order for the coming season.
    e) The Edmonton Symphony Orchestra signs three new violinists to two-year contracts.

8. Is the idea of a right-sized firm a short-run or a long-run concept?

9. If a firm can never operate in the long run, why do economists consider the long run an important concept?

10. How does a firm's capacity output change if the price of a firm's variable inputs fall?

Numerical Questions

11. Assume that Soil Busters Ltd.'s total cost of producing an output of 50 rototillers an hour is currently $8400. If the price of inputs and technology remain unchanged and total costs increase to $16 800, what must happen to the quantity of output under conditions of:

a) Constant returns to scale?
b) Increasing returns to scale ?
c) Decreasing returns to scale?

12. **Table 7.5** contains cost data from four different-sized plants—1, 2, 3, and 4—which are the only four sizes possible.

TABLE 7.5

Output	Plant 1	Plant 2	Plant 3	Plant 4
50	$ 75	$ 95	$120	$140
100	65	80	100	120
150	75	60	75	90
200	90	80	55	80
250	120	100	80	65
300	150	120	105	90

a) What is capacity output for each of the four plants?
b) At what output is minimum long-run average cost achieved?
c) What is the right size of plant to produce an output of 150?
d) What is the right size of plant to produce an output of 50?

13. **Figure 7.14** illustrates a series of short-run average cost curves numbered AC_1 through AC_6, which correspond to six different plant sizes.

FIGURE 7.14

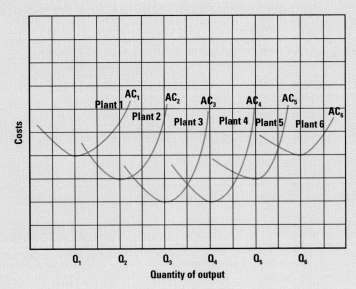

a) Between what levels of output are increasing returns to scale present?
b) At what output levels are decreasing returns to scale present?
c) What is true about all six levels of output, Q_1 through Q_6?

d) What is the best size of plant to produce the output represented by the quantity halfway between Q_4 and Q_5?

14. Assuming that the prices of all inputs remain fixed, decide, in each of the four cases in **Table 7.6**, whether constant, increasing, or decreasing returns to scale exist.

TABLE 7.6

	Total Cost	Output
A	$ 9 800	175
	19 600	370
B	23 260	225
	47 520	450
C	990	77
	1 890	154
D	1 935	7 320
	3 870	14 640

15. **Table 7.7** shows the long-run total costs for three different firms.

TABLE 7.7

JARMO'S		KISH'S		LAGASH'S	
Output	Cost	Output	Costs	Output	Costs
1 000	$ 2 800	100	$18 500	20	$ 400
2 000	5 800	110	18 500	40	680
3 000	8 850	120	18 500	60	900
4 000	12 000	130	18 500	80	1 120
5 000	15 500	140	18 500	100	1 200
6 000	19 500	150	18 500	120	1 440
7 000	23 450	160	18 500	140	1 680
8 000	29 600	170	18 500	160	2 400
9 000	35 100	180	18 500	180	3 240
10 000	40 000	190	18 500	200	5 000

Are each of these three firms experiencing constant, increasing, or decreasing returns to scale?

16. Draw four short-run average cost curves for plant sizes 1 through 4. Indicate the capacity output for plant 1 as 100 and the capacity output of plant 2 as twice that of 1, and of plant 3 as three times that of 1, and of plant 4 as four times that of 1. You are to assume that the quantity of inputs needed to produce the capacity output in 2 are less than twice those needed to produce output 1. Similarly, the quantity of inputs needed to produce capacity output in 3 are less than 50 percent more than those needed to produce the output in 2. Finally, the quantity of inputs needed to produce the output in 4 are exactly $33\frac{1}{3}$ percent more than those needed in 3. Now sketch in the long-run average cost curve. How does this curve illustrate both increasing and constant returns to scale?

17. **Table 7.8** shows data is the New Horizon Circuit Board Company.

TABLE 7.8

Output	100	200	300	400	500	600	700	800
Total cost	$ 1700	$3200	$4500	$5600	$6500	$7200	$9800	$13 600

Would you suggest that New Horizon downsize, upsize, or remain at the present plant size if it believed that its production orders will remain at 300 per month? What about 600 per month? 800?

 Web-Based Activities

1. The University Health System Consortium (UHC) **www.uhc.edu/about/overview.html** is a member-driven alliance of academic health centres (AHCs). Its mission is to help strengthen the competitive position of members and associate members in their respective health care markets. One way in which it is able to do so is by creating economies of scale. Explain how UHC is able to create economies of scale.

2. Go to **www.publicpurpose.com/ut-ecscl.htm#2**. Explain what could cause the economies and diseconomies of scale in the public transportation illustrated in the charts.

Perfect Competition

What's ahead...In this chapter, we take our first look at market structures using what economists call the perfectly competitive model. After describing some examples of perfect competition, we look at the behaviour of the individual firm, how it decides on its production level, and how profits are affected. We derive rules for determining the output level at which the producer breaks even, the level at which it will make the most profit, and the level at which it might be advised to shut down operations. The rest of the chapter shows how the market and the individual producer react to changes in both demand and technology.

A QUESTION OF RELEVANCE...

Market systems are dynamic and always changing. New industries are born, and established industries die, on a fairly regular basis. New firms are continuously entering and leaving both new and established industries. Are new firms guaranteed a profit? Would you be a fool to look for a job in a declining industry, or would you be an even bigger fool to join the multitudes looking for jobs in the growing industries? Is it possible for a firm caught in the drag of a dying industry to redefine itself and became sucessful doing something else? Rather than trying to learn to answer all possible specific questions such as these, is there some kind of common denominator that we can use to study "the market"? This chapter will explore this common denominator.

T his, and the next three chapters, could collectively be called the theory of producer behaviour. We will focus our study on what determines the quantities that firms produce and the price at which they are sold. The previous two chapters provided us with a background for this focus because the costs of production definitely have an effect both on the price of the product and on how much firms will willingly produce. To be able to fully understand price and quantity determination, though, we need to know a bit more about a product than just its costs. We need to know something about the product itself, about other firms in the industry, and about the customers who buy the product. In other words, we need to know more about the market in which the product is sold. Let us be careful about terminology before we go any further: an "industry" is the collective name for all the firms producing a similar product. The different firms in the industry may or may not know each other well, they may or may not be members of some sort of common association, and they may or may not agree on various types of collective action. What they have in common is that they produce a similar product, usually using the same technology. A "market," you will remember from Chapter 2, refers to the interactions of both producers and consumers. In other words:

> **An industry is the name for a group of producers; a market is the name for both producers and consumers.**

Characteristics of Different Markets

Economists see two main ways in which markets differ. One way is in terms of the type of product sold: do the producers sell an identical product, or are there differences between one firm's product and that of other firms? The second difference is in terms of the numbers of buyers and sellers: is the market populated by many firms and consumers, or, conversely, is it dominated by a few big players in the game? The degree of control that a single firm can exercise over the price of its products and the quantity it is able to sell depends very much on the extent of competition between producers and on the relative power of producers and consumers. In addition, it also depends on the degree of difference that exists between its own product and that of the competition. **Table 8.1** shows the range of possible markets. The type of market depends on the number of producers and on whether the firms produce identical or differentiated products.

TABLE 8.1 Matrix of Markets

	Many Firms	**Few Firms**	**One Single Firm**
Identical product	Perfect competition	Undifferentiated oligopoly	Monopoly
Differentiated product	Monopolistic competition	Differentiated oligopoly	NA

perfect competition: a market in which all buyers and sellers are price takers.

As we shall see, the greater the number of firms and the more similar the products, the more competitive the market will be. In later chapters we will look at other forms of competition; this chapter and the next will concentrate on the form known as **perfect competition**.

Perfect Competition

Features of Perfect Competition

Markets are said to be perfectly competitive when no single consumer or producer has any greater power or influence in the market than does any other consumer or producer. In other words, in such a market no single producer or consumer can affect the price or the quantity produced. A competitive market, in other words, provides a level playing field for its participants. This can only happen when four conditions are fulfilled. First, there must be a *large number of buyers and sellers*, and all must be small in relation to the whole market. Since each producer is relatively small, a decision by any particular producer to double its output (or to produce nothing at all) will not have much impact on the market. Similarly, a decision by any particular consumer to increase or decrease her purchases will have no perceptible effect on total sales. Also, a competitive market does not exist if there is any collusion between producers or between consumers, since it is assumed that each person operates separately and independently. Nor is a market considered competitive if producers or consumers form co-operatives or associations that make decisions on behalf of their members. A competitive market, therefore, is one in which the buyers and sellers all act separately and independently and in which each individual producer and consumer has so little market power that no single one of them can affect the quantity bought and sold. As a result, they have no influence on the price of the product. For each of them, the market price is a given. This last point is particularly relevant to perfectly competitive firms, who have no choice but to accept the going market price; that is, they are price takers.

The second feature of a perfectly competitive market is that it is a market in which *there are no preferences shown*. This means that the consumer neither knows nor cares where the product she buys comes from, since the producers all make an identical, or undifferentiated, product. Nor are there any other reasons why a particular producer would be preferred. Similarly, producers show no preference toward any particular consumer. For them, all consumers are the same.

The third defining feature of a competitive market is that *there should be easy entry into and exit from the market*, for both producers and consumers. This is sometimes rephrased to say that there are no significant barriers to entry. For the prospective producer, this implies that it should be reasonably easy to set up in business: the producer does not require a great deal of financial capital; nor does it have to pay a membership fee, licence fee, or any other type of entry fee; nor does the producer have to join any club or organization in order to trade. In this manner, existing firms in an industry have no advantage over newcomers. Easy entry and exit also means that consumers too should not be required to belong to a particular organization or to possess particular attributes in order to buy a certain product.

The fourth and final feature of perfectly competitive markets is that *producers have all the market information necessary to make rational production and purchasing decisions*. This condition ensures that no particular participant in the market has any advantage (or competitive edge) over the other participants. It means, for instance, that we don't have a situation in which only a select few customers are aware of a particular sale going on in town, or in which a firm introduces a superior technology that is unknown to other firms. In other words, if the knowledge is not equally shared, then some people will have an advantage over others; and unless there is equality in the marketplace, it is not perfectly competitive. In summary, the four conditions for a perfectly competitive market are:

- many small buyers and sellers all of whom are price takers
- no preferences shown
- easy entry and exit by both buyers and sellers
- the same market information available to all

If these four conditions exist, the marketplace is said to be perfectly competitive. The result will be that the anonymous forces of demand and supply determine both the price of the product and the quantity traded. Conversely, if these conditions do not exist, it will usually mean that one participant is stronger than the others and can therefore have some degree of influence over the price and quantity. If markets are perfectly competitive, any change in the demand or supply conditions should affect the price; and since presumably demand and supply are almost always changing, we should expect to see the price change quite frequently. We have prima facie evidence that the market is competitive whenever the price in the market changes regularly. Conversely, if the price of a particular product seldom changes, this is prima facie evidence that that market is not competitive. Let us try then to find some examples of competitive markets in our economy.

Examples of Perfectly Competitive Markets

In searching for examples of competitive markets, we should emphasize that the first condition does not require every producer to be small in its scale of operations, but only *small in relation to the total market*. It is just as possible, then, to have some reasonably big competitive firms as it is to have one single, small monopolist. In respect to the second condition, that no preferences be shown, this immediately rules out examples like travel agents, hairdressers, gas stations, and so on, since customers do show preferences, even though the difference between suppliers may seem small. For instance, economists recognize that, from a chemist's point of view, a particular brand of gasoline may well be identical to some other brand, but if consumers show a preference for one over the other, then there is a difference between the two, even if it is only the name of the gasoline. Another important point is that it is not the number of products that makes the market competitive but the number of individual producers. For example, although there are more than a hundred different breakfast cereals on the market, most are produced by just two or three giant firms, which makes it a less than perfectly competitive market.

Given these cautions, are there good examples of competitive markets these days? Well, the closest we will come is a situation in which the market is very big and the product is generic, for example, in the world markets for commodities like aluminum, zinc, cotton, rubber, oil, wheat, and so on. The price of these products often changes hourly in response to changing conditions around the world, and their current prices are published every day in the financial section of most newspapers. A Canadian producer of a particular commodity, however big it may be in Canada, is unlikely to have much impact on the world supply. In most respects, then, world markets for commodities are reasonably competitive. But what about inside Canada—are there any competitive markets domestically? The stock market is often cited as an example of a perfect market, in which the prices of products (stocks and bonds) often change minute by minute. However, on closer inspection it falls short of being truly competitive because the action of a single large buyer or seller can and does affect the price of stocks. This offends our criterion that no single buyer or seller can affect the market price. In addition, you need to use the services of an agent or broker and pay a commission to buy a particular stock, which means that there is not perfectly free access to the market.

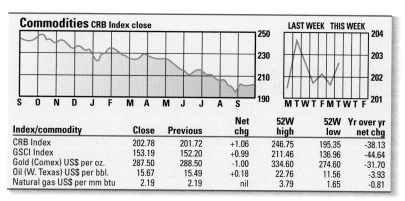

Commodities CRB Index close

Index/commodity	Close	Previous	Net chg	52W high	52W low	Yr over yr net chg
CRB Index	202.78	201.72	+1.06	246.75	195.35	-38.13
GSCI Index	153.19	152.20	+0.99	211.46	136.96	-44.64
Gold (Comex) US$ per oz.	287.50	288.50	-1.00	334.60	274.60	-31.70
Oil (W. Texas) US$ per bbl.	15.67	15.49	+0.18	22.76	11.56	-3.93
Natural gas US$ per mm btu	2.19	2.19	nil	3.79	1.65	-0.81

Source: The Financial Post, September 23, 1998.

At first glance, markets for agricultural products in many countries seem to provide a good example of fairly competitive markets. In Canada, for instance, there are thousands of farmers of wheat and other grain crops, and, though some prairie farms are very big, they are insignificant in relation to the total market. In addition, the products are identical and no consumer knows or, for that matter, cares, which particular farmer grew the wheat or the oats or the potatoes that they purchase. So, on the surface it appears that agricultural markets are fairly competitive. However, as we saw in Chapter 3, the Canadian government has a great deal of involvement in agricultural markets through its establishment of various marketing boards to regulate price and output levels. For this reason, agriculture is not a good example of perfect competition in Canada.

In truth, there are few examples of competitive markets in the modern world, compared with the situation in the eighteenth century, when Adam Smith first wrote about market characteristics. In Smith's day, all producers were small, and the output of most producers was very similar to that of the competition. This is no longer true. Given this fact, it is reasonable to ask why economists continue to talk about and analyze a market structure that hardly exists. The answer is that economists use the construction of the perfectly competitive market structure as an "ideal structure." Then, once we have figured out how perfectly competitive markets work, we have a benchmark with which to judge and compare "real world" markets. In this sense, the economist is no different from the physicist who explains what will happen in ideal situations and then revises his conclusions for other circumstances. Galileo, for example, investigated the behaviour of falling bodies and concluded that they all fall at identical rates of acceleration. It is surprising that many people have learned this snippet of theory, forgetting that it is true only in the *idealized situation of a vacuum*. They will argue vigorously that a kilo bag of feathers and a kilo bag of lead, if thrown from a high building will both hit the ground at the same time! (They don't, as a matter of fact! A kilo bag of feathers is far bigger than a kilo of lead and encounters more air resistance.) In short, the physicists' vacuum is like the economists' "perfectly competitive" market.

Finally, it should be said that the economists' definition of perfect competition differs greatly from the everyday understanding of the term *competition*. Most people, asked to give examples of "vigorous" competition, would cite Pepsi-Cola and Coca-Cola or Reebok and Nike or the competition in the automobile industry. To economists, however, this is about as uncompetitive as you can get, since each of these producers is very powerful and exerts a great deal of influence in its own markets. In economics, true competition exists between a wheat farmer in Alberta and another farmer she has never met in Manitoba, hundreds of kilometres away.

The Rise of Perfect Competition?

European fishers are pioneering a trend that is reshaping the trade in perishables across the globe. By using the Internet, they are able to curb the time spent on paperwork and cut out double handling so as to ensure that fish, produce, flowers, etc. get on their way to the ultimate consumer quicker and arrive fresher. "The availability of advance information and the introduction of e-commerce have revolutionized the turnaround time for highly perishable goods" said a spokesman for a Belgian provider of auction systems which is a unit of Canadian e-Auction Global Trading (**www.e-auctioninc.com**). The potential of this approach is huge since it is capable of putting every fisher and every farmer in touch with the whole world. This is just one example of how the Internet can make competitive markets a practical reality and not just the theoretical construct of economists.

The Competitive Industry and Firm

As we have seen, in perfectly competitive markets the individual producer (and consumer) has no control over the price at which the product is bought and sold. The price is determined by the collective action of thousands, if not millions, of separate, individual participants in the market. The forces of demand and supply determine the price, and once the price is established, it becomes a "take it or leave it" proposition for each individual. Using wheat farming as an example, and assuming no intervention from the government, this is illustrated in **Figure 8.1**.

FIGURE 8.1 The Competitive Industry and Firm

The market demand, D_1, shown in Figure 8.1A, is the total demand from the many buyers of wheat, and the supply of wheat, S_1, comes from thousands of individual farmers. The individual farm depicted in Figure 8.1B produces part of the supply, S_1, but its contribution is such a small part that its actions have little impact on overall supply. The market price of $10 applies to all buyers and sellers, including this particular farm, which can then sell as much or as little as it wishes at this price. Thus the producer faces demand curve D^*.

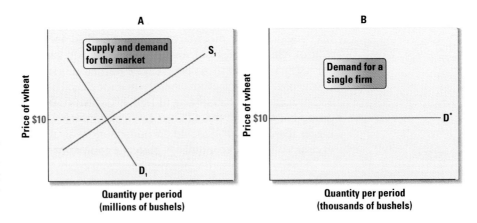

In Figure 8.1A, given the market demand and supply curves for wheat, the equilibrium price is $10 a bushel. This is the market price and is the only price at which wheat will be bought and sold. From the individual farmer's point of view, shown in Figure 8.1B, the price will remain at $10 irrespective of how much or how little this farmer decides to produce. In a sense, to the farmer this price line represents the (perfectly elastic) demand curve, D*, for her wheat. She cannot sell the wheat for a higher price, because nobody will buy it if they can purchase wheat elsewhere for $10; nor would she want to sell it at a lower price, because she can sell as much as she wants at $10. She is very much at the mercy of the market, and should the demand for wheat increase, she will benefit from a higher price. On the other hand, if more farmers are attracted to the wheat industry, the supply of wheat will increase and the individual farmer will lose out because of the lower price. For the individual farmer, the only decision is to figure out what quantity will provide the greatest profit. Before we can do this, however, we need to look a bit deeper at the possible sales revenue for the farmer.

Total, Average, and Marginal Revenues

Suppose that the market price for wheat is $10 a bushel and Farmer Blue is trying to decide how much to produce. **Table 8.2** shows what sales revenues she will receive for different quantities sold.

TABLE 8.2 Deriving Average and Marginal Revenue

Output (Q)	Price (P)	Total Revenue (TR)	Average Revenue (AR)	Marginal Revenue (MR)
0	$ 0	$ 0	$ 0	$ 0
1	10	10	10	10
2	10	20	10	10
3	10	30	10	10
4	10	40	10	10
5	10	50	10	10
6	10	60	10	10
7	10	70	10	10

The total (sales) revenue Farmer Blue receives depends on the quantity she sells and the price at which she sells it, that is:

$$\text{Total Revenue (TR)} = \text{Output (Q)} \times \text{Price (P)}$$

average revenue: the amount of revenue received per unit sold.

The **average revenue** she receives per bushel is simply the total revenue divided by the quantity sold:

$$\text{Average Revenue (AR)} = \frac{\text{Total Revenue (TR)}}{\text{Output (Q)}}$$

marginal revenue: the extra revenue derived from the sale of one more unit.

Finally, the **marginal revenue** is defined as the additional total revenue derived from the sale of an additional unit:

$$\text{Marginal Revenue} = \frac{\Delta \text{ Total Revenue (}\Delta\text{TR)}}{\Delta \text{ Output (}\Delta\text{Q)}}$$

In Table 8.2 you can see that the price, average revenue, and marginal revenue all equal $10. The equality of these three measures of revenue holds for all competitive firms. Stated in the form of an equation, Table 8.2 says that, given a perfectly elastic demand curve,

$$\text{Price} = \text{Average Revenue} = \text{Marginal Revenue}$$

This says nothing more than that the average amount that Farmer Blue receives for selling a bushel of wheat is the price she sells it for, and this remains a constant $10. Similarly, the marginal revenue (the amount she receives for selling an additional bushel) is also a constant $10, that is, the same as the price. Although this might all seem unnecessarily complicated, we shall soon see that the concept of the marginal lies at the heart of economic analysis. In addition, as we shall also see in later chapters, price and marginal revenue are not the same in other market situations.

Let us look at these variables graphically in **Figure 8.2.**

FIGURE 8.2 Revenue Curves

The total revenue curve is upward-sloping, which means that the more wheat sold, the greater the total revenue. It also has a constant slope (it is a straight line) because each additional bushel sold increases the total revenue by the same amount, in this example, by $10.

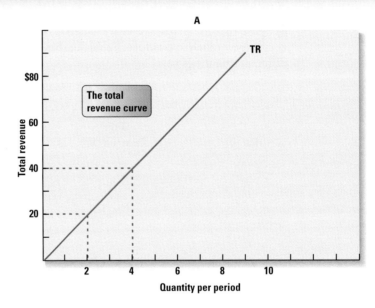

The average revenue, the marginal revenue, and the price are all equal to $10, and all remain constant regardless of the quantity sold. This horizontal line is also the demand curve faced by the individual firm.

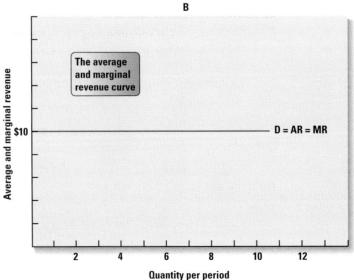

The total revenue curve is a straight, upward-sloping curve whose steepness depends on the marginal revenue (or price) of the product. The greater the price, the steeper will be the slope of the TR curve. Since average and marginal revenues are equal, they are represented by a single curve, as we already saw in Figure 8.1B. This curve is horizontal to the output axis.

Price, Profit, and Output under Perfect Competition

We have seen that the price at which the farmer can sell her wheat is a given; she has no control over it. Her only decision is to decide which output level will produce the maximum profit. (Economists generally assume that profit maximization is the prime goal of the firm. Whether this is a legitimate assumption, and what other goals might be considered, is a discussion we will leave until Chapter 11.) Profit maximization depends on both the revenue and the costs of production. **Table 8.3** repeats the revenue information from Table 8.2 and adds to it the costs of production on Farmer Blue's farm.

TABLE 8.3 Total Revenue, Cost, and Profit for a Perfectly Competitive Producer

Output (Q)	Price (AR = MR)	Total Revenue (TR)	Total Cost (TC)	Total Profit (Tπ)
0	$ 10	$ 0	$ 12	$-12
1	10	10	17	-7
2	10	20	20	0
3	10	30	25	5
4	10	40	34	6
5	10	50	45	5
6	10	60	60	0
7	10	70	78	-8

Total profit is the difference between total revenue and total costs. That is:

$$T\pi = TR - TC$$

The amount of profit—we are talking about economic profit—varies with the output level. When Farmer Blue produces no wheat, she still has to contend with fixed costs of $12 and so would make a loss of $12 at zero output. If she produces an output of one bushel, she would still make a loss (of $7), though it is less than when she produces nothing at all. If she produces 2 bushels, she will just break even, that is, her total costs and revenue are equal so that she makes zero profit. This level of output is referred to by economists as the **break-even output**. Remember, though, that economists regard a normal profit as being part of costs, so that although Farmer Blue is making zero economic profit when she produces 2 bushels, she is still making normal profit and would therefore remain a producer rather than go out of business. If she were to produce an output of more than 2 bushels, she would be making not only normal profit, but also the economic profit shown in the table. She would make maximum economic profit of $6 at an output of 4 bushels. As Farmer Blue tries to increase

break-even output: the level of output at which the sales revenue of the firm just covers fixed and variable costs, including normal profit.

1. Suppose that the total fixed costs of the farmer depicted in Table 8.3 were to increase by $5. What would be the new level of break-even output and the profit-maximizing output?

production above an output of 4, her costs (both marginal and average) start to rise faster than the revenue, so the total profits start to decline. At an output of 6 she would again be breaking even, and at outputs above 6 she would start to encounter losses.

A firm will maximize profit, therefore, when:

(Total Revenue − Total Cost) is greatest.

This idea is illustrated in **Figure 8.3**.

FIGURE 8.3 Total Revenue, Costs, and Profits

If Farmer Blue produces either 0 or 1 bushel, she will make an economic loss because the total costs will exceed the total revenue. The amount of loss is illustrated as the distance between the TR curve and the TC curve and is shown explicitly at the bottom in the total profit curve. At an output of 2 bushels, the two curves intersect, which implies zero profit; that is, this is the break-even output. Any output between 2 and 6 will produce an economic profit, since the TR curve lies above the TC curve. Maximum profits occur at the point where the distance between the two curves is greatest—at an output of 4 bushels. The total profit curve is at a peak at this output. Outputs greater than 6 would result in a loss, since the TR curve is below the TC curve.

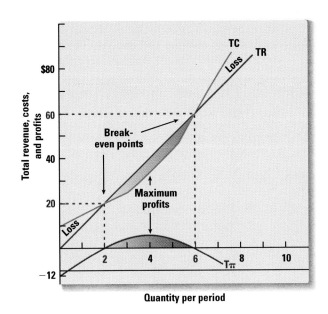

Because of fixed costs, total costs are always higher than revenues at low output levels. Until break-even is reached at an output of 2 bushels, the total cost curve is above the total revenue curve and Farmer Blue would be making a loss; this is shown in the total profit curve at the bottom of the graph. Break-even occurs where the two curves intersect, at outputs of 2 and 6 bushels, and where the total profit curve crosses the horizontal axis. At these two output levels, total profit is zero. At outputs above 6 bushels, Farmer Blue would again be making a loss, but any output between 2 and 6 would produce a profit. Graphically, the distance between the two curves shows the amount of profit or loss, and the greatest profit is realized when the gap between the two curves is greatest, and this occurs at an output of 4 bushels. This is shown explicitly in the total profit curve.

Returning to Farmer Blue, if the price of wheat increases, she will enjoy a higher total revenue at every price. This means that at every output level, total profit will be higher (or total losses lower). In addition, as **Table 8.4A** shows, the range of outputs where she can make a profit is greater.

SELF-TEST

2. Given the following data for Marshall's Meat Ltd., calculate the level of total profits at each output and plot the total revenue, total cost, and profit curves. Indicate the break-even and profit-maximizing outputs:

Output (Q)	Price (P)	Total Costs (TC)
0	$50	$ 40
1	50	115
2	50	160
3	50	190
4	50	210
5	50	250
6	50	280
7	50	350
8	50	450

TABLE 8.4 Total Profit at Different Price Levels

		A Price = $12		B Price = $8.50	
Output (Q)	Total Costs (TC)	Total Revenue (TR)	Total Profit (Tπ)	Total Revenue (TR)	Total Profit (Tπ)
0	$12	$0	−$12	$ 0.00	−$12.00
1	17	12	−5	8.50	−8.50
2	20	24	4	17.00	−3.00
3	25	36	11	25.50	0.50
4	34	48	14	34.00	0.00
5	45	60	15	42.50	−2.50
6	60	72	12	51.00	−9.00
7	78	84	6	59.50	−18.50

If the price increases to $12, it is possible for her to make a profit at any output between 2 and 7, and the amount of profit is higher at every output level than when the price was $10. Her profit-maximizing output level is now at the higher level of 5. In contrast, a drop in the price of wheat to, say, $8.50 a bushel, as depicted in **Table 8.4**, means that the profitable output levels narrow—only an output of 3 bushels is profitable. The level of profit is also lower at every output, and the profit-maximizing output is reduced to an output of 3.

In summary:

> **A higher price implies a wider range of profitable outputs, increased production, and greater profit.**

In contrast, a lower price reduces the range of profitable outputs and results in lower production and smaller profit (or bigger losses) for the producers. Using the numbers from Table 8.4, these ideas are presented in **Figure 8.4**.

FIGURE 8.4 The Effect on Production and Profits of a Change in Price

The higher the price of wheat, the greater the total revenue at each output level. This will mean a steeper TR curve. The lower the price, the flatter the curve. At a price of $12, economic profits can be made at any output greater than 1 bushel. At a price of $8.50, an economic profit can be made only at a single output level of 3 bushels.

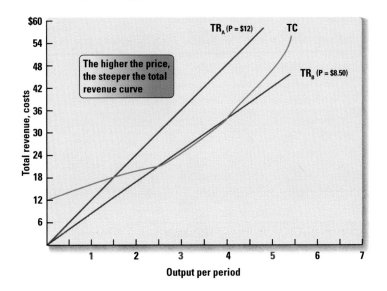

3. Given the data in Table 8.4, calculate the break-even and profit-maximizing outputs if the price of wheat is $14 a bushel.

The Marginal Approach to Profitability

An alternative method of finding the maximum profit level for the producer is in terms of marginals. This marginal approach, though at first glance slightly more daunting than the total approach, is a far more revealing way of looking at profit and also highlights other interesting facets. Let us begin by looking at the average and marginal costs in graphical form, as shown in **Figure 8.5**.

The cost curves are the short-run costs of the firm that we looked at in Chapter 6. You may recall that the average cost curve is U-shaped due to the advantages of the division of labour and diminishing returns. It is an arithmetical relationship between the average and marginal costs that ensures that the two are equal when the average cost is at its minimum.

Let us now begin our analysis with a given price of P_1. Notice that this price (or average revenue) line intersects the average total cost curve at point *a* and at point *b*. These are the break-even outputs we saw in Figure 8.3. This must be so, since if at break-even outputs, total revenue equals total cost, then similarly it must be true that average revenue is equal to average cost. At outputs less than *a* and above *b*, average costs are higher than average revenue, so the firm would make a loss. Between those outputs, the firm can make a profit. But at which is the point of profit maximization? At first glance, it would seem to be at the output where the average costs are lowest, since here the difference between the two curves is greatest. However, this is the point of maximum *average* profit, and we are looking for the point of maximum *total* profit. How do we find this output? This is where an understanding of the marginal cost comes in.

FIGURE 8.5 Average Revenue, Costs, and Profits

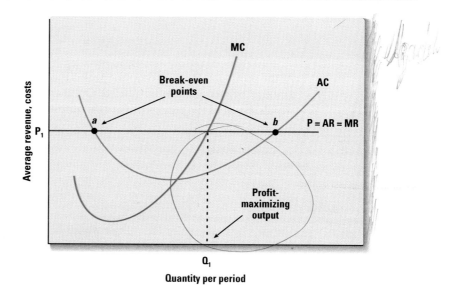

If the price is P_1, then at outputs below *a* and above *b* the firm will incur losses. Outputs *a* and *b* are break-even outputs, at which the firm is making normal profits only. Between *a* and *b*, the firm will make economic profits. The profit-maximizing output occurs at Q_1, where the marginal revenue (= price) is equal to the marginal cost.

The marginal cost represents the additional cost of each individual unit produced. If the firm can sell each unit for more than its marginal cost, then it will do so. If successive units are also profitable, then more should be produced. The firm should produce more and more units so long as the price (the marginal revenue) exceeds the marginal cost. Production should be extended up to the point where the last unit produced just breaks even, that is, where its marginal cost exactly equals the marginal revenue. By the same token, a firm should not produce an item if its marginal cost exceeds the marginal revenue, since that would entail a loss on that item. In terms of Figure 8.5, for every unit of output produced up until output Q_1, the marginal revenue (price) exceeds the marginal cost. Each unit, therefore, is profitable. The amount of profit on each one, called its **marginal profit**, i.e.,

marginal profit: the additional economic profit from the production and sale of an extra unit of output.

$$M\pi = \frac{\Delta T\pi}{\Delta Q}$$

Marginal profit varies because the marginal cost is different for each unit produced. The Q_1-th unit, however, just breaks even. Even so, since the costs include normal profit, even that one is worth producing. However, the firm should not produce more than Q_1 because for outputs in excess of this, the marginal cost exceeds the marginal revenue and would produce a loss (getting successively bigger) on each extra unit. The point of profit maximization therefore occurs when the marginal revenue is equal to the marginal cost. These ideas are important, so let us summarize them:

If marginal revenue > marginal cost → produce more
If marginal cost > marginal revenue → produce less

Therefore, to maximize its total profit, the firm should increase production to the point at which the marginal profit is zero, that is, where:

marginal revenue = marginal cost

average profit: the profit
per unit produced; that is,
the total profit divided by
the output.

In **Figure 8.6**, we can illustrate the amount of total profit by noting that the distance between the *average revenue* and the *average cost* indicates the **average profit**, i.e.,

$$A\pi = \frac{T\pi}{Q}$$

At the profit-maximizing output, Q_1, this is equal to the distance *cd*. If we multiply this amount by the quantity produced, Q_1, then we have the rectangular area P_1cdAC_1, which shows us the total profit at this output.

FIGURE 8.6 Average and Total Profits

Average profit is the difference between the average revenue (or price) and the average cost. Since the average revenue is constant for the perfectly competitive firm, the average profit depends on the average cost. At an output of Q_1, the average cost is AC_1 and the average profit is equal to the distance *cd*. The total profit is equal to the average profit times the quantity produced. This is represented graphically by the shaded area P_1cdAC_1.

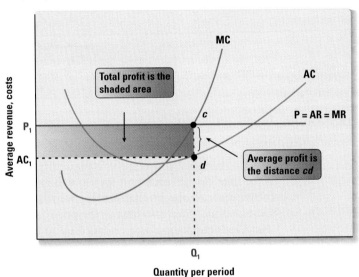

Break-Even Price and Shutdown Price

If the demand for a product increases, the price for the competitive firm will rise. You can perhaps work out for yourself in Figure 8.6 that the effect of an increased price will be that the intersection with the marginal cost curve will now occur at a higher level of output and will result in a higher profit for the firm. But what if the price should drop? Then, the firm will be forced to cut production and accept a lower profit. What we now need to establish is the lowest level to which the price can fall before the firm is producing at a loss. To find this, we need to realize that as long as the price is above the average cost, the firm can be profitable. If it is below, then it does not matter where the firm produces; it will be making a loss. The **break-even price**, therefore, is the price that is just equal to the minimum average total cost curve, as shown in Figure 8.7.

break-even price: the
price at which the firm
makes only normal profits,
that is, makes zero
economic profits.

We can now state that any price above the break-even price P_{BE} in **Figure 8.7** will enable the producer to make an economic profit and any price below P_{BE} will result in a loss. But would a firm ever willingly produce at a loss? In many cases, the answer will be yes. In the *short run*, faced with a *price that is less than average total cost*, the competitive firm has only two choices: continue to produce, but at a loss; or temporarily shut down. In either case, the firm will continue to exist, hoping that the market will eventually pick up. (If it doesn't, in the *long run* it may have little choice but to shut down permanently). So, if the price is below the break-even price, what should it do: produce or shut down?

The answer will depend on whether the loss from producing is bigger or smaller than the loss from shutting down. And what loss will be incurred if the firm decides to shut down? This would be the amount of its total fixed costs. We can thus conclude that:

> **As long as the losses from production are less than its total fixed costs, the firm would be advised to produce.**

FIGURE 8.7 Break-Even Price and Shutdown Price for the Competitive Firm

The break-even price (P_{BE}) is located at the point of minimum average total costs. If the price is above this level, the firm can make a profit; below this, it will make a loss. The shutdown price (P_{SD}) is located at the minimum of the average variable cost curve. If the price is above this, the firm will produce; below this, it will (temporarily) shut down.

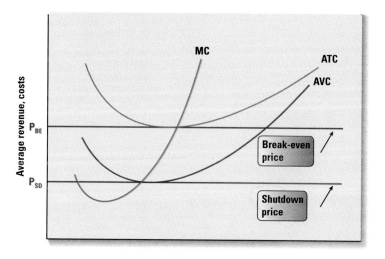

Suppose that the total fixed costs of a firm are $10 000 per week; then the worst loss that the firm can incur is $10 000, which will result from shutting down and producing zero. What this says, in terms of an operational rule, is: since the firm can do little about its fixed costs because these costs have already been incurred, it should at least try to ensure that it can cover its variable costs, such as wages, materials, and so on. If the firm is unable to cover even its variable costs, let alone its fixed costs, it would be foolish to produce at all. However, if it can at least cover the variable costs with a little surplus left over, then this surplus can help to pay for some of the fixed costs. All of this boils down to suggesting that the aim of the firm must always be to at least cover the variable costs, and if it cannot, then it should shut down. In Figure 8.7, this

shutdown price: the price that is just sufficient to cover a firm's variable costs.

means that the **shutdown price** (P_{SD}) is located at the lowest point of the average variable cost curve. If price is above this level, the firm will produce even if it entails a loss because it can more than cover its variable costs. And the best output to produce will be the amount at which the price is equal to the marginal cost. This will at least ensure the smallest loss. If the price falls below the shutdown price, then the firm should shut down temporarily and absorb the loss, which will be equal to its total fixed costs.

Since some of these ideas can seem a little confusing on a first acquaintance, let's summarize what we have said so far in the accompanying graphic.

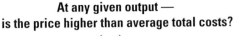

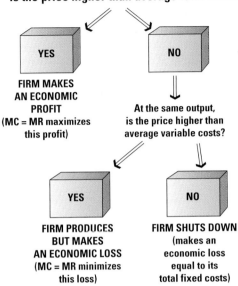

Marginal Pricing in Action

The concepts of marginal costs and marginal profits, far from being esoteric ideas that have no relevance in the business world, play a very important part in determining prices and total profits for many major companies. For example, fixed costs are very high for most airlines. To fly a 747 plane from Toronto to Los Angeles is an expensive proposition, costing tens of thousands of dollars in terms of flight crew, fuel, insurance, landing fees, and so on. The increased variable cost—the marginal costs per passenger—on the other hand, is very low because it consists of a prepackaged meal, perhaps a drink or two, the cost of cleaning a headset, and a lit-

tle more fuel because of the extra weight. Rather than cancel a flight, which an airline cannot do anyway if it is a scheduled flight, it is entirely reasonable for the airline to offer seats below their full costs to at least cover the marginal costs. In other words, as long as the price is above the marginal costs, it will be worthwhile to take on one more passenger.

For a similar reason, many hotels charge room rates far below "total" costs during off-season periods, again on the basis that the important factor is the marginal cost per room, not its average costs.

SELF-TEST

4. The following graph shows the costs of production for Smith Industries, a perfectly competitive firm.

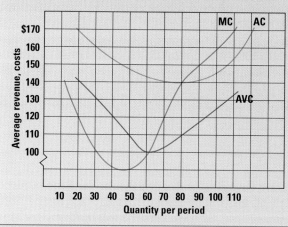

A) What is the break-even price?
B) If the price is $120, what quantity will the firm produce? What will be its average profit or loss at this output? What will be its total profit or loss?
C) If the price is $160, what quantity will the firm produce? What will be its average profit or loss at this output? What will be its total profit or loss?
D) What is Smith Industries' shutdown price?

REVIEW

1. What is the difference between an industry and a market?
2. What are the four main types of markets? In what ways do they differ?
3. What are the four main features of perfectly competitive markets? (For each feature, explain why its absence would make the market uncompetitive.)
4. Why do economists analyze perfectly competitive markets if such markets do not exist in the real world?
5. Why is the demand curve facing the perfectly competitive firm said to be perfectly elastic? Why does this mean that the price for the competitive firm is a "take it or leave it" proposition?
6. Define and explain the difference between *average revenue* and *marginal revenue*.
7. Using the total profit approach, explain the idea of *break-even output* and *profit-maximizing output* for the firm.
8. What is meant by the term *marginal profit*? What is the profit-maximizing rule when using the marginal approach? Explain what the rule means.
9. What is meant by the *break-even price*?
10. What is meant by the *shutdown price*?

The Firm's Supply Curve

Let us now put some flesh on these ideas by working through an example and in doing so help to derive a supply curve for the firm. For a change of pace, let us look at some of the costs of an apple cider producer, as shown in **Table 8.5**. Assume that the output is in quantities of 10-litre jugs.

First of all let us confirm some important benchmarks for this producer. The break-even price is $29, which coincides with the lowest average total cost. If the price is higher than this, he can make a profit; if it is lower, he will make a loss. The shutdown price is $20, which is the lowest average variable cost. If the price is between $20 and $29, the producer will make a loss but the cider is still worth producing; below $20, the producer should, at least temporarily, shut down operations. Given this basic information, let us figure out the supply curve for this producer, relating the quantities he would like to produce at various different prices.

TABLE 8.5 Deriving the Firm's Supply Curve

Output (Q)	Total Costs (TC)	Marginal Costs (MC)	Average Variable Costs (AVC)	Average Total Costs (ATC)
0	$ 40	—	—	—
1	65	$25.00	$25.00	$65.00
2	85	20.00	22.50	42.50
3	100	15.00	20.00	33.33
4	120	20.00	20.00	30.00
5	145	25.00	21.00	29.00
6	180	35.00	23.33	30.00
7	225	45.00	26.43	32.14
8	280	55.00	30.00	35.00

Suppose that the price is $15. We have already decided that he wouldn't produce at this price. By not producing at all, his loss will be equal to his total fixed costs of $40. Now let us see what happens at a price of, say, $25. We know he will make a loss at this price, but let us confirm the best output and the size of the loss. To do this we look down the MC column. As long as the price the cider producer receives can cover the cost of each additional unit, it will be worthwhile producing cider. Bear in mind that the additional costs of producing each unit involve variable costs only. Given this, then, the first five units are definitely worthwhile. However, production of the sixth unit results in a marginal cost of $35, which exceeds the price of $25. The cider manufacturer should therefore produce only 5 units at a total cost of $145 and receive 5 × $25 = $125 in total revenue, thereby making a loss of $20, i.e.,

$$\text{Total Loss } (-\$20) = \text{TR } (5 \times \$25 = \$125) - \text{TC } (\$145)$$

This is certainly preferable to the shutdown loss of $40.

Let's try a third price of $35. We know in advance that the producer should be able to make a profit at this price. Again the profit-maximizing output is where the price is equal to the MC. Looking at Table 8.5, we can see that this occurs at an output of 6, where the MC is also $35. The total cost at this output is $180, and total revenue is equal to 6 × $35 = $210. The profit therefore is:

$$T\pi (\$30) = \text{TR } (\$210) - \text{TC } (\$180)$$

We could continue in similar fashion for other prices, say $45 and $55. The results are tabulated in **Table 8.6**.

TABLE 8.6 The Firm's Supply Curve

Price (P)	Output (Q)	Profit/Loss
$15	0	$–40
25	5	–20
35	6	+30
45	7	+90
55	8	+160

You can see from this table that the higher the price of the cider, the higher the chosen level of production and the more profitable is production. What this table does is relate the various quantities that the producer would produce at various different prices; in other words, this is the producer's supply curve. Since the producer will always equate the price with the MC, the supply curve of the firm is, in fact, identical to its MC curve, as **Figure 8.8** makes clear. Because of the equality between the price and MC:

> **The supply curve for the firm is that portion of its MC curve that lies above its average variable cost curve.**

As we noted before, if the price is lower than the minimum AVC, then the firm would simply not produce.

FIGURE 8.8 The Firm's Supply Curve

The profit-maximizing (or loss-minimizing) output occurs where the MR (or price) equals the MC. At a price of $25, profit maximization is at an output of 5; at $35, it is at an output of 6; at $45, an output of 7; at $55, it is at 8, and so on. These points all occur along the MC curve, which is therefore synonymous with the firm's supply curve; that is, the MC curve is the supply curve. However, if the price is below $20, the firm could not cover its AVC. It would, therefore, be forced to shut down and produce zero. The supply curve is therefore not the whole of the MC curve, but that portion above the AVC curve.

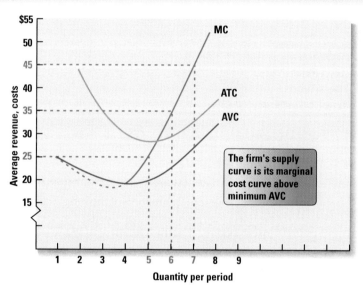

The firm's supply curve is its marginal cost curve above minimum AVC

SELF-TEST

5. Complete the following table of costs for a competitive firm, and derive and plot its supply curve at prices of $25, $35, $45, $55, $65, and $75:

Output	Total Costs	Marginal Costs	Total Variable Costs	Average Variable Costs
0	$ 50	—	—	—
1	90			
2	110			
3	140			
4	180			
5	230			
6	290			
7	360			
8	440			

The Industry Demand and Supply

The total supply of cider for the *whole industry* is derived by adding together the supply of each individual cider producer. For instance, if there were 9 other similar-sized producers in the industry, then the total supply would be equal to 10 times the quantities shown in Table 8.6. This is shown in **Figure 8.9.**

FIGURE 8.9 Industry Supply and Market Equilibrium

The supply of the firm shown in Figure 8.9A is based on Table 8.6. If the industry consists of 10 identical firms, the market supply would be that shown in Figure 8.9B. Given the demand curve shown in that figure, the equilibrium quantity is 60 and the market equilibrium price will be $35. Figure 8.9A shows that at a price of $35, this average firm will produce 6 units, and since there are 10 firms in total, this confirms the industry output of 60.

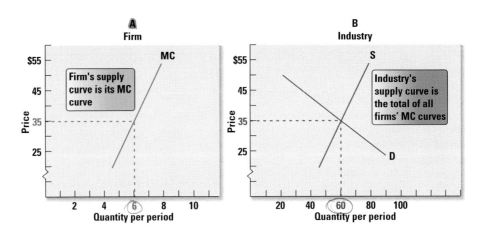

The firm's supply curve is plotted out in Figure 8.9A. The industry supply curve in Figure 8.9B is the summation of the supply curves of the 10 cider producers. Since we have assumed that each firm's supply curve is identical to its MC curve, the industry supply curve is identical to the MC curve of the whole industry. Figure 8.9B also shows the market demand for cider. The equilibrium price for cider therefore is $35 per jug. This price is the same for each cider producer, and we can see in Figure 8.9A at this price the average producer will produce an output of 6 jugs. Table 8.6 confirms that at this output, the average firm will make a profit of $30. (The industry profit is therefore 10 × $30, or $300.) In this way the fortunes of the industry and the individual firm are inextricably entwined. Let us pursue this further by seeing what happens when the demand for cider changes.

Long-Run Effects of an Increase in Demand

We now need to recall what is meant by the ideas of the short and long run from the perspective of both the firm and the industry. As we saw in Chapter 7, the short run for the firm is a period of time during which it can do nothing to affect the size of its premises: the capacity of the firm is therefore fixed. From the industry's point of view, the short run also means that the size of the industry is fixed, because the number of firms in the industry is fixed, and as we said, the size of each firm is also fixed. From the firm's point of view, the long run is the amount of time it takes to change the size of its premises, whereas for the industry the long run is the amount of time it takes to enable present firms to quit or new firms to join the industry. In summary:

> **The short run is a period of time in which the size of both the firm and the industry is fixed; in the long run they are variable.**

Let us now work through the effects of an increase in the demand for cider in both the short and long run. Suppose that new medical evidence suggests that cider reduces cholesterol levels in the body, and the result of this information is a big increase in the demand for cider. From the industry point of view, the effect of this good news is an increase in the price of cider.

Figure 8.10A shows that the increase in demand leads to an increase in price and an increase in the quantity produced. Suppose that the firm shown in Figure 8.10B is a representative cider producer and is initially breaking even, that is, is making only normal profit. As the price of cider starts to rise, this firm as well as the other producers realize they can increase profit by increasing production. The increased production in the industry (from point *a* to *b* in Figure 8.10A) is the result of the present firms producing more (from point *a* to *b* in **Figure 8.10B**) with their present facilities. Each producer, which was previously making only normal profit, now finds itself making economic profit. This situation is unlikely to last indefinitely. New firms will be attracted by the high profit being made in the cider industry and will enter the industry, thus increasing the number of firms. This is shown by a shift in the supply curve from S_1 to S_2 in Figure 8.10A. The effect of this increased competition in the industry will be a fall in the price of cider and a new equilibrium being established at point *c*. From the point of view of the older firms, this drop in the price of cider will force a cutback in production and profit until they are back where they started at point *a* in Figure 8.10B. Although in the long run the price, profitability, and production levels for the average firm are the same as they were previously, there is one big difference: the size of the industry is now much bigger, and the increased industry production is the result of more firms being in the industry.

FIGURE 8.10 The Effects of an Increase in Demand on the Industry and Firm

The industry was initially in equilibrium at point *a* in Figure 8.10A (D_1S_1), and at the equilibrium price P_1, the average firm was breaking even and producing an output of *a* in Figure 8.10B. As a result of the increase in the demand from D_1 to D_2, both the price and the industry output increase to point *b* in Figure 8.10A. The output increases because the higher price induces the average firm to produce more: to point *b* in Figure 8.10B. However, in the long run, new firms enter and the market supply increases from S_1 to S_2. As a result, the market price drops and point *c* becomes the new equilibrium. The average firm finds the price falling and reduces its output back to point *a* in Figure 8.10B.

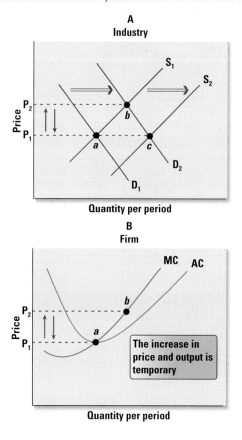

A
Industry

Quantity per period

B
Firm

Quantity per period

The increase in price and output is temporary

Besides the changes analyzed so far, there may well be an additional change to consider. The first effect of the increase in demand was an increase in price, which stimulates firms to produce more. However, the maximum production of each firm is limited by the size of its present premises and by the fact that costs will increase significantly as the firm approaches its physical limits. If the average firm feels that the higher demand is likely to be maintained in the future, it will have every incentive in the long run to increase the size of its facilities. In the long run, the capacity of the industry may increase not only because there are more firms but also because each firm is bigger than it was previously.

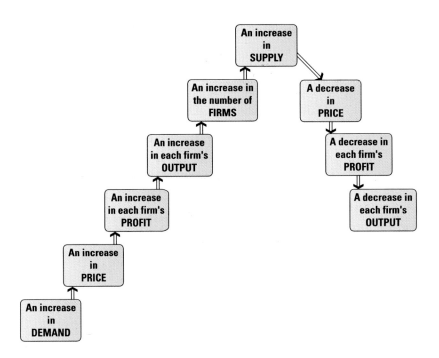

Long-Run Effects of a Decrease in Demand

As in the last example, we will assume that, initially, the average cider producer is just making normal profit. Suppose that new medical evidence suggests that while cider may reduce cholesterol levels in the body, it also causes tooth decay and constipation. Faced with this new information, consumers drastically reduce their purchases of cider. The decrease in demand is shown in **Figure 8.11A**.

FIGURE 8.11 The Effects of a Decrease in Demand on the Industry and Firm

The drop in demand from D_1 to D_2 reduces the output level and the price; that is, there is a movement from point *a* to point *b* in Figure 8.11A. The reason why output drops is that the average firm is forced to cut back production as the price falls. This is shown in the movement from *a* to *b* in Figure 8.11B. Since the average firm is now producing at a loss, in the long run some firms will be forced out of business. This is shown by a leftward shift in the supply curve from S_1 to S_2 in Figure 8.11A. This will cause the price to recover to point *c*. From the existing firm's point of view, the higher price will cause it to return to point *a* in Figure 8.11B, where it again will be breaking even.

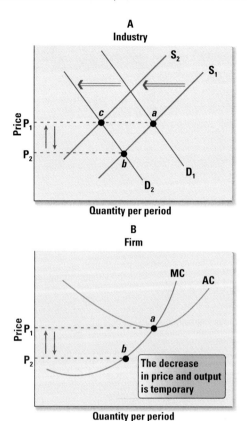

The fall in demand will cause a drop in the price and quantity traded in the industry, as shown in the movement from point *a* to point *b*. This reduction is the result of changes forced on the average cider producer, as shown in **Figure 8.11B**. Here, the drop in price causes a fall in profit and a fall in production from point *a* to *b*. The average firm is now being forced to produce at a loss. This is an untenable situation in the long run. There is a limit to how long firms can continue to incur losses. In the long run, some firms will be forced to close down permanently. The more inefficient ones with higher costs will presumably be forced out of business first. The effect of this exodus from the industry is shown as a decrease in the industry supply curve in Figure 8.11A. The supply curve shifts left from S_1 to S_2. The effect of this will be fewer firms serving the industry with the result that the price will be forced up until the bleeding within the industry stops. This will occur when the representative firm is no longer making a loss; that is to say, when the price level returns to its original level at point *c*. From the firm's viewpoint, Figure 8.11B shows that as the price starts to recover, production and prices will follow suit, so eventually the firm is back at its previous production level at point *a*.

The representative firm in the long run is back where it started, having suffered lower production and profit in the meantime. However, in the long run the size of the industry has shrunk with the exit of a number of firms.

Coal miners leave Phalen Colliery in New Waterford, Nova Scotia, at the end of their shift. This is now a scene from history since the mine was closed in 1999.

Long-Run Supply of the Industry

The analysis we have just done on the long-run effects of a change in the demand for a product suggests that although it may have an impact on the size of the industry and on levels of production, it leaves the price level unchanged. However, this may or may not be true, depending on whether or not changes in the industry size affect the costs of production. For instance, as the industry grows in size with the entrance of new firms, its demand for all sorts of resources, including labour, will similarly grow. The result may be that the price of these resources and therefore the costs of production for the representative firm will increase as a result. If that happens, the marginal cost will be higher as the industry grows, and graphically, it results in the marginal cost curve shifting upward. The result will mean a higher price being charged for the product. If costs of production do tend to rise as an industry expands, then it is known as an increasing-cost industry, and its *long-run supply curve* will look like that in **Figure 8.12A**. If, on the other hand, costs of production were, for some reason, to fall as the industry expands in size, then we have a decreasing-cost industry, and the resulting downward-sloping supply curve is illustrated in **Figure 8.12B**. Finally, the type of industry we have supposed so far—a constant-cost industry with a perfectly elastic long-run supply curve—is shown in **Figure 8.12C**.

FIGURE 8.12 Increasing-Cost, Decreasing-Cost, and Constant-Cost Industries

In all three cases, A, B, and C, the increases in demand from D_1 to D_2 to D_3 are accompanied in the long run by increases in supply from S_1 to S_2 to S_3. If this expansion has no impact on the costs in the industry, as in Figure 8.12C, then the increase in each case exactly matches the increase in demand. Thus, the price is unaffected, with the result that the long-run supply curve is horizontal. In Figure 8.12A, the expansion in the industry is the same as in Figure 8.12C, *but* costs increase as the industry expands. This causes the short-run supply curve to shift back to the left a little, so that the long-run supply curve is upward-sloping. In Figure 8.12B, as the industry expands, the costs of production falls, so that the supply curve shifts a little further to the right each time, resulting in a downward-sloping, long-run supply curve.

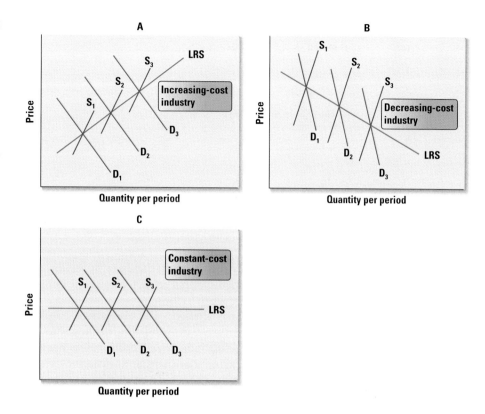

But why would the costs change as an industry expands? The answer, as we suggested, lies in the effect that such an expansion has on the price of resources that a particular industry depends on. If the cider industry consumes a big proportion of all apples sold in the market, then it is likely that as the cider industry grows, and with it the demand for apples, the price of apples and therefore the industry's own costs of production will start to rise.

If that were the case, the cider industry would be regarded as an increasing-cost industry. The long-run supply curve in that case would be upward-sloping, which means that an increase in the size of the industry is accompanied by an increase in the price of cider. If, on the other hand, the cider industry purchased only a very small fraction of the output of the apple industry (or if in general the cost of apples was only a tiny fraction of the total costs of producing cider), then the cider industry could grow without having any impact on apple prices. It would then be categorized as a constant-cost industry, and its supply curve would be horizontal. But what about decreasing costs in the long run? This could happen if, say, the expansion of both the cider and apple industries caused the latter to start to enjoy economies of scale; it could then start to offer apples at a lower price to the cider industry. The cider industry would then be a decreasing-cost industry, with a corresponding downward-sloping long-run supply curve.

SELF-TEST

6. Suppose that initially the market demand and supply for a product are as shown in the following table.

Price	Demand	Supply
$ 2	110	10
4	100	20
6	90	30
8	80	40
10	70	50
12	60	60
14	50	70
16	40	80
18	30	90

A) Plot the curves and label them D_1 and S_1. Identify the equilibrium price and quantity.

B) Suppose that the demand increases by 30 units at every price, and as a result new firms enter, causing the supply to increase by a similar 30 units. Label the new curves D_2 and S_2. Identify the new equilibrium.

C) Assume that as a result of the industry expansion, the costs of production increase by $4 per unit. Label the new supply curve S_3. Identify the new equilibrium, and draw in the industry's long-run supply curve.

In summary, we can see from these examples how dynamic, interrelated, and self-adjusting are competitive markets. A change in demand gets translated into price changes, which affects production, profitability, and the size of the industry. Needless to say, each of these changes will also affect employment and the purchase of resources, which in turn will bring about changes to the suppliers of both complementary and competing industries. Additionally, changes in costs and technology will also affect the profitability of firms and cause the exit or entry of firms and, with it, affect the price, production, and profitability of the industry. In this way, perfectly competitive markets could be called perfectly sensitive markets, because they respond quickly and efficiently to the smallest of changes. In addition, as Chapter 9 will show, they also produce a number of other significant benefits. But that chapter will also point out the ways in which a perfect market can fall down and fail to live up to its billing.

REVIEW

1. "A firm will continue to operate as long as its loss is no greater than its total fixed costs." Explain this statement.
2. What does the term *break-even price* mean?
3. "If the price is below a firm's ATC but above its AVC, the firm will still produce, even though it makes a loss." Explain this statement.
4. Explain why the supply curve for the firm is the part of its MC curve that lies above its AVC curve.
5. Explain the effect on both the industry and the individual firm of an increase in the demand for a product.
6. Explain how a decrease in demand affects both the industry and the average firm in the industry.
7. What is the long-run supply curve of the industry? How might it be upward-sloping? Downward-sloping? Horizontal?

STUDY GUIDE

Chapter Highlights

In this chapter you got an initial look at market structures by focusing on what economists call perfect competition. Using this market structure, you were able to understand and measure the concepts of marginal, average, and total revenue. You were then in a position to compute a firm's profitability using both the total and then the marginal approach. Finally, you were able to work out how an increase or a decrease in demand causes adjustment for both the firm and the industry.

1. *Firms* make up an *industry* and this industry operates within the context of a *market* where both producers and consumers interact.

2. The four conditions that must exist for an industry to be *perfectly competitive* are:
   • many small sellers and buyers all of whom are price takers;
   • no preferences shown by either buyers or sellers;
   • easy entry and exit by both buyers and sellers;
   • the same market information available to all.

3. The *demand curve* for a firm in a perfectly competitive environment is perfectly elastic and is horizontal at the market determined price.

4. *Break-even* output occurs where TR = TC as well as where AC = price (or MR) and this is a situation in which a firm is making normal profits only, with no economic profits.

5. A firm will *maximize* its economic profits where:
   • MC = MR; or
   • TR – TC is the greatest.

6. A firm should *increase* its output if:
   • MR > MC;

   and *decrease* its output if:
   • MR < MC.

7. The *minimum point* of the AVC curve is significant for two reasons:
   • if the market-determined price is below this, the firm should shut down and limit its losses to TFC;
   • the portion of the MC curve that lies above this point is the firm's supply curve.

8. When an industry, which is initially in equilibrium, experiences an *increase in market demand* the following will occur:
   • market price will increase;
   • each firm's profit will increase;
   • output of each firm will increase;
   • new firms will enter the industry;
   • market supply will increase.

9. The *long-run* supply curve for an industry can be:
   • upward sloping, which is called an increasing-cost industry;
   • downward sloping, which is called a decreasing-cost industry; or
   • horizontal, which is a constant-cost industry.

New Glossary Terms and Key Equations

average profit   288
average revenue   281
break-even output   283
break-even price   288
marginal profit   287
marginal revenue   281
perfect competition   276
shutdown price   289

Equations:

1. $TR = Q \times P$

2. $T\pi = TR - TC$

3. $AR = \dfrac{TR}{Q}$

4. $MR = \dfrac{\Delta TR}{\Delta Q}$

5. $M\pi = \dfrac{\Delta T\pi}{\Delta Q}$

6. $A\pi = \dfrac{T\pi}{Q}$

Study Tips

1. Probably the most difficult part of this chapter, for most students, is the derivation of the firm's profit-maximizing output using the marginal approach. Remember, if all else fails, it is always possible to find this output level by using the total approach; that is, for each different price, compare the total revenue and total cost for every output level and see which gives the greatest profit. However, it is worth putting an effort into understanding the marginal approach because it is a far easier and more revealing method.

2. When looking at the marginal approach, bear in mind two things: first, the fixed costs play no part in the decision making, since these costs have already been incurred. You only need to think of them as the amount of the firm's maximum possible loss in the short run. The second thing to remember is that the marginal costs are changes in variable costs and do not need to be incurred, since the firm is not obliged to incur them if it decides not to produce. Given these two facts, you can think of the production process as involving a number of separate, discrete decisions. The owner awakes each day to ask: shall we produce or not today? If not, the fixed costs will still have to be paid, and that will be the total loss. On the other hand, producing just one unit produces both cost (the marginal cost) and revenue (the price). As long as the price exceeds the marginal cost, it pays to produce it, since the excess will help go against the fixed costs. What about a second unit, or a third unit? Are they worthwhile? Yes, as long as the (same constant) price exceeds the marginal cost. That's how we derive the rule that a firm should produce as long as the price exceeds the marginal cost.

3. Another point of confusion for many students is the idea of break-even. They wonder why a firm would ever produce if it is merely breaking even and not making profits. But the firm is making profits. It is making enough to keep the owners in business; that is, it is making normal profits, which economists include in, and regard as, a cost of production. However, at break-even it is true that the firm will not be making *economic profits*. These are an added bonus and are not necessary to the continued existence of the firm. A similar point of confusion, for some, involves the rule that a firm maximizes its profit by pro-

ducing at an output at which the price is equal to marginal cost. Some would ask: doesn't this mean that the firm is just breaking even? No, this is not so. Although the firm does indeed break even on the last item it has produced, it has made profits on each unit up until that last one.

4. Most students can accept the fact that it is often worthwhile for a firm to stay in business in the short run even though it might be operating at a loss, since the alternative is closing down and possibly incurring even bigger losses. Yet, despite this, they still feel that the rule should be that a firm must only cover its fixed costs to avoid shutdown. This is not true. It does not matter whether the firm produces a little or a lot or whether it produces at all; fixed costs remain the same. What it does have control over are the variable costs. These costs must be covered because if they are not, the firm is in "double trouble," being unable to pay all of either the fixed or the variable costs. In this case, it would definitely be better not to produce at all. Therefore, the rule is: cover the variable costs; ignore the fixed costs.

Are You Sure?

Indicate whether the following statements are true or false. If false, indicate why they are false.

1. In a perfectly competitive market, all buyers and sellers are price takers.

    T or **F**   If false: _____

    _____

2. Marginal revenue is the extra income a firm receives above break-even.

    T or **F**   If false: _____

    _____

3. Profit maximization occurs at the output where marginal revenue equals zero.

    T or **F**   If false: _____

    _____

4. A firm will not shut down in the short run so long as it is covering its variable costs.

    T or **F**   If false: _____

    _____

5. In order to maximize its profits, a firm will produce an output at which the marginal revenue equals the marginal cost.

    T or **F**   If false: _____

    _____

6. A firm will maximize its profits at the output at which the difference between its average revenue and average total cost is greatest.

    T or **F**   If false: _____

    _____

7. The supply curve of the firm in perfect competition is that portion of the marginal cost curve above the average variable cost curve.

    T or **F**   If false: _____

    _____

8. An increase in the demand for a product will cause many firms to leave the industry.

    T or **F**   If false: _____

    _____

9. The long-run supply curve of an increasing-cost industry is upward-sloping.

    T or **F**   If false: _____

    _____

10. The reason why the long-run supply curve is upward- or downward-sloping is the result of changes in production costs that accompany any change in the size of the industry.

    T or **F**   If false: _____

    _____

Choose the Best

11. What is the name of the type of market that is dominated by a few firms?
    a) Oligopoly.
    b) Monopolistic competition.

12. Which of the following refers to the perfectly competitive firm?
    a) It is a price maker.
    b) It is a price taker.

13. How is average revenue defined?
    a) It is the extra revenue derived from the sale of one more unit.
    b) It is the total revenue divided by the number of units sold.

14. What type of product is sold by the representative firm in a perfectly competitive market?
    a) The same as is sold by the other firms.
    b) A unique product.
    c) A product similar to that sold by the other firms.

15. What does break-even output mean?
    a) The output at which the price is equal to the average revenue.
    b) The output at which the price is equal to the marginal revenue.
    c) The output at which the price is equal to the average total cost.

16. Which of the following conditions means that the competitive firm is maximizing its profits?
    a) That the price equals average revenue.
    b) That the price is equal to marginal revenue.
    c) That the price is equal to marginal cost.

17. What is the shape of the demand curve facing the perfectly competitive firm?
    a) Downward-sloping.
    b) Horizontal.
    c) Vertical.

18. Which of the following industries provides the best example of a perfectly competitive market?
    a) Insurance.
    b) Hairdressing.
    c) Oil refining.
    d) Agriculture.

19. What will happen graphically if firms exit from a perfectly competitive industry?

a) The market demand curve will shift to the right.
b) The market demand curve will shift to the left.
c) The market supply curve will shift to the right.
d) The market supply curve will shift to the left.

20. What action should a perfectly competitive firm take if, at its present output, MC is both increasing and is greater than the price and the price is greater than the average variable cost?
    a) It should shut down.
    b) It should increase its output.
    c) It should decrease its output.
    d) It should increase the price.

21. What long-run effect will a decrease in market demand have on a constant-cost industry?
    a) The price will stay the same, and the number of firms in the industry will increase.
    b) The price will stay the same, and the number of firms in the industry will decrease.
    c) The price will decrease, and the number of firms in the industry will increase.
    d) The price will decrease, and the number of firms in the industry will decrease.

22. What long-run effect will a decrease in market demand have on a decreasing-cost industry?
    a) The price will increase, and the number of firms in the industry will increase.
    b) The price will increase, and the number of firms in the industry will decrease.
    c) The price will decrease, and the number of firms in the industry will increase.
    d) The price will decrease, and the number of firms in the industry will decrease.

23. What is the correct interpretation of the perfectly competitive firm's supply curve?
    a) It is the same as its average variable cost curve.
    b) It is the same as its total variable cost curve.
    c) It is the same as the portion of its marginal cost curve that lies above the average variable cost curve.
    d) It is the same as the portion of its average variable cost curve that lies above the marginal cost curve.

Refer to **Table 8.7** to answer questions 24, 25, 26, 27, and 28.

TABLE 8.7

Output	Total Costs
0	$10
1	15
2	18
3	20
4	23
5	28
6	38
7	50

24. Refer to Table 8.7 to answer this question. What is the value of the break-even price?
a) $3.60.
b) $5.
c) $5.60.
d) $18.
e) $28.

25. Refer to Table 8.7 to answer this question. What is the value of the shutdown price?
a) $3.25.
b) $4.
c) $5.75.
d) $13.
e) $23.

26. Refer to Table 8.7 to answer this question. What is the profit-maximizing output if the price is $3?
a) 0.
b) 3.
c) 4.
d) 5.
e) 6.

27. Refer to Table 8.7 to answer this question. What is the profit-maximizing output if the price is $10?
a) 0.
b) 3.
c) 4.
d) 5.
e) 6.

28. Refer to Table 8.7 to answer this question. If the price is $10, what profit or loss will this producer earn?
a) 0.
b) -$4.40.
c) +$4.40.
d) +$22.
e) +$32.

Refer to **Figure 8.13** to answer questions 29 and 30.

FIGURE 8.13

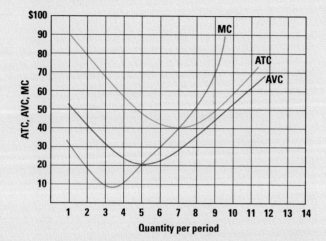

29. Refer to Figure 8.13 to answer this question. If the price of the product is $70, what is the profit-maximizing output, and what is the amount of economic profits?
a) 7 and zero.
b) 7 and $10.
c) 7 and $70.
d) 9 and $180.
e) 11 and zero.

30. Refer to Figure 8.13 to answer this question. What are the values of the shutdown price and the break-even price?
a) $10 and $20.
b) $10 and $40.
c) $10 and $50.
d) $20 and $40.
e) Cannot be determined from this information.

Simple Calculations

31. If the price of oats is $3 per kilo, calculate the total revenue and the total profit (or loss) at the following quantities:

Quantity (kilos)	600	700	800	900	1000
Total revenue					
Total cost	$2000	2150	2400	2650	2910
Total profit					

32. A grummit maker sold 45 grummits last week and received total revenue of $1215. This week he sold 48 grummits and received total revenue of $1296. What is the average and marginal revenue of grummits?

Average: _____ ; marginal: _____ .

33. Complete the following table which shows the total profits from producing grummits:

Quantity	11	12	13	14	15	16
Total profit	$220	$264	$325	$336	$345	$352
Average profit						
Marginal profit						

Problems

34. **Figure 8.14** shows the TC and TVC curves of Galbraith's Globes Inc., a perfectly competitive firm.

FIGURE 8.14

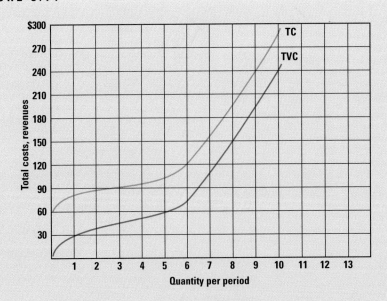

a) If the price is $30, draw in the total revenue curve and label it TR₁. At this price, what is the break-even output(s), the profit-maximizing output, and the level of profits at that output?
Break-even output: _____; profit-maximizing output: _____;
profit: $_____.

b) Draw a total revenue curve, labelled TR₂, which results in Galbraith's Globes, at best, breaking even. What is the value of the corresponding break-even price?
Price: $_____.

c) Draw a total revenue curve, labelled TR₃, which results in Galbraith's Globes, at best, just remaining in operation. What is the value of the corresponding shutdown price?
Price: $_____.

35. **Table 8.8** shows the cost data for Ricardo Runners, a perfectly competitive firm.

TABLE 8.8

Quantity of Output	Total Cost	Marginal Cost
0	$100	—
1	_____	$40
2	_____	30
3	_____	20
4	_____	30
5	_____	40
6	_____	50
7	_____	60
8	_____	70

a) What is the amount of the shutdown loss; that is, what loss will Ricardo Runners incur if it doesn't produce at all?

b) Given that a firm should continue to produce as long as the price exceeds the marginal cost, how much will Ricardo Runners produce, and what will be its profit or loss at the prices in **Table 8.9**?

TABLE 8.9

Price ($)	Quantity of Output	Profit(+)/Loss(−) ($)
25	_____	_____
35	_____	_____
45	_____	_____
55	_____	_____
65	_____	_____

36. **Table 8.10** presents the cost data for three firms that are the only firms in a competitive industry.

TABLE 8.10

Quantity Output	Firm 1 Marginal Cost	Firm 2 Marginal Cost	Firm 3 Marginal Cost
1	$30	$20	$25
2	25	15	20
3	30	10	15
4	35	15	10
5	40	20	5
6	45	25	10
7	50	30	15
8	55	35	20
9	60	40	25
10	65	45	30
11	70	50	35
12	75	55	40
Minimum average variable cost	30	12	10
Total fixed cost	30	45	60

a) In Figure 8.15, graph the supply curves for the three firms and the resulting market supply curve.
b) Given the demand curve shown, what will be the equilibrium price and output in the market?
   Price: $_____; quantity traded: $_____.
c) At this price, how much will each firm produce, and what will be the profit or loss of each? (Fill in your answers in **Table 8.11**.)

FIGURE 8.15

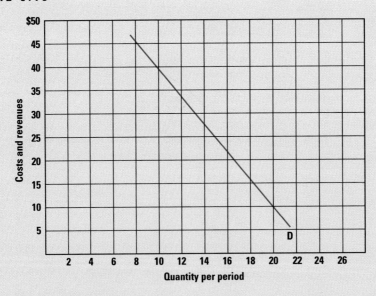

TABLE 8.11

	Firm 1	Firm 2	Firm 3
Output	_____	_____	_____
Profit (+)/loss (−)	_____	_____	_____

37. In **Figure 8.16**, graph A shows the market demand and supply in a competitive market, and graph B shows the cost curves of a representative firm in that industry.

a) What is the value of equilibrium price and quantity in the market?
Price: _____; quantity traded: _____.

b) At equilibrium, what quantity is the firm producing, and what is its total profit or loss?
Quantity: _____; profit (+)/loss (–): _____.
Suppose that the demand were to increase by 600 units.

c) What will be the new equilibrium price and market quantity?
Price: _____; quantity traded: _____.

d) At this new equilibrium, what quantity is the firm producing, and what is its total profit or loss?
Quantity: _____; profit (+)/loss (–): _____.

FIGURE 8.16

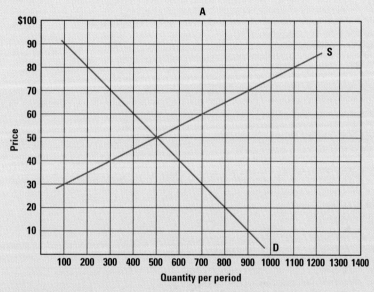

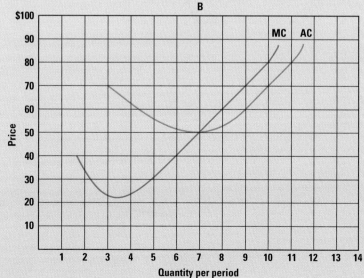

Translations

You are given the following information for the Malthus Mushroom Company, which produces in a perfectly competitive market.

$$\text{TFC} = \$72 \qquad \text{Price} = \$30$$

The marginal cost of each unit produced appears in **Table 8.12**.

TABLE 8.12

Quantity	MC
1	$40
2	25
3	10
4	15
5	20
6	25
7	30
8	35
9	40
10	45

Draw the MC, AVC, ATC, and AR curves in **Figure 8.17**. At the profit-maximizing output, is the firm making a profit or a loss? How much?

FIGURE 8.17

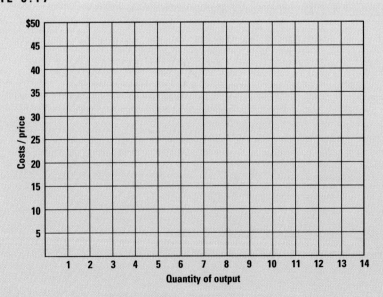

Key Problem

Table 8.13 shows the cost data for Farmer Mill, a barley farmer.

TABLE 8.13

Quantity	Total Cost ($)	Total Variable Cost ($)	Marginal Cost ($)	Average Total Cost ($)	Average Variable Cost ($)
0	6	—	—	—	—
1	____	____	4	____	____
2	____	____	2	____	____
3	____	____	4	____	____
4	____	____	6	____	____
5	____	____	8	____	____
6	____	____	10	____	____
7	____	____	12	____	____

a) Complete the table, and graph the MC, AC, and AVC curves in Figure 8.18.

FIGURE 8.18

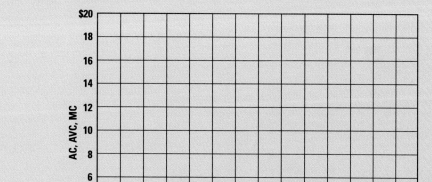

b) Given the prices shown in column 1 of Table 8.14, complete columns 2 and 3, indicating how much Farmer Mill would produce and what profit or loss she would make. (Assume that partial units cannot be produced.)

TABLE 8.14

(1) Price	(2) Output	(3) Profit (+)/ Loss (−)	(4) Total Quantity Supplied 1	(5) Total Quantity Demanded	(6) Total Quantity Supplied 2
$ 2	_____	_____	_____	800	_____
4	_____	_____	_____	700	_____
6	_____	_____	_____	600	_____
8	_____	_____	_____	500	_____
10	_____	_____	_____	400	_____

c) Suppose that there are a total of 100 farms, including and identical to Farmer Mills's, in the barley market. Show the total supply in column 4.

d) If the market demand for barley is as shown in column 5, what will be the equilibrium price and quantity traded?
Price: _____; quantity traded: _____.

e) At the equilibrium price, what quantity will Farmer Mill produce, and what will be her profit? Indicate the price and quantity on your graph. What will be the industry profit?
Quantity: _____; firm profit: _____; industry profit: _____.

f) As a result of your answer in e), will firms enter or leave this industry?
Answer: _____ .

g) Suppose that in the long run, the number of firms increases by 50 percent. Show the new totals in column 6 of the table. As a result, what will be the new equilibrium price? What quantity will Farmer Mill produce, and what will be her profit? Again, indicate the new price and quantity on your graph. What will be the industry profit?
Equilibrium price: $_____; quantity: _____; firm profit:
$_____; industry profit: $_____.

h) Is the industry now in long-run equilibrium? Why or why not?

More of the Same

Table 8.15 contains the cost data for Freidman Product's Inc., a perfectly competitive seller.

TABLE 8.15

Quantity	Total Cost ($)	Total Variable Cost ($)	Marginal Cost ($)	Average Total Cost ($)	Average Variable Cost ($)
0	50	—	—	—	—
1	90	_____	_____	_____	_____
2	120	_____	_____	_____	_____
3	140	_____	_____	_____	_____
4	170	_____	_____	_____	_____
5	210	_____	_____	_____	_____
6	260	_____	_____	_____	_____
7	320	_____	_____	_____	_____
8	400	_____	_____	_____	_____

a) Complete Table 8.15 and graph the MC, ATC, and AVC curves in Figure 8.19.

FIGURE 8.19

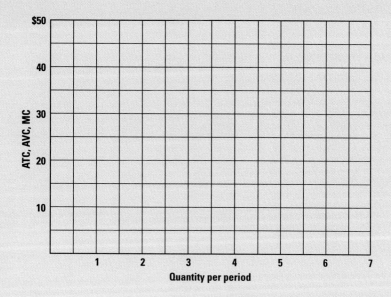

b) Given the prices shown in column 1 of Table 8.16, complete columns 2 and 3, indicating how much the firm would produce and what profit or loss it would make. (Partial units cannot be produced.)

TABLE 8.16

(1) Price	(2) Output	(3) Profit (+)/ Loss (−)	(4) Total Quantity Supplied 1	(5) Total Quantity Demanded	(6) Total Quantity Supplied 2
$25	____	____	____	900	____
35	____	____	____	800	____
45	____	____	____	700	____
55	____	____	____	600	____
65	____	____	____	500	____

c) Suppose that there are a total of 200 firms, including and identical to Freidman Products, in the market. Show the total supply in column 4.

d) If the market demand for this product is as shown in column 5, what will be the equilibrium price and quantity traded in the market?

e) At the equilibrium price, what quantity will Freidman Products produce, and what will be its profit or loss? Indicate the price and quantity on your graph. What will be the industry profit or loss?

f) As a result of your answer in e), will firms enter or leave this industry? Explain.

g) Suppose that in the long run, the number of firms changes by 60. Show the new totals in column 6 of the table. As a result, what will be the new equilibrium price, what quantity will this firm produce, and what will be its profit? Again, indicate the new price and quantity on your graph. What will be the industry profit?

UNANSWERED QUESTIONS

Short Essays

1. A competitive producer either would not, or could not, sell at a price that differs from those of the other producers. Discuss.

2. Explain why the supply curve of the competitive producer is the same as part of its marginal cost curve.

3. Why do the costs of production in certain industries increase as the industry expands, whereas in other industries they fall?

4. Why, in competitive industries, are economic profits equal to zero in the long run?

5. Explain the effect on the price, profits, and number of firms in a competitive market that results from a decrease in the demand for a product.

Analytical Questions

6. If the market is in equilibrium, does this mean that the firms in the industry are making economic profits? Does it mean they are breaking even?

7. Strong competition requires weak competitors. Discuss this statement.

8. It is suggested that, given the demand and costs of production for a product, there is a "right" number of firms for each industry. Can there be such a thing as "too many" or, alternatively, "too few" firms in an industry?

9. Explain what will happen to the output and price of a decreasing-cost industry if there is a fall in demand.

10. Suppose that at a particular output level for a firm, the price of a product is equal to both its average total cost and its marginal cost. Does it follow that the firm will be making economic profits? Will it be making normal profits? Explain.

11. Does the total revenue of a competitive firm need to exceed the total variable costs in order for it to produce in the short run? Does the total revenue of a competitive firm need to exceed the total fixed costs in order for it to produce in the short run?

12. For each of the following cases, a) – g), you are given certain cost and price information for a number of competitive firms at their present output levels. Indicate, based on this information, whether each firm should, in the short run:
    i)   produce more.
    ii) produce less.
    iii) shut down.
    iv) cannot be determined from this information.

a) Average variable cost exceeds price.
b) Price equals marginal cost.
c) Price exceeds both marginal cost and average total cost.
d) Marginal cost exceeds price, and price exceeds average variable cost.
e) Total cost exceeds total revenue.
f) Total variable cost exceeds total revenue.
g) Total fixed cost exceeds total revenue.
   (In all cases, marginal costs are increasing.)

Numerical Questions

13. Figure 8.20 shows the average and marginal costs of Marx's Marbles, a competitive firm.

FIGURE 8.20

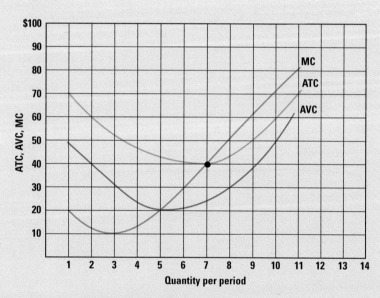

a) If the price is $60, draw in the marginal revenue curve and label it MR_1. At this price, what is the break-even output(s), the profit-maximizing output, and the level of *total* profits at that output?
b) Draw a marginal revenue curve, labelled MR_2, which ensures that, at best, the firm breaks even. What is the value of the corresponding break-even price?
c) Draw a marginal revenue curve, labelled MR_3, which ensures that, at best, the firm just remains in operation. What is the value of the corresponding shutdown price?

14. Figure 8.21 depicts the average and marginal costs of Kandi Keynes, a perfectly competitive firm.

FIGURE 8.21

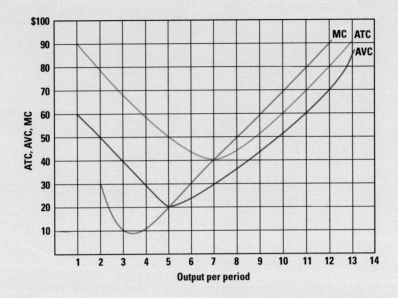

Which of the parts (I, II, or III) of **Table 8.17** is the appropriate supply curve for this firm? Explain.

TABLE 8.17

	(I)		(II)		(III)
Price	Quantity Supplied	Price	Quantity Supplied	Price	Quantity Supplied
$10	0	$10	0	$10	0
20	5	20	0	20	0
30	6	30	0	30	0
40	7	40	7	40	0
50	8	50	8	50	8
60	9	60	9	60	9
70	10	70	10	70	10

15. The cost data in **Table 8.18** is for Veblen's Blinds, a competitive producer:

TABLE 8.18

Quantity of Output	Total Cost
0	$120
1	280
2	370
3	440
4	480
5	500
6	540
7	700
8	960

a) What is the value of the break-even price?
b) What is the value of the shutdown price?
c) If the price of the product is $100, what quantity will Veblen's Blinds produce, and what will be its profit or loss?
d) If the price of the product is $160, what quantity will Veblen's Blinds produce, and what will be its profit or loss?

16. Suppose that the total fixed cost for a particular competitive firm is $80. The marginal cost of the first unit produced is $40 and decreases by $5 for each of the next 3 units produced; thereafter, marginal cost increases by $5 for each additional unit.
a) What is the value of the shutdown price and the break-even price?
b) If the price is $55, what is the firm's profit-maximizing output and the firm's total profit or loss?

17. **Table 8.19** shows the cost data for Say's Sausages, a perfectly competitive firm.

TABLE 8.19

Quantity of Output	AVC	AC	MC
1	$50.00	$122.00	$50
2	45.00	81.00	40
3	35.00	59.00	15
4	33.75	51.75	30
5	35.00	49.40	40
6	37.50	49.50	50
7	40.00	50.30	55
8	45.00	54.00	80

a) Given the prices in **Table 8.20**, indicate how much the firm would produce and what profit or loss the firm would make.

TABLE 8.20

(1) Price	(2) Output	(3) Profit/Loss	(4) Total Supply	(5) Total Demand
$30	_____	_____	_____	700
40	_____	_____	_____	650
50	_____	_____	_____	600
60	_____	_____	_____	550
70	_____	_____	_____	500
80	_____	_____	_____	450

b) Suppose there are a total of 100 firms identical to this one. Show the total supply in column (4) of Table 8.20.
c) If the market demand is as shown in column 5 of Table 8.20, what will be the equilibrium price and quantity traded in the market?
d) At equilibrium, how much will this firm produce, and what will be its profit or loss?
e) As a result of your answer in d) above, will firms enter or leave this industry?

18. You are given the following cost and revenue data for Lipsey's Lemons, a perfectly competitive firm at its current level of output.

$$\text{TR} = \$1200 \quad \text{TFC} = \$300 \quad \text{MC} = \$15 \quad \text{ATC} = \$10 \quad \text{AVC} = \$7$$

a) Is Lipsey's Lemons making a profit or a loss? How much?
b) Is Lipsey's Lemons producing the optimal output? If your answer is "no," should it produce more, less or none at all?

 Web-Based Activities

1. Read **ag.arizona.edu/AREC/WEMC/papers/Today_Tomorrows.html** and determine whether the beef industry is an increasing- or decreasing-cost industry.

2. Perfect competition is generally defined as the absence of barriers to entry – firms can enter into and exit from the market at a reasonably low cost. With the recent explosion of Internet commerce, it is now very easy for existing firms to set up a "virtual shop" and compete in any local market around the world. Review the following articles and determine if "competition" has increased and if markets are, in general, more competitive.
    www.searchz.com/clickz/121697.shtml
    www.techweb.com:80/investor/story/INV19980128S0007
    www.techweb.com/se/directlink.cgi?INW19981019S0083
    www.techweb.com/se/directlink.cgi?INW19981019S0041

An Evaluation of Competitive Markets

What's ahead...This chapter examines the successes and the failures of competitive markets and how with such markets the producer is, to use the words of Adam Smith, "led by an invisible hand to promote an end which was no part of his intention."[1] Out of this comes the concept of efficiency, which we define and explain. We look at some of the other benefits of competition and then examine various situations in which competitive markets fail. Finally, we look at the reasons for the failure and explore some of the ways that these problems can be addressed, either through government intervention or by helping the market to find its own solutions.

A QUESTION OF RELEVANCE...

We are all aware that competition leads to efficiencies and we all benefit as a result. But these benefits come at a cost. Canada is one of the richest countries in the world, and yet it has been estimated that over five million Canadians live in poverty. It is a country blessed with some of the most glorious natural scenery imaginable, and yet its salmon rivers are under constant threat. We live in a society in which new golf courses, executive subdivisions, and corporate highrises are juxtaposed with overcrowded school buildings and inadequate public transportation systems. This poverty, ugliness, and deprivation in the midst of plenty, beauty, and affluence highlights the huge success of the market economy and, at the same time, its abject failure. This chapter may better enable you to understand how this can be.

[1] Adam Smith, *Wealth of Nations* (Edwin Cannan edition, 1877), p. 354.

W e saw in Chapter 8 how competitive firms react to changes in prices and profitability. Each change causes an adjustment by the firm and by the whole industry as well. This chapter will continue to examine this theme of adjustment and will evaluate the results.

Adam Smith popularized the compelling and (at that time) original idea that an economy, and thus a society, functions best if government leaves it alone. The pursuit of self-interest, it seemed to Smith, would lead people, as if directed by an *invisible hand*, to create a harmony of interests. It should be remembered that, in Smith's time, interference by governments in the lives of ordinary people was often arbitrary and despotic. Both of these points led Smith, along with other writers at the time, to suggest that the amount of both political and economic interference by the government should be limited. In other words, he advocated the doctrine of **laissez-faire**.

laissez-faire: the economic doctrine that holds that an economy works best with the minimum amount of government intervention.

For Smith, political and economic liberty went hand in hand. He was arguing that people should be left free to decide their own economic actions, to work wherever and in whatever firm or location they wish, and to produce, sell, and buy whatever products they desire. However, he tried to explain that not only was such a doctrine morally correct but, just as importantly for our purposes, that it was also an economically sound doctrine. An economy works best, he felt, if it is left unplanned, uncoordinated, and undirected. Interference by the government is undesirable because, should a government try to direct you to buy certain types of goods that it feels you want, then you would probably resent its interest in your welfare. After all, you know, better than any government, what you want. Such interference is also unnecessary because you certainly don't need any government to persuade you to buy more of a product if it becomes cheaper, since you will probably do it anyway. Similarly, an entrepreneur does not need to be told that it's a good idea to open a business in a profitable industry rather than in a loss industry; he already knows this. The market works perfectly well, Smith would have suggested, without a manager or a controller or a planning committee to direct it.

Such a doctrine of laissez-faire raises several questions, however. Will the pursuit of self-interest result in the best of all economies? Will it help to generate a good society? Might not the result be a society of greedy and selfish individuals who are unconcerned about their neighbours, a society in which one person's gain is at the expense of another's suffering? And is it possible that an unplanned economy may result in chaos and anarchy?

The major thrust of this chapter is to look at these questions to see how effective a perfectly competitive economy (as envisioned by Smith) is, how well it reacts to economic changes, and how desirable are the resulting changes. Thus, what we need to first look at is how changes are accommodated by a perfectly competitive market.

Technological Improvement and Perfect Competition

If an industry, or an economy, is to grow and prosper, there must exist an atmosphere that encourages and stimulates innovation. Let's see how well perfect competition does this by looking at how it accommodates the most economically important type of change: technological change.

Suppose that Bobby Brewer discovers an improved brewing method that speeds up the fermentation process by 50 percent, so beer can now be produced more quickly and, therefore, more cheaply. The result for Bobby will be higher profits. Will the other brewers (assuming there are no patent laws) be inclined to introduce this new process? Some will, and some won't. Regardless of this, as word of the new process spreads, it's likely that a number of new brewers, sensing the prospect of economic profits, will join the industry. The whole industry will start to grow. However, the result of this influx of new brewers is a long-run increase in supply and a resulting decline in price. And what will happen to the older breweries that didn't introduce Bobby's new technology? Faced with a fall in the price, they will be forced to introduce it; if not, their accumulating losses will force their exit from the industry. Eventually, only firms that use the new process will survive. Producers in competitive markets are forced to be innovative, then, because if they are not, competition from new, more progressive firms will force them to change or go the way of the dodo. That is:

> **Perfect competition ensures *dynamic* efficiency.**

The Effect of Perfect Competition on the Size of the Firm

Next, let's look at the effects of dynamic efficiency on the growth of *individual* firms. In Chapter 8, we observed that in the short run an increase in demand increases both the price and the profitability of the representative firm. This will stimulate the firm to increase production. If the firm believes that the industry is likely to remain a high-demand and high-profit industry, it will be encouraged to grow in size, especially if this leads to economies of scale. This idea is illustrated in **Figure 9.1**.

FIGURE 9.1 Long-Run Equilibrium for the Competitive Firm

Suppose that the firm is operating out of plant 1, and the present market price is P_1. The profit-maximizing output in this case will be quantity Q_1, where in fact the firm is just breaking even. However, if we assume that there are economies of scale to be obtained in this industry, it will pay the firm to move to a bigger plant such as plant 2 and increase its level of production to Q_2 (where P = MC) and thereby earn economic profits.

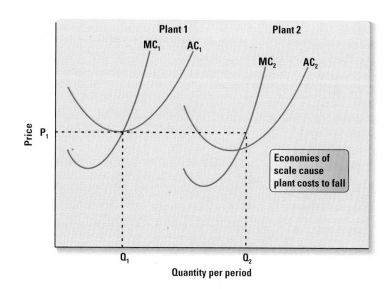

If the firm is operating out of plant 1, the best it can do is break even by producing an output of Q_1. It is not worth trying to produce a higher output than this because the average costs will be higher, and the result will be a loss. If there are economies of scale to be obtained in this industry, however, it will pay the firm to increase the size of its operations in the long run. For instance, if it were to operate out of plant 2 it could now make economic profits because the average costs of production will be lower. In plant 2, profit maximization occurs at an output of Q_2. In time, then, firms will tend to grow in size if there are economies of scale to be enjoyed.

SELF-TEST

1. Exactly why should a firm downsize if it is suffering diseconomies of scale?

Unfortunately from the individual firm's point of view, what is true for it will also be true for *all* firms in this industry: they will all be encouraged to grow in size. The effect on the market would be the same as if new firms entered the industry; that is, the capacity of the industry will expand, which means that market supply increases, and this will result in a reduction in price. The result of this expansion is illustrated in **Figure 9.2.**

FIGURE 9.2 Plant Growth and Its Effect on the Market

The existence of economies of scale will encourage firms to grow in size. Assume that, at present, the price is P_1 and the firm is operating out of plant 1 and is breaking even at a price of P_1 and an output of Q_1. However, in the long run, it will wish to move into a bigger plant, say plant 2, where by increasing the output to Q_2 it can now enjoy economic profits *if* the price stays the same. The problem is that if all firms do the same, the market supply will increase, causing the price eventually to drop to P_2, where the firm is back again making only normal profits, that is, breaking even.

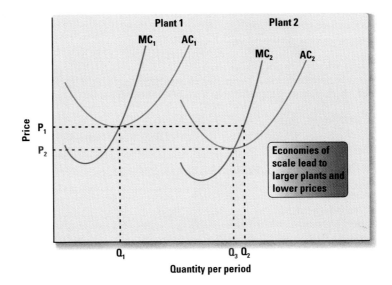

Suppose that the price of the product is initially at P_1 and the average firm's cost curves are shown as AC_1 and MC_1 in Figure 9.2. In the short-run the firm is making only normal profits; that is, it is breaking even. However, there is the prospect of higher profits to be made through growth because of the economies of scale that can be obtained. This will cause the representative firm to move into bigger plants such as plant 2 and, since other firms will do the same this will cause the price to drop as the industry supply increases. In time, the eventual price of the product will drop to price P_2 in Figure 9.2. This is to say that:

In the long run, competitive firms will not make economic profits.

Figure 9.3 extends this idea.

FIGURE 9.3 Price and Long-Run Equilibrium

Over a period of time, competitive firms will tend to grow in size if there are economies of scale to be obtained. However, this causes the price to drop and economic profits to be squeezed out. When the typical firm in this industry has grown to plant size 3, it will have no further incentive to grow because plants bigger than plant size 3 will experience diseconomies of scale. For plant size 3, the optimum output will be Q_3.

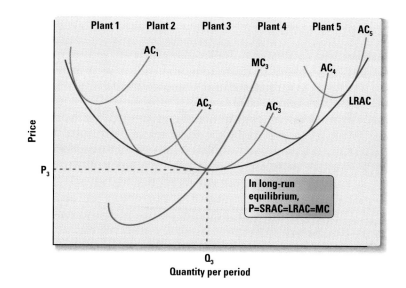

The lure of economic profits will cause firms to continue to grow as long as economies of scale are present, that is, from plant size 1 to 2 to 3. The force of competition, however, means that this growth will result in a drop in price. The two forces combined—firms growing in size and falling market price—will result in the typical firm producing an output of Q_3 in a plant of size 3 in Figure 9.3 and in the price level settling at P_3. This leads to a very important conclusion:

> **In the long run, in perfectly competitive markets, equilibrium price will be equal to the firm's long- and short-run average costs and also to the marginal cost.**

We now need to look at the implications of this important conclusion.

Productive and Allocative Efficiency

Concentrating on the average costs in Figure 9.3 for a moment, we can see that in the long run the firm is forced to produce at the point where price equals short-run average cost and long-run average cost.

productive efficiency: production of an output at the lowest possible average cost.

This conclusion illustrates the concept of **productive efficiency**. This means that a product is being produced at the lowest possible average cost, that is, in the most efficient plant size and at the most efficient level for that size. Furthermore, customers are the main beneficiary of this because they are paying a price just equal to this lowest possible average cost. This means that the firms are making normal profits only.

Productive efficiency is one way in which economists try to evaluate all forms of markets. They ask the question: does this particular system result in goods and services being produced at their lowest costs, and does the price of the product reflect that cost? You can see from our analysis so far that, in the long run, a perfectly competitive market passes this test with flying colours.

But producing products at their lowest costs is not much use if nobody wants to buy those products, or if customers are buying them only because no alternatives are available. There is a second, equally important, test of how well a market performs, and that is to ask: are consumers, given their tastes and incomes, getting the products that they want?

In other words, is the best possible bundle of goods being produced? This is known as the test of **allocative efficiency** and refers to the way that resources are allocated. After all, it is the allocation of resources that determines what and how many products are produced in an economy. Ideally, we would like to ensure that these scarce resources are allocated to various industries in a way that the output of those industries yields the greatest satisfaction to consumers. What the market needs to do is, in a sense, weigh the cost of using the resources in a particular way against the satisfaction the resulting products yield. This means that the marginal cost of production should in some sense be measured against the marginal utility from consumption. As you will recall from Chapter 5, consumers are purchasing their "best bundle" of goods when the MU per dollar spent is equal for all products (the optimal purchasing rule). We also know that, in order to maximize profits, perfectly competitive firms will produce an output at which the price is equal to marginal cost. And what price will ensure both that consumers maximize total utility and firms maximize total profits? The answer is the equilibrium price, where quantity demanded and quantity supplied are equal. Allocative efficiency implies, then, not only the maximization of consumers' utility but also the maximization of producers' profits. Or, put another way:

allocative efficiency: the production of the combination of products that best satisfies consumers' demands.

> **Allocative efficiency exists when prices and quantities are those at which consumers' and producers' preferences coincide.**

In short, allocative efficiency balances the tastes and incomes of consumers against the availability of the economy's resources.

What perfectly competitive markets do is adjust production and consumption between different products until no further gain could accrue to either producers or consumers from any other combination of goods. This is the essence of allocative efficiency and is a major characteristic of perfectly competitive markets. All the adjustments necessary to achieve allocative efficiency occur automatically through changes in price and profits. There is no need for government intervention of any kind. This is the strength of the market that led Adam Smith to advocate the doctrine of laissez-faire. Let's summarize what we have so far. In the long run, firms in perfect competition produce an output:

- from the most efficient plant size for their industry (lowest LRAC)
- at the most efficient level for that particular plant size (lowest SRAC)
- that is productively efficient and at which they make only normal profits (P = AC)
- that is allocatively efficient so that they are producing the right quantity of goods (P = MC)

Other Benefits of Competitive Markets

Productive efficiency and allocative efficiency are the two main standards by which economists try to evaluate markets, but they are not the only benefits that result from competition. As we have previously mentioned, another advantage of the market system (whether competitive or not) has over a planned economy is that *the system is costless.* The market system controls and coordinates itself; it does not require the costly presence of bureaucrats and officials to organize it. In a planned economy, on the other hand, a whole host of officials have to establish the prices and quantities of every single product and resource produced.

A final benefit of the market system is definitely open to debate. Many people would suggest that any idea of freedom is meaningless unless people are guaranteed *economic freedom*. A quote from Adam Smith will help give meaning to the term economic freedom:

> Every man, as long as he does not violate the laws of justice, is left perfectly free to pursue his own interest in his own way, and to bring both his own industry and his own capital into competition with those of any other man, or order of men.[1]

This theme has been taken up in modern days by, among many others, Milton Friedman, the famous economist of the monetarist school. Friedman argues that freedom is impossible in a socialist state because the state, or officers of the state, direct people as to where and how they are to employ their labour and capital. In addition, socialist states usually forbid the private ownership of capital, so the individual has no control over how the country's capital will be used. And, for Friedman, while capitalism does not guarantee freedom, it is a necessary condition for it. He would suggest, then, that all free states are capitalistic, though not all capitalist states are free. In summary, the benefits of the competitive market are that it:

- is productively efficient
- is allocatively efficient
- is a costless system
- offers economic freedom

REVIEW

1. What is meant by the term *laissez-faire*?
2. Explain how competition forces firms to be innovative.
3. To increase profits, a firm may be forced to grow; but if all firms grow, none of them will increase profits. Explain.
4. What is meant by the term *productive efficiency*? If a firm is productively efficient, what condition must be true?
5. What is meant by the term *allocative efficiency*? What condition must exist in order for there to be allocative efficiency in a market?
6. What are the four main benefits of competitive markets?

Market Failures

market failures: the defects in competitive markets that prevent them from achieving an efficient or equitable allocation of resources.

Despite the advantages of the market system, it has been criticized over the years on many grounds. The remainder of the chapter will examine some of these criticisms, called **market failures**. We will look at five types of market failures.

First, it is said that the market is no guarantor of fairness, and *income and wealth inequalities* often seem endemic to competitive markets. Second, *competitive markets are often unstable* and periodically seem to move, without warning, from an expansionary boom to a recessionary slump. Third, competitive markets seem to contain the seeds of their own destruction because they easily admit *forces that work to destroy competition.* Fourth, competitive markets do not ensure the production of a number

---

[1] Adam Smith, *Wealth of Nations* (Edwin Cannan edition, 1877), p. 651.

of important goods and services known as *public goods*. Finally, competitive markets often encourage the overproduction of some products and the underproduction of other products because the marketplace has difficulty in integrating what are known as *externalities.* We will look at each of these criticisms in turn and try to understand why governments feel the need to interfere in the economy in an attempt to correct these deficiencies.

Income and Wealth Inequalities

The question of fairness is particularly pertinent when trying to evaluate how well a particular economic system performs. Critics of competitive markets point out that allocative efficiency, while desirable in some ways, does not guarantee fairness. Allocative efficiency means that resources are allocated in the most efficient manner, *given the tastes and income distribution of the people of that society*.

However, the competitive market system expresses no concern about what that income distribution *actually* is. In other words, if the income distribution were to change in ways that most consider undesirable, the competitive market system would automatically adjust the allocation of resources so as to make the *new* allocation also efficient. Even a society that has a vast number of poor people and a very few very rich people could have an economy that was allocatively efficient. In short, competition is blind to the fate of its participants.

For most people, an important aspect of the concept of fairness is that the rewards should be commensurate with the amount of effort expended. In many respects, competitive markets do reward greater effort with greater incomes. However, the competitive market system does not always guarantee that this will be so. In particular, many people earn great rewards without putting forth any effort because they are owners of resources, and resource ownership is not evenly distributed in competitive societies and is handed down from generation to generation. The result is that the incomes that flow from this wealth are sometimes the result of parentage rather than effort. In short, competitive markets may perpetuate existing inequalities.

There is also the problem of people who possess no marketable resources and who, without government intervention, would be left destitute by the competitive market. This is the case when people do not have even their own labour to sell, perhaps because they are mentally ill or physically infirm, are too young or old, or are in circumstances in which they need to look after family members full-time. The perfectly competitive market would normally fail to provide such people with any income at all.

In summary:

> **The question of what is a fair income distribution is one that the market simply doesn't address.**

Instability of Competitive Markets

Since the dawn of the industrial age, observers have noticed that competitive economies do not grow at a steady pace despite a general upward trend in growth. Instead they seem prone to go through business cycles of booms and slumps. A period of rapid economic growth and full employment eventually comes to an end, followed by a period of low or even negative growth and high unemployment. Such fluctuations are often unpredictable and still not fully understood. They can, and often do, cause great distress for some, and for this reason governments have found themselves forced to intervene in the economy so as to minimize these fluctuations. Such intervention has often been criticized, but the truth remains that the competitive market by itself fails to prevent such harmful booms and recessions. Since the attempts of government policy to manage the economy make up a large part of the subject of macroeconomics, we will not pursue this idea any further here.

The Forces of Uncompetition

Writing at a time when small, independent businesses dominated the economy, Adam Smith looked at the possibility of monopolies flourishing in the future but dismissed the idea as unlikely. But since the competitive market is based on the idea of economic freedom, doesn't this include the freedom of firms to grow or to buy out other firms and, in doing so, to destroy competition? We have seen that large firms do have one great advantage over small firms: the benefit they can get from economies of scale. In the automobile, oil refining, and hydroelectric industries, for instance, the benefits from economies of scale can be enormous. The twentieth century has seen a tremendous increase in the number of very big firms, and many industries today are dominated by a few giant companies. All of this forces us to conclude that the *ideal* of a perfectly competitive market may not be possible given the dynamics of the *actual* market and, therefore, may not produce the benefits that we have looked at.

Provision of Public Goods

Many goods and services consumed in Canada are provided by government. Some of these products could just as easily be provided by the private market. In many other countries, they are. So why do governments in general feel that they should be responsible for providing *any* goods and services, especially when doing so requires the imposition of taxes? In a sense, the provision of public goods is a retreat from the idea of personal freedom because it means, for instance, that you and I do not have complete freedom to choose what we want to buy or not buy.

Nonetheless, there are a number of compelling reasons why, throughout history, governments have felt it desirable to provide certain products. The most obvious case is the one in which private firms would simply not provide them because they would not be able to make a profit in doing so. To understand why this should be so, we need to look in a bit more detail at what exactly economists mean by a public good.

public goods: products that are collectively consumed, so that private firms would be incapable of producing them at a profit, and that therefore must be provided by the government.

private goods: products that can be consumed separately by each individual and are normally provided by private firms.

First let us contrast a **public good** and a **private good**. Private goods, which include all the products supplied by private firms from Cokes to Sony TVs, from Volvos to Heineken beer, are distinguished from public goods on three grounds. Private goods are said to be excludable, divisible, and depletable.

We will define each of these terms in a moment. Public goods, on the other hand, are either non-excludable, non-divisible, or non-depletable. In other words, it is the *nature* of the product itself that makes it a public good—not whether it is produced by the government or by a private firm. Let us look at these three characteristics one at a time.

When you or I buy a private good we expect to have exclusive enjoyment of that product, to dispose of it as we wish. On the other hand, if we are not interested in buying the product, then of course we don't expect to enjoy its benefits. The trouble is, with certain types of products it is impossible (or difficult, without great cost) to prevent people who have not paid for the product from enjoying the benefits of it. If people can

A lighthouse is a public good.

non-excludability: a feature of certain products that makes it impossible to exclude non-purchasers from enjoying the benefits of the product.

non-divisibility: a feature of certain products that means they can only be bought collectively and not in definable units by individuals.

non-depletability: a feature of certain products that makes it possible for additional people to receive benefits without the use of more resources.

get the benefit whether or not they make a purchase, then few people will bother to buy it, and firms could not make a profit from trying to sell it. A classic example of a good which has this characteristic of **non-excludability** is a lighthouse. Imagine a small fishing village where the fishers are often coming to grief because of the hidden presence of a reef just offshore. Someone, quite rightly, decides that the construction of a lighthouse would provide sufficient warning. A lighthouse company constructs the needed lighthouse and charges a fee to all the fishers who are going to use its services. But you can easily see that in this situation there will be no need for individual fishers to pay such a fee, because it will be very difficult for the lighthouse company to exclude non-subscribers from looking at the lighthouse. That being so, the lighthouse company will soon go out of business, and the only way that a future lighthouse could be built is by the government financing it out of tax revenues (or through voluntary contributions). A lighthouse is a public good, therefore, because it has, by its nature, the characteristic of non-excludability.

Other products, although not excludable, are also public goods by dint of being non-divisible. This means that, for some goods, it is very difficult, if not impossible, to sell them in clearly definable units. By contrast, you are able to buy as much or as little as you want of a private good, say, one bottle of pop, or a six-pack or a case. An example of **non-divisibility** is military defence (which is also non-excludable, by the way). It's difficult to see how people could "buy" as much or as little military defence as they felt they personally needed. The same is true of a number of other "products," such as the court system, policing, public health, and so on. For this reason they are, by definition, public goods and must be financed out of the public purse.

The final characteristic of some public goods is that they are non-depletable. Private goods, in contrast, are depletable, which means that the production of more goods involves the depletion of more resources. This would be true of most physical products, such as beer or new housing construction, but is also true of services such as hairdressing or life insurance, in which more clients means more labour expended. However, with certain products, servicing one client or servicing one thousand clients still costs the same in terms of resource use. Think, for instance, of swamp clearance. The clearing of a swamp costs, let's say, $5 million in labour and capital resources, which will benefit a nearby town. However, whether this town has a population of 500 or 500 000 is irrelevant; the cost remains $5 million. It will not cost more to serve more people. The snow clearance of public highways is another service that has to be financed by the government (or done on a strictly volunteer basis), because it too exhibits the characteristic of **non-depletability**.

In short:

> If any product is non-excludable, or non-divisible, or non-depletable it is, by definition, a public good.

Certain products possess all three dimensions: the provision of military preparedness, for instance, is non-excludable, non-divisible, *and* non-depletable. On all three grounds, then, it would be characterized as a public good.

In 1998, HMCS *Ojibwa*, one of Canada's three Oberon-class submarines, ceased sea-going operations and was eventually decommissioned. Canada acquired four modern Upholder-class submarines from Britain to replace the Oberons.

In summary, a private firm will produce a product only if it is profitable and therefore will produce it only if it is excludable, divisible, and depletable. This means that all public goods must be provided by some means other than by the market.

Quasi-Public Goods

It's true to say that public goods must be provided by the government, but not all goods actually provided by the government are public goods—some, in fact, are private goods! In fact, governments today produce a number of goods and services that by our criteria are not strictly public goods. For example, education is not a public good. Indeed, most countries have a private-school sector, since it is easy to exclude non-subscribers. The same is true of private health services (treatment by doctors and hospitals), postal delivery, and the provision of social infrastructure such as highways and harbours. All of these services could be produced by the private sector but are often provided by the government. Such goods are not public goods, as defined by economists. Thus, if they are provided by the government, they are known as **quasi-public goods** (they "look like" public goods). There are three main reasons why governments decide to provide these quasi-public goods.

First, in some cases the costs (to the firm and to consumers) of collecting revenues in a private market might be prohibitive. This is the case with urban roadways, for example. Although a toll charge could be imposed on major highways, it would become a Kafkaesque nightmare if such tolls were introduced on all urban and suburban streets. To prevent this possibility, the provision and maintenance of roads is usually financed from property or gasoline taxes.

A second reason for the provision of quasi-public goods by the government are situations in which it is felt that competition is inefficient because it would involve wasteful duplication. This is particularly true when large economies of scale are involved. Rather than allow a number of competing electricity distribution and public transportation systems, for instance, a government might take sole responsibility for providing such services.

The final, and probably most important, reason why governments provide such services as health and education is that these quasi-public goods are important not only to the people who currently use the services but to society as a whole. These services involve what are known as external costs and benefits, a subject to which we now turn.

quasi-public goods: private goods that are provided by the government because they involve extensive benefits for the general public.

Externalities

externalities: benefits or costs of a product experienced by people who neither produce nor consume that product.

The fifth failure of the competitive market is its inability to take into account external costs and benefits, collectively known as **externalities**. We have already mentioned that in the provision of public goods it is impossible to prevent non-payers from enjoying a benefit. In actuality, in the case of many products it is nearly impossible to ensure that only the users of a product enjoy the benefits and pay the costs. However, with some products the degree of external benefits or external costs are so small that they can be ignored. For instance, if I were to spend money on having my front yard landscaped, I would enjoy a benefit not only in terms of greater aesthetic enjoyment but also because the value of my property would be enhanced. But so too would my neighbours, who would similarly enjoy an increase in property values. My neighbours would therefore enjoy an external benefit. However, this is usually a "free" benefit, unless I go from door to door asking for contributions—not a good idea, in my neighbourhood at least! With other products, though, the external benefits or costs are so great that the market totally distorts the allocation of resources. Let us first take a look at the problem of external costs.

Pollution as an Example of External Costs

When you pay for a product, it is usually assumed that you are paying for the full costs of producing that product. Often, however, this is not the case. Suppose that fishers cast their nets and earn their livelihoods downstream from a pulp mill. What is to prevent the mill from maximizing its profits by discharging its effluent by the cheapest method possible—by simply dumping it into a nearby river? This has enormous implications for the fishers (not to mention the fish). There are any number of examples of external costs besides the obvious ones of water and air pollution. Noise pollution is experienced by anyone living near a major airport or near the lines of an urban railroad. Aesthetic pollution is suffered by anyone whose scenic views from

Water pollution is just one of many examples of external costs.

home or office are suddenly destroyed by a new monster home or skyscraper. It is now acknowledged that these external social costs are as important as the private costs of production. The competitive market, however, does not include these social costs in the overall costs of production. The result of this is that the prices of many products are *lower* than they would otherwise be and the quantity demanded is higher, and thus too much of certain products are being produced. In a sense, then, consumers of these polluting products are enjoying a benefit partly at the cost of other members of society. The present task of policy-makers, given the failure of competitive markets to do so, is to find a way of integrating these costs into the production process—which is what economists term integrating external costs (or internalizing social costs).

We can now summarize the five types of market failures:

- The market may create gross income and wealth inequalities.
- A market economy may be quite unstable.
- Competition, the market's internal regulator, may disappear.
- The market provides no public goods.
- The market ignores externalities.

Limiting Pollution Through Legislative Controls

One method of curtailing the production of pollutants is by way of *legislative controls*. The government could decree quotas on the levels of production or on the level of pollutants; it could set up pollution emission standards and fine or prosecute offending producers who exceed the limits; or it might decree that certain types of anti-pollution devices be installed at the polluters' expense. Each of these methods have been tried, with varying degrees of success. However, sometimes the offences are difficult to detect or to prove or to successfully prosecute. There are many examples of attempts to enforce pollution controls regulations ending up in long courtroom battles that give law firms more business but did not help the environment much at all.

There are, however, other economic methods available to a government to try to reduce pollution.

Limiting Pollution Through Taxation

A second method of integrating the costs of pollution into the overall cost of production (and price) is by *imposing taxes on the polluter*. This could be done by way of an excise tax, or general "pollution tax," which varies with the amount of pollution. Suppose that the marginal costs of production in a particular industry are as shown in **Figure 9.4**. The first curve to note is the total marginal cost curve of the industry (which is the same thing as the supply curve), labelled MPC, which stands for marginal private costs. This curve represents the internal costs of producing the product (which up to now we have simply called marginal costs) and does not include any external costs.

FIGURE 9.4 Marginal Private Costs and Marginal Social Costs

The summation of the marginal private costs of all firms in the industry is shown by the MPC curve. This curve alone gives a market price of P_1 and quantity of Q_1. However, the costs to society include not only these costs but also the external costs labelled *ec*. Adding these costs to the marginal private costs gives us the curve labelled marginal social costs (MSC). If the government imposes a pollution tax of *ec*, which is equal to these external costs, then the new supply curve would be synonymous with the MSC curve and the new price would be P_2 and the new quantity Q_2. The shaded rectangle represents the total tax revenue that the government would receive.

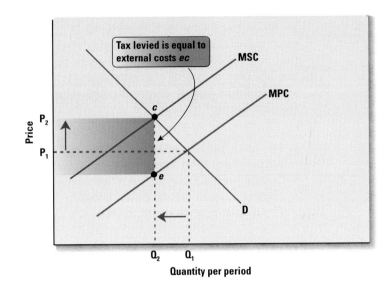

marginal social costs: the additional costs to both the producer (internal costs) and to society (external costs) of producing additional quantities of a product.

Suppose that we were able to measure the costs this industry imposes on the rest of society in the form of air and water pollution. These per unit costs equal the amount *ec* in Figure 9.4. If we add both the marginal private costs *and* the external costs *ec*, then the total costs to society are represented by the higher curve labelled MSC, or **marginal social costs**. These are the true costs of production—the direct production costs and the costs of the associated pollution. If the firms do not have to worry about these external costs, the resulting price, P_1, is too low and the production level, Q_1, is too high from society's point of view. One way to force producers to recognize these costs would be to impose an excise tax equal to the external costs, *ec*.

The effect of the tax will be to increase the price from P_1 to P_2 and reduce production from Q_1 to Q_2. Just how much the price increases or the output decreases will depend on the elasticities of demand and supply. This, in turn, will determine how much of the tax is paid by consumers of this product in the form of higher prices and how much by producers in the form of lower profits. However the tax is split, those people most directly involved with the product are being forced to pay the true cost. In addition, the government will be deriving a tax revenue equal to the rectangular shaded area, which it could use to clean up some of the effects of pollution or help those suffering as a result of pollution.

Limiting Pollution Through Marketing Permits

There is a third way in which the costs of pollution could be integrated into the market process, and that is by what economists call the marketing of pollution permits.

Suppose that a particular lake is the central dumping area for a number of industries and firms, and the government is concerned about the amount of effluents being discharged into the lake. As a result, it decides to employ a research team to determine the maximum amount of pollution this lake could safely endure without serious long-term environmental damage. The scientists come up with a conservative figure of 200 tonnes a year. Given this "supply" of allowable effluent, the government decides to sell, say, 200 one-tonne permits to anybody wishing to purchase them. The price of these licences will depend on the demand for the permits and the supply allowed by government, as shown in **Figure 9.5**.

FIGURE 9.5 Demand and Supply of Pollution Permits

The lower the price of a pollution permit (that is, the right to discharge a tonne of effluent into the lake each year), the greater will be the number of permits that firms wish to purchase. In other words, the demand curve for permits is downward-sloping. The supply of such licences, however, is a fixed amount of 200 permits. The market price, therefore, will be the point at which the demand and supply are equal, that is, at a price per permit of $10 000.

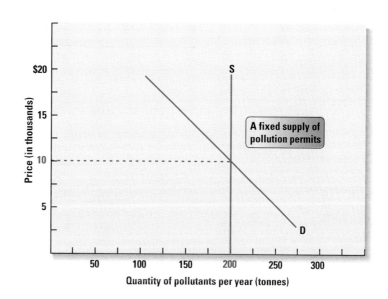

Given the demand and supply illustrated in Figure 9.5, the market price of the pollution permit is $10 000. Purchasing of such a permit will allow the holder to discharge one tonne of pollutants into the lake each year. Those firms who find this figure exorbitant will be forced to find other, cheaper ways of controlling or disposing of their waste.

More significantly, this could also mean that environmental groups, wishing to keep the level of pollution down to a level lower than the 200 tonnes allowed, would be able to purchase permits and not use them, thus preventing others from making use of them. In essence, the market is, in this way, providing private groups with an additional avenue to the decision-making process, which means that such groups don't have to win political elections in order to bring about change. In addition, the government may change the 200-tonne acceptable limit from year to year as circumstances dictate. Moreover, the revenue from the permits could be used to finance other schemes to reduce or eliminate pollution.

SELF-TEST

2. What would happen if, in Figure 9.5, the government were to incorrectly estimate the demand and only charge $5000 for a permit?

External Benefits

An external benefit occurs whenever non-users enjoy a benefit as a result of the production or consumption of a product. A new bridge, for instance, may lower the prices of products for both users and non-users of the bridge. Another example is that of a more effective system for the disposal of sewage in a part of a particular city; the benefits of efficient disposal accrue to everybody in the city, because the system lessens the chances of disease being transmitted. In a similar sense, the external benefits of an educated citizenry are also wide-ranging and include higher productivity and, often, lower levels of crime, poverty, and social unrest.

As with external costs, competitive markets do not account for these external benefits, since the demand for products represents only the private individual benefits that purchasers derive from consumption. The result is that products with extensive external benefits are underpriced and underproduced. Often governments feel the need to intervene in order to encourage more production of such products. We will look at three ways in which the government attempts to integrate these benefits into the provision of goods and services and so increase their production.

Integrating External Benefits: Provision of Quasi-Public Goods

It would be wrong to suggest that the prime reason why most governments provide public education and public medical care is that they recognize the extent of external benefits. The truth is that in many cases the government has not so much granted, as the people over the centuries have demanded, fought, and often rebelled for, the basic "right" to free and public education and medical care. Such services have usually been regarded as necessities, more so than, say, food or housing or clothing. To a certain extent, how well a person is dressed, fed, or accommodated is usually regarded as a matter of private concern, whereas the health and education of people are regarded as being of public concern.

Many governments responded to these demands after World War II and dramatically increased the provision of government services and products. As the public sector increased appreciably, it often extended access from what was considered basic coverage. Public education began to include postsecondary education; health service coverage was extended to dental, chiropractic, and psychiatric medicine; transportation began to include not only the building and maintenance of highways and harbours but also the provision of airports; communication started to include not just postal services but also telephone, radio, and television services. In addition to this, in many countries a number of other industries, including the hydroelectric and mining industries, were nationalized, and in other countries, governments started competing with private industry in the provision of gasoline, concert theatres, and racetracks. This massive proliferation in public services led to a public reaction in the 1980s, and the movement toward "privatization" began. The balance these days between the provision of public and private goods varies considerably from country to country and is in a state of flux generally as countries search for the ideal mixture.

Integrating External Benefits: Providing Subsidies

The direct provision of goods and services is not the only way that the government can encourage more production of certain products; it could do this instead by offering subsidies to private firms. A subsidy is merely a reverse tax, in which the government pays the producer a certain amount for each unit produced. As an example, suppose that the government is convinced that the provision of day-care services involves not only benefits for the children and parents who use them but also external benefits to the rest of society. In **Figure 9.6** the MPB, or marginal private benefits curve, represents the benefits that users of the day-care derive from day-care services. Let's say that in addition, it has been determined that there are external benefits to day-care places that equal an amount of *eb* for each child. The total benefits, both private and external therefore, are shown as the higher curve labelled MSB, or **marginal social benefits**.

marginal social benefits: the additional benefits to both the consumer (internal benefits) and to society (external benefits) of additional quantities of a product.

FIGURE 9.6 Marginal Private Benefits and Marginal Social Benefits

The demand curve for a product, MPB, is a representation of the benefits users derive from it and an indicator of how much they would be prepared to pay for various quantities. In other words, the demand is identical to the marginal private benefits. However, non-users of day-care also enjoy benefits, and this is shown as the amount *eb*. The total of the private and external benefits gives us the marginal social benefits (MSB). Given the supply curve MSC, the equilibrium quantity and price, if external benefits are included, is 60 000 places and $550.

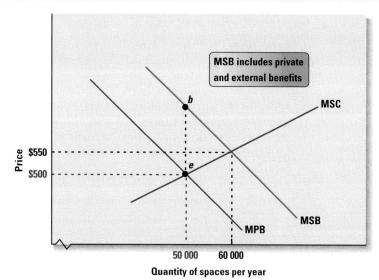

MSC, the supply curve, represents the marginal social costs (which may also be the MPC). If both external and private benefits are considered, giving us the marginal social benefits curve, we have equilibrium prices and quantity of $550 and 60 000 day-care places. On the other hand, if only private benefits are taken into consideration, the result is a lower equilibrium price and lower number of places—50 000 and $500. Thus, ignoring social benefits results in both a quantity and a price that are lower than the socially desirable levels.

One way in which we could achieve the desired increase in the number of places from 50 000 to 60 000 is by offering a subsidy per child to day-care operators. The introduction of such a subsidy would be represented graphically by a rightward shift in the supply curve (the MSC curve)as shown in **Figure 9.7**. This would have the desired effect of increasing the number of spaces to 60 000. But note that it would also lead to a *decrease* in the monthly day-care charge to $450.

FIGURE 9.7 Subsidizing Day-Care Operators

One way in which the government could increase the number of day-care places from 50 000 to 60 000 would be to grant a subsidy to day-care operators sufficient to induce them to build extensions to their premises and to employ additional staff. In this graph, the subsidy amounts to $100 per month for each day-care place. The result of the subsidy will be to increase the number of places and also to reduce the day-care fee from $500 to $450 per month.

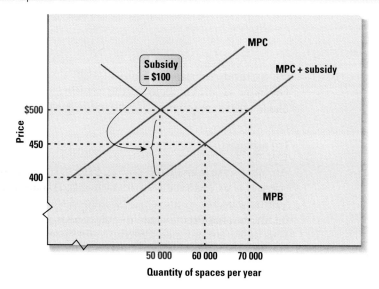

3. In Figure 9.7, after the subsidy has been given, how many spaces would day-care operators offer at $500 per month? Why does the monthly fee drop to $450 after the subsidy?

But there is a problem here. Subsidizing suppliers in this way does not correctly address the fact that because the market ignores externalities, *both* the price and the quantity supplied are too low. Certainly, in our example, a subsidy will increase the amount of day-care spaces, but the result of the subsidy is to make the price even more artificially low. To overcome this problem, some economists suggest that the subsidy should be given, not to the day-care operators, but to the parents of children who use day care. The result would be not only an increase in the number of day-care places but also an increase in the day-care fee. This is shown in **Figure 9.8**.

FIGURE 9.8 Subsidizing Day-Care Parents

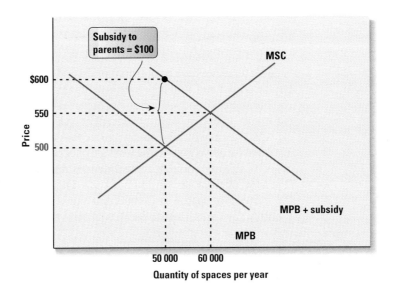

A $100 per child subsidy to parents shifts the demand for day-care places (MPB) to the right, resulting in the MPB + subsidy curve. This results in the socially desirable price and quantity of $550 and 60 000 places.

In Figure 9.8, the unsubsidized demand for day-care places is MPB. A $100 per child subsidy to parents results in MPB + subsidy becoming the new demand curve. Given the supply curve, MSC, the resulting equilibrium price and quantity is $550 and 60 000, which are the socially desirable levels.

Integrating External Benefits: Marketing Benefit Permits

An alternative way of integrating external benefits into the provision of goods and services is to use a method advocated by Milton Friedman some years ago. His suggestion was that, in the area of public education, for example, the government should divide the amount allocated to public education by the number of students attending. This dollar amount per student would be given back to the parents in the form of an educational chit, which they could then use to pay for their children's education at any privately run school of their choosing. If the government wanted to also integrate external as well as private benefits into the scheme, it would have to estimate the marginal social benefits, as illustrated in **Figure 9.9**.

Suppose that we are looking at a competitive market for secondary education and that the market consists solely of private schools. The marginal *private* benefit curve (MPB) is identical to the demand curve. Adding the external benefits of secondary education gives us the marginal *social* benefits curve (MSB).

Suppose that the secondary school population in a particular city is 100 000 students. At that level of attendance, **Figure 9.9** shows that the marginal private benefits are $4000 per student per annum. In addition, the external benefits are estimated at $1000 per student, for a total marginal social benefit of $5000. (The total benefits derived from education in this city are therefore 100 000 times $5000, which equals $500 million.) If the authorities wish to integrate external benefits into the provision of education, then the chit should have a value of $5000 per child in this city. Parents would be provided with one chit per child, to be spent at whichever school they choose.

Marketing the economic benefits of education in this way means not only that every child is guaranteed an education, but also that parents would have the freedom to choose the kind of education they want for their children. It also implies that entrepreneurs would have the right to set up private, independent schools. The choice of schools available would not only include different locations, but also different curriculums, a variety of facilities, and so on. Each school would be paid with education chits, which it would cash in with the government's education board. Poor-quality schools would be unable to attract sufficient students to be profitable and would be forced out of business. It could also mean that a "premium" school would be able to charge "premium" prices; that is, you would tender the education chit plus say, an extra $1000 cash per year for your child.

FIGURE 9.9 Marginal Social Benefits of Secondary Education

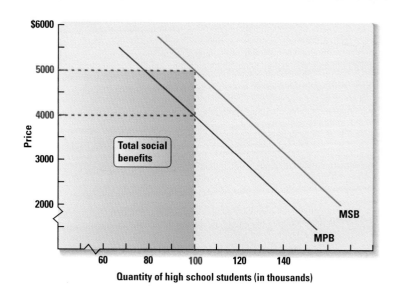

The marginal private benefits from secondary education have been estimated at, say, $4000 per student at the present level of enrolment in this school district, which has a secondary-school population of 100 000 students. In addition, external benefits of another $1000 have been estimated, giving a marginal social benefit per student of $5000. The shaded area shows the total social benefits, which equals $5000 times 100 000, or $500 million.

Understandably, you may have a number of objections to this scheme. The main point of the exercise is to make you aware that there are a number of ways that externalities can be integrated into the provision and pricing of most goods and services. In all cases, however, it does involve the government directing the market in some way so as to encourage the production of those things that society deems important and to discourage the production of those thought to be undesirable.

SELF-TEST

4. According to Figure 9.9, not all parents (or students) in this school district feel that the marginal private benefits of secondary education are worth only $4000 per annum. For example, of the 100 000 households, how many feel that it is worth more than $5000? How many feel that it is worth less than $5000?

REVIEW

1. What is meant by the term *market failure*?
2. List, and briefly explain, five types of market failures.
3. What is one of the major explanations for the inequalities in the amount of income and wealth in a society?
4. In what way are competitive markets said to be unstable?
5. Adam Smith felt that monopolies are unlikely to be successful. Why did he think that?
6. What are three ways in which a *public good* is distinguished from a *private good*? Explain each briefly.
7. What is a *quasi-public good*? Give three explanations of why governments provide quasi-public goods.
8. Explain, and give examples of, *externalities*.
9. Explain three ways in which external costs might be integrated into the provision of privately produced goods and services.
10. What effect does a pollution tax have on the price and quantity produced? Who pays for the pollution tax?
11. Explain three ways in which external benefits might be integrated into the provision of privately produced goods and services.

STUDY GUIDE

Chapter Highlights

In this chapter you first examined the arguments which suggest that competitive markets are both efficient and desirable. Then, the table is turned and you looked at the various ways in which competitive markets can fail to achieve desirable results. Finally, you learned some ways that can be used to try to correct the effects of some of these failures.

1. Competitive markets adjust to *technological change* very well in the sense that those firms that do not keep up with desirable changes will, simply, fail to remain in business.

2. In addition, the direct *benefits* of a competitive market is that it:
   • is productively efficient;
   • is allocatively efficient;
   • is a costless system;
   • offers economic freedom.

3. The ways in which a competitive market can *fail* are:
   • it may create gross income and wealth inequalities;
   • it can be quite unstable;
   • it cannot prevent the rise of monopolies;
   • it is unable to provide certain desirable goods called public goods;
   • it ignores external costs and benefits.

4. Governments sometimes see fit to supply *quasi-public goods*, such as education, even though these goods could be provided privately.

5. The classic example of an *external cost* is pollution, the effects of which can be addressed by:
   • legislative controls on pollution levels;
   • imposing a per unit tax on pollution;
   • setting up a system where pollution permits are sold in the marketplace.

6. The day-care example illustrates how subsidies could be used to incorporate external benefits which the perfectly competitive market would otherwise ignore. This can be done in two ways:
   • a subsidy to day-care operators which would raise the quantity traded and *lower* price;
   • a subsidy to parents which would raise the quantity traded and *raise* price.

New Glossary Terms

allocative efficiency   324
externalities   330
laissez-faire   320
marginal social benefits   334
marginal social costs   332
market failures   325
non-depletability   328

Study Tips

1. Some students confuse the concept of excludability with that of externalities. To sort out this difference, it is important to realize that the production of most products involves both private costs and external costs. The private costs are included in the price of the product and are paid for by the purchaser. The external costs are paid for (though not in money terms) by others who have no part in the production and consumption of the product. Also, most products involve both private and external benefits. The private benefits are the reward of consuming the product, and external benefits are the indirect benefits that non-buyers often receive. It is almost impossible at times to prevent external costs and benefits from occurring, but the chapter analyzes a number of ways in which such externalities can be accounted for and integrated into the market. With certain products, however, it is impossible to prevent some people from enjoying external benefits but, additionally, it is impossible to prevent others from enjoying *private* benefits for free. This last aspect defines the term non-excludability. So for most products, though you can't prevent people enjoying an external benefit, you can, at least, prevent them from enjoying a private benefit (unless they pay for the product). With true public goods this is not true: you can't prevent them from enjoying either.

2. Another possible point of confusion for students is in regard to the three criteria for a public good. A good is a public good and, therefore, must be provided by the government (if it is to be provided at all) if it is non-excludable *or* if it is non-divisible *or* if it is non-depletable. In other words, if a good fails any one of the three tests, it cannot be a private good. You should make sure that you know the definitions of non-excludabilty, non-divisibility, and non-depletability.

3. You should realize that since external costs and benefits are not usually bought and sold in the marketplace, their value is merely an estimate. It is very difficult to put an *exact* valuation on the cost of noise pollution or on the societal benefits of having an educated populace. That doesn't mean that they are unimportant, but on the other hand don't be misled into thinking that a precise figure can be attached to them.

4. Taxes and subsidies are often used by governments to adjust prices and outputs of privately produced goods. Remember that if the seller is responsible for paying the tax, graphically the supply curve will shift left, as it did in Chapter 4 in the sales tax case. On the other hand, if the buyer is responsible for paying, the demand curve will shift left. If the subsidy is given to the seller to encourage more production, it will shift the supply curve right; if the subsidy is given to the buyer to encourage greater consumption, it will shift the demand curve right.

Are You Sure?

Indicate whether the following statements are true or false. If false, indicate why they are false.

1. A market is productively efficient if the price of a product equals the minimum average cost.

   T or **F**   If false: _____

   _____

2. When a competitive market is in long-run equilibrium, the firms will be making economic profits but not normal profits.

   T or **F**   If false: _____

   _____

3. The provision of private goods is an example of a market failure.

   T or **F**   If false: _____

   _____

4. Long-run equilibrium in competitive markets implies that P = MC = AC.

   T or **F**   If false: _____

   _____

5. By non-excludability, economists mean the inability of some firms to prevent certain people from buying a product.

   T or **F**   If false: _____

   _____

6. An externality is a benefit or cost experienced by people who neither produce nor consume that product.

   T or **F**   If false: _____

   _____

7. A subsidy granted to a polluting firm would be one way of integrating external costs.

   T or **F**   If false: _____

   _____

8. Marginal social benefits are the total of both marginal private benefits and marginal external benefits.

   T or **F**   If false: _____

   _____

9. By introducing a pollution licence fee for a lake, the government allows the polluters to decide for themselves the acceptable level of pollution.

   T or **F**   If false: _____

   _____

10. If external benefits are not integrated into the market, insufficient quantities of a product will be produced.

    T or **F**   If false: _____

    _____

Choose the Best

11. When does allocative efficiency occur?
    a) When the price of the product is equal to its average cost.
    b) When the price of the product is equal to its marginal cost.

12. What does the doctrine of laissez-faire mean?
    a) That the government works best with limited market interference.
    b) That the market works best with limited government interference.

13. If the price of a product is less than its marginal costs, then:
    a) Society would prefer more of this product being produced.
    b) Society would prefer less of this product being produced.

14. Which of the following statements is correct regarding marginal social costs?
    a) They include only the private costs of production.
    b) They include only the external costs of production.
    c) They include both the private and the external costs of production.

15. Which of the following is an example of a public good?
    a) A prescription drug.
    b) Postsecondary education.
    c) A lighthouse.

16. What is a quasi-public good?
    a) A public good that also has many characteristics of a private good.
    b) A private good provided by a government.
    c) A public good sold privately to individuals.

17. What does the long-run equilibrium of a perfectly competitive market suggest?
    a) That the price is equal to the lowest SRAC but not necessarily the lowest LRAC.
    b) That the price is equal to the lowest LRAC but not necessarily the lowest SRAC.
    c) That the price is equal to both the lowest SRAC and the lowest LRAC.

18. All of the following, *except one*, are features of a private good. Which is the exception?
    a) Private goods are produced by private firms for a profit.
    b) Private goods are products that could not be produced by the government.
    c) Private goods can be consumed separately by each individual.
    d) Private goods cost more for additional quantities.

19. All of the following, *except one*, are features of a public good. Which is the exception?
    a) Public goods are products that are collectively consumed.
    b) Public goods do not usually cause external costs.
    c) Public goods are provided by the government.
    d) Public goods could not be produced by private firms at a profit.

20. What does the term market failure mean?
    a) The inability of markets to ensure that people get what they want.
    b) The inability of markets to ensure that productive or allocative efficiency is attained.
    c) The inability of the government to ensure that productive or allocative efficiency is attained.
    d) The inability of the government to ensure that people get what they want.

21. Why does the market fail to produce public goods?
    a) Because normally there is no demand for such goods.
    b) Because it is impossible for the producer to exclude non-buyers from enjoying the benefit.
    c) Because such products usually entail large external costs.
    d) Because their production normally leads to increased income inequality.

22. Table 9.1 shows the ridership on a particular toll highway. If the toll is presently $1, by *how much* must the government increase the toll if it wants to reduce traffic by 50 percent?

TABLE 9.1

Toll Charge	Vehicles per Hour
$1	4000
2	3000
3	2500
4	2200
5	2000
6	1800
7	1600

a) $2.
b) $3.
c) $4.
d) $5.

23. All of the following, *except one*, are characteristics of a public good. Which is the exception?
    a) It is non-extendable.
    b) It is non-divisible.
    c) It is non-depletable.
    d) It is non-excludable.

24. All of the following, *except one*, are benefits of perfectly competitive markets. Which is the exception?
    a) Competitive markets promote personal economic freedom.
    b) Competitive markets eliminate externalities.
    c) Ignoring externalities, competitive markets are productively efficient.
    d) Competitive markets are costless to implement.
    e) Ignoring externalities, competitive markets are allocatively efficient.

25. All of the following, *except one*, are examples of market failures. Which is the exception?
    a) Competitive markets do not result in an equitable distribution of incomes and wealth.
    b) Competitive markets do not ensure that the economy will be stable.
    c) Competitive markets do not ensure that competition will continue.
    d) Competitive markets do not ensure that individuals get the type of jobs they would like.
    e) Competitive markets do not take externalities into consideration.

Refer to **Figure 9.10** to answer questions 26 and 27.

FIGURE 9.10

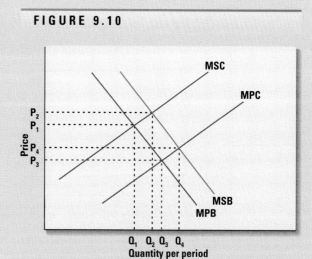

26. Refer to Figure 9.10 to answer this question. Compared with the ideal quantity, which of the following statements is correct regarding an unregulated competitive market?
    a) It would be overproducing at quantity Q_1.
    b) It would be underproducing at quantity Q_2.
    c) It would be overproducing at quantity Q_2.
    d) It would be overproducing at quantity Q_3.
    e) It would be underproducing at quantity Q_4.

27. Refer to Figure 9.10 to answer this question. Which of the following statements is correct regarding an unregulated competitive market?
    a) Its price of P_1 would be lower than a price that included all externalities.
    b) Its price of P_1 would be higher than a price that included all externalities.
    c) Its price of P_2 would be higher than a price that included all externalities.
    d) Its price of P_3 would be lower than a price that included all externalities.
    e) Its price of P_4 would be lower than a price that included all externalities.

Figure 9.11 shows the demand and supply of a product in a competitive market. Refer to this figure to answer questions 28, 29, and 30.

FIGURE 9.11

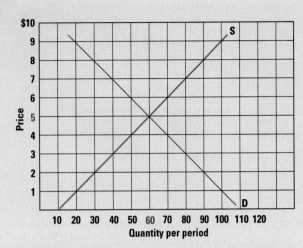

28. Refer to Figure 9.11 to answer the question. Suppose this graph represents a polluting industry and that the government wishes to decrease its output by 10 units. Which of the following will produce this result?
    a) Imposing an excise tax of $2.
    b) Imposing an excise tax of $1.
    c) Granting a subsidy of $2 to producers.
    d) Granting a subsidy of $1 to producers.
    e) Granting a subsidy of $2 to consumers.

29. Refer to Figure 9.11 to answer the question. Suppose that this graph represents an industry with big external benefits and that the government wishes to increase its output by 10 units and lower its price. Which of the following will produce this result?
    a) Imposing an excise tax of $2.
    b) Imposing an excise tax of $1.
    c) Granting a subsidy of $2 to producers.
    d) Granting a subsidy of $1 to producers.
    e) Granting a subsidy of $2 to consumers.

30. Refer to Figure 9.11 to answer the question. Suppose that this graph represents an industry with big external benefits and that the government wishes to increase its output by 10 units and raise its price. Which of the following will produce this result?
    a) Imposing an excise tax of $2.
    b) Imposing an excise tax of $1.
    c) Granting a subsidy of $2 to producers.
    d) Granting a subsidy of $1 to producers.
    e) Granting a subsidy of $2 to consumers.

Problems

31. **Figure 9.12** shows the demand and supply of a certain product.

FIGURE 9.12

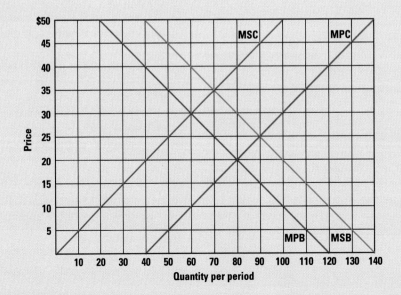

a) In an unregulated market, what would be the equilibrium price and quantity?

Price: $_____; quantity: _____.

b) If this product were taxed by an amount equal to the external costs, what would be the equilibrium price and quantity?

Price: $_____; quantity: _____.

c) Alternatively, if this product were subsidized by an amount equal to the external benefits, what would be the equilibrium price and quantity?

Price: $_____; quantity: _____.

d) Finally, if this product were both taxed and subsidized by an amount equal to the external costs and benefits, what would be the equilibrium price and quantity?

Price: $_____; quantity: _____.

32. Figure 9.13 shows the daily demand for entry into the downtown core of a major city by commuter vehicles and by shoppers' vehicles if they were required to pay a special traffic fee in order to enter.

FIGURE 9.13

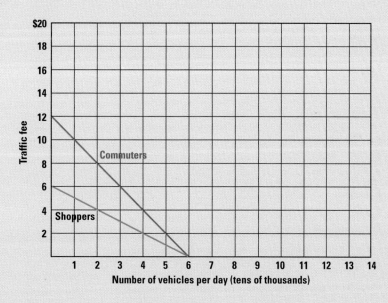

a) Draw the total demand curve.

b) Assuming that there is no charge for entry, what is the total quantity of vehicles entering downtown?

Number of vehicles: _____

c) Suppose that the government, in an effort to reduce the number of vehicles by 50 percent, decides to impose a traffic fee (the same fee for both commuters and shoppers) for entry into the downtown area. What will be the amount of the fee, and how many of each group will enter downtown?

Fee: $_____; number of commuter vehicles: _____;

number of shoppers' vehicles: _____.

d) Assume that the government, alternatively, decides to have a two-fee system but still wishes to reduce the traffic by 50 percent of the no-fee entry level. If it decides to charge shoppers $3, how much will it have to charge commuters?

Commuter fee: $_____.

33. **Table 9.2** shows the demand for pollution permits to emit hydrocarbons in a particular industrial park.

TABLE 9.2

Price per Pollution Permit	Quantity of Pollutants (tonnes)
$4500	100
4000	200
3500	300
3000	400
2500	500
2000	600
1500	700

On **Figure 9.14**, draw the demand curve for pollution permits and label it D_1.

FIGURE 9.14

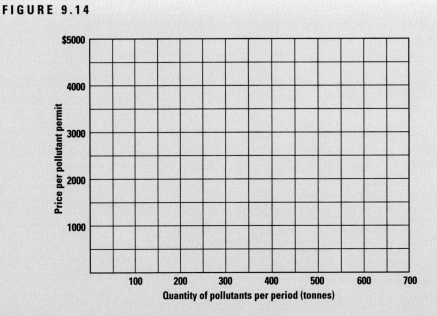

a) If no fee for a pollution right were charged, what quantity of pollutants would be discharged into the atmosphere, assuming a straight-line demand curve?

_____ tonnes.

b) Suppose the government were to set a fee of $3000 per pollution right. Show this fee on your graph. What quantity of pollutants would now be dumped? What is the total revenue received by the government?

_____ tonnes;   Government revenue: $_____.

c) Suppose that a new technology allows for a significant reduction in hydrocarbons at a relatively low cost so that the demand for pollution permits in the industrial park drops by 200 tonnes. Show the new demand on your graph, labelled D_2. Assuming that the government holds the pollution fee at $3000, what quantity of pollutants would now be dumped and what would be the total revenue received by the government?

_____ tonnes;   Government revenue: $_____.

d) After the change in demand in c), what would happen if instead of maintaining the fee of $3000, the government wants to maintain the same level of pollutants as in b). What fee would it have to charge, and what would be its new revenue?

Fee: $_____; Government revenue: $_____.

Translations

Describe Figure 9.15, explaining what each curve means. In addition, explain the reason for, and effect of, taxing this product. Then explain the reason for, and effect of, subsidizing the product.

FIGURE 9.15

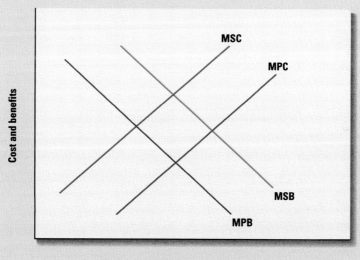

Answer: _____

_____

_____ .

Key Problem

The airport in Tarsus is privately owned and services many types of aircraft and airlines, for which it charges landing and takeoff fees. Over the years, the demand for the use of the runway has increased and so have the fees. The airport owners have categorized the users into two major groups, the "commercials" (which includes international and major domestic airlines offering scheduled flights), and the "privates" (which includes the charter airlines as well as personal plane owners). As a result of the increased demand, the airport authorities have decided to introduce nighttime landings and takeoffs. The demand for the two groups is shown in **Table 9.3**.

TABLE 9.3

Airport Landing Fee	Commercials: Quantity Demanded	Privates: Quantity Demanded	Total Both Groups: Quantity Demanded
$100	160	480	_____
200	124	336	_____
300	100	240	_____
400	80	160	_____
500	70	96	_____
600	64	56	_____
700	58	48	_____
800	52	40	_____
900	46	36	_____
1 000	40	32	_____

a) Complete **Table 9.3**.

   Nighttime usage is between 8 p.m. and 8 a.m., and the airport has a capacity of 20 landing and takeoff time slots per hour.

b) In **Figure 9.16**, graph the total nighttime demand and supply.

FIGURE 9.16

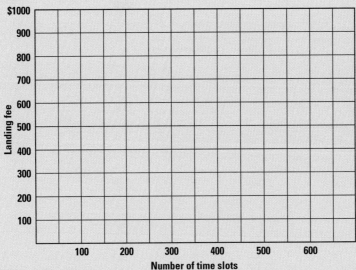

c) What will the airport's nighttime fee be, and how many time slots are being purchased by each group?

Fee: $_____ ;
Number of time slots: Commercial users: _____ ;
Private users: _____ .

Soon after the inauguration of the nighttime flights, local residents become increasingly vocal in showing their displeasure with the external cost of the noise they are forced to endure. Their lobbying of the Tarsus government is successful, so the government decides to impose a $100 tax on all nighttime landings and takeoffs; the tax is to be incorporated into the airport fee.

d) Show the effect of the tax in Figure 9.16. What will be the immediate impact on the landing fee?

After-tax fee: $_____ .

e) Will there be a surplus or a shortage as a result?

f) What will eventually happen to the price?

g) Who will eventually pay the landing tax?

Noting the effects of this tax, a newly elected government in Tarsus decides to repeal it and instead impose a price floor on the nighttime flight with the aim of reducing usage by 50 percent.

h) What should the price floor be to achieve this reduction, and what will be the resulting surplus or shortage of landing opportunities as a result?

Price floor: $_____ ; surplus/shortage: _____ of quantity: _____ .

The following year sees another new government come to power in Tarsus (an annual occurrence). Committed to finding a market solution for the airport problem, the government decides to dismantle the price floor and instead announces to all interested parties, including local residents, community groups, and the noise-abatement society, that they too will now be able to purchase landing fees. Once they have paid the fee they will own the time slot it represents and can therefore prevent any airline from using it.

i) If the nearby residents wish to ensure totally flightless nights for themselves, how much will it cost them to buy all the time slots? (To keep things simple, assume that the demand is the same as in Figure 9.16.)

Total cost of time slots: $_____ .

UNANSWERED QUESTIONS

Short Essays

1. Distinguish between *allocative efficiency* and *productive efficiency*.

2. Explain why competitive markets ensure that, in the long run, prices and outputs are both productively and allocatively efficient.

3. What are the main benefits of a competitive market economy?

4. What is meant by *market failure*? Give examples of four such failures.

5. Explain the main differences between *public goods* and *private goods*.

6. If the production of a certain good involves extensive external costs, explain what methods could be used to reduce such costs.

7. If the production of a certain good involves extensive external benefits, explain what methods could be used to encourage its production.

Analytical Questions

8. The production of each item on the following list involves either an external benefit, or an external cost, or both. Identity which you think it is for each product, and comment on whether you think a competitive market will under- or over-produce each product.
   a) Open-air concerts in a city park.
   b) Public rapid-transit lines to a city's suburbs.
   c) Research and development into an effective quit-smoking product.
   d) Flower baskets on the light posts of busy city streets.
   e) A cancer research laboratory that discharges waste into a nearby lake.
   f) An unrestricted-use city park that is a popular place for owners to walk their dogs.

9. In Canada today, which of the following products is a private good, a public good, or a quasi-public good?
   a) A public park.
   b) Domestic airline flights.
   c) The post office.
   d) Television broadcasting.
   e) Municipal sewage systems.
   f) Professional baseball teams.

10. The elasticity of demand for private long-term care facilities in the country of Hither is far greater than it is in the country of Yon. In which country will a subsidy given to prospective patients have more impact on the amount of spaces available?

11. A political observer once made the following comment: "If the external benefits exceed the external costs in the production of a private good, then it is better that the government doesn't interfere with the market." Do you agree with the observer's comment? Why or why not?

12. In order for an industry to achieve productive and allocative efficiency, three conditions must be fulfilled: a) the firms must be producing at economic capacity; b) the firms must be producing out of plants of minimum efficient scale; c) the firms must be making only normal profits. Explain, using a graph.

13. In what ways are competitive markets part of the problem of income and wealth inequalities, and in what ways are they part of the solution?

14. Although market failures often can be addressed by market solutions, the government must introduce such solutions. Discuss this statement.

Numerical Questions

15. Figure 9.17 shows the market for polio vaccinations in Nania. The present equilibrium price is $16 per vaccination and the quantity (in thousands of vaccinations) is 60. If the marginal external benefit is estimated at an additional $12 per vaccination, what is the optimal price and quantity from society's point of view?

FIGURE 9.17

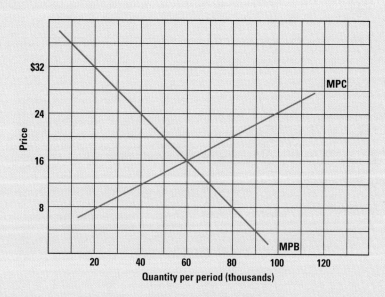

16. The government of Malaca has decided to sell pollution permits to discharge pollutants into its largest freshwater lake. Each permit is a right to discharge one tonne of pollutants. Malaca has determined that the lake will support a maximum of 40 tonnes of pollutants per year and has decided to sell the licences using a Dutch auction. This means that the auction starts at a very high price, which is successively reduced until the price reaches a level that will result in all 40 tonnes of pollution permits being sold. The results of the bidding are shown in Table 9.4.

TABLE 9.4

Price per Pollution Right	Bidder A	Bidder B	Bidder C	Bidder D	Bidder E
$6000	2				
5500	4	6			
5000	6	6	1	1	1
4500	8	7	2	2	2
4000	10	7	4	3	3
3500	12	9	6	3	4
3000	14	10	8	3	5
2500	16	11	9	4	6
2000	18	12	10	4	7

a) What will the price of pollution permits be as a result of this auction?

b) Suppose that Bidder E happened to be an environmentalist group. If this group had not participated in the auction, what would the price of pollution permits have been, and what difference would there have been in the amount of pollutants discharged into the lake?

17. Figure 9.18 illustrates the market for solarium, a product that has both extensive benefits and extensive costs.

FIGURE 9.18

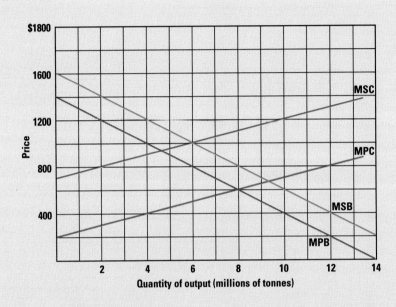

a) In an unregulated market, what would be the equilibrium price and quantity?
b) At the unregulated equilibrium, what is the value of external benefits per tonne? What is the value of external costs per tonne?
c) At the unregulated equilibrium, what is the value of total external benefits? What is the value of total external costs?
d) What is the most desirable price and quantity from society's point of view?

18. Figure 9.19 illustrates the private costs and benefits of producing trisenian.

FIGURE 9.19

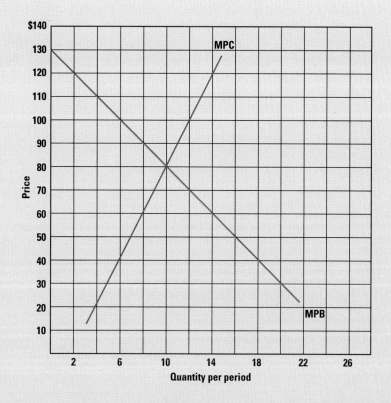

a) Draw the MSC and MSB curves on the graph, assuming that the external benefits are estimated at $50 per unit and the external cost at $20 per unit.

b) What is the most desirable price and quantity from society's point of view?

c) If the government wanted to increase the quantity to the amount in b) above, what subsidy would it need to give to producers?

d) If the government wanted to increase the quantity to the amount in b) above, what subsidy would it need to give to consumers?

19. Table 9.5 shows the market for private long-term care facilities in two countries, Hither and Yon, which have identical demands but different supplies.

TABLE 9.5

Monthly Fee	Demand: Hither and Yon	Supply: Hither	Supply: Yon
$1000	2000	500	0
1200	1800	600	200
1400	1600	700	400
1600	1400	800	600
1800	1200	900	800
2000	1000	1000	1000
2200	800	1100	1200
2400	600	1200	1400
2600	400	1300	1600

a) Graph the demand and supply in each country. What is the present equilibrium fee and number of available spaces used in each country?

b) If the demand were to increase by 300 in each country, what would be the new equilibrium fees and quantity in each country? What explains the different effects in the two countries?

c) From the initial situation in a), suppose that the governments in each country wished to increase the quantity of spaces available in long-term care facilities by 200. They have decided to give subsidies to long-term care residents to encourage this increase. How much subsidy must they give in each country? Explain the difference in the two countries.

20. Given the data for long-term care spaces in Hither and Yon as shown in Table 9.5, suppose that the government wished to increase the number of spaces available by 200. What subsidy would have to be paid to the long-term care operators in each country to produce such an increase?

 Web-Based Activities

1. Governments often step into markets when they believe that unfair competition is taking place. Otherwise, if left alone, the actions of market participants will eliminate productive and allocative efficiencies associated with competition. Review the *Salon* magazine story at **www.salon-magazine.com/21st/feature/1998/05/19featurea.html** and answer the following questions:

    a) What are the basic issues of Netscape's complaint against Microsoft? How does Microsoft respond to this complaint?

    b) Should government intervene to regulate Microsoft's tactics in the Internet software market? Why or why not?

2. Some economists criticize government for creating artificial problems and thereby justifying intervention into the market. One example is the negative externalities associated with energy consumption. For example, read **www.cato.org/pubs/pas/pa-189.html**. Identify the externalities associated with energy consumption. Do you think that governments should intervene in these markets because of the externalities? Why or why not?

Monopoly

What's ahead... This chapter looks at what is meant by monopoly and what conditions lead to its creation. We focus on how a monopoly firm goes about determining the price and output that will ensure the greatest profit. We next compare a monopoly market and a perfectly competitive market to find out which is better and why. In doing this, we also mention some of the social costs and benefits that may result from monopolies. Finally, the chapter looks at various ways in which governments have tried to deal with monopolies, either through taxation, price setting, or outright government purchase.

A QUESTION OF RELEVANCE...

You almost certainly live in an area where there is only one supplier of electricity or natural gas. Have you ever wondered why this is so? What is good about monopolies like these? Is there anything bad about them? Is Microsoft a monopolist? Should Petro Canada have been privatized? Should the government allow large firms to merge? Should the government have any say in questions like these at all? And how do questions like these affect you, a typical consumer? The answers to some of these questions might surprise you.

monopoly: a market in which a single firm (the monopolist) is the sole producer.

From the competitive world of the last two chapters we now turn to look at its opposite: **monopoly**. A firm is a monopolist if it is the sole producer of a product for which there are no close substitutes. The firm not only dominates the industry; the firm *is* the industry. There is no competition for the monopolist, which leaves it in a very powerful position. The study of monopoly, then, is a study in power. People have always been suspicious of monopolies because of the distinct possibility that the monopolist might use its power to exploit its customers, suppliers, and employees. Self-interest might not lead to exploitation in the case of competitive markets because competition itself provides a check and balance on the behaviour of competitors. However, this constraint is largely absent in monopoly markets, and therefore the possibility of abuse is greater.

In a market economy, private ownership allows owners of resources a degree of freedom and gives them licence to exercise very wide discretion in the use of those resources without public input. After all, as members of the public we do not get to vote for the presidents and executives of firms. However, most people do not feel disenfranchised because of this since they can at least vote with their money. We cast votes for the products we like when we buy them. If we do not like a certain product, the "democracy of the marketplace" will mean that the product will not be successful. In addition, we do not feel uncomfortable at this lack of accountability because in the case of the competitive market, the firm represents such a small portion of the industry or the whole economy that any damage it might do is limited. However, none of this is true with monopolies, which replace the democracy of the competitive market with the despotism of the sole producer. As a result, most countries, including Canada, have curtailed the power of monopolies in various ways, which we will look at later in the chapter.

Identifying what is, and what is not, a monopoly may not be quite as straightforward as it sounds. Certainly the monopolist is the sole producer of a product in the market. But what is a product? What is the market? And if there are no close substitutes, what exactly is a substitute, and how close is close? For instance, we need to drink to stay alive, and there are certainly no substitutes for drinkable liquids. Drinkable liquids, however, is a product group, not a product. Pop is a subgroup of drinkable liquids, and cola is a subgroup of pop. And Pepsi is just one type of cola. As we saw when we looked at elasticity of demand in Chapter 4, the wider you define the product, the more inelastic will be the demand. The demand for colas in general will be more inelastic than the demand for any particular brand of cola. (Whether a product has close substitutes or not can be measured in terms of the cross-elasticity of demand for that product.) In general we can say that the demand for the monopoly's product will tend to be fairly inelastic. As for the definition of the market, if a particular small town has only one gas station and the next town is 50 kilometres away, to all intents and purposes that gas station is a monopolist. But in the whole of the province or the country, that gas station is only one of thousands of gas stations. The wider the market, in the sense of accessibility for consumers, the less likely a single firm will be able to dominate. With easier and cheaper transport and communications these days we are able to buy from firms around the world, which means that a Canadian monopolist has to compete with foreign firms. Its power in the domestic market, therefore, is considerably reduced.

Motorists along the Trans-Canada highway pass a Petro Canada station west of Calgary.

Nonetheless, given the above cautions, most people would agree that Ontario Hydro, Rogers Cablevision, and the only gas station in a remote town are examples of monopolies.

E - C O N O M I C S

Is Microsoft a Monopoly?

You are probably aware that the U.S. Department of Justice has taken Microsoft to court for being a monopolist. The government's case is focused on three points: Microsoft monopolizes the market for operating systems for PCs (windows); its bundling of Internet Explorer with the windows operating system is anti-competitive; its contractual arrangements with various vendors of related goods is anti-competitive. To make the first charge stick, the government has to prove that Microsoft *used* its power in some detrimental way such as charging an exorbitant price. However, Microsoft sells their operating system to computer manufacturers for about $40, which is really very cheap. On the second point, the fact is that Microsoft gives Internet Explorer away free. The third point is more murky since the actual contracts between the company and its business associates is not a matter of public record. What is interesting about this whole case is the fact that the supposed "victims" that the government's action is representing are not *consumers* but existing, and potential, *competitors* (e.g., Netscape). One can wonder if this was the original intent of monopoly legislation.

How Monopolies Come into Existence

barriers to entry:
obstacles that make it difficult for new participants to enter a market.

How do monopolies come into existence in the first place, and how are they able to keep out competing firms? The answer lies in the concept of **barriers to entry**, which shelter the monopoly from new competitors in the market. The variety of barriers can be categorized under three headings: technical barriers, legal barriers, and economic barriers.

Technical barriers are those that make it difficult for other firms to duplicate a monopolist's production methods because the monopolist is the sole owner of a resource or technique. For instance, the International Nickel Company (Inco) once controlled most of the world's supply of nickel, and the De Beers Company of Kimberly, South Africa, owns or controls the majority of the world's diamond mines. Sole ownership of a resource confers a monopoly status on the producer. Similarly, a firm is a monopolist if it is the sole owner of the technical knowledge necessary to produce the product. IBM, for instance, had a monopoly on computer expertise for many years, until other companies caught up.

Legal barriers prevent other firms from competing in a particular industry by force of law. In certain instances this is designed to grant a monopoly to the production of a good or service, as is the case with many crown corporations in Canada, such as Canada Post, or provincial-government liquor boards. These are known as public franchises. Other types of legal restriction are designed to give private firms protection from competition and may take the form of a government licence (to fish commercially for salmon, for example) or of a patent or copyright, in which the originator of the idea is given a monopoly for a number of years. For example, the NCR company had the first patent on cash registers, and Xerox held the patent on photocopying using a dry-ink method (xerography).

Economic barriers are present whenever there are extensive start-up costs for new firms. It is difficult to compete internationally with the major automobile firms unless you are ready to invest billions of dollars. It should be noted that this investment needs to encompass not only the fixed costs of the factory buildings and assembly line but also

ADDED DIMENSION

Patents and Exclusive Rights

The rationale for patent legislation is that it provides the original inventor with a period of time during which the invention is protected from competition so that the inventor will be able to make monopoly profits or charge others a royalty, if they wish to use it. In Canada, patents granted prior to 1989 are protected for 17 years; those registered after that are given 20 years' protection. In this way, it is hoped that research and development will be encouraged.

A number of problems associated with patents, however, deserve at least brief mention. For instance, if the registered description of the invention is too narrow, it will allow others to introduce and try to patent something that is merely a slight modification of the original. For this reason, many firms seeking patent protection try to define the patent as broadly as possible (a conveyance with four wheels, for instance) so as to keep out all competition. However, patent offices tend to dismiss patents that are too widely defined, such as "computers," or those in the form of broad ideas or theories, such as "the law of relativity," for example. Additionally, if patent protection was granted only for a short time it would tend to inhibit research, but one that extends the period too much is likely to inhibit competition.

Finally, it should be noted that, in order to register a patent, the inventor must give complete disclosure of the product and the process. But since this might reveal far too much to the competition, a number of inventions (such as the specific formula for Coca-Cola) have never been registered but remain, instead, trade secrets.

the cost of a distribution network and marketing plan, as well as sufficient funds to hire the highly paid design engineers and executives who are able to put all this together. The bigger this initial investment, the more difficult it is for new entrants to join the industry. Automobile firms tend to be large because of extensive economies of scale, which allow big firms to produce at much lower unit costs than can small firms. The existence of the huge corporations and international conglomerates that we see these days is often the result of the drive for higher profits through growth. Sometimes the growth has been "organic," but more often than not, it has been the result of mergers and acquisitions. In summary, barriers to market entry by new firms can take the form of:

- technical barriers, such as sole ownership of a resource
- legal barriers, such as public franchise, licenses, patents, and copyrights
- economic barriers caused by economies of scale

natural monopoly: a single producer in a market (usually with large economies of scale) who is able to produce at a lower cost than competing firms could.

In some industries, in order to make a profit the firm will need to be very big to obtain economies of scale. The required size may be so big that the market can support only a single firm. Monopolies that come into existence in markets where *competing firms simply would not be profitable* are known as **natural monopolies**. This situation is illustrated in **Figure 10.1**.

Suppose the graph illustrates the demand and costs for an urban rail system in a particular city. Because of the very high costs of the railbed and all the rolling stock, the system needs to operate with at least 100 000 users a day to reduce the average cost enough for the system to be profitable. With 100 000 users it can charge a price of $1.50 per ride, and since this is above the average cost of $1.40, the system will be profitable. However, given the size of this particular market, it would be impossible for it to support two competing firms. If each firm had a ridership of 50 000, the average costs would be $2.50 per ride, well above the $1.50 that would result in 100 000 users. Because two firms could not make a profit in this market, we have a natural monopoly. Natural monopolies occur whenever start-up costs in an industry are so high that the market can support only one profitable firm. A small city in Canada simply could not support more than one competing urban rail system, whereas Tokyo possesses a num-

public utilities: goods or services regarded as essential and therefore usually provided by government.

ber of competing rail companies, some privately and one publicly owned. In most small urban markets (and in a number of large ones) such industries as water, electricity, and natural gas supply, urban bus and rail transportation, and telecommunications tend to be natural monopolies. Since they are also extremely important to a community, they may become publicly owned and are often referred to as **public utilities**. The main focus of this chapter is on the operation and control of privately owned monopolies.

FIGURE 10.1 Natural Monopoly

The graph shows that extensive economies of scale result in minimum AC at 100 000 riders. If the rail fare is set at $1.50, then the quantity demanded will be 100 000 and a single transit company could make a profit since, at this level of ridership, the average cost is $1.40 (for the sake of simplicity, the MC curve is omitted). If the market were shared between two rail companies, each serving, say, 50 000 riders each, then the average cost would be $2.50—which exceeds the maximum fare of $2.25 that these riders would be prepared to pay. This would result in both companies experiencing losses.

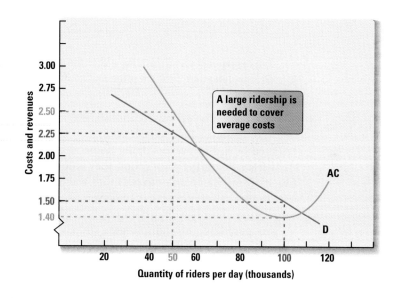

A large ridership is needed to cover average costs

Toronto's GO Train is an example of a natural monopoly.

SELF-TEST

1. In Figure 10.1, suppose there are two competing rail companies, each capturing 50 percent of the market. What would happen if they both charged a fare of $1.50? What would be the total profit or loss of each firm?

Total, Average, and Marginal Revenues

The sole producer of a product is in a very powerful position. That does not mean, however, that it has unlimited power over the market. To a certain extent, the consumer is still sovereign and makes the ultimate decision of whether or not that product will be bought and if, as a result, the monopolist will be successful. Nonetheless, the monopolist, unlike the competitive producer, is a *price maker* rather than a *price taker*, which means that it is able to set the price at whatever level it chooses rather than having to accept the market-determined price. Even so, consumers will decide how much they will buy at that price. Alternatively, the monopolist could determine the size of production and leave it to the market to determine the maximum price at which that output can be sold. Therefore:

> **The monopolist can determine either the price *or* the quantity sold; what it cannot do is to determine *both* the price and quantity sold.**

All this can be expressed another way: since the monopolist and the industry are one and the same, it faces the market demand for the product, and that demand is represented by a downward-sloping demand curve. From the consumers' point of view this means that if the price drops, they will buy more. From the monopolist's perspective, it means that in order to sell more, the monopolist must lower the price. A monopolist cannot sell all it wants at any given price; it is forced to decrease the price in order to sell more. This has important implications in terms of the monopolist's revenues.

Suppose that, through mergers and acquisitions, a monopoly brewer emerged in Canada calling itself Beavertail Brewers. The first two columns of **Table 10.1** show the quantities (in, say, millions of cases per day) that would be sold at various prices of Beavertail Beer; that is, they represent the demand for Beavertail Beer.

TABLE 10.1 Total, Average, and Marginal Revenues of the Monopolist

Quantity (millions)	Price (per case)	Total Revenue (TR)	Average Revenue (AR)	Marginal Revenue (MR)
1	$20	$20	$20	—
2	19	38	19	$18
3	18	54	18	16
4	17	68	17	14
5	16	80	16	12
6	15	90	15	10
7	14	98	14	8
8	13	104	13	6
9	12	108	12	4
10	11	110	11	2
11	10	110	10	0
12	9	108	9	−2

The terms total, average, and marginal revenues were introduced in Chapter 8. Note that, as with the competitive firm, the average revenue is the same thing as the price. Notice also that the total revenue increases with quantity sold but only up to a point. Here that point is a quantity of 10. If Beavertail wishes to increase the number of cases sold to 11, it must drop the price to $10; it will have no effect, however, on the total revenue. The company's total revenue will remain at $110. And should the monopolist wish to increase output and sales to 12, then the price will have to come down to $9, with the result that total revenue will start to fall. Unlike a competitive firm, then, the monopolist is faced with a maximum sales revenue.

Table 10.1 also shows that for the monopolist the marginal revenue is not equal to the average revenue. The extra (marginal) sales revenue that the monopolist receives for selling one more unit is not equal to the price. The reason for this is that when the monopolist sells one more unit, it *gains revenue* equal to the price at which it sells that unit, but it *loses revenue* because it is forced to drop the price not only on the additional unit sold but on *every* unit it sells. Suppose for instance that the brewery is presently selling 5 million cases of beer per week at a price of $16 per case, for a total revenue of $80 million. If it reduces the price to $15, it will be able to sell one million more units and will therefore gain revenue equal to 1 million x $15 = $15 million. However, it will lose revenue because it is dropping the price by $1 on the previous 5 million it was selling; that is, it will lose revenue equal to $1 million x 5 units = $5 million. It gains $15 million but loses $5 million, so that its net gain is only $10 million, which is its marginal revenue. Because the demand curve is downward-sloping, the extra amount of revenue the monopolist gains from an additional sale will always be less than the price. In summary:

> **In order to increase its sales, a monopolist is forced to reduce its price not just on the last units sold, but on the whole of its output.**

These points are illustrated in **Figure 10.2**.

Up to an output of 10 the total revenue curve is upward-sloping, but the slope gets smaller and smaller with increasing output. The slope measures the rate at which total revenue changes, which is the same thing as the marginal revenue. In other words, as the Figure 10.2B shows, the marginal revenue decreases as the output increases. Notice that the total revenue curve rises to a maximum at an output of 10 (and 11), and thereafter declines. Note also that the average revenue curve is the same thing as the demand curve. The marginal revenue curve is consistently below the average revenue curve and is twice as steep; every time the average revenue (price) drops by $1, the marginal revenue drops by $2. As long as the marginal revenue is positive, even though it is falling, then total revenue must be increasing. When it becomes negative, after an output of 11, the total revenue must be falling. Thus:

> **Total revenue must be at a maximum, then, when the marginal revenue is neither positive nor negative, that is, when it is zero.**

This monopolist will never produce an output greater than 11 units, because a higher output will presumably increase the total costs but lower total revenue. Graphically, in Figure 10.2 this means that the monopolist will produce an output of less than 13 or, in other words, on the upper portion of the demand curve. Since the top portion of any demand curve is elastic it means that:

> **All monopolists will produce only where the demand is elastic.**

FIGURE 10.2 Total, Average, and Marginal Revenues

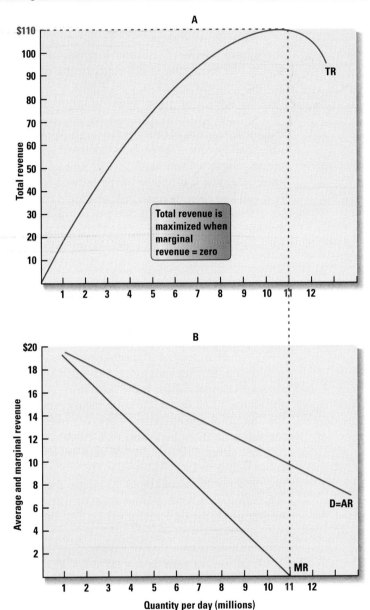

Up to a point, the total revenue of the monopolist increases as more units are sold. However, the rate of increase (the slope of the TR curve) declines throughout. The total revenue reaches a maximum at an output of 10. The 11th unit adds no additional revenue, so the total revenue remains the same. After that, as more units are sold, the total revenue starts to decline.

The average revenue received by the firm is the same thing as the price. The average revenue curve is identical to the demand curve, which means that additional units can only be sold if the price is lowered. The marginal revenue represents the additional revenue derived from selling more units. In this graph, the price must drop by $1 in order to increase sales by one unit; that is, the slope of the demand curve has a value of 1. The slope of the MR curve, however, is 2, since it drops by $2 for each additional unit sold. This means that the MR curve drops twice as steeply as the AR curve and intersects the horizontal axis at exactly half the distance between the origin and the point where the AR curve intersects the horizontal axis.

In order to analyze the behaviour of monopolists a bit more thoroughly, we need to know exactly at what output a monopolist will produce. To do this we need to know not only the revenue, but also the costs and therefore the profitability of the monopolist.

SELF-TEST

2. Suppose a monopolist was charging a price of $50 for his product and was selling 1500 units. He has now lowered his price to $45 and is selling 1700 units. What is his marginal revenue? What is the price elasticity of demand over this price range?

Monopoly and Price Discrimination

One of the interesting aspects of monopoly and other forms of imperfect competition is the fact that, in order to increase sales, a firm is forced to drop the price of its products. And it must normally drop the price not just on additional units sold, but on the whole of its output. The way of avoiding this, as we saw in Chapter 5, is by practising price discrimination. If the monopolist, for example, could somehow divide up and segregate the market so that it could charge every single customer the maximum price that each is prepared to pay, it would be practising perfect price discrimination. In practice, such perfection is impossible. However, any method that allows the firm to charge different prices to different groups *for reasons not associated with costs* is said to practise price discrimination and will generate a higher sales revenue for the firm. As a result, both its output and its profits will be greater.

The practice of price discrimination requires not only that the seller is able to identify and separate groups that have different elasticities of demand, but also that there be no

possibility of reselling of the product in question. There are numerous examples of price discrimination by monopoly and other imperfectly competitive firms. Both telephone and airline companies realize that businesspeople generally have a more inelastic demand for their services than do more casual users. As a result, telephone rates are generally higher during business hours on weekdays than at "off-peak" periods. Similarly, airlines charge more for businesspeople booking last-minute who wish to travel on weekdays than for vacationers who book in advance and are willing to travel on weekends. Electricity companies also discriminate between their customers, charging higher rates to daytime users, whose demand is inelastic, than to nighttime users. In addition, they often discriminate between households and corporate users, charging the former higher rates than the latter because corporate users often have a choice of buying their own generators if necessary, whereas this is not possible for most households.

Profit-Maximizing Output for the Monopolist

In the short run, the cost structure for the monopolist is no different from that of the competitive producer. In the short run, the monopolist similarly enjoys the advantages of the division of labour as it produces more and later faces diminishing returns as it is constrained by the size of its operations. In **Table 10.2** we have added the total costs of Beavertail Breweries to the total revenue data from Table 10.1 to calculate the total profits at the various output levels.

TABLE 10.2 Calculating Total Profits of the Monopolist

Quantity (millions of cases per day)	Price (= AR)	Total Revenue (TR)	Total Costs (TC)	Total Profit (Tπ)
1	$20	$20	$40	$–20
2	19	38	48	–10
3	18	54	54	0
4	17	68	58	10
5	16	80	66	14
6	15	90	76	14
7	14	98	89	9
8	13	104	104	0
9	12	108	121	–13
10	11	110	140	–30
11	10	110	161	–51
12	9	108	184	–76

Given the data in Table 10.2, the profit-maximizing output for Beavertail is either an output of 5 or 6. (For technical reasons we will explain in a moment that the "correct" answer is an output of 6.) The price at this output level would be $15 per case, which will give the monopolist a total profit of $14. These points are shown on the graph in **Figure 10.3**.

Break-even outputs are at 3 and 8. The maximum profit point is at an output level of 6, where the distance between the two total curves is at its greatest. Additionally, the maximum profit point is shown explicitly on the total profit curve, where it occurs at the highest point.

FIGURE 10.3 Total Costs, Revenues, and Profits for the Monopolist

Break-even occurs where the TR and TC curves intersect, that is, at outputs of 3 and 8. Between those two outputs, TR is greater than TC, and therefore any output will be profitable. Maximum profits occur at outputs of 5 and 6. At these outputs, the distance between the two curves is greatest. The total profit curve shows explicitly the amount of economic profit at each output and confirms these points.

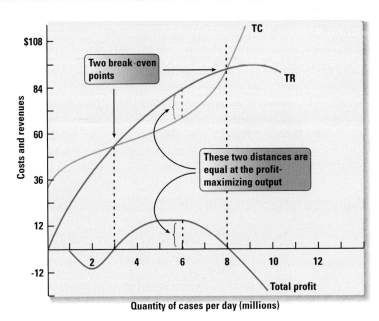

SELF-TEST

3. Complete the following table for Onan the monopolist and indicate the break-even outputs and the profit-maximizing output:

Quantity	Price (= AR)	Total Revenue (TR)	Total Costs (TC)	Total Profit (Tπ)
20	$100	_____	$2060	_____
21	98	_____	2080	_____
22	96	_____	2112	_____
23	94	_____	2142	_____
24	92	_____	2177	_____
25	90	_____	2216	_____
26	88	_____	2257	_____
27	86	_____	2322	_____
28	84	_____	2417	_____
29	82	_____	2530	_____

Now we need to look at things using the perspective of the average and marginal revenues and costs. This view is not quite so straightforward, but it does reveal some interesting aspects. **Table 10.3** shows the average and marginal costs for Beavertail Breweries as well as repeating the revenue data used earlier.

TABLE 10.3 Calculating Total Profits of the Monopolist Using the Marginal Approach

Quantity	Price (= AR)	Total Revenue (TR)	Total Costs (TC)	Average Cost (AC)	Marginal Cost (MC)	Marginal Revenue (MR)	Total Profit (Tπ)
1	$20	$20	$40	$40.00	—	20	$-20
2	19	38	48	24.00	8	18	-10
3	18	54	54	18.00	6	16	0
4	17	68	58	14.50	4	14	10
5	16	80	66	13.20	8	12	14
6	15	90	76	12.67	10	10	14
7	14	98	89	12.71	13	8	9
8	13	104	104	13.00	15	6	0
9	12	108	121	13.44	17	4	-13
10	11	110	140	14.00	19	2	-30
11	10	110	161	14.63	21	0	-51
12	9	108	184	15.33	23	-2	-76

The two columns on which we will concentrate are marginal cost and marginal revenue. The rule for profit maximization, which was developed in the context of perfect competition in Chapter 8, applies regardless of the type of market we are looking at. To make maximum profits (or to minimize losses) a firm should produce to the point where the marginal revenue equals the marginal cost. Looking at those two columns confirms that profit maximization occurs at an output of 6, since at this output both the marginal revenue and marginal cost are equal to $10. (This is why we prefer to identify the output level of 6 rather than 5 as the profit-maximizing output, although both produce the same total profit.) The important difference between a monopoly and a perfectly competitive market is that in a monopoly market the marginal revenue is not the same thing as the price (or average revenue). Indeed, as we have seen, at an output of 6 units, the price will be $15—far greater than the marginal revenue of $10. **Figure 10.4** plots the various average and marginal curves.

FIGURE 10.4 Average and Marginal Costs and Revenues for the Monopolist

Break-even occurs where TR = TC. This must also be where AR = AC, that is, at outputs of 3 and 8. Every output between those two points is profitable. Maximum profit occurs where the MC and MR curves intersect. This is at an output of 6, where MC = MR = $10. This output would be sold at a price of $15, that is, where the vertical line from the output of 6 meets the demand curve.

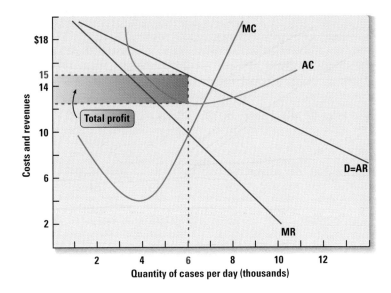

The break-even points occur where total revenue and costs are the same. This is also where the average revenue equals average costs. As we saw before, these points are at an output of 3 and 8. At any outputs between the break-even points, the monopolist will make a profit. Profit maximization occurs where the marginal cost curve intersects the marginal revenue curve, and this is at an output of 6. At that output, the average cost of producing a case of beer is $12.67 and the selling price is $15, so Beavertail Breweries is making an economic profit of $2.33 per case. Since it is selling 6 cases, we can confirm that the total profit is $14. This is the shaded area in Figure 10.4.

Note that, unlike the situation with a perfectly competitive industry, there is no supply and no supply curve for the monopolist. This is because there is no unique relationship between price and quantity. Looking at Table 10.3, you can see it doesn't make sense to ask how much this monopolist would produce at, say, $18 since, given its cost structure, an output level of 3 at a price of $18 is a combination that the monopolist would never choose. For each demand faced by the monopolist, there is only a single price and a single quantity that is appropriate.

We should mention that being a monopolist does not guarantee that profits will be made. If you return to Table 10.3 and assume that average costs were increased by $5 at every output level, you can see that no output would be profitable. It is simply not true, therefore, as many people believe, that almost by definition, monopolists are always profitable. Though many are profitable, monopolists can and do make losses from time to time. This is illustrated in **Figure 10.5.**

SELF-TEST

4. From Table 10.3, calculate the marginal profit at each output level and confirm that the profit-maximizing output does occur at 6.
5. Using the data below, complete the table and:

A) show that at break-even, the average revenue (= price) is equal to the average costs;
B) find the profit-maximizing output and price.

Quantity	Price	Total Revenue (TR)	Total Costs (TC)	Average Costs (AC)	Marginal Costs (MC)	Marginal Revenue (MR)
20	$100	$2000	$2067	___	___	___
21	98	2058	2087	___	___	___
22	96	2112	2112	___	___	___
23	94	2162	2142	___	___	___
24	92	2208	2177	___	___	___
25	90	2250	2216	___	___	___
26	88	2288	2257	___	___	___
27	86	2322	2322	___	___	___
28	84	2352	2417	___	___	___
29	82	2378	2530	___	___	___

FIGURE 10.5 Minimizing Losses for the Monopolist

For this monopolist, its present AC curve is higher than the demand curve at all output levels. Its best option will be to minimize its losses by producing at the point where its marginal revenue equals its marginal costs, that is, where these two curves intersect at a quantity of Q_1. It would charge a price of P_1 and would incur an economic loss denoted by the shaded area, AC_1abP_1.

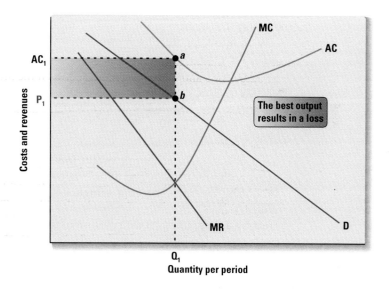

Suppose that, as in Figure 10.5, the once-profitable monopolist now faces a reduced demand for its product. The demand is so low that the demand curve is below the average cost curve at every output. Assuming that it is still able to cover its variable costs, the monopolist will still produce in the short run. Its loss-minimizing output will be the output at which its marginal cost equals its marginal revenue. This occurs at an output of Q_1. The maximum price it can charge for this output is P_1, generating a total loss for the monopolist depicted by the shaded area, AC_1abP_1. Needless to say, this monopolist, like any other firm, will not be able to incur losses indefinitely. If conditions do not improve in the long run, it will be forced out of business.

What's So Bad about Monopoly?

Let's return our focus to a profitable Beavertail Brewers. If this was an example of a competitive firm, we know what would happen in the long run in response to economic profits. As we saw in Chapter 8, the effect would be to attract many new firms into the industry, so that eventually economic profits would be competed away. However, since this is a monopoly market, there is no competition, and because of this a profitable monopolist can continue to make economic profits indefinitely.

Furthermore, the monopolist is reasonably secure because it is protected by various barriers to entry. Of course, like any firm, monopolists might incur losses, which could not be sustained indefinitely and would eventually force the monopolist out of business. However, the existence of monopoly profits do not lead to any change except to make the monopoly owners richer. The implication of this fact is that the monopolist is both productively and allocatively inefficient.

Remember from Chapter 9 that productive efficiency implies that the producer is producing the product at the lowest possible cost. This is not true for the monopolist. A glance back at Figure 10.4 shows that Beavertail Brewers, like all monopolists, will produce at less than economic capacity and therefore at a higher than minimum average cost. Consumers are having to pay a higher price than would be the case in a competitive industry, both because the average cost is higher than it need be and because the monopolist is making economic profits. It is not only the consumers who lose out, but society as a whole, because the existence of monopolies may lead to a more unequal distribution of income and wealth. This must be so, since with competitive industries, the (lower) profits are being spread among many producing firms, whereas with a monopoly the (higher) profits may be concentrated in the hands of only a few owners.

In addition, Figure 10.4 shows that at the profit-maximizing output (where MC = MR), the price is above the marginal cost. This means that the monopoly is also allocatively inefficient and that consumers' desire for this product at the margin, as measured by the price, is higher than its cost. In other words, consumers would prefer that more of this beer be produced and that its price be lower. Such results would be achieved in the long run *if* this market was competitive. In summary, monopolies are criticized for:

- being able to make economic profits indefinitely
- being both productively and allocatively inefficient
- producing less and charging a higher price than would occur in a competitive industry
- creating a more unequal distribution of income and wealth within society

REVIEW

1. Define the term *monopoly*.
2. Explain why the definition of monopoly hinges on the definitions of product and market.
3. What is meant by *barriers to entry*? What are the three types of barriers? Give examples of each.
4. What is a *natural monopoly*? Give examples.
5. Explain why the average revenue of the monopolist is not the same thing as the marginal revenue.
6. In terms of both totals and averages/marginals, define and explain how the profit-maximizing output is obtained for the monopolist.
7. Explain why monopolies are productively and allocatively inefficient.

Monopoly and Perfect Competition Contrasted

We can show the comparison between a perfectly competitive industry and a monopoly graphically. Suppose that **Figure 10.6** illustrates a perfectly competitive mushroom industry that consists of 100 small mushroom growers all producing identical mushrooms. The supply curve represents the total supply of mushrooms from these growers, and the demand curve is the total market demand from millions of mushroom eaters.

The competitive price of mushrooms, as shown in Figure 10.6, is $4 per kilo and the total production is 200 000 kilos per month.

Suppose now that a monopolist were to buy out all the mushroom growers in the area. Having consolidated all the farms into one big combine, the monopolist sets out to maximize profits. How does it do this? The answer is, by finding the output at which the marginal cost is equal to the marginal revenue. This will be the profit-maximizing point. Graphically, the supply curve of the perfectly competitive industry, you may remember, is synonymous with its marginal cost curve. Deriving the marginal revenue curve is reasonably straightforward because the demand curve is the same thing as the average revenue curve. Given the straight-line demand curve in Figure 10.6, the marginal revenue can be drawn as a curve falling twice as steeply.

FIGURE 10.6 Monopoly and Perfect Competition Contrasted

The competitive market's equilibrium occurs where the quantities demanded and supplied are equal. This occurs at a price of $4 and an output of 200 000 kilos. This would be the price for each mushroom grower who would collectively produce 200 000 kilos. If, on the other hand, this were a monopoly industry, the monopolist would produce at the point where the MR equals MC. (The MR curve is twice as steep as the demand curve; the MC curve is the same thing as the supply curve.) The profit-maximizing output for the monopolist, then, is at an output of 150 000 kilos, which could be sold at a price of $5.50 per kilo.

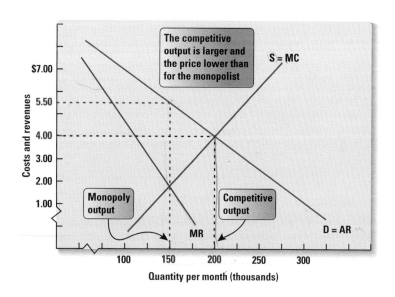

The intersection of the marginal cost and revenue occurs at an output of 150 000 kilos. To find the maximum price at which this quantity could be sold, we graphically extend the output up to the demand curve, which establishes that this quantity could be sold at a maximum price of $5.50 per kilo.

In simple terms, the monopolist can make maximum profits by restricting the output, thereby pushing up the price of the product. In summary:

> **A monopolist will produce a lower output and charge a higher price than those of a competitive industry.**

No wonder then that governments have often interceded in the market and have often outlawed private monopolies or broken up existing ones. While this may be true at times, it is fair to say that the history of anti-monopoly legislation and its enforcement in North America over the past century shows a singular lack of consistency. In certain periods, even the slightest suggestions that some firms were seeking to merge or were thought to be behaving in an uncompetitive way has been greeted by a chorus of protests and has prompted vigorous action by legislators. In other periods, trusts, monopolies, and mergers have been greeted with benign indifference by governments. Why this ambivalence from governments, even allowing for the fact that other political considerations may be at work? One major explanation is that many people—and that includes economists—are not convinced that monopolies are necessarily all bad. They point out that monopolies possess a number of advantages over competitive markets. So let us take a look at some of these benefits.

SELF-TEST

6. In Figure 10.6, what would be the total revenue earned by the perfectly competitive industry? What would be the total revenue earned by the monopolist industry? In the light of your answer, explain why the monopolist isn't charging the same price as the competitive industry.

7. Complete the following table of revenue and costs for an industry.

Output	Price (= AR)	Total Revenue	Marginal Revenue	Total Costs	Average Costs	Marginal Costs	Total Profit
10	$30	___	___	$258	___	___	___
11	29	___	___	268	___	___	___
12	28	___	___	280.3	___	___	___
13	27	___	___	293	___	___	___
14	26	___	___	306	___	___	___
15	25	___	___	319.5	___	___	___
16	24	___	___	334	___	___	___
17	23	___	___	350	___	___	___
18	22	___	___	368	___	___	___
19	21	___	___	389	___	___	___
20	20	___	___	414	___	___	___
21	19	___	___	444	___	___	___
22	18	___	___	482	___	___	___

A) Suppose that the data depicts a monopoly industry. What will be the monopoly price, output, and profits?

B) Suppose, instead, that the data depicts a perfectly competitive industry. What will be the competitive price, output, and profits? (Hint: Remember that the MC of an industry is the same as its supply.)

C) What general conclusions can you come to as a result of your answers?

In Defence of Monopoly

We can focus on one of the possible benefits of monopoly by returning to our illustration of the mushroom industry and the effects of its becoming monopolized. Some would argue that the conclusions, with their negative implications, made earlier are not valid because, if a competitive industry were monopolized, the costs of production would likely change. This is because a monopolist is unlikely to preserve 100 separate mushroom farms, each one a replica of the others, with the resulting duplication of many functions. More likely, the monopolist would rationalize the industry in an attempt to achieve *economies of scale*. It certainly would not require a hundred managers, a hundred accountants, a hundred crating machines, and so on. If it is true that costs are lower under monopoly, then graphically this would mean that the whole average cost curve will be lower, resulting in a correspondingly lower price and a higher output than is shown in Figure 10.6. In fact, if costs were significantly lower, the profit-maximizing price could be lower and the output higher than under perfect competition.

A second suggested benefit of being big (and many monopolies are very big) is one that accrues to both the monopolist and to society as a whole and occurs because of more extensive *research and development*. A number of economists, including Joseph Schumpeter and John Kenneth Galbraith, have written extensively on the advantages that big firms have in terms of research and development. Small competitive firms simply do not have the capability of doing extensive research and development, the scale and costs of which tend to be prohibitive. Many innovations have been brought about by big businesses this century. As just one example, AT&T (American Telephone and Telegraph) in the United States, which at the time was a monopolist, has been given the major credit for the development of transistors and of lasers, both of which have been major technological breakthroughs. Against this, critics suggest that while big firms may have the *ability* to do research and development, they do not always have the *desire*; in fact the bigger and more dominant they are, the greedier and more complacent they may become. As a result, instead of using their energies and resources to improve technology, they are diverting them to creating bigger barriers to entry in an effort to keep out competition.

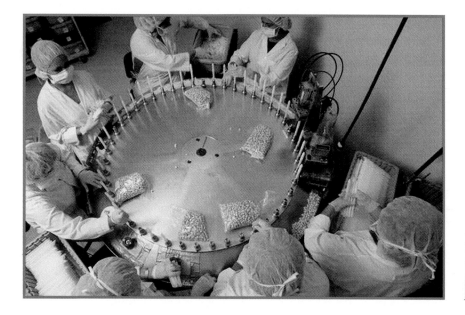

Joseph Schumpeter and John Kenneth Galbraith both felt big firms have advantages in terms of research and development.

ADDED DIMENSION

John Kenneth Galbraith: Iconoclast

John Kenneth Galbraith (1908–) is an economist who has earned a reputation as a critic of orthodox economic theory. Born in rural Ontario, Galbraith was educated at the University of Toronto and the University of California, Berkeley. During his varied careers he has had several roles, including that of adviser to the U.S. government during World War II, member of the board of directors of *Fortune* magazine, and U.S. ambassador to India in the Kennedy administration. He was, for decades, also a respected teacher at Harvard University. In addition, he is a recognized expert on Far Eastern art. His prolific writings include *The*

Affluent Society and *The New Industrial State*, in which he criticizes American big business for creating consumer demand through advertising rather than simply satisfying existing demand.

Galbraith sees today's multinational corporations as being controlled by a small elite, which he terms the technostructure, rather than by shareholders or directors. Some of his colleagues have attacked his work for being fuzzy-minded social criticism, yet his elegant writings enjoy the rare status of being widely read by both economists and the general public.

A third and final advantage that large corporations, like monopolies, may have over smaller firms is that they can *offer better salaries and conditions to their employees* and as a result attract a higher quality of staff. In addition, perhaps because their size makes them so conspicuous or because they have the finances to do so, big corporations often have better labour practices and are more consumer-aware than are their smaller cousins.

Many observers, recognizing these benefits of monopoly, suggest that the government should take a laissez-faire attitude toward monopolies. There are, they suggest, other ways of curbing any possible excesses of the monopolist. Monopolists are not all-powerful, because they will always be at the mercy of their consumers, who may simply choose not to buy the product. The fear of the possible public scrutiny of their operations and the surrounding bad publicity that will accompany it often serve as a sufficient brake on any possible abuses. In addition, while the monopoly, by definition, does not have to worry about any present competition, it does have to worry about possible future competition. In other words, the barriers to entry are seldom totally insurmountable, and the attraction of high profits may be a sufficient incentive to newcomers to try to overcome these barriers. In summary, the existence of monopolies can be defended on the grounds that:

- they capture large economies of scale in production
- they engage in extensive research and development into new techniques of production and new products
- they offer relatively good wages and working conditions for their employees

Controlling the Monopolist

In the past, governments have seldom been persuaded that public scrutiny or the threat of competition are, in themselves, sufficient to redress the possible damage that can be caused by monopoly. They therefore feel impelled to take more direct action. We will consider three possible courses of direct action: taxation, price setting, and nationalization.

What a government is often trying to do in regulating monopoly is bring about a more competitive result. This means that, ideally, the aim of policy is to force the monopolist to reduce its price and profits, and to increase its output. As we shall see, the specific measures that are often attempted have varying degrees of success. Let's look at the first of these measures: the taxation of the monopolist.

FIGURE 10.7 Profits Tax Levied on a Monopolist

Before the imposition of the profits tax, the monopolist was maximizing its profits at the point where MC = MR, producing an output of 1 million units at a selling price of $80 per unit. The effect of a fixed tax of $10 million will be to increase the average costs of the monopolist, which increases from $60 to $70 at the 1 million level of output. However, this tax has no effect on the MC. As a result, the monopolist will continue to produce 1 million units at a price of $80. However, its profits will decline by the $10 million tax.

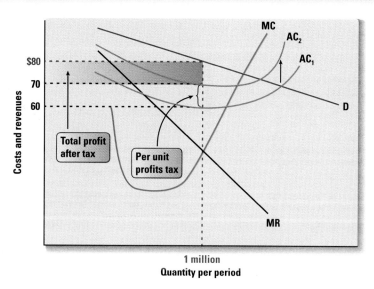

Taxing the Monopolist

Two major types of tax could be levied on the monopolist: a profits tax and a monopoly sales tax. We will look at both. Suppose, for instance, as in Figure 10.7, the government allows the monopoly to exist and to control its own affairs in return for the payment of an annual lump-sum profits tax of $10 million. What effect will this have on the monopolist? In particular, will the monopolist end up paying this tax, or will it simply pass this tax on to its customers? Let us look at the results graphically.

Suppose that before the imposition of the tax, the monopolist was producing a profit-maximizing output of 1 million units, which were being sold at $80 per unit. What effect will the lump-sum tax have on output and price? The important point to bear in mind is that the monopolist must pay this $10 million tax regardless of the level of profits or output. In other words, the tax represents a fixed cost to the monopolist and will increase the average costs of production *while leaving the marginal cost unaffected.* In Figure 10.7, the average cost curve will reflect this new tax by shifting up $10 at the present 1 million output. However, since the variable costs are unaffected by this tax, the marginal cost curve does not change. As a result, the profit-maximizing output remains unaffected. Given the new costs, the best output level is still 1 million and the best price is still $80 per unit. The only thing that has been affected is the profitability of the monopolist.

Since the output and price levels are unaffected by a lump-sum profit tax, such a policy is not a particularly effective policy, though it does at least return some of the excess profits to society by way of increased tax revenue to the government.

Instead of a profits tax, a government might decide to introduce a *monopoly sales tax* on the monopolist's output. In this case, what effect, if any, will this tax have on the monopolist, and will the tax be passed on to the consumer?

Since a monopoly sales tax is a tax on each unit sold, unlike the lump-sum profits tax, it will affect the marginal cost as shown in Figure 10.8.

FIGURE 10.8 The Effect of a Monopoly Sales Tax on a Monopolist

Prior to the tax, maximum profit was obtained by the monopolist producing an output at the point where the marginal cost equals the marginal revenue, that is, where the MC and MR curves intersect—at an output of 50 this gives a selling price of $32. Imposing a $5 per unit sales tax means that the MC increases by $5 at every output level. This is shown by an upward shift in the MC curve from MC_1 to MC_2. The new profit-maximizing equilibrium now occurs at the point where the MC_2 curve intersects the MR curve, that is, at an output of 42. The resulting price at which this output can be sold is $34.

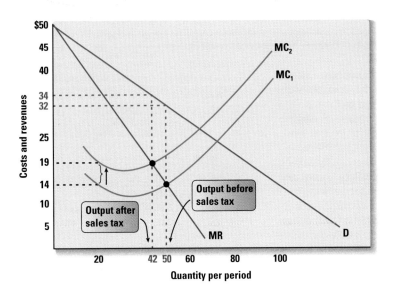

The average cost curve has been omitted in the graph because we don't need it to bring out the main points. Prior to the tax, the output level is 50, the marginal cost and revenue equal $14, and the price is $32. Suppose that the government now imposes a monopoly sales tax of $5 per unit. The result will be that the marginal cost curve will shift upward by $5 at every level of output, from MC_1 to MC_2. As a result, the new profit-maximizing output is reduced to 42 and the new price will be $34. Part of the new tax of $5 does get passed on to the customer, since the price has increased by $2. The other $3 is absorbed by the monopolist. The extent to which the monopolist is able to shift the tax onto the consumer depends in good part on the price elasticity of demand. In most cases the cost is shared between the producer and consumer, and as a result the total profit of the monopolist will be reduced. However, this type of tax fails abysmally to get the price reduced and the output increased, and in fact has exactly the opposite effect.

Government Price Setting

We can now see why governments, particularly in Canada, have seldom used taxation to control monopolists. Instead they usually prefer the more direct method of *price setting*. Governments, in theory, have the power to force the monopolist to sell at any price as long as this does not impose losses on the monopolist (and thus go out of business). However, some prices are better than others. From society's point of view, the most allocatively efficient solution would be to force the monopolist to charge a price that is equal to the marginal cost of production. This is known as the **socially optimum price** and is illustrated in **Figure 10.9**.

socially optimum price: the price that produces the best allocation of products (and therefore resources) from society's point of view, that is, P = MC.

Suppose that without government regulation, the monopolist would produce the quantity Q_{UM} (unregulated monopolist) at a price P_{UM}. Assume now that the government decides to regulate the monopolist and forces it to charge a price equal to its marginal cost. If you think of the demand curve as being the price curve, then it is easy to find the socially optimum price because it is located at the point where the MC curve cuts the demand curve. (You might recall from an earlier discussion that if this were a perfectly competitive industry, then the marginal cost is the same as the supply, so that the socially optimum position is the equivalent to the equilibrium between demand and supply.) The socially optimum price therefore is P_{SO}, and at this price the quantity purchased will be Q_{SO}. This regulated price will have the desired effect of reducing the price (and profits) of the monopolist and inducing an increase in output.

FIGURE 10.9 The Socially Optimum and Fair-Return Prices

With no interference by the government, the monopolist would maximize profits where MC = MR. This occurs at the output marked Q_{UM} and at a price of P_{UM}. The socially optimum price is where the price is equal to the MC. This occurs where the MC curve intersects the demand curve, producing a socially optimum output of Q_{SO} and a price of P_{SO}. In the situation depicted here, however, this price is below the AC, so the monopolist would be forced to incur a loss. As a result, the government might instead impose a fair-return price at which the price is equal to the AC. This occurs at the point the AC intersects the demand curve and produces the output Q_{FR} and a price of P_{FR}.

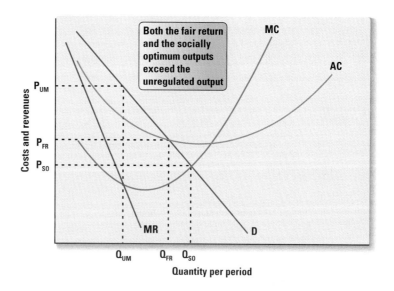

Wherever possible, the socially optimum price is the best. In certain circumstances, however, the imposition of such a price might result in the monopolist operating at a loss. This is particularly true where, as in Figure 10.9, the costs of production are high relative to the demand at the relevant price. A price of P_{SO} in the above example is below the average costs of production regardless of the output produced. In circumstances like this it would not be possible for the government to force the monopolist to incur losses. In other words, the government will need to ensure that the monopolist is able to earn at least a reasonable profit. And what is a reasonable profit? Presumably, it is an amount sufficient to keep the company in business and to prevent owners from looking for other avenues for their financial investment. This is what economists mean by normal profits, and if you remember, normal profits are regarded as a cost of production and are therefore included in the average cost shown in Figure 10.9. A **fair-return price**, in other words, is a price that allows the monopolist to earn a normal profit and no more. This means that the price should be set equal to average costs. To find it in Figure 10.9, we need to locate the point at which the AC curve cuts the demand curve. This occurs at a price of P_{FR}, and at this price the quantity purchased is equal to an output of Q_{FR}. You can see that the fair-return price tends to be something of a compromise between the unregulated monopolist's position and the socially optimum position. In many cases, however, a government may have no choice but to compromise.

One issue associated with guaranteeing a fair return for the monopolist is what is called the extravagance problem. Since the return is based on average costs, it may be to the advantage of the monopolist to pad its costs by spending extravagant amounts on facilities, amenities, and salaries.

fair-return price: a price that guarantees that the firm will earn normal profits only, that is, where P = AC.

ADDED DIMENSION

Government and Monopolies: An Uneasy Relationship

Since monopolies produce both benefits and costs, governments have often differed in their approach to them. Unlike the United States, Canada has tended to look at monopolists not so much as problems in themselves but as part of a wider problem of restrictive practices, in which firms often combine to restrain competition. As such, the first anti-combines legislation was passed in Canada in 1889 and sought to prevent the formation of monopolies or near-monopolies, but also forbade collusion by firms to raise prices or restrict supplies to their customers, or to do anything which would "unduly lessen competition." Over the years, this legislation has been revised and updated, the last revision coming in the form of the 1986 Competition Act. This act forbids things that would lessen competition but does not outlaw mergers or monopolies; it forbids only the "abuse of dominant position." In fact, it explicitly recognizes that some mergers may be warranted as being in the public interest if, for example, this would allow Canadian firms to better compete in world markets.

SELF-TEST

8. The following table gives the cost and demand data for a monopolist. What would be the price, output, and profit of the monopolist if it were:
   A) unregulated?
   B) regulated and required to charge a socially optimum price?
   C) regulated and required to charge a fair-return price?

Output	Price	Marginal Revenue	Average Cost	Marginal Cost
0	$175	—	—	—
1	160	$160	$240	$100
2	145	130	150	60
3	130	100	116.7	50
4	115	70	105	70
5	100	40	100	80
6	85	10	97.5	85
7	70	−20	96.40	90
8	55	−50	96	93
9	40	−80	95.9	95

Nationalization

A final way in which governments attempt to deal with monopolies is to remove them from private ownership by nationalization. This means that the state acquires the monopoly reluctantly (sometimes) or eagerly (often), either by compulsory and uncompensated acquisition (seldom) or by a buyout of the owners (usually). The state then operates the enterprise (as a crown corporation in Canada) on whatever terms it sees fit. It may or may not operate the enterprise to make a profit; it may or may not charge the socially optimum price. There is no guarantee, however, that simply because the monopoly is operated by the state it is likely to be any more efficient or socially responsible than if it was privately owned.

ADDED DIMENSION

Nationalization or Regulation?

In efforts to ensure that certain monopoly and oligopoly industries act in the public interest, some countries have taken the extreme measure of taking over the industry completely (either with or without compensation). Supposedly, the government can then appoint its own managers, who will therefore have full knowledge about the costs of production and can ensure that "fair" prices and a "proper" level of production is maintained. In the United Kingdom after the World War II, a number of industries, such as coal mining, steel, and railways, were nationalized by the then-ruling Labour government and run by government-appointed boards. In contrast, in the United States, these and other industries were left in private hands but regulated by government-appointed bodies.

In Canada, as might be expected, some firms and whole industries have been nationalized, whereas some are still privately owned but regulated and others remain privately owned and unregulated. The nationalized firms (called crown corporations in Canada) include federally controlled corporations like the CBC and Canada Post, and until recently, Canadian National (CN), Air Canada, and Petro Canada. In addition, most provinces have crown corporations producing electricity, while at the municipal level, urban transit, the water system, and garbage collection are usually public enterprises.

REVIEW

1. Contrast monopoly and perfect competition in terms of the profit-maximizing price and output.
2. Explain three major benefits that a monopoly market might have over a perfectly competitive one.
3. Why would a lump-sum profits tax have no impact on either the price or output produced by the monopolist?
4. To what extent will an excise tax be passed on to the customer by a monopolist?
5. What are the three major ways in which the government attempts to control monopoly?
6. What is the *socially optimum price*? Is it higher or lower than the unregulated monopolist's price?
7. What is the *fair-return price*? Is it higher or lower than the unregulated monopolist's price? From society's point of view, which is preferable?

STUDY GUIDE

Chapter Highlights

In this chapter you learned that defining what is and what is not a monopoly, and whether monopolies are a good or a bad thing for society in general, is not as clear cut as it might at first appear. In addition, the concept of the profit maximizing output and price was extended from the equality of P and MC under perfect competition to the equality of MR and MC under monopoly.

1. Since a monopolist is a single seller its demand curve is the market demand curve and, for a straight-line demand curve, its marginal revenue (MR) curve is twice as steep as the demand curve.

2. The existence of monopolies is a result of barriers to entry which come in three types:
   - technical barriers such as sole ownership of a resource;
   - legal barriers such as government legislation or patents;
   - economic barriers which result from the existence of extensive economies of scale.

3. The profit maximization output for a monopolist is where:

$$MC = MR;$$

   and the price the monopolist will charge for this output is the maximum possible price, given the market demand curve.

4. Monopolies can be criticized for:
   - being able to make economic profits even in the long run;
   - being both productively and allocatively inefficient;
   - producing a lower output and charging a higher price than would be done in a competitive industry;
   - creating a more unequal distribution of income.

5. On the other hand, monopolies can be defended on the grounds that:
   - they capture large economies of scale and are, therefore, efficient;
   - they engage in extensive research and development into new technology and new products;
   - they offer relatively good wages and working conditions for their employees.

6. Governments can attempt to change the behaviour of monopolies in three ways:
   - taxing the monopolist;
   - requiring that they sell at a specific price, either a socially-optimum price (where $P = MC$) or a fair return price (where $P = AC$);
   - converting a privately-owned monopoly into a crown corporation.

New Glossary Terms

Study Tips

1. Students initially have problems understanding why the marginal revenue is less than the price. The best way to understand the difference is to make up a few tables for yourself, with quantities increasing by 1 unit and price decreasing by any constant amount. Work out the total and marginal revenues, and think out what is happening. Now put it into words. If you are able to do this, then you understand the concept.

2. Figure 10.4 is probably the single most complicated graph that you have encountered so far. It is also very important that you are able to draw it for yourself and understand what it says. It's probably a good idea to first draw a smooth, saucer-shaped average cost curve with a clearly identifiable lowest point. Now draw the marginal cost curve intersecting this lowest point. Next put on the demand curve so that it intersects the average cost curve to the right of the lowest point. Finally, draw in the marginal revenue curve. Strictly, this is supposed to be twice as steep as the demand curve and should cut the horizontal axis at the halfway point between the origin and the demand curve's intersection with the horizontal axis. But don't worry if it's not exact and you find you have to cheat a little. Once you have located the intersection between the marginal cost and revenue curves, draw a vertical line down to the quantity axis to get the profit-maximizing output. Then continue this vertical line upward until you hit the demand curve. Go across to the price axis to get the profit-maximizing price.

3. The other difficult graph to draw in this chapter is Figure 10.9, which shows the effect of government price setting. Since you want to set up a situation in which the socially optimum price involves a loss for the monopolist, proceed as you would for the normal monopoly diagram. However, when you come to draw in the demand curve, make sure that it intersects the average cost curve to the *left* of the latter's lowest point.

Are You Sure?

Indicate whether the following statements are true or false. If false, indicate why they are false.

1. A monopolist is free to charge any price it wishes for its product.

   T or F   If false: _____

   _____

2. A patent is an example of a barrier to entry.

   T or F   If false: _____

   _____

3. The marginal revenue of the monopolist may be equal to, greater than, or less than its average revenue.

   T or F   If false: _____

   _____

4. A natural monopoly exists when a single producer is able to produce at a lower cost than competing firms could.

   T or F   If false: _____

   _____

5. At the profit-maximizing output of the monopolist, the price will be equal to the marginal cost.

   T or F   If false: _____

   _____

6. A monopolist will only be able to make a profit if, at some output level, the average revenue exceeds the average cost.

   T or F   If false: _____

   _____

7. A lump-sum profit tax imposed on a monopolist will cause the monopolist to increase the price and reduce output in order to maximize its profits.

   T or F   If false: _____

   _____

8. A fair-return price is a price set equal to a firm's lowest average cost.

   T or F   If false: _____

   _____

9. A socially optimum price is a price set equal to a firm's marginal cost.

   T or F   If false: _____

   _____

10. A monopolist will break even if it is producing an output at which the average revenue is equal to the average cost.

    T or F   If false: _____

    _____

Choose the Best

11. Since a monopolist faces a downward-sloping demand curve, which of the following statements is true?
    a) Its average revenue is equal to the price.
    b) Its average revenue is equal to its marginal revenue.

12. Sole ownership of a particular resource is an example of what?
    a) A natural monopoly.
    b) A barrier to entry.

13. Which of the following is true?
    a) A monopolist cannot make economic losses in the short run.
    b) A monopolist cannot make economic losses in the long run.

14. All of the following, *except one*, are true statements about a natural monopoly. Which one is the exception?
    a) It is able to produce at a lower cost than competing firms could.
    b) It faces increasing returns to scale and a declining LRAC over the relevant range of demand.
    c) The demand for its product is perfectly elastic.

15. Which of the following statements regarding the definition of a monopoly market is incorrect?
    a) Whether a certain market is regarded as a monopoly depends upon the definition of the demand.

b) Whether a certain market is regarded as a monopoly depends upon the definition of the market.

c) Whether a certain market is regarded as a monopoly depends upon the definition of the product.

16. Under what circumstances will a monopolist be forced to shut down?
   a) If the average revenue exceeds the average costs of production.
   b) If the average revenue exceeds the average variable costs of production.
   c) If the average variable costs of production exceeds the average revenue.

17. What will be the effect of a sales tax imposed on a monopolist's product?
   a) It will lead to an increase in the price and a reduction in the output.
   b) It will lead to an increase in the price but will have no effect on the output.
   c) It will have no impact on the price nor on the output.

18. All of the following statements, *except one*, are true. Which is the exception?
   a) A monopolist is able to control the price of the product but not also the quantity purchased.
   b) A monopolist is able to control the quantity purchased of the product but not also the price.
   c) A monopolist can control both the price and the quantity purchased.

19. Which of the following statements is true regarding the marginal revenue curve of the monopolist?
   a) It is twice as steep as the average revenue curve.
   b) It is equal to the price.
   c) It is a horizontal line.
   d) It is the same as its average revenue curve.

20. All of the following, *except one*, are examples of barriers to entry. Which is the exception?
   a) Economies of scale.
   b) Minimum-wage legislation.
   c) Copyrights.
   d) Government licences.

21. Which of the following is a correct statement of the socially optimum price?
   a) It is a price equal to the average cost.
   b) It is a price equal to the marginal cost.
   c) It is a price equal to the lowest average cost.
   d) It is a price equal to the marginal revenue.

22. All, *except one*, of the following statements regarding the profit-maximizing output of the monopolist are correct. Which is false?
   a) At that output, the marginal cost will be equal to the price.
   b) At that output, marginal profit is zero.
   c) At that output, the difference between the total revenue and the total cost will be at a maximum.
   d) At that output, marginal cost will equal marginal revenue.

23. Suppose that a perfectly competitive industry is monopolized. If the costs of production remain unchanged, which of the following statements is correct?
   a) Both the price and the output of the perfectly competitive industry will be higher than those of the monopoly industry.
   b) Both the price and the output of the perfectly competitive industry will be lower than those of the monopoly industry.
   c) The perfectly competitive price will be higher, and the output will be lower.
   d) The perfectly competitive price will be lower, and the output will be higher.

Table 10.4 outlines the cost and revenue data for a monopolist. Use it to answer questions 24 and 25.

TABLE 10.4

Quantity Demanded	Price	Total Cost
0		$40
1	$45	58
2	40	73
3	35	87
4	30	100
5	25	118
6	20	143

24. Refer to Table 10.4 to answer this question. What are the profit-maximizing level of output and price respectively?

a) 3 and $35.
b) 4 and $30.
c) 5 and $25.
d) 5 and $30.
e) 6 and $20.

25. Refer to Table 10.4 to answer this question. What is the level of profits at the profit-maximizing output?
    a) 0.
    b) $7.
    c) $15.
    d) $20.
    e) $120.

Refer to Figure 10.10 to answer questions 26 and 27.

FIGURE 10.10

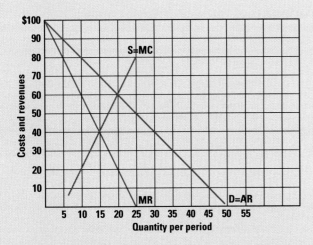

26. Refer to Figure 10.10 to answer this question. Suppose this graph depicts a perfectly competitive industry. What will be the equilibrium price and output respectively?
    a) $40 and 15.
    b) $40 and 30.
    c) $60 and 20.
    d) $60 and 25.
    e) $70 and 15.

27. Refer to Figure 10.10 to answer this question. Suppose this graph depicts a monopoly industry. What will be the profit-maximizing price and output respectively?
    a) $40 and 15.
    b) $40 and 30.

c) $60 and 20.
d) $60 and 25.
e) $70 and 15.

Figure 10.11 depicts the cost and revenue curves for a monopolist. Use it to answer questions 28, 29, and 30.

FIGURE 10.11

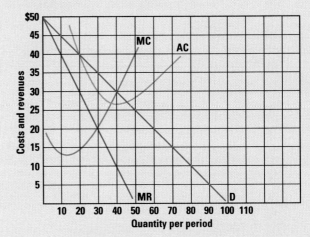

28. Refer to Figure 10.11 to answer this question. What are the profit-maximizing level of output and price respectively?
    a) 30 and $20.
    b) 30 and $35.
    c) 35 and $27.50.
    d) 40 and $30.
    e) 42 and $28.

29. Refer to Figure 10.11 to answer this question. At the profit-maximizing level of output, what is the amount of total costs?
    a) $20.
    b) $600.
    c) $900.
    d) $1200.
    e) Cannot be determined from this information.

30. Refer to Figure 10.11 to answer this question. What is the level of profits at the profit-maximizing output?
    a) 0.
    b) $20.
    c) $150.
    d) $450.
    e) $600.

Problems

31. a) Complete **Table 10.5**, which shows the costs and revenues of Solo the monopolist, assuming that the demand curve is a straight line.

TABLE 10.5

Quantity per Period	Price	TR	MR	MC	TC	ATC
0	—	—	—	—	25	—
1	___	___	___	___	___	60
2	___	___	46	30	___	___
3	___	___	___	___	115	___
4	___	___	___	___	135	___
5	___	210	___	___	___	32
6	___	___	___	30	___	___
7	38	___	___	___	225	___
8	___	___	___	40	___	___
9	___	___	18	___	310	___
10	___	___	___	___	___	36

b) What are the values of the profit-maximizing output?

Price: $_____; output: _____ units; total profit/loss $_____.

c) At what output will sales revenue be maximized, and what will be the value of sales revenue?

Output: _____ units; total revenue: $_____.

32. Figure 10.12 shows the demand for Primo the monopolist's product.

FIGURE 10.12

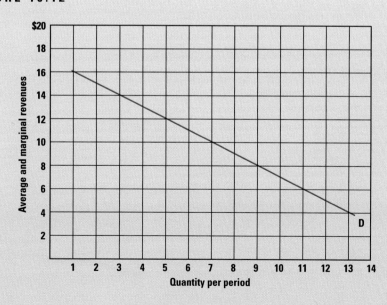

a) From this information, complete **Table 10.6** and add the MR curve to Figure 10.12.

TABLE 10.6

Quantity Demanded	Price = AR ($)	TR ($)	MR ($)
1	_____	_____	_____
2	_____	_____	_____
3	_____	_____	_____
4	_____	_____	_____
5	_____	_____	_____
6	_____	_____	_____
7	_____	_____	_____
8	_____	_____	_____
9	_____	_____	_____
10	_____	_____	_____
11	_____	_____	_____
12	_____	_____	_____

b) At what output level is total revenue maximized? What is the marginal revenue at this output?

Output of: _____ units; marginal revenue: $_____.

c) What is the elasticity of demand between outputs of 8 and 9?

Elasticity: _____.

d) What is the maximum output that this monopolist would produce?

Output of: _____ units.

e) Is the demand elastic or inelastic for outputs less than this maximum?

_____

f) What general rule can you derive from these observations?

_____

33. **Figure 10.13** shows the cost and revenue information for Shitotsu the monopolist.

FIGURE 10.13

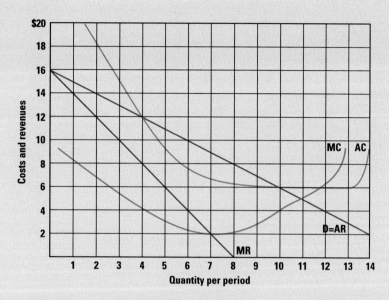

What are the levels of (1) price; (2) output; (3) total (sales) revenue; and (4) total profits if the monopolist were to produce at the positions a) through d) in **Table 10.7**?

TABLE 10.7

	(1) Price ($)	(2) Output	(3) Total revenue ($)	(4) Total profits ($)
a) Sales revenue maximization	——	——	——	——
b) Profit maximization	——	——	——	——
c) Socially optimum price	——	——	——	——
d) Fair-return price	——	——	——	——

34. Figure 10.14 depicts the cost and revenue curves for a particular industry.

FIGURE 10.14

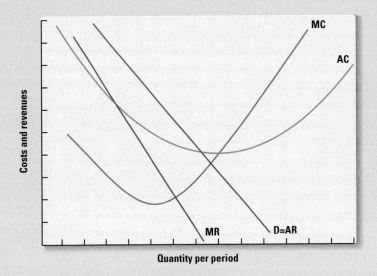

a) Assume that this industry is perfectly competitive. Identify the equilibrium, and mark on the graph the price (P_C) and the quantity (Q_C).

b) Suppose instead that the graph depicts a monopolistic industry. Identify the profit-maximizing price and output and label them on the graph as P_M and Q_M.

c) Now suppose that the government were to regulate this monopoly so that it was required to charge a socially optimum price. Identify this on Figure 10.14, and label the price P_{SO} and the corresponding quantity Q_{SO}.

d) Finally, suppose that the government were to regulate this monopoly so that it was required to charge a fair-return price. Identify this on the graph and label the price P_{FR} and the corresponding quantity Q_{FR}.

Translations

Tom, a steel drum manufacturer (the only one in Narnia), can sell a single drum for $30. However, for every extra drum he wants to sell, he is forced to reduce the price (for all his customers) by $2. The total fixed costs in his workshop are $15, and the variable cost of the first drum produced is $25. For each extra drum thereafter, the cost drops by $5 until the fifth drum. After that, the cost of each extra drum increases by $5. Draw the AR, MR, ATC, and MC curves in **Figure 10.15** and identify the profit-maximizing output and the amount of profits.

FIGURE 10.15

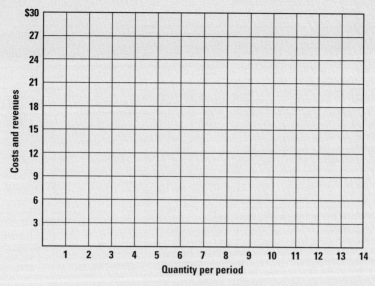

Key Problem

Corona is a military dictatorship whose most important industry is the production of (empty) metal beer kegs. The industry is *perfectly competitive* and has the costs and demand shown in **Table 10.8** (all units, apart from the price are in thousands per week).

TABLE 10.8

Price ($)	Quantity Demanded	TR ($)	MR ($)	MC ($)	TC ($)	Tπ ($)	ATC ($)
30	0	___	—	—	28	___	—
28	1	___	___	___	48	___	___
26	2	___	___	___	59	___	___
24	3	___	___	___	67	___	___
22	4	___	___	___	83	___	___
20	5	___	___	___	100	___	___
18	6	___	___	___	118	___	___
16	7	___	___	___	138	___	___
14	8	___	___	___	163	___	___
12	9	___	___	___	193	___	___

a) Complete the table and, in Figure 10.16, draw in the demand and supply curves for the industry. (Recall that the supply curve for a perfectly competitive industry is the same as its MC curve.)

FIGURE 10.16

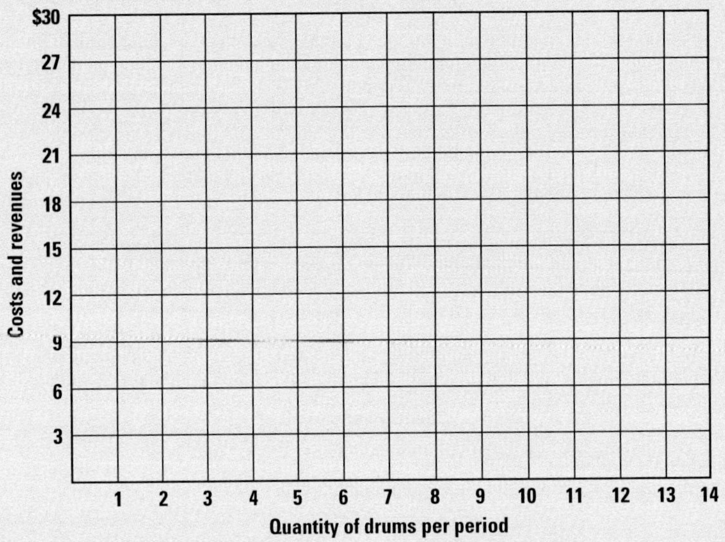

Quantity of drums per period

b) What are the equilibrium values of price, quantity traded, and total profit (or loss) in the industry? Label the competitive equilibrium as e_1 on the graph.

Price: $_____; quantity: _____; profit/loss $_____.

Suppose that Irina, the sister-in-law of Corona's president, is given the metal keg industry as a birthday present. She immediately amalgamates all the firms into one large monopoly.

c) Assuming that Irina wishes to maximize her profits from the industry, what price and quantity will she produce, and what will be her total profits? (*Hint:* Draw in the ATC and the MR on your graph in Figure 10.16.)

Price: $_____; quantity: _____; profit/loss $_____.

The following year, the president becomes concerned with the big profits being made by Irina and informs her that, if she wishes to remain in business, she has a choice. She can either pay a tax of $5000 per period to the government or not pay a tax but have the government determine what price she will be allowed to charge. If she chooses the latter option, then the government will require her to charge either a price equal to her average cost or a price equal to her marginal cost.

d) Locate the two price choices available to Irina and identify them on Figure 10.16.

e) Summarize the results of the three options in Table 10.9.

TABLE 10.9

	Price ($)	Quantity Traded	Profit/Loss ($)
1. Tax of $5000	_____	_____	_____
2. P = AC	_____	_____	_____
3. P = MC	_____	_____	_____

Given the three options, which is the best one, from Irina's point of view? From the government's? From the people of Corona's?

Irina's choice: _____

Government's choice: _____

Coronans' choice: _____

More of the Same

Nopoli's major export is golf bags, which are produced in a perfectly competitive industry. **Table 10.10** outlines the industry's costs and demand (all units, apart from the price, are in thousands per month).

a) Complete the table and graph the demand and supply curves for the industry on the grid in **Figure 10.17**.

TABLE 10.10

Price ($)	Quantity Demanded	TR ($)	MR ($)	MC ($)	TC ($)	Tπ ($)	AC ($)
50	0	—	—	—	64	_____	—
48	1	_____	_____	_____	97	_____	_____
46	2	_____	_____	_____	124	_____	_____
44	3	_____	_____	_____	148	_____	_____
42	4	_____	_____	_____	168	_____	_____
40	5	_____	_____	_____	192	_____	_____
38	6	_____	_____	_____	220	_____	_____
36	7	_____	_____	_____	252	_____	_____
34	8	_____	_____	_____	286	_____	_____
32	9	_____	_____	_____	326	_____	_____
30	10	_____	_____	_____	376	_____	_____

FIGURE 10.17

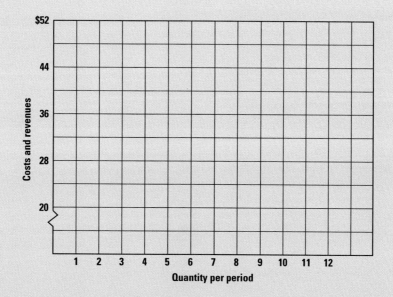

b) What are the equilibrium values of price, quantity traded, and total profit (or loss) in the industry? Label the competitive equilibrium with an *a* on your graph.

Suppose that the golf bag industry is taken over by Norman Greg (known as the brown dolphin in Nopoli's golfing circles). Norm immediately sets about amalgamating all the firms into one large monopoly.

c) Add the marginal revenue curve and the average cost curve to your graph. If he wishes to maximize his profits from the industry, what price and quantity will Norman produce, and what will his total profits be?

The government, however, concerned with the fact that its major export industry is controlled by a single person, decides to levy a lump-sum monthly tax of $6000 on Norm's firm.

d) What will be the new price, quantity, and profits of the firm as a result of the imposition of the tax?

e) Suppose, alternatively, that the government decides to impose a socially optimum price on the firm. What will be the new price, quantity, and profits of the firm as a result?

f) What if, instead, the government decides to impose a fair-return price on the firm? What will be the new price, quantity, and profits of the firm now?

UNANSWERED QUESTIONS

Short Essays

1. Explain why a monopoly market is not as beneficial to consumers as a competitive market.

2. What are some of the advantages a monopoly industry might have over a competitive industry?

3. Explain why the marginal revenue of the monopolist is always less than the average revenue.

4. Explain, with examples, the meaning of barriers to entry. In what way do they lead to the creation of monopolies?

5. What conditions must exist in order for a monopolist to practise price discrimination?

6. What methods are available for a government wishing to regulate a monopoly? How successful are such methods likely to be?

Analytical Questions

7. Suppose that the average variable costs for a monopolist remained constant regardless of how much it produced. What would then determine the profit-maximizing output of the monopolist?

8. Comment on the validity of the following statements regarding an unregulated monopolist.
   a) A monopolist charges the highest possible price.
   b) A monopolist tries to maximize its sales revenue.
   c) A monopolist cannot make economic losses in the short run.
   d) A monopolist cannot make economic losses in the long run.
   e) A monopolist can make economic profit in the long run.

9. Since a monopolist can increase its total revenue by decreasing the price of the product, why doesn't it continue to reduce the price indefinitely?

10. A monopolist would never produce in the price range at which the demand was inelastic. Why not?

11. Suppose that there is a single monopoly fishing vessel in a small town. Once the catch is landed for the day, the supply of fish cannot be adjusted. How is the price of fish determined? What difference would it make if the industry was competitive and there were many competing fishing boats?

12. What are the implications of a government forcing a monopolist to charge a price equal not just to its average costs but to its *minimum* average costs?

13. There is no such thing as the supply curve for a monopolist because there is no unique relationship between the price of the product and the quantity produced. Explain.

14. Suppose that a monopolist could practise perfect price discrimination and charge each consumer the maximum that each is prepared to pay. Draw the monopolist's new demand and marginal revenue curves. How do they compare with those for the non-discriminating monopolist? (Hint: Try using some actual numbers.)

Numerical Questions

15. **a)** Complete **Table 10.11** for Uno the monopolist:

TABLE 10.11

Quantity	P = AR	TR	MR
1	___	___	24
2	23	___	___
3	___	___	20
4	___	84	___
5	___	___	16
6	19	___	___
7	___	126	___
8	___	136	___
9	___	___	8
10	15	___	___
11	___	154	___
12	___	___	2

b) At what output is total revenue maximized? What is marginal revenue at this output?
c) What is the maximum output that this monopolist would produce?
d) What is the price elasticity of demand over the range of prices shown in the table?

16. **Figure 10.18** shows the demand and marginal cost curves for Meanie the monopolist. Draw in Meanie's marginal revenue curve and identify the following points:
a) The profit-maximizing output and price.
b) The sales-maximization output and price.

FIGURE 10.18

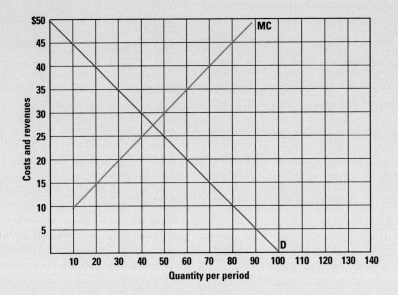

17. Clay Monopoly is considering whether it is worthwhile producing an additional 10 units of his terra cotta pots, which will cost him an additional $80. He is selling 120 pots a week at $18 each. In order to increase his sales by 10 units, however, he would need to reduce the price of all his pots to $17. What would you recommend?

18. Unisel is the sole automobile manufacturer in Concordia, which prohibits the importation of cars. Figure 10.19 depicts the demand and the costs for Unisel.

FIGURE 10.19

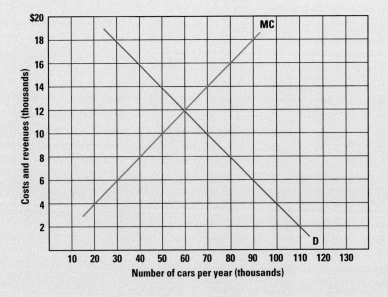

a) What is Unisel's profit-maximizing output and price?

b) Suppose that the government of Concordia imposes a price ceiling of $10 000 per car. What is Unisel's profit-maximizing output now?

c) What would be the output if this were a perfectly competitive market?

19. Table 10.12 outlines the cost and revenue data for Mo the monopolist.

TABLE 10.12

Quantity per Period	Price	Total Cost
0	$21	$18
1	20	40
2	19	50
3	18	58
4	17	62
5	16	70
6	15	80
7	14	91
8	13	105
9	12	123
10	11	148

a) Graph Mo's demand, MR, and MC curves. What is Mo's profit-maximizing price and output, and what will be the amount of his profits?

b) Suppose that the demand for Mo's products increased by 3 units at every price level. Graph Mo's new demand and MR curves. What will be Mo's new profit-maximizing price and output, and what will be the amount of his profits?

20. Table 10.13 shows the costs and demand for the Primrose Oil industry.

TABLE 10.13

Quantity	Price	Total Cost
0	$95	$50
1	90	90
2	85	120
3	80	135
4	75	160
5	70	210
6	65	265
7	60	325
8	55	400

a) If this were a perfectly competitive industry, what would be the price, output, and total industry profit?

b) If, alternatively, this were a monopoly industry, what would be the price, output, and total profit?

21. Figure 10.20 shows the demand curve facing Max the monopolist.

FIGURE 10.20

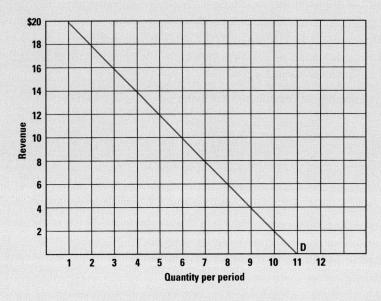

a) Using Figure 10.20, construct a table showing AR_1, MR_1, and TR_1.

b) Draw the MR curve labelled MR_1.

c) Assuming that partial units cannot be sold, what is the monopolist's maximum revenue?

d) Suppose that the monopolist could practise perfect price discrimination by selling each unit at a difference price (the first unit at \$20, the second at \$18, the third at \$16, and so on). Add additional columns AR_2, MR_2, and TR_2 to your table. Draw the AR_2 and MR_2 curves.

 Web-Based Activities

....

1. Up until very recently, the telephone industry was a monopoly. It was also argued that this industry was a natural monopoly. Read **www.indcom.gov.au/research/other/teleeco/ch02.pdf** and **www.cato.org/pubs/journal/cjv14n2-6.html** and determine if the telephone industry was in fact a natural monopoly.

2. In your text, it is asserted that the government often provides public utilities that are regarded as essential. In **www.cato.org/pubs/journal/cj18n1-3.html** the author argues that water supply need not necessarily be supplied by a governmental monopoly. Do you agree with the author? Why or why not?

Imperfect Competition

What's ahead...This chapter looks at the behaviour of firms operating in two types of imperfectly competitive markets, referred to as oligopoly and monopolistic competition. We begin by looking at the common features of both. In particular, we look at how firms try to distinguish their products from the competition through advertising and other types of product differentiation. We then explore the conditions for equilibrium in both types of markets and evaluate how the results compare with perfect competition. In the case of the monopolistically competitive firm, we show why the distinction between the short run and the long run is important. In the case of the oligopoly firm, we emphasize the important characteristic of interdependence between firms. This feature results in there being no single theory of oligopoly, but instead a number of variants, of which we examine three.

A QUESTION OF RELEVANCE...

Baseball caps, video cameras, haircuts, beer, books, TV programs, cell phones, cigars, calculators, and airline flights. What do all these products have in common, apart from the fact that they are of interest to most students and their professors? The answer is that they are all produced by firms that are neither perfect competitors nor monopolies. Instead, all the firms associated with these products operate in a market structure that economists call imperfect competition.

S o far we have examined two market structures: monopoly and perfect competition. There are only a few examples of a pure monopoly, and, as we have seen, the model of perfect competition is more of an abstraction (albeit a very useful abstraction) than a description of our present world. Lying between these two extremes is the marketplace for a multitude of products with which we are all familiar and that millions of people buy. The term **imperfect competition** is used by economists to refer to these more familiar market situations, and it describes much of modern capitalism reasonably well. Many of the ideas in this chapter were developed independently in the 1930s by Edward Chamberlin at Harvard University and Joan Robinson at Cambridge University.

imperfect competition: a market structure in which producers are identifiable and have some control over price.

ADDED DIMENSION

Joan Robinson: Filling the Void

Joan Robinson (1903–1983) was a long-time professor of economics at Cambridge University and a student of Alfred Marshall's. Although she was neither a member nor a founder of any particular school of thought, she made an important contribution to economic theory. She wrote a critique of Marxist economics, but her position was as a friendly detractor. Her most important contribution, however, was her work entitled *Economics of Imperfect Competition (1933)*. This book filled a huge void in economics: the analysis of market structures that lie between the two extremes of monopoly and perfect competition.

Her work was published at the same time as that of the American economist Edward Chamberlin, who wrote on the same theme. The two provided similar, though not identical, analyses. While Chamberlin praised imperfect competition for adding increased consumer choice, Robinson was critical of it for leading to the waste of underutilized resources. She concluded that firms in imperfect competition are likely to reduce output in order to maintain price, and this results in a great deal of idle capacity and underutilized resources. Consequently, she believed that government should intervene to discourage this form of market structure.

Roadside signs are one way in which sellers try to differentiate their products.

Product Differentiation

product differentiation: the attempt by a firm to distinguish its product from that of its competitors.

Imperfect competition is characterized by firms often competing with each other on a basis other than price. As a result, what economists call product differentiation is common. **Product differentiation** involves the attempt by a seller to offer a product that is *seen* by the consumer as different and presumably better than the others on the market. There are several ways this may be done. A recognizable logo is a popular form of product differentiation. Nearly everyone recognizes the Nike "swoosh" symbol that is seen on television ads, T-shirts, baseball hats, and billboards. To many consumers the widely recognized symbol adds to the desirability of owning a pair of Nike shoes. This increases the demand for Nike products and enables the company to charge a higher price than its rivals do. Perhaps the world's most recognizable symbol is McDonald's golden arches. The success of this company speaks volumes about the rewards of effective product differentiation.

Besides using a logo, firms try to create a special image for their products through the use of a distinctive brand name. There are several highly successful examples that one could think of: a Hoover is a vacuum cleaner; Kleenex is really facial tissue; a Band Aid is an adhesive dressing; Saran Wrap is quite ordinary plastic sheeting; and Scotch tape is just one of many types of adhesive tape. However, in each of these cases the generic product has come to be commonly identified with a brand name. Besides the use of recognizable symbols or brand names, firms sometimes try to differentiate their product through distinctive packaging. Infants, for instance, can recognize their own favourite brands of cereal or candy long before they are able to read.

ADDED DIMENSION

Rebranding Britain

Opinion polls show that most foreigners regard Britain as backward-looking and stodgy. The British government, starting in 1998, decided to try to change this perception by "rebranding" Britain and creating the impression of "Cool Britannia." Foreign dignitaries are being served meals prepared by British cooks who really can cook. High-tech British products, as well as horseguards, are being put on display. "God Save the Queen" has been jazzed up (it is reported that the Queen winced upon her first hearing). A new souped-up vacuum cleaner received a mention in a prime minister's speech. So we can see that the concept of a recognizable brand can extend to countries as well as products.

Product differentiation may take a different form. Think of a business such as a retail outlet, in which location and service are often significant ways to differentiate itself. This explains, for example, why some dry-cleaning shops do a brisk business while others do not, or why a supermarket chain retains a strong presence in older neighbourhoods because it has long-established, attractive locations and a reputation for service.

Another type of product differentiation occurs when firms redevelop their product by introducing a new and supposedly improved version. A prime example of this occurs annually in the auto industry, where new models are introduced every fall and each new version is reported to be an improvement that will better meet customer needs. This same phenomenon has now spread to other industries, resulting in, for example, the annual new model of television sets or, almost unbelievably, of mattresses.

Finally, let's look in some detail at the way firms attempt to differentiate their products through advertising. There may, in fact, be no difference between two brands of motor oil, but if people think there is a difference then product differentiation has occurred. Successfully convincing consumers that one motor oil is better than another often involves extensive advertising effort.

Advertising by rival firms can be thought of as a very expensive and very important form of non-price competition. The word "advertising" conjures up in most people's minds images of expensive television commercials, which only very large firms can afford. However, advertising comes in other forms as well—from flyers delivered directly to households to sign boards in a mall. One way that smaller firms attempt to differentiate themselves from their rivals is to use this type of advertising. Larger firms, on the other hand, can afford national television exposure.

There is debate within the discipline of economics over the benefits of advertising to society as a whole. We will try to sort through the highlights of this debate by presenting the in-favour view, which focuses on the positive aspects of advertising, and the contrary view, which is much more critical of advertising as a method of competition.

The in-favour view points out that advertising provides the consumer with vital information about the availability, quality, and location of products, which helps greatly to cut down on the consumers' search time in acquiring products. For instance, it would be very time-consuming if, because of the lack of advertising, you could obtain information about buying a car only by driving from dealer to dealer.

A second argument put forward by the in-favour view is that advertising increases the degree of competition in the market because new firms are better able to enter an industry when they can announce their entry through advertising. For example, you can imagine the near impossibility for a firm like Hyundai to break into the North American car market without the benefits of national advertising. An extension of this argument is that the development and introduction of new products is also greatly enhanced by the presence of advertising. Further, the point is sometimes made that advertising creates an atmosphere that encourages new-product development so that technological change is encouraged.

The third argument in the in-favour view is that advertising can actually lower the price of many products that are extensively advertised. There are two reasons for this. The first is that increased competition, mentioned above, would be expected to heighten consumer knowledge about prices and thereby force down prices and lower profit margins for the representative firm. In addition, it has been argued that advertising enables a firm to expand its size and thereby enjoy economies of scale in production, which lower average costs, and thus, ultimately, lead to a lower price for the final product.

Lastly, another benefit credited to advertising is the increased availability of the magazines and television shows financed by sponsors' ads. Whether this improves our overall standard of living is a value judgement best left to the reader.

In summary, the in-favour view is that advertising is beneficial in that it:

- provides the consumer with vital information
- enhances competition between firms
- lowers the prices of products
- finances magazines and television shows

In rather dramatic contrast, the contrary view argues that advertising is wasteful because even if all advertising were eliminated tomorrow, total consumption expenditures in the economy would not decline. Expenditure patterns may well change as fewer products that were highly advertised are bought, but more of other products would be bought, so total consumer spending would be little affected. This argument continues by stating that the billions of dollars spent on trying to *persuade* consumers to buy a certain brand of product could then be spent in much more socially desirable ways. This argument discounts the informational value of advertising by pointing out that most advertising (TV in particular) is aimed at persuasion, and its effectiveness is cancelled out by a rival firm's large expenditures with the same goal in mind. For instance, millions of dollars are spent by both Procter and Gamble and its rival Johnson and Johnson as they go head-to-head in the shampoo wars on television. It might be questioned, after all is said and done, whether the consumer is any better off as a result.

Proponents of the contrary view also challenge the idea that advertising increases competition by arguing that it is just as likely that huge advertising budgets used to promote brand loyalty in a product can create a barrier to entry that could, in fact, encourage the emergence of monopoly tendencies.

Finally, the contrary view holds that expenditures on advertising must raise the price of products. Someone pays for the billions of dollars spent every year on advertising, and that someone must be either the producer of the product or the consumer of it. If the producer in fact ended up paying, it would seem logical for it to not advertise. But, the argument goes, producers don't pay and thus the consumer does, and it is very unlikely that anyone's hair is any cleaner or more beautiful because of advertising—but the shampoo is probably more expensive than it would otherwise be.

In summary, the contrary view is that advertising:

- is mostly non-informative and wasteful
- encourages concentration within industries
- raises prices to the detriment of consumers

As you can see, points on both sides of this argument seem quite valid, and empirical studies have not succeeded in putting an end to this argument. One clear observation remains, however, which is that huge expenditures on advertising continue to be made every year, especially by large firms who are locked in direct competition with one another. Suppose that in the following example two large competing firms dominate an industry. One question that faces both firms is how much to spend on advertising. To a great extent, the answer to this question depends on how much the rival firm spends. We will use what economists call **game theory** to explore this further.

game theory: a method of analyzing firm behavior that highlights mutual interdependence between firms.

Figure 11.1 shows the pay-off matrix (total profits) that each firm can expect, depending on its own action and on the reaction of its rival. We need to point out that these pay-off figures are hypothetical and are not derived in any way. The absolute numbers do not matter but their comparative levels are important. There are four possible outcomes. If both firms—Western and Eastern—agree to maintain a strategy of a small advertising budget, the outcome is shown in cell A of Figure 11.1, which shows that each firm receives $500 million in profits per year. There is, however, an enormous potential reward involved if either firm decides to cheat on the agreement, as can be seen by examining the results in cells B and C. If either firm chooses a large budget strategy and its rival chooses a small budget strategy, then its profits will increase significantly while its rival's profits decrease. For example, if Western goes with a large budget and Eastern goes with a small budget, then Western's profits will rise to $800 million while Eastern's profits will fall to $150 million (cell B).

FIGURE 11.1 Rival Firms' Advertising Strategies

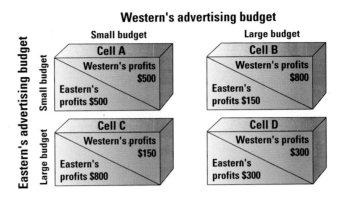

The reason for this is not hard to understand. If Western greatly increases the advertising expenditure on its product while Eastern does not, then Western will gain market share at its rival's expense. The demand for Western's product will increase while Eastern's demand will decrease, with the result that profits will rise in the one case and fall in the other. Cell C illustrates the situation in which Western chooses a small advertising budget while Eastern goes with a large one. From this we can see that each firm, being aware of the possible disaster that could result from choosing a small budget strategy, reasons that it has no choice but to go with a large budget strategy, and the result of this reasoning is represented in cell D, in which each firm ends up with $300 million profit. This helps to explain the large expenditures on advertising in today's market economy. Now, you may well ask: wouldn't it be advantageous for the two firms to get together and agree with each other not to use the large-budget strategy? On the surface the answer to this question would seem to be yes, but for this solution (represented by cell A) to persist, as we shall see, both firms must trust each other. We will do more on this theme later in this chapter.

Let's bring this discussion on product differentiation to a close by summarizing the ways that firms attempt to do this:

- developing a recognized brand name, product logo, or packaging
- securing a superior location or developing a reputation for exceptional service
- engaging in product redevelopment and improvement
- developing an effective advertising strategy

SELF-TEST

1. Assume that two firms dominate the running-shoe industry. One of these firms hires a high-profile sports figure to endorse its product by appearing in its advertising.

A) What would you expect the other firm to do in response, and why?

B) After the second firm has reacted in the way you said it would above, what do you think the relative share of the market that each firm enjoyed would be?

C) Given your answer in B) above, what might these two firms be tempted to try to do?

The Difference Between the Two Types of Imperfect Competition

monopolistic competition: a market in which there are many firms who sell a differentiated product and have some control over the price of the products they sell.

oligopoly: a market dominated by a few large firms.

concentration ratio: a measurement of the percentage of an industry's total sales that is controlled by the largest few firms.

We now need to distinguish between two types of market structures that come under the general heading of imperfect competition. **Monopolistic competition** is a market containing many relatively small firms, whereas **oligopoly** is a market with a few large firms. One way of emphasizing this distinction is to compare industry concentration ratios. These **concentration ratios** measure the percentage of an industry's total sales that the largest few (for example, four) firms control. High concentration ratios would occur in industries dominated by a few large firms producing, between them, a big percentage of total output. This often occurs when large output levels are required to capture economies of scale. The automobile, steel, oil refining, beer, soft drink, and airline industries are all oligopolies. On the other hand, industries in which economies of scale are not significant tend to have low concentration ratios. These industries, such as real estate agencies, brake and muffler shops, travel agencies, hair salons, and dry-cleaning shops, contain many small firms and are therefore monopolistically competitive.

Table 11.1 provides some data on selected Canadian industries that are highly concentrated and whose markets are therefore oligopolistic. The figures indicate the percentage of total industry output produced by the largest four firms in the industry.

TABLE 11.1 Highly Concentrated Canadian Industries

Industry	Concentration Ratio (%)
Tobacco products	99.4
Breweries	97.7
Motor vehicles	95.1
Asphalt roofing	86.1
Major appliances	85.0
Cement	81.7
Distilleries	77.0
Petroleum products	64.0
Steel pipe and tubes	63.7

Source: Statistics Canada, *Industrial Organization and Concentration in the Manufacturing, Mining and Logging Industries, 1985* (Ottawa, June 1989).

Monopolistic Competition

Monopolistic competition is the third type of market structure we study. Some examples of monopolistic markets were mentioned above. Others include almost all retailing, from ladies' clothes stores to gasoline retailing; almost all the services that are provided directly to the retail consumer, including travel agents, hairdressing, shoe repair, and tax accounting; almost all services aimed at the home owner, such as roofers, plumbers, carpet layers, and painters; most of the growing cottage-industry sector, from software designers to authors and proofreaders; and some manufacturing markets, such as the textile, footwear, and furniture industries.

A monopolistically competitive industry has four characteristics. The first is that the industry is made up of *many relatively small firms* that act independently of each other. Across any metropolitan area are dozens of shops, agencies, and small businesses, each of which tries to distinguish itself from its competition. Similarly, across the whole economy are dozens of T-shirt or chair manufacturers acting in the same way.

Second, there is *freedom of entry* into the industry for new firms. This is analogous to the perfect-competition model. Free entry does not mean that entry requires no money. What it does mean is that there are no significant barriers to entry, as discussed in the previous chapter.

Third, firms within a monopolistically competitive industry have *some control over the price* of the products they sell. This is unlike the firms in a perfectly competitive industry. Despite such control, there often is very little price competition between firms. Instead, competition centres on attempts by individual firms to differentiate the products they sell.

The fourth characteristic of a monopolistically competitive industry is the fact that firms sell a differentiated product.

In summary, the characteristics of a monopolistically competitive industry are:

- many small firms
- freedom of entry
- some control over price   *monopolistic*
- differentiated products

The Short-Run Equilibrium for the Firm

The costs of production of firms in a monopolistically competitive industry tend to be very similar—the cost of running one hair-cutting salon isn't much different from the cost of another. On the other hand, the presence of non-price competition and product differentiation does result in the possibility that the demand faced by one firm can be quite different from that facing another. This is why our analysis of this type of market structure focuses on the role of the demand faced by the individual firm. Usually, the individual firm faces a highly elastic demand curve, although it is not perfectly elastic as in the case of the perfectly competitive model.

To launch the analysis of the monopolistically competitive model, let's imagine a trendy restaurant that is currently doing well. Could this firm be making economic profits? **Figure 11.2** will provide us with an answer.

In this figure, we have an elastic demand curve (D_1) that the restaurant faces, along with its associated marginal revenue curve (MR_1). The demand curve for a representative firm is more elastic than the market demand curve for the whole industry, because it is so easy for customers to stop coming to this establishment and go to a competitor instead. In fact, the firm's elasticity of demand will depend on the amount of competition as well as the degree of product differentiation it has achieved.

FIGURE 11.2 The Monopolistically Competitive Firm in Short-Run Equilibrium

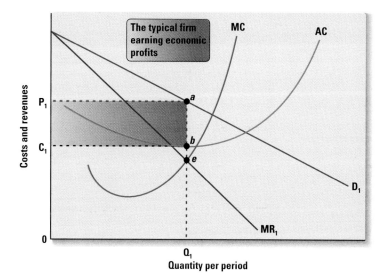

D_1 is an elastic demand curve with its associated marginal revenue curve MR_1. AC and MC are the normal U-shaped cost curves. The area P_1aQ_10 represents total revenue. Similarly, C_1bQ_10 represents total costs. If we subtract costs from revenue, we get economic profits, which is represented by area $P_1\ ab\ C_1$.

Also on the graph is the average cost curve (AC) and its associated marginal cost curve (MC). These two curves are the same as those developed in Chapter Six.

Next, recall the two basic questions that any firm must answer: what is the right output level at which to operate, and what is the right price to charge? The answer to the first question is: the output level that maximizes total profits, which in Figure 11.2 is quantity Q_1. This is the point where the marginal cost equals marginal revenue (point e). The right price is the highest price that can be charged and still sell the optimum quantity—in this case, price P_1.

To find out the amount of total profit the restaurant is making, remember that total revenue equals price times quantity. This is represented on the graph by the area P_1aQ_10. Similarly, average cost times quantity equals total costs, and this is represented by the area C_1bQ_10. Total revenue less total cost is total profit, and this is represented by the area P_1abC_1. Remember that these are economic profits, since normal profits by definition are incorporated in the costs.

We now come to the crucial point in understanding how monopolistically competitive industries function. What will be the response of outsiders not yet in the industry to the fact that this restaurant is making economic profits? The answer is that some of these outsiders will want their share of these profits and will enter the industry as new firms. And what will be the effect of this entry?

The first indication of this change will be that the restaurant will notice that business just isn't as good as it used to be. At its current price it will find that it now has fewer customers. In graphical terms, the demand curve that the restaurant faces (the one in Figure 11.2) shifts to the left and also becomes more elastic. The reason for this is simply the fact that the restaurant in question must now share the market with new competitors. **Figure 11.3** illustrates the eventual result of this entry.

FIGURE 11.3 The Long-Run Equilibrium for the Firm

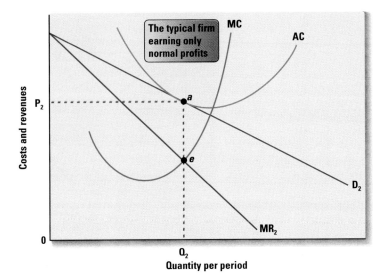

The equilibrium price and quantity are P_2 and Q_2. Further, since the demand curve and the average cost curve are tangent to each other at point a, the area P_2aQ_20 represents both total revenue and total cost. This is the case of zero economic profit.

Again, the firm's best output level is at the point where marginal cost equals marginal revenue (point e), which occurs at quantity Q_2. The best price is the highest that can be charged and still sell quantity Q_2. This is price P_2. The crucial thing to notice about the graph is that the new demand curve (D_2) faced by the restaurant has shifted to the left (because of the entry of new firms) and has become more elastic, so that it is now tangent to the average costs curve at point a. Given this point of tangency between the AC curve and the demand curve (which is also the average revenue curve), the area P_2aQ_20 represents both the restaurant's total revenue and its total cost. Therefore economic profits are zero. Another way of stating this is that the firm is making only normal profits.

How can we be sure that economic profits will end up at zero in the long run? Well, as long as even some economic profits continue to be made by the representative firm, then more entry will occur, and this additional entry will mean that the demand curve faced by that representative firm will continue to shift back until it is eventually tangent to the average total costs curve and economics profits are eliminated. In short, the existence of economic profit triggers a reaction that continues until that profit disappears.

Can too many firms enter the industry? To answer this question, let's look at **Figure 11.4**.

FIGURE 11.4 The Effect of Too Much Entry

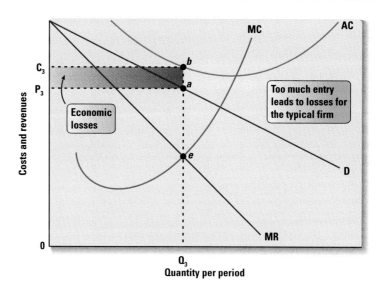

Entry by too many firms results in the demand curve shifting so far to the left that it cannot be tangent to the AC curve. Equilibrium price and quantity are P_3 and Q_3. As a result, the total revenue, area P_3aQ_30, is smaller than the total cost, which is area C_3bQ_30. Thus, area C_3baP_3 represents the loss.

Quantity Q_3 is the profit-maximizing output level, and price P_3 is the maximum price possible at that output. Entry has been so great that the demand curve for the representative firm has shifted so far to the left that an economic loss occurs. The area P_3aQ_30 represents total revenue and the area C_3bQ_30 is total cost, with area C_3baP_3 representing the size of loss.

Can this be long-run equilibrium? The answer is no, since in the long run a firm must earn at least normal profits to remain viable. What will happen here is that some firms will exit from the industry. This means that each remaining firm will experience a slight increase in demand, represented by its demand curve shifting somewhat to the right. This will result, once again, in the normal profit we saw in Figure 11.3.

We are now ready for the main conclusion from our analysis of the monopolistically competitive industry model:

> **In the long run, the representative firm in a monopolistically competitive market makes only normal profits.**

Another way of saying the same thing is that there are no economic profits to be made in, say, the dry-cleaning business or in shoe repair, or in the hardware retailing business or in textile manufacturing. Think of it this way: if there were economic profits to be made in doing something as simple as running a dry-cleaning shop, wouldn't some of you start doing that? And if enough of you did open your own shop, what would happen to those economic profits? They would surely disappear.

Now, this last point should not be interpreted to mean that there are *no* monopolistically competitive firms that make economic profits in the long run. We are probably all aware of some travel agent or gas station or convenience store that seems, even in the long run, to be so busy it must be making an economic profit. Such exceptional firms do exist, and usually the reason for their success can be summed up in two words: product differentiation. This could be the result of an excellent location, exceptional service, or some other similar reason. However, for every one of these kinds of success stories, there are three or four other stories of firms who, over the previous years, have entered the same industry, hung on until the owner's money was gone, and then gone out of business. If we subtract these firms' losses from the profits of the successful firms, we would more closely approximate zero economic profits in the long run in the *whole industry*.

SELF-TEST

2. What would be the effect on any individual restaurant's demand curve if thousands of new restaurants entered the industry and product differentiation was impossible?

3. Assume that a representative firm in monopolistic competition is experiencing economic losses. What series of events will occur to return this firm to its long-run equilibrium?

Excess Capacity

You may recall from Chapter 6 that economic capacity is achieved by the firm when output is produced at minimum average cost. This is an automatic result for the representative firm in the long run in perfect competition because the firm's demand is perfectly elastic. However, the monopolistically competitive firm faces a less than perfectly elastic demand. The result is that the point of tangency between the demand curve and the average total costs curve cannot be at the latter's minimum point. **Figure 11.5** illustrates this point.

FIGURE 11.5 Excess Capacity

The long-run equilibrium for a perfectly competitive firm with a perfectly elastic demand curve, D_1, is at point *a*. This is the point of minimum average total cost. The long-run equilibrium for a monopolistically competitive firm with a downward-sloping demand curve, D_2, is not at the point of minimum average cost, as can be seen by point *b*. The difference in the two outputs $Q_C - Q_M$ is referred to as excess capacity.

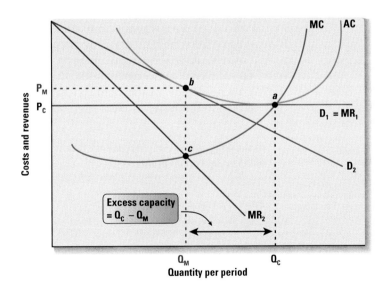

In Figure 11.5, the perfectly elastic demand curve, D_1, is tangent to the average cost curve at point *a*, which is its minimum point and is referred to as economic capacity. This is the long-run output of the competitive firm. Demand curve D_2 is the demand curve of the monopolistically competitive firm. Since it is not perfectly elastic, the point of tangency with the average cost curve must be to the left of, and above, its minimum—such as at point *b*.

The conclusion from this analysis is that monopolistically competitive firms, unlike firms in perfect competition, do not produce at economic capacity and consequently do not achieve *productive efficiency* because the long-run equilibrium price does not equal minimum average total cost. This difference between output Q_M, which is produced, and Q_C, which would be produced given productive efficiency, is excess capacity.

In addition, the price that the monopolistically competitive firm will charge is P_M, which is greater than marginal cost (measured by the distance $Q_M c$) and is also above the perfectly competitive price of P_c. Since this price exceeds marginal cost, we can also conclude that the firm does not achieve *allocative efficiency* as defined in Chapter 9.

This is the same excess-capacity concept discussed earlier in Chapter 6. At the root of this excess capacity is product differentiation. Each firm's attempt to differentiate itself, or its product, from all the others in the market results in the overall market being fragmented. Excess capacity is the result.

The result of this fragmentation is that the representative firm in each industry finds its profit-maximizing output to be one at which average total costs are not at the minimum. This means, in effect, that the total output of a monopolistically competitive market could be produced by fewer firms and at a lower cost. Examples of excess capacity are seen in the large number of hairdressing salons, gas stations, and travel agencies that dominate the urban landscape, all working at less than capacity.

Does this then mean that public policy should somehow restrain firms from fragmenting the market by attempting to differentiate themselves? The answer to this is almost certainly no, because, apart from its being very difficult to do, there are benefits from differentiation. The most important is the fact that consumers have a wide choice of variations of the same general product, which makes it more likely that diverse consumer tastes will be fully satisfied. There are many gasoline stations, convenience stores, and shoe styles available to choose from in our economy. Most people see this as a strength of the market system. However, this wide choice does come with a cost to the consumer, which is that production could be technically more efficient if the representative firm could raise its output to the level at which average costs are at a minimum.

SELF-TEST

4. Given the following data:

Quantity	MC	AC	MR
140	$80	$99.57	$86
160	84	97.62	84
180	89	96.67	82
200	95	96.50	80
220	102	97.00	78
240	111	98.08	76

A) What output will this firm produce?

B) How much excess capacity exists at this output level?

Explaining the Franchise Phenomenon

It should be clear from the discussion so far that there are no economic profits in a monopolistically competitive industry in the long run because of the easy entry of new firms into the industry. We can turn this observation around and deduce that if entry could somehow be blocked, then the chances for most firms to experience economic profits would be greatly enhanced. How would it be possible to block entry, that is, to make a monopolistically competitive industry less competitive? If a product could be successfully differentiated so as to redefine what constitutes an industry, then it might be possible to partially block entry into it. This is the explanation for the enormous growth in nationwide groupings of franchised firms. We find such groupings in the fast-food industry, real estate agencies, auto repair specialists, and convenience stores, among others.

The many potential advantages to franchising include bulk purchasing, national advertising, and, in particular, brand identification. In addition, it allows individuals to own their own businesses without having to accumulate the large sums of money it would take to get started on a national level. If such brand identification becomes strong enough that going out for a hamburger is redefined as going out to McDonald's, then the meaning of the term industry is changed. This means that entry can be controlled, since each franchise holder has a contractual commitment from the franchiser that entry into his territory is blocked. Now, of course, there is no guarantee that a rival grouping will not enter the same territory, but, nonetheless, entry by a new firm selling the same differentiated product is controlled. Proof that even this limited blocking of entry is valuable is found in the fact that the price to purchase an established franchise firm is often quite high. Professional associations also try to redefine the industry in which their members practise. They do this by trying to create the perception in the public's mind that members of the association are better qualified to do a certain kind of work than are non-members. If hiring an accountant is redefined, through advertising, to mean hiring a certified general accountant, then the demand for CGAs will increase. If, in addition, the professional association is able to limit the number of new certifications that it issues (so restricting entry), then those who already hold certification receive benefits in the form of higher fees.

Blocked Entry as a Result of Government Policy

Entry into a monopolistically competitive industry may be blocked by government law or regulation. For example, several things are required to enter the taxi cab business in Vancouver. One would, of course, need a special driver's licence, a car, a kilometrage meter, and a sign. But that is not all; one would also have to obtain a taxi licence. This is unlike any ordinary business licence, however, because the city of Vancouver limits the quantity issued. Therefore, usually the only way to buy a licence is to purchase one from an existing holder. This, of course, can be done, but the price is rather steep—approximately $140 000 (in the spring of 2000). How can the holders of existing licences get away with such a price? The answer is because entry is blocked by the policy of the city government to allow only limited increases in the total number of cabs. Government-regulated quotas on such agricultural products as chickens, cheese, and milk have the same effect—the existing holders of such quotas can sell their quota for a (sometimes high) price. If such entry ceased to be blocked because of a change in government policy, then the price of an existing licence or quota would immediately drop to the government's new licence fee.

In summary, a purely monopolistically competitive industry will experience zero economic profits in the long run. Free entry by new firms ensures this. If successful product differentiation and a redefinition of what is an industry is successful, then what was free entry becomes controlled entry and economic profits could exist in the

E - C O N O M I C S

A More Competitive Economy?

One of the more interesting questions that comes to mind as one watches the emergence of what is being called the new economy, is whether all this means that the market place will become more, or less, competitive as a result. Evidence of a more competitive market includes, for example, the insurance industry that was, not long ago, a very stable industry with a distribution system of local insurance agents. Now banks have been given permission to sell insurance and new competition is growing from companies who sell insurance over the telephone or on the Internet. The number of companies listed on U.S. stock exchanges has nearly doubled in the last twenty years and the percentage of price mark-up/cost ratio in U.S. manufacturing industries has dropped from 19 to 15 percent in the last few years. On the other hand, evidence to the contrary can be found in the fact that the frequency of collaboration among competitors has been increasing through mergers, the formation of new partnerships, and various types of innovative alliances. Just how all of this will sort out is something worth keeping an eye on.

long run. Similarly, if government pursues a policy of limiting entry by new firms into a particular industry, then this too will result in long-run economic profits.

Oligopoly

Let us now turn to the last of our four market models, oligopoly. As mentioned earlier, an oligopoly is characterized first of all by the fact that the industry is made up of a *few large firms*, which means that the concentration ratio is high.

Oligopolies can be found both in industries that produce differentiated products and in industries that produce a standardized product. Examples of oligopolistic industries in which the products are differentiated include tobacco, breweries, automobiles, major appliances, electronic goods, and batteries. Examples of industries in which the few firms produce a standardized product include steel, lumber, and pulp. Individual oligopolistic firms are generally large enough to be commonly known by most people. They include all the "Generals"—General Motors, General Foods, General Tire, General Electric, General Paint—plus a host of other household names from Phillips to Nikon to Air Canada.

New firms do occasionally enter an oligopoly industry. Yet, and this is our second characteristic, *entry is difficult*—much more so, for example, than in a monopolistically competitive industry. Let's examine why this is so. Notice that the firms mentioned above concentrate on the production of a physical product such as a car, a tire, a TV set, or a box of cereal. This is no coincidence, because the production of almost any physical product involves economies of scale, and such economies result in falling average cost as output is increased. Thus, at the early stages of a new industry, those firms that are first able to increase their size of operations will gain a tremendous advantage over their rivals, who lag behind. This leads to the dominance of an industry by the few firms who grew fastest in the beginning. Thus, once the industry has grown beyond its early stages, barriers to entry become more significant.

REVIEW

1. Explain four methods of product differentiation.
2. What are some of the arguments for and against advertising?
3. What is a concentration ratio?
4. What are the four characteristics of a monopolistically competitive industry?
5. In the short run, is it possible for the typical monopolistically competitive firm to make economic profits?
6. What reaction will be triggered if the average firm in a monopolistically competitive firm is making economic profits?
7. What can be said about a firm's average total cost if it is experiencing excess capacity?
8. If entry into a monopolistically competitive industry can be, at least partially, blocked, then the possibility of firms' making economic profits is increased. True or false?

mutual interdependence:
the condition in which a firm's actions depend, in part, on the reactions of rival firms.

As discussed earlier in the chapter, oligopoly firms like those in monopolistic competition engage in a great deal of *non-price competition*. This is especially so when product differentiation is present. This can be considered the third characteristic.

The fourth characteristic is the ability of the firm to have significant *control over the price* that it charges for its product. However, in addition to the effect of consumer demand in determining the price, the oligopolist's control is also circumscribed by a phenomenon called **mutual interdependence**, which is the fifth characteristic of this market structure. Mutual interdependence exists when one firm, contemplating a course of action, must consider the reaction of rival firms. It is this phenomenon of mutual interdependence that, more than any other characteristic, distinguishes oligopoly from the other types of market structures. For example, let's imagine a typical oligopolistic industry in which a large percentage of the total output is produced by only two firms (the soft-drink industry in North America is a typical example). Each firm is large and powerful and would, presumably, be able to set the price of its own product. Yet, any pricing decision that either firm might decide on could generate a response from the rival firm. Thus, the power of firm A is very much constrained by the anticipated reaction of firm B. Such interdependence plays a crucial role in any oligopoly environment. In summary then, an oligopoly industry has five characteristics:

- It is dominated by a few large firms.
- Entry by new firms is difficult.
- Non-price competition between firms is widely practised.
- Each firm has significant control over its price.
- Mutual interdependence exists between firms.

Collusion or Non-collusion

To a large extent the world of oligopoly is a struggle between cooperating and competing. It pays for oligopoly firms to cooperate, because that's how they can make the most *joint* profits. But even when they cooperate, there is still the incentive to compete and outdo the rival, which could result in even greater *individual* profits for one of the firms. Cooperation between rivals is called collusion, which is a secret agreement or understanding between firms for the purposes of setting prices and/or dividing up the market.

Such collusion is illegal in most countries, but, nonetheless, there are obvious potential benefits to the firms who do successfully collude. This makes such action tempting, despite its illegality. Collusion between firms reduces the intensity of competition between them and thereby enhances their profitability and greatly reduces the risks and uncertainty they face. In addition, colluding firms are better able to block any possible entry by new firms.

The existence of interdependence and the possibility of collusion between firms results in oligopoly theory being complex and rather messy. For this reason, there is not a single oligopoly model but, rather, several possible variants, each of which has a different focus. We will look at three variants: one that assumes collusion between firms and two that assume non-collusion.

The Cartel Variant

Our first variant assumes the presence of collusion, which, as we mentioned, is illegal in Canada and the United States. However, in some parts of the world collusion is not illegal and, in fact, is openly practised. This collusion can take any one of several forms, such as firms dividing up the market on the basis of geography (you stay south of the river and we will stay north). Alternatively, the whole market could be divided up based on existing client lists or, simply, by general agreement on an output quota for each firm. The most obvious form of collusion, of course, is for the colluding firms to simply agree on a fixed price. When both price fixing and quotas are used, the several firms are acting as if they were a single monopolist. This means that they need to determine the profit maximizing output for the group as a whole and then divide up this output in some agreed on fashion. Whether the collusion is out in the open or secret, the term *cartel* is used to describe a formal agreement of cooperation among firms.

The classic example of an openly practised cartel arrangement is that of the Organization of Petroleum Exporting Countries, OPEC, which came into existence in 1961. Within a few years it controlled over 85 percent of the world's oil exports, but it did not draw much worldwide attention until 1973, when the member countries decided to intensify their cooperation by restricting their (combined) output, thereby decreasing the market supply of oil. This was accomplished by setting a total output target and then assigning each member a quota based on that (restricted) quantity. This had a dramatic effect on world markets, and some straightforward elasticity analysis will help us understand why. Prior to this point in OPEC's history, the demand faced by any of the twelve individual member countries was undoubtedly elastic. However, the world demand for oil is inelastic, and once member countries agreed to act in concert, the organization created a near-monopoly on oil exports. Thus OPEC, as an organization, faced a highly *inelastic demand.* **Figure 11.6** shows the effect of OPEC's policy of restricting the output of oil.

The decision to restrict oil output is represented by a shift to the left in the supply curve from S_1 to S_2. Remember that our definition of supply is the amount that producers are able and *willing* to put onto the market at various different prices. What we are saying here is that the OPEC producers were, at each and every price, only willing to put onto the market less than before. The inelastic demand curve in Figure 11.6 means that a relatively modest 20 percent restriction in quantity (from 30 million barrels a day to 24 million) causes a dramatic 400 percent increase in price (from \$2 a barrel to \$8). Notice what happened to OPEC's revenues—they rose from \$60 million a day (30 million × \$2) to \$192 million a day (24 million × \$8). Each of the twelve member nations was selling less oil than before, but combined, they were receiving over three times the previous revenue. This was the beginning of a very significant shift in the wealth between the world's economies, and it all came about through former rivals acting cooperatively and treating the market as if they were a monopoly. How long could this last? Seemingly, as long as each of the twelve stuck to their assigned quotas and *trusted* that others were doing the same.

FIGURE 11.6 The Effect of OPEC's Policy on the World Market for Oil

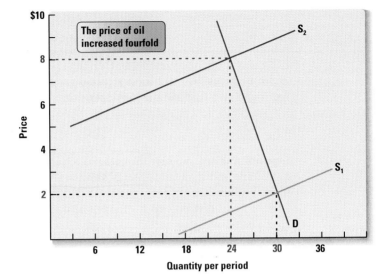

The twelve members of OPEC were able, by forming a cartel, to reduce the world's supply curve of oil which resulted in the supply curve shifting to the left from S_1 to S_2. Since the world demand for oil is inelastic, this resulted in a dramatic increase in the price of oil from $2 to $8.

However, like most things, OPEC's oil-export stranglehold on the world markets changed. On the supply side of things, the high price of oil (it peaked at about $35 a barrel in the early 1980s) brought new productive capacity onto the market by countries not in OPEC who were keen to enter the market at these high prices. In addition, the world's demand for oil was reduced as a result of conservation efforts that often involved new technology and by some success in developing alternative sources of energy. All of this caused the world price of oil to start to drop. Then, when the worldwide recession of 1981–83 hit, the price of oil began to plummet even further and the OPEC countries found that cutting their quotas again and again did not stop the trend toward much lower prices. Oil revenues to the OPEC twelve fell dramatically, which was quite a shock, given that these countries had come to assume that they would enjoy fantastic revenues forever and had begun to spend accordingly. In the face of falling revenues and growing excess capacity, various members of OPEC began to cheat. They started to sell their quota at the official (agreed-upon) price and then also tried to sell additional quantities under the table at a reduced price. The net effect of this was a further increase in the world's supply of oil and an even greater downward pressure on the price.

The choice that faced each member country was between cooperating (sticking to the agreement) or competing (breaking the agreement). We can, again, analyze this fundamental dilemma using game theory. In **Figure 11.7**, we set up a simple payoff matrix in which we assume there are only two countries, Rani and Raqi.

The figures in each cell show the (hypothetical) total revenues resulting from the four possible outcomes. (Once again, these figures are simply made up and it is the way in which they change that matters.) Joint revenue between the countries is maximized at $1600 million ($800 million each), as seen in cell A, and can be achieved if both countries cooperate and stick to the agreement. The payoff matrix tells us, however, that this will not be the case. Consider Rani, for example. It can see that if it cheats, the best possible outcome is $1000 million in revenue (cell B), which is better than $800 million (cell A). Similarly, the worst possible outcome is better if it cheats, $700 million (cell D), than if it doesn't cheat, which would result in $500 million (cell C). Looking at things from the point of view of Raqi would, of course, result in the same conclusion. Competing (cheating), it seems, is better than cooperating (not cheating).

FIGURE 11.7 Rani and Raqi's Payoff Matrix

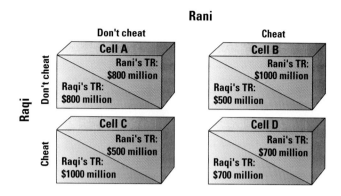

This gives you some idea why cartels are difficult to hold together. The temptation to cheat is just too great. As a result, by 1985, OPEC officially abandoned its system of quotas, and the power of the most significant cartel of the century was weakend. In summary, we can say that:

> **Cartels work to the advantage of their members only if there is no cheating between the participants.**

In the spring of 2000, OPEC was again able to flex its muscle and succeeded in increasing the price of oil to over $30 a barrel. Whether this is the early stages of a new era of high oil prices or just a temporary aberration is something that only time will tell. Our theory, however, predicts that these high prices won't prevail in the long run.

The Price Leadership Variant

Both the OPEC example and the advertising example in this chapter suggest that although cooperation through collusion produces the greatest joint rewards, individual rivals still end up competing because the incentive to cheat is so strong. Will this always be the result? No, not necessarily. Certainly it will not be the result if rivals learn from bitter experience. This is particularly true when competition takes the form of price cutting. Often such activity has led to an outright price war. Such price rivalry leads to "death by a thousand cuts," causing great losses and bankruptcies. To avoid this in the future, firms often come to practise price leadership. This is the situation in which rival firms engage in what amounts to price fixing without overt collusion taking place. Here, industrial history and a process of trial and error lead to the firms in an industry conceding the role of price leader to a single firm—usually the largest or most efficient firm. The leader then monitors its cost and revenue patterns with the long view in mind—ignoring the day-to-day fluctuations in demand and costs. When conditions change sufficiently that a price increase seems urgent, the leader will balance the advantages of a large increase with the risks of creating a tempting opening for a new entrant into the industry. Having decided on a price increase that is profitable but not too high to risk new entry, the leader announces this price increase in some very public way and the rival firms in the industry quickly follow suit by also increasing their prices by a similar amount. As far as prices go, this

In 1996, Montreal police had to unsnarl traffic as motorists waited in line for an hour to tank up when a gas station owner slashed his prices to 29.9 cents a litre in a price war.

has the same effect as would overt collusion, but it is accomplished without technically doing anything illegal. This also allows firms in the industry to adjust prices without triggering a price war. It is generally recognized that Canada Cement Ltd. was a price leader in the 1940s; Canadian General Electric was a price leader in light bulbs in the 1950s; and, in their respective industries, US Steel was in the 1960s and American Airlines was in the 1970s.

The Kinked Demand Curve Variant

In certain circumstances the choice of action by an oligopoly firm is not clear cut. In some cases rival firms may want to compete, and at other times they might wish to cooperate. This is the case with the model known as the kinked demand curve. The basic proposition of this model is that any one interdependent firm, say Wonder Inc., will reason that if it increases the price of its product, rival firms will see this as a golden opportunity to gain market share at the expense of Wonder by simply *not* increasing their price. Thus, in effect, the demand curve that Wonder faces for all prices above the prevailing price is quite elastic, and we know that increasing the price of a product that has an elastic demand is not advantageous to the firm because its total revenue would fall. At the same time, Wonder Inc. reasons that if it were to lower its price, its rivals may well interpret this as a very aggressive move on Wonder's part to attempt to steal customers from them. They would have no option, Wonder reasons, but to compete by matching the lower price and, thus, the overall distribution of market share between firms wouldn't change. This means that Wonder's lower price would attract very few new customers. Thus, in effect, the demand curve that Wonder faces for all prices below the prevailing price is inelastic. And, of course, lowering the price of a product with inelastic demand is also not advantageous, because this too would decrease total revenue. This leads to the conclusion that the demand curve faced by Wonder Inc., given its view of the way that rivals would react to any price change it might initiate, is kinked at the prevailing price. This is illustrated in **Figure 11.8**.

FIGURE 11.8 The Kinked Demand Curve

Wonder Inc. thinks that any price decrease that it might initiate will be matched by its rivals, which will result in inelastic demand below the prevailing price. Further, it thinks that if it raises the price of its product its rivals will not raise their prices, which will result in elastic demand above the prevailing price. Thus, Wonder Inc. views its demand curve as kinked at the prevailing price of P_1.

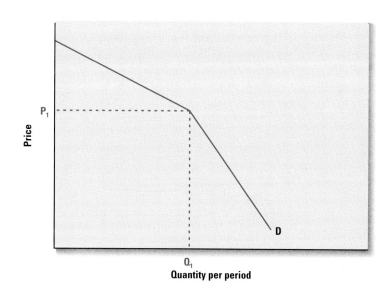

Given this, then, it's a case of "damned if you do, and damned if you don't." The best action that Wonder Inc. could take is no action at all. This is an explanation of the often-observed phenomenon of oligopoly rivals charging very similar prices for competing products. Furthermore, these prices don't change often. What is of additional interest about the kinked demand curve is that the marginal revenue curve associated with this peculiar demand curve has a discontinuity in it, as shown in **Figure 11.9**.

FIGURE 11.9 The Kinked Demand Curve and Marginal Revenue Curve

The discontinuity in the marginal revenue curve is the result of the kink in the demand curve. MC_1 is the original marginal cost curve. Quantity Q_1 is the profit-maximizing output which results in price P_1. An increase in marginal cost from MC_1 to MC_2 results in no change in equilibrium price or quantity.

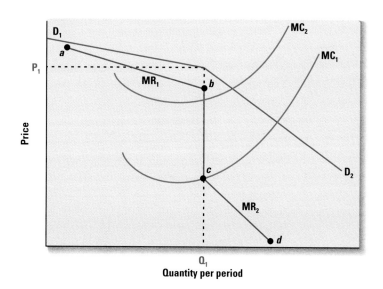

The marginal revenue curve associated with the kinked demand curve D_1D_2 is *abcd*. It turns out that this discontinuity in the marginal revenue curve could be of some significance. The intersection of MC_1 with the marginal revenue curve, *abcd*, at *c* confirms that the prevailing price of P_1 is the profit-maximizing price. Next, observe what happens if Wonder Inc.'s marginal cost rises to MC_2. Wonder's profit-maximizing price and quantity remain P_1 and Q_1.

Now, in normal circumstances an increase in a firm's cost of production will be (at least partially) passed on to the customer in the form of a higher price. But this does not happen here, because the firm is afraid of the loss of business from increases in its price and will be forced, reluctantly, to absorb the higher costs. This means that it is common to observe very stable prices in oligopoly industries despite changes in demand and cost conditions. For example, prices of some cars or fridges can remain unchanged for months, if not years, at a time.

One rather serious qualification about the kinked demand theory needs to be added before we leave it. If you go back and quickly reread this section, you will notice that nowhere in the analysis did we explain how the prevailing price of P_1 originally got established! Thus, although it is a rather neat and logical explanation for price rigidity, it cannot explain how that price came about in the first place.

SELF-TEST

5. Given the following graph:

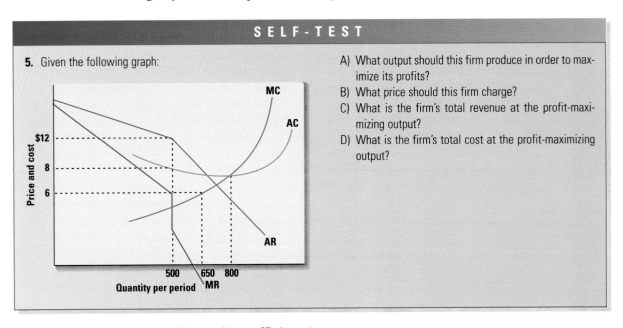

A) What output should this firm produce in order to maximize its profits?

B) What price should this firm charge?

C) What is the firm's total revenue at the profit-maximizing output?

D) What is the firm's total cost at the profit-maximizing output?

Are Oligopolies Efficient?

From an overall economic point of view, how do oligopolies measure up—are they an efficient form of market structure? The typical oligopoly firm possesses a degree of market power, which means that its demand curve is downward-sloping. Thus it will not operate on the minimum point of its average cost curve. This means that it will not achieve economic capacity. Moreover, an oligopoly firm will charge a price that exceeds average total cost. These two points lead us to our first conclusion: an oligopoly firm does not achieve productive efficiency. Second, an oligopoly firm will charge a price higher than its marginal costs. Thus, it will also not achieve allocative efficiency. When we compare these realities with that of the firm in perfect competition, we see that oligopolies do not stack up very well at all.

Some people have even gone so far as to argue that monopolies are preferable to oligopolies. At least it is politically feasible to regulate monopolies, whereas oligopoly industries, which often produce very similar outcomes to those in a monopoly industry, go unregulated.

On the other hand, it has been argued that oligopolies operate in an environment that is very conducive to the vital research and technological change that our economy needs to remain competitive by world standards. John Kenneth Galbraith is a leading proponent of this view and points out that modern research is very expensive. For this reason, large oligopoly firms are the most likely firms to be able to finance research. In addition, the barriers to entry that they enjoy give them some assurance that they will be able to recover the cost of research before the new technology or new product is imitated by others.

If this view is correct, it will mean that an oligopoly industry, over the long haul, will foster technological change and improvement. This would reduce its average cost, with the result that prices would fall and output levels would rise. On the other hand, many suggest that oligopoly industries, because they are protected by barriers to entry, may well become greedy and complacent and lose their competitive edge. In addition, they often spend their time and energy in non-price competition like advertising (thereby creating even higher barriers to entry), rather than in initiating research and development.

Once again, you can see a sharp point of debate within the discipline:

> **Some believe that oligopolies are too powerful and produce inefficiently; others take the view that oligopolies are at the cutting edge of new technology development and, in the long run, push the average costs of production down.**

Pricing Strategies for Firms with Market Power

We discussed in Chapter 5 how firms would like to be able to capture some, or all, of the consumer surplus in the market place through some form of price discrimination. Oligopoly firms often have enough market power to achieve this, at least to some degree. Let's examine several techniques that are used.

First, we have *peak-load pricing* where the seller is able to charge a higher price when demand for its product peaks at certain times and a lower price at other times. Examples would include the demand for roads and tunnels at rush hour, for electricity in the late afternoon of hot summers, or weekend attendance at a ski resort or an amusement park. Closely related to this is *intertemporal price discrimination* where consumers are separated into different groups with different elasticities of demand. Think of the pricing of new technologically advanced electronics equipment where a high initial price does not deter enthusiasts from buying immediately. A few months later the price is reduced in order to appeal to those with higher demand elasticities. We see the same pattern in the hard cover edition of a new book being priced well above the soft cover price that comes out a year later. In other instances, firms use a *two-part tariff* where consumers are required to pay an up front fee for the right to buy a product. Examples here include an annual membership fee to a golf or tennis club that gives you the right to buy time on the course or court, or the sale of a Polaroid camera which gives you the right to buy Polaroid film.

Next, let's consider what is called *mixed bundling* such as we see on many restaurant menus. The restaurant owner knows that most of her clientele expect to spend

ADDED DIMENSION

The World's Largest Economic Entities

Following is a list of the world's eighty largest economic entities. Countries are ranked by 1997 GDP and corporations by 1999 revenue, both in billions of U.S. dollars.

Rank	Entity	Value ($ billions U.S.)	Rank	Entity	Value ($ billions U.S.)
1.	United States	$7783	41.	**Mitsubishi** (Japan)	$107
2.	Japan	4812	42.	Singapore	102
3.	Germany	2321	43.	**Exxon** (U.S.)	101
4.	France	1542	44.	**General Electric** (U.S.)	100
5.	United Kingdom	1231	45.	**Toyota** (Japan)	100
6.	Italy	1160	46.	Malaysia	98
7.	People's Republic of China	1055	47.	Israel	94
8.	Brazil	784	48.	**Royal Dutch/Shell** (Netherlands/UK)	94
9.	Canada	595	49.	**Marubeni** (Japan)	94
10.	Spain	570	50.	**Sumitomo** (Japan)	89
11.	South Korea	485	51.	Philippines	88
12.	Netherlands	403	52.	Colombia	87
13.	Russia	395	53.	**IBM** (U.S.)	82
14.	Australia	383	54.	Venezuela	79
15.	India	357	55.	**AXA** (Europe)	79
16.	Mexico	349	56.	**Citigroup** (U.S.)	76
17.	Argentina	319	57.	**Volkswagen** (Germany)	76
18.	Switzerland	305	58.	**Nippon T&T** (Japan)	76
19.	Belgium	272	59.	Egypt	72
20.	Sweden	232	60.	Chile	71
21.	Austria	225	61.	**BP Amoco** (U.K.)	68
22.	Indonesia	222	62.	**Nissho Iwai** (Japan)	68
23.	Turkey	199	63.	**Nippon Life Insurance** (Japan)	66
24.	Denmark	184	64.	**Siemens** (Germany)	66
25.	Thailand	166	65.	Ireland	65
26.	Hong Kong	164	66.	Pakistan	65
27.	**General Motors** (U.S.)	161	67.	**Allianz** (Europe)	65
28.	Norway	159	68.	Peru	64
29.	**Daimler-Chrysler** (Germany/U.S.)	155	69.	**Hitachi** (Japan)	62
30.	**Ford** (U.S.)	144	70.	**U.S. Postal** (U.S.)	60
31.	Saudi Arabia	143	71.	**Matsushita** (Japan)	60
32.	**WalMart Stores** (U.S.)	139	72.	New Zealand	60
33.	Poland	139	73.	**Phillip Morris** (U.S.)	58
34.	South Africa	130	74.	**Ing Group**	56
35.	Finland	127	75.	**Boeing** (U.S.)	56
36.	Greece	122	76.	Czech Republic	54
37.	Portugal	110	77.	**AT&T** (U.S.)	54
38.	**Misui** (Japan)	109	78.	**Sony** (Japan)	53
39.	**Itochu** (Japan)	109	79.	Ukraine	53
40.	Iran	109	80.	**Metro**	52

Source: Compiled from "The Global 500," *Fortune Magazine,* 1999, and "Size of the Economy," *World Development Indicators* 1999.

about $20 when they visit. She also knows that people value the appetizer, the main course, and dessert differently. Thus, she might charge, for example, $5 for an appetizer, $14 for a main course, and $4 for dessert. At the same time she would also bundle all three into a single price of $20. In this way whether people buy two or three of the options, they all spend about $20. Finally, we have the case of *coupons and rebates*, where sellers of products like breakfast cereals and cameras, in effect, offer more price sensitive consumers a lower price than those who simply can't be bothered with clipping the coupons or mailing in the rebate requests.

Are Firms Profit Maximizers?

John Kenneth Galbraith's work is also at the centre of another point of debate within the discipline. All four market models—from perfect competition to oligopoly—contain an underlying assumption that we need to examine. This is the assumption that the firm behaves in a way that maximizes its profits. If the demand changes or if costs change or if taxes change, then the firm will adjust its output level and (if it can) its price level in response, so as to continue making maximum profits. This assumption underlies the concept of firm equilibrium and is at the heart of microeconomics. This can be seen by the following quote from the University of Chicago's George Stigler:

> [Profit maximization is] the strongest, the most universal, and the most persistent of the forces governing entrepreneurial behaviour.[1]

Galbraith challenged this fundamental assumption in his work *The New Industrial State* (1967), in which he pointed out that a characteristic feature of the large multinational corporation of today is that management and ownership have become divorced. Ownership of publicly traded companies is typically very diverse and unknown to the hired managers that make up the decision-making corps, whom Galbraith calls the technostructure. Galbraith goes on to say:

> So long as earnings are above a certain minimum it would be agreed that management has little to fear from the stockholders. Yet [the discipline of economics assumes that] it is for these stockholders, remote, powerless and unknown, that management seeks to maximize profits.[2]

Most would find, argues Galbraith, that the proposition that individual managers seek to maximize their own return—to make as much income for themselves as possible—is reasonable and sound. For managers to maximize the profits of the corporation, they would have to show great restraint in what they pay themselves. In effect, they would have to forgo personal reward in order to enhance it for others. Galbraith says:

> Accordingly, if the traditional commitment to profit maximization is to be upheld, they [the managers] must be willing to do for others, specifically the stockholders, what they are forbidden to do for themselves.[3]

If the behaviour of today's modern corporations is not driven by profit maximization, how might one understand their behaviour? Galbraith sees the *multiple* goals of today's corporations as including the earning of sufficient profits to keep the

[1] George J. Stigler, *The Theory of Price*, rev. ed. (New York: MacMillan, 1952), p. 149.
[2] John Kenneth Galbraith, *The New Industrial State* (Boston: Houghton Mifflin Co., 1967), p. 115.
[3] Ibid., p. 117.

stockholders happy, as well as other goals such as obtaining autonomy of decision making, developing state-of-the-art technology and achieving high rates of growth, and even social goals such as the design and manufacture of a superior space vehicle, which would greatly enhance the company's image and give the corporation's management a great sense of pride. There need not be a particular hierarchy in such a list of possible goals, because one corporation's ranking of goals may not be the same as another corporation's. The point is that modern management is often motivated to pursue a number of goals rather than the single one of attempting to maximize profit.

Again, we do not feel any particular ability, or see any particular need, to try to resolve this issue. We do, however, find it important and interesting that something as fundamental as the assumption of profit maximization has not gone without challenge. This is evidence that the discipline of economics is alive and that its ideas continue to be debated and developed.

SELF-TEST

6. A) Explain how one might argue that the existence of oligopolies means *higher* prices for consumers.

B) Explain how one might argue that the existence of oligopolies means *lower* prices for consumers.

REVIEW

1. List four characteristics of an oligopoly industry.
2. What is meant by *mutual interdependence*?
3. What is a cartel?
4. Explain how the demand curve for an oligopoly firm might be kinked.
5. What is the main deficiency of the kinked demand curve variant of oligopoly theory?
6. On what aspect of firm behaviour does game theory focus?
7. What might be some of the goals of the technostructure?

STUDY GUIDE

Chapter Highlights

In this chapter you examined the two remaining types of market structure which come under the general heading of imperfect competition. Monopolistic competition, which is representative of the hundreds of retail shops seen in any major city, was looked at first and the model used to analyze it is straightforward. Then you looked at oligopoly which is representative of any of the scores of large, often multinational, firms with which most of us are familiar. Because of the phenomenon of firm interdependence, oligopoly theory is not so clean cut.

1. Product differentiation distinguishes all of the monopolistic competitive market structure and most of the oligopoly market structure (though some oligopoly industries are made up of firms that sell identical products).

2. There is debate within economics about the benefits of advertising. The in-favour view is that advertising:
   - provides the consumer with vital information;
   - enhances competition between firms;
   - lowers prices of products;
   - finances magazines and television shows;

   while the contrary view holds that it:
   - is mostly non-informational and wasteful;
   - encourages concentration within industries;
   - raises prices to the detriment of consumers.

3. Game theory is a method of analyzing firm behaviour that highlights the mutual interdependence between firms. Its first application in the chapter was to analyze two possible advertising strategies between two firms.

4. Monopolistic competition is a market in which:
   - there are many small firms;
   - there is freedom of entry by new firms;
   - firms have some control over price;
   - firms sell differentiated products.

5. In the long run, the typical firm in monopolistic competition:
   - makes no economic profit;
   - charges a price above minimum average cost and is therefore not productively efficient;
   - charges a price above minimum marginal cost and is therefore not allocatively efficient.

6. Oligopoly is a market in which:
   - there is domination by a few large firms;
   - entry by new firms is difficult because of barriers to entry;
   - non-price competition between firms is widely practiced;
   - each firm has significant control over price;
   - mutual interdependence exists between firms.

7. The three variants to oligopoly theory that we looked at are the:
   - cartel variant which involves overt collusion between firms and can be analyzed effectively using game theory;
   - price leadership variant which involves tacit collusion between firms;
   - kinked demand curve variant which is effective in explaining the often observed phenomenon of stable prices within oligopoly industries.

8. Pricing strategies for firms with market power include:
   - peak-load pricing;
   - intertemporal price discrimination;
   - two-part tariffs;
   - mixed bundling;
   - coupons and rebates.

New Glossary Terms

concentration ratio   401
game theory   399
imperfect competition   396
monopolistic competition   401
mutual interdependence   410
oligopoly   401
product differentiation   397

Study Tips

1. Students often relate well to this chapter because it is able to explain some observations they make about the real world. If this is your reaction, this has probably been an enjoyable chapter. Don't think that you must be missing something because "it seems so obvious."

2. The following is to remind you of two important concepts used in this chapter to evaluate market performance:

   Productive efficiency occurs when the firm is producing at an output that results in minimum ATC and is charging a price equal to ATC.

   Allocative efficiency occurs when the firm is charging a price equal to MC.

3. The chapter's Figure 11.3 is the one key to your understanding of firm equilibrium under conditions of monopolistic competition. In stark contrast, oligopoly theory comes in three variants.

4. When you are asked to draw a graph illustrating the long-run equilibrium of a monopolistically competitive firm, you need to ensure that the demand curve is just tangent to the ATC curve and that this point of tangency is at the same output level where MR = MC. Therefore, leave the drawing of the marginal revenue curve until last.

5. Key Problem I (like the one in Chapter 9) asks you to use knowledge from earlier chapters as well as this one to find solutions. This is done to emphasize that the quantity produced and the price of any product depends on the type of market structure in which that production takes place.

Are You Sure?

Indicate whether the following statements are true or false. If false, indicate why they are false.

1. Imperfect competition is characterized by firms competing on price.

   T or F   If false: _____

   _____

2. One characteristic of monopolistic competition is the existence of many firms operating in the same industry.

   T or F   If false: _____

   _____

3. Monopolistically competitive firms typically make economic profits in the long run.

   T or F   If false: _____

   _____

4. The franchise system attempts to limit the entry of new firms into an existing industry.

   T or F   If false: _____

   _____

5. Mutual interdependence is a significant characteristic of a monopolistically competitive industry.

   T or F   If false: _____

   _____

6. Both the kinked demand curve and the price leadership variants of oligopoly theory assume that firms collude with each other.

   T or F   If false: _____

   _____

7. Productive efficiency occurs when firms charge a price that is equal to ATC.

   T or F   If false: _____

   _____

8. Allocative efficiency is absent if price exceeds marginal cost.

   T or F   If false: _____

   _____

9. Galbraith argues that oligopoly firms can be efficient because of the research they engage in and the technological change they foster.

   T or F   If false: _____

   _____

10. The assumption that firms attempt to maximize sales revenue underlies much of the analysis in microeconomics.

   T or F   If false: _____

   _____

Choose the Best

11. What does product differentiation mean?
    a) It is the attempt by the firm to offer a product similar to that of its rivals.
    b) It is the attempt by the firm to offer a product seen to be different from that of its rivals.

12. In which of the following two market structures is entry easiest?
    a) Monopolistic competition.
    b) Oligopoly.

13. What price does a monopolistically competitive firm charge?
    a) A price equal to marginal cost.
    b) A price greater than marginal cost.

14. What is the level of economic profits earned by a firm operating in the short-run under conditions of monopolistic competition?
    a) It is positive.
    b) It is likely to be positive, but could be negative.
    c) It is zero.

15. Graphically, what will be the effect of entry by new firms into a monopolistically competitive industry?
    a) It will shift the firm's demand curve to the right.
    b) It will shift the market's demand curve to the right.
    c) It will shift the market's supply curve to the right.

16. What might be the result of many new firms entering a monopolistically competitive industry?
    a) The price charged by the representative firm will be equal to marginal cost.
    b) The representative firm will certainly incur losses.
    c) While the representative firm will not make economic profits, it will be able to make normal profits.

17. What is meant by the term "allocative efficiency"?
    a) When a firm is producing an output that equals minimum ATC.
    b) When a firm is producing an output and charging a price that equals minimum ATC.
    c) When a firm is charging a price equal to MC.

18. Which of the following would measure excess capacity?
    a) The difference between what is being produced and the level of production that achieves minimum efficient scale.
    b) The difference between what is being produced and economic capacity.
    c) The difference between what is being produced and the level of production that minimizes short-run marginal cost.

d) The difference between the level of production that minimizes short-run average cost and that which achieves economic capacity.

19. All of the following *except one* are oligopoly industries. Which is the exception?
    a) The manufacture of automobiles.
    b) The manufacture of cigarettes.
    c) The provision of accounting services.
    d) The provision of long-distance telephone services.

20. Which of the following statements is correct about price and quantity when comparing a monopoly market and competitive duopoly market?
    a) Both price and quantity would be higher in the monopoly market than in the duopoly market.
    b) Both price and quantity would be lower in the monopoly market than in the duopoly market.
    c) The price would be lower and the quantity would be higher in the monopoly market than in the duopoly market.
    d) The price would be higher and the quantity would be lower in the monopoly market than in the duopoly market.

21. All except one of the following statements about the kinked demand curve theory of oligopoly are correct. Which is the exception?
    a) It explains why the prices charged by rival firms are often similar.
    b) It explains why rival firms that charge similar prices may not be in collusion.
    c) It explains why the prices charged by rival firms sometimes go for months, or even years, without changing.
    d) It explains, particularly well, how the prevailing price in the industry first got established.

22. If we assume that price leadership prevails in a particular industry, what might prevent the leader from announcing a dramatic increase in the price of the product sold?
    a) The fear that the ATC of the firms within the industry would decrease.

b) The fear that new firms would be tempted to enter the industry.

c) The fear that one of the other firms would break ranks and increase their price even more.

d) The fear that such action would provide proof that the firms are engaged in overt collusion.

23. All of the following statements, *except one*, are correct concerning the cartel variant of oligopoly theory. Which is the exception?
a) An effective cartel restricts the supply of the product being sold.
b) The individual members of the cartel must agree to and respect quotas on their output.
c) The primary threat to the success of a cartel is government regulation.
d) The output and the price of the cartel is often similar to that of a monopoly.

24. All of the following statements, *except one*, are correct about game theory analysis of oligopoly theory. Which is the exception?
a) It has led some economists to conclude that the likelihood of cheating is a more effective barrier to collusion than government legislation.
b) It emphasizes the importance of mutual interdependence.
c) It is an attempt to explain firm behaviour.
d) It shows that it is rational for each firm to trust the other.
e) It is able to predict a likely outcome of two firms engaged in considering a specific action.

25. All of the following, *except one*, could be an explanation of a price war between firms. Which is the exception?
a) A breakdown in the collusive agreement between firms.
b) The intense competition that one finds in a perfectly competitive industry.
c) An aggressive young firm challenging the established price leadership of a rival firm.
d) The action taken by established firms to ward off the possible entry of a new firm.

26. Which of the following statements is correct about oligopoly firms?
a) They typically achieve economic capacity.
b) They may or may not charge a price higher than marginal cost.
c) They maximize profits by equating marginal revenue and marginal cost.
d) They operate in an intensely competitive atmosphere in which the market dictates price.
e) They produce an output that puts them graphically on the rising portion of the ATC curve.

27. All of the following statements, *except one*, are valid arguments for barriers to entry and the existence of large profits in an oligopoly industry. Which statement is not valid?
a) Barriers to entry enable firms to spend large sums on research that can then be recovered in future sales.
b) Barriers to entry and the large profits enable the introduction of various kinds of non-price competition.
c) The large profits enable firms to finance the development of new technology.
d) The barriers to entry help maintain large-size firms within the industry, which enhances the ability of these firms to capture economies of scale.
e) The barriers to entry increase the prospect of downward shifts in the short-run average cost curves.

28. All *except one* of the following statements are valid arguments in favour of advertising. Which one is the exception?
a) Advertising provides consumers with information.
b) Advertising reduces the search time needed by consumers to acquire products.
c) Advertising increases the barriers to entry into an industry and thereby enhances competition.
d) Advertising can lower the prices of products by reducing the firms' average cost through increased output levels.
e) Advertising increases the availability of radio and television program choices for the consumer.

29. Most economic theory is based on the assumption that firms have one goal. Which of the following is that goal?
    a) Profit maximization.
    b) Continued growth of the corporation's sales and size of operations.
    c) The achievement of management autonomy in decision making.
    d) Development of state-of-the art technology.
    e) Enhancement of the company's image and the management's pride.

30. All of the following statements, *except one*, are correct about a firm operating under conditions of either monopolistic competition or oligopoly. Which is the exception?
    a) Graphically, it faces a downward-sloping demand curve.
    b) It charges a price above marginal cost in both the short run and the long run.
    c) It charges a price equal to average cost in both the short run and the long run.
    d) It fails to achieve economic efficiency.
    e) It fails to achieve productive efficiency.

Problems

31. The graph in **Figure 11.10** is that of Do Drop In, a shop in the dry-cleaning industry.

FIGURE 11.10

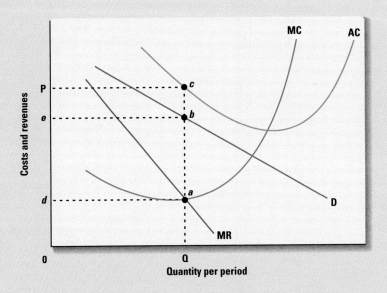

a) Identify Do Drop In's total revenue, total cost, and losses.

   TR: _____; TC: _____; total loss: _____.

b) If this firm made a rational decision to continue to produce, despite the losses, average variable cost at output Q must be below what level?

   AVC must be less than _____.

32. Aruna owns a small firm, Pottery Plus, that produces terra cotta pots, which are sold in the Edmonton area. Pottery Plus has two rival firms, and the current price that each firm charges for a dozen pots is $12. Aruna is convinced that she dare not raise her price because her rivals will not and that she dare not decrease price because her rivals will simply match her lower price. On the graph in **Figure 11.11**, sketch in the demand and marginal revenue curves that fit Aruna's perception of the market (Aruna is currently

producing 8 dozen pots per period). Next, sketch in two marginal cost curves, MC_1 and MC_2, that are at different levels but still indicate that Aruna is maximizing profits at the current $12 price.

FIGURE 11.11

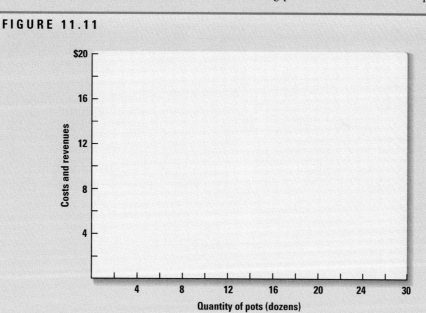

33. **Table 11.2** is the demand faced by The Tienshan Company, a monopolist, which enjoys zero variable cost in its production.

TABLE 11.2

Price	Demand
$5	30
4	60
3	90
2	120
1	150
0	180

a) What is the price Tienshan will charge, and what quantity of output will it produce?

Price: _____; output: _____.

b) Suppose that Endless Journey Inc., which also has zero variable cost, enters this industry and assumes that Tienshan will continue to produce its current output. What output will Endless Journey choose to produce, and what will be the new market price, given both firms' output?

Endless Journey's output: _____; new price: _____.

c) If Tienshan responds to Endless Journey's action assuming that Endless Journey will continue to produce at its current output, and then Endless Journey responds again to Tienshan, and so on, what will be the equilibrium price and quantity for the each of the two firms, assuming that they share the market equally?

Price: _____; output: _____.

34. Assume that the only two firms in an industry, Sundance Inc. and Moondance Ltd., have agreed to restrict their output to 300 units per day (for each firm).

   a) Fill in the matrix in **Figure 11.12**, assuming that any possible increase in output contemplated by either firm is 500.

FIGURE 11.12

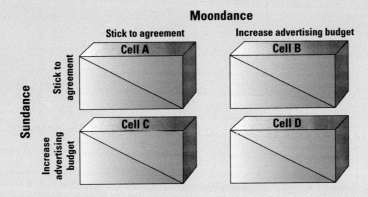

   b) Explain what quantity you think both firms will end up producing and why.

_____

_____

_____

Translations

On the grid in **Figure 11.13**, draw a demand curve for firm A that indicates a current price of $12 and an output of 300, and reflects the fact that this firm thinks rivals will match any price decrease and ignore any price increase. Then sketch in the associated marginal revenue curve. Finally, sketch in two marginal costs curves, MC_1 and a lower MC_2, so that the same output would be produced regardless of which of the two curves was being referred to.

FIGURE 11.13

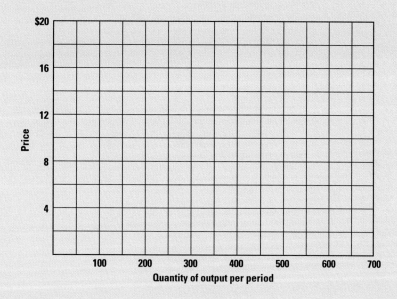

Key Problem I

The graph in **Figure 11.14** is for Chic and Sharpe Ltd., a firm in the women's garment industry, which is monopolistically competitive.

FIGURE 11.14

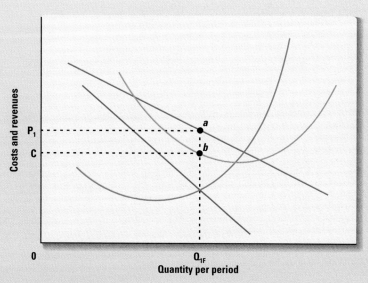

a) Label the four curves in Figure 11.14.

b) What area in Figure 11.14 represents:

   Total cost: _____; total revenue: _____; economic profit: _____.

The graph in **Figure 11.15** represents the market supply and demand for the women's garment industry.

FIGURE 11.15

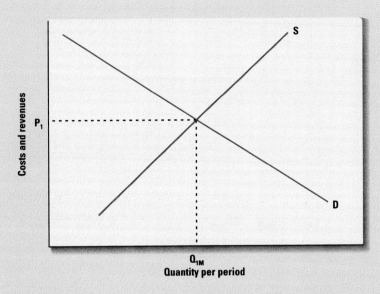

Costs and revenues

P_1

Q_{1M}
Quantity per period

c) On Figure 11.15, sketch in the effect of entry by new firms into this industry, and label the new price and quantity traded as P_2 and Q_{2M}.

d) Using the average/marginal cost curves in **Figure 11.16** (which are the same as in Figure 11.14), sketch in the firm's new demand and marginal revenue curves that would be consistent with zero economic profits. Label the equilibrium price and quantity traded as P_2 and Q_{2F}.

FIGURE 11.16

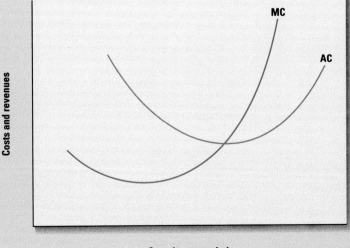

Costs and revenues

MC

AC

Quantity per period

e) What area in Figure 11.16 represents:

Total revenue _____; Total costs_____.

f) Indicate, with Q_C, the capacity output for the firm.

g) What is the amount of this firm's excess capacity?

Answer: _____ .

Key Problem II

Figure 11.17 shows the demand for nectar in Gardenia.

FIGURE 11.17

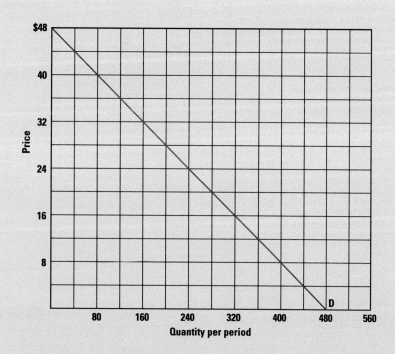

Suppose that there are only two firms, Ace and Pace, producing nectar, and they decide to collude and share the market equally.

a) What price and quantity will maximize their joint total revenue, and what amount is that?

Price: _____;   Quantity: _____.

Show the price and quantity on the graph.

b) In the pay-off matrix in **Figure 11.18**, show in cell A the amount of total revenue each will receive if they stick to the agreement.

FIGURE 11.18

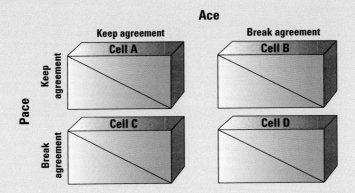

c) Suppose that Ace believes that Pace will honour the agreement by maintaining his present output. What output should Ace produce in order to maximize his revenue? (Try increases of 20, 40, 60, and so on.) Show Ace and Pace's results in cell B.

d) Now assume that the positions are reversed and that Pace decides to cheat while assuming that Ace will stick to the agreement. Show Ace and Pace's resulting revenue in cell C.

e) Finally, in cell D show the total revenue of Ace and Pace that would result when they finally reach the outputs at which further cheating is not rewarding. Show this price and quantity in Figure 11.18.

UNANSWERED QUESTIONS

Short Essays

1. Product differentiation plays no role in perfect competition or monopoly. Discuss.

2. Although there are social advantages to advertising, some economists remain critical of it. Explain.

3. Describe the four characteristics of monopolistic competition and the five characteristics of oligopoly. What are the main points of difference between the two types of markets?

4. What role does mutual interdependence play in oligopoly theory?

5. Explain the two ways in which oligopolies are not efficient.

6. What other goals, besides profit maximization, might be important to a firm?

Analytical Questions

7. How would your analysis of a monopolistically competitive industry be altered if the government were to block the entry of new firms?

8. In long-run equilibrium, a monopolistically competitive firm's ATC equals price. Given this, why hasn't it achieved productive efficiency? How is excess capacity related to your answer?

9. Productive efficiency is impossible to achieve, except under conditions of perfect competition. Explain.

10. The chapter demonstrates that if marginal cost is zero, a monopolist would produce one half the output of a perfectly competitive market and that duopolists would jointly produce two thirds. How much do you think would be produced if there were three firms? Five firms? One hundred firms?

11. Popsi and Cuke entered into an agreement whereby each will reduce the amount of advertising by 50 percent. After a year of partial success, Popsi is uneasy about the agreement and begins to wonder whether it should continue to abide by the agreement or, instead, go back to its pre-agreement level of advertising. The payoff matrix, expressed in million of dollars of profits per year, for Popsi and Cuke's choices is shown in **Figure 11.19**.

FIGURE 11.19

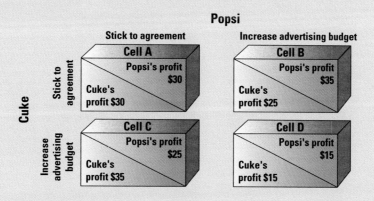

What do you think Popsi should do, and why?

12. You are the consultant to three firms, Tic, Tac, and Tow, each of which belongs to a different cartel. Each firm is trying to decide whether it is better to honour its present agreement or to cheat. The numbers in the payoff matrix in **Figure 11.20** show the total profits the three companies can make and the profits of each of their rival firms.

FIGURE 11.20

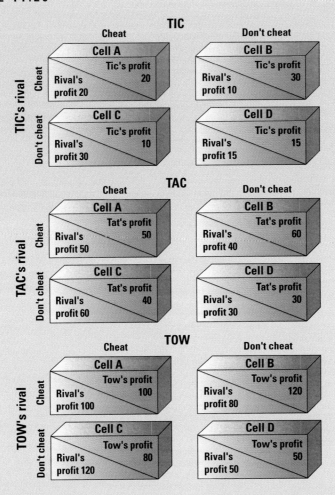

What would you recommend to Tic, Tac, and Tow?

Numerical Questions

13. Air Supply Unlimited, a zero-marginal-cost monopolist, is currently maximizing profits by producing an output of 36. What output would you expect to be produced by each firm if a second zero-marginal-cost firm appeared on the scene and the two firms collude to maximize joint profits?

14. Suppose that there are (only) two identical firms in an industry, Hickory Dick and Hickory Dock, and that there is no collusion between them. Currently, neither firm is spending anything on advertising and each is making a profit of $15 million a year. If Dick advertises and Dock does not, Dick will increase its profits to $22 million and Dock will suffer a loss of $2 million. The opposite will be true if Dock advertises and Dick does not. If both advertise, each will have profits of $6 million.
a) Construct a payoff matrix illustrating these circumstances.
b) Explain what you think will be the outcome of these circumstances.

15. The graph in **Figure 11.21** shows the demand for Cosmic shampoo.

FIGURE 11.21

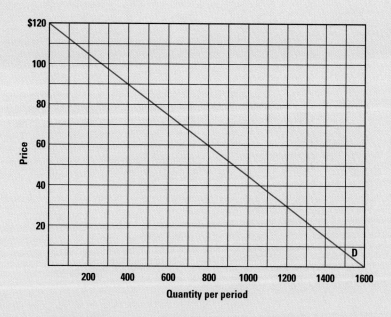

Suppose there are no fixed costs and marginal cost is a constant $60.
a) What is the perfectly competitive price and quantity?
b) What is the monopoly price and quantity?
c) What is the price and quantity of each firm if three firms collude to maximize joint profits?

16. Assume that an oligopoly industry is composed of three identical-cost firms, Ram, Ren, and Rim, who share the market equally. **Table 11.3** contains the cost data for one of the firms, along with its demand.

TABLE 11.3

Price	Quantity Demanded	Total Revenue	Marginal Revenue	Total Cost	Marginal Cost
$70	0	$—	$—	$ 0	$—
65	1	___	___	15	___
60	2	___	___	25	___
55	3	___	___	40	___
50	4	___	___	60	___
45	5	___	___	85	___
40	6	___	___	115	___
35	7	___	___	155	___
30	8	___	___	205	___

a) Complete Table 11.3.
b) What price would Ram, Ren, and Rim each charge in order to maximize profits?
c) What would be the total output produced in the industry?
d) What would be the total industry's profit/loss?

17. **Table 11.4** contains some revenue and cost data for the Rising Moon T-shirt Company (quantities for packets of a dozen shirts).

TABLE 11.4

Price	Quantity Demanded	Total Revenue	Marginal Revenue	Marginal Cost	Total Cost
_____	0	$_____	$_____	$_____	$28
_____	1	_____	64	_____	60
_____	2	_____	60	_____	90
_____	3	_____	56	_____	122
_____	4	_____	52	_____	156
_____	5	_____	48	_____	192
_____	6	_____	44	_____	230
_____	7	_____	40	_____	270
_____	8	_____	36	_____	312
_____	9	_____	32	_____	356
_____	10	_____	28	_____	402

a) Fill in the Marginal Cost, Total Revenue, and Price columns.
b) What price will Rising Moon charge, and what output will it produce?
c) What is the firm's profit or loss?

Assume that entry into the industry results in this firm's demand decreasing by 3 at every price. Construct new TR and MR columns.
d) What price will the firm now charge, and what output will it produce?
e) What is the firm's new profit or loss?

 ## Web-Based Activities

1. The Organization of the Petroleum Exporting Countries (OPEC) is one of the most successful cartels in history. Still, at times, some members have cheated on the cartel and offered "under the table" discounts. A description of several export cartels is contained in a report prepared for the Canadian Department of Foreign Affairs and International Trade entitled "Competition Policy Convergence: The Case Of Export Cartels," at **www.dfait-maeci.gc.ca/english/foreignp/dfait/policy_papers/1994/94_03_e/94_03_e.html#s21**
   Review section 2 of this report and answer the following questions:
   a) What is an export quota and what is its main purpose?
   b) Certain conditions are required for the continued viability of an export cartel arrangement. What are they?
   c) Review the two case studies found in section 2.4 and answer the following questions:
   i. How did each cartel impose restrictions on producers of diamonds?
   ii. The author makes the point that De Beers is a low-cost producer. Why is this important for a cartel leader?
   iii. What problems did the tin cartel face that ultimately caused its dissolution?

2. Read **www.dfait-maeci.gc.ca/english/geo/europe/constb-e.htm**, which describes the retail hardware market in Belgium, and answer the following questions:
   a) Describe the market structure that currently exists.
   b) How have firms in the independent retail outlets differentiated their product?
   c) If a firm wishes to enter this market, how should they differentiate their product to be most successful?

The Factors of Production

What's ahead...In this chapter we shift our focus from the structure of the market for goods and services to that of the market for the factors of production. The key concept here is the productivity of those factors, whether labour, land, or capital. You will learn that it is both productivity and the prices of the output produced that lie behind the demand for any factor. We also examine the supply of each of the factors, putting particular emphasis on the supply of labour, and we explain the reasons behind different wage rates.

A QUESTION OF RELEVANCE...

You, like most students today, probably spend a lot of time wondering about what kind of job you will end up with and even more energy worrying about whether the job will be satisfying and well paid. There are a number of other questions students sometimes wonder about as well. Is it a good idea to chase the elusive dollar, or should you sacrifice some income to gain a satisfying career? You might also wonder if it makes sense to take risks while you are young and leave caution for middle age. Or, perhaps, you wonder why professional athletes get paid so much while day-care workers get paid so little. This chapter will give you some insights into these questions and others like them.

product market: the market for consumer goods and services.

factor market: the market for the factors of production.

The first eleven chapters of this book wove their way through the topics of supply and demand, costs, and market structure. There was a common theme to all of this discussion. The focus was on the **product market,** for example, the demand for orange juice and gasoline, the supply of automobiles by oligopoly firms, and the supply of or demand for shoes from a monopolistically competitive firm.

We now shift the focus to the **factor market** and look at the supply of and demand for the factors of production—labour, natural resources (land), capital, and enterprise—as well as at some of the more interesting issues that arise from this discussion. One comment about the demand for factors can be made now. Factor demand is a derived demand; that is, since people want automobiles, there is a demand for auto workers.

The Labour Market

The Demand for Labour

To ask what determines the demand for labour is equivalent to asking: what factors does an employer consider when deciding whether or not to hire one more employee or pay for more hours of labour? The discussion in Chapter 6 on marginal productivity is key to formulating an answer. What the employer has to keep in mind in making such a decision is the benefit derived from one more hour of labour, which is called the marginal product of labour, compared with the cost of employing that person, which is called the hourly wage rate. If the benefit appears to outweigh the cost, then the additional hour will be bought. If, however, the cost outweighs the benefit, no new work will be created.

Actually, this cost–benefit comparison is a little more complicated, because you will recall that productivity is measured in physical units (of output), that is, marginal product, whereas cost is measured in money units. To emphasize the fact that marginal product is measured in physical units, economists sometimes use the term marginal physical product (MPP), which is defined in the same way as was marginal product earlier. We need to find the value of marginal product in money terms. This is done by multiplying marginal product (or marginal physical product) by the price the employer receives from the sale of each unit of output. This gives us the **marginal revenue product**, which is formally defined as the change in total revenue as a result of using one more unit of input—in this case, one more hour of labour, i.e.,

marginal revenue product: the increase in a firm's total revenue that results from the use of one more unit of input.

$$\text{Marginal revenue product (MRP)} = \frac{\Delta \text{total revenue (TR)}}{\Delta \text{inputs}}$$

We can envision the employer balancing the cost of one more hour of hired employment, which is the wage rate, with the marginal revenue product of the person supplying that extra hour. **Table 12.1** will help clarify this.

TABLE 12.1 Marginal Revenue Product of Labour Data

Hours of Labour	Total Product	Marginal Product of Labour	Unit Price of Product	Total Revenue	Marginal Revenue Product of Labour
0	0	—	$1.50	0	—
1	10	10	1.50	$15.00	$15.00
2	25	15	1.50	37.50	22.50
3	45	20	1.50	67.50	30.00
4	75	30	1.50	112.50	45.00
5	100	25	1.50	150.00	37.50
6	120	20	1.50	180.00	30.00
7	130	10	1.50	195.00	15.00
8	138	8	1.50	207.00	12.00
9	140	2	1.50	210.00	3.00
10	140	0	1.50	210.00	0

The first three columns in the above table are from Table 6.3 in Chapter 6 and need no comment. The fourth column indicates that the per unit price of the product is $1.50 and, further, that this price does not change as more and more output is produced and sold. (We are assuming that the producer is selling its output in a perfectly competitive market.) The figures in the Total Revenue column are obtained by multiplying the total product by the $1.50 price per unit. The marginal revenue product of labour figures can be obtained by either calculating the change in total revenue or by multiplying the marginal product by price, i.e.,

$$MRP = \frac{\Delta TR}{\Delta inputs} \quad or \quad = \quad MP_L \times price$$

For instance, when seven hours of labour are employed, the MRP is equal to:

$$MRP = \frac{\$195 - \$180}{1} = \$15 \quad or \quad 10 \times \$1.50 = \$15$$

Having identified the marginal revenue product of labour, we will now ask the question: in our hypothetical example, how many hours of labour would an employer hire if the wage rate is, for example, $15 per hour? The answer can be read directly from Table 12.1. Seven hours of labour would be hired. The reason is that each of the seven hours hired add more to total revenue—each has a marginal revenue product that either equals or exceeds the $15 wage rate. The eighth hour of labour would not be hired because its marginal revenue product ($12) is less than the hourly wage of $15.

We are now in a position to make a significant generalization. An employer, operating under conditions of a perfectly competitive labour market, will hire up to the point at which the marginal revenue product of labour equals the wage rate. This can be expressed as:

$$MRP_L = W$$

In fact, we can generalize by saying that *any* factor (capital, labour, or land) will be bought up to the point where its MRP just equals its price. If the marginal revenue product of capital, for example, is $600 per unit and its price is $550, it will be bought. If, however, its marginal revenue product is only $500, it will not be bought. Generally, as long as the marginal benefit (MRP) of employing or purchasing an additional unit of a factor exceeds its marginal cost (price), the firm should employ it. This idea is analogous to the optimal purchasing rule we saw in Chapter 5, where we concluded that consumers would maximize utility by equating the marginal utility per dollar spent on each product with its price. Here, the firm, not the consumer, is maximizing profits, rather than utility.

Now let's return to the data in Table 12.1 and ask: how many hours of labour would be hired if the wage rate decreased to $12? We can see that the MRP_L of the eighth hour of labour is also $12 and, applying the equation above, eight hours of labour would be hired.

Let's now turn to **Figure 12.1**, where we graph the marginal revenue product data from Table 12.1. If the wage rate was, say, $15, the firm would hire seven hours of labour. An eighth hour of labour would be hired only if the wage rate dropped to $12. In general, the demand by firms for *any* factor depends on that factor's marginal revenue product, which is illustrated by the downward-sloping portion of its MRP curve. In short:

> **The downward-sloping portion of the MRP curve is the firm's demand curve for that factor.**

FIGURE 12.1 The Firm's Marginal Revenue Product of Labour

The downward-sloping portion of the firm's MRP_L curve represents its demand curve for labour. For instance, when the wage rate is $15, seven hours of labour will be hired. At a wage rate of $12, eight hours of labour would be hired.

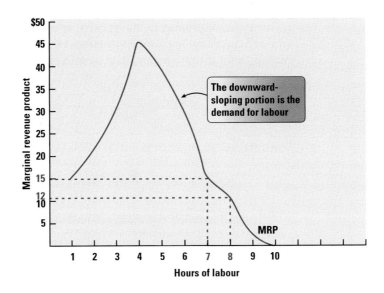

The above illustration of the firm's demand for labour assumed that the firm was selling its output in a perfectly competitive product market. Would our analysis change if the firm operated in, say, an oligopolistic product market? The basic answer is no, since the only change would be that the marginal revenue product of labour would decline faster. This is because using more of any factor always increases output, and this increase in output would mean that the firm would be forced to decrease price in order to sell the increased quantities. That is to say, the marginal revenue for competitive firms is constant and equal to price, whereas for imperfectly competitive firms it declines with output, driving marginal revenue product down faster.

The Supply of Labour

labour force: the total number of people over the age of 15 who are willing and able to work.

An economy's **labour force** is, simply, the number of people over the age of 15 who are willing and able to work for paid employment. The total amount of hours that these people are willing to work is the **labour force supply**.

labour force supply: the total hours that those in the labour force are willing to work.

We know that the labour force supply tends to expand as the wage rate increases. There are two explanations for this upward-sloping supply of labour. First, as the wage rate increases, the rate at which the population is willing to participate in the labour force increases because the higher wage rate makes employment more attractive. For example, younger people enter the labour force sooner, older workers tend not to retire as quickly, and others who were previously not participating in the labour force are more likely to enter it.

How would those already in the labour force respond to a higher wage rate? Wouldn't everyone be willing to work more hours through taking on overtime work or a second job? Some would, and some would not. The reason for this is that such decisions involve more than just the maximization of income. For instance, either of your authors could work weekends at McDonald's and increase his income. Why don't we? The answer involves what economists call the income effect and the substitution effect. It is certainly true that a higher wage will make working additional time more attractive. However, working more time also means less leisure. As one's income rises there is a point reached where leisure becomes more valuable and, at this point, a further increase in the wage rate means that the same level of income can be obtained with *less* work and more of the valuable leisure time can be enjoyed.

The net effect of these two opposing alternatives is that economists know that the supply curve for labour is upward-sloping but relatively inelastic so that, say, a 10 percent rise in the wage rate will result in something less than a 10 percent increase in the quantity of labour supplied. This is illustrated in **Figure 12.2**.

FIGURE 12.2 The Labour Force Supply Curve

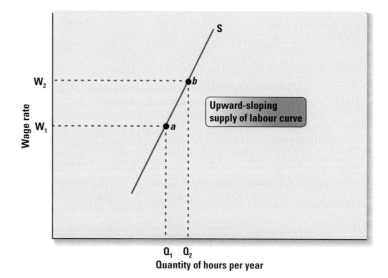

An increase in the wage rate from W_1 to W_2 results in the quantity of labour supplied rising from Q_1 to Q_2, that is, from point *a* to *b*. This indicates that the supply of labour curve is upward-sloping with a relatively steep slope.

Theoretically, if we were to imagine a very high wage rate, so that a majority of people weighed more leisure over more income, then the number of hours people would be willing and able to work would, in fact, decline. Graphically, the labour force supply curve would, as a result, start to bend back to the left as it continued to rise. However, we will ignore this possibility.

As Figure 12.2 shows, an increase in the wage from W_1 to W_2 results in an increase in the quantity of hours that the population is willing to work, as indicated in the movement up on the labour force supply curve, S_1, from point *a* to point *b*.

Figure 12.2 illustrates the *market* supply of labour curve. We know from our earlier discussion that a single firm's demand for labour curve is determined by that firm's marginal revenue product. Just as we did in Chapter 2, we could sum each firm's demand for labour to obtain a *market* demand for labour curve. When we put the market demand for labour curve together with market supply of labour curve, as we do in **Figure 12.3**, we get the equilibrium wage, W_1, for labour.

FIGURE 12.3 The Market Equilibrium Wage Rat

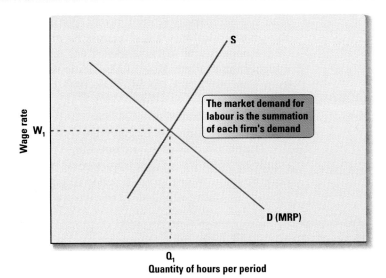

Given the upward-sloping supply of labour curve and the downward-sloping demand for labour curve, the equilibrium wage rate is W_1 and the equilibrium quantity is Q_1.

Market Equilibrium

Given the market demand for labour, D_1, and the market supply of labour, S_1, we obtain the equilibrium wage rate, W_1, and the equilibrium quantity of hours, Q_1, that are bought and sold.

The answer to the very important question of what determines the wage rate for labour is the rather conventional answer: the supply of and demand for labour. We do not mean to imply that this general answer has universal application. There are, after all, many wage rates for labour, not just one, and as we will soon see, labour markets are not always competitive. However, we have uncovered something significant.

> **There are both supply and demand elements underlying every wage rate.**

If the labour market is competitive, the market-determined wage rate will be the wage rate applicable to each individual firm. As a result, the firm is able to hire as much labour as it wishes, up to the point where the wage rate equals the marginal revenue product of labour. Graphically this is illustrated in **Figure 12.4**.

FIGURE 12.4 The Firm's Equilibrium Quantity of Labour in a Competitive Labour Market

In a competitive labour market, the wage rate is determined by the forces of market supply and demand. Given this market-determined wage rate, W_1, the individual firm faces a perfectly elastic supply of labour curve, S_1. The quantity of labour this firm would hire is determined by the intersection of the firm's MRP_L curve with the perfectly elastic supply curve, resulting in quantity Q_1 being hired.

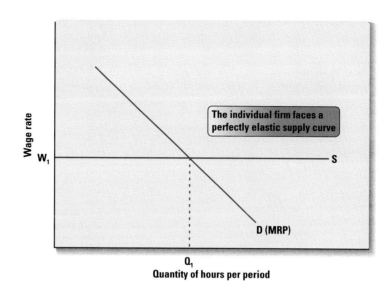

In a competitive labour market, the market supply and demand for labour determines the market wage rate of W_1. The individual firm operating within this market faces a perfectly elastic supply curve for labour, S_1, at this market wage rate. This means that it is able to hire as much, or as little, labour as it wants without affecting the market wage rate. The quantity of labour that this firm will hire is determined by the equality of its marginal revenue product for labour and the market wage rate. This quantity, Q_1, is illustrated in Figure 12.4 by the intersection of the supply curve and the demand curve, labelled D (MRP).

The Case of Monopsony

monopsony: a market structure in which there is only one buyer.

Next, we need to ask what happens if the firm is operating in a **monopsony** labour market, that is, a market in which it is the only buyer of labour. For instance, imagine a firm that was the only employer of some highly specialized labour. It would need to pay a higher wage to attract additional workers. In other words, the firm would face an upward-sloping supply of labour curve. Recall that the firm operating within a competitive labour market can hire *additional* labour at the going market wage rate. This is not true for the monopsonist. Additional labour could be hired only if a higher wage rate were offered. Furthermore, it would have to pay that higher wage rate not only to additional workers but also to all the previous labour that it has already hired. The net result is that a firm operating in a monopsony labour market faces an escalating total wage bill as a result of hiring additional labour, compared with the firm that operates in a competitive labour market.

SELF-TEST

1. A) Given the following data, and assuming that the output of Sparky the Plug Maker can be sold for $3 per unit, fill in the table below:

Hours of Labour (thousands per week)	Total Product (thousands of units)	Total Revenue (thousands of dollars)	Marginal Revenue Product of labour (per hour)
0	0	—	—
1	80	_____	_____
2	180	_____	_____
3	260	_____	_____
4	320	_____	_____
5	360	_____	_____
6	380	_____	_____
7	390	_____	_____
8	395	_____	_____
9	398	_____	_____
10	400	_____	_____

B) If the firm can hire all the labour it wants for $9 an hour, how many hours per week will it hire, and what output will it produce?

The Long-Run Supply of Labour

The size of Canada's labour force has grown considerably over the last 30 years, as can be seen in **Table 12.2**. There are two distinct explanations for this growth. The first is the growth in population. This influence was most significant in the late 1960s and 1970s, reflecting the high birth rate in the years immediately following World War II. In addition, Canada has experienced a great deal of immigration over the last few decades. As a result of these factors, Canada's population has grown from just over 16 million in 1956 to over 30 million in 1999.

TABLE 12.2 Canada's Labour Force for Selected Years

1966	7 493 000
1976	10 530 000
1986	13 378 000
1996	14 900 000
1999	15 721 000

Source: Statistics Canada, *Historical Labour Force Statistics* (Ottawa, 1999).

The second reason for the very strong growth in the labour force supply is an increase in the rate at which the population participates in the labour force. Since 1950, the percentage of the female population in the labour force supply has steadily grown, from under 30 percent to approximately 60 percent by the 1990s, while the male participation rate has declined, in the same period, only slightly from nearly 80 percent to about 75 percent.

In explaining the cause of the growth in the labour force, we raise the question of exactly how to define the labour force supply. Since we earlier defined the supply as total hours worked rather than as the number of individuals working, the average number of hours per week worked also is relevant. It is interesting to note that the average hours per week worked has been increasing in the last few years, reversing a downward trend of many decades.

The overall increase in an economy's supply of labour will not fall evenly across every industry in the economy. Some industries will experience a larger increase in the supply of labour than others will. For example, young people today seem to put a great deal of importance on maximizing their chances for getting a good entry-level job. Thus, more high school graduates are choosing to extend their formal education in colleges, universities, and technical institutes. And the areas they are choosing to focus on tend to be the more "practical" subjects, such as accounting, dental assisting, or computer studies. At the same time, most people want a chance to be creative in their work and to enjoy good working conditions. Thus, the supply of labour for any industry that seems to offer a good prospect for getting started as well as being interesting will be high. Examples of these industries include the software, medical services, and petroleum industries. Meanwhile, the supply of labour for the more traditional industries that aren't growing much, such as mining, forestry, and fishing, will be lower.

The Long-Run Demand for Labour

We have established the importance of the marginal revenue product of labour in determining the demand for labour. Our discussion so far has assumed that technology and the size of the economy's capital stock remain unchanged. Yet, of course, technology improves and the capital stock grows over time. The effect of this can be seen in the growth of labour productivity, which has the effect of increasing each firm's marginal product and thus graphically shifting its MRP_L curve out to the right.

In addition to an increase in productivity, the demand for any factor is a derived demand. This means that an increase in the demand for an industry's product will, in the short run, cause an increase in its price and, in the long run, an increase in the number of firms in that industry. Both will result in an increase in the demand for labour.

Therefore, an increase in the demand for labour in any industry could occur because of increases in labour productivity in that industry or, simply, because demand for the product is growing.

We can put these trends together in **Figure 12.5**, where we see a shift to the right in the demand for labour curve (D_1 to D_2) because of increases in overall labour productivity or in the demand for the industry's product. In this figure, we also show an increase in the supply of labour, which could have been a result of people being attracted to the industry because they know it is a growing one and offers the possibility of interesting jobs with attractive working conditions. As shown in the figure, if the demand for labour increases more than the supply does, then both the equilibrium quantity of labour and the wage rate will rise. This, for example, could illustrate what is happening in the computer software industry. Recent graduates, trained in management information systems, are being offered entry-level jobs at several thousand dollars more per year than are students whose major was in the more conventional subjects.

Does training in computer science mean better job prospects?

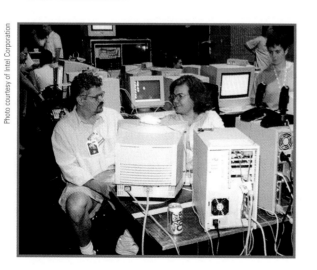

Photo courtesy of Intel Corporation

FIGURE 12.5 The Long-Run Trend in Labour Force Supply and Demand

Increases in labour productivity and the growth in overall output for this industry cause the demand for labour curve to shift to the right, as illustrated by D_1 to D_2. The supply of labour curve also shifts to the right, as illustrated by S_1 to S_2. Since the demand for labour increased more than the supply, both the equilibrium quantity of labour and the wage rate rise.

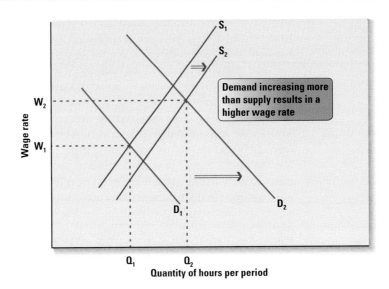

Demand increasing more than supply results in a higher wage rate

---

SELF-TEST

2. The economy's supply and demand for labour is as follows:

Wage Rate	Supply of Labour (billions of hours)	Demand for Labour (billions of hours)
$12	12	16
14	13	15
16	14	14
18	15	13
20	16	12

and data for Ruby's Rhubarb is as follows:

Hours of Labour Hired	MRP_L
180	$18
220	16
260	14
300	12
340	10

A) How many hours of labour will Ruby's hire?

B) If the supply of labour increased by two billion at every wage rate, what effect would this have on the quantity of hours that Ruby's hires?

Productivity and the Real Wage

real wage: the purchasing power of the nominal wage; i.e., nominal wage divided by the price level.

nominal wage: the wage rate expressed as a dollar-and-cents figure.

To extend the discussion of the importance of productivity, let's ask the question: what was (the famous fictional castaway) Robinson Crusoe's real wage? By **real wage**, we mean the purchasing power of any given wage. In contrast, the **nominal wage** is the dollar-and-cent figure received from work. That is to say:

$$\text{real wage} = \frac{\text{nominal wage}}{\text{price level}}$$

Returning to the question above, Robbie's real wage is whatever he is able to produce for himself. If he produces nothing, his real wage would be nothing. If he produced more this month than he had produced the previous month, his real wage would have risen.

What is true for Robinson Crusoe, who lived alone on an uninhabited island, is also true for a whole economy. Given the labour force supply, the real wage for Canadians depends on how much is produced by Canadians, and, generally speaking, the more Canada produces, the higher will be Canadians' real wage. This inevitable relationship between productivity and the real wage is illustrated in **Figure 12.6**.

FIGURE 12.6 Trend in Business-Sector Real Hourly Compensation and Productivity, Canada, 1946–96

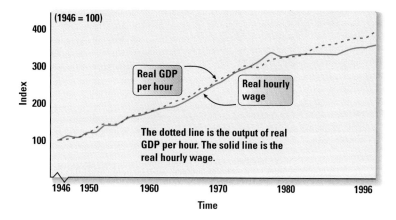

What is really being said here is that:

> **An economy's real output and real income are the same thing.**

Thus, an economy's real income (real wage rate) per worker can only increase at about the same rate as its output per worker.

In summary:

- Both supply and demand are involved in determining how much labour is paid.
- There are distinct long-run trends of growth in both the labour supply and demand.
- The average real wage for labour for the whole economy has increased over time, and this increase is closely related to increases in labour productivity.

Having established these quite general, but important, points, we now need to examine some explanations of why wage rates for specific groups of individuals differ. In other words, we need to examine what explains the wage rate differentials between pipefitters and nurses, or between medical doctors and helicopter pilots.

The Effects of Trade Unions and Professional Associations

Many individuals who earn a living by selling their labour belong, in association with their fellow workers, to a trade union such as the Canadian Autoworkers' Union or to a professional association such as the Nova Scotia Medical Association. From an economist's point of view, the broad objectives of such groups are to: (a) increase the work available to their members; (b) increase the compensation received by their members; and (c) improve the working conditions of their members. If such unions and associations have any influence on how labour markets perform, then their existence forces our analysis to go beyond the context of perfectly competitive markets.

At a demonstration in front of the Quebec Federation of Labour offices in Montreal on March 20, 1998, about 50 McDonald's employees gathered to voice their opposition to being unionized.

As far as increased work and increased compensation are concerned, organizations use three basic approaches to achieve these objectives. **Figure 12.7** looks at the first approach—the attempt to increase the demand for the type of work their members perform.

FIGURE 12.7 The Effects on Wage Compensation of an Increase in Demand for Tailors

The non-unionized demand and supply for clothing makers is D_1 and S. Equilibrium occurs at an equilibrium wage of $8 and quantity of 10 000. Effective unionization could result in the demand for labour shifting to the right, as illustrated by D_2. This would increase the wage rate to $10 and the quantity to 13 000.

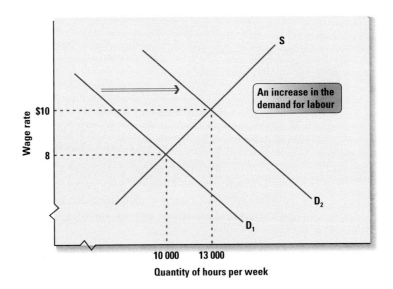

Figure 12.7 could refer to any type of work, such as that of a medical practitioner, gas-line plumber, or tailor. Let's choose the latter for our illustration. D_1 and S are the demand for and supply of labour in a non-unionized environment. This yields a wage of $8 and an equilibrium quantity of 10 000 hours per week.

Now, suppose that the clothing workers become unionized, and their union is able to increase the demand for this type of work. The result is that the demand curve shifts out to D_2. This results in the wage rate increasing to $10 and the equilibrium quantity increasing to 13 000 hours. This is obviously to the advantage of the organization and its members.

But how might the organization achieve this increase in demand for its members? One way is by the union spending its own funds to advertise the employer's product. An ad campaign to encourage people to buy only clothes with a "union-made" label would increase the demand for union-made clothing and thus increase the demand for the union members that make it. Another example would be a "Hire a CGA" campaign paid for by the organization aiming to increase the demand for its members.

Some organizations may not be able to use the above method to increase the demand for their members. Instead, a second approach to improving pay or employment is to restrict the supply of those who are qualified to do the work. **Figure 12.8** illustrates this situation.

FIGURE 12.8 The Effects on Wage Compensation of Supply Restriction

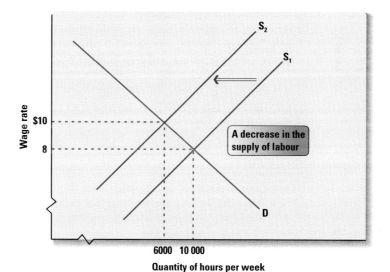

Restricting the supply of labour shifts the supply curve from S_1 to S_2. As a result, the wage rate rises to $10 but equilibrium quantity declines to 6000.

The effect of restricting the supply of labour as shown by the shift from S_1 to S_2 is to cause the wage rate to rise from the non-unionized $8 an hour to $10 an hour. However, in this case the equilibrium quantity declines from the original 10 000 hours per week to only 6000. This approach is not as desirable to the organization and its members as was the one of increasing the demand, which raised both the equilibrium wage rate and quantity hired.

How might an organization restrict the supply of labour? One way is for the organization to successfully lobby for the passage of laws that restrict those who can perform a certain task; for example, only those who are certified as brokers can legally sell stock, or only licensed pipefitters can work on gas plumbing. The most effective way for an organization to restrict the supply of labour is to gain control of the certification (or licensing) process itself. Examples of this are the medical associations, which control the licensing of new doctors, or the bar associations, which do the same with new lawyers, or university professors, who influence the future supply of their own kind by having a say in how many students successfully complete graduate studies.

We should also point out that any organization that can both increase the demand for its members *and* restrict the supply of them will succeed in raising the wage rate even higher than the $10 used in our example.

Many individuals who sell their labour to an employer do unskilled work that cannot be easily licensed or certified, so the methods discussed above are not open to the organizations that represent them. Is there any other way that these organizations might increase the wage rate of those they represent? The answer is yes, and this brings in the third way in which unions can improve things for their members. This is the situation that most students probably think of when the word "union" is used. Many (but not all) trade unions are well enough organized to have sufficient bargaining power in negotiating contracts of employment to *simply impose* a wage rate that is above what would otherwise be market equilibrium. **Figure 12.9** illustrates this case.

As in the previous figure, Figure 12.9 illustrates a market equilibrium wage rate of $8 an hour and a quantity of 10 000. If, through bargaining power, the union negotiates a contractual wage rate of $10 an hour, we would have the situation as shown here. This is analogous in many ways to price setting by a government, which we examined in Chapter 3. Here the price setting is being done (with agreement from employers) by trade unions. Note that the quantity of labour demanded has declined to 6000 hours per week at point *a* while the quantity supplied has increased to 14 000 at point *b*. The result is that 8000 more hours per week are supplied than are demanded—the distance *ab* in Figure 12.9. This is essentially the phenomenon that occurs when an outsider looks enviously at a job that someone else has and says to himself that he wished that he too had one of those jobs.

FIGURE 12.9 A Negotiated Wage Rate Above Equilibrium

A union may succeed in obtaining a $10 wage rate in contract negotiations, but the consequence of an imposed wage settlement above equilibrium is that the quantity of hours supplied exceeds the quantity demanded by the horizontal distance *ab* which, in this case, is 8000 hours per week.

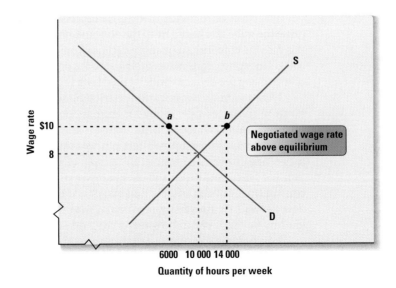

How successful are attempts such as this to raise the wage rate above what would be market equilibrium? Studies that attempt to measure the effect of trade unions on wage rates seem to agree that union organizations do increase the wage rate by anywhere from 10 percent to as much as 30 percent. It is interesting to note, however, that this same evidence seems to conclude that the total payment going to labour (as opposed to going to the factors land or capital) does not change despite the influences of organizations aimed at increasing the wage of their members. This implies that to the extent that such organizations are successful, it is at the expense of workers who have no organization to represent them or those members who are consequently thrown out of work.

In summary, unions can attempt to raise the wages of their members by:

- increasing the demand for their members by advertising the employer's product or their members' skills
- restricting the supply of labour into certain types of jobs by convincing the government to establish legal qualifications for the work and then affecting the number of people who would obtain such qualifications
- negotiating a fixed wage rate above equilibrium

Explanations of Wage Differentials

Conceptually, if all people and all jobs were the same, and if we had a competitive labour market with no trade unions or professional associations, we would have only a single equilibrium wage rate. People are not the same, however, and this results in differences in the supply of different kinds of labour. Similarly, all jobs are not the same, and this results in differences in the demand for different types of labour. Further, as we just saw, trade unions and professional associations do alter wage compensation in different occupations. The result is that we have many different wage rates. Let's take a closer look at the wage differentials that exist in our economy.

human capital: the accumulation of all skills and knowledge acquired by individuals.

The accumulation of skills and knowledge that each individual has acquired is known as **human capital**. All individuals have some human capital—the ability to read, write, count, and perceive—but it is obvious that some people possess much more than others, either because of natural gift or because of much greater investment in formal education or training and experience. Usually, a greater level of human capital means a more productive individual, and we have already established that higher productivity means a higher wage.

Next, we should recognize that some jobs involve considerable risks that are absent in other jobs, and we usually find a higher wage being paid as compensation for such risks. Examples here would be power-line construction jobs or the work of deep-sea divers, which pay commensurately higher than equivalent low-risk jobs.

Third, some jobs have unpleasant characteristics that must be compensated for in order to get enough people to do them. This is why we often find a higher wage rate being paid, for example, for the night shift or for dirty, exposed work such as that on an oil exploration rig, especially if that rig is 200 kilometres northeast of Aklavik.

Fourth, some jobs have very attractive non-pecuniary benefits that result in the wage rate being lower than it would otherwise be. These benefits range from lots of time off (for example, for school teachers) to flexible working hours (for example, for a self-employed writer) to the opportunity to be creative (for example, for a landscape architect).

As a fifth explanation we need to mention that discrimination in the labour market results in some jobs being difficult to obtain by members of certain groups, such as women or visible minorities. This restricts the supply of labour into these kind of jobs, which raises the wage rate paid in them. In addition, the supply of labour into jobs traditionally held predominantly by women (day-care workers) or visible minorities (janitorial work) and requiring relatively low skills is greater than it might otherwise be, with the result that wage rates are lower.

This is not an exhaustive list of the reasons for wage differentials. There is, for example, an aspect of luck in all this. Some people seem to have just "lucked into" a job that they really love, and as a result they do the job very well and get better compensation for doing so than others who do the same work—imagine the really happy gardener or hairdresser. But the point is that people are different, and jobs are different, so wage rates differ despite the impersonal forces of supply and demand, which underlie every wage rate. In summary, wage differentials can exist because:

- the level of human capital varies between individuals
- some jobs involve more risks than others
- some jobs have unpleasant characteristics
- some jobs have attractive non-pecuniary benefits
- there is discrimination in labour markets

ADDED DIMENSION

Education and Earning Power

It has long been established by economic research that individuals with more formal education enjoy, on average, higher earning capacity throughout their lives. The following data illustrate this point. The dollar figures are average incomes for males in the age category of 45 – 54 years.

Level of Formal Education	Median Annual Income
Elementary school only	$31 308
Some high school	36 502
High school graduation	40 278
Some postsecondary	53 763
Postsecondary degree	60 691

Source: Statistics Canada, *Earnings of Men and Women, 1993* (Ottawa, 1994).

REVIEW

1. What is another term for marginal product?
2. What is *MRP*?
3. How is the demand curve for labour derived?
4. What effect would an increase in the wage rate have on the quantity of labour supplied?
5. Give an example of how a union can increase the demand for its members' services and how it can decrease the supply of such services.
6. Distinguish between the *real wage* and the *nominal wage*.
7. What is the consequence of a negotiated wage rate that is above the market equilibrium wage?
8. What are the reasons for differences in wage levels?

Good Service Is Becoming More Expensive

Many people have observed that the prices of tickets to a concert or the theatre have become almost prohibitive. There is an explanation for this. Live performances require direct contact between those who consume the service and those who provide it. In contrast, the consumer (buyer) of, say, a VCR has no idea who worked on it or how much labour time went into its production; that is, there is no contact between producer and consumer.

Next, consider the fact that technological change saves labour time in producing the VCR and often results in a lower price. However, this is not at the cost of a reduction in product quality. On the other hand, few such innovations are possible in providing live theatre or musical perfor-

mances, and therefore it is difficult to increase the productivity of a live performer.

The possible increases in labour productivity in manufacturing that come from technological change increase the wage rates paid throughout that sector. When wages for common labour in manufacturing rise, musicians and actors expect to receive an increase too. Such increased labour costs must be paid for from increased ticket prices because they cannot come from increased productivity.

This general point, that the service sector faces rising (real) costs of production, can be extended to include most public services as well, such as firefighters, teachers, and social service workers.

The Concept of Economic Rent

economic rent: the return to any factor of production that has a perfectly inelastic supply.

The original concept of economic rent is rooted in the work of the nineteenth-century classical economist David Ricardo. Ricardo assumed that land had a single use: agriculture. Since the quantity of land is fixed, he went on to argue that it was perfectly inelastic in supply. Therefore, Ricardo saw the price of land as being purely demand-driven. If land is in high demand, its price will be high, as was the case in Ricardo's England. However, if the demand for land is low, as it was in nineteenth-century North America, its price is very low (in many cases it was free). Whatever the price of land might be, this is the price that the owners of land earn. Ricardo called this return to land that has a perfectly inelastic supply **economic rent**.

If we do suppose that the supply of land is perfectly inelastic, as shown in **Figure 12.10**, and demand is relatively high, as with D_1, then the rent will be R_1. A decrease in demand, as illustrated by D_2, will result in the rent decreasing by exactly the same amount—to R_2. Even if the price of land is zero, its supply is the same. Because land has this unique aspect, Ricardo considered the return to land, the economic rent, a surplus and not a cost. What this means is that the rent rate of, say, wheatland on the prairies will increase as a *result* of a higher price of wheat rather than being the *cause* of the higher wheat price.

FIGURE 12.10 The Concept of Economic Rent as Applied to Land

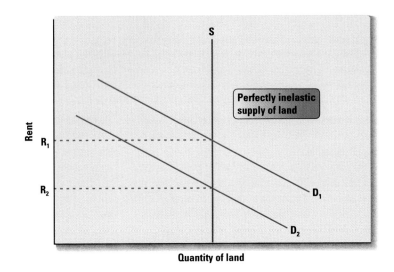

If we assume that land has only one use, then its supply is perfectly inelastic, as illustrated by S. Given this, the price of land, or the rent that it receives, is purely demand-driven. If demand is high, as in D_1, then rent is R_1. Low demand, as illustrated by D_2, results in the lower rent of R_2.

We know today, however, that land has other uses besides agriculture. The larger the number of alternative uses that land might have, the less inelastic the supply of land for any one use. Because the supply curve of any factor is less than perfectly inelastic, we need to distinguish between rent and **transfer earnings** when discussing the return to the factor. Transfer earnings are defined as the necessary payment that a factor of production must earn in order to remain in its present use. Let's take the concept of transfer earnings and apply it to the example of another factor of production that has a very inelastic supply.

transfer earnings: a necessary payment that a factor of production must earn in order for it to remain in its present use.

Economic Rent and Professional Athletes

We are all aware of the fact that there are many well-paid professional athletes who love the game so much that they would continue to play even if they received only a fraction of what they are currently earning. The wage rate that would be necessary to ensure that they continued to play is their transfer earnings. The difference between the transfer-earnings wage and the actual wage received is the economic rent. **Figure 12.11** will help us understand this concept better.

FIGURE 12.11 Economic Rent and Transfer Earnings

At wage rate W$_1$, our athlete will play for only four years. At wage rate W$_2$, he will play for six years. The red-shaded area is the pay that is necessary to induce him to commit to the full eight years. Given the wage rate W$_3$, the entire rectangle is what he actually receives. Therefore, the blue-shaded area is his economic rent.

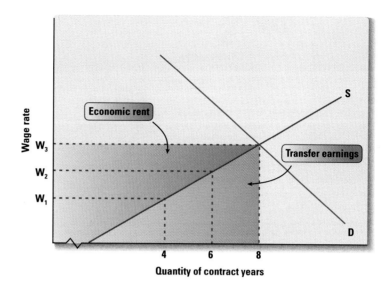

To really understand this concept of economic rent, we need to view the supply curve, S in Figure 12.11, as showing the minimum price at which a given quantity is willingly supplied. Let's consider the case of a young athlete who is currently working hard but struggling in the minor leagues, yet the hope of making it into the big time of the majors is still alive. If the wage rate is W$_1$, our young athlete will play for a total of four years because he loves to play. Yet, he knows that most of his kind will not make the big time, and the promise of riches will go unfulfilled. Therefore, he is not willing to play more than four years because the current wage is not sufficient for him to postpone getting on with his life any longer. To get him to agree to play for a fifth and a sixth year, a higher wage rate, W$_2$ for example, would have to be offered. Similarly, he will willingly play for eight years only if the wage offered is again increased, this time to W$_3$. The red-shaded area under the supply curve, therefore, is the transfer earnings necessary to induce our would-be pro to play for the full eight years. On the other hand, if our athlete is paid wage rate W$_1$ for each of the eight years, his total pay is the entire rectangle. Thus, the blue-shaded area represents his total pay less his transfer earnings, that is, his economic rent. This economic rent is a real bonus for him; it is the pay he receives over and above what he would have been willing to accept in order to continue doing what he is already doing.

Next, look back at Figure 12.11 and imagine, first, a supply curve that is drawn with much greater elasticity and, second, one that is drawn with even greater inelasticity. It should be clear to you that the more inelastic the supply curve, the greater the economic rent that any particular wage rate will generate. Now, ask yourself: what is likely to be the elasticity of supply of an exceptionally good athlete who is a star in the major leagues of any professional sport? The answer is, of course, that it is *very* inelastic. This means that the majority of his earnings is an economic rent; the transfer earnings (what he could earn in the next-best alternative occupation) is small.

In addition, the demand for professional athletes, some of whom are very good and some not so good, has increased dramatically in the last several years due to the expansion of the number of teams in all four major sports in North America.

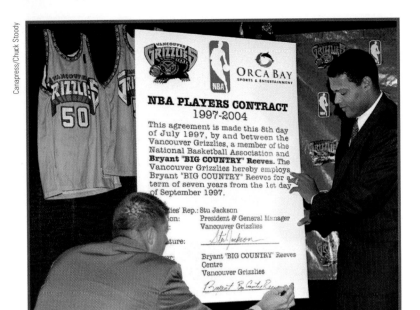

Canapress/Chuck Stoody

In 1997, Bryant "Big Country" Reeves signed a six-year contract extension with the Vancouver Grizzlies. Reeves is believed to have signed the six-year deal for $50 million.

Furthermore, these leagues have enjoyed rapidly escalating revenue from television contracts. If you combine this increase in demand with the inelastic supply of the really good athletes we have just mentioned, you get a good explanation for the great increases in the wages paid to professional sportsmen and sportswomen.

What we are really saying here is that the high pay many athletes today enjoy is *demand driven*. To clinch this point, let us point out that the world's very best squash players are paid only about $150 000 a year. Although this is a high salary, it is far lower than the salaries received by even average players in the major North American professional sports. Is this because there are so many of them, or because they really aren't as skillful as a football linebacker, or that they don't really work as hard as a baseball outfielder? The answer to all these questions is, of course, no. So why does David Wells, a baseball pitcher, get paid 20 times more than Jansher Khan, one of the world's best squash players? The answer is because the ticket sales and television contract revenue earned by a baseball team are so enormous that the demand for good baseball players is much greater than the demand for good squash players. This demand-side phenomenon explains Tiger Wood's tens of millions of dollars; and the concept of economic rent explains the sense, shared by many, that maybe he doesn't deserve all of it. In addition, Wells has a union representing his interests, whereas Janshar Khan does not.

As we all know, the very high salaries of athletes in major sports have led to the attempt by team owners to impose salary caps (maximums) in one form or another on individual players. The players' unions have, of course, resisted these attempts. What this dispute boils down to is a question of who (the team owner or the athlete) is entitled to what percentage of the economic rent that exists.

SELF-TEST

4. Draw a normal downward-sloping demand curve and a perfectly inelastic supply curve for labour. Label the axes wages and quantity of labour. Indicate the equilibrium wage as W_1 and quantity as Q_1. What portion of the pay that goes to this labour is economic rent?

The Natural-Resource Market

Natural resources are both renewable (trees and wild fish) and non-renewable (minerals). The use of one more unit of a non-renewable resource reduces, forever, the supply with which nature has endowed this planet. For this reason, non-renewable resources are a topic of particular interest to both economists and the public in general. As an example, oil is non-renewable. Does this mean that the supply of the world's oil is perfectly inelastic, as illustrated by S_1 in **Figure 12.12**?

FIGURE 12.12 The World's Supply of Oil

Given the facts that not all of the oil in the world has been discovered and that not all the discovered oil is for sale at the present price, say P_1, the supply curve for oil is upward-sloping, as illustrated by S_2. Only in the very long run can we think of the supply curve of oil as being perfectly inelastic, as in the curve S_1.

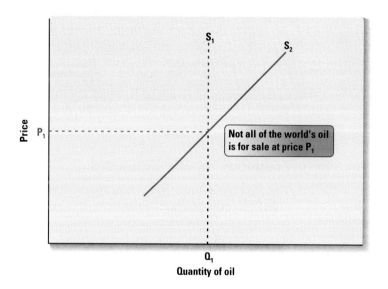

Not all of the world's oil is for sale at price P_1

Given that there is only so much oil on our planet, some people assume that a perfectly inelastic supply curve, such as S_1 in Figure 12.12, represents the circumstances facing humankind. In some grand sense, over the very long run, this is valid. However, it must be recognized that not all of the earth's oil has been discovered. Furthermore, much of the oil that has been discovered is not for sale at current prices. Therefore, the present supply curve of oil is much more like S_2 and represents not so much the total quantity that exists, but the amount currently available for sale.

Given that in the very long run there is only a finite amount of oil available, we need to ask if the price system leads to an overly rapid exploitation of oil. Or is it possible that the future will prove our current rate of use to be too conservative?

This is a highly politicized question, but economists do have something to say about it. Let's try to follow an argument that can get rather complex. The current value of oil to consumers is the amount they are willing to pay for one more barrel. Let's assume this figure is $20. Further, let's assume this is also the current market price for oil. An additional barrel extracted and sold now will yield $20 in revenue to the oil producer, which can be held and earn interest that we will assume is 5 percent, so that the producer would have a value of $21 a year from now. Alternatively, he could leave the barrel of oil in the ground in order to extract and sell it one year from now. Which is better, to extract and sell it now or in one year from now? The answer depends on what the price of the barrel of oil turns out to be in one year. If, one year from now, its price is $21.50, the producer will realize that he should have left it in the ground. If, however, the price turns out to be $20.50, the producer will realize that he should have extracted and sold it a year ago. Understanding this little conundrum leads us to a very usable conclusion:

> **The rate of extraction of oil depends on the difference between the change in the price of oil and the interest rate.**

To nail this down, again assume that the present rate of interest is 5 percent and that it remains unchanged, so that extracting a barrel of oil today and selling it for $20 would give us (approximately) a revenue of $25.50 in five years. If, five years from now, the price of a barrel of oil is also exactly $25.50, then our rate of extraction is exactly correct. On the other hand, if the price of oil turns out to be only $24, then we have been extracting oil far too fast. Similarly, if the price of oil turns out to be $27, then we have been conserving oil too much. Interesting, isn't it?

Let us hasten to say that we are not proposing this idea as the complete solution to the complex question of how quickly we should use up non-renewable resources. We do, however, wish to emphasize the point that economists do have some ideas in this area.

Common Property Resources

common property resource: a resource not owned by an individual or a firm.

There is also an interesting question concerning (some) renewable resources that are called **common property resources**. This term means that no one individual or firm (or government, for that matter) owns the resource. Wild fish in the ocean are the classic example of a common property resource.

As we saw in the case of non-renewable resources such as oil, the question here is: what is the correct rate of exploitation of a common property resource? If this question is not addressed and answered by some regulatory body, we can be certain that the resource will be overextracted and, possibly, destroyed. Consider the cod stocks in the Grand Banks, off the coast of Newfoundland. From a social point of view, these fish should be harvested at a rate that does not exceed their natural rate of reproduction. This will ensure that there are fish to catch next year and 10 years from now and 100 years from now. However, from an individual fisher's point of view, the more fish he can catch now, the greater his income. But isn't a sound conservation policy to that individual's long-term benefit? Yes, but *only if all* other fishers don't do what each and every one is strongly tempted to do—fish intensively before the stocks are all gone. You can see the need for the social regulation of a common property resource. Given the state of the East Coast cod fisheries today, one can conclude that such regulation was not done well.

Let's now leave the natural-resource market and turn to the capital goods market.

The Capital Goods Market

In a sense, the market for capital goods—whether they are machines used in a factory, or a computer system for an office, or a simple carpenter's tool—is very similar to the market for any *product*, as discussed in Chapter 2. There is a quite conventional demand for and supply of capital goods, as illustrated in **Figure 12.13**.

FIGURE 12.13 The Market for Capital Goods

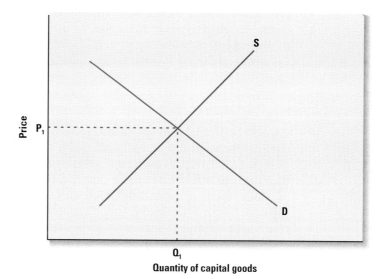

The equilibrium price for capital goods occurs at the intersection of the supply and demand curves, that is, at a price of P_1 and a quantity of Q_1.

In the figure, the interaction of the demand for and the supply of capital goods yields an equilibrium price and quantity of P_1 and Q_1. We don't have anything more to say about the supply of capital goods than we have already said in reference to the supply of any particular product such as orange juice—as the price increases, the quantity supplied rises.

It is the demand for capital goods that is more interesting. First, we need to point out that the demand for capital goods is in fact derived from the marginal revenue product of capital, just as the demand for labour depended on its marginal revenue product. In this case, the MRP of capital is the additional benefit accruing to the firm from the employment of the last unit of capital and is equal to the marginal physical product it produces multiplied by the price of the product. Second, we need to recognize that the purchase of capital goods almost always needs to be financed with borrowed money. Even large firms are not able to lay out several hundred thousands of dollars in cash for a new computer system. Instead, they arrange for a loan to finance the purchase, which is then paid back over time. They must, of course, pay interest on this loan, and it is because of this that the demand for capital goods is (inversely) related to the cost of financing capital purchases, which is the interest rate. In other words, the higher the interest rate, the lower will be the amount of borrowed funds and, therefore, the lower the amount of spending on capital goods. The factors that determine the rate of interest are more a matter for discussion in a macroeconomics course.

The demand side of the capital goods market is also interesting because an improvement in technology can certainly affect the demand for such goods. Significant improvements in technology can render existing capital goods obsolete and require that they be replaced by the newer versions. This increases the demand and is illustrated graphically by a rightward shift in the demand curve for the new capital goods.

Just as technological change increases the marginal revenue product of labour, it also increases the marginal revenue product of new capital goods that incorporate the new technology, and this can result in (the newer) capital goods being more productive *relative* to labour. Firms will then be very tempted to substitute the now more-productive capital for labour, which has become relatively less productive and, therefore, relatively more expensive. In other words, when deciding on amounts of substitutable factors like capital and labour, a firm would take into account both productivity and the price of the factors. Thus, if

$$\frac{MP_K}{P_K} > \frac{MP_L}{P_L}$$

it would be profitable to substitute capital for labour. In a sense, what the firm does is compare the value received for each dollar spent on labour with each dollar spent on capital. If a dollar spent on capital yields a greater return than a dollar spent on labour, then the firm will invest in more capital. This ratio of the marginal product of capital per dollar spent on capital compared with the marginal product of labour per dollar spent on labour is analogous to the equation we saw in Chapter 5 when exploring a consumer's attempt to maximize total utility. By equating the marginal product per dollar of the two factors, we know that the firm is maximizing total profits.

Such substitution of capital for labour is something that we witness almost every day. One of your authors, as a teenager, used to work after school unloading cases of beer from railway cars—one case at a time. Today, one person, using a forklift, does the work that half a dozen kids used to do. As another example, think of the labour saved at a supermarket because of the use of the conveyor belt and the bar-code reader. A third example is the use of computerized test banks in economics courses, which have replaced student graders.

The phenomenon of capital being substituted for labour raises the question of whether or not such automation destroys jobs and is therefore something that society needs to be concerned about. Many misconceptions about this issue can be easily cleared up. There is no question that automation does indeed eliminate certain types of jobs—the days of young people unloading beer from railway cars are gone. Economists call this the **factor substitution effect** of technological change. But, if technological change causing the substitution of capital for labour was the whole story, we would have to wonder how it is that anyone is still working, given the fact that our economy has experienced over 200 years of dramatic changes in technology.

In fact, the substitution effect is not the whole story. Capital substitution increases labour's productivity (the labour that was not replaced by capital) and thus lowers the cost of production. This, in turn, lowers the price of the final products being produced, which increases both the quantity demanded for those products and, thus, total output. This increase of total output increases the demand for labour, and thus the **output effect** of technological change *creates* jobs. Given the fact that there are more people working in our society today than ever before, the output effect of technological change must have been stronger than the substitution effect over the last two centuries or so.

factor substitution effect: the phenomenon of one factor replacing another factor as a result of technological change.

factor output effect: the phenomenon of rising total output leading to an increased demand for labour.

The Luddites and the Fear of Machines

Although the twentieth century has seen a quantum leap in the amount of machines used by society, it has generally not resulted in mass unemployment. In the short run, however, the replacement of labour by machines can result in a loss of specific jobs. In the early days of the Industrial Revolution, these short-term effects were devastating the lives of many workers. The rapid introduction of machines led, in Karl Marx's phrase, to a an "industrial army of unemployed workers." Small wonder then, that, working people at the time, still more used to country ways rather than city ways, feared and hated the introduction of machines. A group of them, inspired by a mythical figure called Ned Ludd, swore to fight the invasion of the machines. In the textile areas in the north of England, Luddites went on a rampage of burning and wrecking factories. These riots peaked in 1811 and 1812 but were eventually brought to an end by the authorities. A mass trial in 1816 led to the hanging of some of the group's leaders and the deportation of others, resulting in an abrupt end to the reign of "King Ludd."

5. Given its current output, Rally Rackets Ltd. is experiencing a marginal product of capital of 60 and a marginal product of labour of 10. If the price of capital is $100 a unit and the price of labour is $25 a unit, how should this firm substitute factors?

The Entrepreneurial Market

The fourth of our four factors of production is enterprise, or entrepreneurial talent. No economist explored the role of entrepreneurial talent in the market economy more than Joseph Schumpeter, who taught at Harvard University in the first half of the twentieth century. Schumpeter saw the entrepreneur as an innovating doer who bridged the gap between a mere idea and a productive application. Eccentric minds invented, and common businesspeople managed, but it was the risk-taking entrepreneur who had the vision and the chutzpah to take truly new and revolutionary *action*. The entrepreneur, in Schumpeter's eyes, is the engine of economic growth and development in a capitalist economy.

From the time of Adam Smith, economists have argued that competition within a capitalist economy would tend to result in (economic) profits being competed down to zero—a process we explored in the context of both the perfectly competitive and the monopolistically competitive market models. What then explained the continued existence of economic profits nearly two centuries after capitalism took root in the western European and North American economies?

Surely, Schumpeter argued, it was the innovations of the entrepreneur that were the source of economic profits in capitalism. New innovation created unique situations in which profits could be made. In time, the swarm of imitators of the innovation would become established, and such profits would be driven to zero. However, in a dynamic and growing economy, another wave of innovation would have already occurred and new profit opportunities would be continuously created.

While entrepreneurs create profits, they are often not long the beneficiaries of them. As John Kenneth Galbraith points out in *The New Industrial State*, the risk-taking entrepreneur sometimes loses control of his growing business to the impersonal forces of what he calls the technostructure, which is at the heart of the modern transnational corporation. When this happens, more conservative and more bureaucratic managers take over from the risk-taking entrepreneur.

Before we leave this topic, we should point out that there is an alternative explanation for profits: the existence of oligopoly and monopoly influences that inhibit the natural tendency for profits to be competed away. However, this explanation, while valid, just doesn't have the same zing to it as Schumpeter's.

REVIEW

1. List five explanations of wage differentials.
2. Define *transfer earnings*.
3. What is *economic rent*?
4. What economic variable is relevant when considering the right rate of extraction of a non-renewable resource?
5. What is a *common property resource*?
6. What is the price of finance?
7. What is the *factor substitution effect*?
8. What is the *factor output effect*?
9. What, according to Schumpeter, might prevent profits from being driven to zero in a competitive world?

STUDY GUIDE

Chapter Highlights

In this chapter you studied the factor markets for labour, land, capital, and entrepreneurial activity. You learned that it is the productivity (marginal product) of each factor that underlies the rate of return that it earns and the rate that it is employed.

1. The *demand for labour* is a derived demand which is determined by the marginal product of labour which, when converted to money terms, becomes:

$$MRP_L = \frac{\Delta \text{total revenue}}{\Delta \text{ labour inputs}} \quad or \quad = \quad MP_L \times P$$

2. The downward sloping portion of the MRP_L curve is the demand for labour curve while the *supply of labour curve* is upward sloping since increases in the wage rate increase the quantity supplied of labour. The *equilibrium wage rate* is determined by the point of intersection of these two curves.

3. In a competitive factor market, the individual firm is able to hire all the labour it wishes at the market determined wage rate and will, in fact, *hire labour* up to the point that the:

$$MRP_L = W$$

4. A firm operating in a *monopsony* labour market will find that if it wants to hire more labour it will have to offer a higher wage rate to new employees which increases the average wage rate that it must pay.

5. Canada's *long-run supply of labour* has been growing steadily as a result of increased population and an increase in labour force participation rates.

6. Increases in *labour productivity*, which depends on technological change and increases in the nation's capital stock, is closely related to:
   - the long-run demand for labour;
   - the real wages of Canadians which is measured by:

$$\text{Real wage} = \frac{\text{nominal wage}}{\text{price level}}$$

7. *Trade unions and professional associations* attempt to benefit their members by increasing the demand for their work; raising their nominal wage rates; and improving their working conditions. This is done by:
   - shifting the demand curve for the members' labour to the right;
   - shifting the supply of labour curve to the left;
   - imposing a negotiated wage rate above the market equilibrium rate.

8. Wage rate *differentials* exist because:
   - of variations in the level of human capital between individuals;
   - some jobs involve more risks than others;
   - some jobs have unpleasant characteristics;
   - some jobs have attractive non-pecuniary benefits;
   - there is discrimination in labour markets.

9. The concept of *economic rent* was originally conceived as the return to land (which was assumed could only be used for agriculture) and was perfectly inelastic in supply. The modern view of rent is that it is the return to a factor which is over and above that factor's transfer earnings.

10. The two interesting questions in the *natural-resource market* are:
    • what is the best rate of exploitation of a non-renewable resource such as oil;
    • how best to regulate common property resources such as wild fish.

11. The demand for *capital goods*, like the demand for all factors, depends on the productivity of capital which is determined by technological change and which lowers the price of capital goods and leads to the substitution of capital for labour so as to maintain the equality:

$$\frac{MP_K}{P_K} = \frac{MP_L}{P_L}$$

12. The two views of *economic profits* are that they are the result of:
    • entrepreneurial activities *à la* Schumpeter;
    • imperfect competition in the product markets.

New Glossary Terms and Key Equations

common property resource   458
economic rent   453
factor market   438
factor output effect   460
factor substitution effect   460
human capital   451
labour force   441
labour force supply   441
marginal revenue product   438
monopsony   443
nominal wage   446
product market   438
real wage   446
transfer earnings   454

Equations:

1. $MRP = \dfrac{\Delta TR}{\Delta \text{inputs}}$

2. $MRP = MP_L \times \text{price}$

3. Profit maximization: $MRP = P$

4. $\text{Real wage} = \dfrac{\text{nominal wage}}{\text{price level}}$

Study Tips

1. This chapter is about the demand and supply of factors, not products. In short we have shifted our focus from the product market to the factor market. Most of the chapter assumes a perfectly competitive factor market. This concept means that a firm can buy all it wants of a particular factor, say labour, at the going wage rate; that is, the firm's hiring practices will not drive the wage rate up. Another way of looking at this is that the price of a factor remains constant because the actions of individual sellers and buyers do not affect the price. This is analogous to the perfectly competitive product market we studied in Chapter 8, in which the price of the product remains constant regardless of the action of individual buyers and sellers.

2. You may recall that in Chapter 6 we stressed the importance of the relationship between the costs of production and productivity of inputs. Productivity plays a key role in this chapter also, in that it determines, in the long run, the real return received by the factor; for example, the real wage of labour is determined by labour's productivity.

3. The calculation of the MRP of any factor can be done in one of two ways. The first is by multiplying the MP of the factor times the price of the product sold. The second way is to simply determine the change in total revenue resulting from the use of one unit of the factor in question.

4. Students tend to confuse the effect of a change in the price of a competitive firm's product with the effect of a change in the price of a factor that the firm hires. The former shifts the factor demand curve, while the latter results in a movement along the demand curve for the factor.

5. Even though it may seem like a small point, make sure you understand the distinction between the real wage and the nominal wage. This will be essential when you take on the study of macroeconomics.

6. You should not assume that the concept of economic "rent" applies only to land. Under the right conditions, any factor can receive economic rent.

Are You Sure?

Indicate whether the following statements are true or false. If false, indicate why they are false.

1. Although supply and demand analysis can be used to analyze the product market, it cannot be used to analyze the factor market.

   T or F   If false: _____

   _____

2. Marginal revenue product is the increase in a firm's total revenue that results from the use of one more unit of input.

   T or F   If false: _____

   _____

3. An employer operating under conditions of a perfectly competitive labour market will hire labour up to the point where the marginal product of labour equals the wage rate.

   T or F   If false: _____

   _____

4. If the product market is imperfectly competitive rather than perfectly competitive, the marginal revenue product curve declines faster.

   T or F   If false: _____

   _____

5. The fact that neither of the authors works weekends at McDonald's demonstrates that they both value an extra hour of leisure over the added hourly income that they could earn.

   T or **F**   If false: _____

   _____

6. The size of Canada's labour force has doubled over the last 30 years.

   T or **F**   If false: _____

   _____

7. The typical range for the annual increase in labour productivity in Canada over the last 30 years has been between 3 and 5 percent.

   T or **F**   If false: _____

   _____

8. The real wage is defined as the nominal wage divided by labour productivity.

   T or **F**   If false: _____

   _____

9. Often, trade unions have the same effect as do professional associations on the labour market.

   T or **F**   If false: _____

   _____

10. Some form of regulation is needed to ensure that a common property resource is not over extracted.

   T or **F**   If false: _____

   _____

Choose the Best

11. The argument that technological change creates jobs assumes that:
    a) The factor substitution effect outweighs the factor output effect.
    b) The factor output effect outweighs the factor substitution effect.

12. Which of the following is assumed in Ricardo's concept of economic rent?
    a) A perfectly inelastic supply curve.
    b) A perfectly inelastic demand curve.

13. The world's supply of oil is:
    a) Perfectly inelastic at all prices.
    b) Elastic at prices up to a certain level, and then becomes perfectly inelastic.

14. Which of the following statements best describes Schumpeter's view of profits?
    a) Profits come in a steady stream in a capitalist economy as long as full employment is achieved.

    b) Economic profits are zero in a capitalist economy in the long run.
    c) The source of profits, whatever level they may be, is the entrepreneur.

15. What is the most likely consequence if a monopsonist hires more labour?
    a) A decrease in the wage rate.
    b) An increase in the wage rate.
    c) A wage rate that neither increases nor decreases.

16. What is the most likely effect of an increase in the demand for a particular type of labour?
    a) The wage rate for that type of labour will rise, and the quantity hired will decrease.
    b) The wage rate for that type of labour will rise, and the quantity hired will also increase.
    c) The wage rate for that type of labour will rise, but the quantity hired will remain unchanged.

17. Which of the following would be most advantageous to a trade union or professional association?
    a) The supply of labour is restricted.
    b) The demand for labour is decreased.
    c) The supply of labour increases by more than the demand increases.
    d) The demand for labour increases by more than the supply increases.

18. The average wage rate in Canada has increased over the last 30 years. Which of the following is the most likely explanation?
    a) The demand for labour has decreased.
    b) The supply of labour has decreased.
    c) The demand for labour has increased more than the supply of labour has decreased.
    d) The demand for labour has increased more than the supply of labour has increased.

19. All *except one* of the following statements are correct concerning the explanation of wage rate differentials. Which is the exception?
    a) All individuals possess the same amount of human capital.
    b) Different jobs involve different degrees of risk.
    c) Some jobs have unpleasant characteristics that are absent in other jobs.
    d) Some jobs have very attractive non-pecuniary benefits.

20. All *except one* of the following statements are correct concerning the labour market for high-profile professional athletes. Which is the exception?
    a) The supply is inelastic.
    b) The wage rate is demand-driven.
    c) There is an element of economic rent in their pay.
    d) There is no transfer earnings involved in their pay.

21. What do most economists think is the socially optimum extraction rate of a natural resource such as oil?
    a) One that equals the MRP of the resource.
    b) A rate that ensures that the price of oil increases at the same rate as the interest rate.

    c) One that is less than the rate of discovery of new sources.
    d) One that is less than 2 percent of known reserves so as to guarantee at least 50 years' supply at all times.

22. If the MP_K/P_K is greater than the MP_L/P_L, which of the following is correct?
    a) The firm should substitute labour for capital.
    b) The firm should substitute capital for labour.
    c) The firm should raise the wage rate of its labour.
    d) The firm should decrease its output.

23. Suppose that the MRP_L for a competitive firm is currently $50 and the hourly cost of labour is $40. Which of the following is the correct action for the firm?
    a) Since the firm must be profitable, it need not do anything.
    b) The firm should hire more labour.
    c) The firm should substitute labour for capital.
    d) The firm should raise the wage rate of its labour.

24. At what point will a competitive firm stop hiring additional labour?
    a) When its total product is maximized.
    b) When the marginal product of labour is maximized.
    c) When the marginal revenue product of labour is maximized.
    d) When the marginal revenue product of labour is just equal to the wage rate.

25. Which of the following would cause graphically a shift to the right in the demand curve of a factor?
    a) A decrease in the price of that factor.
    b) An increase in the price of a substitute factor.
    c) A decrease in the price of the product produced by the factor.
    d) An increase in the marginal product of a substitute factor.

26. If most people's desire for leisure increases, which one of the following statements is correct ?
    a) The wage rate would fall, and the quantity of products produced would rise.

b) Both the wage rate and the quantity of products produced would fall.
c) The wage rate would fall, and the demand for labour would increase.
d) The wage rate would rise, and the quantity of products produced would fall.
e) Both the wage rate and the quantity of products produced would rise.

27. All *except one* of the following statements concerning the concept of economic rent are correct. Which is the exception?
a) The more inelastic the supply of a factor, the more economic rent that factor earns.
b) A factor that has a perfectly inelastic supply will earn no transfer earnings.
c) It is possible for a factor to receive both economic rent and transfer earnings.
d) If we assume that land has only one use, such as agriculture, then all of its return is economic rent.
e) The higher the transfer earnings of a factor, the higher its economic rent will be.

28. When is the marginal revenue product of a factor at a maximum?
a) When its marginal product is at a maximum.
b) When the firm's total product is at a maximum.
c) When its marginal product is at a minimum.
d) When both its marginal product and the firm's total product are at a maximum.
e) When average product is at its maximum.

29. If a firm is operating in a monopsony market, which of the following statements is correct?
a) The firm can hire additional labour at the same wage rate it is currently paying.
b) The firm would hire more labour in the monopsony situation than in the competitive situation.
c) The firm faces an upward-sloping supply of labour curve.
d) The MRP_L declines faster in the case of the monopsony situation than in the competitive one.
e) The firm's demand for labour curve is downward-sloping in the situation of the monopsony market and horizontal in the case of the competitive one.

30. All *except one* of the following statements are correct when a trade union successfully imposes a wage rate above equilibrium. Which is the exception?
a) There will be more workers willing to work than are hired.
b) The firm's total wage bill will definitely be higher.
c) The average firm is not operating in a competitive factor market.
d) The quantity of workers hired will be less after the imposition of the higher wage than it was before.
e) Neither the demand for nor the supply of labour has changed.

Simple Calculations

31. Complete the following data for Gimlets Inc.:

Quantity of labour	1	2	3	4	5	6
Total product	10	28	45	60	70	78
Marginal product						
Price	$6	$6	$6	$6	$6	$6
Total revenue						
Marginal revenue product						

32. The following data is for Gumbles Ltd.:

Quantity of labour	1	2	3	4	5	6	7
Marginal revenue product	$10	$15	$14	$12	$10	$8	$5

How many workers should Gumbles hire at the following wage rates?
a) $15 per hour: _____; b) $12 per hour: _____; c) $9 per hour: _____; d) $6 per hour: _____ .

33. Suppose that in the country of Gardenia the nominal wage rate is $18 per hour and the price level is 1.2.
   a) What is the value of the real wage rate? _____ .
   b) If the nominal wage rate increases by 10 percent, what will be the new value of real wages?
      _____ .

   c) If instead, the price level were to increase by 10 percent, what will be the new value of real wages?
      _____ .

Problems

34. The demand for film animators is illustrated in Figure 12.14.
   a) Draw in a supply curve from the origin showing that the quantity increases by 100 for each $10 increase in the wage rate.

   b) What are the total earnings per period of the animators as a group?

      Answer: _____ .

   c) How much of the earnings in b) are transfer earnings, and how much is economic rent?

      Transfer earnings: _____; economic rent: _____ .

   d) If the supply of animators increased, would the total earnings for the group increase or decrease?

      Increase: _____; decrease: _____ .

FIGURE 12.14

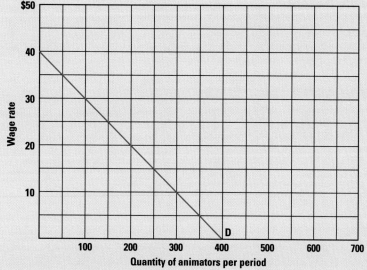

35. Some data for the country of Valhalla is presented in Table 12.3.

TABLE 12.3

Wage	Demand for Labour 1	Supply of Labour	Demand for Labour 2
$12	600	0	900
14	500	200	800
16	400	400	700
18	300	600	600
20	200	800	500
22	100	1000	400

a) If the demand is Demand 1 and the firm Odin is operating in a perfectly competitive labour market, what wage will it have to pay for labour?

Answer: _____.

b) If, instead, Odin was a monopsonist, would it hire more or less labour, and would the wage rate be higher or lower?

Quantity hired: _____; wage rate: _____.

Now assume that the demand for labour increased as illustrated by Demand 2 in Table 12.3.

c) Given the same conditions as in a) above, what is your answer now?

Answer: _____.

36. Table 12.4 lists some productivity data for the firm Omir in the country of Hanu.

TABLE 12.4

Units	$MP_K 1$	MP_L	$MP_K 2$
1	23	11	50
2	21	10	45
3	18	8	38
4	14	6	30
5	10	3	11
6	5	0	10

a) Assume that both the price of capital and labour is $1 per unit. If the present MP of capital is the column $MP_K 1$, what is the right capital–labour ratio for Omir to use?

Ratio: _____.

b) Assume that the price of capital remains at $1 but the price of labour increases to $2. Now what is the right capital–labour ratio for Omir to use?

Ratio: _____.

c) Assume, again, that the price of both capital and labour is $1 a unit. If the present MP of capital is shown as column $MP_K 2$, what is the right capital–labour ratio to use?

Ratio: _____.

Effect on the number of workers: _____.

Effect on the wage rates: _____.

Translations

FIGURE 12.15

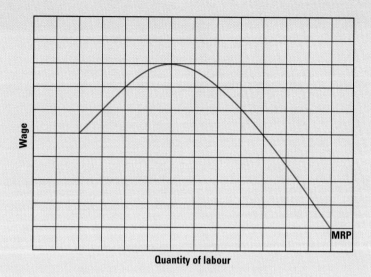

Quantity of labour

Describe the meaning of the graph in Figure 12.15. In doing so, make reference to marginal product, the law of diminishing returns, and marginal cost. You may assume that this firm operates in a competitive factor market as well as a competitive product market.

_____

_____

_____

_____

Key Problem

Heavenly Bubbles is a small soap company whose main product is hand soap, which sells in a competitive market for $2 a bar. The bars are produced at autonomous workstations that feature a specially designed machine. The output per hour of each workstation varies with the amount of labour used, as the data in **Table 12.5** indicates. Labour costs $16 per hour.

a) Fill in the marginal product, total revenue 1, and marginal revenue product 1 columns in Table 12.5.

b) How many workers should the firm assign to each workstation?

Number of workers:_____

c) Assuming the firm has 6 workstations, construct the firm's demand for labour curve (and label it D_1) on the graph in Figure 12.16. Indicate, with the letter a, the total amount of labour that the firm will hire at a wage rate of $16.

TABLE 12.5

Quantity of Labour	Output per Hour	Marginal Product	Total Revenue 1	Marginal Revenue Product 1	Total Revenue 2	Marginal Revenue Product 2
0	0	—	—	—	—	—
1	24	___	___	___	___	___
2	44	___	___	___	___	___
3	60	___	___	___	___	___
4	72	___	___	___	___	___
5	80	___	___	___	___	___
6	84	___	___	___	___	___

d) Now, assume that there is an increase in employment taxes (the employers share of UIC and CPP), which raises the cost of labour to $24 an hour. Now, how many workers per hour should the firm assign to each workstation, and how many should it hire in total?

Number of workers: _____; number of workers in total: _____.

e) On the graph in Figure 12.16 indicate, with the letter *b*, the effect of this increase in the cost of labour.

f) Suppose the price of each bar of soap rises to $3. Fill in the total revenue 2 column and marginal revenue product 2 column, and indicate the effect of this change on the graph in Figure 12.16 by drawing in the new demand curve and labelling it D$_2$.

FIGURE 12.16

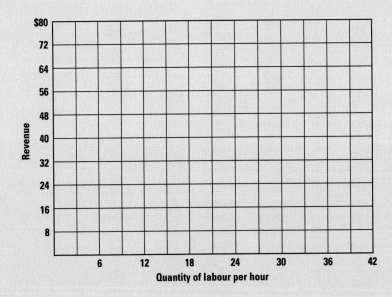

g) Assuming that the cost of labour remains at the $24 an hour level, how much labour per hour will the firm now hire? Label it *c* on the graph.

Number of workers:_____

h) Suppose that, instead, there is a 25 percent increase in labour productivity (that is, the MP of labour increases by 25 percent) over that shown in Table 12.5. If the price of soap is $2, fill in **Table 12.6**.

TABLE 12.6

Quantity of Labour	Output per Hour	Marginal Product	Total Revenue	Marginal Revenue Product
0	_____	—	—	—
1	_____	_____	_____	_____
2	_____	_____	_____	_____
3	_____	_____	_____	_____
4	_____	_____	_____	_____
5	_____	_____	_____	_____
6	_____	_____	_____	_____

i) On the graph in Figure 12.16, draw in the demand for labour curve that reflects the increase in productivity and label it D_3.

j) Compare the changes in d), f), and h).

_____

_____

_____

_____

More of the Same

Rainbow Sky is a small company that sells packages of scented incense in a competitive market. The daily output of each worker is given in **Table 12.7**. The firm sells the incense for $2.50 a packet, and labour costs $30 a day.

a) Fill in the marginal product, total revenue 1, and marginal revenue product 1 columns in Table 12.7.

b) How many workers per day should the firm hire?

c) On the grid in **Figure 12.17**, construct the firm's demand for labour curve (label it D_1). Indicate, with the letter *a*, the total amount of labour the firm will hire.

FIGURE 12.17

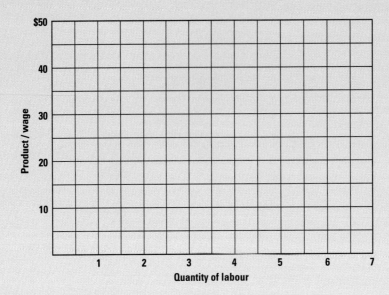

d) Now assume that wages decrease to $25 per day. How many workers per day will Rainbow Sky hire now?

e) On your graph, indicate with the letter *b* the effect of this decrease in wages.

TABLE 12.7

Quantity of Labour	Output per Hour	Marginal Product	Total Revenue 1	Marginal Revenue Product 1	Total Revenue 2	Marginal Revenue Product 2
0	—	—	—	—	—	—
1	22					
2	40					
3	56					
4	70					
5	82					
6	92					

f) Next, assume that the price at which Rainbow Sky can sell its product decreases to $2. Fill in the total revenue 2 and marginal revenue product 2 columns in Table 12.7. Now draw in a new demand curve for labour and label it D_2.

g) Assuming that the cost of labour remains at the $25 a day level, how much labour per day will the firm now hire?

h) Now assume a 25 percent decrease in labour productivity, along with the original $2.50 price for incense, and construct a new demand for labour curve and label it D_3 on your graph.

i) Does your graph verify that an increase in the cost of labour is a movement on the demand curve for labour, whereas both a decrease in the price of the incense and in the productivity of labour will shift it?

UNANSWERED QUESTIONS

Short Essays

1. Describe three ways in which a union might be able to increase the wage rate received by its members. Make reference to the quantity of members that would be hired in each of the three instances.

2. What does Schumpeter see as the key to economic growth in a capitalist economy? Do you think that Schumpeter's idea is likely to become more or less relevant in the next 20 years?

3. Although the use of a common property resource must be regulated, that of a non-renewable resource need not be. Discuss.

4. An individual worker's productivity is increased by giving her more capital to work with. Yet, the process of increasing the capital–labour ratio results in labour being replaced by capital. Surely, this means that as labour's productivity increases, fewer people will have jobs. Discuss.

5. Comment on the following observation: "I know of an economics professor who spent 9 years in university to prepare for his profession, and now earns $60 000 a year. I also know a stockbroker who did not attend college or university and who is making over $60 000. Obviously, the professor is underpaid or the stockbroker is overpaid."

Analytical Questions

6. On a graph, draw a supply and demand curve for a factor that illustrates the idea that all of the earnings are in the form of economic rent.

7. Discuss the following statement: "The Canadian Medical Association is perhaps the most powerful union in the country."

8. The government of Canada subsidized the oil industry to the tune of billions of dollars in the 1970s to encourage the exploration of oil in the Arctic and off the coast of Newfoundland. Oil was found, lots of it, in fact. Why are we then extracting only small quantities of it?

9. The price of a ticket for a good seat at a professional hockey game in some cities in Canada is now over $80. The long-run consequences of this will be that the pay earned by professional hockey players will surely fall. Discuss.

10. Any owner of a major sports team in North America could pay her players considerably less and still get them to play. Discuss.

11. Kant Skatte and his agent are considering three contract proposals being offered by his current team. Each proposal is for a 5-year term. The three proposals are summarized in **Table 12.8**.

TABLE 12.8

Year	Proposal A	Proposal B	Proposal C
1	$3 million	$1 million	$5 million
2	$3 million	$2 million	$4 million
3	$3 million	$3 million	$3 million
4	$3 million	$4 million	$2 million
5	$3 million	$5 million	$1 million

Which of the three proposals is preferable, from Kant's point of view? Why?

12. "Since rent is a surplus and not a cost of production, a tax on land will have no effect on the annual rent." Comment on this statement, using a graph in your analysis.

13. Use the theory of marginal productivity and the concept of the real wage to discuss whether you think Robinson Crusoe's standard of living increased or decreased as a result of Friday coming onto the scene.

Numerical Questions

14. **Table 12.9** shows the daily production of window frames by Willi Wider Windows Ltd.

TABLE 12.9

Number of Workers	Total Production
1	5
2	12
3	20
4	26
5	31
6	35
7	37
8	38

The firm is able to hire labour at $10 per hour and can sell frames for $2 each. How many workers will the firm employ?

15. Assume that the current equilibrium price for a barrel of oil is $18 and the interest rate is 6 percent.
   a) What does the price of oil need to be two years from now to justify extracting it now?
   b) What will happen if oil producers think that the price of a barrel of oil in two years will be more than this figure?

16. The graph in **Figure 12.18A** shows the demand and supply of nurses in the long-term-care hospital industry. The graph in **Figure 12.18B** is the MRP (demand for labour) by a single hospital that employs the nurses.
   a) In a perfectly competitive labour market, what will be the market wage, and how many workers will the hospital employ?
   b) Suppose that the nurses' trade union is able to negotiate a $5 per hour wage increase for its members. What will be the resulting surplus of labour, and how many workers will the hospital now employ?

FIGURE 12.18

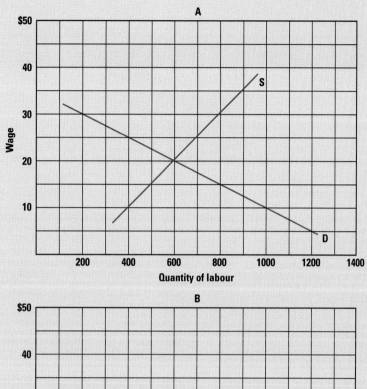

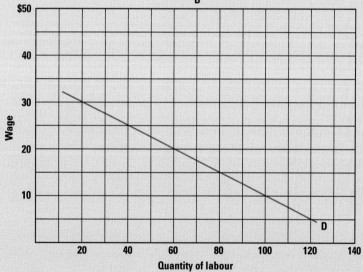

17. **Table 12.10** shows data for a small company, Soft Pine, that makes wooden stir sticks. The marginal product figures are for kilos per day.

TABLE 12.10

(1) Units of Labour	(2) MP$_L$	(3) MRP$_L$ A	(4) MRP$_L$ B
1	12	___	___
2	9	___	___
3	8	___	___
4	7	___	___
5	6	___	___
6	5	___	___

a) Fill in column 3 in the table, assuming that Soft Pine sells its product in a competitive market for $30 a kilo (situation A). Then fill in column 4, assuming that the price of sticks increases to $36 (situation B).

b) If labour costs $180 a day, how much labour will Soft Pine hire in each of the two situations, A and B?

c) On a graph, sketch in the two demand curves and indicate the quantity of labour hired.

18. **Table 12.11** lists some data for the economy of Onlyoneland, in which all labour is identical. All labour figures are in millions.

TABLE 12.11

(1) Wage	(2) Supply of Labour 1	(3) Demand for Labour 1	(4) Supply of Labour 2	(5) Demand for Labour 2
$6	12	16	___	___
$7	13	15	___	___
$8	14	14	___	___
$9	15	13	___	___
$10	16	12	___	___

Table 12.12 lists data for the firm Oneofmany, which operates in a competitive labour market.

TABLE 12.12

Hours of Labour Used	MRP$_L$
2000	12
3000	10
4000	8
5000	6
6000	4

a) Given Supply 1 and Demand 1, how many workers will Oneofmany hire, and what wage will it pay?

b) Now fill in columns 4 and 5 in Table 12.11, assuming that both the supply of and the demand for labour increases by 2 million at each wage rate.

c) What will be the quantity of labour hired by Oneofmany and the wage rate it pays after this change?

19. Table 12.13 shows the supply of labour for Big Inc., a monopsonist.

TABLE 12.13

(1) Quantity of Daily Labour	(2) Wage (equals average wage cost)	(3) MRP
1	$70	180
2	80	190
3	90	200
4	100	190
5	110	180
6	120	170
7	130	160
8	140	150
9	150	140
10	160	130

a) Calculate the total wage cost of employing each of the 10 units of labour.

b) Calculate the marginal wage cost for the monopsonist (that is, what is the increase in the total wage bill as a result of hiring one more unit of labour?).

c) How many units of labour will be employed, and what will be the daily wage?

Web-Based Activities

1. In general, workers should be paid an amount that reflects their contribution to profits. If individuals increase the profits of the firm because they are more productive, then their compensation should increase. Are corporate CEOs overpaid, in as far as their total compensation is out of line with how corporate profits are changing over time? Read **www.pioneerpress.com/archive/ceopay/index.htm** and look at the top 25 paid executives. What do you think—are they overpaid? (Look at how profits are changing, and then look at how the CEO's salary is changing.)

2. The entrepreneur is the engine of economic growth. How does one become an entrepreneur? Is it related to genes, or can the skills be learned? Take the quiz at **www.cnnfn.cnn.com/1997/03/12/busunu/entrepreneur_quiz** to find out if you have the necessary skills to be an entrepreneur.

International Trade

What's ahead... We start by looking at the reasons why individuals and countries trade with each other, and discover that the reason in both cases is differences in endowment: some are endowed with attributes not available to others but often lack things possessed by others. These differences lead to the cost advantages over others that some producers enjoy and is at the heart of Ricardo's theory of comparative advantage, which we investigate in the first part of the chapter. We then look at the concept of the terms of trade and show how this determines who gets what share of the increased production that results from trade. The chapter then looks at some of the arguments against free trade and ends with an investigation of how and why trade has often been restricted and impeded.

A QUESTION OF RELEVANCE...

Have you looked at the little tag on your jeans lately? Were they made in Canada? What about your camera? Your fishing rod? Your tennis racket? Your CD player? Does it concern you that they all might well have been made abroad? It probably won't come as a surprise to you that Canada imports approximately a quarter of all its products. Is this good for the country? Surely it would be in Canada's interest to produce its own goods. Or would it? This chapter looks at the question of whether Canada is better or worse off as a result of international trade.

P eople have traded in one form or another since the dawn of time, and most of the great powers in history have also been famous traders: the Phoenicians and the Greeks; medieval Venice and Elizabethan England; the early American colonies and modern Japan. It seems obvious that great benefits are obtained from trading, but there has always been the underlying suspicion that someone also loses as a result. For many, a great trading nation is one that consistently, and through shrewd practice, always manages to come out on top during trade negotiations. This "beggar thy neighbour" attitude was the cause of no great concern for writers immediately preceding Adam Smith, who thought it was part of the natural state of affairs that there are always winners and losers in trade. It was the job of policy-makers, they felt, to ensure that their own country was always on the winning side.

It took the mind of Adam Smith, however, to see that whenever two people enter into a voluntary agreement to trade, both parties must gain as a result. If you trade a textbook in exchange for your friend's new Guns 'n Butter CD, you obviously want that CD more than the textbook, and your friend must want the textbook more than the CD. Trade is to the advantage of both of you, otherwise it would not take place. When we look at international trade between nations, all we are doing is simply looking at this single transaction multiplied a billionfold. It is not really nations who trade, but individual people and firms who buy from other foreign individuals and firms. In many ways the reason you trade with a friend is the same reason you buy products from a Toronto brewery or Winnipeg car dealer or Tokyo fishing rod manufacturer: you hope to gain something as a result, and what you give up in return (usually money) is of less value to you than the thing you obtain in return.

All of which raises the question of why you personally (or a whole nation for that matter) would want to buy something rather than make it at home. In other words, why are people not self-sufficient? Why do they not produce everything that they personally consume? Well, Adam Smith had an answer for this (as for many things):

> It is the maxim of every prudent master of a family, never to make at home what it will cost him more to make than to buy.[1]

There, in essence, is the main argument for trade: why make something yourself if you can buy it cheaper elsewhere? If it takes Akio three hours to make a certain product but he can buy it elsewhere from the income he gets from one hour's work in his regular job, then why would he bother? It would pay him to do his own job for three hours; he could afford to buy three units of the product. An additional consideration is the fact that there are many things that Akio is incapable of making (actually, most things), or that he could make only after extensive training and with the help of very expensive equipment.

Specialization and Trade

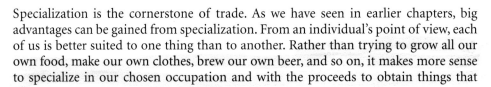

Specialization is the cornerstone of trade. As we have seen in earlier chapters, big advantages can be gained from specialization. From an individual's point of view, each of us is better suited to one thing than to another. Rather than trying to grow all our own food, make our own clothes, brew our own beer, and so on, it makes more sense to specialize in our chosen occupation and with the proceeds to obtain things that

---

[1] Adam Smith, *Wealth of Nations* (Edwin Cannan edition, 1877), p. 354.

other people can make better and cheaper. Similarly, firms will be far more productive if they specialize in the production process, that is, make use of the division of labour. As we shall see in this chapter, there are also great benefits to be enjoyed by countries that specialize rather than try to be self-sufficient.

It follows that the result of more specialization is more trading. Specialization and trade go hand in hand. Modern nations, firms, and individuals have become increasingly specialized, and with this has come a huge increase in the volume of trade, domestically and internationally. But is there a limit to specialization? From a technical point of view, Smith thought not; but he did believe that specialization would be limited by the size of the market. The smaller the market, the less output and therefore the less opportunity or need for extensive specialization. The bigger the size of the market, the more specialization that can take place and the lower will be the cost of producing goods. The prime driving force behind the expansion of markets is that it enables firms to produce in higher volumes and at a lower cost. All things being equal (including demand), it is the cost of production and therefore the price of the product that induces trade. If you can produce a product cheaper than I can, then it will make no sense for me to try to produce it myself. And why are you able to produce certain products cheaper than I can? The answer presumably is that you possess certain advantages over me. Let us look at these advantages.

ADDED DIMENSION

Canada, the Great Trader

Canada is certainly one of the world's great trading nations, at least in relative terms. In 1999, for example, Canada exported $410 billion worth of goods and services and imported $383 billion from abroad. These figures represent nearly 40 percent of Canada's GDP. Only a few countries, such as Germany and the Netherlands, trade a larger fraction. The United States and Japan, in comparison, trade only about 10 percent of their GDPs (though, of course, in actual dollars this represents a lot more). In terms of Canada's trading partners, the United States is far more dominant than all other countries combined (buying approximately 80 percent of our exports). In fact, Canada sells three times as much to the United States as it does to all other countries combined and buys approximately 76 percent of all its merchandise from our neighbour to the south.

Factor Endowment

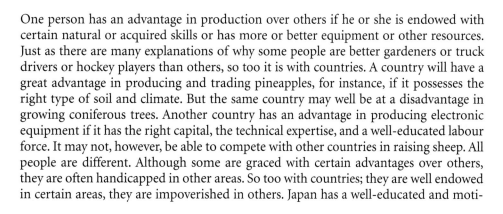

One person has an advantage in production over others if he or she is endowed with certain natural or acquired skills or has more or better equipment or other resources. Just as there are many explanations of why some people are better gardeners or truck drivers or hockey players than others, so too it is with countries. A country will have a great advantage in producing and trading pineapples, for instance, if it possesses the right type of soil and climate. But the same country may well be at a disadvantage in growing coniferous trees. Another country has an advantage in producing electronic equipment if it has the right capital, the technical expertise, and a well-educated labour force. It may not, however, be able to compete with other countries in raising sheep. All people are different. Although some are graced with certain advantages over others, they are often handicapped in other areas. So too with countries; they are well endowed in certain areas, they are impoverished in others. Japan has a well-educated and motivated work force, possesses great technical expertise, and is highly capitalized, yet it is very poorly provided with arable land and possesses very few mineral resources.

It is often suggested that the prime reason a country trades is in order to buy resources that it does not naturally possess. Although there is some truth in this, it often obscures the main motivation. Canada, for instance, is not endowed with a warm and sunny climate throughout the year and is unable to produce bananas commercially. However, through the use of geodesic domes with artificial light and heating, it could grow its own bananas, but the cost would be enormous. The reason it does not grow bananas is not because it cannot, but because it is cheaper to buy them from countries that possess the necessary resources at lower cost. Most countries, then, can often overcome a resource deficiency by using different methods or other resources, but it would not make sense if this production method results in more expensive products than those obtainable from abroad.

Theory of Absolute Advantage

A country will tend to gravitate to producing in those areas where, because of its own factor endowments, it possesses a cost advantage over other producing countries: Canada produces wheat, lumber and minerals; Colombia produces coffee; Malaysia produces rubber; Japan produces electronic equipment, and so on. This is no more or less than what Adam Smith proposed when he put forward his *theory of absolute advantage*. Nations, like firms and individuals, should specialize in producing goods and services for which they have an advantage, and they should trade with other countries for goods and services in which they do not enjoy an advantage. Let us work through a simple example of this theory. We will concentrate on just two countries and suppose that they produce just two products. We will assume that the average cost of producing each product remains constant. In addition, to begin with, we will further assume that each country is self-sufficient and that no trade is taking place. **Table 13.1** shows the productivity per worker (average product) of producing wheat and beans in Canada and Mexico.

TABLE 13.1 Output per Worker by Country and Industry

	NUMBER OF BUSHELS PER DAY	
	Wheat	**Beans**
Canada	3	2
Mexico	1	4

We can see at a glance in Table 13.1 that Canada is more productive than Mexico at producing wheat, whereas Mexico is more productive than Canada at producing beans. Let us examine the possibility of gains if both countries were to specialize— Canada in wheat and Mexico in beans. Since the table shows output per worker, let's move a single worker in Canada out of the bean industry and over to the wheat industry. In Mexico, the transfer is in the opposite direction: one worker goes from the wheat industry to the bean industry. Table 13.1 has already shown us what each country will gain and what it will lose. Canada would gain an additional 3 bushels of wheat, since that is the average productivity in that industry, but lose 2 bushels of beans. In Mexico, the gain would be 4 bushels of beans at a loss of 1 bushel of wheat. (To keep things simple here, we are assuming that the average and marginal products are equal; that is, each worker in Canada, for instance, produces three bushels of wheat regardless of the number of workers employed.) The movement of workers is summarized in **Table 13.2**.

TABLE 13.2 Gain/Loss of Output

	NUMBER OF BUSHELS PER DAY	
	Wheat	**Beans**
Canada	+3	−2
Mexico	−1	+4
Total	+2	+2

It is possible, then, with just the transfer of one worker in each country, for there to be a net increase in the production of both products. These are what are known as the *gains from trade*. Strictly speaking, they are the gains from specialization. It would seem to be the case from this example that if more workers were to shift industries in this manner, then the gain would be commensurately higher. Presumably, the greater the specialization, the bigger the gains. Note that if a country is not to end up consuming just a single product, it will be forced to trade.

SELF-TEST

1. Suppose that the productivity per worker in the beer and wine industries of Freedonia and Libraland are as follows:

	Output in Hundreds of Litres	
	Beer	**Wine**
Freedonia	4	1
Libraland	3	4

A) Which country should specialize in which product?
B) Suppose that a single worker in each country is transferred from the less- to the more-productive industry. What will the total gains from specialization be?

Theory of Comparative Advantage

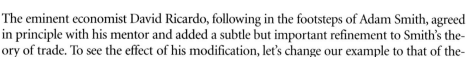

The eminent economist David Ricardo, following in the footsteps of Adam Smith, agreed in principle with his mentor and added a subtle but important refinement to Smith's theory of trade. To see the effect of his modification, let's change our example to that of theoretical trade between the United States and the Philippines, but keep the same two products, wheat and beans. The output per worker in each country is shown in **Table 13.3**.

TABLE 13.3 Output per Worker by Country and Industry

	NUMBER OF BUSHELS PER DAY	
	Wheat	**Beans**
United States	6	4
Philippines	1	2

If we compare the United States' productivity in wheat, you can see from the table that it is six times as great as that of the Philippines; similarly, the United States is twice as productive as the Philippines in producing beans. If we were to follow Smith's dictum, then presumably the United States should produce both products itself. After all, how can it possibly be of any advantage to that country to trade with the Philippines, since it could produce both products cheaper? The heart of Ricardo's idea is that it is not *absolute* but **comparative advantage** that provides the mutual gains from trade. Let us see exactly what this means, through an example.

Suppose you happened to be the absolutely best lawyer in town. Not only that, but you are also its greatest secretary. Given this, why would you bother to hire a secretary to do your clerical work, since you are faster and, by all measurement, more efficient than anyone you could possibly hire? The answer is that you would still hire a secretary because you couldn't afford not to. The reason for this is that you are so productive. Your high productivity is both a blessing and a curse. It is a blessing because you earn a great deal as a lawyer; it is a curse because you sacrifice a great deal in not being a secretary. In other words, your opportunity cost of being a lawyer is the lost salary of not being a secretary. Your opportunity cost of being a secretary is your lost earnings as a lawyer. But because you can earn *comparatively* more as a lawyer than as a secretary, you would be advised to concentrate on that career and hire someone (admittedly less productive than yourself) to act as your secretary.

What Ricardo did with his idea of comparative advantage was, in a sense, to direct attention away from making comparisons between countries and instead focus attention on the comparison between products. In Table 13.3, for instance, what is the cost for the United States of producing wheat? One way to answer this would be to express it in dollars and cents. Knowing that the value of money varies over time and that it is often misleading to translate one currency into another, Ricardo was at pains to express costs in more fundamental terms. One way of doing this would be to express costs in terms of the number of hours it takes to produce something. For instance, if in our example the average worker in the United States can produce 4 bushels of beans in an average 8-hour day, then the cost of 1 bushel of beans would be 8/4, or 2 hours. In contrast, the cost of one bushel of beans in the Philippines would be 8/2, or 4 hours. So, it is twice as expensive in the Philippines. However, a better and more illuminating way of measuring costs is in terms of *opportunity costs*. This is the method Ricardo chose.

You will remember that the opportunity cost of producing one thing can be measured in terms of another thing that has to be sacrificed in order to get it. As far as the United States and the Philippines are concerned, the cost of producing more wheat is the sacrifice of beans, and the cost of increased bean production is the loss of wheat. Let us work out these costs for each country. The cost of employing a worker in the wheat industry is what that worker could have produced in the bean industry, assuming that the country is fully employed. In other words, for every 6 bushels of wheat that an American worker produces, the country sacrifices 4 bushels of beans. In per unit terms in the U.S.:

since 6 bushels of wheat costs 4 bushels of beans,
then, 1 bushel of wheat costs 4/6 = 0.67 bushels of beans,
and since 4 bushels of beans costs 6 bushels of wheat,
then, 1 bushel of beans costs 6/4 = 1.5 bushels of wheat.

Similarly, in the Philippines: the cost of 1 wheat is 2 beans and the cost of 1 bean equals 1/2 wheat. Let us summarize these figures in **Table 13.4.**

TABLE 13.4 Opportunity Costs of Production

	COST OF PRODUCING ONE UNIT	
	Wheat	**Beans**
United States	0.67 beans	1.5 wheat
Philippines	2 beans	0.5 wheat

Hopefully, you can now understand the significance of comparative costs. Whether you measure the costs in absolute terms using hours or dollars, beans are cheap to produce in the United States. But in comparative terms they are very *expensive*. Why is that? Because to produce beans, the United States has to make a big sacrifice in the product in which it is even more productive: wheat. Similarly, although beans in absolute terms are very expensive in the Philippines, in comparative terms they are cheap, since to produce them the Philippines doesn't have to make much sacrifice in wheat production because productivity in the wheat industry is so low.

In this example then, as Table 13.4 suggests, the United States should specialize in producing the product in which it has the comparative advantage, wheat; and the Philippines should specialize in beans, where it has the comparative advantage.

Let us extract some further insights by showing the production possibilities of the two countries on the assumption that the size of the labour force in the United States is 100 million, that of the Philippines is 80 million, and that unit costs are constant. Their respective production possibilities are shown in **Table 13.5.** The 600 wheat, under option A in the U.S., is the maximum output of wheat if all of the 100 (million) workers were producing 6 wheat each. Similarly, if the 100 million U.S. workers produced only beans, and no wheat, then they would produce 400 beans (100 million times 4 beans each) as seen under option E. The figures for B, C, and D are derived by calculating the output if 75, 50, and 25 million workers are employed in wheat production while 25, 50, and 75 million workers are, correspondingly, employed in bean production. The figures for the Philippines are similarly obtained, this time changing the number of workers by 20 million for each new option.

TABLE 13.5 Production Possibilities

UNITED STATES: OUTPUT (millions of bushels per day)					
	A	**B**	**C**	**D**	**E**
Wheat	600	450	300	150	0
Beans	0	100	200	300	400

PHILIPPINES: OUTPUT (millions of bushels per day)					
	A	**B**	**C**	**D**	**E**
Wheat	80	60	40	20	0
Beans	0	40	80	120	160

Suppose that initially the countries are self-sufficient and that both are producing combinations B. Before specialization and trade, therefore, their joint totals are as shown in **Table 13.6.**

TABLE 13.6 Output of Both Countries before Specialization and Trade

| | TOTAL OUTPUT (millions of bushels per day) | |
	Wheat	Beans
United States	450	100
Philippines	60	40
Total	510	140

If the two countries now specialize, the U.S. producing wheat and the Philippines producing beans, their output levels would be as shown in **Table 13.7.**

TABLE 13.7 Output of Both Countries after Specialization and Trade

| | TOTAL OUTPUT (millions of bushels per day) | |
	Wheat	Beans
United States	600	0
Philippines	0	160
Total	600	160

You can see by comparing the before and after specialization positions of the two countries that production of both products is now higher. **Table 13.8** outlines the gains from trade.

TABLE 13.8 Gains from Specialization and Trade

| | TOTAL OUTPUT (millions of bushels per day) | |
	Wheat	Beans
	+90	+20

Before we try to figure out which country will get what portion of this increased production, let us look at the production possibilities graphically. **Figure 13.1** shows the production possibilities of each country on the same graph.

As we saw in Chapter 1, the slope of the production curve measures the cost of production. In Figure 13.1 this is the cost of beans measured in wheat. The slope of the U.S. production possibilities curve is 3/2, reflecting the fact that beans are relatively expensive at 1.5 wheat per unit of beans. The Philippines' production possibilities curve, in contrast, is much flatter. Its slope is 1/2, which means, as we have seen, that the cost of beans is only 0.5 wheat per unit of beans.

FIGURE 13.1 U.S. and Philippines' Production Possibilities Curves

The slope of the production possibilities curve is determined by the average cost of wheat production in terms of beans. In this figure, the slope of the U.S. production possibilities curve is equal to 3/2 (wheat production drops by 3 for every increase of 2 beans); that is, the cost of 1 bean in the U.S. is $1\frac{1}{2}$ wheat. In contrast, the cost of beans in the Philippines is cheap because it sacrifices only $\frac{1}{2}$ wheat for each 1 bean produced; that is, the slope of the Philippines' production possibilities curve is $\frac{1}{2}$.

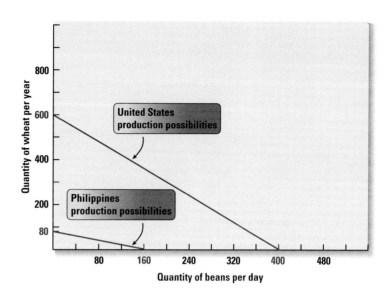

SELF-TEST

2. Suppose that the labour force in Freedonia is 10 million, of whom 6 million are producing apples, one of the two crops it produces; the other is pears. In contrast, Libraland's labour force is 16 million, half of whom are producing apples, and the rest, pears. The labour productivity in the two countries is as follows:

	Output per Worker (bushels per day)	
	Apples	**Pears**
Freedonia	5	2
Libraland	1	3

Assuming constant costs, draw the production possibilities curves of the two countries on the same graph. Mark on it the present production combinations and the quantities that each would produce, were they to specialize according to their absolute advantages.

Thus, we can conclude that

> **As long as there are differences in comparative costs between countries, regardless of the differences in absolute costs, there is a basis for mutually beneficial trade.**

What these examples show is that it is possible for both countries to gain from trade, but the remaining questions are: Will they? How will the increased production be shared? Will it be shared equally, or will one country receive more than the other? Discussion of the terms of trade will help answer these questions.

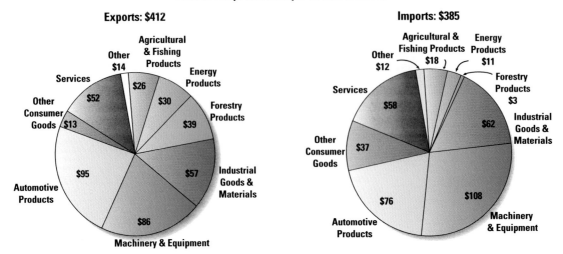

Canada's Exports and Imports, 1999 (billions)

Exports: $412

Imports: $385

Source: Compiled from Statistics Canada, CANSIM Matrix 3651

Terms of Trade

terms of trade: the average price of a country's exports compared with the price of its imports.

The **terms of trade** refers to the price at which a country sells its exports compared with the price at which it buys its imports. StatsCan regularly measures Canada's terms of trade using the following formula:

$$\frac{\text{Average price of exports}}{\text{Average price of imports}} \times 100$$

If the worldwide demand for Canadian softwood lumber were to increase, for example, it would increase the average price of Canadian exports, with the result that the terms of trade would be said to have moved in Canada's favour. The result would be the same if Canadian prices remain the same but the price of imports drops. In either case, the sale of our exports would enable us to purchase more imports. On the other hand, the terms of trade would shift against Canada if Canadian export prices dropped and/or the price of imported goods rose.

In our previous United States–Philippines example, the simple answer as to which country gains most from trade is that it all depends upon the terms of trade. But let us look at what would be acceptable prices from the two countries' point of view. Remember that the United States is the wheat producer and exporter. A glance back at Table 13.4 shows that: *in the U.S. 1 bushel of wheat costs 0.67 bushels of beans.* Given this we can ask: what price would it be willing to sell its wheat for? Presumably for as high a price as it can get, but certainly not for less than 0.67 beans. What about the

Philippines: how much would it be willing to pay for wheat? Remember, Table 13.4 tells us that: *in the Philippines 1 bushel of wheat costs 2 bushels of beans.* Therefore, we can conclude that the Philippines would certainly not pay any higher than this price and would be happy to buy it for less. You can see that as long as the price is above the U.S. minimum and below the Philippines' maximum, both countries would be willing to trade. In other words, trade is possible if the price of one unit of wheat is anywhere between 0.67 and 2 units of beans. We could have just as easily expressed things in terms of beans, and a glance back at Table 13.4 shows that feasible terms of trade would be anywhere between 0.5 wheat to 1.5 wheat for 1 bushel of beans. Where the actual terms of trade end up will depend on the strength of demand in the two countries for these products.

Let us choose one particular rate among the many possible terms of trade and work out the consequences. Suppose, for instance, that the terms end up at: *1 bushel of wheat = 1 bushel of beans.* Let us now assume that the Philippines is quite happy consuming the 40 million bushels of beans that it was producing before it decided to specialize, as shown in Table 13.5. However, because of specialization it is now producing beans only and will have therefore 160 − 40 = 120 million bushels of beans available for export, which it sells to the United States at a rate of 1 bean for 1 wheat. It will receive back 120 million bushels of wheat and will finish up with 40 million bushels of beans and 120 million bushels of wheat. Because of trade, it will have gained an additional 60 million bushels of wheat, compared with its self-sufficient totals shown in combination B of Table 13.5. The United States will also gain. It was the sole producer of wheat, and of the total of 600 million bushels produced, it has sold 120 million bushels to the Philippines in exchange for 120 million bushels of beans. It will end up with 480 million bushels of wheat and 120 million bushels of beans, which is 30 million bushels of wheat and 20 million bushels of beans more than when it was producing both products as shown in combination B. All the numbers above can be a bit overwhelming, so let's summarize what we have just done in the graphic below. Recall that we are assuming that the Philippines consumes the same 40 million bushels of beans before and after trade.

Terms of Trade

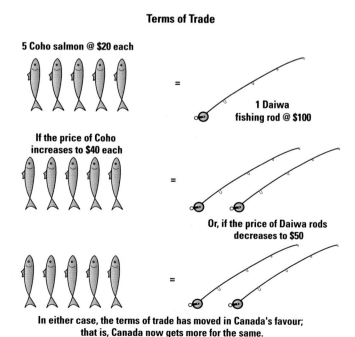

In either case, the terms of trade has moved in Canada's favour; that is, Canada now gets more for the same.

PHILIPPINES

		Before Trade	After Trade
	Beans produced	40	160
	Beans exported	0	−120
Beans consumed		**40**	**40**
	Wheat produced	60	0
	Wheat imported	0	+120
Wheat consumed		**60**	**120**

Gain = 60 Wheat

UNITED STATES

		Before Trade	After Trade
	Beans produced	100	0
	Beans imported	0	+120
Beans consumed		**100**	**120**
	Wheat produced	450	600
	Wheat exported	0	−120
Wheat consumed		**450**	**480**

Gain = 20 Beans and 30 Wheat

SELF-TEST

3. Suppose that the average productivity in Freedonia and Libraland is as follows:

Assuming the two countries wish to trade, would terms of trade of 1 pear = 2.5 apples be feasible? What about 1 pear = 1 apple? 1 pear = 1.75 apples?

	Output per Worker (bushels per day)	
	Apples	Pears
Freedonia	6	3
Libraland	3	2

Terms of Trade and Gains from Trade, Graphically

Let us now look at each country's trading picture separately. **Figure 13.2** shows the production possibilities curve for the United States. Before it decided to trade, this was also its consumption possibilities curve, since it could obviously not consume more than it produced. The slope of the curve is 1.5, which is the cost of 1 bean (that is, it equals 1.5 wheat). The curve to the right is its trading possibilities curve, which shows how much the United States could obtain through a combination of specializing its production and trading. Note that the slope of the trading possibilities curve is equal to 1. This is the terms of trade of 1 wheat for 1 bean, which the United States can now obtain from the Philippines. You can see from this graph that the United States, at one extreme, could produce the same maximum quantity of 600 million bushels of wheat as before and keep all of it. However, before trade, the maximum amount of beans available was 400. Now, if it wished, the United States could produce 600 million bushels of wheat and trade *all* of it, and receive in exchange 600 million bushels of beans. More likely, of course, it will opt to have a combination of both products, such as 480 million bushels of wheat and 120 million bushels of beans as in our numerical example above.

FIGURE 13.2 U.S. Production and Trading Possibilities Curves

The slope of the production possibilities curve shows the cost of producing beans in the United States and is equal to 1.5 wheat per bean. The slope of the trading possibilities curve shows the cost of buying beans internationally; that is, it is the terms of trade and equals 1 wheat per bean. The previous maximum obtainable quantity of beans was 400 million bushels, when the United States was self-sufficient. Its new maximum, as a result of trading, is now 600 million bushels because it could produce, if it wished, a maximum amount of 600 million bushels of wheat and trade this output for 600 million bushels of beans.

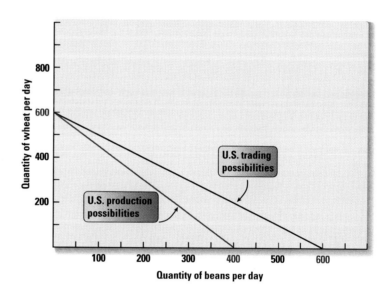

Figure 13.3 shows the position from the Philippines' point of view. The inside curve is its production (and therefore its consumption) possibilities curve, representing the maximum of both products that can be produced when the country is self-sufficient. The slope of the curve represents the cost of 1 bushel of beans and is equal to 0.5 bushels of wheat. The outer curve is the trading possibilities curve based on the terms of trade: 1 bean = 1 wheat. You can see that trading allows the Philippines also to enjoy increased consumption. After specialization, the maximum amount of beans remains unchanged at 160 million bushels. However, the maximum amount of wheat has increased from 80 (if produced in the Philippines) to 160 (by trading away all its 160 million bushels of beans for this quantity of wheat).

FIGURE 13.3 Philippines' Production and Trading Possibilities Curves

The Philippines specializes in the production of beans, and its trading possibilities curve lies to the right of the production possibilities curve. In other words, irrespective of whether it trades or not, the cost of beans remains the same; the cost of wheat, however, is now lower as a result of trade, since it can now obtain wheat at a cost of 1 bean per 1 wheat, whereas producing its own wheat costs 2 beans per 1 wheat.

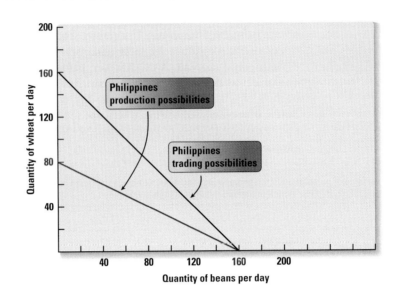

SELF-TEST

4. From the data contained in Figure 13.2 and Table 13.5, how many beans can the United States obtain if it is self-sufficient and is producing 450 million bushels of wheat? If, instead, it specializes in wheat production and can trade at terms of 1 wheat = 1 bean, how many beans could it have to accompany its 450 million bushels of wheat? What if the terms were 1 wheat = 2 beans?

The Benefits of Free Trade and Some Important Qualifications

Ricardo's theory of comparative advantage, which we have been looking at, is very important because it clearly highlights the major benefits of trade. Free and unrestricted trade allows nations and individuals the opportunity to sell in world markets, and this will, as a result, enable them to specialize in the products in which they enjoy an advantage over others. The result will be that products will be produced and sold at a *lower price* and in higher volumes, which translates into *higher incomes* and standards of living for all. In addition, the *variety of products* available when the world becomes one big market would presumably increase. A final benefit of free trade is the fact that it is more difficult to be a world monopolist than it is to be a monopolist in the home market. In other words, it is often suggested that free trade *increases competition*. In summary, free trade has the following advantages:

- lower prices
- higher incomes
- a greater variety of products
- increased competition

Canada's minister for international trade, Art Eggleton, shakes hands with Israel's minister of industry and trade, Natan Sharansky, after the signing of the Canada–Israel Free Trade Agreement in 1996.

These are indeed powerful arguments in favour of free trade, but before we leave the topic let us look at some of the qualifications that need to be introduced. First, free trade is never free, because there will always be transport, insurance, and other freight charges, which must be added to the cost of production and which will usually reduce the trading advantage of foreign sellers. (However, in a country as extensive as Canada, it is often cheaper to transport products to American states bordering the country than it is to transport them from one end of the country to the other.) In addition, selling in a foreign country is always going to be more difficult (and usually, therefore, more expensive) than selling in the domestic market because of the differences in language, culture, taxation, regulations, and so on. Besides cost differences, the analysis we have presented so far has assumed constant costs. This leads to the result in our examples that countries should specialize in, perhaps, a single product and produce that product to a maximum. However, as we learned in Chapter 1, if any country tries to concentrate on a single product, its production is subject to the law of increasing costs. This means that one country only enjoys a cost advantage over others *up to a point*. As it tries to push production levels higher, its cost will start to increase so that it no longer enjoys a competitive advantage. This is the reason why few countries specialize entirely and why many countries both produce *and* import the same product. The presence of increasing costs will also lessen the advantages that one country enjoys over another in trade.

Even allowing for these cautions, it is still true that there are a number of benefits to be obtained from trade. This leads us to ask: why then does free trade tend to be the exception rather than the rule throughout history? Why does the question of free trade still divide countries and lead to such acrimonious debate? To understand part of the reason, let us look at the consequences of trying to restrict trade.

Trade Organizations and Treaties of the World

Several international organizations exist today. The more important ones include the following.

WTO

The World Trade Organization (WTO) was established on January 1, 1995, and consists of more than 100 nations. It was formerly known as GATT (General Agreement on Tariffs and Trade) and is devoted to liberalizing world trade by reducing tariffs and quotas between nations. WTO regularly issues publications that document every aspect of its activities. Its secretariat is in Geneva.

OECD

The Organization for Economic and Cooperative Development (OECD) grew out of the Marshall Plan, which was designed to aid war-ravaged Europe at the end of World War II. This Paris-based intergovernmental organization's main purpose is to provide its 29 members with a forum in which governments can compare their experiences, discuss the problems they share, and seek solutions that can then be applied in their own national contexts. Each member is committed to the principles of the market economy and pluralistic democracy.

NAFTA

The North American Free Trade Agreement (NAFTA) is an agreement between Canada, the United States, and Mexico, implemented in 1989, whereby barriers to trade between the countries would be phased out over a 10-year period. In addition, it promotes fair competition and increased investment and provides protection of intellectual property rights. An important aspect of the treaty is a final and binding dispute-resolution mechanism that can be triggered by any one of the parties.

EU

The European Union (EU) currently has 15 member countries and grew out of the former European Economic Community,

which was established in 1957. By 1993 it had evolved into a true common market, within which there is free movement of goods and service, capital, and labour. It is moving toward greater monetary union with the establishment of the euro currency in 1999 and, some believe, eventual political union.

G8

This group of eight nations consists of Canada, the United States, Japan, the United Kingdom, France, Germany, Italy, and, recently, Russia. It represents (along with China and Spain) the ten largest economies in the world. The heads of state of these eight countries hold summits in which the world's pressing economic, political, and social issues are discussed. Often a summit meeting is followed by the release of a position paper on policy objectives that each has agreed to pursue.

APEC

The Asia-Pacific Economic Cooperation (APEC) was formed in 1989 and includes Canada among its 18 members. Its goal is to advance Asia-Pacific economic dynamism and sense of community by encouraging the region's economic growth and development; encouraging the flow of goods and services, capital, and technology; and encouraging the reduction of barriers to trade in goods and services in a manner consistent with WTO principles.

MAI

The Multilateral Agreement on Investment (MAI) was a failed attempt by the OECD to negotiate a new agreement that would do for investment what had already been achieved for trade in goods and services: create a set of global rules that would liberalize international investment, ensure fairness, and replace a patchwork of over 1600 bilateral investment agreements. Many believe that the WTO will make a similar effort in the near future.

Trade Restrictions

Let us set up a scenario in which, initially, we have two self-sufficient countries, France and Germany, each producing wine. The demand and supply conditions in the two countries are very different, of course, with both the demand and supply being greater in France than in Germany, as is shown in **Table 13.9**.

TABLE 13.9 The Market for Wine in France and Germany (millions of litres per month)

	FRANCE			GERMANY	
Price ($ per litre)	Demand	Supply	Price ($ per litre)	Demand	Supply
3	24	13	3	12	2
4	19	14	4	11	3
5	**15**	**15**	5	10	4
6	12	16	6	9	5
7	10	17	7	8	6
8	9	18	**8**	**7**	**7**

The equilibrium price in France is $5 per litre and the equilibrium quantity is 15. In Germany, the equilibrium price and quantities are $8 and 7 respectively. These are shown in **Figure 13.4**.

FIGURE 13.4 Demand and Supply of Wine in France and Germany

In France, the demand and supply of wine are both higher than in Germany. The consequence is a greater quantity of wine traded in France: 15 million litres, compared with 7 million in Germany. The price of wine, however, is lower in France than in Germany.

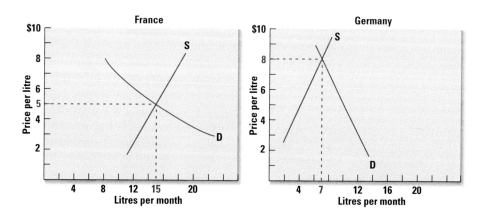

Now suppose that the two countries decide to engage in free trade. To keep things simple, let's assume there are no transport costs. If free trade is now introduced, what will be the price of wine in the two countries? Well, we know that at $5 per litre, the French winemakers were making a profit, so they should have no difficulty in competing with the German producers and presumably could easily undercut the German price of $8. Since we've assumed there are no transport costs, the price in the two countries should be the same. To find this price, all we need to do is look at the combined market of France and Germany. In other words, we need simply to add the demands and supplies of the two countries, as shown in **Table 13.10**.

TABLE 13.10 Deriving the Total Market Demand and Supply of Wine for France and Germany (in millions of litres per month)

	FRANCE		GERMANY		TOTAL MARKET	
Price ($ per litre)	Demand	Supply	Demand	Supply	Demand	Supply
3	24	13	12	2	36	15
4	19	14	11	3	30	17
5	15	15	10	4	25	19
6	12	16	9	5	**21**	**21**
7	10	17	8	6	18	23
8	9	18	7	7	16	25

The total market demand is obtained by adding together the French demand and the German demand at each price. For instance, at $3 per litre, the quantity demanded in France is 24 and in Germany it is 12, giving a total for the two countries of 36. Similarly, the quantity supplied at $3 is 13 in France and 2 in Germany, giving a total market supply of 15. This is done for all prices. The new market price (let's call it the world price) then, will be $6 per litre, and at that price a total of 21 million litres will be produced and sold.

Now let us look at the effect in each market. French winemakers are delighted at the situation because they are getting a higher price now that free trade has opened up a new market in Germany and their volume of business is higher. French winemakers are now producing 16 million litres, up from the 15 million litres produced before trade. Note also that in France the quantities produced (16) exceeds the demand from French consumers (12). What happens to the surplus of 4 million litres? The answer is that it is being exported to Germany. And what is the situation in that country? Well certainly, German consumers are delighted, because the new world price of $6 is lower than the previous domestic price of $8. But we can imagine that the German winemakers are far from happy. The new lower world price has caused a number of producers to cut back production, and presumably some producers are forced out of

Bottled wine ageing in storage.

business. At the world price of $6, German producers are only producing 5 million litres, below the German demand of 9 million litres. How is this shortage going to be made up? Answer: from the import of French wine. This simply means that the French export of 4 million litres equals the German import of 4 million litres. These points are illustrated in **Figure 13.5**.

FIGURE 13.5 Demand and Supply of Wine in France and Germany with Free Trade

The new world price of wine is above the previous French price but below the previous German price. The result is a surplus of wine in France of 4 million litres but a shortage in Germany of 4 million litres.

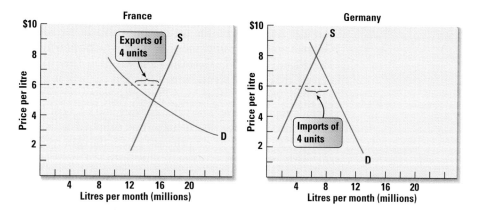

SELF-TEST

5. In Table 13.10, if the demand for wine in Germany increased by 5 (million litres) at every price, how much wine would now be produced in Germany, and how much would be imported from France?

So who are the losers and who are the gainers as a result of markets being opened up? The answer in our example is that both German wine consumers and French wine producers gain and French wine consumers and German wine producers lose. Free trade has cost French consumers $1 a litre, and it has cost German winemakers $2 per litre. Previously these winemakers were selling 7 million litres at $8 per litre, for a total revenue of $56 million. Now, they are selling only 5 million litres for $6 per litre, for a total revenue of $30 million. In total, then, these producers, of whom there may be fewer than 100, have collectively lost $26 million in revenue. It is easy to see why these producers may not be in favour of free trade! In fact, it would pay them to lobby their own parliament and to launch publicity campaigns in an attempt to keep out "cheap" French wines. As long as their efforts do not cost more than $26 million, they will be ahead of the game.

It is easy to see why powerful lobby and special interest groups have been very vocal throughout history in trying to persuade parliament and the public that it is in the country's interest to ban or curtail foreign imports. This is an activity that economists call *rent seeking*. Such **protectionism** can take many forms, which we need to look at.

protectionism: the economic policy of protecting domestic producers by restricting the importation of foreign products.

Imposition of Quotas

quota: a limit imposed on the production or sale of a product.

The most obvious restriction of imports is to ban them either entirely or partially, and this is exactly what is meant by a **quota**. A quota can take a variety of forms, ranging from a total restriction to a maximum limit being placed on each individual foreign exporter, or perhaps the requirement that each foreign exporter reduces its exports by a percentage of the previous year's sales. The essence of a quota is to reduce or restrict the importation of certain products. And what will be the effect of such restriction? Suppose in our wine example that German winemakers were successful in their efforts to keep out French wines, and the German government imposed a total ban on French wines. At the current price of $6 per litre, there will be an immediate shortage in Germany. The result of the shortage is to push up the price of wine. It will continue to rise, encouraging increased German production until the price returns to the pre–free-trade price of $8. In France, the immediate effect of the German quota will be to cause a surplus of French wine, which will depress the price of French wine until it too is back at the pre-trade price of $5 per litre.

Let's move on from our France/Germany example and look at trade from the Canadian perspective. The price of wine and of most products traded internationally is determined by the world's demand and supply. That is to say, for any one small country, such as Canada, the world price is a given; the country's action will have little impact on the world price. This situation is illustrated in **Figure 13.6**.

FIGURE 13.6 The Effects of a Quota

Initially the Canadian demand and supply is D_d and S_d and the world price is P_w. The quantity demanded in Canada at the world price P_w, equals c, of which Canadian producers would produce a and foreign producers would export ac to Canada. A quota of ab would raise the price to P_q. As a result, domestic production will increase, and imports would drop to the amount of the quota.

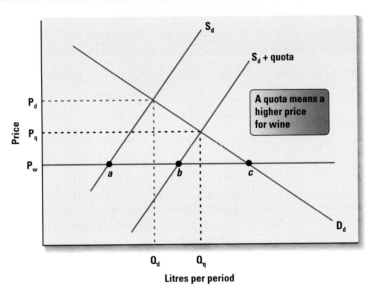

Figure 13.6 shows the domestic demand (D_d) and supply (S_d) of wine in Canada. P_d is the domestic price and Q_d is domestic production. Suppose that the world price is P_w and that Canada now freely allows imports into the country. At the world price of P_w, the amount produced by domestic Canadian producers is a and the amount demanded is c. Since Canadian consumers want to purchase more than Canadian producers are willing to produce, the difference of ac represents the amount of imports. Now suppose that the Canadian government yields to pressure from Canadian wine producers and imposes a quota of ab on imported wine. In effect, the total supply is equal to the domestic supply plus the amount of the quota. This is represented by the

new supply curve, S_d *plus quota*. Since the total available has now been reduced, the price will increase to P_q and the quantity will fall to Q_q.

From this, it can be seen that the losers will be Canadian consumers (who are paying a higher price and are having less quantity and variety of wines) and foreign winemakers whose exports are being restricted. The winners will be Canadian winemakers, who are producing more wine and receiving a higher price.

The Imposition of a Tariff

tariff: a tax (or duty) levied on imports.

A second way of restricting imports is by the use of a **tariff**, which is a tax on imports. It is a more frequently chosen method than quotas, because governments can derive considerable revenue from tariffs. The effects of a tariff are much the same as those of a quota because, in both cases, the price of the product will increase. With a quota, however, the domestic producers get the whole benefit of the higher price, whereas with a tariff, the benefit is shared between the domestic producers and the government. An additional benefit of a tariff over a quota is that a quota tends to treat foreign producers indiscriminately because each and every producer is treated in the same way, whereas with a tariff only the more efficient producers will continue to export, since only they will be able to continue to make a profit. A tariff discriminates against the less efficient producers, and therefore, from an efficiency point of view, it is superior to a quota. These points are illustrated in **Figure 13.7**.

In Figure 13.7, suppose again that we are describing the Canadian wine market. At the world price of P_w, Canadian producers are supplying a and Canadian consumers are buying b. The difference ab is the amount of imported wine. Suppose that the Canadian government imposes a tariff of t per unit. The price in Canada will rise to P_t. Note that at the higher price, Canadian producers, who will receive the whole price P_t, will increase production to Q_f. Canadian consumers will reduce consumption to Q_g. In addition, imports will fall to $Q_g - Q_f$. The result is very similar to what we saw in the analysis of quotas. Again, it is Canadian consumers and foreign producers who lose out, and Canadian producers who gain.

FIGURE 13.7 The Effects of the Imposition of a Tariff

The imposition of a tariff, *t*, will increase the price of wine in Canada to P_t from P_w. As a result, Canadian production will increase from Q_e to Q_f and imports will drop to $Q_g - Q_f$. The tax revenue to the government is equal to *t* times the quantity of imports, $Q_g - Q_f$, the shaded area.

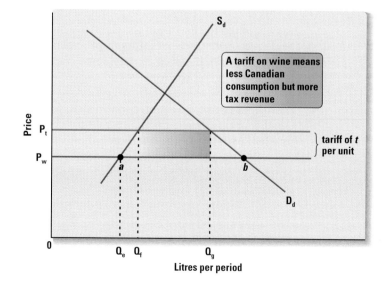

The other gainer in this scenario will be the Canadian government, which will receive tax revenue equal to the shaded rectangle in **Figure 13.7**.

Other Trade Restrictions

exchange controls: restrictions imposed by a government limiting the amount of foreign currencies that can be obtained.

Besides the two popular protectionist measures of tariffs and quotas, a number of other available methods deserve mention. **Exchange controls** are similar to quotas, but instead of a restriction being placed on the importation of a good, the restriction is placed on the availability of foreign currencies (that is, foreign exchange). The effect is the same because, since foreigners wish to be paid in their own currencies, if an importer is unable to get his hands on the appropriate currency, he will not be able to buy the foreign goods. The controls might be across-the-board restrictions or restrictions on particular currencies or on particular products or industries. The effect in all cases will be to increase the domestic price of the products affected, which will be to the benefit of the domestic producer at the expense of the domestic consumer. Another more subtle but often equally effective way of cutting imports is by way of *restrictions and regulations*. A government might make trade so difficult or time-consuming for the importer that the amount of trade is significantly reduced. For instance, the customs department of a particular country might tie the importer up with red tape by requiring that all imports must be accompanied by 10 different forms (all in triplicate) obtainable from 10 different government departments. Or perhaps the product must comply to certain very unrealistic standards of safety, or packaging, or hygiene standards that are not required for domestically produced items.

voluntary export restriction (VER): an agreement by an exporting country to restrict the amount of its exports to another country.

A more recent type of trade restriction is known as **voluntary export restrictions (VERs)**. Rather than imposing, say, tariffs and quotas, the importing country requests that the exporting country itself voluntarily restrict the amount being exported. In this way, the exporting country is given the power to administer the quotas, which will also prevent the importing country from receiving tariff revenue on the imports. Since the restrictions are voluntary, the exporting country does not have to comply. However, since the importing country has other weapons at its disposal, then...

Free Trade and Protectionism

In this chapter we have tried to avoid making an outright declaration in favour of free trade, though the flavour of the chapter would suggest that there are many benefits to be derived from trade, and probably the majority of economists feel that the freer the trade, the better. But even a notable free-trader like the astute Adam Smith recognized that there *may be* occasions when a degree of protectionism in the way of tariffs and quotas might be called for. He suggested, for instance, that a country's strategic industries should be offered protection so that, for instance, the country does not become dependent on foreign manufacturers for the production of military hardware. The problem with this *strategic industry argument*, however, is that most industries would claim that they are of "strategic importance" to a nation and therefore deserve similar protection from foreign competition. Also, the idea of hindering the production of military goods has appeal to many.

In addition, Smith suggests that in order for there to be a level playing field for both domestic and foreign producers, if the produce of domestic industry is being taxed, then foreign imports should be taxed by a similar amount. He also felt that if a foreign country is placing tariffs and quotas on your country's exports, then you should do likewise to its exports, but not, it should be noted, just for retaliation, but to help the foreign country to recognize the folly of its actions and to persuade it to restore free trade. Finally, Smith was prescient enough to realize that if a country has had a long history of protectionism, then the sudden arrival of free trade is likely to cause dramatic shifts of labour and capital away from industries that can no longer compete to those industries that find themselves growing. This dislocation may cause a great deal of suffering in the short term, so Smith felt that a wise government would introduce free trade gradually and would try to mitigate the suffering. This caveat is of particular importance in terms of the North American Free Trade Agreement discussions. Although many feel that there will be great long-term benefits for all the participating countries, it is equally certain that in the short term a great deal of suffering will be experienced by those industries, firms, and individuals who, through no fault of their own, find themselves unable to compete. Some type of government assistance may be needed to help in the adjustment process.

In addition, it ought to be mentioned that some economists feel that certain "infant" industries should be given a helping hand by the government until they are sufficiently mature to compete with foreign competition. This *infant industry* argument is strongest when the government feels that undue reliance on the exportation of a few staple products would leave the country in a vulnerable position if a future change in demand or technology were to occur. In order to diversify the economy and develop other industries, many feel that these "infants" should be sheltered from competition. However, the trouble is, these infant industries often never grow up! In addition, even if there are persuasive arguments in favour of protecting or assisting certain industries, it may be better for the government to give this aid in the form of direct subsidies rather than by interfering with normal trading patterns through the imposition of tariffs and quotas.

A final argument against free trade is the *cultural identity* argument. This one is difficult to dismiss solely on economic grounds. Many commentators feel that free trade brings with it mass production and standardization, which may harm the importing country's sense of individuality and cultural identity. As a result, some are totally against free trade while others feel that it should not extend into areas like communications, health, and education. They firmly believe that a country's radio and television stations, its newspapers and magazines, its educational institutions and hospitals, should not be foreign-owned or -controlled. In summary, three arguments against free trade are:

- the strategic industry argument
- the infant industry argument
- the cultural identity argument

REVIEW

1. **What is meant by *terms of trade*? Explain how the terms of trade can change.**
2. **In general, what could cause the terms of trade to move in Canada's favour?**
3. **What does the slope of the production possibilities curve indicate? What does the slope of the trading possibilities curve indicate?**
4. **Give three major advantages of free trade.**
5. **What does *protectionism* mean? Mention five ways in which governments control trade.**
6. **Who is helped and who is hurt by the imposition of quotas and tariffs?**
7. **Explain three arguments against free trade.**

STUDY GUIDE

Chapter Highlights

In this chapter you learned that the benefits of free trade are rooted in specialization and that a nation's comparative advantage determines what products it should export. The way that the gains from trade are divided between trading partners is determined by the terms of trade between them. You also learned that when a nation embraces free trade there are both winners, usually consumers, and losers, usually inefficient producers of certain products.

1. If trade is voluntary, then *both parties* to the trade must *benefit*.

2. Differences in factor endowments between nations and the *theory of absolute advantage* explain why, for example, Canada exports lumber and imports bananas.

3. The *theory of comparative advantage* explains why one nation is willing to trade with another nation even though it may be more efficient in producing both (all) the products involved.

4. The trade in any two products between any two nations will result in there being gains from trade unless the *opportunity costs* of production happen to be exactly the same in each country.

5. The way in which the gains from trade are divided between the trading partners is determined by the *terms of trade* which is calculated as the average price of exports divided by the average price of imports times 100.

6. The major *benefits of free trade* are:
   • lower prices;
   • higher incomes;
   • a greater variety of products;
   • increased competition.

7. The two most common forms of *trade restrictions* are tariffs and quotas both of which:
   • increase the domestic price of a product that is imported;
   • reduce the quantities traded of that product.

   While the other two types of restrictions are:
   • exchange controls;
   • voluntary exports restrictions.

8. Three arguments *against free trade* are the:
   • strategic industry argument;
   • infant industry argument;
   • cultural identity argument.

New Glossary Terms and Key Equations

comparative advantage   486
exchange controls   502
protectionism   499
quota   500
tariff   501
terms of trade   490
voluntary export restriction (VER)   502

Equations

$$\text{terms of trade} = \frac{\text{average price of exports}}{\text{average price of imports}} \times 100$$

Study Tips

1. The argument for free trade is based on Ricardo's theory of comparative advantage. It is important that you fully understand the basic idea of opportunity costs that lies behind this theory. A good way to test yourself is to make up your own figures for a two-country, two-product world, draw the corresponding production possibilities curves, and work out which country has an advantage in which product and why.

2. Some students have difficulty understanding that if we are dealing with only two products and if a country has a comparative advantage at producing one product it must, by definition, have a comparative *disadvantage* in the other product.

3. To get an understanding of the terms of trade, again try to make up some numbers for yourself and plot them on a production possibilities diagram. For instance, start off with a country that could produce 30 units of wool or 20 computers and has an advantage in wool production. If it could trade at 1 wool = 1/2 computer, what combinations could it have? Try 1 wool = 1 computer, 1 wool = 2, 3, 5 computers and so on. Draw each resulting trading possibilities curve. Note that both the trading and production possibilities curves reflect opportunity costs. The former case shows what must be given up in trading; the latter case shows what must be given up in production.

4. To understand the idea behind world markets, note, as in Figure 13.5, that what one country is exporting, another country must be importing. This means that if one country produces a trade surplus, then the other country must be experiencing a trade deficit. In the exporting country, the world price must be higher than the domestic price. In the importing country, the world price must be lower than the domestic price.

5. You will get a good grip on the effects of tariffs and quotas by drawing a simple demand and supply curve and noting, first, the effect of a price set above market equilibrium (which is what a tariff produces) and second, a quantity below market equilibrium (which is what a quota produces). This approach suggests that the effect of both tariffs and quotas is to produce higher prices and lower quantities.

Are You Sure?

Indicate whether the following statements are true or false. If false, indicate why they are false.

1. A country has a comparative advantage over another only if it is able to produce all products more cheaply.

   T or F   If false: _____

   _____

2. David Ricardo first introduced the theory of comparative advantage.

   T or F   If false: _____

   _____

3. If a country chooses to specialize its production, it will want to engage in trade.

   T or F   If false: _____

   _____

4. If a country is able to produce all products more cheaply than any other country can, then there is no advantage in trade.

   T or F   If false: _____

   _____

5. The terms of trade relate to the laws and conditions that govern trade.

   T or F   If false: _____

   _____

6. If the price of both a country's exports and its imports decrease, then the terms of trade will move in its favour.

   T or F   If false: _____

   _____

7. If a country's trading possibilities curve lies to the right of its production possibilities curve, there are no gains from trade.

   T or F   If false: _____

   _____

8. Protectionism is the economic policy of protecting domestic producers by restricting the exportation of products.

   T or F   If false: _____

   _____

9. A tariff is a tax on exports; a quota is a tax on imports.

   T or F   If false: _____

   _____

10. Domestic producers gain and domestic consumers lose as a result of the imposition of tariffs or quotas.

    T or F   If false: _____

    _____

Choose the Best

11. To what does the term "gains from trade" refer?
    a) The surplus of exports over imports.
    b) The increase in output resulting from international trade.

12. What is a tariff?
    a) It is a tax imposed on an import.
    b) It is a tax imposed on an export.

13. Who was the originator of the theory of absolute advantage?
    a) Adam Smith.
    b) David Ricardo.

14. What is the definition of "the terms of trade"?
    a) It is the average price of a country's imports divided by the average price of its exports.
    b) It is the average price of a country's exports divided by the average price of its imports.
    c) They are the rules and regulations governing international trade.

15. What does it mean if the opportunity costs differ between two countries?
    a) Then comparative costs must be the same.
    b) There can be no gains from trade.
    c) It is possible for both countries to gain from specialization and trade.

16. On what basis are the gains from trade divided between countries?
    a) According to the terms of trade.
    b) According to international trade agreements.
    c) According to the quantity of resources possessed by each.

17. Under what circumstances will there be no opportunity for mutually advantageous trade between two countries?
    a) When the terms of trade are the same.
    b) When comparative costs are the same.
    c) When comparative costs are different.

18. Suppose that originally the average price of Happy Island's exports was 180, and the average price of its imports was 120. Now, the price of its exports drops to 160, and the price of its imports drops to 100. What effect will this have on Happy Island's terms of trade?
    a) There will be no change in the terms of trade.
    b) The terms of trade have moved in Happy Island's favour.
    c) The terms of trade have moved against Happy Island.

19. Suppose that the cost of producing 1 unit of wine in Happy Island is 2 units of rice and in Silly Island, 1 wine costs 4 rice. What does this mean for the two countries?
    a) Happy Island should specialize in and export rice to Silly Island.
    b) Happy Island should specialize in and export wine to Silly Island.
    c) Happy Island should specialize in rice but export wine to Silly Island.
    d) Happy Island should specialize in wine but export rice to Silly Island.

20. Suppose that the cost of producing 1 unit of wine in Happy Island is 2 units of rice; in Silly Island 1 wine costs 4 rice. What might be possible terms of trade between the two countries?
    a) 1 rice = 3/8 wine.
    b) 1 rice = 3 wine.
    c) 1 rice = 6 wine.
    d) 1 wine = 1 rice.

21. All the following, *except one*, are forms of protectionism. Which is the exception?
    a) Import subsidies.
    b) Tariffs.
    c) Exchange controls.
    d) Quotas.

Figure 13.8 shows the market for cloth in Smith Island. Refer to it to answer questions 22, 23, and 24.

FIGURE 13.8

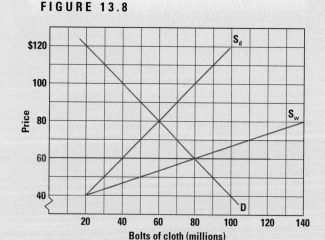

22. Refer to Figure 13.8 to answer this question. At the world price how much is Smith Island trading?
    a) It is importing 30 units.
    b) It is importing 40 units.
    c) It is exporting 30 units.
    d) It is exporting 40 units.

23. Refer to Figure 13.8 to answer this question. If Smith Island introduced an import quota of 20, what would be the new price in Smith Island?
    a) $55.
    b) $60.
    c) $70.
    d) $90.

24. Refer to Figure 13.8 to answer this question. If Smith Island introduced a tariff of $10 on cloth, how much would be imported?
    a) 0 units.
    b) 10 units.
    c) 20 units.
    d) 40 units.

25. What is the difference between a tariff and a quota?

    a) A tariff causes an increase in the price, whereas a quota does not affect the price.

    b) Both a tariff and a quota will affect the price, but a tariff has no effect on the quantity, whereas a quota will lead to a reduction.

    c) Both a tariff and a quota will affect the price, but a tariff has no effect on the quantity, whereas a quota will lead to an increase.

    d) A quota affects all foreign producers equally, whereas a tariff does not.

    e) A tariff affects all foreign producers equally, whereas a quota does not.

Refer to **Figure 13.9** to answer questions 26, 27, 28, and 29.

FIGURE 13.9

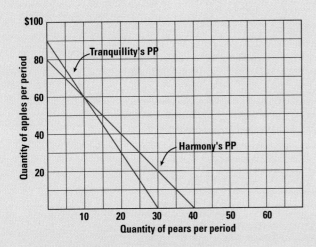

26. Refer to Figure 13.9 to answer this question. What is the opportunity cost of producing 1 apple in Harmony and in Tranquillity?

    a) 2 pears in Harmony and 3 pears in Tranquillity.

    b) 1/2 pear in Harmony and 1/3 pear in Tranquillity.

    c) 2 pears in Harmony and 1/3 pear in Tranquillity.

    d) 1/2 pear in Harmony and 3 pears in Tranquillity.

    e) 3 pears in Harmony and 2 pears in Tranquillity.

27. Refer to Figure 13.9 to answer this question. What do the comparative opportunity costs in the two countries suggest?

    a) That there are no advantages to be gained from trade.

    b) That Harmony should specialize in apples but export pears.

    c) That Tranquillity should specialize in apples but export pears.

    d) That Harmony should specialize in pears but export apples.

    e) That Harmony should specialize in pears and Tranquillity should specialize in apples.

28. Refer to Figure 13.9 to answer this question. Suppose that both Harmony and Tranquillity are producing 20 pears; what will be the total gains from trade for the two countries?

    a) 20 apples and 0 pears.

    b) 30 apples and 10 pears.

    c) 20 apples and 10 pears.

    d) 20 apples and 30 pears.

    e) 0 apples and 20 pears.

29. Refer to Figure 13.9 to answer this question. What could be possible terms of trade between the two countries?

    a) 1 apple = 0.25 pears.

    b) 1 apple = 2.5 pears.

    c) 1 apple = 3 pears.

    d) 1 pear = 0.5 apples.

    e) 1 pear = 2.5 apple.

Table 13.11 shows the output of kumquats per month. Refer to this table to answer question 30.

TABLE 13.11

Price ($ per kilo)	SMITHLAND Demand	SMITHLAND Supply	IMPORTS INTO SMITHLAND Supply
3	100	40	30
4	90	50	40
5	80	60	50
6	70	70	60

30. Refer to Table 13.11 to answer this question. What is the world (free trade) price, and what quantity of this product is being consumed domestically?

a) $4 and 50 kilos consumed.
b) $4 and 90 kilos consumed.
c) $5 and 80 kilos consumed.
d) $6 and 70 kilos consumed.
e) $6 and 130 kilos consumed.

Simple Calculations

31. If the terms of trade for the country of Onara equals 90 and the average price of its imports is 1.4, what is the average price of its exports? _____ .

32. In Onara, the average worker can produce either 5 bags of pummies or 3 kilos of clings whereas in Traf the average worker can produce either 4 bags of pummies or 6 kilos of clings. Which country can produce pummies cheaper and which can produce clings cheaper? Show the cost in each country.

pummies: _____ ; cost: _____

clings: _____ ; cost: _____

Problems

33. The following shows the maximum output levels for Here and There:

	Cloth		Computers
Here	100	or	50
There	60	or	120

a) What is the cost of a unit of cloth and a computer in Here?

1 unit of cloth: _____ ; 1 computer: _____ .

b) What is the cost of a unit of cloth and a unit of computers in There?

1 unit of cloth: _____ ; 1 computer: _____ .

c) In what product does each country have a comparative advantage?

Here: _____ ; There: _____ .

d) What would be feasible terms of trade between the two countries?

1 unit of cloth: _____ ; 1 computer: _____ .

34. **Table 13.12** shows the production possibilities for Canada and Japan. Prior to specialization and trade, Canada is producing combination D, and Japan is producing combination B.

TABLE 13.12

CANADA'S PRODUCTION POSSIBILITIES

Product	A	B	C	D	E	F
Compact disc players	10	8	6	4	2	0
Wheat	0	4	8	12	16	20

JAPAN'S PRODUCTION POSSIBILITIES

Product	A	B	C	D	E	F
Compact disc players	30	24	18	12	6	0
Wheat	0	6	12	18	24	30

a) On the graph (**Figure 13.10**), draw the production possibilities curve for each country, and mark their present output positions.

b) Suppose that the two countries specialize and trade on the basis of 1 CD player = 1.5 wheat. Draw the corresponding trading possibilities curves.

FIGURE 13.10

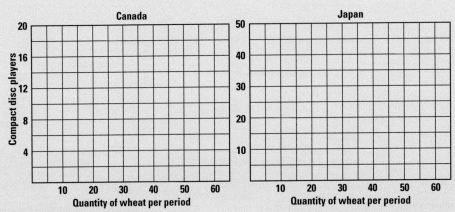

35. The following incomplete table (**Table 13.13**) shows the productivity levels of producing beer and sardines in Canada and Mexico.

TABLE 13.13

Production per Worker (average product)	Beer	Sardines
Canada	6	4
Mexico	3	?

In order for there to be no advantage to be gained from trade, what does the Mexican productivity per worker in the sardine industry need to be?

36. Suppose the Canadian demand for and the Japanese supply of cars to Canada is shown in **Table 13.14** (quantities in thousands).

TABLE 13.14

Price ($)	Quantity Demanded	Quantity Supplied (before tariff)	Quantity Supplied (after tariff)
$12 000	180	60	_____
13 000	160	80	_____
14 000	140	100	_____
15 000	120	120	_____
16 000	100	140	_____
17 000	80	160	_____
18 000	60	180	_____
19 000	40	200	_____

a) The present equilibrium price is $_____ and quantity is

_____ (thousand).

b) Suppose that the Canadian government imposes a $2000 per car tariff on imported Japanese cars. Show the new supply in the last column above. The new equilibrium price is:

$_____ and quantity is _____ (thousand).

c) The total revenue received by the government will be $_____.

d) Assume, instead, that the government imposes an import quota of 100 000 cars. The new equilibrium price is $_____ and quantity is _____ (thousand).

e) The total revenue received by the government will be $_____.

Translations

Latalia has a labour force of 12 million, one third of whom work in the wool industry, the remainder being employed in rice farming. The labour productivity in the wool industry is 40 kilos per worker per year, and in rice farming it is 100 kilos per worker per year. Latalia has discovered that the international terms of trade are 2 kilos of rice per kilo of wool. It is happy with its current consumption of rice but would like to obtain more wool.

FIGURE 13.11

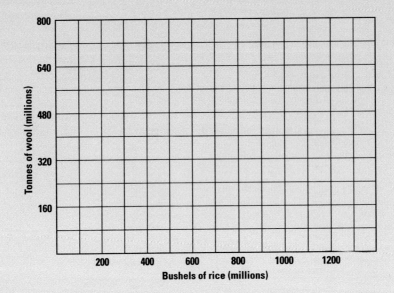

Assuming constant per unit costs, on the graph in Figure 13.11, draw a production and a trading possibilities curve for Latalia. Explain what product it should specialize in and show the gains, if any, it could receive from trade.

Explanation:

_____

_____

Key Problem I

Suppose that Peaceland and Prosperity have the output figures shown in Table 13.15.

TABLE 13.15

	AVERAGE PRODUCT PER WORKER	
Country	Wheat	Wine
Peaceland	4 bushels	2 barrels
Prosperity	4 bushels	3 barrels

Assuming that costs and productivity remain constant:

a) What is the opportunity cost of producing 1 bushel of wheat in Peaceland? _____

b) What is the opportunity cost of producing 1 barrel of wine in Peaceland? _____

c) What is the opportunity cost of producing 1 bushel of wheat in Prosperity? _____

d) What is the opportunity cost of producing 1 barrel of wine in Prosperity? _____

e) In what product does Peaceland have a comparative advantage? _____

f) In what product does Prosperity have a comparative advantage? _____

Suppose that the labour force in Peaceland is 10 million, and it is 20 million in Prosperity.

g) Fill in the missing production possibilities data for both countries in **Table 13.16**.

TABLE 13.16

PEACELAND'S PRODUCTION POSSIBILITIES (millions of units)

	A	B	C	D	E
Wheat	40	30	20	10	0
Wine	___	___	___	___	___

PROSPERITY'S PRODUCTION POSSIBILITIES (millions of units)

	A	B	C	D	E
Wheat	___	___	___	___	___
Wine	0	15	30	45	60

Suppose that both countries are presently producing combination D.

h) Show the joint totals below:

Total output in millions of units:

	Wheat	Wine
Peaceland	___	___
Prosperity	___	___
Total: both countries	___	___

Now suppose that each country specializes in the product in which it has a comparative advantage.

i) Show the new totals below:

Total output in millions of units:

	Wheat	Wine
Peaceland	___	___
Prosperity	___	___
Total: both countries	___	___

j) As a result, the joint gain from trade is equal to:

_____ wheat   _____ wine.

Suppose that the two countries establish the terms of trade at 1 wine =1.5 wheat, and Prosperity decides to export 15 wine to Peaceland.

k) As a result the two countries will gain as follows:

Gains for each country in millions of units:		
	Wheat	**Wine**
Peaceland	_____	_____
Prosperity	_____	_____
Total: both countries	_____	_____

Key Problem II

Table **13.17** shows the market for wool in Australia, which is closed to trade.

TABLE 13.17		
Price per Tonne ($)	**Domestic Demand**	**Domestic Supply**
1700	145	45
1800	140	60
1900	135	75
2000	130	90
2100	125	105
2200	120	120
2300	115	135
2400	110	150

a) What is the present equilibrium price and domestic production?

Price: _____;   domestic production: _____.

b) Suppose that Australia now opens to free trade and the world price of wool is $2000. How much wool will Australia produce domestically, and how much will it import?

Domestic production: _____;   imports: _____.

c) Assume that the Australian government, under pressure from the Australian wool industry, decides to impose an import quota of 20 tonnes. What will be the new price, and how much will the Australian industry produce?

Price: _____;   domestic production: _____.

d) Now suppose that the Australian government, wishing to benefit from the trade restriction, decides to replace the import quota with a tariff. If it wishes to maintain domestic production at the same level as with a quota, what should be the amount of the tariff and how much tariff revenue will it receive?

Tariff: $_____;   tariff revenue: $_____.

More of the Same

Suppose that Hopeland and Faithland have the output figures contained in **Table 13.18**, shown in terms of productivity per worker.

TABLE 13.18

AVERAGE PRODUCT PER WORKER

Country	Wheat	Wine
Hopeland	3 Bushels	1 barrels
Faithland	1 Bushels	2 barrels

Assuming that the costs and productivity remain constant:

a) What is the opportunity cost of producing wheat and wine in Hopeland and Faithland?

b) In which product does each country have a comparative advantage?

Suppose that the labour force in Hopeland is 20 million, and it is 10 million in Faithland.

c) Show the production possibilities data for both countries in a table.

Assume that both countries are now producing 5 million wine.

d) What are their present joint output totals?

Now suppose that each country specializes in the product in which it has a comparative advantage.

e) What will be the new output totals, and what will be the gains from trade?

Suppose that the two countries establish the terms of trade at 1 wine = 2 wheat, and Hopeland decides to trade 15 wheat to Faithland.

f) What will be the consumption totals for the two countries?

UNANSWERED QUESTIONS

Short Essays

1. Explain the difference between Adam Smith's and David Ricardo's theories of trade.

2. Explain what is meant by comparative costs and why there are no advantages to trade if nations have identical comparative costs.

3. Explain Adam Smith's dictum that the division of labour is limited by the extent of the market.

4. What are "terms of trade," and how can they be measured for nations that generally trade in more than two products?

5. Explain the main advantages of free trade.

6. Discuss the main arguments against free trade.

7. What are the main methods used by governments to protect domestic industries? Which do you think are the more successful methods?

8. Who gets helped and who gets hurt by the imposition of a tariff?

9. In what way are a tariff and a quota similar, and in what way are they different? Which is preferable, and why?

Analytical Questions

10. Why do some countries enjoy a cost advantage over others in the production of certain products? To what extent do these advantages remain constant? How may they disappear over time?

11. In what way is a direct subsidy from the government preferable to a tariff or quota as a way of assisting an infant industry?

12. What circumstances would make a country an exporter of a product? What would make it an importer?

13. If comparative cost is the basis for trade, why are Third World countries, which have very low wage rates, not the world's greatest trading nations?

14. If Third World countries are unable to compete in world markets, why are so many North American corporations locating plants in these countries?

15. The analysis in this chapter suggests that if a country produces only two products, and if it has a comparative advantage in one, it must have a comparative disadvantage in the other. How is this affected if a country produces three, or four, or a thousand products?

16. To what extent are the conclusions of the theory of comparative advantage affected if unit costs increase, rather than remain constant, as output increases?

Numerical Questions

17. The graph in **Figure 13.12** shows the domestic supply of and demand for mangos in India.

FIGURE 13.12

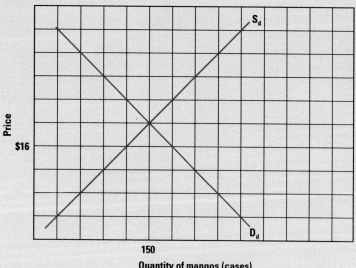

The world price is $16 a case and India has free trade.
a) Will India export or import mangos?
b) What quantity will domestic producers supply?
c) What quantity will India export or import?
d) What will be the price in India?

18. **Table 13.19** shows the (hypothetical) annual demand and supply of cellular phones in Canada (in tens of thousands annually), where D is the quantity demanded by Canadian consumers, S_C is the quantity supplied by Canadian manufacturers, and S_J is the quantity supplied to the Canadian market by Japanese manufacturers.

TABLE 13.19

Price	D	S_C	S_J
$200	28	4	0
300	26	6	2
400	24	8	4
500	22	10	6
600	20	12	8
700	18	14	10
800	16	16	12
1000	14	18	14

a) Add a final column showing the total quantity supplied in the Canadian market, labelled S_T. Graph D, S_C, and S_T.

b) If Japanese imports were totally banned, what would be the price and quantity of cellular phones in Canada?

c) If Canada was open to Japanese imports, what would be the price and quantity of cellular phones in Canada as a result?

d) Suppose that the Canadian government were to impose a quota on Japanese imports limiting them to 4 (tens of thousands) per year. What would be the price and quantity of cellular phones in Canada now?

e) To produce the same result as in d), alternatively what amount of tariff would the Canadian government have to impose on Japanese imports?

19. The graph in **Figure 13.13** shows the domestic demand and supply of apples in Canada.

FIGURE 13.13

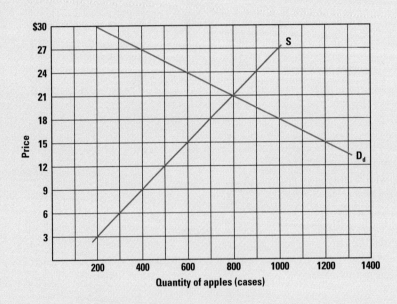

The world price is $15 per case and Canada is open to free trade.

a) How many cases per period will Canada import from abroad?

Suppose the government wishes to reduce imports by 300 cases per period.

b) What import quota should it impose, and what will be the effect on the price?

c) Alternatively, what tariff should the government impose, and what will be the total revenue from the tariff?

20. **Figure 13.14** shows the production possibilities for the countries of Kinell and Kenrick.

a) What are the costs for the two products in each country?

b) What products should they each specialize in and export?

FIGURE 13.14

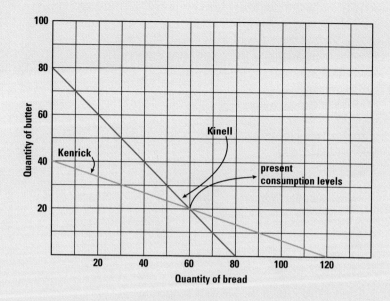

c) Suppose that terms of trade are established at 1 unit of butter = 2 units of bread. Show the trading possibilities curve for each country.

d) Assuming that each country is happy consuming the same quantity of its specialized product as it did before trade, show the amount of the imported product now available to it.

21. **Table 13.20** shows the production possibilities curves for Concordia and Harmonia.

TABLE 13.20

CONCORDIA'S PRODUCTION POSSIBILITIES

Product	A	B	C	D	E
Pork	4	3	2	1	0
Beans	0	5	10	15	20

HARMONIA'S PRODUCTION POSSIBILITIES

Product	A	B	C	D	E
Pork	8	6	4	2	0
Beans	0	6	12	18	24

a) What are the costs of the two products in each country?

b) What products should each country specialize in and export?

c) If, prior to specialization and trade, Concordia produced combination C and Harmonia produced combination B, what would be the total gains from trade for the two countries?

d) What would be feasible terms of trade between the two countries?

22. Given the production possibilities in question 21, suppose that before trading Concordia experienced a doubling of productivity in the pork industry but continued to produce 15 units of beans. From this initial position, answer the following questions:

    a) What are the costs of the two products in each country?

    b) What products should each country specialize in and export?

    c) If, prior to specialization and trade, Concordia produced combination D and Harmonia produced combination B, what would be the total gains from trade for the two countries?

    d) What would be feasible terms of trade between the two countries?

23. Suppose three countries have the productivity figures shown in **Table 13.21**.

TABLE 13.21		
Productivity per Worker	**Wheat**	**Beans**
Alpha	1	2
Beta	4	2
Gamma	2	2

Show the calculations used to arrive at the answers to the following questions.

   a) Which country can produce wheat comparatively more cheaply? Which country can produce beans comparatively more cheaply?

   b) Suppose that the international terms of trade were 1 wheat = 3/4 beans. Which countries would export wheat? Which countries would import wheat?

   c) Suppose instead that the international terms of trade were 1 wheat = $1\frac{1}{2}$ beans. Which countries would export wheat? Which countries would import wheat?

 Web-Based Activities

1. Is free trade a good idea? What are the arguments for and against free trade? Read the following articles and summarize the case for and against free trade: **www.fraserinstitute.ca/media/media_releases/ 1998/19980504.html** and People's Global Action Manifesto at **www.agp.org/agp/en/index.html**

2. Go to **www.tradecompass.com** and enter "softwood lumber" into the search box. Then read the latest articles on the possible renewal (or not) of the softwood lumber agreement between Canada and the U.S. Do you think that this issue is an example of broad consumer gain versus small special interest loss that was discussed in this chapter?

Glossary

allocative efficiency: the production of the combination of products that best satisfies consumers' demands.

average fixed cost: total fixed cost divided by the quantity of output.

average product: total product (or total output) divided by the quantity of inputs used to produce that total.

average profit: the profit per unit produced; that is, the total profit divided by the output.

average revenue: the amount of revenue received per unit sold.

average total cost: total cost divided by quantity of output.

average variable cost: total variable cost divided by total output.

barriers to entry: obstacles that make it difficult for new participants to enter a market.

break-even output: the level of output at which the sales revenue of the firm just covers fixed and variable costs, including normal profit.

break-even price: the price at which the firm makes only normal profits, that is, makes zero economic profits.

capital: all human-made resources that can be used to produce goods and services.

capital goods: things used to aid in the production of other goods, such as buildings, tools, equipment, and machinery.

ceteris paribus: all things being equal, or all things remaining the same.

change in demand: a change in the quantities demanded at every price, caused by a change in the determinants of demand.

change in supply: a change in the quantities supplied at every price, caused by a change in the determinants of supply.

change in the quantity demanded: the change in quantity that results from a price change. It is illustrated by a movement along a demand curve.

change in the quantity supplied: the change in the amounts that will be produced as a result of a price change. This is shown as a movement along a supply curve.

concentration ratio: a measurement of the percentage of an industry's total sales that is controlled by the largest few firms.

constant returns to scale: the situation in which a firm's output increases by the same percentage as the increase in its inputs.

consumer goods: goods used by consumers to satisfy their wants and needs.

consumer surplus: the difference between the consumer's evaluation of a product and the price paid for it.

common property resource: a resource not owned by an individual or a firm.

comparative advantage: the advantage that comes from producing something at a lower opportunity cost than others are able to do.

complementary products: products that tend to be purchased jointly and whose demands therefore are related.

cross-elasticity of demand: the responsiveness of the change in the quantity demanded of product A to a change in the price of product B.

decreasing returns to scale: the situation in which a firm's output increases by a smaller percentage than its inputs.

demand: the quantities that consumers are willing and able to buy per period of time at various prices.

demand schedule: a table showing the various quantities demanded per period of time at different prices.

depreciation: the annual cost of any asset that is expected to be in use for more than one year.

diseconomies of scale: bureaucratic inefficiencies in management that result in decreasing returns to scale.

division of labour: the dividing of the production process into a series of specialized tasks, each done by a different worker.

dumping: the sale of a product abroad for a lower price than is being charged in the domestic market or for a price below the cost of production.

economic capacity: that output at which average total cost is at a minimum.

economic profit: revenue over and above all costs, including normal profits.

economic rent: the return to any factor of production that has a perfectly inelastic supply.

economies of scale: cost advantages achieved as a result of large-scale operations.

elastic demand: quantity demanded that is quite responsive to a change in price.

elasticity coefficient: a number that measures the responsiveness of quantity demanded to a change in price.

elasticity of supply: the responsiveness of quantity supplied to a change in price.

enterprise: the human resource that innovates and takes risks.

equilibrium price: the price at which the quantity demanded equals the quantity supplied such that there is neither a surplus nor a shortage.

equilibrium quantity: the quantity that prevails at the equilibrium price.

excess capacity: the situation in which a firm's output is below economic capacity.

exchange controls: restrictions imposed by a government limiting the amount of foreign currencies that can be obtained.

explicit cost: a cost that is actually paid out in money.

externalities: benefits or costs of a product experienced by people who neither produce nor consume that product.

factor market: the market for the factors of production.

factor output effect: the phenomenon of rising total output leading to an increased demand for labour.

factor substitution effect: the phenomenon of one factor replacing another factor as a result of technological change.

factors of production: the productive resources that are available to an economy, categorized as land, labour, capital, and enterprise.

fair-return price: a price that guarantees that the firm will earn normal profits only; that is, where P = AC.

game theory: a method of analyzing firm behaviour that highlights mutual interdependence between firms.

human capital: the accumulation of all skills and knowledge acquired by individuals.

imperfect competition: a market structure in which producers are identifiable and have some control over price.

implicit cost: a costs that does not require an actual expenditure of money.

income effect: the effect that a price change has on real income, and therefore on the quantity demanded of a product.

income elasticity: the responsiveness of quantity demanded to a change in income.

increasing returns to scale: the situation in which a firm's output increases by a greater percentage than do its inputs.

inelastic demand: quantity demanded that is not very responsive to a change in price.

inferior products: products whose demands will decrease as a result of an increase in income and will increase as a result of a decrease in income.

interest: the payment made and the income received for the use of capital.

labour: human physical and mental effort that can be used to produce goods and services.

labour force: the total number of people over the age of 15 who are willing and able to work.

labour force supply: the total hours that those in the labour force are willing to work.

laissez-faire: the economic doctrine that holds that an economy works best with the minimum amount of government intervention.

land: any natural resource that can be used to produce goods and services.

law of diminishing marginal utility: the amount of additional utility decreases as successive units of a product are consumed.

law of diminishing returns: as more of a variable input is added to a fixed input in the production process, the resulting increase in output will, at some point, begin to diminish.

law of increasing costs: as an economy's production level of any particular item increases, its per unit cost of production rises.

long run: the period of time during which all inputs are variable.

long-run average cost curve: a graphical representation of the per unit costs of production in the long run.

macroeconomics: the study of how the major components of an economy interact; it includes the topics of unemployment, inflation, interest rate policy, and the spending and taxation policies of government.

margin(al): the extra or additional unit.

marginal cost: the increase in total variable costs as a result of producing one more unit of output.

marginal product: the increase in total product as a result of adding one more unit of input.

marginal profit: the additional economic profit from the production and sale of an extra unit of output.

marginal revenue: the extra revenue derived from the sale of one more unit.

marginal revenue product: the increase in a firm's total revenue that results from the use of one more unit of input.

marginal social benefits: the additional benefits to both the consumer (internal benefits) and to society (external benefits) of additional quantities of a product.

marginal social costs: the additional costs to both the producer (internal costs) and to society (external costs) of producing additional quantities of a product.

marginal utility: the amount of additional utility derived from the consumption of an extra unit of a product.

market: a mechanism that brings buyers and sellers together and assists them in negotiating the exchange of products.

market demand: the total demand for a product by all consumers.

market failures: the defects in competitive markets that prevent them from achieving an efficient or equitable allocation of resources.

market supply: the total supply of a product offered by all producers.

microeconomics: the study of the outcomes of decisions by people and firms through a focus on the supply and demand of goods, the costs of production, and market structures.

minimum efficient scale: the smallest-size plant capable of achieving the lowest long-run average cost of production.

minimum wage: the lowest rate of pay per hour for workers, as set by government.

monopolistic competition: a market in which there are many firms who sell a differentiated product and have some control over the price of the products they sell.

monopoly: a market in which a single firm (the monopolist) is the sole producer.

monopsony: a market structure in which there is only one buyer.

mutual interdependence: the condition in which a firm's actions depend, in part, on the reactions of rival firms.

natural monopoly: a single producer in a market (usually with large economies of scale) in which it is able to produce at a lower cost than competing firms could.

non-depletability: a feature of certain products that makes it possible for additional people to receive benefits without the use of more resources.

non-divisibility: a feature of certain products that means they can only be bought collectively and not in definable units by individuals.

non-excludability: a feature of certain products that makes it impossible to exclude non-purchasers from enjoying the benefits of the product.

normal products: products whose demand will increase as a result of an increase in income and will decrease as a result of a decrease in income.

normal profit: the minimum profit that must be earned to keep the entrepreneur in that type of business.

nominal wage: the wage rate expressed as a dollar-and-cents figure.

oligopoly: a market dominated by a few large firms.

opportunity cost: the value of the next-best alternative that is given up as a result of making a particular choice.

optimal purchasing rule: in order to maximize utility, a consumer should purchase the product that yields the greatest marginal utility per dollar spent.

perfect competition: a market in which all buyers and sellers are price takers.

price ceiling: a government regulation stipulating the maximum price that can be charged for a product.

price controls: government regulations to set either a maximum or minimum price for a product.

price discrimination: the selling of an identical product at a different price to different customers for reasons other than differences in the cost of production.

price elasticity of demand: the responsiveness of quantity demanded to a change in price.

price floor: a government regulation stipulating the minimum price that can be charged for a product.

private goods: products that can be consumed separately by each individual and are normally provided by private firms.

product differentiation: the attempt by a firm to distinguish its product from that of its competitors.

product market: the market for consumer goods and services.

producers' preference: an allocation system in which sellers are allowed to determine the method of allocation on the basis of their own preferences.

production possibilities curve: a graphical representation of the various combinations of maximum output that can be produced.

productive efficiency: production of an output at the lowest possible average cost.

profits: the income received from the activity of enterprise.

protectionism: the economic policy of protecting domestic producers by restricting the importation of foreign products.

public goods: products that are collectively consumed, so that private firms would be incapable of producing them at a profit, and that therefore must be provided by the government.

public utilities: goods or services regarded as essential and therefore usually provided by government.

quasi-public goods: private goods that are often provided by the government because they involve extensive benefits for the general public.

quota: a limit imposed on the production or sale of a product.

rationing: a method of allocating products that are in short supply by the use of ration coupons issued by the government, guaranteeing a certain quantity per family.

real income: income measured in terms of the amount of goods and services that it will buy. Real income will increase if either actual income increases or prices fall.

real wage: the purchasing power of the nominal wage.

rent: the payment made and the income received for the use of land.

rent control: a government regulation making it illegal to rent accommodation above a stipulated level.

shutdown price: the price that is just sufficient to cover a firm's variable costs.

short run: any period of time in which at least one input in the production process is fixed.

socially optimum price: the price that produces the best allocation of products (and therefore resources) from society's point of view, that is, P = MC.

subsidy: a payment made by the government to a firm (or others), which may be a lump-sum grant or depend on the amount produced.

substitute products: any products whose demand varies directly with a change in the price of a similar product.

substitution effect: the substitution of one product for another as a result of a change in their relative prices.

sunk costs: the historical costs of buying plant, machinery, and equipment that are unrecoverable.

supply: the quantities that producers are willing and able to sell per period of time at various prices.

supply schedule: a table showing the various quantities supplied per period of time at different prices.

tariff: a tax (or duty) levied on imports.

technological improvement: changes in production techniques that reduce the costs of production.

terms of trade: the average price of a country's exports compared with the price of its imports.

total cost: the sum of both total variable cost and total fixed cost.

total fixed costs: costs that do not vary with the level of output.

total product: the total output of any productive process.

total revenue: the total amount of income a firm receives from its sales; formally, it is price multiplied by the quantity of the product sold.

total variable cost: the total of all costs that vary with the level of output.

transfer earnings: a necessary payment that a factor of production must earn in order for it to remain in its present use.

unitary elasticity: the point where the elasticity coefficient is equal to 1, that is, where the percentage change in quantity is exactly equal to the percentage change in price.

utility: the satisfaction or pleasure derived from the consumption of a product.

voluntary export restriction (VER): an agreement by an exporting country to restrict the amount of its exports to another country.

wages: the payment made and the income received for the use of labour.

Index